Untrodden Ground

Untrodden Ground

How Presidents Interpret the Constitution

HAROLD H. BRUFF

THE UNIVERSITY OF CHICAGO PRESS   CHICAGO AND LONDON

HAROLD H. BRUFF is the Rosenbaum Professor of Law at the University of Colorado Law School. He is the author, most recently, of *Bad Advice: Bush's Lawyers in the War on Terror*.

The University of Chicago Press, Chicago 60637
The University of Chicago Press, Ltd., London
© 2015 by The University of Chicago
All rights reserved. Published 2015.
Printed in the United States of America

24 23 22 21 20 19 18 17 16 15   1 2 3 4 5

ISBN-13: 978-0-226-21110-7 (cloth)
ISBN-13: 978-0-226-21124-4 (e-book)
DOI: 10.7208/chicago/9780226211244.001.0001

Library of Congress Cataloging-in-Publication Data

Bruff, Harold H., 1944– author.
    Untrodden ground : how Presidents interpret the Constitution / Harold H. Bruff.
        pages cm
    Includes bibliographical references and index.
    ISBN 978-0-226-21110-7 (cloth : alkaline paper)—ISBN 0-226-21110-X (cloth : alkaline paper)—ISBN 978-0-226-21124-4 (e-book)—ISBN 0-226-21124-X (e-book)
    1. Executive power—United States—History. 2. Implied powers (Constitutional law)—United States—History. 3. Presidents—United States—History. I. Title.
    JK511.B78 2015
    342.7302'9—dc23

                                                                    2014025164

♾ This paper meets the requirements of ANSI/NISO Z39.48–1992 (Permanence of Paper).

In our progress toward political happiness my station is new, and if I may use the expression, I walk on untrodden ground. There is scarcely an action, the motive of which may not be subject to a double interpretation. There is scarcely any part of my conduct which may not hereafter be drawn into precedent. Under such a view of the duties inherent in my arduous office, I could not but feel a diffidence in myself on the one hand, and an anxiety for the Community . . . on the other.

PRESIDENT GEORGE WASHINGTON, 1790

Contents

INTRODUCTION: Only a Necessity   1

PART I.   **Durable Consequences**

CHAPTER 1.   Responsibility: The Constitution   11

CHAPTER 2.   Summoned by My Country: Washington and Adams   25

CHAPTER 3.   The Fugitive Occurrence: Jefferson and Madison   57

PART II.   **A New Nation**

CHAPTER 4.   Independent of Both: Jackson, Tyler, and Polk   83

CHAPTER 5.   A Rough Time of It: Lincoln   120

CHAPTER 6.   Unmindful of the High Duties: Andrew Johnson   157

PART III.   **Steward of the People**

CHAPTER 7.   Facing the Lions: McKinley, Theodore Roosevelt,
and Wilson   187

CHAPTER 8.   What Must Be Done: Franklin Roosevelt   223

PART IV.   **One Single Man**

CHAPTER 9.   Going to Hell: Truman and Eisenhower   261

CHAPTER 10.   Bear Any Burden: Kennedy and Lyndon Johnson   293

CHAPTER 11.   Not Illegal: Nixon, Ford, and Carter   325

PART V.   **A New Era**

CHAPTER 12.   First a Dream: Reagan   359

CHAPTER 13.   The Vision Thing: George H. W. Bush and Clinton   376

PART VI.   **Deciders**

CHAPTER 14.   No Equivocation: George W. Bush   401

CHAPTER 15.   The Last Mile: Obama   427

CONCLUSION: The Stream of History   456

Acknowledgments   467

Notes   469

Index   551

Introduction

Only a Necessity

It ought always to be remembered that historical continuity with the past is not a duty, it is only a necessity.—Justice Oliver Wendell Holmes[1]

American presidents are creatures of law. They all know this because they begin by taking the constitutionally prescribed oath to "preserve, protect, and defend" the Constitution.[2] The obvious purpose of the oath is to impose legal obligations. But what is the content of those obligations? The process of answering that question has gone on for more than two and a quarter centuries and will continue as long as the Republic exists. Perhaps surprisingly, many answers have been provided by the presidents themselves. Presidential actions that depend on interpretations of the Constitution have infused its grand generalities with concrete meaning.

Thus presidents are at the same time creatures of law and creators of law. George Washington intuitively understood this dual role. When he had been in office less than a year, he remarked that he stood on untrodden ground and that everything he did would become a precedent. Knowing that his actions would bind his successors in some way, he stepped forward carefully, leaving tracks in which others would follow.

Most Americans do not think of the president as the nation's most important interpreter of law, but he is.[3] This role is a necessary consequence of the Constitution's creation of three separate branches. In daily operation, each branch interprets the Constitution constantly, independent of the views of the other two. Since the beginning of the nineteenth century, the Supreme Court has exercised the power of judicial review to invalidate statutes as unconstitutional. At times, the Court has wielded this power

quite vigorously, earning the hostility of the other branches and the astonishment of many foreign observers. The Court has ruled on the scope of
the president's constitutional power much less often.[4] Presidential statutory interpretations are, however, frequently reviewed in modern times.
Within the executive branch, responsibility for interpreting the Constitution and statutes is assigned to the president by the opening clause of
Article II, which vests the "executive Power" in the president, and by the
oath, which bonds the incumbent to the document. Many others advise,
but the president decides.

Depending on their temperament, our forty-four presidents have interpreted the Constitution in ideological or pragmatic ways that have
built on the precedents set by their predecessors. Presidents have always
had lawyers who support proposed actions with theories that encapsulate
the precedents, combining arguments from history and law. The constitutional meaning that matters results from what presidents have *done*.
Official bureaucratic explanations of these actions matter only when they
have become an important part of the precedent. Freestanding assertions
of power that are not tied to actual decisions do not form precedents with
any punch, because they do not induce the kinds of reactions that test a
precedent's worthiness.

Presidential constitutional interpretation is a process very similar to
generation of the traditional common law upon which so much American
law rests. In judicial hands, the common law consists of the accretion of
precedent on the basis of past decisions in similar cases, adjusted for the
facts of the case at hand and present conditions. When a common law
judge decides that it is time to alter an ancient doctrine to reflect present
realities, his or her decision of a case becomes a proposal to the legal community that may then be accepted, rejected, or modified by later court
decisions in similar cases.[5] Similarly, presidents find guidance and comfort
in what their predecessors have done successfully and are comfortable asserting the legality of present action based on past example. Where there
is no nearby past example, they know the legality of their action will be
more doubtful.

Although thick legal and policy bureaucracies prepare today's presidential decisions, the ultimate interpretive choices remain highly personal
in nature. Presidential constitutional interpretation differs from that of
any lawyer or judge, because it reflects a unique level of personal responsibility that shapes the president's judgment. Harry Truman once said
that the responsibility is "so personal as to be without parallel"; Abraham

Lincoln warned that the president has "no moral right to shrink from" it or "even to count the chances of his own life" against it.[6] Presidents turn to their predecessors for guidance precisely because these are the only other Americans who have experienced the pressure of presidential decision making firsthand.

In these pages, I examine five main factors that appear to drive presidential interpretation; they lie more in history and politics than in law as conventionally understood. First, each president sees the Constitution through the lens of his own character and experience. Presidents approach the document in ways that reflect their temperament (for example, Buchanan's cowardice, Lincoln's courage, Andrew Johnson's rigidity). Therefore, I sketch the aspects of each president's personality that seem salient to interpretation.

Second, a president's political values and priorities affect his view of the Constitution in fundamental ways. Each incoming president encounters the political opportunities and constraints of the day. Sometimes the scope of available political choice is wide, sometimes narrow.[7] Some of our presidents have reconstructed the politics of their day by their behavior in office—Jefferson, Jackson, Lincoln, Franklin Roosevelt, Reagan. In doing so they find a wide scope for constitutional interpretation as well. Thus politics and law move together, guided with varying degrees of success by presidents. Whatever their capacities, all presidents have interpretive options. For example, the core constitutional duty to faithfully execute the laws has received widely variant interpretation depending on which groups a president wishes to benefit, as in the choice between supporting management or labor during strikes. More broadly, whether a president believes in a vigorous or restrained role for the federal government affects his constitutional interpretations comprehensively.

Third, incentives built into the presidency steer presidents once they assume the office, whatever their prior views may have been. For most presidents, a broad view of the powers of the office is essential to achieving political goals. Hence, the Whig presidents of the nineteenth century often found themselves abandoning party orthodoxy, which favored a quite restrained presidency, in favor of the vigorous views that other incumbents have adopted.[8]

Fourth, the practical problems of the day drive interpretation. Of course, no president controls his own agenda more than partially. Fate intervenes. As Lincoln remarked, events control presidents to an important extent.[9] Perceived necessity demands a solution that works today, whatever its implications for tomorrow or its basis in yesterday.

Fifth, presidents view themselves in historical perspective and want to be compared with their most illustrious predecessors, not the least of them. Therefore they rummage among the available precedents that could be invoked to lend both legitimacy and luster to a new decision. They avoid precedents that invite comparison to the presidency's worst moments.

Presidents are likely to take any action they consider necessary if it is unlikely to prompt serious resistance in the form of an impeachment effort, reactive legislation, judicial invalidation, or debilitating public outcry. Thus the law of presidential power depends on the operation of our national political process. Whenever the courts cannot be expected to decide contested constitutional issues, the necessary condition on legitimacy is that the president seek what I call "political ratification," the assent of Congress and the people.[10] Acquiescence in a precedent can cement it; rejection can eliminate it. In this relationship, presidents hold the vital advantage of the initiative—they can select the action to which the nation will react. This means that presidents can often present the nation with a fait accompli that is very difficult to modify or undo. (Presidential war making provides the most vivid examples.) Conventional legal materials are never irrelevant to decisions; they are always cited in the debate, but it must be understood that it is always possible to tie an action (however loosely) to some fragment of the constitutional text.

The practice of generating constitutional law in the executive branch is similar to but distinct from the parallel practices of the other two branches of the federal government. When Congress legislates, it asserts the constitutionality of its product. When courts interpret the Constitution, they assert the validity of their decisions. Whenever a presidential action rests on constitutional interpretation, it asserts the legitimacy of that reading. Hence the executive's law-generating capacity is inherent; the problem is one of limits. The distinctive feature of presidential lawmaking is its performance by a single individual (although with varying levels of institutional support from within the executive branch). This characteristic makes it comparatively flexible, speedy, and dangerous.

Constitutional law generation by all three branches is responsive to public opinion. Congress is built to register it sensitively. Presidents ignore it at their peril. And even the Supreme Court, atop the most insulated of the branches, has generally reflected broad currents in American public opinion.[11] Thus all of our constitutional law is "historically conditioned and politically shaped."[12] This is not a reason for alarm. It was understood early in our history that if interpretation of the written text of the Constitution were not informed by practice, nothing would ever be settled—there could be endless and debilitating reargument of any issue.[13] Happily, however, the generation of precedent by actual practice is flexible enough to respond to changing conditions. History, like law, is always contested ground.

Most of the precedents that I examine concern a president's interpretation of his own powers. I also consider some presidential interpretations of the powers of the other branches and of the Bill of Rights that have had important effects on how the Constitution actually operates. For example, today the power of the federal government depends on the extent of Congress's power to regulate interstate commerce and on the scope of its power to take actions that are "necessary and proper" to implement its specified powers. Presidential interpretations of these two clauses have affected the federal government's powers compared to those of the states. Presidential interpretations of the First Amendment have affected the rights of the people to know what their government is doing and to criticize it without fear.

My historical approach should persuade the reader that three recently fashionable approaches to constitutional law are flawed. First, those who advocate an "original intent" approach to constitutional interpretation would strip away the rich accretion of meaningful precedent that has occurred since the founding.[14] Second, those who advocate a "unitary executive," a president who possesses plenary power to dismiss and supervise all the officers who execute the law, slight the important and accepted role of Congress in controlling executive officers by both statutes and informal practices.[15] Third, those who advocate broad and exclusive executive power in the national security realm envision a presidency shorn of controls that our history has shown to be indispensable.[16]

The portrait of the presidency that emerges from these pages has several prominent features. First, there has been immense overall growth in presidential power since the framing. The expansion has not been continuous, however. It has occurred episodically, sometimes but not always in the hands of great presidents, often but not always during periods of crisis, and has been offset by periods of retreat and uncertainty. The impact of new activities that presidents have developed depends on the power of the other two branches of the federal government, which have also developed important new powers over the years. The question of overall balance of power among the three branches, which was vitally important to the framers, thus demands a continuous comparative inquiry.

Second, within this pattern of overall growth of power, presidential constitutional interpretation has been remarkably stable in some vital ways. By the time the founding generation left the White House in 1825, many precedents had been set that still endure. By the dawn of the twentieth century, the early modern presidencies were emerging and were resolving constitutional issues with analysis that is familiar today. By the end of World War II, the emergence of the national security state was under way, setting a framework of constitutional issues that Americans still confront. Great presidents led the nation through its two gravest crises, the Civil War and the Great Depression, without inflicting lasting damage on the constitutional framework.

Stability in both constitutional interpretation and our national life has been enhanced by the usual concession of presidents that they are bound by statutes, a stance that is essential to maintaining the rule of law in the United States. Wide discretion often remains within statutory boundaries—I will show that presidents possess ample power to do great good for or great harm to the nation under a formulation of their power that does not ordinarily allow them to contravene statutes. Instead, the dominant historical pattern, especially in foreign affairs, has been for presidents to exercise wide powers of initiative under existing constitutional and statutory text, leaving Congress to exert statutory or funding controls after the fact.[17]

The third prominent feature of presidential power as it has matured is a consequence of broad powers of executive initiative: the American people must tolerate initial and perhaps fateful decisions made by presidents who possess strong incentives to adopt legal interpretations that will expand their own power. The Cuban missile crisis is the classic example of such a moment of peril. I see no way to eliminate this problem and its attendant dangers if there is to be sufficient executive power to protect the nation. If the problem cannot be eliminated, can it be controlled?

The vital and continuously operative constitutional control on presidents is their knowledge of the need for subsequent political ratification of their actions. For that process to operate, two preconditions exist. First, enough information must be available to allow accountability.[18] Second, every president must accept that although he or she makes the initial decision, it is "We the People" who will make the final one. Happily, this book describes few outright collisions between presidents and the other two constitutional branches, and many techniques for avoiding confrontations. This avoidance pattern fosters legal indeterminacy, preserving flexibility in the system.

As presidents form and adapt constitutional precedents, they are generating law in the full sense of the term. I define law in a standard modern way, as consisting of practices that have become normatively binding in the affected community, whether their source be in legal text, judicial decisions, or behavioral conventions that have achieved general acceptance.[19] Thus constitutional law includes any "rule of behavior accepted as obligatory by those concerned in the working of the constitution."[20] This definition does not sharply distinguish law from politics, nor do presidents sharply distinguish these related realms. Instead, a feedback loop exists in which constitutional text, presidential behavior, and political response produce enduring precedents that operate as constitutional law.[21] Just as American political culture is especially attuned to law, American constitutional law is especially attuned to politics.[22] This relationship has preserved the Constitution for more than two centuries.

Unlike some observers who think our constitutional system is fundamentally broken, I do not favor major revision by constitutional amendment.[23] After reviewing our constitutional history, I will suggest some limited alterations in the document. My caution reflects the view that avulsive constitutional change through amendments risks making our polity worse, not better. The interpretive stability that I have mentioned suggests that evolved constitutional law has met the needs of the nation. Developments after World War II that led to the much-criticized "imperial presidency" have produced important statutory responses. Although the efficacy and wisdom of these responses are questionable, statutes, unlike constitutional amendments, can be altered fairly readily to reflect experience.

Justice Oliver Wendell Holmes qualified his observation that historical continuity is "only a necessity." Fearing the "pitfall of antiquarianism," he urged Americans to "spend our energy on the study of the ends sought to be attained and the reasons for desiring them."[24] I share Holmes's endorsement of a pragmatic interpretive approach that is informed but not dictated by history. In the constitutional history that I recount here, presidents often have their worst moments when they are most ideologic and their best when they are most pragmatic. The difference lies in that elusive quality, statesmanship.

With these considerations in mind, let us proceed to a very rich history. First, let us see what decisions the framers of the Constitution made about the presidency and what questions they left for the future to answer.

PART I
Durable Consequences

Many things which appear of little consequence in themselves and at the beginning, may have great and durable consequences from their having been established at the commencement of a new General government.— George Washington, 1789

CHAPTER ONE

Responsibility

The Constitution

[Vesting executive power in a single person would provide] energy, dispatch, and responsibility.—James Wilson at the Constitutional Convention[1]

The Constitution that presidents swear to defend is known for its brevity and occasional obscurity. Article II, which creates and empowers the executive branch, exemplifies both characteristics. To interpret the document, presidents and their legal advisers consult standard sources of constitutional history: the records of the Constitutional Convention, the *Federalist Papers*, records of the ratification process, other statements by the framers, and general histories of the time. From this enterprise emerges some clarity but enough doubt to justify a wide range of potential development in the presidency.

Staking Out the Ground: Conceptions of an Executive

When the framers set out to create a chief executive, they could agree most readily on what they did *not* want.[2] On one hand, having just fought a successful revolution against the kingly oppressions that they had decried in their Declaration of Independence, most of them were determined to avoid creating a new monarch (who would be all the more dangerous an ocean closer than the old one). The colonists, having felt deeply betrayed when King George III sent troops to suppress their liberties, had reacted viscerally against executive power.[3] On the other hand, painful memories lingered from conducting the Revolutionary War under a cobbled-together government that lacked any formal chief executive. The postwar

Articles of Confederation, resolutely eschewing kings and therefore having no executive branch, operated badly through committees of the states. Plainly, something between a king and a committee would be requisite, but that covers a lot of ground.

Fortunately, the framers had a common fund of knowledge about government to guide them.[4] Their education had covered the histories of England and of the ancient republics.[5] They were also conversant in political philosophy.[6] Even more important was their shared experience in colonial government, revolutionary war making, and the new state governments. The document they drafted reflected all of these influences but was not simply a patchwork of old elements—it was an original creation that would set a new example for the world.

The separation of powers, the most distinctive contribution of the framers to the art of governance, had ancient roots.[7] Both the Greeks and Romans had defined a republic as an "empire of laws not men."[8] To secure the rule of law against the whim of rulers, they employed offsetting powers with some success. Yet the conventional lesson from ancient history was that republics were fragile and quite vulnerable to usurpation by whoever held the executive power.

A more modern example, one with a happier outcome, followed the English Civil War in the seventeenth century.[9] England entered that turbulent century with a rudimentary division of functions among Parliament, the Crown, and the common law courts. This triad provided a rough model for later ideas of formal separation of powers. Parliament possessed most of the power of the purse; the Crown held various ill-defined prerogatives; the common law judges claimed the power to articulate law that could bind even a monarch. As viewed from eighteenth-century America, seventeenth-century England had experienced monarchical absolutism, a military dictatorship during the Interregnum, more monarchical abuses after the Restoration, and a final Glorious Revolution that deposed another king and confirmed the ascendancy of Parliament.

Americans drew much of their political philosophy from a group of great synthesizers of the English revolutionary experience, among whom John Locke and Baron de Montesquieu took primary importance. Locke's *Two Treatises of Government* (1690) built a model of government on the Revolution settlement.[10] He advocated some elements of a system of separation of powers. He thought that Parliament could limit the monarch's internal, "executive" functions but could not limit external, "federative" ones regarding foreign relations and war. He supported some judicial independence.

In an analysis that has been important ever since, Locke defined the nature and limits of executive power. His grasp of both human nature and the essential workings of government have commended his thoughts to the ages—and to American presidents. He began with the general proposition that those who make laws should not execute them as well, because the combined powers might be "too great a temptation to human frailty."[11] Yes indeed. Nevertheless, he saw a need for executive lawmaking in some circumstances. He articulated what is now known as the "Lockean prerogative," the power "to act according to discretion, for the publick good, without the prescription of the Law, and sometimes even against it."[12] His rationale was that the legislature was too slow to meet all needs of execution, that it could not foresee everything, and that laws would do harm if executed too rigidly. These are all true, but what would control this dangerous power? Locke thought that the acquiescence of the people to an extraordinary executive action would legitimate it.[13] He was less clear about ratification by the legislature, perhaps because legislatures were not yet viewed as indirect embodiments of the people's will.

Locke also made a prescient observation: that the prerogative would always be largest in the hands of the "wisest and best" princes, because the people would see the benefits of their actions and would not contest them. Ironically, these reigns would be the most dangerous to liberty, because wicked successors would cite these precedents to justify their own bad actions.[14] Here Locke conceded the essential flaw in his scheme: at least initially, whether to invoke prerogative would lie in the hands of the prince, with all the attendant incentives to abuse power.

An alternative scheme for emergencies, one well known to the American founding generation, traced from the Roman Republic through to the work of Niccolò Machiavelli: "constitutional dictatorship."[15] The essential idea is that because a republic designs its institutions for ordinary times, some provision must be made for military or economic emergencies that threaten the state. The structural solution is for the nation's lawmakers to delegate nearly absolute power to someone to meet the emergency, but only temporarily. In the most famous example, the Roman Republic conferred a temporary constitutional dictatorship on Cincinnatus, a farmer-statesman who put down his plow, took up arms to save the republic from invasion, and then immediately put down the arms and picked up the plow again.[16]

Unfortunately, not all constitutional dictators relinquish power as readily as did Cincinnatus. Nevertheless, the operative constitutional judgment underlying such a scheme is that the risk is worth taking as a trade-off for an effective way to meet emergencies, and one that is within the rule of law. Machiavelli emphasized this element of constitutional regularity.[17] By contrast, Locke located prerogative outside the bounds of ordinary constitutional authority, with the consequence that its legitimacy is constantly in question.[18] The American framers would struggle with this problem and would ultimately finesse it, leaving future generations to struggle with it as well.

Montesquieu's celebrated *The Spirit of the Laws* (1748) became, along with Locke's *Second Treatise*, the political authority most widely cited by our founding generation.[19] Montesquieu advocated a set of checks in a system of separated powers. He articulated the triad of legislative, executive, and judicial powers that is familiar today.[20] He prescribed a bicameral legislature and a separate executive consisting of a single monarch possessing veto power over legislation and commanding the army. An independent judiciary would provide a vital bulwark against tyranny. Montesquieu's thinking provided important guidance at the Constitutional Convention.

In addition to their education, the framers relied on their intense practical education in politics. Most of them were veterans of the Revolutionary War. Many had served in the new state governments or in the rudimentary national government under the Articles of Confederation. In private life, they were farmers, merchants, or lawyers. All were men, and many were slave owners. As colonists sitting in the colonial assemblies, they had battled with the royal governors and had learned to favor restricting executive power. James Wilson noted that in the colonies both the executive and judicial powers were placed in foreign (British) hands, remote from the people in a way the assemblies were not.[21]

Abandoning the British model for their own governments, Americans turned to separation of powers.[22] The new state constitutions often contained ringing endorsements of separation of powers principles, but in practice they vested power almost entirely in the legislatures and especially in the lower houses. The resulting structures were prone to an unanticipated problem—majoritarian legislative abuse of the other branches and of the people.

Nothing in their experience or in traditional theories told Americans how to select an executive. It was obvious, though, that the mode of selection was crucial to the authority of the office. Except for New York, the state constitutions of 1776–78 subordinated the executive to the legislature.[23] These weak governors were consistent with strict separation of powers theory but not with effective government, as war pressures demonstrated.

The Articles of Confederation, drafted during a war against a central government accused of abusing its tax and commerce powers, were fatally (and understandably) weak in those particulars. The Articles omitted any permanent executive, providing only for a committee of states to sit while Congress was in recess. No one could mistake this ramshackle construct for an effective and vigorous government. Eventually, patience ran out, and delegates convened in Philadelphia to repair the deficiencies of the existing system.

Constructing the Edifice: The Constitutional Convention and Ratification

Given this background, it would be difficult to claim that when the Constitutional Convention convened in 1787, any particular version of executive power was likely. At the outset James Madison's "Virginia plan" set the agenda.[24] It did not provide for a strong executive branch. Instead, an executive of undetermined number would be elected by the legislature without possibility for reelection. In debate about the plan, James Wilson argued that the executive should consist of a single person who would be independent of the legislature and eligible for reelection. This proposal produced an uneasy pause as delegates glimpsed ghosts of kings. After some sharp discussion, the Convention preliminarily chose legislative election of an individual to a single, seven-year term; impeachment for "malpractice or neglect of duty"; and executive powers to veto legislation, to execute the laws, and to make appointments (except for judges, who were to be appointed by the Senate).

When the Convention turned to the relationship of Congress to the executive, they exuded fear of what they called "corruption," a term with a special historic meaning. English kings had developed a technique that jeopardized legislative independence. They "corrupted" Parliament by granting lucrative offices to its members, in a successful effort to sway their loyalties and maximize power. This practice was controversial for many decades on both sides of the Atlantic, amid much condemnation of executive domination of the legislature.[25] Ironically, in Britain holding offices in both branches would eventually have the reverse effect—it would allow the development of parliamentary control of the ministry. The essential point, that having the same officers in both branches might allow either branch to control the other, was not clearly seen at the time of the framing. Instead, the framers banned "corruption" in a traditional move to limit executive power. In the process, they would insulate each branch from the other and foreclose the development of a parliamentary system in the United States.

After extended preliminary discussions, the Convention recessed while a Committee of Detail drafted a document embodying the decisions so far. The committee adopted an enumeration of executive powers that would remain mostly unchanged. It specified that the "executive power" would be in a single person. The title of "president," derived from the Latin term *to preside*, was considered familiar and reassuring.[26] The president's powers would include being commander in chief, receiving ambassadors, appointing executive officers, exercising a conditional veto, and issuing pardons. The Senate was to have exclusive power to make treaties and to appoint ambassadors and justices.

Debate on the draft began. The Convention had not seriously addressed the president's relation to administration. Gouverneur Morris and Charles Pinckney called for a council of state to assist and advise the president and for a specified group of executive departments for agriculture, manufacturing, foreign affairs, and war.[27] The president would appoint and remove the ministers. Thus the executive branch would have had a constitutional composition. The Convention eventually rejected the Morris-Pinckney plan, keeping only a clause that authorized the president to call for written opinions from his subordinates.

The Convention finally broke a long deadlock over selecting the executive by inventing the Electoral College, a solution that "almost satisfied almost everybody."[28] The small states gained weighted minimum representation, while the large ones gained proportionality otherwise. This device reflected "the indispensable necessity of making the Executive independent of the Legislature" and gave those anxious for popular choice half a loaf.[29] As it turned out, the positive contribution of the Electoral College to American history would consist solely of creating the potential for a presidency tied to the people. The creaky mechanism it created for choosing presidents has caused repeated trouble otherwise.

A spirit of compromise also shaped relations between president and Senate. The executive received appointment and treaty powers—with the Senate's concurrence. The president had gained power in foreign affairs and had lost some in appointments. Both kinds of power were to be shared between the executive and the Senate, in contrast to the British concentration of them in the monarch. Not noticed at the time but important afterward was the framers' failure to provide for any mechanism to resolve disputes between presidents and the Senate over appointments and treaties. By contrast, the president's power to veto legislation was subject to override by Congress; if that effort failed, the president's veto would prevail.

Now the shift from congressional government to a balanced system was complete. The president's term was to be four years, with reelection allowed. Impeachments were to be tried in the Senate, on a two-thirds vote. The major decisions having been made, Gouverneur Morris, an accomplished stylist, "wrote" the Constitution.[30] After adopting the draft, the Convention appended a resolution recommending that it be submitted to conventions in the states, with delegates chosen by the people, not the legislatures. With this procedural step, "the distinction between a constitution and ordinary law became the fundamental doctrine of American political thinking."[31]

The document that the Convention produced contained as much political art as political science. Much was left to the future for resolution. For example, the "necessary and proper" clause, enabling Congress to enact legislation to implement both its own constitutional powers and those of the other two branches, was adopted unanimously without debate. This "sweeping provision," as opponents would later call it, left Congress remarkably free to structure the executive and judicial branches as it liked.

By 1787, both separation of powers and checks and balances were widely accepted as general principles. Madison provided the key link by arguing that checks maintain separation—they bulwark a constitution's parchment barriers.[32] There was spirited disagreement, however, over the institutional arrangements that would satisfy these principles.

In the end, the Constitution employed three main separation of powers techniques. First, it allocated particular functions to specified branches. For example, Congress would raise revenue, and the courts would decide cases. Second, it guaranteed each branch particular attributes of autonomy that experience had suggested. Congress received control over its elections, its membership, and its meetings, and its members received an explicit privilege for what they said in debate. The executive would have an assured term, absent stated grounds for impeachment. Equally important was the creation of an independent political base for the presidency.

Severing the executive from dependence on Congress created three truly independent branches.

The third major means of separating the branches was a ban on the joint holding of legislative and executive offices. Under the incompatibility and ineligibility clauses of Article I, section 6, the very delicate issue of "corruption" was compromised. No one could hold office in both branches at the same time, but former legislators could serve in the executive unless their offices were new or carried increased salaries. Hence Congress could not create or fatten offices and then induce appointment of its members to them. Requiring that the two political branches be staffed by different people was meant to create the Madisonian competition between the branches that explains much of our law and politics.

Executive power remained vague in the minds of the framers. Constitutional controversy in seventeenth-century England had sharpened understanding of some executive powers. For example, kings had arbitrarily suspended statutes; the framers forbade that abuse by requiring the president faithfully to execute the laws. At the Convention, Madison identified faithful execution as the "essence" of the presidency.[33] The constitutional nature of powers over war and foreign affairs had not been contested with the Crown in the revolutionary period. Consequently, they remained especially vague in the Constitution.[34]

The framers were much too leery of executive power to provide any explicit mechanism for constitutional dictatorship on the Roman model. Instead, they created an approximation by granting Congress and the executive various emergency powers if they acted together. When Congress had not authorized emergency action, the vague potential for exercises of Lockean prerogative lay in the background. The only explicit emergency power they put in the Constitution is the authority to suspend the writ of habeas corpus in cases of "Rebellion or Invasion."[35]

The most important limitations on executive power were Congress's control of the purse, its power to override vetoes by two-thirds majorities in both houses, and the senatorial check on appointments and treaties. The president's veto, which partially intruded the executive into legislation, was reconciled with separation of powers principles as a limited check that could only force reconsideration. Madison viewed the veto as "a check to precipitate, to unjust, and to unconstitutional laws."[36] Since the Crown had not dared veto a bill for nearly a century, however, some wondered if it would be a dead letter.

The structure of the Constitution, combining separation of powers, checks and balances, and federalism, appears to have been designed to serve three overall purposes. First, the framers meant to diffuse and offset power in hopes of achieving an overall balance, or at least of avoiding a tyrannical concentration in one place. This effort to achieve balanced government was instrumental to the ultimate goal of securing the rule of law. Second, as their (ultimately unsuccessful) resistance to a bill of rights demonstrates, they hoped that structural techniques would protect individual liberties. And third, through the interrelation of structure with multiple bases of political representation, they hoped the new government would promote the broad public interest, not narrow faction. These goals are no less important today than they were in 1787. Realizing them has been the challenge.

Both the Constitution and its supporting arguments display the Enlightenment's interest in social mechanics.[37] The *Federalist Papers* appeared in an effort to obtain ratification in the critical state of New York. Their pseudonymous and correctly republican author Publius argued that the Constitution used republican institutions to foster the best elements of human nature, or public virtue, while including devices for "supplying, by opposite and rival interests, the defect of better motives."[38] Madison's famous argument in *Number 10* claimed that a large republic could diffuse and offset faction. In *Number 51*, he added a layer of competing officeholders to the competing interest groups. He argued that for self-interest to serve social utility, "ambition must be made to counteract ambition." Having the officers check each other would let private interest "be a sentinel over the public rights."[39]

The new constitution would alter the underpinnings of separation of powers doctrine by making the executive a representative of the people. Because the legislature was no longer the sole representative branch, accountability arguments would have to shift to promoting overall balance.[40] Thus, in *Number 51* Madison would defend the conditional veto by arguing that the alternative of an absolute veto could be either too blunt an instrument to be useful (if recent English history were any guide) or an excessive power for the executive (if its potential were realized). Madison argued that the president would be weaker than even a limited monarch, lacking power either to dissolve the legislature or to corrupt it.[41]

Ratification was a close battle, its outcome far from assured.[42] Political manipulation was intense.[43] The debates did not focus on the potential power of the presidency except for some concern (ironically, shared by Thomas Jefferson) about the potential for incipient monarchy in the president's eligibility for reelection.[44] Instead, debate centered on such issues as the absence of a bill of rights and the presence of a federal power to tax. Sadly, there was little stated opposition to the Constitution's endorsement of slavery—everyone knew this compromise was essential to formation of the Union.[45] The nation and its presidents have struggled with the consequences of that decision ever since. Once ratification had succeeded, the new nation embarked on an unknown future.

Legacy: The Constitutional Text and the Presidency

Article II of the Constitution spells out detailed procedures for electing presidents but lapses into generalities when identifying the powers of the office. Plainly, the framers were more comfortable specifying process than substance. Hence, it has often been observed that constitutional clauses on powers and rights are usually open ended; those on organization and procedure are often specific.[46] The consequence is to confer the most interpretive latitude where the stakes are highest. Presidents and their opponents have taken advantage of this opportunity throughout our history. Consider the range of possible interpretations of the most commonly debated elements of presidential power.

Article II begins by providing that "the executive Power shall be vested in a President," to serve a four-year term with eligibility for reelection. This clause confirms that the framers chose a single, not a plural executive. If it means no more than that, it confers no substantive power. Alternatively, the use of the phrase "executive power" might be a substantive grant of, well, whatever power is executive in nature. It would not be long before this debate was joined.

Article II's designation of the president as commander in chief of the military could conceivably be a grant of power to "do anything, anywhere, that can be done with an army and a navy."[47] The narrowest view would be that the president is merely the "first general and admiral," the senior military administrator awaiting instructions from Congress on war making.[48] There is vast ground between these positions. We no longer inhabit the eighteenth-century world, in which oceans were wide and time for response to threats was plentiful. Under the pressure of circumstance, the meaning of this clause has evolved substantially over the years. The textual wedge that presidents have used to expand their power is the Convention's deletion of a provision authorizing Congress to "make" war in favor of the power to "declare" war. The change was designed to allow presidents to "repel sudden attacks."[49] Hence, sometimes the president must act unilaterally to defend the nation. More than two centuries into American constitutional history, it remains unclear just when those times might be.

The broadest view of the clause that requires the president to "take Care that the Laws be faithfully executed" emphasizes that the president oversees the entire executive branch, unlike an administrator charged to implement a particular statute. Perhaps, then, the president has Lockean discretion to harmonize conflicting policies in the welter of statutes that may touch upon a national problem. The narrowest view is that the clause simply imposes a duty to obey and enforce the statutes. If so, the president must make do with the tools Congress gives, without trying to adapt them to changing times or emergencies.

In addition to these oft-contested grants of power, the president received the conditional veto, the power to enter treaties with the concurrence of two-thirds of the Senate, the power to nominate executive and judicial officers (this time with the concurrence of a majority of the Senate), the power to receive ambassadors from foreign nations, and the power to issue pardons. The executive bureaucracy appears in only two shadowy references. Congress may vest the appointment of inferior officers in the heads of departments, and the president may ask administrators for written opinions about their duties. Closing Article II with a warning, the framers provided that the president and other officers could be removed on impeachment and conviction for "Treason, Bribery, or other high Crimes and Misdemeanors."

From an initial standpoint, then, two potentialities were clearly present. First, the vague assignments of power would allow substantial fluctuation or evolution over time and with the character of particular presidents. Today, one can plausibly portray the vastly divergent activities of James Buchanan and Abraham Lincoln as consistent with the Constitution's text and history. Second, Congress had substantial legislative powers that could result in too much or too little control of presidents. On the one hand, Congress might try to exert close control over the executive branch, to avert tyranny or to serve its own interests. On the other, presidents would hold substantial institutional advantages (including the veto) that might frustrate legitimate statutory controls.

The nature of the presidency also created two great complexities that were seen dimly or not at all by the framers. First, the president would be both chief executive and head of state. Although the Constitution located ultimate sovereignty in "We the People" and then delegated parts of it out to three semi-independent branches and to the states, only one person could represent and speak for the nation, and that would be the president. Accordingly, the real powers of the presidency would always exceed its paper powers and would rest to some uncertain degree on the head of state role. Claims to exercise any kind of prerogative power are much easier to credit when the personal embodiment of the nation is speaking.

The head of state dimension would also affect particular powers and limitations of the presidential office, sometimes obviously, sometimes subtly. In foreign affairs, the head of any nation derives substantial power from the function of performing its communications with other nations. From the earliest days, presidents would exercise broad discretion in the foreign realm without much support from constitutional text. A more subtle effect of this dimension has surfaced in its discouragement of the impeachment of miscreant presidents, who can remind everyone that the dignity of their office must not be tarnished. In appraising particular presidential actions, then, the intrinsic duality of the office must always be taken into account.

A complexity that Americans initially denied (but soon would embrace) is the president's role as head of a political party. The Constitution ignores parties as it constructs a republic of virtue, but parties were a fact of life before George Washington left office. The duality of the president as both constitutional officer and chief partisan politician means that presidential attempts to lead the nation are automatically vulnerable to a partisan critique. Knowing this, presidents try to legitimate their actions by invoking what their predecessors have done, especially if someone from the other party generated a pertinent precedent. The role of party chief also soon drew presidents into the internal affairs of Congress, notwithstanding traditional concerns about "corruption."

Thus the operation of the new Constitution would be affected by developments in both American political life and the governmental imperatives the Constitution itself created. James Madison anticipated the inevitability of evolution when he remarked at the Convention that "in framing a system which we wish to last for the ages, we [should] not lose sight of the changes the ages will produce."[50] Here he was suggesting that the Constitution should not be read by posterity through eighteenth-century spectacles but as a living document, that is, "one that evolves, changes over time, and adapts to new circumstances, without being formally amended."[51] This attitude would certainly be consistent with the nature of common law reasoning as the framers had imbibed it.[52] The principal legal guide for early Americans, William Blackstone, had emphasized the need to read statutory text according to its spirit and with guidance from principles of equity.[53]

In addition, there was a practical reason for flexible interpretation that presidents would soon turn to their advantage. Unwittingly, the framers had made it extremely difficult to amend their document. The requirement that three-quarters of the states ratify proposed amendments has doomed many a proposal. For presidents, this has meant that their constitutional interpretations are usually safe from textual override. Instead, the ordinary political process has provided or withheld approval for what they do.

For the first 140 years of the nation's existence, a structural quirk in the original Constitution gave each newly inaugurated president nine months to govern without Congress in session. During this period, which I call the "presidential window," new presidents had time to put their stamp on the nation and its Constitution within the limits set by existing legislation and funding. Article I of the Constitution called for Congress to meet at least once every year, ordinarily beginning in December. In the early life of the nation, an extraordinary meeting pattern arose and persisted because it took considerable time for Congress to assemble. Each Congress held a long session of about six months beginning in December of odd-numbered years, a full year after its election. It would then hold a shorter, lame duck session from December of even-numbered years to the next March, adjourning as the inaugural date for the president approached.

Therefore, unless a new president called Congress into special session, he had the presidential window of opportunity all to himself (and other substantial periods as well). The Twentieth Amendment finally remedied this bizarre sequence following the inauguration of Franklin Roosevelt in 1933. Henceforth, Congress would convene in January of each year and would soon be meeting much of the time.[54]

The constitutional description of the presidential office was undoubtedly affected by the framers' anticipation that George Washington would be the first president and would take the first steps onto untrodden ground. Washington's astonishing relinquishment of power at the end of the Revolution had made him the American Cincinnatus, the very exemplar of a restrained republican executive. The fate of the Constitution, like that of any constituent document, would necessarily depend on how it was administered. The framers' trust in Washington allowed them to create an office with great potential to evolve and to grow. Happily for all of us, their confidence was not misplaced.

CHAPTER TWO

Summoned by My Country

Washington and Adams

I was summoned by my country, whose voice I can never hear but with veneration and love, from a retreat which I had chosen with the fondest predilection. — George Washington, first inaugural address, 1789[1]

A s George Washington traveled to New York in the spring of 1789 for his inauguration, a wide range of possibilities lay before him. Having presided at its drafting, he well knew that the new Constitution sketched only the broad outlines of an executive branch.[2] He also knew that whatever he did would go far toward defining the enduring nature of his office. That certainly proved to be the case.[3] Like the other framers, he treated the Constitution not as a document with a meaning forever crystallized in Philadelphia but as a work in progress whose meaning would emerge in application to concrete problems of governance.[4]

The Character of a Man Shapes an Office

Once in office, Washington made choices that were guided by his character and values. His contributions to the law and politics of the presidency, like those of all of his successors, were determined by what he was as a person. His political values were a distillation of eighteenth-century classical conservative republicanism. He was such an exemplar of his age that his dignified death in the last days of the century signified its passing as well as his own.

Washington wanted to create a "constitutional republic on a continental scale."[5] Its characteristics would include adherence to the rule of law, identification and pursuit of an essentially unitary public interest, promotion of civic virtue among the people and their representatives, and a commitment to liberty within a stable and orderly polity. He could never admit, to himself or to others, the unavoidable rowdiness of the partisan politics that had characterized the colonies and would soon emerge in the new republic. Instead, he would preside grandly over a harmonious scene. His first inaugural promised that "no separate views, nor party animosities" would distract his "comprehensive and equal eye."[6]

At some level, this claim (or aspiration) would be stated by all American presidents. Yet as Washington approached New York, the discerning eye might have spied the fault line across which the two great American parties would form. The value system competing with classical republicanism was Lockean liberalism, and under the aegis of Thomas Jefferson it would soon dominate American politics.[7] The underlying philosophical differences were not extreme—Jeffersonian liberals displayed a greater emphasis on individual liberty, a readiness to believe that factions would pursue private interest, and a resulting desire for checks on government power.

In actual practice, differences about particular government policies would soon produce an embittered political debate that initially surprised and always dismayed Washington, who was sure he knew what was best. His extended lament about faction in the Farewell Address conceded that his world was ending even as he prepared to leave it. But in the meantime, he instilled elements of his vision in the office he would bequeath to posterity.

Washington's character and personality determined many of the early precedents about the presidency.[8] Honor was everything to him. He was cautious and restrained in the use of power yet committed to creating a strong, effective presidency. He was deliberate about making decisions, possessed of excellent judgment, and resolute in implementing policy.[9] Above all, he was devoted to the rule of law. If he had tried to aggrandize himself and the office he held, he might have damaged the new republic irreparably.

Washington's progress to New York for the inauguration, attended by a constant outpouring of adulation, would have loosed the incubus of dictatorship in many other men. Instead, he self-consciously set about to convert his own deep well of popularity into support for the new national government, the Constitution, and the presidency. Today, "there is a symbolic, ritualistic, almost mystical quality that inheres" in the presidency, flowing from the president's role as head of state.[10] It may be that Washington's greatest contribution was endowing the office with the dignity it needed to protect the new nation from enemies foreign and domestic. He was the only public figure who could fulfill the nation's need for an icon, a safely temporary republican monarch. To play that intrinsically conflicted role was a delicate and difficult task.

Arriving in New York, Washington was embarrassed to discover that in the new Senate a debate had broken out about the appropriate form of address for the chief executive.[11] Presiding over the Senate, Vice President John Adams pontificated about the need to foster the dignity of the presidential office by creating appropriate rituals. Adams promoted the egregious title "His Highness the President of the United States and Protector of the Rights of the Same." Those who would soon become high Federalists liked the ring of that. In the House of Representatives, however, those who would soon become ardent Republicans objected, and to the nation's everlasting benefit James Madison engineered approval for the Constitution's simple title, "President of the United States." It was also fortunate that if Washington lacked anything it was not gravitas. His innate sense for dignified, restrained behavior set a personal standard for all of his successors to emulate.

More was going on here than an early outbreak of pomposity in the Senate. The debate revealed that the emerging division between republicanism and liberalism had produced two competing visions of the presidency. One was essentially monarchical, an independent and powerful executive at the helm of a modern nation like Great Britain. Adams and Hamilton held these hopes. Some even thought the presidency might evolve into an actual monarchy. The strongest opposing view, associated with Jefferson (and soon with Madison), saw a modest republican officer at the head of a limited government that would not displace much of the authority of the states.[12] At the Constitutional Convention, this difference of opinion had been papered over with the laconic text of Article II to produce a proposal that could be ratified. Now, however, with a flesh and blood president in office, it was time to start filling in the blanks. Washington himself instinctively leaned toward the Hamiltonian position but drew back from its most extreme implications.

One way to see Washington's importance to the nature of the presidency is to imagine what the early precedents might have been had the first oath of office been administered to Hamilton or to Jefferson. Hamilton would have pushed toward the British model (and did so as secretary of the treasury).[13] Jefferson would have promoted the decentralized agrarian utopia that glimmered in his romantic visions. It is doubtful that Congress would have wholly accepted either alternative, but a path would have been blazed that would have been difficult to erase later on.

Executive Branch Architects

Trusting President Washington not to abuse power, the First Congress was prepared to construct an executive branch that gave broad scope to presidential discretion. Surprisingly, once the often bitter fight over ratification of the Constitution had been decided, the new nation largely acquiesced in the outcome—the First Congress had heavy Federalist majorities. This reaction and the unanimous selection of Washington by the Electoral College submerged the presence of party divisions during the critical period needed to construct a government. The edifice that Congress and the president created together in 1789 still stands.

As the First Congress created the architecture of the executive branch, Washington remained in the background, believing that his role was to execute the laws, not to make them.[14] Here he was reflecting the traditional Whig sensitivity about "corruption" in the form of executive manipulation of the legislature. Washington's only suggestion for Congress in his inaugural, drafted by James Madison, was for a bill of rights to redeem the promises that Federalists had made to secure ratification. Serving as the president's ally in the House of Representatives, Madison wanted to control the amendment process closely to forestall anything that might "mutilate" the Constitution.[15] Washington shared the fear that the new government might be "shipwrecked in sight of the port." Thanks largely to Madison's political skill in steering the amendment process, no wreck occurred.

As the proposed amendments that would become the Bill of Rights emerged from Congress, Washington made no claim that they should be submitted to him for his signature or veto. Article V of the Constitution, which specifies the amendment process, does not mention a presidential role, but the analogy to ordinary legislation, which is exposed to the veto, might have implied one. Washington's restrained view of his role was later confirmed by the Supreme Court.[16]

Washington was quite reluctant to employ his power to veto bills. He shared the then dominant opinion that only very serious objections to a bill, ordinarily constitutional ones, should prompt a veto.[17] Washington resorted to the power only twice in his two terms of office. The first veto was on constitutional grounds concerning composition of the House of Representatives; the second was based on a policy objection to a bill reducing military personnel, which Washington thought would threaten the safety of the western posts.[18] Congress accepted both.

The veto power remained dormant until Andrew Jackson breathed fire into it. Either employing or threatening a veto would eventually become a crucial check on Congress for presidents, but the time was not yet ripe for such confrontations. Before the development of political parties and outright clashes between the branches over policy, interbranch relations proceeded more delicately than would later be the norm.

Washington could not forgo executive management of legislation entirely, however. It soon became clear that the content of statutes is vital to the success of every president. Early presidents, needing to appear to be above politics, managed legislation through surrogates in their administration and in Congress. For Washington, Hamilton took a very active role in Congress, where the president's friends, led by Madison in the House, ensured that presidential discretion was preserved as the first administrative agencies were created.

This was the time of the framers in government. The First Congress had ninety-one members, many of whom had been in Philadelphia. Those who had written the Constitution now worked out fundamental issues concerning its implementation. Because so much of the structure they built has endured, decisions taken in the early years have had a lasting influence on constitutional interpretation. Hence, our nation's founding was not a moment but a process that continued at least through the end of the Federalist era in 1801.[19]

The central constitutional issue was the president's relationship to administration. The Constitution's text provided clues but not answers. The clause vesting executive power in the president surely determines who is the head of the executive branch, but it does not define supervisory relationships within the branch. The requirement that the president take care that the laws be faithfully executed is phrased in the passive, implying that someone else will do the actual administering of statutes. That surely makes sense—even the infant federal government could not have sent every statutory decision by every customs inspector in every port to the president's desk. The faithful execution clause also clearly assigns the ultimate responsibility for execution of the law to the president. But how does that responsibility relate to the vesting clause? The Constitution does not say. Finally, the clause allowing the president to require written opinions from his subordinates about their duties certainly presumes that the president is to be no stranger to administration. Still, once he receives an opinion, if he disagrees with the officer's interpretation of a statute, may he countermand the officer's decision? May he fire the officer? The First Congress initiated the process of answering these questions. Perhaps surprisingly, we are still engaged in it today.

The First Congress created three cabinet departments—State, Treasury, and War—along with a part-time attorney general. These original four offices still form the core of the executive branch. I call them the "constitutional cabinet" because they implement the president's constitutional powers over foreign affairs, spending, war, and law. Hence the president's claim of plenary supervisory powers over them is at its maximum compared to other entities, such as the post office that Congress also empowered.

These early legislative decisions showed how Congress can control the president's discretion by crafting the tools it gives him. The statutory design of the three departments revealed an understanding that presidential supervision was more appropriate for some government functions than others.[20] Overall, the executive was mostly unified under presidential command.[21] State and War received minimal internal organization and were instructed to perform duties that the president might assign. Treasury was constructed rather differently, with more links to Congress than the other departments. In addition to performing the executive function of spending, the department would help Congress exercise its own constitutional powers of taxing and appropriating. Because Congress was touchy about executive influence in its realm, it gave Treasury a detailed internal architecture and carefully specified its statutory duties.[22]

Congress debated the constitutional issues about presidential supervision of administrators in the context of deciding whether the president could remove them from office. Notice that this issue is not coterminous with the broader topic of presidential supervision of the executive branch. Obviously, removal authority implies some supervisory power, but presidential power to fire an officer for making bad decisions does not necessarily mean that the president can direct the decisions themselves if statutes assign them to the officer.

The Constitutional Convention did not discuss the subject of removing executive officers except for the question of impeachment. Resolution of the issue by the First Congress has been called the "decision of 1789," a label that hides substantial uncertainty about just what the decision was.[23]

The question of removing the secretary of state produced a thoughtful and wide-ranging debate in which policy and constitutional considerations intertwined.

In the House, James Madison moved the creation of departments of war, treasury, and foreign affairs, each to be headed by a secretary who would be "removable by the president." Some representatives objected that this language suggested that removal power was a matter of legislative grace rather than constitutional executive prerogative. Others took the opposite position that the Senate must consent to removals, as it was empowered to do for appointments. Madison thought that removal was an exclusively executive power, serving the "great principle of unity and responsibility in the Executive department."[24]

The House, beset by disagreement and uncertainty, eventually crafted substitute text referring ambiguously to the officer who would run the department "whenever the principal officer shall be removed" by the president. Representatives who believed either that the Constitution created an executive removal power or that Congress could do so could vote for the substitute. It passed the House. In the Senate, after consideration in secret session, it passed when the vice president's vote broke a tie on the question of deleting the controversial provision. President Washington signed the bill. Both branches had finessed the underlying constitutional issue and deferred it to the future.

Congress did, however, consider limiting removal of a subordinate officer, the comptroller of the treasury.[25] Madison, who at this time was generally a strong supporter of executive responsibility, thought that the comptroller's duty to settle accounting disputes partook of "a Judiciary quality."[26] Therefore he concluded that the comptroller should not serve at the pleasure of the executive. Congress once again produced a muddled resolution: it rejected a set term for the comptroller but made accounting decisions "final and conclusive," suggesting that the president could not overrule them.[27] Over the years, the broader principle that officers who adjudicate cases can be protected from political removal has become embedded in constitutional law. To the extent that presidents have lost some supervisory power over execution, the competing constitutional value of due process has been protected.

Thus, rather than a single "decision of 1789," the First Congress made several different judgments, all of which Washington accepted by signing the bills. It placed State and War under close presidential control, creating responsive bureaucracies to conduct foreign affairs and war. Treasury, however, was tied more closely to Congress because of its support of taxing and appropriations. This theory that Treasury had a unique place among the departments would persist well into the nineteenth century. Hence the overall "decision of 1789" was that the responsiveness of principal officers to the president should vary, depending on the nature of their statutory duties. This flexible principle suited an infant government and could adapt to a mature one as well.

Equally important was what Congress did *not* do in 1789. In *Federalist Number 77*, Hamilton had tried to assuage fears about the power of the presidency by arguing that the Constitution would require the Senate's advice and consent for removal of executive officers (although the text was silent on that point).[28] He explained that this rule would lend stability to the executive by reducing turnover as administrations changed. Congress considered this position but did not adopt it; nor did Washington commend it to them. The wisdom of its choice would soon be demonstrated when John Adams became president and made the mistake of retaining Washington's cabinet instead of appointing officers whose loyalty ran to him. The holdovers constantly undermined and frustrated Adams, who finally removed two of them near the end of his term.

Adoption of the Hamiltonian position on removal would have made the executive branch more stable, but at great cost to the president's constitutional power. Madison argued that if the president had to share the removal power with the Senate, the government would be a "two-headed monster."[29] Indeed. The consequence could have been to move our government toward a parliamentary system, with some executive officers holding a direct allegiance to Congress, not the president. The balance of power in the government would have depended on party alignments in the Senate. Instead, Congress created a clean chain of command and responsibility for most of the offices it created in 1789.

Seizing the Reins

Once the new departments were created, the next task was to operate them. Experience would flesh out the concrete meaning of constitutional "executive power." Early presidents could establish their own administrative practices without much oversight from Congress, which was in session less than half the time. These presidents took their lead from the gifted manager who first held the office.

George Washington took immediate command of the executive branch—there would be no government by committee. Thus norms of collective ministerial responsibility that would later emerge in some parliamentary systems never gained traction in the United States. Washington established an initial tradition of direct presidential involvement in decision making. Important issues of policy and law were hammered out in discussions among the handful of executive officers and were usually decided personally by the president.[30]

Secretary of State Thomas Jefferson called Washington the "hub of the wheel" for administration, seeing and passing on everything important but often deferring to the secretaries' choices.[31] There was a constant flow of paper back and forth between the president and the secretaries, as Washington actively employed his constitutional power to demand opinions from his officers in order to build a tradition of bureaucratic regularity and to cement his own supervisory power. Washington initiated the practice of issuing "executive orders," which are commands to executive officers to do this or stop doing that in pursuance of their statutory duties.[32] As the federal government grew over the years and presidents could no longer supervise their subordinates by speaking directly with them, executive orders would become an essential means for presidents to instill their policies in the bureaucracy. Overall, Washington's policies evolved in a pragmatic, deliberative manner—he was not an ideologue like Hamilton or Jefferson.

Washington's style of governing owed much to his military experience. During the Revolutionary War, he had consulted carefully with his subordinate generals in councils of war before making his decisions. This hierarchical method of decision making transferred readily to the simple structure of the new executive branch. Washington decided issues of foreign policy and war with a confidence born of experience. In economic matters, where he was not comfortable, he usually deferred to Hamilton's expertise. Sharing the judgment of Congress that Treasury was distinct from the other departments, Washington did know that establishing the young nation's credit and economic stability were crucial to its success. Hence he fully supported Hamilton's financial program and the secretary's skilled efforts to persuade Congress to adopt it.

In the early years, the federal government performed only a few tasks.[33] A tiny defense establishment dealt with the Indians, with internal disorders such as the Whiskey Rebellion, and with the ominous superpowers (Britain, France, and Spain).[34] There was some economic regulation in the form of customs duties and occasional trade embargoes against the superpowers. Finally, there were some housekeeping functions—delivering the mail, surveying and selling the public lands, collecting a few taxes. The federal service—not yet a civil service with entry and promotion controlled by statute—consisted mostly of customs agents in the ports and postmasters scattered around the countryside.[35]

Who Selects the Officers?

Staffing this small and decentralized federal bureaucracy fell to the president and the Senate through the appointments power in Article II.[36] From a practical standpoint, appointments are much more important than the removal issue that the First Congress debated. If a president is to control the executive branch, the power to fill vacancies with compatible people is vital. Removal of those who turn out to be unfit or uncooperative is often blocked by political considerations, whatever the law might be.

President Washington found himself with about a thousand federal offices to fill. He saw that these offices provided the new federal government a way of reaching into the states—an opportunity to exert a nationalizing influence.[37] Throughout the Federalist era, no one could admit to a party affiliation in the modern sense. Washington operated on a nonpartisan basis, choosing people he knew or who were recommended by those he knew, and insisting only that nominees be "friends of the Constitution"— that is, no antifederalists need apply.[38] He consulted both senators and representatives about appointments within their constituencies. Washington was trying to maximize his influence in both Congress and the states. Delicacies about "corruption" were yielding to power politics. By 1801, the practice of consultation would be firmly established.[39]

The critical question about senatorial confirmation was whether it would be confined to a check on presidential discretion or instead would expand into a sharing of the initial power of choice. The laudable constitutional premise of confirmation is that it will produce better officers by installing a check on unilateral presidential selection. The possibility of deadlock was built in, however, since the Constitution provided no referee for a clash of presidential and senatorial wills. The political imperatives of patronage increased the natural interbranch tension because control of patronage builds power.

No one should be surprised that the Senate immediately found a way to allow its members to control presidential nominations in their home states. The practice now known as senatorial courtesy, in which the entire Senate defers to one of its member's objections to an appointment, emerged immediately. In August 1789, at the instance of a Georgia senator the Senate rejected a Washington nominee for port collector in Savannah. Boiling with frustration, the president entered the Senate chamber, rebuked the senators, and later said he regretted having gone there at all.[40] Surrendering to necessity, he then nominated someone else. Already the potential that individual senators might control the selection of nominees was manifest. The presence of the confirmation check, by dividing appointment power, had created the "two-headed monster" that Madison averted for removals.

The Senate as an Executive Council

During the process of forming the Constitution, concerns surfaced that the role of the Senate in advising and consenting to nominations and treaties would blur the separation of powers between the branches. For nominations, the practice of senatorial courtesy soon had that effect for some officers. For treaties, the blending of power might be more justifiable, because the Senate might be a wise advisory council on foreign relations, perhaps even playing an active role in negotiating treaties as well as approving them. Early in his presidency, George Washington explored this possibility. The results foreclosed an active role for the Senate in advising on treaty negotiations, shifting that power into the executive branch exclusively.

In the summer of 1789, President Washington and Secretary of War Henry Knox were formulating the new nation's initial policy regarding the Indian tribes. The two men shared a view that would later seem relatively advanced and humane, that Indian relations should be managed through purchase or treaty acquisition of land and not through brutal and uncompensated conquest.[41] They were also attempting to seize the initiative in forming Indian policy, leaving Congress in a reactive role.

Secretary Knox informed the president that he had drafted a treaty providing for a three-person commission to negotiate peace between the Creek Indians and Georgia.[42] Washington thought he should consult the Senate regarding the instructions for the envoys. Both the president and the Senate expected consultation to occur before the final terms of a treaty were set.[43] What ensued would foreclose any formal prior consultation of the Senate by presidents.

Armed with a message containing seven complex questions for the Senate, Washington proceeded to its chamber.[44] He gave the treaty papers to Vice President Adams (sitting in his constitutional role as president of the Senate). Adams read them, trying to make himself heard over street noise. The senators, who were unprepared to respond, began asking questions. More ominously, Senator Maclay, an early and determined opponent of Washington's, made a series of motions to obstruct or delay the provision of advice.

Eventually, after much discomfort all around, a proposal arose to refer the questions to a committee. This triggered an outburst of Washington's famous (and usually suppressed) temper. Declaring that "this defeats my every purpose in coming here," Washington stormed out of the chamber. He did return some days later and obtained the Senate's approval of sending the commissioners, but he never again sought its advice on treaty negotiations. Henceforth, presidents have communicated with the full Senate only in writing and usually only for its consent to treaties already negotiated.[45]

For institutional reasons, even the early Senate of twenty-six members was unsuited to a role as an advisory council. Four intrinsic problems were evident in the Creek treaty fiasco. First, the quality of advice depends on the information available to the adviser, but the executive branch cannot bring the Senate fully into its everyday activities. Second, because the Senate has always been far less hierarchical than the larger House of Representatives, harnessing it to a particular task is notoriously difficult. Third, the presence of the "loyal" opposition, personified by Maclay in 1789, makes confidentiality difficult to preserve and offers ample opportunities for obstructionism. Fourth, because senators have political bases independent of the president, he cannot control them as he can an executive council.

Washington was used to hierarchical military advice from generals who were loyal to him and fully acquainted with the facts. He could replicate that system within the executive branch but not in the Senate. Today's Senate, four times as large as the original body and a deeply fractured institution, cannot provide reliable, confidential, and cogent advice in advance of negotiations, even with the organizational advantages of the committee system. Washington had made a misstep, but he rapidly learned his lesson.

Creating the President's Legal Adviser

The process of creating, staffing, and operating the executive branch required a steady flow of constitutional interpretation within both Congress and the executive. (During the Federalist era, the Supreme Court was too weak and peripheral to provide more than occasional interpretive guidance.) As a many-headed institution, and one that soon exhibited party divisions, Congress has always found it difficult to formulate and follow a single, coherent line of legal analysis. A president can adopt a consistent legal theory, although maintaining it amid the stress of politics is a feat. The nature and quality of the legal advice that presidents consider has always depended on the internal structure of the executive branch.

While setting up the federal courts in the Judiciary Act of 1789, Congress gave the president an official legal adviser, the attorney general, who has always been charged to render legal advice to the president and other executive officers regarding the performance of their duties.[46] Modern Americans think of the attorney general as a member of the constitutional cabinet, the president's chief legal officer. Surprisingly, the creation of the office was ambiguous enough that it could have evolved quite differently than it has, with important changes in the nature of the legal advice that presidents receive. Before long, though, some decisions by George Washington placed the attorney general at his side, there to remain. The consequence was to assure presidents that their legal powers would be interpreted sympathetically, thereby encouraging presidents to view their powers broadly.

At first, it was not even clear whether attorneys general were exclusively executive officers or instead were legal officers for the entire government, who might report to all three branches. In separation of powers law, a fundamental way to determine which branch an officer serves is to identify who appoints the officer. The Judiciary Act did not say who would appoint the attorney general, and a draft of the bill that became the act would have assigned appointment authority to the Supreme Court.[47] In addition, the act neither labeled the office "executive" nor instructed the attorney general to take orders from the president, nor addressed the removal issue. Did Congress intend that legal advice to the executive branch be provided from outside the direct chain of command, to foster its objectivity? We cannot know, because Washington immediately moved to take custody of his legal adviser.

Washington asserted the constitutional power to appoint the attorney general by nominating his trusted personal lawyer, Edmund Randolph, to the office.[48] The Senate acquiesced by confirming him. Ever since, the attorney general has been treated as a principal executive officer to be nominated and confirmed in accordance with Article II of the Constitution. The selection of Randolph began a practice that has continued to the present: presidents ordinarily choose attorneys general from among their close personal and political supporters, obtaining the benefits of loyalty at the cost of bypassing distinguished strangers. This practice has increased the likelihood that presidents will rely on the advice of their attorneys general and has diminished the likelihood that the advice will be dispassionate.

Washington's assertion of the power to nominate the attorney general was a critical step in assuring the unity, autonomy, and vigor of the executive branch as a whole. When presidents propose to take actions that are constitutionally controversial, they need a supporting legal rationale to present to the nation. Official legal advice would now come from a sympathetic, "in-house" source and not from a disinterested outsider who might neither understand nor sympathize with the president's legal position. As we shall see, whether they are lawyers or not, presidents have proved quite willing to make constitutional judgments on their own, sometimes without asking anyone's advice. The nation is best served when the president receives legal advice in advance of a decision that is sympathetic and expert, yet within the bounds of the lawyers' professional responsibility.[49]

On issues of great importance Washington (like most of his successors) was prepared to seek the best legal advice he could get without worrying about departmental protocol, for the Judiciary Act did not obligate the president to ask the attorney general's advice about anything. This fact has led to an enduring delicacy in the relationships between presidents and their attorneys general. The cabinet is never short of able and aggressive lawyers who head other departments and are quite ready to provide legal analysis supporting presidential initiatives if the attorney general should resist.

Both of the two greatest legal issues of the Washington administration, the constitutionality of a national bank and of a proclamation of neutrality, illustrate these dynamics. In both cases, the president outlined the issues to his cabinet and patiently elicited and considered the competing arguments. Then Washington decided each of the controversies in favor of Alexander Hamilton's position (and in line with his own inclinations). Both decisions fundamentally expanded presidential power.

Constitutional Interpretation: Creating a Bank

Alexander Hamilton's proposal for a national bank was integral to his plan to place the finances of the new nation on a secure footing. In early 1790, he had proposed assuming the war debts of the states and fully funding them along with the federal debt. Here he was trying to tie the business community to the federal government, in the process building up both of them and pouring the foundations for a modern industrial nation. Hamilton succeeded to a remarkable extent. The funding plan passed after the famous deal in which the South agreed to support it if the new national capital were located on the Potomac. Next was the proposal for a national bank, which was to be a mixed public/private entity, with the government owning part of the stock. In an era of primitive banking, a national bank could secure federal funds, allow borrowing against expected revenues, and speed fund transfers. It would also serve Hamilton's broader goal of building a modern economy linked to the government.

The very idea of a national bank horrified Jefferson, who never understood banks and always hated them as a symbol of the kind of nation he was trying *not* to build. It was all much too British for his tastes. Moreover, as an advocate of limited federal power he knew that the constitutional argument that would be necessary to support the bank would support an indefinite and threatening expansion of national power. The enumerated powers of Congress do not include creating corporations. Therefore, a bank could be formed only if it were "necessary and proper" to serve Congress's explicit powers to tax, to regulate commerce, and so on.

This raised the great issue of the implied powers of the entire federal government. For wherever Congress could legislate, the courts could adjudicate and the executive could administer. And if Congress had enough implied power to create a bank, where would the argument stop? Questions about the constitutionality of federal support of internal improvements in the states would soon be debated, with a profoundly divisive question lurking in the background—the extent of federal power to interfere with slavery. The new nation had scarcely begun operations, and already the central issue of the reach of its powers was inescapably presented.

When the bill to incorporate the bank reached President Washington, he was troubled that James Madison had opposed it in the House of Representatives as not necessary and proper to implement Congress's enumerated powers. This was the moment of breach between the two men. Madison had played a critical role in building the new executive branch, but that did not entail controversial substantive choices about what the government would do. This project did.

Washington first asked the opinion of Attorney General Randolph, who produced two "rather rambling" and not very persuasive papers concluding that the incorporation of a bank would be unconstitutional.[50] Jefferson concurred. Washington then turned to Hamilton, who quickly produced a powerful forty-page opinion favoring a broad interpretation of the implied powers of Congress and supporting the bank bill.[51] Two days later, Washington signed the bill.

By approving the creation of the Bank of the United States, this president who was so conscious of precedent formed one of the most important ones in our history. He endorsed a broad view of national legislative powers under the necessary and proper clause, one that has dominated our history. Equally important, Washington's broad-construction approach to constitutional powers could be applied to executive as well as congressional powers and soon would be. A precedent of strict interpretation of the Constitution could have shipwrecked both political branches "in sight of the port."

Washington's decision to reject the legal advice of his attorney general did not result in Randolph's resignation over this basic issue of constitutional interpretation. If it had, there might have developed a tradition of resignations over principle by executive branch legal advisers in the United States. In Great Britain and other parliamentary nations, traditions of such resignations have evolved. The absence of this tradition in the United States has two effects. First, legal advisers have remained tied to the president, whose control over the executive is thereby enhanced. There are obvious associated costs, however, to general values of the rule of law and the transparency of presidential decisions. Second, and paradoxically, when such a resignation does occur (as during the Watergate scandal in 1973), its power to influence events is greater because of its rarity.

The history of the Bank also demonstrates how a precedent set by one president can affect decisions of his successors and decisions of the other branches as well. The Bank came up for reauthorization while James Madison was president. Despite his earlier constitutional opposition as a representative, he signed the bill, explaining that all three federal branches had treated the Bank as constitutional and it was too late for him to object.[52] Chief Justice Marshall then adopted the Hamiltonian view of implied powers in the course of his famous decision upholding the constitutionality of the Bank.[53] And when President Andrew Jackson later had the nerve to disagree with the constitutional opinions of Washington, Madison, and Marshall in explaining his famous veto of another bill to reauthorize the Bank, he expanded the president's veto power while dealing the government's legislative powers a sharp setback.[54]

The Emergence of Political Parties

The clash within the Washington administration over the bank bill stimulated the rise of open political parties in America.[55] The starkly differing visions of the nation's future between the main protagonists, Hamilton and Jefferson, could no longer be papered over by a pretense that all officers pursued a unitary public interest. Washington, however, still clung stubbornly to his republic of virtue. He never took partisan positions regarding congressional elections, and only in the second term would his cabinet reflect personal loyalty to him instead of collecting the leading figures of the day. But the new order was rising all around him.

Hamilton, a brilliant operator in the style of the new politics, saw that when Congress brought Treasury close to its operations, an opportunity arose for *him* to dominate *it*. To Jefferson's horror, he openly favored "corrupting" Congress by dealing in influence and reciprocal favors.[56] Jefferson, increasingly paranoid over Hamilton's supposed "phalanx" of the money interest, joined with Madison to begin organizing their Republican Party. Emerging Federalists responded heatedly. Each side saw the other as an illegitimate attempt to wreck the Revolution by creating either a British monarchy or a Jacobin democracy. All of the attributes of a modern nation like Great Britain went together in the minds of both sides: a substantial bureaucracy, a standing army, a large debt, a strong executive.

The possibility of an institutional political opposition to the administration was new to everyone, but Jefferson soon took a critical step to create one. In 1791 he sponsored a newspaper, the *National Gazette*, to articulate antiadministration arguments in opposition to the pro-Hamilton *Gazette of the United States*. Jefferson, who was always protected against his hypocrisy by the shield of his self-righteousness, thus sowed division from within the administration. The president, hating the conflict and knowing its sources, nonetheless appealed to Jefferson to stay on as secretary, to retain what Jefferson called the "check of my opinions in the administration."[57] In addition to this statesmanlike reason, Washington likely thought that Jefferson would be less an opponent inside than outside his cabinet. Eventually the stress became too great, and Jefferson resigned at the end of 1793 to await his time to seek the presidency under his own banner.

Neutrality and Presidential Direction of Foreign Policy

George Washington's greatest contributions to constitutional precedent concerned the constitutional allocations of power in foreign policy.[58] Above all, he "sure-handedly established the principle of Presidential direction of foreign policy."[59] He faced the challenge of leading a weak new nation with a miniscule army and navy in a world dominated by great powers. Washington had to balance the nation's treaty ties to France against its economic ties to Britain. Fortunately, he had an initial chance to put the new government on a secure footing—the period spanning the Constitution's framing and his first term was a rare interlude of peace in Europe. But from 1793 to 1812 the United States groped for a policy of workable neutrality in the Napoleonic Wars, while every step the administration took angered either Britain or France. Plainly a confrontation with either power would be extremely dangerous.

Washington quickly established precedents that would empower his direction of foreign policy. His reaction to the episode of the Creek Indian treaty prompted him to claim the power of initiative. Henceforth, the executive would negotiate with other nations and would present the Senate with a deal to accept, reject, or modify. The disadvantage of this sequential relationship was that the Senate would not be precommitted and could react unpredictably according to the politics of the moment.

Controlling negotiations requires controlling who negotiates. Washington set precedents that not all diplomatic agents have to be appointed with the Senate's consent. In October 1789, he made a unilateral decision to send Gouverneur Morris to Britain to sound out prospects for a commercial treaty. And when Congress formulated the first appropriation for the new State Department, the president had Secretary Jefferson argue that the executive, not Congress, should decide what grade of diplomat to send where. Jefferson articulated a strong view of foreign policy as executive in nature, and Congress acquiesced.[60] Eventually, presidents would unilaterally send all sorts of envoys overseas. If they could not do so, the effectiveness (and especially the secrecy) of executive branch initiatives in foreign policy would be greatly reduced.

Washington directed foreign policy personally, as would most of his successors. The neutrality crisis that broke out soon after revolutionary

France beheaded its king and went to war with Britain in 1793 provided him an opportunity to assert presidential power to develop foreign policy without asking for congressional directions in advance.[61] In the course of resolving the crisis, Washington set several fundamental precedents. He steered a careful middle course amid sharply conflicting arguments about both policy and law.[62]

On receiving reports of the war in April, Washington "inclined instantly toward neutrality."[63] Congress had adjourned until the new Third Congress would convene in December, however, and unless Washington called a special session he was on his own. Taking advantage of the window of opportunity, he did not call them. His reluctance to involve Congress doubtless stemmed from his unhappy memory of the Creek Indian consultation.

The European war presented a stark dilemma. The treaty with France dating from the Revolution required that the United States both protect French interests in the West Indies and allow the fitting out of privateers to raid British commerce. But the United States could not risk provoking Great Britain, the greatest naval power in the world. The Constitution did not specify which branch of the federal government should resolve the dilemma. Nothing in its text or history clearly authorized the president to make general determinations of foreign policy. Congress had the power to declare war, but could the president declare peace? Washington asserted no power to override any decision that Congress might later make, but he saw an immediate need to advise Americans and others about the stance of the executive branch, which could affect various legal rights and duties.

Inflaming the situation was the behavior of one of the least subtle diplomats in world history, the minister from the new government of France, Citizen Edmond Genet. He arrived in America in April 1793 and proceeded noisily toward Philadelphia, issuing calls for the United States to join the grand fight for liberty and giving out privateering commissions. He was trying to present the United States with a fait accompli, thrusting the nation into the war.

The rapidly shifting events impelled the president to change his method of consulting the cabinet. In the first term he had usually spoken with the members separately; now he convened them as a group, having circulated thirteen "sundry questions" about law and policy that had been drafted by Hamilton.[64] Everyone agreed that calling Congress into session was not necessary and that a proclamation preventing American citizens from interfering in the conflict was needed. With the two most important questions settled, Washington asked for written opinions on the remaining questions, which included the nation's obligations under international law and the status of the treaty with France.

The Anglophile Hamilton and the Francophile Jefferson clashed immediately. Neither thought the United States should go to war. Hamilton argued that the president should suspend the treaty with France and declare neutrality immediately. Jefferson held back, arguing that only Congress could decide—that the power to declare war included the power to determine neutrality. Hamilton and Jefferson debated in several intense meetings of the cabinet.

Washington took a characteristically cautious tack. He initially decided that the treaty remained in effect, thereby avoiding the tricky question of the president's power to suspend treaties, regarding which the Constitution is silent. At the same time, though, he was asserting an important kind of authority—to interpret treaties as part of his duty to implement them. Later presidents have continued to claim this interpretive authority, and within wide limits. In this case, Washington interpreted the treaty loosely enough to allow him to deny France any right to host privateers in America on grounds that it would be too provocative.

But what to do about Genet? Receiving ambassadors was among the president's explicit powers, but the constitutional text and history were ambiguous regarding whether this was simply a ceremonial power to receive diplomatic credentials or a substantive power to decide whether the United States would recognize the government issuing the credentials as legitimate.[65] Washington decided to receive Genet and to recognize the Republic as the government of France, as opposed to its royal predecessor. Ever since, presidents have successfully asserted that the reception power embodies full and exclusive authority to determine which claimant is the legal government of another nation, without asking Congress.[66]

Washington then settled on an immediate declaration of neutrality. Attorney General Randolph wrote the proclamation, avoiding the term "neutrality" to avoid offending Jefferson.[67] Instead, the president simply urged Americans to "pursue a conduct friendly and impartial toward the belligerent powers" and threatened prosecution of those who disobeyed. With publication of the proclamation, a disorderly public controversy erupted. Francophile newspapers charged Washington with violating the Constitution. Citizen Genet tried to appeal to the people over Washington's head, but by now he had thoroughly worn out his welcome. In August, Washington asked the French to recall him, and they made him a date with the guillotine.[68]

As the controversy boiled, Hamilton wrote seven "Pacificus" letters in the *Gazette*, defending Washington's actions.[69] He argued that the president is "the organ of intercourse between the nation and foreign nations" and is therefore the "interpreter of the national treaties." Hamilton carefully tied this conclusion to the various executive powers in Article II relating to foreign policy: the authority to negotiate treaties, to receive ambassadors, to command the military, and to execute the laws. He concluded sensibly that although Congress possesses the power to declare war, the executive has the duty "to preserve Peace till War is declared."

Hamilton also threw in a broader argument that was only loosely tethered to the actual text and structure of the Constitution. He claimed that Article II of the Constitution vests all power that is "executive" in nature in the president, limited only by specific provisions in the article, such as the Senate's right to consent to treaties. This "vesting clause" argument was unnecessary to Hamilton's case, but it has been invoked ever since when a president takes action without statutory authorization. The seductive power of the argument is that one can characterize almost any presidential action as executive, and if that power is exclusive, congressional power must be minimized lest it interfere with the president. This potential did not pass unnoticed at the time.

At Jefferson's prompting, Madison responded with five "Helvidius" articles, arguing that treaties are essentially legislative in nature and emphasizing the president's duty of faithful execution of all laws, including treaties. Madison's argument was a bit wooden—he did not recognize that powers can be concurrent, that the president might be allowed to take the initiative until Congress intervenes. Displaying his underlying concern, Madison urged prophetically that war is the "true nurse of executive aggrandizement." Hence Madison's fear was not that presidents would rush into neutrality but the opposite, that they would rush into war.

This exchange in the press overlaid the political debate with a constitutional one. The essential positions of Hamilton and Madison on the issues of implied and exclusive executive powers have framed the debate ever since. President Washington did not say what his theory was in issuing the proclamation (nor had he done so in signing the bank bill). He did display a cautious adherence to international law by declining to suspend the treaty. In fact, Washington never took an action that could have rested only on Hamilton's loose vesting clause argument.[70]

Issuing the Neutrality Proclamation created as many legal problems as it resolved regarding the duties of impartiality. In July, Washington had

Secretary of State Jefferson write a letter to the Supreme Court, asking a series of twenty-nine questions about treaty interpretation.[71] The letter assured the justices that they could decline to answer any particular questions that the prospect of future litigation might "forbid them to pronounce on." Chief Justice Jay knew that the Constitutional Convention had rejected a proposal to grant the federal courts an advisory opinion power like those of some states. Moreover, answers to hypotheticals might bind the Court in later cases. When the Court met, it turned down the request, pointing to its own role as the court of last resort and to the president's explicit power to obtain opinions from his department heads.[72] Subsequently, the president issued detailed executive orders interpreting the nation's international obligations.[73]

Ever since the neutrality controversy, the Supreme Court has adhered to the doctrine that it will not issue advisory opinions, that it will only decide concrete cases. Thus the possibility that the Court might become an advisory council to the executive on legal issues disappeared. It was a mistake for Washington to have asked for the Court's advice. He had already seen the Senate's capacity to be a captious advisor about policy. It is hard to believe that the Supreme Court, lacking political sensitivity, would have become a good sounding board for abstract questions of law, which are never free of political ramifications.

When the new Congress convened the following December, it praised Washington's conduct in the crisis. The president came over and delivered a speech to both houses explaining that the Neutrality Proclamation reflected his duty to keep the peace, summarizing his other actions, calling delicately for legislation to address the various consequences of the war in Europe, and promising his "warmest co-operation."[74] The Senate purred that it "contemplate[d] with pleasure the proclamation you promulgated, and give it our hearty approbation."[75] While ratifying the proclamation, Congress was also asserting its right to approve and control executive action, albeit retrospectively. The centerpiece of its legislative response was the Neutrality Act of 1794, which made neutrality violations federal crimes.[76] Washington's resolution of the neutrality crisis had received a full airing and ratification both among the people and in Congress, thereby setting a solid, enduring precedent.

The European war that initiated the neutrality crisis also resulted in the first prominent example of another presidential constitutional power, the executive agreement.[77] Although the Constitution provides an explicit process for entering treaties, it says nothing about less formal pacts between the United States and other nations. Nonetheless, it has always been necessary to arrange some international relations through simple exchanges of correspondence that are not submitted to the Senate for ratification. For example, the first executive agreements under the Constitution provided for the international delivery of mail. If all such matters were submitted to the Senate, that body would be overwhelmed, and the speedy and flexible conduct of foreign relations would be impossible.

Hence, all American presidents have made many executive agreements with other nations. The problem is one of limits—when does this technique impair the Senate's right to consider treaties? That question would eventually arise, but not at the nation's outset. The potential for agreements to affect the rights of American citizens was soon evident, however. During the war, an American ship, the *Wilmington Packet*, was seized by a Dutch privateer, raising issues of the ownership of her cargo under international law.[78] The American owners persuaded the Washington administration to press their case for return of their property with the Dutch, and the Adams administration finally reached a settlement. It was the first of many claims settlements by executive agreement.

Protecting Presidential Papers

When one of the houses of Congress requests documents in the hands of the executive branch, may the president refuse to provide them? The Constitution is silent regarding both congressional powers of investigation and presidential power to control documents. George Washington set precedents about this delicate aspect of congressional relations that still provide essential guidance. In some early episodes, the president asserted that he possessed discretion to withhold especially sensitive documents, although he gave Congress what it had requested.[79] Congress appeared to agree with the principle that the president could withhold some secret documents, such as selected correspondence relating to treaty negotiations, but it also displayed a willingness to use its levers regarding appropriations and treaty ratification to force disclosure.

The first prominent controversy over the executive privilege issue concerned the Jay Treaty in 1796. Washington had dispatched Chief Justice Jay to London to try to reach a settlement of issues that had festered ever since the peace treaty that ended the Revolutionary War.[80] Because Republicans were outraged at the very idea of a deal with the hated British, Jay's return with a treaty caused a political crisis even before its terms were known. The Senate debated and ratified it in secret. To show its irritation at being excluded from the treaty's negotiation, the Senate deleted some provisions. Ever since, the Senate has felt free to do so, and presidents take or leave what is left, adopting or abandoning the altered treaty as they see fit.

Jay, in a weak bargaining position, had extracted few concessions from the British. As Washington considered whether to sign the treaty, the terms leaked. Amid the furor, Jay's effigy burned brightly in many places. Washington then signed the treaty to restore peace abroad and at home. He had bought the nation "the priceless commodity of time."[81]

Hoping to embarrass the president, Republicans in the House of Representatives adopted a resolution calling for all documents relating to the Jay Treaty except for "such papers as any existing negotiations may render improper to disclose."[82] Of course, the House lacks any formal role in the treaty process. Therefore, the basis of the inquiry was the need for appropriations to implement the treaty. There were two distinct issues: whether papers held in confidence by the executive could be forcibly obtained by anyone, and the narrower question of the special institutional interests of the House. Washington's response touched on both issues, but wisely emphasized the latter.

Washington's message denied that the House had power to "demand, and to have as a matter of course, all the Papers respecting a negotiation with a foreign power."[83] This, said Washington, "would be to establish a dangerous precedent," because of the need to preserve the secrecy of negotiations. He was, however, willing to share the papers with the Senate, and did so. Later presidents have consistently tried to shield the secrecy of treaty negotiations.

President Washington also argued that it would be unconstitutional to give the House a role in the treaty process. He claimed that Congress had already acquiesced in this position, because the House had not previously asserted any right to participate in treaty formation. Perhaps realizing the weakness of an acquiescence argument so early in the nation's history, he added an interesting argument invoking the original intent of the Constitution's framers. His message reminded the House that he had presided at the Convention and asserted that the absence of an explicit role for the House in the treaty process was intentional. Madison, responding in the House, rejected the relevance of the Convention: it had produced "nothing but a dead letter, and life and validity were breathed into it by the voice of the people." There is a rich irony here. While the framers inhabited our government, they sometimes cited their own recollection of the Convention and sometimes denied the relevance of what occurred there to constitutional interpretation. They were quite inconsistent in doing so—they tended to support the position that advanced their political needs of the moment.[84]

For a time, the House continued to threaten to use its plenary power to deny appropriations for the treaty. The Senate, strongly Federalist, countered by threatening to delay other business until the House cooperated. Eventually a political sea change in favor of the treaty occurred, and the House voted narrowly to appropriate the funds. No definitive resolution of the underlying constitutional issue had occurred.

To this day the question of the constitutional status of executive privilege as a defense to congressional demands for information remains unresolved. The outcome of any particular controversy depends, as did the one over the Jay Treaty papers, on the ebb and flow of political power. Sometimes the president prevails; sometimes Congress extracts the papers. In our system, some relationships endure for a long time. This early controversy also revealed both the characteristic protectiveness of presidents toward their institutional prerogatives and the hesitancy that Congress often displays about both its entitlement to executive papers and the wisdom of pressing hard to obtain them.

Internal Security

On two subjects involving the internal security of the nation, Washington set precedents by exerting executive power in a restrained way. Not all of his successors would be so careful. Washington's most serious domestic crisis was the Whiskey Rebellion in 1794, a reaction to the first serious federal tax, which was imposed on whiskey as part of Hamilton's funding plan.[85] On the frontier, whiskey was a basic article of both consumption and exchange. Farmers in western Pennsylvania counties defied the hated tax, terrorized the revenue officers, closed the courts, and marched on Pittsburgh with about seven thousand men. The challenge to the authority of the federal government was direct.

President Washington proceeded cautiously. He issued two proclamations condemning the unrest and threatening strict enforcement of the law. He also sent out a futile peace commission. After it failed, his patience exhausted, Washington invoked his statutory powers and called up fifteen thousand militia, a very large force at the time, to serve under his personal command. He was drawing on his own immense military prestige. He explained that the rebellion threatened "the very existence of Government, and the fundamental principles of social order."[86] He was not willing to trifle with *that* challenge. With Washington personally at its head, the Army quickly quelled the rebellion.

The president's cautious and incremental response to the Whiskey Rebellion stemmed from his appreciation of the sensitivity of the states to receiving orders from the new federal government. Before he could call up the state militias, he had to assure himself that they would come. The new national government could not easily have withstood a confrontation with the state governments.[87]

In the wake of the rebellion, two of its leaders were convicted of treason and pardoned by Washington. This was an initial instance of a common use of the pardon power—to bind the nation together by forgiving rebels against its authority.[88] John Adams would do the same thing with the leaders of Fries's Rebellion some years later. In both cases, citizens had been convicted of treason for armed resistance to federal statutes. If that use of the treason statute had become accepted, it might have led to broad suppression of civil liberties in times of unrest. Thus the pardon power can confine the reach of the criminal law in ways essential to the health of the nation.[89]

In another effort to heal the wounds left by the Whiskey Rebellion, President Washington supported and signed legislation to compensate those who had suffered property damage in the disruptions.[90] This began a long national tradition of providing relief to Americans who had suffered disasters through no fault of their own. The constitutional basis was congressional power to tax and spend to "provide for the . . . general Welfare of the United States."[91]

The second important issue of internal security was Indian policy. In partnership with Secretary of War Henry Knox, Washington made Indian policy and varied its stringency.[92] Although Congress sometimes participated, the president felt quite free to set a general course without its authorization. Sadly, the Creek Indian treaty of 1789 presaged the sorrows to come. The treaty's promise to protect remaining Creek lands in return for the lands surrendered was soon undone by the Yazoo frauds and the refusal of either Georgia citizens or their state government to abide the treaty's terms. The federal government was never able to control either settlers on the frontier or recalcitrant states like Georgia, and the harsher policies of Andrew Jackson lay not far ahead.

Legacy

Historians often say that among George Washington's many legacies, his "most important act" was his decision to relinquish the presidency at the end of two terms.[93] Certainly his decision voluntarily to retire produced astonishment around the world and joy for friends of limited government. The history of the world is dark regarding the renunciation of power. With Washington's retirement, it might even be that the new nation would become what it claimed to be, a republic of limited and distributed powers. The two-term tradition immediately became firm enough that no successor dared defy it until Franklin Roosevelt did so in 1940, in the midst of a world war. Of course, no one who knew Washington well should have been surprised. All Americans have benefited in some unknown measure from his example of voluntarily surrendering power.

Preparing to retire, Washington issued his Farewell Address to stress themes he wanted his countrymen to consider.[94] He emphasized the duty of all Americans to obey the rule of law. His presidency had adhered carefully to the Constitution as he best understood it.[95] This was an absolutely vital precedent, because no later president would feel free to abandon the duties of law and to seize all power based on some vague claim of the national interest. Too many republics with bright beginnings have suffered that fate.

The address also stressed Washington's hopes to bind the newly independent republic into a genuine nation. In his time—and until the Civil War—the term "United States" was conventionally treated as a plural noun: "the United States are . . ." He had done all he could to foster nationhood. As would many later Americans including Abraham Lincoln, he used the term "Union" as a synonym for nation—the closest one could come without offending states' rights sensitivities.[96] He knew the project was unfinished but was clear about his hopes.

Regarding nationhood, Washington and all of his successors until Lincoln suffered a tragic failure. Above all, it was slavery that stood between a plural and a singular United States. No antebellum president had the courage or the capacity to address this fatal flaw in the nation's composition. (Washington himself and all of his slave-owning successors brought household slaves to their official residence until 1850.) All of the various compromises about the admission of new states merely deferred the slavery question to the future. Of course, the original Constitution clearly allowed and protected slavery, although it never used that repellent word.

During Washington's presidency, there was a moment of opportunity that tantalizes us. In 1790, the first antislavery petitions reached Congress. The dying Benjamin Franklin had signed one from the Quakers. Washington's cautious response was that they were premature—the issue was too sensitive in a fledgling government.[97] It is easy to understand his judgment on this point, but one wonders, what *could* he have done—what precedent could he have set for his successors that would have ameliorated slavery for the present and set it on the way to extinction? Many of the framers naively allowed themselves to believe that slavery would naturally expire in an expanding republic, at the very time that the institution was becoming too entrenched to eliminate short of war. If a man of Washington's immense prestige lacked the courage to address this issue in any other way than freeing his own slaves in his will, we cannot be surprised that his successors would do no better.

Limited War

As president, John Adams found himself in the unenviable position of succeeding an icon. Adams was a proud and prickly man, full of principle and integrity, but without great political gifts.[98] He had no executive experience prior to the presidency and was out of the loop in the Washington administration. He was the most prolific writer about political theory among the framers. He began with the British model of mixed government and adapted it to a republic. He saw the need for a strong executive to mediate between the representatives of the few and the many in the legislature. Because of his Anglophilia, a reputation as a monarchist dogged him.

The two most important precedents of the Adams presidency involved the successful conduct of limited war overseas and an unfortunate attempt to suppress domestic dissent. The quasi war with France occurred because once the Jay Treaty became public, France retaliated by seizing American ships and cargoes.[99] Adams called the first special session of Congress to respond. Eventually, Congress would lay an embargo on trade, grant authority to attack French ships, build a navy, and raise a temporary army.

Together, these actions amounted to a declaration of limited war against France. The Constitution contemplates such hostilities by empowering Congress to "grant letters of Marque and Reprisal," a now archaic phrase that refers to authorizing privateers to attack enemy ships, a step short of full national engagement. Limited wars have occurred ever since, in many cases solely at presidential initiation. This initial one was a joint effort.

Fearing a possibly unlimited war in 1797, Adams followed the example of the Jay mission to Britain by sending a delegation to France to repair the breach. Washington's leftover cabinet, which Adams had unwisely retained, undermined him by pressing for war at the urging of Hamilton, who was then in (not very) private life. Adams's vice president, Jefferson, also undermined him by supporting the French. Adams grimly resisted escalating the hostilities.

When the delegation (which included John Marshall) returned without a deal, Republicans in Congress gleefully demanded the papers of the failed mission. Adams sprung a trap by handing over the papers. They revealed that the ineffable French foreign minister, Talleyrand, had demanded bribes through agents listed as X, Y, and Z in the records. The Americans had refused; they were immediately hailed as heroes. The XYZ episode showed how presidents can manipulate the release of secrets in their possession for political advantage. The lesson would not be lost on Adams's successors. Eventually, another mission succeeded in obtaining a treaty. Adams had successfully defended American interests short of outright war.

President Adams also resolved a ticklish controversy with Great Britain. In the process he created a precedent about presidential power that has been debated in modern times.[100] In 1800, the British requested extradition of one Jonathan Robbins, whom they alleged to be a deserter from the Royal Navy. Adams had to make two kinds of routine and important determinations. First, he had to determine the facts in a preliminary way: was there enough evidence against Robbins to confirm the bona fides of the British request? Second, he had the legal task of interpreting the extradition provisions of the Jay Treaty. Adams decided that he should return Robbins to the British.[101]

A partisan furor erupted in the House. John Marshall, then a representative, articulated the Adams administration's argument in a famous speech in which he referred to the president as "the sole organ of the nation in its external relations, and its sole representative with foreign nations."[102] In context, this statement merely asserted that it is the president who communicates with other nations, after making the determinations of mixed fact and law that Adams had made in this instance. Lifted from context, however, the statement can be read to claim that the president enjoys hegemonic control of foreign policy, free of constraint by Congress. Lifted it would be, as we shall see. For present purposes, it is enough to say that Marshall made no such claim and that the president's actions in the Robbins affair were well within existing precedents set by the Federalist administrations.

Sedition

A less happy story is the enactment and enforcement of the Alien and Sedition Acts of 1798.[103] This legislation, which surrendered to hysteria about alien plots and domestic subversion at the height of the French crisis, has been regarded by posterity as unconstitutional and a great blot on the nation's record of protecting civil liberties. At the time, the constitutionality of repressing dissent was unsettled. Federalists loathed both the swarming French and Irish immigrants and the abusive Republican press. It does Adams no credit that he supported the legislation in the interests of protecting national security. In his defense, however, it is true that the nation was in the throes of defining the nature and limits of dissent as part of its adjustment to the reality of party politics. Also, the likelihood of irrational fears of foreign-inspired plots to subvert the government should not be dismissed by anyone who recalls the Cold War.

The legislation allowed the president to summarily expel any alien he deemed to be "dangerous" to America's peace and safety. There was some objection in Congress to giving the president this arbitrary power and to the due process violations it threatened. In the event, no one was deported, but some aliens fled the country. It thus appeared that in times of perceived crisis, Congress might be receptive to writing blank checks for presidents.

More notorious, and more vigorously employed, was the Sedition Act. It responded to the first mass media in our history, the Republican papers that organized political opposition to the administration and ran inflamed articles condemning its policies. Benjamin Bache of the *Aurora* understood what the Adams administration did not, the role of the press as a "constitutional check upon the conduct of public servants."[104] We now take that role for granted as a fundamental control on democratic government. At the end of the eighteenth century, Americans from the president on down were just beginning to glimpse it.

The Sedition Act was both oppressive and obviously partisan. It prohibited "false, scandalous, and malicious" speech that defamed various high government officials, including the president and Congress (but not the vice president, who was the Republican Jefferson!). This definition codified the common law doctrine of seditious libel, with the improvement that it required proof of falsity, as the common law did not. The act was to expire the day before the next inaugural. Its enforcement produced seventeen indictments and ten convictions. Some Republican newspapers were shut down, but more sprang up and opposition soared. Clear signs emerged that suppression is not an effective tool for controlling the press in a republic.

At the end of his term, John Adams set two kinds of lasting precedents on the power to nominate judges. In its last months the Adams administration rushed "midnight" legislation expanding the federal judiciary through Congress, and Adams then filled all the new posts.[105] This initial use of the nomination power in a partisan fashion set an example that some but not all of Adams's successors would emulate.

More important, by one of his late choices Adams unwittingly demonstrated the potential for judicial appointments to let a president's constitutional values throw a very long shadow into the future. After casting around for a while, Adams nominated John Marshall, his secretary of state, to be chief justice. The president was certainly aware of Marshall's brilliance, but he could not know that he had selected the nation's greatest chief justice, who would serve for thirty-four years and die in office in the age of Jackson. His successor, Roger Taney, then nearly matched that tenure and died during the Civil War. These two legal giants had more influence on American law and history than many a president (for both good and ill) and far longer tenures than any of them. Given the stakes, what is surprising is not that modern confirmation battles over Supreme Court nominations are so sharp but that it took so long for them to become so.

Overall, the two Federalist presidents gave the office they held a sound and honorable basis. They represented a dying era of elitist politics, though. Strong democratic forces unleashed by the Revolution and the stunning growth and development of the nation swept the Federalists aside. How would a Republican president redefine the office? The immensely gifted and complex Thomas Jefferson turned to that task at the dawn of the nineteenth century.

CHAPTER THREE

The Fugitive Occurrence

Jefferson and Madison

The Executive in seizing the fugitive occurrence which so much advances the good of their country, have done an act beyond the Constitution. The Legislature in casting behind them metaphysical subtleties, and risking themselves like faithful servants, must ratify & pay for it, and throw themselves upon their country for doing for them unauthorized, what we know they would have done for themselves had they been in a situation to do it. . . . But we shall not be disavowed by the nation, and their act of indemnity will confirm & not weaken the Constitution, by more strongly marking out its lines.—Thomas Jefferson's justification for the Louisiana Purchase[1]

A s a simply dressed Thomas Jefferson strolled from his boarding-house to the new Capitol for his inauguration in March 1801, there was much on his deep and intricate mind.[2] His careful emphasis on proper republican simplicity symbolized his genuine view that the federal government in general and the presidency in particular should be limited in power, especially as compared to the monarchical Federalists who had preceded him. Yet his conduct in office would oscillate between actions that did implement his vision and other actions that expanded both the government he headed and the office he held beyond anything in his predecessors' imaginations. Except for Washington, "Jefferson was more aware than any other president of the importance of precedent."[3] Therefore, it would undoubtedly have dismayed him deeply to know that among the precedents he set, those expanding executive power have endured and the limitations have withered.

The reason for this precedential asymmetry lies in the nature of both Jefferson's theories and his actions. His theories, even when employed temporarily for limited ends, contained the seeds of much broader assertions of power, as his successors would realize. And his actions were often substantially more aggressive than they seemed at the time, so that repetition by others expanded presidential power.

Confirming the Revolution

The constitutional crisis that followed Thomas Jefferson's election in 1800 led to a fundamental transformation of the presidency, one that went largely unappreciated at the time—except by Jefferson himself. The election of 1800 produced an accidental tie in the Electoral College between Jefferson and vice presidential candidate Aaron Burr. After some drama, the House of Representatives settled the issue in favor of Jefferson.[4] During the crisis, Jefferson made the accurate claim that he was the people's choice for president—a claim pregnant with the suggestion that presidents represent the American people generally (rather than a majority of the Electoral College) and are uniquely positioned to embody their wishes.[5]

The underlying defect, the failure of the original Constitution to require electors to designate separate candidates for the presidency and vice presidency (so that the two victorious Republican candidates tied), was speedily repaired by the Twelfth Amendment.[6] The nature of the repair would link future presidents more directly to the American people, increasing presidential power and decreasing that of Congress. The framers had supposed that the Electoral College would be an actual deliberating body and that electors in the states would likely cast their two votes for some local favorite and a distinguished national figure, whereupon the House of Representatives would often make the final selection among several leading contenders.

Once the Twelfth Amendment required designation of a presidential preference by the electors, the way was clear for a candidate to campaign nationally, seeking a mandate of the people in defiance of the elitist eighteenth-century expectations of the framers.[7] Jefferson, understanding this potential, began transforming the presidency into the tribunate of the people, with all the augmentation in the power of the office that the change implied.

The Twelfth Amendment contained a latent flaw regarding the vice presidency, however. As the party system matured in the years after Jefferson left office, presidential candidates acquired an incentive to pick running mates who were not political clones of themselves, in order to appeal to broad segments of their party and the public. This meant that when a president died, he would likely be replaced by someone with a different political orientation, and perhaps markedly so. Thus the unhappy transition at the time of the death of a president might lead to a much different constitutional orientation in the successor as well.

A Republic of Virtue

Three features of Thomas Jefferson's first inaugural address strike the eye today; each requires a bit of explanation to recover his full meaning.[8] First, he said that the United States would have the "strongest" government on earth—not because it would be the most powerful but because, unlike foreign despotisms, it would possess a virtuous government drawing strength from the people. Second, both at the beginning and the end of the address, he clearly tied his presidency directly to the people as a whole, in a way no Federalist would have done (because in their view the Constitution refracted the people's will through several layers of representation).[9] This explains the third and most famous feature of the address, the claim that "we are all republicans; we are all federalists." This arresting statement, often understood as an olive branch for the defeated opposition, was in fact an assertion that Jefferson intended to return to the first principles of the Revolution as he saw them—that a limited federal government should receive everyone's allegiance.[10]

Paradoxically, Jefferson thought that only a strong chief executive could produce an appropriately restrained federal government that would serve the agrarian empire of liberty he envisioned.[11] (Two of his transformative successors, Jackson and Reagan, would see the same need for strong executive activity in pursuit of individual liberty.) He "aimed to devise a government too weak to aid the wolves, but strong enough to protect the sheep."[12] All of this was in service of a rather gauzy political philosophy that engaged in a pragmatic search for the public good, freed of the Federalist emphasis on adhering to tradition.[13]

Jefferson treated the Constitution as an evolving document. In 1816, years after his presidency ended, he praised the framers but remarked that the era "was very like the present, but without the experience of the present: and 40 years of experience in government is worth a century of book-reading: and this they would say themselves."[14] He was also explicit about his efforts to shape the presidential office by the precedents he generated. By 1805, he was saying that he would not seek a third term as president, noting that Washington had set the example and that "a few more precedents will oppose the obstacle of habit" to anyone tempted to go on.[15]

What Jefferson never admitted to anyone (including himself) was the internal contradiction at the heart of his vision.[16] As Americans spread across a continent that remained largely wilderness in 1800, they needed the aid of an active federal government to protect them from internal and foreign hazards, even if the government was performing relatively few functions other than protecting national security. As president, Jefferson was drawn into an active role despite his conflicted reaction to it. (Jackson, in contrast, would heartily embrace it.)

The needs of the people as Jefferson saw them induced him to take bolder actions than either of his predecessors. More darkly, Jefferson showed much less respect for the rule of law than had Washington or Adams. He thought his political goals must be lawful, since they were so evidently in the public interest. The views of judges on such large matters rarely impressed him. Instead, the constraint that mattered was Jefferson's own sense of limits, one always subject to his characteristic "willingness to put aside his scruples to achieve his goals."[17]

Modifying Practices, Reversing Policies

Once he took office, Jefferson continued the firm and decisive managerial style that Washington had successfully initiated.[18] Having been in the Washington administration at the outset, he had absorbed its organizational lessons.[19] Like his great predecessor, Jefferson kept himself fully informed about government policy and held the reins of the executive branch in his own hands. Having also witnessed the chaos of Adams's disloyal cabinet, he exerted close control over his own and kept its original membership stable during his presidency. Although he relied greatly on his secretary of the treasury, Albert Gallatin, and his secretary of state, James Madison, it was always clear that the president was in charge.

At the same time, Jefferson struck out beyond Federalist precedents on a number of fronts that would enhance later presidencies. On two related topics, patronage and congressional relations, the developing political system required Jefferson to deploy all of his considerable subtlety. Because frankly partisan political activity was still forbidden by the fiction of a unified public interest, Jefferson could not simply remove all existing Federalist officers and replace them with Republicans. He understood, though, that time was on his side. Therefore, he left most Federalists in place, at least if they had the good sense to avoid opposing him openly.[20] As vacancies occurred, he chose his adherents to fill them, saying he was seeking only a "proportionate share" of the spoils of office.[21]

Jefferson's allies in Congress were also interested in patronage but had to press their views quietly and did not always get their way.[22] Soon enough, good Republicans abounded in the executive branch. The first, tentative step had been taken away from the elitist meritocracy of the Federalists and toward a spoils system that would tie the bureaucracy to the president with threads of loyalty.

Jefferson understood the importance of presidential management of legislation, but had to avoid traditionalist charges of "corrupting" Congress. (Indeed, he had made just that charge against Alexander Hamilton during passage of the nation's initial fiscal program.) Tension existed between the Constitution's explicit empowerment of the president to "recommend to [Congress's] Consideration such Measures as he shall judge necessary and expedient" and the formalities that the framing generation thought were required by the separation of powers more generally. The Federalist presidents had been quite passive, pointing out problems but not making specific proposals except through surrogates, such as Treasury Secretary Hamilton.

To approach this problem, Jefferson made best use of his nonconfrontational and secretive character.[23] He honored the formalities by remaining aloof from Congress as a body, never appearing before it in person and confining himself to written communications. Meanwhile, he quietly began to develop the important presidential role of party leader for the legislative agenda.[24] He worked with congressmen in small groups, for example by hosting a series of dinners for the leaders. He wanted to hold a "constant conversation" with the lawmakers.[25] This hidden-hand technique proved very effective in steering legislation through Congress: "Congress not only passed virtually all of his recommendations; it passed virtually no bills of any significance without his recommendation or tacit approval."[26]

Turning the Hamiltonian precedent to his own advantage, Jefferson had Treasury Secretary Gallatin draw up legislation for submission through friends in Congress. Eventually, Jefferson influenced Congress through a combination of a powerful Speaker of the House, friendly floor managers, and party caucuses. He developed these techniques because he sought fundamental alteration in federal policy, and that required legislative revision. No future president could hope to be powerful if he or she failed to maximize the recommending power that Jefferson energized for the first time.

Ironically, after Jefferson left office, the changes he sponsored in Congress were turned against his weaker successors in a period of congressional dominance. It is risky for those who invent tools to lay them down. Later presidents would pick them back up.

Thus Jefferson replaced the old personal politics of the Federalists with the initial mechanisms of a party machine.[27] Reviled or not, parties were necessary to operating the government of a nation that was evolving from an elitist republic to a popular democracy. Building and controlling the party was also essential to making the president a direct representative of the people in more than the ceremonial capacity that attended the role of head of state. Jefferson, by initiating and invigorating the role of the president as head of party, took a long step toward creating the modern presidency.

Meanwhile, Jefferson's substantive policies pointed to a diminished executive at the head of a much-shrunken government.[28] Here the elements of his thinking that emphasized distrust of government and the pursuit of liberty dominated.[29] He immediately set out to reduce the size of the government toward the old Confederation model instead of the British one that the Federalists had admired. In general, he wanted everything except external affairs and matters common to all states to be left to the state governments, which he admired. Therefore, in partnership with Congress he reduced the federal bureaucracy and cut the military budget in half. Fearing future executive adventuring, he disliked the offensive capacities of armies and navies but trusted the defensive tools of militias and gunboats. He eliminated the despised excise taxes, leaving the federal government with almost no impact on the daily life of citizens except for the post office. He shrank the public debt for the same reason that Hamilton had created it—that it built an industrial nation and the federal government simultaneously. All Jefferson could see was that the debt fed the "corrupt" practices of entwined governmental and private interests that he so detested. (Republican successors all tried to retire the debt until Jackson finally did so in his last year in office.) By the time Jefferson left office, the government was "weaker than at any other time in its history."[30]

All of this vigorous pruning was fundamentally transitory, however. Because the changes were made by ordinary legislation, they could be undone when national needs changed—as would happen in Jefferson's second term. Moreover, the essential structure of the executive branch, which the Federalists had created, was left intact for later reinvigoration.[31] Jefferson had demonstrated that with a supportive Congress, a new president can grow or shrink the government and his own branch and can reverse policy within broad limits. Thus, with the rise of parties and informal links between the branches, the American government became more parliamentary in operation than it is in theory whenever the same party holds both political branches.

Departmentalism in Action

As Jefferson turned to reversing the most hated Federalist legacy, the Sedition Act, he developed a theory that has justified broad presidential power ever since. The act expired as Jefferson took office as president—no retaliation against Federalist "sedition" would be possible.[32] Unfinished business remained, however. Ten Republican newspapermen had been convicted and fined under the act, and one prosecution was still pending. Jefferson ordered the federal district attorney to stop the prosecution, pardoned those convicted, and convinced Congress to repay the fines. He argued that the act was a constitutional "nullity" because the First Amendment forbade Congress to legislate regarding the press.

A lot was going on in this seemingly simple episode. First, Jefferson was viewing the pardon power as plenary in nature—his to use as he chose, free of interference from anyone in government. Precedents like this one have led modern Americans to view pardons that way.[33] The ameliorative effect of the pardon power on the rigors of the criminal law had already shown itself in pardons by the Federalist presidents. The attractiveness of the Sedition Act pardons to later sensibilities about freedom of the press has buttressed an unhindered form of the power.

Second, Jefferson's refusal to enforce the Sedition Act on grounds that it was unconstitutional has been vindicated. The act's notoriety as a historical precedent has led the modern Supreme Court to declare that although the act "was never tested in this Court, the attack against its validity has carried the day in the court of history."[34] Thus Jefferson's use of his powers to negate enforcement of the act is an important precedent demonstrating the capacity of presidents to instruct the nation about constitutional values generally, shaping constitutional law through the verdicts of history.

Third, presidential intervention in a pending criminal prosecution has always been a very sensitive matter, and for good reason. It is true that the faithful execution duty requires presidential oversight of federal prosecution generally. Yet intervention in a particular case carries a strong potential for improper influence from political pressures that are extraneous to the legitimate grounds for prosecution. Here Jefferson was on solid ground because of his strong claim that any prosecution was unconstitutional. Had that claim been absent, the people's interest in effective prosecution would have weighed much more in the balance.

Presidential intervention in prosecution is most damaging when it is used to hound individuals, infringing their constitutional right to due process. Late in his presidency, Jefferson amply demonstrated this potential in his pursuit of Aaron Burr for treason.[35] The president announced Burr's guilt in advance of the trial and actively pressed the prosecutors forward without much regard for the evidence (which remains inconclusive to this day). Only the firmness of Chief Justice Marshall, presiding at the trial, prevented a possible miscarriage of justice and a dangerous precedent for using the law of treason to punish a president's political enemies.

Jefferson's resistance to the Sedition Act revealed his stance on the president's power to interpret the Constitution independently of Congress and the judiciary. He well knew that President Adams and the enacting Congress believed the act to be constitutional, as did the federal judges who upheld convictions under it. None of that mattered to him. In a famous letter to Abigail Adams, Jefferson explained himself:

> You seem to think it devolved on the judges to decide on the validity of the sedition law. But nothing in the Constitution has given them a right to decide for the Executive, more than to the Executive to decide for them. Both magistracies are equally independent in the sphere of action assigned to them. The judges, believing the law constitutional, had a right to pass a sentence of fine or imprisonment; because that power was placed in their hands by the Constitution. But the Executive, believing the law to be unconstitutional, was bound to remit the execution of it; because that power has been confided to him by the Constitution. That instrument meant that its co-ordinate branches should be checks on each other. But the opinion which gives to the judges the right to decide what laws are constitutional, and what not, not only for themselves in their

own sphere of action, but for the Legislature & executive also, in their spheres, would make the judiciary a despotic branch.[36]

This is a classic statement of "departmentalism," the theory that each of the three branches has the right—and the obligation—to interpret the Constitution for itself. As the Sedition Act controversy demonstrates, some version of departmentalism is intrinsic to any system of semiautonomous branches sharing power. That is, before any branch can take its assigned role in resolving any problem of public policy, it must generate an internal opinion about its own constitutional duty in the matter. This had happened with the Sedition Act: Congress enacted it, President Adams signed it, and the federal courts enforced it. If any of the three branches had thought the act unconstitutional, it would never have gone into effect.

Now we can see the implications of Jefferson's argument to Abigail Adams. He was declaring independence (he was good at that) in a limited way from all three branches—Congress, the courts, and his own predecessor. His declaration was limited because he was asserting it only for his own set of assigned powers. He could pardon someone, but he did not assert that he could simply decree that the act and all actions under it were void. Limited or not, this assertion of power was profoundly important. It meant that until and unless one of the other branches conclusively exercised one of *its* own powers, such as a congressional override of a presidential veto or a Supreme Court decision in a civil case (where no pardon power existed), a president would be free to take some undefined range of actions based on his own interpretation of his power.

Jefferson's reference to the judiciary as possibly a "despotic branch" revealed his underlying fear. He was a consistent enemy of judicial supremacy, which he considered deeply antithetical to republicanism. In resisting that bugbear on behalf of his own branch, he was freeing the executive from both other branches to an important extent. For Jefferson's strong departmentalist position assumed that the presidency was not an essentially administrative office that would rest on prior grants of authority from legislation or court decisions but was instead a powerful and independent constitutional entity that could act vigorously within its assigned sphere.

For departmentalism to become an official position of the Jefferson presidency, it would need articulation in a more formal context than a letter to a trusted friend. The need for official legal opinions from the attorney general provided the opportunity. For attorney general, Jefferson chose Levi Lincoln, who was an able lawyer and a strict constructionist. A legal controversy was left over from the "quasi war" with France. An armed French ship, the *Schooner Peggy*, had been captured by an American privateer and claimed as a prize under a federal statute that awarded part of the value to the captors. During the litigation to condemn the ship as a lawful prize, a treaty settled outstanding differences between the United States and France. Secretary of State Madison asked Lincoln whether the treaty required restoration of the ship to its owners. While this question was pending in the Supreme Court, the attorney general advised the secretary that the capture was valid and had become final before the effective date of the treaty.[37]

A few days later, the Court ruled to the contrary.[38] Doubtless with President Jefferson's guidance, Lincoln promptly wrote another opinion to the secretary.[39] He began by making it clear that he disagreed with the Court's legal reasoning. Conceding that the Court's decision was binding in the particular case, Lincoln denied it any broader effect, declaring that in other cases executive officers must obey "their own convictions of the meaning of the laws and constitution of the United States, and their oaths to support them." In the particular context, this statement meant little, because the validity of a capture would depend on the facts of the case. Hence the attorney general was really staking a claim for another day and other, more important issues. The opinion was a preemptive strike against another branch that had not yet asserted power to confine the executive in any serious way.[40]

As Jefferson himself so often did, this opinion pointed in two directions at one time. It conceded the Supreme Court's power to bind the executive branch by deciding litigation over which it had jurisdiction. The rule of law surely required that much. Yet the opinion also denied the Court any power to set general legal principles going beyond the decision of particular cases, to which the executive must defer. On this broader issue of required executive deference to judicial precedent, debate persists to the present. In this early instance, the Jefferson administration was trying to confine judicial supremacy as closely as possible.

The implications of aggressive departmentalism for presidential power are sweeping. Jefferson's stance as articulated by his attorney general would support any executive action not clearly forbidden by the text of the Constitution, a treaty, or a statute. That is a wide swath of territory, especially in foreign relations, where the courts are less often willing to test executive actions even after the fact.

Pirates!

As President Jefferson took office, a foreign crisis tested his views about executive war power.[41] The Barbary pirates had resumed a practice of seizing American merchant ships and holding their crews hostage for failing to pay tribute. Congress was out of session, and the new president had his window of opportunity. Ever since his time in the Washington administration, though, Jefferson had consistently decried executive war making as the incubus of monarchy. Our first president, lacking a navy, had paid off the pirates. Like Washington, Jefferson felt quite free to determine American foreign policy within the limits set by the Constitution and existing treaties and statutes, without asking Congress for advance authority to act. From the outset, Jefferson's foreign policy was "more belligerent and assertive than [that of] his predecessors."[42]

Jefferson discussed the crisis with his cabinet. Attorney General Lincoln wrote an opinion trying to reconcile the Constitution's placement of the power to declare war in Congress with the framers' recognition that the president should nevertheless be allowed to repel attacks. Reflecting republican principles that Jefferson could be expected to endorse, Lincoln decided that the Navy could act defensively, repelling attacks by the pirates on its ships, but could not mount a general offensive against them.[43] Led by Treasury Secretary Albert Gallatin, the rest of the cabinet disagreed with this narrow and unrealistic interpretation of presidential war powers.

Jefferson chose a course of practicality first and principle later, using a bit of deception to mask the difference. (He would not be the last president to do that.) On his own authority, the president dispatched a naval squadron to the region to "search for and destroy" the pirates.[44] He justified unilateral action on grounds that Tripoli had declared war on the United States. Jefferson authorized the Navy to "protect our commerce and chastise their insolence" by "sinking, burning, or destroying their ships and vessels."[45] An American frigate then disabled a pirate ship but released it to pursue another errand. Once Congress convened, Jefferson described this convenient episode and misleadingly explained to Congress that the Constitution forbade him "without the sanction of Congress, to go beyond the line of defense." He requested and speedily obtained broad authority to take offensive measures to subdue the pirates. After another two years of fighting on and around the "shores of Tripoli," the mission was accomplished, and the Marines had a phrase for their hymn.

Presidents Washington and Jefferson displayed two basic assumptions about their role in the episodes involving neutrality and pursuit of the Barbary pirates. First, they thought that they possessed discretion to take initial action within the bounds of existing statutory authority. Second, they conceded that Congress could respond by issuing definitive instructions if it chose to do so. This appears to have been the dominant early understanding among the framers in government. It is captured in the maxim that "the President proposes, but Congress disposes."[46] This maxim recognizes substantial power in both of the political branches and does not necessarily exclude the courts from playing a role should litigation arise. Equally important, it does not provide firm answers to too many questions. Politics, rather than law, predominates. Under this general understanding, the new republic was free to evolve along its own historical path.

In the Barbary pirates episode, once there had been a clash of arms between American forces and the enemy, it was not likely that Congress would refuse to endorse the president's action in dispatching the Navy, or even that it would inquire too closely into the background facts. Later presidents would certainly absorb these lessons from the episode as they deployed the American military in harm's way. The next time the choice between principle and practicality was presented to Jefferson, however, the simple expedient of dissimulation would not quite solve the problem.

The Louisiana Purchase

Thomas Jefferson dreamed no small dreams. Once president, he began planning the Lewis and Clark expedition to explore what might someday become an extensive agrarian "empire of liberty."[47] A major obstacle stood in the way of westward expansion, however: Napoleon Bonaparte. Spain had ceded Louisiana to France in 1800 in hopes of building a strong buffer between Mexico and surging American settlements in the old Southwest. This transaction substituted a strong bordering nation for a weak one and risked blocking the access of American farmers to markets via New Orleans. To Jefferson, who immediately grasped the strategic value of Louisiana, the dreaded consequence was that "we must marry ourselves to the British fleet and nation."[48] Since he would have been a most reluctant groom at *that* wedding, he sought another solution, one that would preserve his dreams.

Jefferson sent James Monroe as a personal envoy to France to help his ambassador, Robert Livingston, try to buy West Florida and New Orleans. Monroe knew Jefferson very well and could judge what deal the faraway president would accept. The timing of the mission was propitious. A revolt in Haiti soured Napoleon on dreams of American empire, and he also needed cash. On April 30, 1803, Monroe and Livingston signed a treaty to buy all of Louisiana for about $15 million. The deal doubled the size of the nation, removed the French threat to expansion, and freed commerce on the Mississippi. Its merits were obvious to everyone except the Federalists, who generally resisted expansion into territory that would likely produce new Republican states.[49]

News of the treaty created an acute dilemma for the president. His expansionist vision and the strategic interests of the nation impelled him to accept this stupendous opportunity. Yet his principle of strict construction of the Constitution forbade a simple push for treaty ratification, because the Constitution was silent about acquisition of new territory.[50] With some relish, the Federalists opposed the Louisiana treaty as unconstitutional, echoing Jefferson's own earlier objections to the Bank of the United States by arguing that the treaty was not necessary and proper to the execution of any power vested in the federal government by the Constitution.

In private, Jefferson agreed: "The general government has no powers but such as the constitution has given it, and it has not given it a power of holding foreign territory, and still less of incorporating it into the Union."[51] Attorney General Lincoln shared his doubts, but Treasury Secretary Albert Gallatin did not, arguing that the nation has an inherent right to acquire territory.[52] Gallatin's memo supporting the purchase argued that national sovereignty implied the necessary power to acquire territory. From outside the government, the old revolutionary warhorse Thomas Paine chimed in with the appealing theory that the treaty "makes no alteration in the Constitution, it only extends the principles of it over a larger territory."[53] These were strong arguments that Jefferson could quite honorably have embraced—except for their Hamiltonian implications about federal power generally.

After dithering a bit, Jefferson went to work on a draft of a constitutional amendment to address the problem. This activity stopped abruptly in August 1803, when urgent messages arrived from the American negotiators in France. Livingston and Monroe warned that Napoleon was suffering seller's remorse and was looking for a pretext to undo the deal. They urged that Congress speedily and unconditionally ratify the treaty. Jefferson understood that public expression of doubts about the legality of the treaty would encourage Napoleon to renounce it. The president immediately reversed course and adopted a new strategy. He told Madison that "the less we say about the constitutional difficulties respecting Louisiana the better. What is necessary for surmounting them must be done *sub silentio*."[54] Jefferson then called Congress into an early session to ratify the treaty before the deadline it contained.

Anticipating the congressional session, Jefferson wrote Virginia senator Wilson Cary Nicholas:

> Whatever Congress shall think it necessary to do should be done with as little debate as possible, and particularly so far as respects the constitutional difficulty. . . . I had rather ask an enlargement of power from the nation, where it is found necessary, than to assume it by a construction which would make our powers boundless. Our peculiar security is in possession of a written Constitution. Let us not make it a blank paper by construction.

Accordingly, Jefferson's annual message to Congress finessed the constitutional issue. Having the needed votes in the Senate, Jefferson apparently saw "nothing to be gained, and much to be lost, by spinning dangerous webs of constitutional theory." When Congress met in October, the Senate speedily ratified the treaty. The House, where appropriations to pay the price had to be sought, was less compliant. Jefferson's floor managers overcame opposition by making Hamiltonian arguments about the necessary and proper and general welfare clauses of the Constitution.[55] No wonder Jefferson wanted to remain silent.

As Jefferson's letter to Senator Nicholas revealed, the president's silence avoided any explicit endorsement by him of Hamiltonian approaches to the Constitution, but the justification that he did put forward took him to an even more radical position, whether he could admit it or not. In the epigraph to this chapter, Jefferson referred to the purchase as an act "beyond the Constitution," for which he and Congress had to seek the people's ratification, which in turn "more strongly marked out" the Constitution's lines. This was an explicit invocation of the Lockean prerogative to exceed or even contravene the limits of the law.[56] Jefferson repeatedly claimed that he possessed such a prerogative.[57] He argued that "on great occasions every good officer must be ready to risk himself in going beyond the strict line of the law, when the public preservation requires it; his motives will be a justification."[58] Similarly, "a strict observance of the written laws is doubtless *one* of the high duties of a good citizen, but it is not *the highest*. The laws of necessity, of self-preservation, of saving our country when in danger, are of a higher obligation."[59]

Clearly Jefferson thought that an ad hoc invocation of prerogative was preferable to a general acceptance of the Hamiltonian approach. He seems to have believed that he could reduce the formal constitutional powers of the presidency for ordinary circumstances while retaining the option to invoke extraconstitutional powers in extraordinary situations.[60] But he could not have it both ways.

Tracing the implications of Jefferson's position reveals its defects. In general, he wanted to appeal to the people to support narrow constructions of the Constitution.[61] Of course, the direct presidential link to the people that he had already asserted was a precondition to this activity. And the people duly assented to the Louisiana Purchase by reelecting Jefferson and his party overwhelmingly in the election that followed the next year.[62] Yet the lines to be marked out by acceptance of the Louisiana Purchase would necessarily expand, not contract, national power. And where national power went, executive power would follow. Perhaps Jefferson thought that the Louisiana Purchase was a unique national opportunity, one not likely to be repeated. To use his own terminology, the occurrence was a fugitive one, in which speedy action was imperative for the good of the country. But the precedent of unauthorized action in the interests of the nation had been set, and Jefferson could exert no control over its historical course.

Jefferson's rationalization for the Louisiana Purchase, taken as a general theory about constitutional interpretation, would allow the two political branches to do almost anything that might earn public approval. The result would be a common law Constitution that could be amended as needed by the informal consent of the people. It is possible, of course, that in any particular case the main alternative, a real constitutional amendment, would expand presidential power more than the uncertain support that is provided by a historical precedent. Any such amendment, though, might contain limitations, whereas a precedent can be offered later on to legitimate any executive action that seems either comparable on the facts or a less robust exercise of power.

Hence Jefferson's invocation of the Lockean prerogative was more radical than a practice of broad interpretation of existing constitutional text, however he might have wished to characterize it. In one way, though, the Louisiana precedent had a limited impact.[63] The effect of Jefferson's prerogative was to fill one of the many gaps in the original Constitution, not to override apparently controlling text. It would fall to Abraham Lincoln to grapple with the latter kind of problem as he contemplated emancipation of the slaves.

Jefferson's argument for submitting the constitutionality of the Louisiana Purchase to the approval of the people conspicuously omitted another and more conventional mode of determining legality—submittal to the judgment of the courts.[64] Because Jefferson resisted judicial supremacy as wholly inconsistent with republican principles, he would never willingly have submitted to the authority of his despised Federalist cousin, Chief Justice John Marshall. If he had, one of two bad outcomes would have ensued. Marshall and the Court might have struck down the treaty and the purchase with it. To do that, the Court would have to override the joint action of both other branches in a highly important matter. That was not an assertion of power Jefferson would happily tolerate. More likely, the Court would have upheld the treaty, but by doing so it would certainly have written the dangerous Hamiltonian position into the constitutional law of the land.

Assailing the Citadel

As it happened, although the legality of the Louisiana Purchase was never litigated, both of the larger outcomes that Jefferson feared came about, partly as a result of his unsuccessful attempt to control the judiciary. Early in his first term, President Jefferson initiated a confrontation with the federal courts.[65] He had certainly been provoked—he saw the "midnight" legislation on the judiciary by the Adams administration as a naked power grab meant to preserve Federalist power. Jefferson fumed that the Federalists had "retired into the judiciary as a stronghold, and from that battery all the works of Republicanism are to be beaten down and erased."[66] Against so fundamental a threat to his dreams, Jefferson was impelled to fight back. He did so in a characteristically indirect fashion, but the threat he mounted to judicial independence was very real.

Advancing on multiple fronts, Jefferson began by quietly having his congressional friends sponsor a repeal of the Federalist statute expanding the judiciary. He won an important victory when the Supreme Court upheld the constitutionality of the repealer against an argument that it deprived the new circuit judges of their lifetime jobs.[67] It appeared, then, that partisan manipulation of the size of the judiciary—court packing or unpacking—was a tool available to presidents whenever Congress would acquiesce.

The president also encouraged the ultimately unsuccessful impeachment of Justice Samuel Chase for some overbearing and partisan activities on the bench that were not unusual for the time.[68] Jefferson orchestrated the Chase impeachment from behind the scenes, pressing hard for the principle that even judges should reflect the will of the people.[69] After the effort failed, Jefferson called it a "farce which will not be tried again."[70] He had discovered that impeachment was not a practical constitutional weapon against justices who disagreed with him. In retrospect, we can see that the risks of destabilizing the constitutional system were simply too great. Jefferson's proposed interpretation of the impeachment power had been rejected. No later president, whatever the provocation, would turn to that device as a way to limit the power of the Supreme Court.[71] John Marshall and his colleagues and successors were safe in their citadel.

Equally important, in the landmark case of *Marbury v. Madison* Jefferson declined to recognize judicial authority to issue orders to high executive officers.[72] In *Marbury*, John Marshall won a brilliant and enduring victory over both of the other branches of government, and not incidentally over Thomas Jefferson as well. Marbury had been one of the midnight appointments as a justice of the peace, but by mistake he had not received his commission. Marbury brought a "mandamus" action (a traditional common law action ordering an officer to perform a legal duty) in the Supreme Court against Secretary of State Madison, who had custody of the commission.

Sending a clear warning shot to the Court that he might defy a mandamus order, Jefferson declined to have the executive appear in the litigation. Could—and would—the Court order the executive to deliver the commission? Marshall asserted the Court's power to hold both other branches to their duties under law but issued no order that Jefferson could defy. He did that by holding that Marbury had a legal right to the commission that a court having jurisdiction could enforce but that Congress's attempt to confer statutory jurisdiction on the Supreme Court to issue mandamus was unconstitutional because it did not comply with a technical provision of Article III of the Constitution.

Predictably, Jefferson detested the *Marbury* decision. He also detested Marshall's subsequent decisions that took a Hamiltonian view of national powers and the necessary and proper clause, but he could only fume and complain.[73] After all, the courts could make their own departmentalist claim to powers of judicial review—and did. Marshall's great opinion in *Marbury*, tracking Hamilton in *Federalist Number 78*, asserted blandly that a court presented in litigation with both a statute and a written constitution had the duty to compare them and to give controlling power to the constitution. Thus, although the other branches could make constitutional interpretations as their own duties demanded, the courts held the final power of resolution whenever a case was properly before them.

After many decades, the *Marbury* decision would become the cornerstone of judicial review of both executive and congressional action in American constitutional law. This process took time, in part because in the early nineteenth century the courts were still in the process of becoming clearly separate from the executive or legislature, to one of which they had traditionally been attached.[74] Marshall sped the process by guiding the justices to abandon old political roles and to claim only legal powers—which he then expanded by his deceptively simple departmentalist analysis. Still, until the mid-twentieth century, presidents had little to fear from the courts, where litigation challenging their actions rarely appeared.

Embargo and Overreach

Toward the end of Jefferson's presidency occurred his one "unmitigated failure," the sponsorship and enforcement of the Embargo Act of December 1807 and its increasingly draconian successors.[75] By the end of this dismaying episode, Jefferson had abandoned almost all restraint in an effort to force the people to comply with his policies.[76] His actions cannot be squared with his lifelong devotion to a limited government that respects the liberties of the people. Looking back, we see the dangers that perceived necessity will detach presidents from their principles and that civil liberties are most at risk when a president suppresses them with the active aid of Congress rather than unilaterally. Jefferson's conduct of the embargo intruded far more into the lives and liberties of Americans than had the Sedition Act of 1798, which he had so eloquently deplored.

The embargo crisis began in June 1807, when a savage British attack on the frigate *Chesapeake* triggered war fever. With Congress not in session, the president decided to take immediate action in response.[77] Without an appropriation, he ordered the purchase of munitions and supplies. Knowing that he lacked constitutional support for this action, he trusted that Congress would approve "what they would have seen so important to be done, if then assembled."[78] Here was the Lockean prerogative in its traditional form. Congress assented.

For the longer term, Jefferson was inclined as usual to seek economic sanctions rather than the executive-expanding consequences of war. In addition, his earlier deep reductions in the nation's military capacity left war making an unavailable option. The initial embargo legislation barred American ships and goods from international trade in an effort to compel both Britain and France to recognize the rights of the United States as a neutral nation. Both Britain and France were seizing American ships carrying cargoes that they claimed were destined for the other belligerent. The embargo's restrictions savaged the American economy, sparking fierce resistance among American merchants, especially in New England. There was some impact on the two superpowers, but they were immersed in their struggle and took little notice of the embargo. "Perhaps never in history has a trading nation of America's size engaged in such an act of self-immolation with so little reward."[79]

President Jefferson reacted to the frustrations caused by evasion of the embargo by seeking and obtaining increasingly repressive enforcement legislation.[80] When trade with Canada continued in defiance of the embargo, Jefferson employed the military to police the border. "This was the only time in American history that the President was empowered to use the army for routine or day-to-day execution of the laws."[81] Ignoring the limits on search and seizure in the Fourth Amendment and the trial guarantees of the Fifth Amendment, the enforcement legislation authorized summary seizure and condemnation of ships on suspicion of intention to violate the embargo.

As both the ineffectiveness of the embargo and the arbitrariness of its enforcement became clear, Congress finally yielded to popular resistance and humiliated the president by repealing the most draconian provisions, effective on his last day in office. Even then, however, the Non-Intercourse Act of 1809 replaced the general embargo with a ban on trade with the belligerents and gave the president broad discretion to release the ban against France or Britain if he determined that either nation had improved its behavior toward the United States.[82]

The embargo did not go unchallenged in court.[83] One litigation raised fundamental issues about the president's duty to comply with statutes and court orders. In *Ex Parte Gilchrist*, a customs officer acting on the president's instructions had refused to clear a ship to leave port.[84] The shipowner obtained a writ of mandamus ordering the officer to grant the clearance. Sitting in a lower federal court, Justice William Johnson held that the statute required the officer to exercise his own judgment in the matter and not to defer to the president's instructions.[85]

Since the Supreme Court had already established the principle that the president had to obey statutes and had asserted its own power to decide what actions statutes required, the lower court's decision might have seemed noncontroversial.[86] Not so, however—it ran headlong into President Jefferson's departmentalist point of view. Believing that the executive branch could read a statute as well as a federal judge, Jefferson obtained an opinion from his attorney general, Caesar Rodney, concluding that the court lacked jurisdiction and that its order was "taking the executive authority out of the hands of the president." The president then instructed local officers to follow his instructions and ignore the court's opinion.[87]

Although Jefferson's reaction to the court order in *Gilchrist* initially seems high-handed, he initiated a practice that the executive branch still follows today, and for good reason. Jefferson explained why he took the action: the president needs the capacity to give uniform instructions to subordinate federal officers, so that they can act consistently everywhere in the nation.[88] The decentralized federal judiciary lacks that capacity until a case reaches the Supreme Court. Thus federal courts scattered around the new nation could have given conflicting orders to the customs officers. Accordingly, ever since Jefferson objected to Justice Johnson's order, presidents have felt free to follow a policy of "nonacquiescence" in lower federal court orders that conflict with their own readings of statutes.[89]

The effect of this departmentalist practice is to empower presidential supervision of the executive branch and to disable the lower federal judiciary from disrupting systematic execution of the law. Nonacquiescence is a central feature of the autonomy of the executive branch and therefore of the president's capacity to control it.

Jefferson's excesses and frustrations during the embargo warned future presidents about the practical limits of government power over recalcitrant citizens. At the same time, his successors could learn that principled statements about the need to minimize executive discretion can yield to the perceived imperatives of events. Better, then, to claim broad power in case it is ever needed and never to disclaim it in advance.

Congress Rebounds

Jefferson's presidency initiated an unparalleled period of single-party rule in America, lasting through the time of Andrew Jackson. During this era, it was schisms within the dominant Republican Party that mattered, not the views of the faded Federalists. Ironically, one consequence was to weaken all of Jefferson's successors prior to Jackson in relations with Congress. The party nominee (and presumptive president) was chosen by the party's congressional caucus until conventions appeared in the age of Jackson.[90] Hence the majority in Congress might dominate any of its selections who lacked Jefferson's qualities of leadership, as all of them did. For the time being, the framers' creation of the Electoral College to prevent congressional control of the executive had been circumvented informally but successfully. Moreover, because cabinet members were often interested in the presidency, their need to seek favor in Congress tended to vitiate the president's effective control over the executive branch.[91]

Madison's Principled Purity

As president, James Madison amply demonstrated the disadvantages for the presidency and the nation of an overly constrained view of the executive's constitutional powers.[92] Adhering carefully to republican principles of executive restraint, he was "faithful to principle to the point of folly."[93] He did not use patronage as a lever to control his own branch; nor did he think it appropriate to manage legislation actively. Madison could not even secure the confirmation of his own choice for secretary of state, Albert Gallatin, who remained in his old post at Treasury. As a consequence of Madison's diffidence toward the Senate, his cabinet was very weak—the critical positions at State and War were in the hands of mediocrities or worse during much of his tenure. (Throughout American history, the strength of the cabinet correlates well with the strength of the president.) Power flowed to congressional committees and leaders, who eventually pressed Madison toward war with Great Britain. The famous triumvirate of Clay, Calhoun, and Webster was entering Congress.

Showing a bit of vigor, Madison did bully the Spanish out of West Florida on grounds that it was part of the Louisiana Purchase. Sharing Jefferson's Anglophobia, he ignored British objections to his action. Still, as war loomed in 1811, Madison was unable to prepare the nation to fight it. Republicans in Congress prevented reauthorization of the Bank of the United States, although it was the best vehicle for borrowing and financing the war. This action was "disastrous for the war effort," which relied on borrowed money rather than new tax revenues.[94]

Madison's position on the unsuccessful reauthorization of the Bank before the war and on a successful one that followed the war was the same—he favored it, notwithstanding his opposition to the creation of the First Bank in the Washington administration. Here he was more consistent than he appeared. Recall that in *The Federalist* Madison had taken the position that the meaning of the Constitution would be settled by practice. As the new government matured and he found himself at its helm, he came to the conclusion that a "national judgment" in favor of the Bank had occurred.[95] "When an authoritative, uniform, and sustained course of decision or practice received 'public sanction,' Madison believed that the Constitution evolved in meaning, and the old must give way to the new."[96]

Madison's belief in a living, evolving Constitution limited the departmentalism he shared with Jefferson. But where constitutional meaning was unsettled, he demonstrated a more departmentalist outlook in an effort to solidify practice and thereby control the evolution of meaning. At the end of his tenure he vetoed a national roads and canals bill, finding no authority for it in any of Congress's enumerated powers—not even in the vague power to tax and spend for "the . . . general Welfare of the United States."[97] He argued that treating the general welfare clause as a freestanding power would render the enumeration "nugatory" by granting Congress "a general power of legislation" to advance the public good.[98] On this point, Madison differed from Hamilton, who thought that congressional power under the general welfare clause was not limited by the other enumerations. Many years later the Supreme Court would side with Hamilton.[99]

The Jeffersonian and Jacksonian presidents, however, often vetoed spending bills for internal improvements as unsupported by either the general welfare clause or the necessary and proper clause. Hence the effective constitutional law regarding internal improvements was generated by presidents during this period, whatever Congress and the Supreme Court might think. These presidents did, however, rely on the general welfare clause to continue Washington's precedent of spending for disaster relief. For example, Madison supported a bill to provide compensation for losses suffered in the War of 1812.[100]

A less martial president than James Madison is hard to imagine. Yet he presided (quite badly) over the first war conducted under the Constitution. Given the vast mismatch in military power between Great Britain and the United States in 1812, it is difficult to understand the bellicosity of the "war hawks" in Congress or the confidence with which Americans, including the president, eventually went to war. Madison, however, "was not pushed into war—he backed into it."[101] Britain had the world's dominant navy and a large veteran army. The United States had a few frigates and almost no soldiers. The war was also pointless in any real sense, because just as it was declared, the British repealed the policies that most interfered with American commerce.

The actual reason for the War of 1812 appears to have been the pursuit of national dignity—the question whether the United States would be treated like a colony or an independent and sovereign nation.[102] Accordingly, the War of 1812 was often called the "second war for independence" at the time. New England Federalists, who resisted it to the point of threatening disunion, called it "Mr. Madison's war." Federalist opposition to the war sank the party as a national force, partly because Federalist members of Congress voted against supplying the troops in wartime. History took immediate note. Ever after, presidents have known that no one in Congress will lightly oppose supporting the military in combat. As the Federalists' power waned, they gave unilateral presidential war making an indirect but precious gift.

Madison proved to be the most feckless commander in chief in American history.[103] He and his cabinet managed to let the British burn Washington despite plenty of warning about their intentions. American dignity was saved by the victory of Andrew Jackson at New Orleans after the peace treaty had been signed. Since the treaty simply restored the prewar status quo, the war produced nothing except some American pride at fighting a great power to a draw. With peace in Europe, the underlying causes of the war finally ended. Americans, their national existence now secure, could turn to the realization of their "Manifest Destiny," as the next generation would call it. Meanwhile, poor Madison had amply demonstrated the perils of presidential diffidence. His war had, however, produced an American military hero who, as president, would be accused of many things, but never of excessive diffidence.

PART II
A New Nation

Four score and seven years ago our fathers brought forth on this continent a new nation, conceived in liberty and dedicated to the proposition that all men are created equal.
—Abraham Lincoln, Gettysburg Address

CHAPTER FOUR

Independent of Both

Jackson, Tyler, and Polk

The Congress, the Executive, and the Court must each for itself be guided by its own opinion of the Constitution. Each public officer who takes an oath to support the Constitution swears that he will support it as he understands it, and not as it is understood by others. It is as much the duty of the House of Representatives, of the Senate, and of the President to decide upon the constitutionality of any bill or resolution which may be presented to them for passage or approval as it is for the supreme judges when it may be brought before them for judicial decision. The opinion of the judges has no more authority over Congress than the opinion of Congress has over the judges, and on that point the President is independent of both.
— Andrew Jackson's message vetoing the Bank bill[1]

In the period between the War of 1812 and Andrew Jackson's delayed acquisition of the presidency in 1828, Presidents James Monroe and John Quincy Adams followed most precedents they had inherited, while adding a few of their own. Monroe presided over the end of the Virginia Dynasty in an honorable, efficient, and cautious fashion.[2] His geniality may have contributed to the misleading label for his time, the Era of Good Feelings.[3] Those feelings had dissipated by the time Monroe's gifted secretary of state, yet another prickly and virtuous Adams, received the presidency by a vote of the House of Representatives in early 1825, after he had run second to Jackson in an inconclusive popular vote.[4] The "corrupt bargain" by which Henry Clay threw his support to Adams in return for the position at State and the presumptive succession poisoned Adams's presidency from the outset. His lack of any grounding in a popular mandate further debilitated him and foreshadowed the coming shift to a presidential politics that would rely vitally on that grounding.

The time from Jefferson through Jackson's successor, Martin Van Buren, has been the only period of single-party rule in our history. The basic fault line in American politics remained, of course, just below the surface. All serious politicians called themselves Republicans. The heirs of the disintegrating Federalists, capitalizing on the nationalistic spirit that followed the War of 1812, continued to favor a strong central government that would fund internal improvements, protect industry through a tariff, and regulate the currency through the Bank of the United States. These factions would coalesce as the National Republicans and succeed in placing John Quincy Adams in the White House. By the end of Jackson's presidency, they had morphed into the Whigs. The intellectual heirs of Jefferson, soon called the Old Republicans, sought a decentralized governmental and economic system that eschewed national banking, tariffs, and federal internal improvements. Under Jackson, they would evolve into the Democrats. Until the new party alignment matured, presidents wobbled between National and Old Republican policies as they sought to hold a governing coalition together. The confusion was such that James Monroe, reflecting elements of both factions in his own thinking, even conducted a simultaneous debate both with himself and with Congress over internal improvements, eventually adopting an essentially incoherent view that some spending for them could be justified.[5]

As the "second party system" emerged in American life, all three branches of the federal government protected slavery: presidents represented bisectional coalitions, Congress was overweighted toward the South by the three-fifths clause, and the federal courts contained many southern sympathizers.[6] A tenuous balance persisted on the most explosive issue in American life.

Creating Institutional Memory

In the person of James Monroe, the founding generation retired from the presidency in 1825.[7] For knowledge of what his predecessors had done, no future president could simply rely on personal memories formed from having been in or around the government since its inception. Even John Quincy Adams, the son of a framer, had limited personal memories of the early days, and Andrew Jackson had spent many of them in the rude frontier communities of Tennessee. Nor could future presidents easily tap the memories of earlier ones. In 1826, the senior Adams and Thomas Jefferson had their famous mutual date with mortality—and immortality. James Madison, who would live on for another decade, still kept his immensely valuable notes of the Constitutional Convention among his personal papers, not to be released to guide posterity until 1840. Nor could a president simply turn to the official papers of his predecessors. From George Washington through Richard Nixon, presidents leaving office took their papers with them. Eventually they began to deposit their papers in special libraries scattered around the nation.

More by luck than by design, the problem of creating an institutional memory for the presidency was solved by Monroe's selection of an attorney general who transformed the office.[8] William Wirt was a distinguished Supreme Court advocate who served for twelve years under Monroe and Adams, the longest tenure to date. Once confirmed, Wirt was astonished to discover that the office had no system of records whatever.[9] He had no way of knowing whether any opinion he gave was consistent with what prior presidents and attorneys general had said and done. Wirt immediately set up an opinion book and a letter book. Attorneys general have had a continuous body of precedent to draw on ever since.

A respect for precedent that has been generated within the executive branch is a corollary of departmentalism. Any claim by a branch that its interpretation of the Constitution deserves deference from anyone must rest on the soundness of the opinion given, which is a function of its consistency with prior ones. Thus the attorney general's emergent precedent-gathering function held the potential to mimic the way that judges respect the precedents of their own and other courts. Past presidents and their executive advisers might have found wise answers to problems. At least their opinions deserved respect—and demanded explaining away if they were to be discarded. Thus, once records were kept, it was natural to treat them as precedents having at least some constraining effect. Now the attorney general had become a bureaucrat rather than an essentially private lawyer for the executive who might care little for what predecessors in that role had done.

Stepping onto the World Stage

The rapidly growing and maturing nation that emerged from the validating experience of the War of 1812 and took a full role in international affairs by the end of Andrew Jackson's presidency deserves to be called an "assertive republic."[10] Presidents Monroe, Adams, and Jackson cautiously increased their branch's primacy in directing foreign policy and wound up doing much of the Republic's asserting. They consistently worked to remove foreign obstacles to American expansion across the continent. Congress insisted on being part of the enterprise, while conceding to presidents a role in initiating policy that it was institutionally ill suited to play.

In 1818 President Monroe took up the project of separating the Floridas from Spain, as Madison had tried halfheartedly to do.[11] This time he employed a weapon adequate to the task: Andrew Jackson.[12] Under weak Spanish rule, the area was a violent no-man's land full of escaped slaves and Creek and Seminole Indians displaced by white settlements—and by Jackson's earlier Indian wars. Congress had not authorized any action, but Monroe proceeded anyway without consulting it, on grounds that the action was defensive in nature. General Jackson would soon prove that he could "conduct defense so aggressively that those on the receiving end might well be pardoned if they mistook it for aggression."[13] The content of Monroe's instructions to Jackson remains unclear. Certainly Jackson was to "pacify" the Indians and was given discretion to do that "in the manner he may judge best."[14] Monroe may have agreed to Jackson's request to take the Floridas.[15] Monroe denied ever having sent that signal, but he did not move directly and forcefully to control Jackson, whose aggressiveness and tendency to disregard his orders were well known. Thus Monroe set the example of a commander in chief issuing lax instructions to a subordinate so that he could take credit for all successes while denying responsibility for any excesses. The effect of this precedent would be to blur the accountability of the president to both Congress and the people for military action.

General Jackson descended on the Floridas, battered the Seminoles, occupied two Spanish forts, and executed two British subjects for aiding the Indians. With considerable skill, Monroe and Adams calmed the resulting furor by returning the forts, conciliating the British, and negotiating the Transcontinental Treaty with Spain. Jackson's foray had convinced the Spanish that they could not long hold the Floridas. Adams took advantage of their duress; the treaty gave the United States clear title to the Floridas and waived Spanish claims to western North America above the present northern border of California. Two important barriers to the continental nation that existed in Adams's vision had fallen. To assuage the Spanish, the United States waived claims to Texas—for the time being. The Senate, after fulminating about Jackson's misdeeds for a time, happily ratified the treaty.

The famous second stage of Monroe's foreign policy, articulation of the doctrine that bears his name and John Quincy Adams's fingerprints, arose as the Spanish Empire in the Americas continued to disintegrate and the European powers eyed the spoils. A more important menace to American interests was British and Russian activity in the Northwest. As articulated in Monroe's 1823 annual message to Congress, the doctrine had two major components. First, Monroe warned European powers not to place new colonies in the Americas. Second, he warned them not to interfere in the internal affairs of existing governments in the hemisphere.[16]

The Monroe Doctrine, crafted largely by Adams but with Monroe's guidance, was breathtaking in its implications. In this "Magna Charta of Manifest Destiny," the United States was claiming ownership of most of North America and implying hegemony over Latin America.[17] The doctrine was the brainchild of these two executive officers, who did not involve Congress in its formulation. Happily for Monroe and Adams, the doctrine would not be tested for a while. Its announcement sparked some celebration in the United States and some condemnation in European capitals but no clash of arms.

For the remainder of the Monroe, Adams, and Jackson administrations, presidents followed an essentially consistent foreign policy that emphasized national expansion and the removal of barriers to burgeoning American trade. As president, Jackson surprised the international community, which justly feared that he would be a wild man, with his skill and overall moderation. Notwithstanding his inexperience in foreign affairs (except for fighting), he kept a close watch on administration policy with the help of an able succession of secretaries of state. He was particularly successful at negotiating treaties to resolve trade disputes that had festered for years.[18] He did bluster as needed, especially toward the French. He was careful to respect congressional prerogative concerning international trade, for which Congress has explicit constitutional regulatory authority.

Nevertheless, Jackson, holding a surprisingly global outlook considering his background, felt free to project American power around the world on his own responsibility. He engaged in some vigorous gunboat diplomacy against perceived miscreants overseas, without Jefferson's purported punctiliousness about obtaining advance authority from Congress.[19]

Closer to home, the president was more cautious. Jackson hungered to acquire Texas, but he held back because of the extreme sensitivity of the issue in Congress (largely owing to slavery).[20] He remained ostensibly neutral as Texans fought for independence but did not try to prevent Americans from aiding the rebellion. He knew that any attempt to annex Texas or even to recognize the revolutionary republic could sunder his party and doom the prospects of his anointed successor, Martin Van Buren. After Van Buren was safely elected, Jackson carefully obtained a resolution from Congress urging him to extend recognition to the Republic of Texas, and he did so as he eased into retirement.

The Old Hero

Andrew Jackson's popularity while in office and his later stature among presidents rest mostly on his domestic achievements, not on his foreign policies. As he took office, he knew that he had very broad popular support. His tally of 56 percent of the popular vote would not be exceeded until the twentieth century. Modern Americans know his nickname as Old Hickory, but in his presidential years he was more often called the Old Hero. That reference could readily be understood in the street without including his name. Jackson was always willing to rely on his connection to the people and to invoke it explicitly in times of adversity in ways no predecessor would have dared.

Jackson used the theory that he alone represented the majority of the American people to transform the presidency in both politics and law.[21] In politics, the president would no longer stand at one remove from the people, subordinated to the claims of Congress that it was the primary representative branch. Even more, the presidential claim to be the tribune of the people implied that members of Congress, each representing only a part of the whole nation, were inferior voices for the people unless they joined together in legislation. Consequently, in separation of powers law the executive branch moved into a position at least equal to that of Congress, and superior wherever the incumbent could make it so.

In both good and bad ways, Andrew Jackson was an extraordinary human being.[22] His principal biographer stresses his very "dynamic, charismatic, forceful, and intimidating personality." He "simply dominated everyone around him." Fortunately, he was "a pragmatic, determined, clever, resourceful, and extremely popular politician" who instinctively knew how to use his enormous popularity to lead.[23] His world and his character were starkly Manichean. To his friends and supporters, he was gracious, kind, loyal, and forgiving. To his opponents and enemies, he was vindictive, relentless, violent, and cruel. A product of the old frontier who had imbibed its code of honor and agrarian values, he had fought eight duels, killing one opponent, and as president still carried two bullets in his body. Throughout his life, he showed a willingness to disregard legal authority when it conflicted with his policy goals.[24]

Jackson presided over a nation that was in the midst of a revolution in transportation, communications, and finance, some of which he tried to hold back in pursuit of Jefferson's old agrarian vision. The nation's population was doubling every generation, creating immense pressure for expansion, even as the steamboat, the railroad, and the telegraph were shrinking distance. Jackson arrived in the capital in a carriage; eight years later, he left on a train. He had achieved most of his domestic agenda: destruction of the Bank of the United States, Indian removal, tariff reform, and elimination of the debt. What made his presidency transformational was not this list of substantive achievements, which is short and includes at least as much harm as good. Instead, it was the way he went about working his will that altered the office he held.

To the Victor

Andrew Jackson's presidency was the product (and not the catalyst, as is often claimed) of a vital sea change in American politics.[25] Recall that the Jeffersonian presidents were creatures of Congress because they were chosen by the Republican Party's congressional caucus. By the time of the disputed congressional election of John Quincy Adams, this system was obviously breaking down, to be replaced by the convention system by the time of Jackson's reelection in 1832. The underlying causes of the breakdown were the broadening of the voting franchise toward universal white male suffrage and the associated movement toward direct popular choice of presidential electors. The replacement of the original American politics of indirect choice of presidents by elites with the current one of (almost) direct choice by the people was complete enough to catapult Jackson to the presidency. He never forgot who put him there.

Lashed to the prow of the steamboat that took Andrew Jackson on the first stage of his journey to Washington were two hickory brooms, symbolizing his campaign promise (almost the only one he made) to sweep incumbent civil servants out.[26] He had an outsider's distrust of the capital, having spent only about a year there, mostly as a senator in 1823–25. His first annual message to Congress called for "rotation" in office, explaining that long tenure fostered corruption. The duties of officers, he said, were "so plain and simple that men of intelligence" could easily perform them.[27] Opponents immediately charged that he intended a spoils system, but the charge was inaccurate as applied to Jackson himself (although it was on target as applied to his lieutenants).

Jackson's presidency was transitional regarding patronage. He thought in personal terms of supporters and opponents, not coalitions and parties. He appointed friends and people he knew to office, distrusting others. Only toward the end of his time did he begin to use appointments to promote the interests of a party organization. He had been elected by a loose agglomeration of diverse interests that included many of the Old Republicans as well as some of the National Republicans who had supported Adams. By his second term these fragments had coalesced into a new Democratic Party.

The new politics needed new politicians, and Jackson's eventual successor, Martin Van Buren, showed the way with his pragmatic style, organizational gifts, and reliance on patronage to tie the people to the party. Van Buren and his acolytes turned the politics of the framing generation on its head by arguing that parties were not a menace to the public interest but rather a positive good, because they allowed the people to take part in their government and to defend it against the selfish abuse that the framers had styled faction. (It was one of Van Buren's people who made the famous statement that "to the victors belong the spoils of the enemy.")[28] That pointed the way to the future. For presidents, the use of party structure to forge a direct bond with the people would give departmentalism a new grounding. Now every constitutional executive power could be deployed in what the incumbent declared to be the people's interest.

Before starting to rotate anyone out of office, the new president needed to rotate his own cabinet in. For this he relied on the advice of a close friend, Senator John Eaton of Tennessee. Jackson made Eaton secretary of war and placed Van Buren at State. The rest of the cabinet was weak— Samuel T. Ingham at Treasury and John M. Berrien as attorney general. The group was designed to reflect the various elements in Jackson's coalition. Amos Kendall received a sinecure as fourth auditor of the Treasury, a perch from which he could play his real role as adviser to Jackson.

For the most trivial of reasons, the cabinet soon became highly dysfunctional.[29] Secretary Eaton had married the scandalous Peggy O'Neale, after the two had an affair while she was married to a naval officer. The wives of other cabinet members spurned Peggy Eaton socially; an enraged Jackson rose chivalrously to her defense; the squabble consumed vast amounts of Jackson's and the cabinet's time and attention until the president finally cut the knot by restructuring the cabinet wholesale in 1831.

Jackson's replacement of his cabinet after the Eaton affair remains the most extensive cabinet turnover in American history. The overall effect was to send a clear signal about who was the boss of the executive branch. The cagey Van Buren offered to resign to make it easy to displace the others, and Jackson then induced resignations from everyone except the postmaster (an accomplished spoilsman). The new cabinet for the second term was much stronger: Louis McLane came in at Treasury, Lewis Cass at War, Edward Livingston at State, and Roger Taney as attorney general. Van Buren's reward was the vice presidency. After the reorganization, Jackson convened his cabinet more than in his first term. He never asked for a vote in the cabinet—his instincts were too military for that. Nonetheless, Jackson allowed his cabinet to disagree with him and gave them wide latitude to do their jobs. Like George Washington, he understood the value of hearing differing points of view, at least from his supporters.

Toward the end of Jackson's first term, opposition newspapers started complaining about informal presidential advisers, the famous "Kitchen Cabinet," which was an unstructured group of people whom Jackson trusted. It included Kendall, Van Buren, and Francis Blair Sr., a newspaper editor who published Jackson's house organ, the *Globe*, through which the group manipulated the news. The Kitchen Cabinet also included members of Congress—Thomas Hart Benton in the Senate and James K. Polk in the House. Jackson was displaying a trait that is common to his modern successors. Whatever the composition of his official advisers in the cabinet, he felt the need to seek advice from trusted friends wherever they might be found. The importance of this development is its capacity to expand a president's mental horizons by evading formal bureaucratic structures that might prove confining. It is far easier for a president to control and trust a Kitchen Cabinet than the real one, the members of which often have political bases and ambitions of their own.

When Jackson began his program of rotating executive officials below the cabinet level, he encountered the Senate, which held the power to confirm many of them. Dealing with the Senate was never easy for him, because the supremely formidable triumvirate of Clay, Webster, and Calhoun was assembling there (Calhoun was vice president in the first term but was always unruly).

Jackson began his rotation program right away, sending seventy-six names to a special session of the Senate called in March 1829 to confirm appointments.[30] It was not surprising that Jackson nominated his supporters to office; earlier presidents had done that. The new element was mass removal of incumbents. As promised, Jackson made some effort to seek out corruption, but few scoundrels were identified. Jackson removed 45 percent of the presidential appointees, most of them in his first year. The removals did not sweep away the existing bureaucracy, though: the gross removal figure for all civil servants was only 9 percent.

What mattered most was the animating vision of an executive branch that selected its senior bureaucrats not by merit but by political loyalty to the president's party. That vision endures today, although civil service statutes have cabined it. It provides political accountability at the price of danger to the neutral and effective administration of the law. Jackson's practice of removing presidential appointees certainly took root with his successors—in the antebellum years it was often over 50 percent. Ironically, an effect of the rotation system was to increase the need for rules within the executive to guide the changing personnel: "democracy begat bureaucracy."[31]

The Senate was ready to resist presidential nominations. In Jackson's eight years, forty-nine executive nominations were rejected, four times the rate of his predecessors.[32] His tendency to nominate members of Congress and newspaper editors raised concerns about old-style corruption of the legislature and manipulation of public information. The relationship between Jackson and the Senate was quite confrontational at times. Characteristically, he did not shrink from combat, explaining: "Whenever the Senate rejected a good man, on the ground of his politics, I gave them a hot potatoe [sic]" by sending up someone they might like even less.[33] The president evidently understood what modern observers would call game theory. If the Senate would not cooperate, neither would he, and no one ever stared him down.

Underlying these battles was a primal issue about separation of powers, the question of the locus of control over the executive branch. By splitting the appointment power between president and Senate, the framers had invited a battle for custody of the executive. Jackson and the Senate fired some early salvoes in that battle, which rages still. Resolute presidents like Jackson have done well in the battle; their weaker colleagues have not.

Indian Removal and Faithful Execution

The president's constitutional duty to "take Care that the Laws be faithfully executed" has often been called the core idea of the office. Unfortunately, the removal and resettlement of Indian tribes that occurred during and just after Andrew Jackson's presidency provides a sad example of the potential for presidential neglect of this duty to render great harm to vulnerable people.[34] As this episode confirms, presidential failures of faithful execution are very difficult for Congress, the courts, or the people to police. The actual meaning of this duty, then, lies almost entirely in the discretion of the president.

Andrew Jackson took office with a record of removing Indian tribes from the path of white settlement, and he intended to complete that task.[35] The obstacle was a group of relatively civilized tribes occupying the Old Southwest, the region from western Georgia to the Mississippi River. The tribes had firm treaty rights (which they had earlier negotiated with General Jackson), but neither white settlers nor the State of Georgia had any intention of honoring the treaties. Only a very firm stance by the federal government and especially the president could have had any hope of stemming the tide, but both political branches of the government aided the expropriation. Only the Supreme Court gave the Indians any aid.

President Jackson's chief legislative priority in his first year was the Indian removal bill. With Jackson's prodding, Congress passed legislation granting him power to set aside land west of the Mississippi that tribes could "choose" to accept in exchange for their eastern lands. Tragedy attended the subsequent removals. Jackson "personally intervened frequently, always on behalf of haste, sometimes on behalf of economy, but never on behalf of humanity, honesty, or careful planning."[36] Initially, the Choctaws were pressured to move west in the winter of 1831–32. The ubiquitous Tocqueville captured the misery of their passage over the Mississippi:

> It was then the middle of winter, and the cold unusually severe; the snow had frozen hard upon the ground, and the river was drifting huge masses of ice. The Indians had their families with them, and they brought in their train the wounded and the sick, with children newly born and old men upon the verge of death. They possessed neither tents nor wagons, but only their arms and some provisions. . . . No cry, no sob, was heard among the assembled crowd; all were silent.[37]

In 1832, the Creeks started moving west with prodding from federal troops. Jackson, wanting the Indians out, did nothing to protect them from the settlers. The culminating "Trail of Tears" was a movement of sixteen thousand Cherokees in 1838, after Jackson's departure from office. During his time, he moved about forty-six thousand Indians west. Jackson, who routinely called the Indians his "children," always argued that removal was in their best interest. Humanitarian objections to the removal were voiced in and out of Congress but never gained enough traction to prevent the abuses.

The Indians and their allies twice brought litigation to the Supreme Court to enforce their treaty rights. They received the cold comfort of sympathetic treatment without a court order that would protect them much. In the first case, *Cherokee Nation v. Georgia*, the tribe tried to restrain the state from exercising jurisdiction over it.[38] Chief Justice Marshall, finally nearing the end of his tenure, avoided reaching the merits of the claim by holding that the tribe was a "domestic dependent nation" rather than a foreign nation that could bring suit directly in the Supreme Court. Ironically, Marshall's theory indirectly undermined the executive's traditional use of the treaty power to govern relations with the tribes. If Indian tribes were not foreign nations for purposes of federal court jurisdiction, how could they be foreign nations for purposes of the treaty power? For forty years, presidents solved this dilemma by the simple expedient of ignoring this implication of *Cherokee Nation*. They continued making treaties with the tribes until 1871 on the theory that they were independent nations.[39] Presidents undoubtedly took this tack because, except for the treaty clause, the Constitution fails to give the executive branch power to deal with Indians in peacetime, while the Indian commerce clause suggests that Congress should control relations with the Indians by ordinary legislation.

A second opportunity for Supreme Court intervention occurred when Georgia tried to eject some missionaries from Indian territory for resisting the removal. The Court held that Cherokee treaty rights and not Georgia law governed the territory.[40] Invalidation of the Georgia law gave the Indians a hollow victory, since the state ignored the decision. President Jackson may have reacted by saying, "John Marshall has made his decision; now let him enforce it."[41] The story may be apocryphal, because Marshall's order required nothing directly of the president. Whether or not Jackson made the statement, he acted as if he had, doing nothing to protect the federal rights of the Cherokees from further depredations at the hands of Georgia and its citizens. (In the later nullification crisis, when a state challenged Jackson's authority directly, it drew a much different response.)

The War against the Bank

Andrew Jackson's successful battle against the Second Bank of the United States, the "Monster" as he called it, had two phases, which expanded different aspects of executive power.[42] First, Jackson's veto of a bill to recharter the Bank fundamentally altered the presidential veto power. Second, when Jackson decided to withdraw government deposits from the Bank to speed its demise, he removed a treasury secretary for defying his instructions, thereby solidifying presidential control of executive branch subordinates.

Early in his presidency, Jackson experimented with the veto power in a way common to his Republican predecessors, by invoking constitutional grounds to justify vetoing a bill funding an internal improvement (the Maysville Road in Kentucky).[43] Madison, Monroe, and Jackson all did this occasionally to establish their Old Republican credentials by taking a narrow view of the general welfare and necessary and proper clauses.[44] They argued that in the particular cases the benefits from the projects would be local, not national, and therefore were beyond federal power. There was also a sectional advantage to the vetoes: southerners feared that a federal government that could build a canal might someday free a slave. Still, having advertised their principles, all of these presidents also signed numerous bills funding internal improvements, discovering national benefits in these cases.

In another experiment with the veto power, Jackson issued the first important "signing statement" to explain his reservations about a bill he was nonetheless signing. In 1830, he signed an appropriation for a road to be built from Detroit to Chicago but forbade its construction beyond the border of Michigan Territory on grounds that Congress's power to legislate for the territories extended no farther.[45] In the House, critics responded that this action amounted to an unconstitutional line-item veto, but Jackson prevailed. The framers had not empowered presidents to veto items in bills, and no prior president had claimed such a power. Jackson was asserting both an independent power to decide on the constitutionality of the bill and a corollary power to execute the provisions that he deemed constitutional and ignore the rest. In the future, this technique of partial enforcement of enacted law would grow in tandem with the importance of legislation and would create enduring tensions with Congress.

Overall, presidential vetoes before Jackson had been sporadic, and only a few had produced controversy.[46] Jackson shattered existing precedent. The Second Bank of the United States had a perfected constitutional pedigree. The First Congress and President George Washington had created its predecessor after carefully considering its constitutionality. When a later Congress created the Second Bank after the War of 1812 proved the need for one, President Madison signed the bill, having changed his mind on the constitutional issue because the nation had accepted national banking. And in an opinion by Chief Justice John Marshall, the Supreme Court upheld the constitutionality of the Second Bank in its landmark decision in *McCulloch v. Maryland*.[47]

The political history of the Second Bank was less appealing, however.[48] The Bank exerted great power over the economy yet was only loosely controlled by the federal government through ownership of 20 percent of its stock.[49] The notes it issued formed 20 percent of the nation's currency. It held a quarter of all deposits. By calling in notes of state banks it could manipulate the nation's currency. In its early years, the Bank suffered bad management. First it conducted an orgy of speculation; then it abruptly contracted its obligations to survive, thereby incurring widespread blame for the Panic of 1819.[50] By the time Andrew Jackson became president, Nicholas Biddle, the Bank's president, had put the Bank on a firm foundation, but no one could be sure that financial mismanagement would not recur. The Bank also had a deserved reputation for extending favors to its political friends that it denied to its opponents. Jackson thought it had used corrupt means to oppose him in 1828. Signs of its political influence always infuriated him because it lay beyond his control.[51]

Andrew Jackson was viscerally opposed to everything the Second Bank represented. He had been an advocate of hard money and an enemy of aggressive banking ever since narrowly escaping financial ruin after accepting some bad paper obligations in Tennessee. Also, the Bank triggered Jackson's instinctive revulsion for monopoly and special privilege. He had campaigned to purify the nation from corruption, and the Second Bank had some sorry history on this score.

In his first annual message to Congress, Jackson fired a warning shot at the Bank. He complained about it but said he would let Congress decide how to restructure it.[52] As the years went by, the rumblings continued.

Then Nicholas Biddle made the major miscalculation of challenging the president. Biddle was inclined to seek an early recharter to reduce financial uncertainty. Both Daniel Webster and Henry Clay advised him to go ahead on the premise that Jackson would not dare veto the bill in an election year. The bill, which limited the Bank's power somewhat, passed both houses in early July. Now the two great streams of American politics, Hamiltonian and Jeffersonian, collided at Jackson's desk. No one who knew him well could have doubted the outcome.

The president vetoed the Bank bill without consulting with his cabinet.[53] The cabinet, except for Roger Taney, favored the Bank, while the Kitchen Cabinet generally opposed it. In any event, by now the issue had become a crusade with Jackson. Taney and Kendall helped the president compose the veto message. It was an unprecedented document, sounding themes of both constitutionality and economic policy. The Jeffersonian states' rights vision of America was explicit. There was even some raw democratic invective attacking monopoly and privilege.

The constitutional analysis (supplied by Taney) contained the declaration of independence from the other two branches that forms the epigraph to this chapter. Given the Bank's constitutional pedigree, this was the strongest statement of departmentalism yet made, and it was advanced unapologetically. Jackson's deep devotion to majority rule explains the vigor of the argument. He would not concede judicial primacy even on the Constitution. Intermediary institutions did not impress him. For example, he was certainly no fan of the Electoral College after his 1824 experience, in which his plurality was ignored.[54]

On the merits of the constitutional issue, the message conceded that the necessary and proper clause could justify some financial agent for the government—but not this monopoly bank with too much control over state banks. This was a plausible enough argument, although it flew in the teeth of Marshall's opinion in *McCulloch*. It did fit within the erratic pattern of the vetoes of internal improvement bills by Republican presidents (and Jackson himself) based on a narrow view of the clause.

The message's invocation of policy grounds implied that presidents would participate freely in the legislative process before a bill's enactment instead of exercising a final and limited check. Prior presidents had honored Washington's sensitivities about congressional independence, resorting to Jefferson's hidden-hand technique when they wanted to influence legislation. Jackson's opponents in Congress perceived the threat immediately. Daniel Webster objected that the veto message "proceeds to claim for the President, not the power of approval, but the primary power, the power of originating laws."[55] There soon appeared a famous political cartoon of King Andrew I, crowned, robed in ermine, and clutching a scepter and a veto message.[56] Plainly an important shift of power from Congress to the president had occurred. Jackson's enemies showed their concern about this in their choice of a name for the new party they formed—the Whigs, evoking the traditional opponents of royal excess in Britain.

At one point, Webster's fury over the Bank veto carried him away. He fumed: "If these positions of the President be maintained, there is an end of all law and all judicial authority. Statutes are but recommendations, judgments no more than opinions."[57] Here Jackson was right and Webster was wrong. Jackson's position was that the president's veto power is plenary—that is, exclusive of control by the other two branches. Jackson was asserting that he was entitled to act upon his own view of the Constitution, no matter what anyone else thought. He was also claiming the right to form his own policy views, however inconsistent with those of congressional majorities. Essentially, the veto message was an appeal to the people to agree that the Bank was fundamentally inconsistent with American institutions. Upon receipt of the message, Congress had the right to override the veto and enact the bill into law on any constitutional theory that a court would later accept. Nonetheless, the supermajority requirement for overriding presidential vetoes meant that the president's weight in the legislative process now equaled that of two-thirds of both houses of Congress.[58]

In the bank bill veto message, Jackson was also asserting a right to judgment independent of his own predecessors Washington and Madison. As presidents generate law by deciding what actions to take, they are free to overrule their predecessors' precedents, as Jackson established by overturning the dominant and long-standing interpretation of the veto power as limited to being based on constitutional grounds. The Supreme Court, understanding that constitutional meaning cannot be frozen, often overrules its own precedents as its judgments about the Constitution change. Jackson understood that presidents need the same capacity to break new ground, within the limits that the American political system will tolerate.

Because a president's power is often shared with the other two branches, however, there are structural limits to this power of constitutional interpretation. If a president takes an unauthorized action that Congress can overturn with a statute or that a court will enjoin as inconsistent with an existing statute or the Constitution, his interpretation is not final in the way that a veto is (if not overridden). It is easy to confuse these two kinds of presidential action, as Webster did in his reference to overturning statutes and judgments. The president was claiming no such power.

Andrew Jackson intended the election of 1832 to be a referendum on his banking and Indian removal policies.[59] The election featured the first third-party candidate (the Anti-Masons nominated Wirt) and the first nominating conventions, replacing the defunct caucus. Jackson won the vindication he sought by drubbing Clay and Wirt, receiving a slightly lower percentage of the vote than in 1828. Modern historians think that the victory may have been despite, not because of, the bank veto, that it was driven by the Old Hero's personal popularity. Election mandates are necessarily blurred messages, but Jackson found what he wanted in this one.

Now began the second and final phase of Jackson's war against the Monster.[60] He warned Representative Polk that "the hydra of corruption" was "only scotched, not dead."[61] With Blair and Kendall urging him to remove federal deposits from the Bank to kill it, Jackson inserted a passage in his 1832 annual message to Congress questioning whether government deposits were safe in the Bank. The House of Representatives responded by passing a resolution that they were entirely secure. Undeterred, the president gathered the cabinet and asked them questions about the safety of the deposits. Treasury Secretary McLane responded by questioning the safety of the state banks and pointing out that the statute creating the Bank placed the power to remove the deposits in the secretary, not the president.[62] Frustrated, Jackson shifted McLane to the state department and replaced him with William Duane, who was a past opponent of the Bank.

It turned out, however, that Duane was shocked by the plan to remove the deposits, because he doubted the solvency of the state banks and worried about the inflationary effects of a funds transfer. He and Jackson began an extended debate in both letters and meetings. Duane interpreted the statute to allow him to withdraw deposits only if he found that they were unsafe in the Bank, although this condition was not explicit. Certainly the deposits were safe in the Bank. Duane also thought that the statute required him to rely on his own judgment and told the president that he feared impeachment if he removed the funds. "A secretary, sir," said Jackson, "is merely an executive agent, a subordinate, and you may say so in self-defense." Duane replied: "In this particular case, Congress confers a discretionary power, and requires reasons if I exercise it. Surely this contemplates responsibility on my part."[63]

Jackson continued unsuccessfully to seek harmony in the cabinet. In September 1833, the president informed the cabinet that he would remove the deposits, and a final confrontation within the executive branch began.[64] Jackson said that he wanted to withdraw government deposits gradually and that new revenues would go to selected banks in the states (which were soon called the "pet" banks by the opposition). Attorney General Taney supported the plan. Secretary Duane still thought it was both unwise and illegal to remove the funds without authorization from Congress. No one was certain whether the president or the secretary had the power to resolve this issue.[65] Jackson and Duane argued the withdrawal issue again at some length. Jackson instructed Duane to "take the [attorney general's] opinion and pursue it, he being our legal adviser, his opinion of the law, where there were doubts, ought to govern the heads of the Departments as it did the President."[66] Taney prepared an opinion supporting Jackson, but Duane would not budge.

In this controversy, the president claimed the ultimate authority within the executive branch to decide what the relevant statute meant. He sent the cabinet a long memorandum arguing his view of the law and concluding:

> The President could not, in justice to the responsibility which he owes to the country, refrain from pressing upon the Secretary of the Treasury his view of the considerations which impel to immediate action. Upon him has been devolved by the Constitution and the suffrages of the American people the duty of superintending the operation of the Executive Departments of the Government and seeing that the laws are faithfully executed. . . . Far be it from him to expect or require that any member of the Cabinet should at his request, order, or dictation do any act which he believes unlawful or in his conscience condemns.[67]

In a sideshow that revealed the heated political atmosphere, the Senate demanded a copy of the memo, and Jackson adamantly refused, even though versions had been published in the newspapers. This is the first instance of a claim of "deliberative privilege" for internal White House discussions.[68]

When Duane remained recalcitrant, Jackson summarily removed him from office, sending him a curt letter saying his services were "no longer required."[69] Taney took temporary control of the department and began the withdrawals. Jackson's annual message said that removal was forced by the Bank's attempts to influence elections.

That was not the end of the matter, however. In the Senate, John C. Calhoun, by now an enemy of the administration, objected to this effort "to unite in the President the power of the sword and the purse."[70] Daniel Webster argued that Congress could place independent authority in the hands of the secretary. Webster distinguished the president's power to dismiss Duane, which he conceded, from the power to direct the performance of the secretary's statutory duties, which he denied:

> The law charges the officer, whoever he may be, with the performance of certain duties. The President, with the consent of the Senate, appoints an individual to be such an officer; and this individual he may remove, if he so please; but, until he is removed, he is the officer, and remains charged with the duties of his station, duties which nobody else can perform, and for the neglect or violation of which he is liable to be impeached.[71]

The Senate then passed the only resolution censuring a president in American history. It said that the reasons given by Taney for removing the funds were "unsatisfactory and insufficient" and that the president had "assumed upon himself authority and power not conferred by the constitution and laws, but in derogation of both."[72] In the House, Polk secured passage of resolutions supporting the president.

In the controversy between Taney and the Senate over legal authority for removing the deposits, fair arguments can be made for each side.[73] Since Taney had a plausible if not conclusive defense for his action, the Senate was left to punish him politically, as it did by twice rejecting his later nominations to office.

Jackson responded to the Senate by sending it a "Protest."[74] He claimed the power to remove subordinates and defended his own role as custodian of the public funds. He protested that he had no way to defend himself against these charges unless an impeachment were brought. More broadly, Jackson asserted that he was "the direct representative of the American people," elected by them and "responsible to them." Webster strongly objected that the Constitution "nowhere calls him the representative of the American people; still less, their direct representative."[75] The Senate refused to receive the protest. It also refused to confirm Taney's nomination to serve as treasury secretary, obliging Jackson to find a replacement.

Andrew Jackson was not one to abandon a campaign after a reverse, however. His nomination of Taney for a Supreme Court opening was spurned by the Senate, but Jackson later successfully nominated him for chief justice after John Marshall's death. And when the time seemed right as Jackson neared the end of his term, his friends in the Senate engineered a vote that expunged the censure. The president said that it "healed the wound."[76] More important, expunging the censure resolution ratified Jackson's interpretation of presidential power.[77] Together with the veto of the bank bill, this victory sealed Jackson's liberation of the presidency from the preexisting tradition of congressional supremacy.[78]

The drama attending removal of the Bank deposits was not confined to Congress. Both Jackson and Biddle took actions contracting the economy. In 1835, Jackson proudly paid off the public debt, eliminating a stable medium of monetary exchange. And in 1836 Jackson issued the Specie Circular, requiring hard money for public land purchases. Meanwhile, Biddle contracted the Bank's obligations in a failed effort to save it and to bully Congress into a recharter. The resulting Panic of 1837 was followed by a five-year depression that consumed the entire presidential term of the unfortunate Van Buren and stood as the worst in American history for a century.[79]

The central banking functions that the Bank performed were necessary but would not be restored until formation of the Federal Reserve System in 1913. The Jacksonians made no real effort to find an effective way to regulate the currency. But the Bank war was never really about banking—it was about power. Jackson's removal of the funds in favor of the state banks confirmed that his veto had shifted "enormous" power from the Bank to the executive branch.[80]

The controversy over Jackson's removal of Secretary Duane resulted in the establishment of several fundamental principles about the president's supervisory relationship with subordinate officers who are charged with statutory duties. Recall that the First Congress did not designate Treasury as an "executive" department explicitly subject to presidential direction as it did State and War. The notion that Treasury had a special relationship with Congress and stood at some distance from the president persisted until Jackson's time.[81] Hence, if there were to be legal limits on removing any cabinet officer, they would have applied to the treasury secretary. When the first departments were formed in 1789, Congress had finessed the question whether the president had constitutional power to remove an officer whom the Senate had confirmed. Jackson emphatically claimed that power, and eventually prevailed over the Senate's effort to negate the claim.

In the internal battle within the Jackson administration over the bank deposits, everyone seemed to agree that the claim of legal right to withdraw the funds was to be made by the officer who was empowered by statute to make the decision. Even so headstrong a president as Andrew Jackson never simply tried to assume the authority that the statute had placed in the Secretary. Instead, he jawboned the Secretary with all of his considerable might. This understanding that presidents may supervise but not displace authority vested in other officers by statute remains dominant today, although it has been vigorously contested at times.[82] An important effect of the understanding is to empower the subordinate officer to enter a dialogue about legal right, as happened with Duane and Jackson, instead of merely awaiting orders. If the two come into agreement, the chances that the rule of law will prevail are enhanced, and the ethical conscience of the officer is honored.

Still, when a president's will is not to be denied, the Bank war demonstrates that a cabinet officer who cannot acquiesce must resign or be fired. The president must then persuade the Senate to accept a replacement, as Jackson eventually did after the Senate rejected Taney. This reciprocal process leaves the president in command of the legal interpretations that the executive branch makes, subject to the oversight of the Senate as it considers whether to confirm an officer who will do the president's bidding.

Important as the precedent of the Duane removal was, however, it did not settle all questions about the scope of congressional power to restrict presidential removal of executive officers.

In the Bank controversy, President Jackson asserted broad authority to supervise a subordinate's exercise of statutory duties, with removal for noncompliance as the sanction. Jackson found his supervisory authority in his responsibility to the people. During this era, attorneys general issued opinions reflecting a belief that the president's supervisory power is variable. Thus one opinion advised the president that he could not countermand the adjudicative decisions of accounting officers about the amount owing a particular claimant.[83] This opinion was correct, and would probably be required by due process principles today. Another opinion encouraged the president to direct a federal attorney to drop a proceeding that was interfering with foreign policy.[84] Again, the correct result: the president, and not a local prosecutor, makes our foreign policy.

These instances of legally analyzed supervisory efforts were, however, un-usual. More commonly, presidents just went ahead and instructed their subordinates as seemed necessary, as in Jackson's supervision of Indian removal.

Nullification and Union

The nullification crisis of 1832–33 was a "fire bell in the night," warn-ing of the disunion to come.[85] It is no accident that the crisis occurred in South Carolina, where politics were far to the right of any other state. South Carolina's hero was John C. Calhoun, who wrote the bible of nullification, his "Exposition." Calhoun relied on the theory that the Constitution was a compact of sovereign states that could nullify un-acceptable federal laws and, if necessary, secede from the Union. This theory was anathema to Andrew Jackson's majoritarian instincts and had been emphatically rejected by John Marshall in his great decisions, such as *McCulloch*.

The stated occasion for the nullification effort was the federal tariff, although as usual slavery was not very far in the background. The crisis came to a boil after the election of 1832. The South Carolina legislature called for a convention, which then declared the existing tariffs null and void in the state, threatened secession if the federal government used force, and called for draconian measures to punish any federal attempt to collect the tariff.[86]

President Jackson handled the crisis with a superb combination of firmness and conciliation. His annual message called for "moderation and good sense" but promised to suppress the revolt. In private, Jackson fulminated about hanging traitors to nearby trees; coming from him, no one would have dismissed such threats as bluster. Jackson then issued his Nullification Proclamation.[87] With help from his advisers, he produced a "forceful, moral statement," one to rival his Bank veto message.[88]

The proclamation informed the people of South Carolina that nulli-fication was "in direct violation of their duties as citizens of the United States" and that it was "subversive" of the Constitution. Jackson stressed that the American people, not the states, made the Constitution and were represented in the presidency and the House of Representatives. He pre-pared to use force. He made clear that he was ready to ask Congress for volunteers and to arrest the state's leaders for treason. At the same time, he tried to avoid confrontation by moving federal troops to island forts so that they would not fire the first shot.

Thus pressured by the president and discovering that no other states had come to their aid, the South Carolinians wavered, and a compromise emerged in Congress. On the same day, Congress passed a tariff reduction bill and a force bill to authorize the president to suppress rebellion. South Carolina then reopened its convention and repealed the ordinances nullifying federal tariffs (but passed another purportedly nullifying the force bill). With enough restraint on both sides, the crisis had passed. Nullification was dead as a politically viable option for the South. Secession would be the remedy next time.

In the nullification crisis, Jackson did not expand the president's own constitutional powers in any significant way. Washington had taken a firm hand against the Whiskey rebels, and Jackson was following in his footsteps. Instead, the important constitutional precedent in Jackson's approach to nullification concerned his interpretation of the constitutional nature of the Union. He was quite prepared to use force to establish that the Constitution created a perpetual Union through ratification by the people. No constitutional principle has been more important to our history. Nevertheless, Jackson was sensitive enough to the role of the states in the federal system to avoid pressing South Carolina too hard and to welcome compromise when it came.[89]

Of course, Andrew Jackson did not settle the question of the constitutional nature of the Union. That task would fall to Abraham Lincoln (and to General Ulysses S. Grant). But Jackson's proclamation provided Lincoln vital support for his own constitutional position when it declared that the Constitution "forms a government, not a league," a "single nation" that is perpetual and does not provide any right of secession except by duly ratified constitutional amendment.[90] As the first president to publicly deny a unilateral right of secession, Jackson formed an important precedent about the Constitution as a whole. Moreover, he was successfully claiming that it would be the president and not the leaders of any state government who would authoritatively interpret the document.

In the tradition of his time, Jackson made his arguments to the people in the form of official statements such as his annual messages and the Nullification Proclamation rather than by giving speeches.[91] This formalized process allowed presidential positions on the Constitution to be fully vetted with advisors and crafted for widespread consumption.

Jackson's Third Term and the Whig Experiment

The presidency of the "sly fox," Martin Van Buren, is sometimes called "Jackson's Third Term" (sans Jackson).[92] Together, Jackson and Van Buren formed the Democratic Party as an alliance between small merchants and farmers in the North and West and slave-owning planters in the South. This awkward alliance would sustain the party until the Civil War.

Van Buren, the first president to have been born a United States citizen rather than a British subject, was everything Jackson was not: urbane, evasive, unassertive, a master of indirection.[93] These qualities brought him to the presidency, but ill suited him to fill it. Van Buren shared Jackson's political values and continued his policies, such as Indian removal. A former slaveholder himself, Van Buren had "no moral feelings" about the subject.[94] Hence he was happy to continue the illegal policy of refusing to deliver abolitionist literature through the mails to the South, which Jackson and his postmaster Kendall had begun.

Van Buren's presidency was wrecked by the depression he inherited from Jackson and his weak response to it. He thought the Constitution gave the federal government little power to respond to an economic crisis by actions such as printing paper money.[95] Shackled by his own view of his powers, he could only look on as the depression played itself out.

With Van Buren's ascension, a period of weak presidencies began that extended to the Civil War, with the notable exception of James Polk's single term. Perhaps, then, Jackson's expansion of executive power had been personal, not institutional. As Polk's example would show, however, Jackson had set precedents that were available for later assertion, tools that were ready for hands strong enough to wield them. The greatest variable in the power of the presidency is always the personal character of the incumbent. Precedents set by strong presidents have never lain disused long enough to rust away.

The Whig Party, born in resistance to Andrew Jackson and nurtured as an opposition party, naturally took a restrictive view of presidential power. They favored a weak, essentially administrative presidency that would be dominated by Congress. The Whig theory envisioned a single-term president who would rarely use the veto power, would defer to the Senate regarding patronage, and would even allow the cabinet to determine administration policy by majority vote.[96]

In 1840 and 1848, the Whigs captured the presidency. How would Whig presidents behave—would they be faithful to party theory, or would they succumb to the temptations of office? The 1840 election provided a good chance to find an answer, because the Whigs took not only the presidency (with 53 percent of the vote) but also both houses of Congress. Yet as Madison had stressed at the time of the framing, one's stand on separation of powers issues depends on where one sits: congressional and presidential perspectives differ in predictable ways. Whig presidents would have to renounce multiple precedents that their predecessors had developed and would have to limit their own power systematically if they were to remain faithful to theory. Nevertheless, perhaps a new era was dawning.

William Henry Harrison's inaugural address was a Whig manifesto, and not a short one. After delivering it for ninety minutes on a cold day, Harrison took sick and died a month later. (It cannot be surprising that all subsequent inaugural addresses have been shorter.) The address contained a lengthy warning about the dangers of a powerful executive.[97] Condemnations of Caesar and Cromwell were thinly veiled references to Andrew Jackson. The speech included promises to serve only a single term and to abjure the spoils system, along with an endorsement of old-fashioned nonpartisan civic virtue.

Harrison died before he could work out the relation of theory to practice.[98] Before his demise, though, he had refused to subject himself to control by his party leaders. From his perch in the Senate, Henry Clay repeatedly pressed for particular cabinet nominations. Finally, Harrison rebuked him: "You forget that I am the President."[99] Whiggish restraint was already yielding to the incentives every president experiences to control those who will fill the cabinet.

Harrison's successor, John Tyler, was another Virginia aristocrat, but there the resemblance ended. An "eccentric Virginia states-righter," Tyler had left the Democrats for the Whigs in reaction to Andrew Jackson's forcefulness.[100] Now the latent defect in the Twelfth Amendment would be revealed. The Whigs, in search of a combination of candidates that would win, had created a politically incompatible ticket. Tyler governed like a Democrat, was ejected from the party by the furious Whigs, and wound up fruitlessly pursuing an independent candidacy for his own election to the presidency (which would have violated the single-term principle). The Whig experiment in executive restraint would have to be postponed to another day.

His Accidency

John Tyler's first decision after Harrison's death formed an important constitutional precedent that was not consistent with Whig theory. Because no prior president had died in office, no one was sure about Tyler's exact status.[101] Article II of the Constitution unhelpfully says that in case of a president's death or "inability to discharge the powers and duties of the said office, the same shall devolve on the Vice President." The ambiguity in "the same" is obvious: does the office of president devolve, or only its powers and duties? In other words, would Tyler be only an "acting president," with the sharply diminished authority of an interim officer? Legal treatises provided esteemed academic authority on each side of the question.

John Tyler provided a definitive answer. He proceeded to Washington and convened his cabinet of Whigs. Tyler told them emphatically that he believed the presidency devolved on him the moment Harrison died. The new secretary of state, Daniel Webster, mentioned that Harrison had intended to make decisions by majority vote of the cabinet. The whiff of a Whig regency was in the air. Tyler would have none of it:

> I, as President, shall be responsible for my administration. I hope to have your
> hearty cooperation in carrying out its measures. . . . When you think otherwise,
> your resignation will be accepted.[102]

This Jacksonian statement brought the cabinet around; they agreed he was president and abandoned hopes for cabinet government. Tyler took the presidential oath and issued an "inaugural address" explaining his position. He then moved into the White House and met with some foreign ministers to cement his new role.

Congress, where each party thought Tyler belonged to the other, was initially doubtful, but both houses passed resolutions that Tyler was president. Although detractors continued to refer to Tyler as "His Accidency," he had won the battle. Many years later, in 1967, the Twenty-Fifth Amendment to the Constitution ratified Tyler's interpretation by providing that when the president no longer serves, "the Vice President shall become President." In the interim, whenever presidents died, their vice presidents took the constitutional oath and became presidents free to realize the entire potential of the office.

Tyler's initial triumph in office was almost his last. He immediately departed from Whig orthodoxy by enthusiastically pursuing a spoils system, removing officers and putting in his supporters to try to build his own base for the election of 1844.[103] By this time, the link between patronage and presidential power as head of a party was evident to all. The struggle between presidents and Congress over appointments had settled into a test of political strength, as it remains today. The developing custom of senatorial courtesy, by which the entire Senate defers to a member's objection to a nominee, dramatically reduced presidential power in this struggle.[104] A single senator who can wield the power of the entire body through courtesy stands on an even plane with the president, who loses his usual power to play off the senators against each other in search of a majority vote.

In an effort to work his way around Senate obstruction of his nominations, Tyler made frequent use of his recess appointments power. Article II of the Constitution empowers presidents to "fill up all Vacancies that may happen during the Recess of the Senate" by making appointments that "expire at the End of their next Session." This housekeeping provision of the Constitution was useful in the early days, with Congress out of session much of the time. Not surprisingly, Jackson had used recess appointments in his battles with the Senate. Tyler interpreted the power broadly, to extend not only to vacancies occurring during a recess but to preexisting ones not filled when the Senate rose.[105] The broad view is preferable—presidents have a good claim under their faithful execution duty to ensure full staffing of the executive, and recess appointments are temporary. The Senate, however, was not amused.

Tyler was forced onto the defensive generally by a Whig Congress that was determined to enact its program. Reduced to governing by the veto, he may have reconsidered his opinion of Andrew Jackson. In fact, he not only emulated Jackson's use of the veto but extended it.[106] Although Jackson made his famous claim of a plenary veto power, his rejection of the bank bill also included more traditional assertions that the bill was unconstitutional. Although Tyler frequently stated constitutional objections, he also clearly claimed the power to veto a bill for political reasons, thus cementing the broader view of the Jacksonian practice. Tyler suffered the first successful congressional override. Wholly undeterred, he vetoed both a bill to recharter a rather constricted federal bank and an even weaker successor bill to form a "fiscal corporation" (not a bank, to be sure). He vetoed two tariff bills and then signed one.

Constantly confronting Congress, Tyler successfully asserted executive privilege against congressional attempts to obtain some diplomatic correspondence and to learn the names of congressmen who had applied for executive positions, but he wound up handing over some papers regarding an investigation of Indian land frauds. Meanwhile, his frustrated Whig cabinet had all resigned save Webster, who was enmeshed in some diplomatic negotiations.

President Tyler's restrained conception of federal power came under stress when the "Dorr Rebellion" broke out in tiny, cranky Rhode Island.[107] Two groups claimed to constitute the legitimate government of the state; violence threatened. Article IV of the Constitution obliges the United States "to guarantee to every State . . . a Republican form of government" but does not say which branch should do the guaranteeing. After initially declining the governor's request to intervene, Tyler responded to the onset of violence by issuing an executive order threatening to call out the militia in neighboring states if the rebels did not disperse. That quashed the insurrection, except for some later litigation that eventuated in a Supreme Court decision holding that authority to enforce the guarantee clause lay with the political branches, not the judiciary.[108]

Tyler's deadlocked presidency had one remaining achievement: the annexation of Texas.[109] As a good Jeffersonian Republican, Tyler believed in expansion of the agrarian republic (and not incidentally, the expansion of slavery). The way Tyler accomplished the annexation created an important precedent about constitutional power, giving presidents a new tool to use. The history of the Louisiana Purchase strongly suggested that treaties were the exclusive constitutional mechanism for acquiring new territory for the United States. Other treaties, such as the Transcontinental Treaty with Spain, had confirmed the practice.

Forging ahead without a political base to stand on, Tyler secretly negotiated a treaty to annex Texas. He submitted it to the Senate with an extremely impolitic justification penned by his secretary of state, none other than John C. Calhoun, arguing that acquiring Texas would protect the beneficial institution of slavery from British interference. This was a bit blunt for the Senate, which rejected the treaty resoundingly. The episode demonstrated that when a president negotiates a treaty in secret, without preparing the ground by consulting senators, the risk of rejection rises.

Tyler bided his time and was encouraged to try again by Polk's election to the presidency in late 1844 on a platform that included acquiring Texas. Now the Old Hero, in his last year of life, offered a suggestion that

Tyler adopted: ask Congress to annex Texas by joint resolution (that is, by the equivalent of a statute), which would require only simple majorities in both houses, instead of by treaty. Article IV of the Constitution says that new states "may be admitted by the Congress into this Union," but does not specify the method.[110] This time Tyler presented the argument for annexation more tactfully, emphasizing the need to bring Texas under the protection of the United States and to create secure borders. After a debate over slavery, Congress narrowly passed the resolution, and the president signed it.

Together, Congress and the president had created a new constitutional method for annexing territory. Because the annexation evaded the two-thirds supermajority requirement for Senate ratification of treaties, however, constitutional doubts lingered. No matter—once the joint resolution had passed and the president had signed it, there was no obvious way to undo the action. Bitter political opposition to the annexation soon subsided—the nation had ratified the annexation.[111] Perhaps the election of Polk had provided a form of prior public consent to the acquisition of Texas; otherwise it was the kind of fait accompli that aggressive presidents can present the nation. This one would exacerbate political opposition to the coming war with Mexico.

As his term expired, Tyler invited Texas to enter the Union. Mexico had said that it would consider annexation equivalent to a declaration of war. In response, Tyler ordered the Navy to patrol the Gulf of Mexico and the Army to patrol ground near but not in Texas. He was warning but not provoking Mexico. His successor would intensify the signals.

Manifest Destiny

James K. Polk was narrowly elected in 1844 on an expansionist platform calling for the annexation of Texas and Oregon.[112] He was Andrew Jackson's protégé from Tennessee, and an apt one—serious, shrewd, tenacious, willful, a bit sanctimonious. His inaugural address sounded the appropriate notes from Jefferson and Jackson. Once president, he happily vetoed internal improvements bills, believing they fostered "a rich and splendid government" that would oppress the people.[113] He opposed abolition, national banking, national debt, and protective tariffs. Most important, he gave the overture for Manifest Destiny by warning that Texas would be protected against any outside power and by claiming that the United States had "clear and unquestionable" rights to take Oregon (this in the face of an existing joint occupancy agreement with Great Britain).[114]

In order to secure his nomination as a dark horse candidate, Polk had renounced any intention of seeking reelection, so that rivals might unite temporarily around him.[115] When a president becomes a lame duck either by renouncing reelection or by becoming ineligible for it, his control over the cabinet and the party diminishes as other leaders subordinate their loyalty to the president to their own ambitions. Yet Polk overcame this initial handicap and accomplished his goals in a stunningly complete fashion. He wanted to secure Texas, obtain Oregon and California, reduce tariffs, and stop putting government funds in private banks.[116] He immediately declared that "I intend to be *myself* President," so that party leaders would understand there would be no regency.[117] Polk dominated his cabinet but did use it as a constant sounding board to test his ideas and to present a unanimous executive branch to the outside world. Disinclined to delegate responsibility, he worked constantly, admitting, "I prefer to supervise the whole operations of the Government myself . . . and this makes my duties very great."[118] This devotion to duty and dominance eventually exhausted him. At the end of his term of office, he retired to Tennessee and was dead in less than four months.

Before the development of a substantial White House staff in the twentieth century, presidents had to run the executive branch through the cabinet, whatever its fragmentation of loyalties might be. Polk's secretary of state was a constant thorn in his side—James Buchanan, an erratic politico possessed of terrible judgment and loyal only to his own presidential ambitions.[119] Polk tolerated him and kept him under control but did not fire him despite ample reason to do so. The uneven cabinet also included William Marcy at War and Robert Walker at Treasury. Secretive by nature, Polk often kept his own views to himself so that he could strategically dole out information about his intentions both within the cabinet and to supporters in Congress.

Intent on managing the press as a link to public opinion, Polk established his own house organ, the *Washington Union*.[120] Buchanan once remarked that when the organ fell out of tune, the president adjusted its pipes. During the Mexican War, when the Senate rejected some of Polk's legislation, he had the *Union* thunder away at it, which produced complaints that he was using the paper to destroy the separation of powers. Tellingly, Polk won the legislative victory.

Patronage was the bane of Polk's existence as president.[121] It had become a three-way scramble among the president, senators, and party organizations. He removed few officers—mostly partisan Whigs—because vacancies were such a mixed blessing. Polk repeated the observation that presidents since Jefferson had made, that each appointment produced one ingrate and twenty enemies. This multiplier effect meant that patronage disputes fed party divisions. In Polk's view patronage therefore weakened the presidency by impeding reelection. It was becoming clear that unless a president could dominate his party, patronage would erode his power by fragmenting his control over the executive. Struggling, Polk accepted some senatorial demands for patronage and resisted others. Everything else he did was more fun.

President Polk took a more moderate approach to Oregon than his strident inaugural address suggested he would. The most radical expansionists wanted the entire northwest part of the continent up to the tip of the Alaska Panhandle. (Thus the campaign slogan "Fifty-four forty or fight.") But presidents since Monroe had offered the forty-ninth parallel as a dividing line, and Polk was happy with that. He and Buchanan quietly made that offer to the British and were rebuffed. Characteristically, Polk responded aggressively. Telling a congressman that "the only way to treat John Bull was to look him straight in the eye," Polk claimed the entire territory.[122]

After December 1845, with Congress finally in session, Polk involved it in the Oregon question by inducing it to pass a resolution authorizing his termination of the joint occupancy agreement.[123] Considering the looming war with Mexico, this aggressive approach to the British was quite dangerous. To defuse the situation, Polk had Buchanan tell the British that an offer by them of the forty-ninth parallel would be welcome. This time they agreed. Concerned about criticism from the fifty-four forty crowd in Congress, Polk took the unusual step of obtaining the Senate's formal consent to Britain's proposal before he formally concluded the treaty. It was finished in 1846, after the Mexican War had begun. With the northwestern border of the United States settled at last, Polk could turn his gaze elsewhere.

Taking California had been on the president's mind all along, although he did not share his goal widely. His first annual message to Congress in December 1845, restated the Monroe Doctrine to ward off supposed British and French interest in California (and to keep everyone out of Texas).[124] Settling the Oregon question helped by confining British activity along the Pacific Coast. Now Polk needed only to detach California from its tenuous control by Mexico. He was ready to buy it or to foment revolution there or to take it by war if necessary. Without congressional authorization, he dispatched naval patrols to California and General John C. Fremont's overland expedition to survey a route to the California coast. As with Jackson's earlier adventure in Florida, aggressive local commanders might make conquests the president could embrace.

Polk pressured Mexico with both military and diplomatic steps. He was less circumspect than Tyler had been in deploying the military in contested territory. He accepted the thin claim of Texas to the area between the Nueces and the Rio Grande and ordered General Zachary Taylor to cross the Nueces and to regard any Mexican incursion over the Rio Grande as an act of war.[125] If this provocation resulted in war, Polk was ready to wage one.

Meanwhile, the president dispatched a diplomatic mission to accomplish his ends peacefully. Without asking for senatorial confirmation, he sent John Slidell to Mexico with instructions to try to buy California and New Mexico. The Mexican government, understandably feeling unduly pressured, prepared to reject the mission. Hearing this, Polk ordered Taylor to move forward to the Rio Grande, within territory long claimed by Mexico. For a while, nothing happened.

In May 1846, boiling with frustration, Polk had his cabinet vote in favor of a request for a declaration of war. The next day he learned of the first combat. Provoked by Taylor's blockade of the Rio Grande, a Mexican force had crossed the river and attacked American troops, killing eleven of them and capturing others. Polk then sent a message to Congress calling for a declaration of war, saying with more passion than justification that Mexico "has invaded our territory and shed American blood on the American soil."[126]

Polk's message (and more important, the violence he had instigated) had the desired effect. The House took a half hour to pass the declaration by a substantial margin; the Senate readily concurred the next day. Opposition came from significant quarters, however. In the House, John Quincy Adams voted against this "most unrighteous war."[127] In Massachusetts, Henry David Thoreau protested by refusing to pay his taxes and went to jail. His "On Civil Disobedience" followed. Dissent, often bitter, persisted throughout the war, but to his credit Polk never made an effort to suppress it.

As "Mr. Polk's war" became costly in both treasure and lives, opposition mounted. The Whigs took a majority in the House in 1846 and passed a resolution stating that the war had been "unnecessarily and unconstitutionally begun by the President." Abraham Lincoln, in his single term in Congress, challenged the honesty of the president's actions by unsuccessfully introducing his "Spot Resolutions," demanding to know the "spot" on American soil where blood was shed.[128] Lincoln also disputed the constitutionality of Polk's initiation of the war. With his characteristic sense for the heart of an issue, Lincoln protested that if a president could provoke war by placing the troops in harm's way, the constitutional decision to go to war was placed in the hands of "one man," evading the assignment of the war power to Congress by the Constitution.[129] (In 1861, he may have ruefully recalled this argument.)

The initiation of the Mexican War formed a precedent permanently altering the distribution of war powers between presidents and Congress. As Lincoln saw so clearly, presidents can invoke their commander in chief power to deploy American forces in ways that can be expected to trigger a violent response. General Taylor's march to the Rio Grande did just that. Congress has very little practical power to prevent such actions if it desires to fund an effective and flexible military. Presidents can then present Congress with a fait accompli once American forces are attacked. As the speedy congressional votes to commence the Mexican War illustrate, it does not take an attack on the scale of Pearl Harbor or 9/11 to trigger a furious patriotic response from legislators.

Once the war got under way, President Polk generated his own strategic aims. He then obtained support from his cabinet but did not involve his generals in the strategy-planning process. Disinclined to seek expert military input, he approached his responsibilities as commander in chief in the same way he supervised the executive branch generally. Ever the micromanager, he even instructed General Taylor regarding whether to transport supplies in wagons or on mules.[130]

Pursuant to his strategy of occupying regions he hoped to detach from Mexico, Polk quickly sent American forces to take control of New Mexico and California. The campaign against Mexico proper, which was designed to force concession of this territory, presented greater problems of both a military and a political nature. Polk's suspicion of the political ambitions of his generals interfered with his performance as commander in chief. Senator Thomas Hart Benton captured the problem with his observation that Polk wanted "a small war, . . . not large enough to make military reputations, dangerous for the presidency."[131]

Throughout the war, Polk machinated against both of his senior generals, considering them Whigs (he appointed only Democrats to new general officer openings). Initially, he was justifiably reluctant to give command in the field to Winfield Scott, his most senior and most gifted general. Scott's unbounded vanity and ambition led to his exquisite nickname of "Old Fuss and Feathers" and to a troubling tendency to challenge civilian authority. Distrusting Scott's Whiggish political ambitions, the president kept him close by in Washington and entrusted the Mexican campaign to Zachary Taylor. Soon Polk also felt the need to keep Taylor in check, as "Old Rough and Ready" enjoyed enough success in northern Mexico to open speculation about his presidential prospects in 1848. (Had Polk not renounced running at the outset of his term, this talk might have diminished.)

Seeing that Taylor was at a strategic dead end in northern Mexico, Polk had the idea of opening a second front through Veracruz to attack toward Mexico City. Winfield Scott, offered the command, loved the prospect of being a second Cortés. After Scott took Mexico City in a brilliant campaign and then resumed irritating the president, Polk summarily relieved him from command. Comprehensively suspicious, Polk also resisted efforts of members of Congress to get executive appointments, especially in the military, echoing old concerns by citing a "corrupting" tendency if he yielded.[132]

Victory in the "Halls of Montezuma" gave the Marines another line for their hymn and raised the problem of deciding what territory to extort from the defeated Mexicans. Polk secretly sent Buchanan's able chief assistant at State, Nicholas Trist, as his envoy to press American claims and end the war. Trist concluded the Treaty of Guadalupe Hidalgo, acquiring California and the Southwest for $15 million and the assumption of some claims. Although he was inclined to press for even more, Polk knew that the war was increasingly deadly and unpopular and decided to accept it, as did the Senate in 1848.

Now the United States was truly a continental nation, thanks largely to the efforts of James K. Polk. He had "successfully discovered the latent constitutional powers of the commander in chief to provoke a war, secure congressional support for it, shape the strategy for fighting it, appoint generals, and define the terms of peace."[133] He skillfully brought such congressional leaders as Benton into enough of his confidential plans to convert them into legislation. To keep Congress compliant, Polk sent it even highly confidential documents when they were demanded, such as the negotiating instructions to Nicholas Trist.[134] This strategy left both members of Congress and the public in a reactive stance, forever trying to catch up to what Polk had already done. He was crafting history and letting the nation learn about it after the fact.

Thus a majority in Congress had, however reluctantly, ratified Polk's theory of his constitutional powers. At the close of the war, there was a perfect opportunity for the Whigs to take the constitutional issues to the nation in the election of 1848. But the antiwar party squandered the opportunity by nominating war hero Zachary Taylor in an effort to capture the White House by any means necessary. Taylor's nomination and his electoral victory show how rapidly the United States moved on from disputes about the war to squabbles over its booty. Later presidents could deduce from the Mexican War that stretching executive power works whenever the people approve of the ultimate result.

The United States would discover that the ultimate price of the territory acquired in the Mexican War was far higher than the money specified in the treaty. Ralph Waldo Emerson had predicted that "Mexico will poison us" like a dose of arsenic.[135] Indeed it did—the vast new acquisitions deranged the careful compromises about slavery that had patched the nation together over the years, shifted national politics to sectionalism and the future of slavery, and led to civil war.[136]

Modern historians sometimes wonder why James Polk, whose presidency was entirely successful on its own terms and left the United States the legacy of much of its current map, has not been more revered. The narrow compass of his character provides the explanation. For an instructive contrast, consider John Quincy Adams, whose presidency was so disappointing but who rose to greatness in his later career in the House of Representatives. In 1848, while still waging his fierce battles against slavery and the Mexican War, Adams collapsed on the floor of the House and died soon after. His longtime opponent Senator Benton gave the perfect eulogy: "Death found him at his post of duty; and where else could it have found him?"[137] Benton was responding to the moral dimension that enlarged Adams but not Polk (who was no less devoted to his own, narrower, sense of duty). Great presidents are revered for placing a moral stamp on the nation, maximizing their contribution as head of state. This achievement expands the overall legal powers of the presidency by increasing the people's regard for the office and their willingness to accept broad presidential claims of power.

After the Polk presidency, the Whigs had one more try at their experiment in reducing executive power. In 1848, they nominated Zachary Taylor because he had the considerable virtue of a blank political record.

A southern slaveholder, he had never voted and had no known political views. He did wish to be president, however. So he declared himself a Whig and promised to take the lead of Congress on the usual issues such as the tariff and internal improvements. That sufficed for his election along with his running mate, Millard Fillmore of New York, who was a genuine Whig but no Henry Clay. Of course, the bad luck of the Whigs held: after only sixteen months, a second Whig general-president was dead, and Fillmore was president (thanks to Tyler, not "acting president").[138]

Ironically, the slaveholding Taylor had been a nationalist who disappointed both the South and the Whigs. He endorsed a strong presidency by threatening to send federal troops to stop Texas from invading the territory of New Mexico in an effort to expand slavery.[139] At odds with Congress, he granted many recess appointments, taking the broad view of the power as applying to all vacancies in existence when the Senate recessed.

Taylor's "doughface" successor Fillmore pleased the South by supporting the Compromise of 1850, an agonized set of trade-offs that temporized with the issue of slavery in the territories and included the notorious Fugitive Slave Act. Fillmore then proceeded to overenforce the act's draconian provisions for returning runaway slaves. He overcame spirited and sometimes violent resistance in the North in an inverted replay of Jackson's nullification crisis. Like Jackson before him and Lincoln after him, Fillmore was willing to use both the militia and the armed forces to enforce federal law.[140] Fillmore showed, however, none of Jackson's wise admixture of conciliation, a quality that was especially needed given the odiousness of this law. A president's duty faithfully to execute the law, which is so difficult for Congress or the courts to control, requires presidential sensitivity as well as vigor.

Fillmore emphasized a corollary of Manifest Destiny, the desirability of opening trade with the Far East. The opening of Japan by Matthew Perry and his fleet demonstrated aggressive initiative in executive control of foreign policy. Secretary of State Daniel Webster authorized Perry to negotiate with the Japanese and to punish them if resistance were encountered, but only in "self-defense," since the president could not declare war—reminiscent of Jefferson and the Barbary pirates.[141] The expedition was a success, and commercial treaties followed. As advocates of Manifest Destiny had long dreamed, American power now stretched across the Pacific.

A Democrat, Franklin Pierce was very much in the mold of his predecessor Millard Fillmore. Another northern doughface, Pierce stuck to a strict construction of the Constitution that protected slavery and states' rights.[142] His view of the role of the federal government was so cramped that he vetoed a bill to set aside public lands to fund institutions for the insane, saying that the Constitution did not make the government "the great almoner of public charity."[143] He ineffectively pursued Manifest Destiny in the Caribbean in hopes of adding more slave territory. He vigorously enforced the Fugitive Slave Act. In 1854 he signed the Kansas-Nebraska Act that abandoned the old Missouri Compromise line, which had restricted slavery in the territories. The available avenues for avoiding disunion were narrowing.

CHAPTER FIVE

A Rough Time of It

Lincoln

These rebels are violating the Constitution to destroy the Union; I will violate the Constitution, if necessary, to save the Union; and I suspect, Chase, that our Constitution is going to have a rough time of it before we get done with this row.—Abraham Lincoln, conversation with Salmon P. Chase[1]

A rough time it was. The question for us now, a century and a half later, is what lessons to draw about the Constitution from the most extraordinary and sustained crisis in American history. Perhaps the Civil War era remains so unique that its constitutional history should be regarded as a temporary aberration leaving little residue for today's conditions. I do not think so. While the particular stresses that the era placed on the Constitution do not bear close repetition, some of the interpretations that emerged from them do have modern utility in times of crisis. The challenge is to determine which elements of the Civil War experience are now graven on the Constitution and which remain graven only on haunting daguerreotypes.

Mr. Buchanan and Mr. Scott

The final crisis of the Union began in the spring of 1857 with two nearly contemporaneous events. First, James Buchanan was inaugurated president, remarking happily in his speech that the great question of slavery in the territories would soon be put to rest by the Supreme Court. When the decision in the *Dred Scott* case was announced two days later, it was soon apparent that, far from settling this deeply vexed political issue, the

Court had reduced the possibility of further sectional compromise.[2] Perhaps chastened by the furious reaction to its decision in the North, the Supreme Court then receded from the great constitutional battles over the nature of the Union, leaving them almost entirely for the president and Congress to decide.

Dred Scott, a slave, had been brought by his master into Illinois and the Minnesota Territory, neither of which allowed slavery. The issue in the case was whether these sojourns freed him. For the Supreme Court, Chief Justice Roger Taney wrote a long and tortured opinion in an effort to end controversy about the legality of slavery in the territories. The question actually presented in the case was comparatively easy, and the Court decided it correctly. The Constitution's pervasive recognition of slavery and its explicit provision for the return of escaped slaves powerfully implied that the temporary presence of Scott in a free state or territory did not end his bondage.[3]

Nonetheless, Taney went on (and on) to argue unnecessarily that blacks could not be American citizens and that Congress had no power to exclude slavery from the territories. True to his roots in the time of Jackson, Taney was trying to forge a new sectional compromise along Jacksonian lines, empowering the slaveholding elements of the old bisectional coalition.[4] But the political effects of this theory were as devastating as its premises were inhumane. The North could no longer compromise by acceding to the presence of slavery in some territories but not others; the South, no longer having to rely on popular sovereignty theories to extend slavery, turned toward intransigence.[5]

As president-elect, Buchanan had played a highly improper role in the decision of the case. At the time, five of the nine Supreme Court justices, including Taney, were southerners. In an effort to persuade at least one of the northern justices to join Taney's opinion, Buchanan wrote a letter to Justice Robert Grier of Pennsylvania, urging him to join the majority, and he did.[6] Then as now, presidents had no power to intervene in pending Supreme Court litigation. Such an action very likely violates the constitutional rights of litigants to due process. Buchanan's unseemly action was kept secret at the time and remained so for many years, until discovered in his papers.

No one should be surprised, though, that James Buchanan would sacrifice principle to expediency. He had the revealing nickname of the "Old Public Functionary," in part because he had spent time in both houses of Congress, as a minister abroad, and as Polk's erratic secretary of state.

At the core he was an insubstantial, weak man who served only his own advancement.[7] The only political value that he consistently adhered to— and one that drove his constitutional interpretation—was the interest of the slaveholding South. Buchanan never forgot that he owed his election to southern support for his doughface stance.[8] By the time of his inaugural, his intervention in *Dred Scott* had made a down payment on recompense to his supporters.

The aftermath of the *Dred Scott* decision reawakened a long-standing, important, and still unresolved debate about the extent to which a Supreme Court decision has any binding effect upon the executive branch beyond the parties who litigated it. In 1857, many American politicians entered that debate, among them Abraham Lincoln. He vehemently denounced Taney's opinion. Lincoln conceded that since the Court had held that Dred Scott was a slave, the executive could not set him free. But Lincoln urged every possible method of political opposition to the decision, such as the election of legislators who would seek ways to overturn or undermine it.[9] This much was certainly appropriate.

The trickier issue is whether Congress and the president are under an obligation to adhere to the principle that underlies a particular decision in other cases to which the principle fairly applies.[10] Andrew Jackson would certainly not have recognized any such obligation; his bank veto message explicitly rejected it. Ever since Jefferson, executive branch departmentalism has tried to minimize the collateral effects of judicial decisions. *Dred Scott* illustrates the justification for doing so. Ranging far beyond the issues presented in the case, much of Taney's decision deserved no deference from anyone.

The principle for which the outcome of the case stood is that temporary sojourns into free territory did not free slaves. At the most, the rest of the federal government should have honored that, but it was under no obligation to abide by the Court's broadest statements. Thus, after Lincoln became president, he was following the lead of Jefferson and Jackson when he directed federal agencies to treat free blacks as citizens for such statutory purposes as patent eligibility.[11] He was correct that the Court had not needed to decide any such question and that it remained open to his resolution in the course of his duties.[12]

President Buchanan's administration was a prelude to tragedy. He set the table for secession. His unrelenting support for the South aggrieved the North, encouraged southerners' sense of being wronged by abolitionist or containment spirit in the North, increased the impact of *Dred Scott*, and squandered whatever opportunity remained for reconciliation. His disastrous support for attempts to foist a proslavery constitution on the new state of Kansas despite a local majority against it hardened lines of sectional opposition and indirectly loosed the whirlwind, physically embodied by John Brown.[13]

The fact that Buchanan's proslavery political views drove his constitutional analysis was not unusual. In the antebellum years, no southern sympathizer would be in favor of either strong federal power in general or strong executive power in particular (except for enforcing the Fugitive Slave Act). To earn his spurs as a constitutional heir of Jefferson and Jackson, Buchanan even vetoed some internal improvements bills.

Buchanan managed the executive branch poorly.[14] He was fussy, disinclined to delegate decisions, and thin-skinned. He formed a cabinet of southern sympathizers, who reinforced his insulation from the dominant political views of the North. His command of the executive was weak enough to engender claims that the administration was actually run by a prosouthern "Directory" consisting of Howell Cobb at Treasury, Jacob Thomson at Interior, and Senator John Slidell of Louisiana. Whatever the truth of these claims, Buchanan's lax supervision of the executive allowed an outbreak of corruption that featured graft in government contracts, diversion of public funds to Democrats, and even bribery of congressmen.

Buchanan's cabinet was no ornament. Secretary of State Lewis Cass was senile, leaving Buchanan to craft his own rather captious foreign policy, which pursued the southern dream of acquiring Cuba. At the War Department, Virginian John Floyd made clear that he would do nothing that might offend the South. A congressional committee investigated him for the scandals about contractors and tarred him considerably. Lacking the courage to fire Floyd, Buchanan kept him on until nearly the end of his term and then had Vice President Breckinridge ask for the resignation.

The most serious default in Buchanan's duty to ensure faithful execution of the laws occurred during the secession crisis that followed Lincoln's election.[15] During the crisis, Buchanan met with the cabinet almost daily. All were inclined to blame the North and to sympathize with secession. They did not think there was a legal right to secede, though, and Buchanan agreed. None were ready to fight for the Union. Buchanan took advice from no one who held contrary views and even consulted Jefferson Davis. Eventually, Buchanan asked his able attorney general, Jeremiah Black, for an opinion on presidential power to collect customs

duties, defend federal property, and enforce the laws in the South. The
opinion said that the president could take all these steps and could call
out the militia but that going beyond "defensive" measures to an "offensive" war to enforce federal supremacy was beyond the power of the
government.[16]

Buchanan cobbled these various elements into a highly muddled and
untenable constitutional stance. His annual message to the lame duck
Congress that convened in December 1860 revealed his unwillingness to
take effective action to preserve the Union. He began by denying that
states had any constitutional right to secede but immediately vitiated
that statement by asserting that the Constitution gave the government
no power "to coerce a State into submission which is attempting to withdraw." If any further signal of his acquiescence to secession be needed, he
went on to blame northerners and abolitionists for the crisis and to call
for steps to protect slavery in the South.

Although Buchanan doubtless considered himself a true political heir
to Andrew Jackson, the real Jackson would have tolerated none of this.
His vision of a decentralized republic stopped where threats to the Union
began, as he proved in the nullification crisis. Abraham Lincoln was Jackson's true heir on this point. He pronounced secession the "essence of
anarchy."[17] Yet president-elect Lincoln was in no position to engage in
Jacksonian bluster: only the lower South seceded during the winter, and
Lincoln kept quiet, hoping to hold both the upper South and the border
states in the Union.

Because the Constitution is silent regarding whether a state may secede and whether the federal government may coerce it to remain, antebellum presidents could plausibly adopt either Buchanan's passive theory
or the active one that Lincoln inherited from Jackson (no antebellum
president conceded the legitimacy of secession). The difference between
these positions depends on an underlying theory about the nature of the
Union and whether it creates a league or a nation. No more important
interpretive question could come before a president. In the antebellum
years, a president's answer to it would determine many particular issues
related to federalism, especially questions relating to slavery. In 1860, the
answer would determine whether the Union would be preserved at the
cost of civil war.

As a matter of pure theory, a state could assert a plausible right to secede. After all, the Constitution's framers had essentially seceded from the
"perpetual" union declared by the preceding Articles of Confederation,

which clearly required unanimous state consent to alterations.[18] Disobeying this requirement, the eleven states that initially ratified the Constitution formed a new union that left North Carolina and Rhode Island isolated, wondering where their sisters had gone. If the technique was acceptable in 1788, why not now?

The answer to this question had to go beyond dry webs of theory and enter the realm of statesmanship—a president's vision of what the American nation (or nations) had been and could become. Buchanan's essential failing was inconsistency between an abstract duty to preserve the Union, which he asserted, and his unwillingness to assert the powers of his office as a means to that end. In other words, he was delegating the issue to Congress and the states, awaiting events rather than shaping them.

By replacing Buchanan with Lincoln, whose views on the permanence of the Union were clear, the election of 1860 brought the long-simmering issue of secession to a boil. Lincoln was elected with 40 percent of the popular vote in a four-way race. He had 54 percent in the North, but in parts of the Deep South he received no votes at all. The operation of the Electoral College transformed this fragmented result into a clear victory for Lincoln.[19] With his majorities in the populous states of the North, Lincoln received 60 percent of the votes in the Electoral College.

The initial spate of secessions was not caused by anything Lincoln had recently said or done—he had always said he wanted to stop the spread of slavery but would leave it alone where it existed. Instead, the lower South seceded because the executive branch would no longer be in the hands of a supporter of slavery. The election results appeared to foreclose the alternative of trying to continue the politics of sectional compromise that preceded 1860. Southerners understood that even without confronting slavery directly, an unsympathetic president could use his patronage powers to put federal officers in the South who would threaten it. For example, Republican postmasters might deliver abolitionist tracts through the mails.

While Lincoln awaited his inauguration, President Buchanan dithered. He said that resolution of the crisis was for Congress, where some efforts were made to patch things together. These included a proposed thirteenth amendment protecting slavery; it went to the states and had one ratification when the war started.[20] The trickiest issue for Buchanan concerned the federal forts in the South, which were symbols of national authority. The president's faithful execution duty surely meant that he should protect federal military property. Buchanan never said he would abandon the forts and even mounted a halfhearted expedition to relieve Sumter that was turned back by Confederate gunfire.

But Buchanan would not press War Secretary Floyd to take sufficient action to secure the forts. As the crisis deepened, the cabinet started departing. A new attorney general, the redoubtable Edwin Stanton, reflected fierce northern opinion by exerting pressure to save the forts. Toward the end, buffeted by clashing pressures, Buchanan fell back on assertions that preserving the status quo was principled. He would not fire the first shot and was trying to avoid provoking the Confederates into doing so. Having escalated the crisis of the Union, Buchanan finally escaped it and his office together.

Perhaps it is idle or cruel to task James Buchanan overmuch for his grave failures of faithful execution of the law. His weakness of character and devotion to slave interests left him incapable of the kinds of action that his far stronger successor would take. And once the election had produced a president-elect who was prepared to preserve the Union by force of arms, there may have been no peaceful path to saving it. In any event, Buchanan leaves us a stark example of how a president can fail his faithful execution duty through inaction. Ironically, Lincoln's successor, Andrew Johnson, would provide an equally stark example of how a president can fail this duty through aggressive action. In the interim, winning the Civil War would require the more subtle and effective interpretation of the duty that Lincoln was prepared to provide.

The Spark of a Constitutional Revolution

Like the great statue that graces his monument, Abraham Lincoln can strike us as an enigma frozen in marble. His contemporaries would have understood our fascination with him and our frustration at probing his inner self. David Davis, who knew him well, called Lincoln the "most reticent, secretive man" he had known, hidden behind his iron self-control.[21]

As many historians have noted, "the hallmark of Lincoln's greatness was his capacity for growth."[22] He constantly learned in office, both following and shaping public opinion as it evolved. Lincoln was "the last Enlightenment politician," believing in reason (not revelation), natural rights, prudence, a fatalistic deism, and human progress.[23] Like his best general, Ulysses S. Grant, he moved constantly forward to meet the challenges before him, never retreating from the essentials of his values. He was committed to stopping the spread of slavery. As he took office, he had to decide how to do that while preserving the Union. He was determined to achieve both goals.

Abraham Lincoln believed in our constitutional system and the rule of law more deeply than Thomas Jefferson or Andrew Jackson ever did.[24] From the Declaration of Independence Lincoln drew a national commitment to civil and political equality that he saw as informing the later Constitution. He believed that the normal processes of government could eventually excise the Constitution's great flaw, slavery. To begin that project, it would be necessary to recast national politics, rejecting the sordid bargains of the Kansas-Nebraska Act in favor of a return to the first principles of the nation's founding as he saw them.[25] The constitutional legacy that he inherited included precedents for forceful action from Washington, Jefferson, Jackson, and Polk. He rejected the competing legacy (from the other side of Thomas Jefferson), which interpreted the Constitution narrowly to create a quite limited federal government that needed explicit grants of authority for acting.

Having been nurtured on Henry Clay's ambitious American System, Lincoln was never sympathetic to narrow constitutional analysis. His nationalistic politics had always favored federal internal improvements and the broad style of constitutional interpretation that was necessary to support them.[26] Although the tension between broad and narrow constitutional interpretation would long survive him, Lincoln's presidency set a new, more nationalistic, baseline for it.

The linchpin of all Lincoln's constitutional analysis was his unshakeable devotion to the concept of the Union. Like Jackson, he drew it from the central political and constitutional value of majority rule. More emotionally, he could feel—and would invoke in his first inaugural—the "mystic chords of memory" that had tied Americans together since the Declaration of Independence. Gazing at what others saw as a confederation of sovereign states, he saw a nation. He would not abandon it, no matter what.

Old Institutions, New Responsibilities

In 1861, neither the United States nor its government was ready to conduct the world's first major industrial war. Notwithstanding the improvements in transportation and communications since Jackson's time, America was still predominantly a nation of farmers who were accustomed to weak government. Four years later, having accelerated its industrial revolution under strong executive governance, a newly *United* States began its climb toward world economic dominance.

The new president was bereft of executive experience. He would head an executive branch that lacked both the organizational and operational capacity to conduct a great civil war. The Army of sixteen thousand troops was scattered around on Indian duty; the Navy of forty-two ships was mostly off on patrol or under repair.[27] Four years later the Grand Army of the Republic would parade in its teeming numbers; a Navy that could effectively blockade the long southern coastline would boast the world's first fleet of ironclad warships.

Lincoln had to rely on rudimentary existing mechanisms for controlling the executive branch. In 1861, the incoming president had authority to hire a personal staff consisting of one private secretary.[28] Lincoln hired three gifted young aides (placing two formally in the Interior Department). John Hay was a recent college graduate who would go on to become a distinguished secretary of state at the end of the century. John Nicolay was a journalist. William Stoddard, the third, was not as close to Lincoln as the other two.

Lincoln's personal secretaries displayed remarkable versatility, loyalty, and honesty. They screened the many requests for meetings with him, managed the flood of his mail, and greeted the various dignitaries such as members of Congress, the cabinet, and the military who simply showed up at the White House expecting to see the president. Lincoln also used them as his eyes and ears, sending them on confidential assignments to serve as observers and informal envoys in situations demanding secrecy and discretion. With such a skeleton staff, Lincoln could barely handle his workload. Much was left to his own vast stamina, devotion, and patience.

Especially at the outset, the White House was inundated by office seekers crowding the halls and seeking to importune Lincoln and the secretaries directly. The resulting chaos made Lincoln feel like "a man letting lodgings at one end of his house, while the other end was on fire."[29] The president saw no alternative to the loathsome tasks of patronage, however. Needing to ensure that the civil service would be loyal to him and to the Union, he replaced almost 90 percent of serving presidential appointees, almost all of whom were Democrats.[30] Lincoln worked with members of Congress on the new appointments, deferring to their preferences on minor offices to build alliances in his new party.

When Lincoln took office, he brought into the cabinet his principal rivals for the Republican presidential nomination: William Seward at State, Simon Cameron at War, Salmon Chase at Treasury, and Edward Bates as attorney general.[31] He followed this astonishingly self-confident action by gently but firmly squashing Seward's attempt to install himself as a kind of premier to supervise the less experienced president. After the incompetent and dishonest Cameron had been squeezed out in early 1862 in favor of the dynamic and upright Edwin Stanton, Lincoln had a superb cabinet that also included Gideon Welles at the Navy Department.[32]

In Seward, Stanton, and Chase, Lincoln found that he had three fine lawyers in addition to his attorney general. All four of them advised Lincoln generally throughout the Civil War on the mixed issues of military policy and law that the war presented. As they came to realize, though, Lincoln himself was a supremely gifted lawyer who was inclined to rely on his own counsel.

For the president, the cost of bringing his rivals into the cabinet was that they never functioned as a unit. Of course, the diversity of departmental responsibilities always limits the potential unity of the cabinet. But these were not Lincoln's own people, although Seward and Stanton came to revere him. Each department proceeded on its own for most issues. The cabinet was not used as a coordinating body. Instead, Lincoln dealt directly with each officer and let them run their departments.[33] Having no significant personal staff, Lincoln left many matters to Seward and Stanton, so that he could spend his time deciding major issues himself.[34] The rest of the cabinet, feeling left out, bickered and sometimes complained to allies in Congress about drift in the administration. For Lincoln, the compensation for tolerating considerable disarray was that he received advice from several viewpoints.

The presidential ambitions of Lincoln's erstwhile rivals never entirely stilled. In the dark days of late 1862, Chase tried to eliminate Seward as a future rival by entering a cabal with Republican senators to force Lincoln to reorganize his cabinet.[35] The president, knowing both that the congressional displeasure was really aimed at him and that his control of the executive branch was at risk, would have none of it. With great skill, he parried the move against himself and solidified control of the cabinet. First he patiently listened to the complaints of the senators. He then called a joint meeting of the senators and the cabinet, in which he asked each cabinet member individually whether he supported the president's decisions. Having no alternative, all did so, and Lincoln had held control of the executive branch—for the time being.[36] For Lincoln, managing his cabinet presented constant difficulties, just as did managing his generals.

"And the War Came"[37]

In his first inaugural address, Lincoln avoided statements that might provoke the South except for a pledge to "hold, occupy, and possess" federal facilities located in seceding states. He conditioned that statement, however, with a clear promise not to fire the first shot in a civil war. The tension between these two promises would soon become apparent.

Lincoln's constitutional arguments in the address drew on the views of Andrew Jackson and Daniel Webster that the Union was perpetual and not subject to secession. He made clear that he intended to decide constitutional questions himself, without much deference to the courts. In a clear rebuke to Roger Taney's Supreme Court, Lincoln argued that if the Court could settle all constitutional issues, the people "will have ceased, to be their own rulers, having . . . practically resigned their government, into the hands of that eminent tribunal."[38] Throughout the war, Lincoln would follow his own constitutional course without significant judicial intervention except for one confrontation with Taney that occurred right away.

When Abraham Lincoln was inaugurated in March 1861, Congress was not scheduled to convene until December under the leisurely schedule of the original Constitution. Presidents have constitutional power to convene one or both houses of Congress "on extraordinary Occasions."[39] Conditions in March 1861, were certainly extraordinary in any sense of the term, but all previous presidents had treated the convening power as lying in their sole discretion and were loath to invoke it unless they needed new legislation, appropriations, or confirmations. There was a powerful incentive to begin a presidency with the long window of opportunity to guide events under existing authorities.

For several reasons the new president did not call a special session right away. First, it was not clear who all the members of the new Congress would be. Following the uncoordinated election practices of the times, several northern states would be holding congressional elections throughout the spring. Still, an uncompleted Congress would be better than none at all were legislation to be sought.

Second, a probably decisive consideration was Lincoln's strong reluctance to put early pressure on the wavering slave states of the upper South and the border, which would have had to decide whether to send their delegations or secede. Here Lincoln's determination to maintain the Union impelled him to try to hold it together through his own unilateral actions, without forcing the secession issue unnecessarily.

Proceeding unilaterally held several political advantages for Lincoln as well. He was not yet in full command of the Republican Party and did not want fractious Democrats sniping at him as he tried to deal with the crisis. Within Congress, pressure might have arisen to let the South go; there had been signs of that impulse during the winter. Thus Lincoln wanted some time to get the situation under control before dealing with Congress. Republican leaders in Congress assented to the strategy of waiting and promised ratification of his actions.

The day after his inaugural, Lincoln discovered that Fort Sumter in Charleston Harbor was fast running out of supplies. He knew that Buchanan's supply ships had been driven away from Charleston by shore batteries. The president's dilemma was acute. If he sent a fleet to fight its way into the fort, he would be blamed for violating an inaugural promise and starting a civil war. Moreover, aggressive action would undoubtedly trigger secession in the upper South. If he abandoned the fort, he would violate his other inaugural promise, encourage southern radicals, and lose all credibility in the North at the very outset of his presidency.

Obviously mindful of the start of the Mexican War, Lincoln adopted suggestions for a course of action that was subtler than Polk's had been, one that would place the onus for beginning any war on the South. As Polk had done, he would use his constitutional power to deploy the armed forces to force the other side to choose between war and peace. He informed South Carolina's governor that Sumter would be resupplied with provisions but no munitions and sent ships to carry out the mission. The Confederates responded to the imminent arrival of the relief force by cannonading the fort and forcing its surrender. Whether he wanted it or not, Mr. Lincoln had his war.[40]

As reports of the fall of Fort Sumter sped around the nation, events moved quickly. Lincoln convened the cabinet to ask its advice on two issues. The first was how many militia troops to call up under the venerable 1795 statute, which called for a determination that an insurrection "too powerful to be suppressed" by criminal proceedings existed.[41] That condition was certainly met. The second question was what date to set for a special session of Congress. The two issues were related, because the militia statute limited service of the troops to thirty days after the next convening of Congress. The president needed enough time from the militia to protect the Union until the Army could mobilize. Doubtless this fact confirmed his earlier decision to postpone an immediate call for a special session of Congress.

This initial meeting typified Lincoln's approach to his cabinet: he had already decided to call up the militia and to delay calling Congress into session until he could devise initial responses to the rebellion and wanted advice only on the details. The president then set July 4 for a special session of Congress and called on the states for seventy-five thousand militia. The upper South, responding to Lincoln's call for troops and to war fever prompted by the echoes of cannon from Charleston, joined the new Confederacy.

In the absence of Congress, the president soon ran out of steps that he could take under existing statutory authority. He ordered several actions that were unauthorized by any existing statute.[42] He was counting on later congressional ratification to save him from charges that he had violated his duty of faithful execution of the laws either by ignoring statutory limits or by acting without statutory support. He was following the precedent of Jefferson's reaction to the attack on the *Chesapeake*. The Lockean prerogative now extended to the context of civil war.

Citing his power as commander in chief, Lincoln called for thousands of volunteer soldiers and sailors and an expansion of the regular Army and Navy. Although justified by the depth of the emergency, this action was illegal because the Constitution explicitly assigns the power to raise armies and navies to Congress in order to forestall unilateral executive war making. As had Jefferson, Lincoln then transgressed another fundamental limit on executive power by paying funds out of the Treasury without a prior appropriation, which is an explicit constitutional condition on spending that ensures congressional control of the purse. Unsure of the loyalty of the federal bureaucracy, he took this step secretly to facilitate assigning some government functions to private individuals whom he trusted.

Finally, Lincoln issued a proclamation that treated the burgeoning rebellion as a war in the full legal sense of the term, thereby trenching deeply on the constitutional power of Congress to declare war and altering fundamental rights of private citizens in the South. After Confederate president Jefferson Davis authorized privateers to prey on the Union's sea commerce, Lincoln responded by proclaiming a naval blockade of the Confederacy and seizing ships that violated it.[43] Throughout the Civil War, property confiscations such as these raised constitutional issues under the protections for private property that the due process clause provides.

Lincoln always took care to articulate a connection between his actions and constitutional text. Because his objection to secession was that it violated the Constitution, he always had to maintain a plausible stance that his own actions were lawful. Notwithstanding his critics' caricatures of him as a tyrant, he never claimed general dictatorial powers in wartime. He spent too much time trying to induce his nominal subordinates to obey him to tempt him to set up as a tyrant. Nor did he embrace tactless Jacksonian arguments that he was the tribune of the whole people as compared to the local constituencies of members of Congress. No matter how aggressive his actions, he took a lawyerly approach to justifying them.

While awaiting congressional ratification of his actions, Lincoln justified them by stressing the duty his inaugural oath gave him to "preserve, protect, and defend" the Constitution.[44] He took the oath very seriously, as witness the repeated references to it in his inaugural address. The oath, however, can be interpreted in two very different ways. On one hand, it may contain no substantive empowerment at all. It may simply refer to the particular powers and duties contained elsewhere in the Constitution. On the other hand, because the language of the oath does state a duty but contains no limits, treating it as a substantive empowerment might justify any conceivable action.

Here, Lincoln was invoking the oath for a temporal patch until Congress convened and not as an excuse to ignore statutes generally. Thus constrained by context, the argument merely invokes the Lockean prerogative to act beyond statutory authority until the legislature assembles. Although Lincoln often mentioned his oath during the war, he had the wisdom not to rely on it as an omnibus justification. Nor was he attracted to available Hamiltonian arguments that the vesting clause gave him all powers that anyone might consider executive in nature. Instead, he was stressing the uniqueness of the nation's situation—and his own. He was not thinking about executive power generally or presidential war power generally but about what his power was in a *civil war*. For that, existing precedents served him poorly, so he felt his way along as both the war and his thinking about it evolved.

From the outset, the insurrectionary nature of the war suggested two lines of expansion of presidential power. In the North, internal security measures that would be extreme for a foreign war might be appropriate. In the South, executive action might deprive citizens of property they used to support the rebellion, including slaves. Lincoln's actions eventually followed both of these avenues.

Suspension of Habeas Corpus

The most important of the early emergency actions was Lincoln's suspension of the writ of habeas corpus in order to protect the capital. In the aftermath of Fort Sumter, federal troops rushed toward Washington to defend it against threats from the Confederacy, which was soon located immediately across the Potomac. When the soldiers marched through Baltimore to connect from one rail line to another en route to the capital, a mob attacked them, and the first significant bloodshed of the war occurred among the troops and rioters. The emergency was grave. The railroad link through Baltimore was the only one connecting Washington to the northern states. If it were cut, only seaborne relief could arrive with any speed.[45]

Both the governor of Maryland and the mayor of Baltimore had authorized burning bridges to keep federal troops out. Consequently, Lincoln was unsure that he could rely on the loyalty of any Maryland authorities, including the judges and juries. Lacking any federal police force, Lincoln ordered federal troops to seize the rail and telegraph lines between Baltimore and Washington to prevent the loss of the capital at the outset of the war.

The president also considered whether to suspend the writ of habeas corpus in Maryland. The traditional purpose of the writ is to require the executive to show a judge sufficient justification for detaining a person. The Constitution authorizes suspension of the writ "when in Cases of Rebellion or Invasion the public Safety may require it" but does not say whether it is Congress or the president who takes the action.[46] Before deciding, Lincoln consulted Attorney General Bates, who provided a summary of authorities on the subject that was "not encouraging."[47] Nevertheless, in late April Lincoln ordered suspension of the writ in the endangered areas, initially along the "military line" between Philadelphia and Baltimore.

A legal challenge soon followed. Military officers arrested John Merryman, a prominent secessionist Marylander, for aiding the rebellion by sabotaging the rail and telegraph lines. Merryman sought and obtained a writ of habeas corpus from Chief Justice Taney in his auxiliary role as federal circuit judge for Maryland.[48] Taney certainly gave every indication that he was spoiling for a confrontation with Lincoln. Without inviting the executive's lawyers to argue their side of the case, Taney issued an elaborate opinion void of any concession that emergency executive action might be necessary. Instead, Taney characterized the president's authority in the crisis as limited to executing existing laws through normal court process. With more justification, his opinion asserted that only Congress and not the president could suspend the writ.[49] When the military refused to deliver up Merryman, the frustrated Taney sent the record to Lincoln, who bore ultimate responsibility for the refusal.[50]

Normally, the president's next step would have been to appeal Taney's order to the full Supreme Court. In 1861, however, the Court was still dominated by the southerners who had decided *Dred Scott*. It could be expected to uphold Taney and rebuke the president. While refusing to yield to Taney, Lincoln took another tack by appealing the *Merryman* order to Congress rather than to the Supreme Court.[51] Here he was on quite uncertain ground. After *Dred Scott*, Lincoln had conceded the Court's power to bind the executive with its determination that Scott remained a slave. Both before and after the Civil War, presidents have routinely obeyed court orders as they apply to the litigants themselves.[52] Hence Lincoln should either have let Merryman go or appealed the order to release him. But the president was unwilling either to encourage the filing of more habeas petitions by releasing Merryman or to file an appeal that would very likely have led to a Supreme Court order against him, which he might have found it necessary to disobey. Turning to Congress probably seemed the least unpalatable option.

In his message to Congress as it convened in July 1861, the president sought ratification for all of his emergency actions since the war began.[53] Regarding the suspension, Lincoln denied that he had violated his constitutional duty of faithful execution, as Taney's supporters had charged. Instead, he argued that he possessed constitutional power to suspend the writ and had done so "very sparingly." After noting that the Constitution did not specify which branch had suspension authority, he stressed the gravity of the crisis—that a third of the states were in rebellion and Congress could have been prevented from assembling. The suspension clause, he said, "was plainly made for a dangerous emergency, it cannot be believed that the framers of the instrument intended, that in every case, the danger should run its course, until Congress could be called together." Here he was not making a broad argument that the suspension power belonged exclusively to the executive but only that the power was concurrent in emergencies. He concluded that the nature of the crisis gave him authority to act and stressed that every action he had taken was supported by constitutional power in the government—that he had done nothing "beyond the constitutional competency of Congress." Thus he claimed no free-ranging emergency power.

Lincoln then added a rhetorical flourish that has misled its readers ever since about the argument he was making: "Are all the laws, *but one*, to go unexecuted, and the government itself go to pieces, lest that one be violated?"[54] But Lincoln had not conceded that he had violated any law, and he had clearly and persuasively claimed legal authority for his suspension of habeas corpus. Here he was really arguing in the alternative: if Congress thought he had lacked authority for the suspension, it should recognize a residual emergency power in the president to preserve the nation *and* its Constitution.

The Lockean prerogative's arguments from necessity are very seductive. Justice Robert Jackson, aware of the problems, once said that inherent emergency power "either has no beginning or it has no end."[55] Yet the crisis at the beginning of the Civil War was without precedent in its severity, and if a president's ultimate sources of authority were ever to be invoked, that was the time. The difficulty is that later presidents have been tempted to argue that if Lincoln could do what he did, they may take less drastic actions that seem necessary to them. The plausibility of such arguments depends on the similarity of the underlying facts to those Lincoln faced.

While preparing his address to Congress, Lincoln had called on Attorney General Bates to provide an opinion "to present the argument for the suspension."[56] Bates complied, making a broader argument than was needed by adopting an extreme version of departmentalism reminiscent of Andrew Jackson. At one point he stated that each branch was wholly independent of control by the others and that the president "must, of necessity, be the sole judge" of how to suppress the rebellion.[57] That argument suggests that neither Congress nor the courts could control presidential actions, a position that Lincoln never took. Somewhat inconsistently, Bates conceded that the president's suspension power was "temporary and exceptional" and that Congress could regulate suspensions of the writ.[58] The arguments that Lincoln advanced for his action were more limited and nuanced than those of Bates, as befits the better lawyer of the two. As in other contexts, the president argued only that he could act

without prior statutory authority, not that his power excluded congressional control. Outside the government, constitutional lawyers engaged in a
vigorous and extended debate about the suspension.[59]

As Congress convened, Lincoln was calling on it to share in the responsibility for his actions. By asking Congress for a retroactive grant of authority, Lincoln was implicitly conceding that Congress held the ultimate
power to set the course for the Civil War. Congress responded by ratifying Lincoln's actions generally.[60] Yet it was not until 1863 that Congress
addressed habeas corpus specifically, passing legislation worded ambiguously regarding whether Congress was approving the president's actions
or exercising its own suspension powers.[61]

The Habeas Corpus Act of 1863 required release of civilians detained
by the military where the judicial systems were "unimpaired" by the war.
Lincoln interpreted this provision narrowly, not to cover "aiders or abet-
tors" of the enemy.[62] After the war was over, the Supreme Court rejected
this interpretation in *Ex parte Milligan*, holding that a resident of Indiana
could not be tried by military commission for aiding the rebels.[63]

By the slimmest of margins, in 1863 the Supreme Court upheld Lincoln's blockade and its seizures of private property in the *Prize Cases*.[64] The
Court relied in part on the ratification statute and said that in the period
before its passage the question whether the rebellion merited a response
as drastic as a blockade was committed to the president's discretion by the
Constitution. This part of the Court's rationale suggested that the power
to suspend habeas corpus might similarly have been within the president's
emergency power to respond to rebellion, but the Court never ruled on
that issue. This state of affairs left the power to suspend habeas corpus, like
the opinion of Chief Justice Taney in *Merryman*, in legal limbo.

A robust modern debate concerns whether Lincoln's actions during
the eleven weeks between his inaugural and the convening of Congress
constituted a "constitutional dictatorship."[65] If so, his behavior was "constitutional because the ultimate checks of elections and impeachment remained, but a 'dictatorship' because he disregarded the proximate checks
and balances in an emergency."[66] The essential feature of a constitutional
dictatorship is advance authorization by constitutional or statutory provision. That authorization was incomplete in this instance. Lincoln could
make plausible constitutional arguments for many of his actions, even
the blockade and the suspension of habeas corpus. But his expansion of
the military and spending of unappropriated funds were simply illegal for
lack of statutory support.

Where Lincoln lacked the needed statutory delegations of power, he claimed that the Constitution itself filled the gaps: "It became necessary for me to choose whether, using only the existing means, agencies, and processes which Congress had provided, I should let the Government fall at once into ruin or whether, availing myself of the broader powers conferred by the Constitution in cases of insurrection, I would make an effort to save it, with all its blessings, for the present age and for posterity."[67]

This was not quite correct. Insofar as Lincoln's actions exceeded all prior precedent or contravened constitutional limits, they were exercises of Lockean prerogative, which meant that they were only *contingently* legitimate, depending on congressional and popular ratification.[68] Lincoln did recognize ultimate constraints by tying all his actions either to particular constitutional executive powers or to the capacity for Congress to ratify them once assembled. Thus the persuasiveness of his argument rests partly on the sufficiency of his grounds for declining to call Congress into special session before July. I think they were adequate, in which case the Constitution did contain enough flexibility to support Lincoln's initial responses to the war.

President Lincoln's actions during his eleven-week window of opportunity established the basic strategies that would govern conduct of the war (except for emancipation). It is not that Congress was supine—after it had assembled and ratified Lincoln's initial decisions, it played an active role in setting policy and overseeing the executive throughout the war. But the president had charted the course.

Lincoln as Commander in Chief

Abraham Lincoln reached the presidency with negligible military experience, having served briefly in the Illinois militia during the Black Hawk war. His predecessors had compiled some precedents in dealing with local insurrections, such as the Whiskey Rebellion, but the Civil War was on a wholly new scale. Operating with very little guidance, Lincoln presided over the transformation of the nation's military into a massive fighting machine and won a civil war against a determined foe that needed only to avoid defeat to achieve victory. He could not have done so without following a robust interpretation of his powers as commander in chief and obtaining the full support of Congress.

For the president, as for Congress and the people of the Union states, the strategic purpose of the Civil War evolved as it increased in fury and slaughter. What began as a war to restore the Union as it was, with slavery where it was, became a struggle to subdue the South that would strip away slavery in the process. As befits a civil war, domestic politics affected both the composition of the mobilizing armed forces and the president's relationship with his generals.

As in America's prior wars, mobilization involved adding a large volunteer force to the small regular Army. The regular officer corps was dominated by Democrats, just as the rest of the executive had been in the 1850s. To leaven this mix, the president had the power to nominate the many new generals that were needed, subject to Senate confirmation. Lincoln immediately encountered the problem of pressure to appoint politicians to military commands, regardless of their qualifications. Knowing that the support of local leaders was critical to the war effort, Lincoln often yielded to the pressure. This practice exacerbated the problems he faced through the first half of the war in finding generals who could win.

Lincoln's most debilitating difficulties with a general involved George McClellan, whose skills in creating and training an army were exceeded only by his inability to bring himself to use it. Politics as well as psychology affected McClellan's famous case of the "slows." One of the president's secretaries once observed acutely that McClellan and Lincoln were really heads of rival political parties.[69] McClellan wanted to restore the Union with slavery intact and minimal damage to southern institutions. Lincoln battled constantly against his insubordination, which was sometimes outright.

In the wake of his failure on the Virginia Peninsula in 1862, McClellan wrote the president a presumptuous letter arguing about war aims. Yet the general had enough support in the Army and the nation to make it difficult or even dangerous for Lincoln to displace him, and the president lacked capable replacements. In the wake of McClellan's partial victory at Antietam, the general's tendency toward barely concealed criticism of his civilian superiors infected his staff, and he actually had to order them to respect civil authority.[70] He did not, however, respond to the president's repeated entreaties to pursue Lee's army into Virginia. Once the midterm elections were over, Lincoln justifiably relieved McClellan from command, and the general went on to show his stripes by becoming Lincoln's Democratic opponent in the 1864 election, running on a peace platform.

Abraham Lincoln gave himself a crash course in military strategy, reading everything he had time to absorb. This study combined with Lincoln's common sense to make him an excellent strategic leader. From the beginning, the president understood what many of his generals did not, that to defeat the Confederacy it was far more important to destroy its armies than to occupy particular places. Whenever his generals were in disarray, Lincoln served as his own general in chief, even taking operational control at times. By midwar, he was usually able to let Secretary of War Stanton and General Henry Halleck run the Army.

Once it had convened in July 1861, Congress took an active role in both supporting and supervising the president's discharge of his duties as commander in chief.[71] The war aims of both branches evolved substantially as time passed; under Lincoln's skillful leadership, they operated harmoniously enough to secure victory.

The special session of Congress in 1861 lasted about a month. With the president's support Congress passed the Johnson-Crittenden resolutions, reciting that the war was not being fought to subjugate the South or to demolish slavery. Thus hopes for a restoration of the old Union remained until the changing nature of the war destroyed them. Accelerating that change, in the wake of the defeat at Bull Run Congress passed an authorization for a half-million volunteers, and then another. Then Congress adjourned until its usual December meeting, leaving another window for presidential action.

A very long session of the Thirty-Seventh Congress that extended from the end of 1861 until 1863 enacted most of the important legislation of the war. Lincoln consulted with Congress but often let it take the lead on legislation. He wanted to keep the great issues of war strategy in his hands and was willing to defer on lesser matters. Congress was prepared to contest this division of authority, however. It formed the powerful Joint Committee on the Conduct of the War to investigate early defeats and to prod McClellan. The committee, chaired by Senator Benjamin Wade, was dominated by radical Republicans who constantly pressed Lincoln to assail the enemy aggressively.[72] The president cooperated with the committee and never tried to withhold information from it.

The emerging scale of the war effort required fundamental changes in the operation of the federal government. Shorn of its southern members, Congress could finally take a broad view of its power under the necessary and proper clause of the Constitution. It did not waste the opportunity. No national currency existed in 1861; Congress authorized the paper money, greenbacks, that we use today. To support the currency and the war, the first federal income tax was imposed. Internal improvements statutes also had enduring effects on the nation (especially in the West), creating homesteads, land-grant colleges, and the transcontinental railroad. For Lincoln, it was natural to support broad congressional power to develop the nation and bind it together.

For the Lincoln administration, foreign policy was essentially an extension of the conduct of the Civil War.[73] The president, as bereft of diplomatic as military experience, learned quickly. He skillfully managed his gifted but volatile secretary of state, William Seward. The Union's primary foreign policy goal was to prevent Britain or France from either recognizing or aiding the Confederacy. Here, emancipation eventually became as much an asset to the president as slavery was a liability to the Confederates. A skillful combination of warnings to the other powers with conciliatory conduct accomplished the goal and gave the Union room to subdue the rebellion.[74]

Apart from protecting its European flank, the executive branch proceeded with caution in foreign policy. For example, wishing to recognize the black governments of Haiti and Liberia for domestic political purposes in 1862, Lincoln asked the assent of Congress before proceeding. And while the Civil War lasted, the administration tolerated the massive violation of the Monroe Doctrine created by European intervention in Mexico.

Civil War, Civil Liberties

In 1861, the nation lacked any significant civilian apparatus for internal security. Lincoln addressed the unprecedented security problems of a civil war ad hoc, assigning them to the State Department at the outset of the war and then shifting them to the War Department (the nation's diplomats lack any enforcement capacity but the soldiers are amply endowed with one). Yet entrusting this responsibility to military officers always risks unnecessary infringement of civil liberties—military training does not emphasize the kind of restraint that domestic protection of national security demands. Lincoln supervised his generals as best he could, but he also lacked a civilian apparatus in the White House or the War Department that was adequate to control the uniformed military. The result was a wavering, inconsistent approach that included both some overprotectiveness of security interests and some surprising toleration of dissent.[75]

Lincoln always weighed the political disadvantages as he authorized suspensions of habeas corpus. Constant opposition from Democrats "helped keep the army and the Republicans honest."[76] By the end of the war, there had been eight suspensions of the writ. Like the initial one along the rail lines, most of the orders applied locally, but two had nationwide application. All of the suspensions responded to military problems that seemed urgent. From the start, Lincoln delegated decisions to suspend the writ to local commanders who would know the facts. Of course, some commanders were sensible and some were not. Unable to control implementation of his own orders closely, the president often found himself defending actions that he would never have approved in advance.

Merryman's arrest was not an isolated incident. During the war, military officers arrested and held more than twelve thousand civilians on a variety of charges and usually let them go within days after they took an oath to support the Union.[77] Many of the arrests were of the routine sort that a civil war would occasion, such as southerners found behind Union lines, smugglers, fraudulent contractors, and draft evaders. The cauldron of Missouri, where guerrilla warfare raged throughout the Civil War, produced a large proportion of the total arrests.

In 1862, many states turned to the first conscription efforts in American history to fill their militia quotas for the Army. In four states, widespread violent resistance required use of federal troops to restore order. Lincoln responded by issuing a proclamation in September that suspended habeas corpus nationwide and invoked martial law against "all persons discouraging volunteer enlistments, resisting militia drafts, or guilty of any disloyal practice, affording aid and comfort to the Rebels."[78] The president argued that the suspension was for prevention, not punishment, and that the threat was nationwide, existing wherever resistance might occur.[79] If enforced in a draconian fashion, this order would have threatened a police state. Fortunately, by the time the order was issued, interference with recruiting had diminished. The several hundred draft evasion arrests that were made resulted in a few criminal charges.[80]

In 1863, when federal conscription began, New York City erupted in the most violent riot in American history, which was suppressed by the Army. In the wake of the draft disorders, state courts harassed Union commanders with writs of habeas corpus to release soldiers who had been conscripted or who were being held for desertion. Lincoln's second nationwide suspension order forbade use of the writ in such cases.[81] Desertion cases remained within the military. Lincoln reviewed all death sentences personally so that he could consider exercising his pardon power. Although tormented by the cases and inclined toward clemency, the president often did order executions.

Martial law is nowhere mentioned in the Constitution. Throughout American history, principles drawn from the international law of war have governed its use. Lincoln, as had his predecessors, thought the law of war constrained his conduct of the war generally; he promulgated regulations for the military codifying the applicable principles, such as the decent treatment of prisoners.[82]

Trials by military commission have been used to punish violations of the law of war (spying, for example), to control populations in occupied foreign territory (as in Mexico), and domestically where civil authority does not function (as in some border states like Missouri). In the Civil War, military commissions provided basic procedural regularity, if not all the protections of the Bill of Rights. Defendants were allowed lawyers, witnesses, confrontation of their accusers, and appeals. In the disruptions of a civil war, this rough-and-ready form of justice was usually acceptably fair.

Some arrests were particularly sensitive, however, in terms of protecting democratic processes during the war. Political prisoners, who made up a small subset of the total number of arrests, fell into three categories: state legislators, prominent critics of the war, and newspaper editors. Lincoln was cautious in politically charged cases, because he knew of the potential to inflame opposition to the war, which often focused on his unilateral actions as president. He once cautioned Stanton: "While we must, by all available means, prevent the overthrow of the government, we should avoid planting and cultivating too many thorns in the bosom of society."[83] Unfortunately for the president, his subordinates were more inclined to take precipitate action.

In the first year of the war, the Maryland legislature twice met amid speculation it would enact an ordinance of secession.[84] The first time, in April, Lincoln refused to arrest the legislators, and they did no harm. In September, however, spurred on by McClellan's usual fears of rebels behind every fence post, Lincoln ordered Union troops to seal off the meeting and to arrest secessionist members along with others suspected of conspiring to detach Maryland from the Union and to raise insurrection in Baltimore. The legislators were held for two months until a more compliant legislature had been elected; some of the others were held through most of 1862.[85] Lincoln was prepared to hold strategically critical

Maryland in the Union by force if necessary. Only a theory that secession was unconstitutional combined with a military judgment that the capital could not be isolated could justify so deep an intrusion on traditional states' rights values.

The most notorious prosecution of a war opponent concerned former congressman Clement Vallandigham, a gubernatorial candidate in Ohio as a peace Democrat.[86] His noisy criticism outraged General Ambrose Burnside in 1863. Having produced a military disaster the past winter at Fredericksburg, Burnside produced a civil one by arresting Vallandigham and charging him with "implied treason" before a military commission. Lincoln, presented with a fait accompli, supported his general but stemmed the controversy by commuting Vallandigham's sentence of imprisonment and expelling him to the Confederacy.

The president defended the prosecution in an open letter that emphasized the direct damage to the war effort that Vallandigham's speeches were causing. Lincoln asked a rhetorical question that captured the dilemma surrounding wartime dissent: "Must I shoot a simple-minded soldier boy who deserts, while I must not touch a hair of a wily agitator who induces him to desert?"[87] The wily agitator made his way to Canada and then returned to Ohio, again running for governor and losing badly. Despite fear that Vallandigham might win the election, Lincoln left him alone this time. Notwithstanding the fierce rhetoric he had deployed in defense of his misguided general, the president had little appetite for arresting those who abused him or opposed the war.

There were some scattered arrests of newspaper editors during the war.[88] The most controversial case involved closing the *New York World* and arresting its editors in 1864 for the publication of a false presidential proclamation calling for renewed conscription. In the city that had witnessed the severe antidraft riots of 1863, this was incendiary behavior. Nevertheless, Lincoln's order to close the paper was rash and unnecessary, given the alternative of a prompt and public denunciation of the hoax.

An even less justifiable action was the decision of General Burnside (again) to close the *Chicago Times*, a venomously anti-Lincoln paper. Lincoln told the errant general to reconsider, and he desisted. Lincoln rejected a later appeal to close the *Times* for a second time, stressing the "danger of abridging the *liberties* of the people" and affirming that the government should go to "the very extreme of toleration."[89] The closures by local commanders continued, however. Altogether, the military temporarily interrupted publication by about three hundred opposition newspapers. Lincoln was unable effectively to transmit his policy of restraint to his military subordinates.

Today, no one would think that the Constitution's First Amendment permits silencing dissenters or closing newspapers in wartime. In the Civil War era, however, there was little judicial precedent protecting freedom of speech. Following no general theory other than the need to preserve the Union, Lincoln pressed hard enough against civil liberties to raise a considerable outcry by his opponents, who made repression a campaign issue in 1864. Nevertheless, Lincoln did tolerate a torrent of abuse, much of it unfair, and never considered stopping wartime elections, even though he was convinced for a time that he would be defeated for reelection. Lincoln's infringements of civil liberties were milder in nature and based on more substantial justification than the abuses presidents would commit in the wars of the twentieth century.

Emancipation

When Abraham Lincoln wanted to make a point, he would often tell one of his homely little stories. The one he used when pressed to take positions he thought were premature had the punch line, "I never cross a river until I come to it."[90] The story of the Emancipation Proclamation, his most important single action as president and perhaps the most important action any president has taken, is of his being brought to the river by the progress of the Civil War, crossing it, and never looking back.

Always Lincoln knew that emancipation complexly mixed deep issues of law, politics, strategy, and morality. As the war began, no one could doubt that the Constitution supported slavery. Two specific provisions stood squarely in the way of any unilateral executive emancipation. The due process clause of the Fifth Amendment forbade the federal government to take anyone's private property, such as slaves, without compensation. The fugitive slave clause required that a slave escaping across state lines be returned to his or her owner. Surely the president's faithful execution duty included the Fugitive Slave Act, which implemented the latter provision. More generally, the original Constitution exuded acquiescence in slavery by forbidding an end to the slave trade for at least twenty years and by counting each slave as 60 percent of a person for purposes of apportioning the House of Representatives.

By the end of 1860, all three branches of the federal government had generated mounds of precedents treating slavery as a property right governed exclusively by state law and beyond federal regulatory power (except perhaps in the territories). Against all this the president could cite his power as commander in chief of the military, and Congress held various war powers with which it could empower executive action, but no one knew what these authorities meant in a civil war. Time would tell.

In politics and strategy, the crosscurrents roiled. The fiercest abolitionists raged against slavery and condemned Lincoln for his every hesitation. (After the fall of Fort Sumter, Representative Thaddeus Stevens marched into Lincoln's office and demanded that the president immediately emancipate the slaves as a war measure.)[91] The abolitionists touched a sympathetic chord in Lincoln, who knew that slavery had created the "house divided," sapping the nation's great potential and bringing on the war. Yet some Democrats supported the war effort and might turn away if slavery were threatened. More important, the border slave states were the hinge on which the Union turned. Lincoln saw no way to win the war—or even to hold the District of Columbia—if they were lost. And like many other leaders in the North, he held out hope that there was a substantial minority of Unionist southerners who might induce the seceded states to reconsider their departure if slavery were left alone.

On the moral issue, Lincoln saw clearly that "if slavery is not wrong, nothing is wrong."[92] But he never conflated his moral views with his legal powers as president. And sadly, as a child of the border regions he knew the depth of the racism that infected most white Americans, northerners and southerners alike. He knew that opposition to allowing slavery in the territories was prompted by resistance to black migration there. Northern states usually denied free blacks the right to vote and often tried to exclude them entirely. As a man of his times, Lincoln did not think blacks were in all respects equal to whites, but his generous nature held none of the animosity that many of his countrymen felt, and he believed deeply in equality of basic civil rights.

As the war began, events quickly overtook the assumptions of the past. In May 1861, the Union commander at Fortress Monroe in Virginia, Ben Butler (a political general if ever there was one), heard pleas for freedom from escaping slaves who were arriving at the fort.[93] Butler's response was inspired. He decided that he was governed not by the Fugitive Slave Act but by the international law of war, which allowed the confiscation of "contraband" war supplies belonging to an enemy. Butler promptly designated the fugitives "contrabands," who were subject to confiscation from their owners. The brilliance of this stance was that it required no precise determination either about the viability of southern laws recognizing slavery or about the legal status of the fugitives themselves. Were they free? Butler so treated them, and Lincoln quietly approved his action, saying there would be no reenslavement of the runaways. For the rest of the war, slaves reaching Union lines would be "contrabands" and would be put to work aiding the war effort. By 1864 about 10 percent of the Confederacy's slave population had reached freedom through what Lincoln called the "friction and abrasion" of war.

There were, however, both legal and practical difficulties with Butler's action and Lincoln's approval of it. Legally, the law of war required a conflict between independent nations for confiscation to apply. Yet no branch of the federal government ever admitted that the seceding states had gained even temporary independence as legal entities. (This problem beset the naval blockade as well.) Lincoln finessed the problem (as would the Supreme Court in the *Prize Cases*). Practically, the need for circumspection meant that the president issued no clear guidance to his generals. Not surprisingly, military practice varied in the early days of the war, with some commanders welcoming runaways and others turning them away.

Two of Lincoln's generals were prepared to go beyond his cautious stance. When the grandiose general John Charles Fremont issued an emancipation order within his Missouri command in 1861, the president ordered him to rescind it.[94] The need to retain the allegiance of the border states remained paramount. In 1862, Lincoln revoked another emancipation order, this time issued by General David Hunter for some southern seacoast territory that was under Union control.[95] The president emphasized that "I reserve to myself" the emancipation question.[96]

Throughout the war, Congress wanted to play a role in emancipation, but it struggled to speak consistently. Without southern Democrats, the Congress meeting in the summer of 1861 was under solid Republican control. The first tentative step, the Johnson-Crittenden resolutions, took a restorationist stance that was inconsistent with emancipation. Yet the same session enacted the First Confiscation Act, which supported Lincoln's contraband policy by allowing confiscation of property (including slaves) actually used for Confederate military purposes (but without clarifying whether they were free).[97] Given the presence of the Constitution's due process and fugitive slave clauses, the legislation had to rely on the war powers of Congress, the extent of which remained unclear.

In the spring of 1862, the carnage at Shiloh, where more Americans died than in all prior wars, signaled the onset of total war.[98] That summer, Congress enacted a group of statutes that partially supported emancipation.[99] At long last, Congress responded to abolitionist dreams by prohibiting slavery in the territories and abolishing it in the District of Columbia. An amendment to the Articles of War forbade Army officers to return runaways to their owners, negating the Fugitive Slave Act to that extent. The Senate ratified a treaty with Britain to suppress the slave trade. The Militia Act authorized the president to enroll blacks for war service, even as soldiers, and gave slaves who enlisted their freedom. The Second Confiscation Act took the property of all rebel "traitors" including slaves, who, upon reaching Union lines "shall be forever free."[100] Both Confiscation Acts, though, contained cumbersome judicial enforcement provisions that kept them from having much effect.[101]

Lincoln signed the Confiscation Acts despite serious concerns about their constitutionality.[102] The president always thought that the constitutional powers of Congress concerning the war differed from his own because the text empowering and constraining the branches differs. This distinction became critical regarding emancipation, because Lincoln thought that although he could invoke his military powers to free particular slaves owned by rebels, Congress had no power to override state laws that recognized slavery as an institution and could not exceed constitutional limits to statutory punishments for treason.

Lincoln's concern for the legality of his own and congressional actions never abated. Fearing the intervention of Taney's Supreme Court, he sought the best available legal bases for the government's actions. In 1861, he denied that he had any power to free any slaves.[103] Therefore, he repeatedly pressed the border states to adopt his proposals for compensated emancipation, because state-initiated emancipation was clearly legal. He turned to his own proclamation only after frustration with these efforts changed his mind in the summer of 1862. By then it was also clear that the Confederacy would fight to the finish and could not be lured to desist by promises to protect slavery. Moreover, emancipation would buttress the economic war against the Confederacy that the blockade had initiated and would help meet the Union's manpower needs as black troop levels increased.

Abraham Lincoln made the most important legal decision of his presidency, and the one for which he is most revered, essentially on his own. The idea of freeing the slaves grew in Lincoln's mind during the difficult summer of 1862. He was under immense pressure regarding this deeply divisive issue. In July, he told Seward and Welles that he intended to issue an emancipation proclamation because it was a military necessity: "We must free the slaves or be ourselves subdued."[104] He brought the cabinet together and read them his draft of a proclamation. He told them that he "had resolved upon this step, and had not called them together to ask their advice," although he welcomed suggestions.[105] After general discussion, which did not alter Lincoln's mind on the essentials, the president accepted Seward's suggestion that promulgation should follow a victory on the battlefield.

As the president held his proclamation ready and awaited the victory that would come with the battle of Antietam in September, he signaled his intentions in an open letter to newspaper editor Horace Greeley:

> My paramount object in the struggle *is* to save the Union, and is *not* either to save or to destroy slavery. If I could save the Union without freeing *any* slave I would do it, and if I could save it by freeing *all* the slaves I would do it; and if I could save it by freeing some and leaving others alone, I would also do that.[106]

Lacking any power to free slaves in the border states, he chose the third option. His deep underlying determination could not be doubted. He had said that he expected "to maintain this contest until successful, or till I die."[107] Almost two years later, his success and his death would occur in the same week.

Shortly after Antietam, Lincoln released his preliminary proclamation, which would apply only to states still in rebellion on January 1, 1863. After that date, the Confederacy would be subject to a war of liberation, not restoration. In the agonizing hundred days between the preliminary and final proclamations, the president closely monitored military and political developments, saying that he was studying "the plain physical facts of the case" while awaiting the time for a final decision.[108] In the fall midterm elections, peace Democrats made substantial gains in the House of Representatives as the voters registered disquiet with both the progress of the war under the sluggish McClellan and the effects of anticipated emancipation. Lincoln's annual message to Congress in December stressed the moral foundation that buttressed his military order: "The fiery trial, through which we pass, will light us down, in honor or dishonor, to the latest generation. . . . In *giving* freedom to the *slave*, we *assure* freedom to the *free*."[109] Now the president was leading the nation in a direction it had begun to take but had not fully accepted. In December, both houses of Congress, voting along party lines, passed a resolution "approving the policy of the President in setting slaves free in insurrectionary districts."[110]

In the final Emancipation Proclamation, the president freed all slaves who were held in areas still in rebellion within the Confederate states. By restricting emancipation to regions not yet controlled by the Union Army, Lincoln crafted his proclamation as a military order. The proclamation crystallized Lincoln's thinking by describing itself as "an act of justice, warranted by the Constitution upon military necessity," resting on the president's power "as commander-in-chief . . . as a fit and necessary war measure for suppressing . . . rebellion."[111] It could also derive some indirect authority from the Confiscation Acts and the other 1862 legislation. Lincoln later said that military necessity was the only legal justification for the proclamation.[112] Accordingly, when Chase pressed him to extend the order to areas already under Union control, Lincoln responded that such an action would "give up all footing upon Constitution or law" and enter the "boundless field of absolutism."[113]

Lincoln's detractors reacted to the proclamation by calling it a useless gesture that freed only those slaves the government could not reach. Of course, this complaint ignored the proclamation's legal basis. More important, it missed the proclamation's latent force. Quite simply, it *worked.* Emancipation had direct military effects. It impaired the South's economic base, increased the flow of runaways, encouraged blacks to join the Union Army, and improved the nation's relationship with Britain and France.

Some observers saw the proclamation in a broader context. Karl Marx said that emancipation shifted the war from a "constitutional" to a "revolutionary" struggle; Frederick Douglass hoped that it would form the "first chapter" in a new American history, as it did.[114] These statements recognized that although the military effects of the proclamation would be limited to the war's duration, the moral impulse that it embodied could endure. Meanwhile, the Union Army became an army of liberation.

A spirited legal debate about the proclamation broke out in the newspaper articles and pamphlets that were the mass media of the day.[115] Against objections that the proclamation was an unauthorized taking of private property without just compensation, supporters urged that the powers of the government as a belligerent in war included the right to free an enemy's slaves.[116] Supporters also pointed out the asymmetry of the legal arguments that opponents made by claiming the full protections of the peacetime Constitution for those who were resisting it by force of arms.

Emancipation remained at the center of American political debate about the war, along with Lincoln's other unilateral actions, through the election of 1864 and beyond. Under constant pressure from peace Democrats as the 1864 election approached, Lincoln consistently declared that he had two preconditions for peace: preservation of the Union and emancipation.[117] Because the Democratic platform called for peace without emancipation and condemned the military arrests and the suppression of freedom of speech and of the press, Lincoln's conduct of the presidency was the issue on which the election would turn. Trying to broaden his base of support, the president ran on a "Union" ticket that aimed at adding to the Republican base. Reaching across the aisle, he chose Andrew Johnson, a war Democrat from Tennessee, as his vice presidential candidate.[118] Once again, considerations of electoral success led a president to choose a vice president who might veer off in an unexpected direction if the president were to die.

Following the practice of the times, Lincoln did not campaign for reelection, except for the public letters that he so often used to communicate with the people.[119] In these, he vigorously defended all he had done. The people of the North endorsed him by a 55 percent majority that carried all but three states and gave the Republicans a three-fourths majority in the next Congress.[120] It must have gratified Lincoln that where soldier votes were tabulated separately, he received a 78 percent majority.

The ultimate question about the legality of the Emancipation Proclamation is difficult to think about today, repelled as we are by claims of constitutional rights to property in human beings. Yet we know that the original Constitution recognized just such rights, leading the abolitionist William Lloyd Garrison to condemn it as a "Covenant with Death and Agreement with Hell."[121] Perhaps *this* is the place for Lincoln's argument for a residual power to ignore part of the Constitution to save the rest— and the soul of the nation.[122] Lincoln made just that argument in a letter he wrote in 1864. After reviewing his own moral opposition to slavery and asserting that, as president, he could not use his powers of office merely to implement his private values, he continued:

I did understand however, that my oath to preserve the constitution to the best of my ability, imposed upon me the duty of preserving, by every indispensable means, that government—that nation—of which that constitution was the organic law. Was it possible to lose the nation, and yet preserve the constitution? . . . I felt that measures otherwise unconstitutional, might become lawful, by becoming indispensable to the preservation of the constitution, through the preservation of the nation.[123]

Nothing short of the cauldron of the Civil War and the desperate need to win it could have justified the proclamation in law.[124] But justified it was, based on the "plain physical facts of the case" and as a "fit and necessary war measure."

Nowadays, emancipation is easier to justify as a matter of conscience. Lincoln spoke directly to us as he prepared to sign the proclamation, saying, "If my name ever goes into history it will be for this act, and my whole soul is in it."[125] Yes.

Lincoln's Constitutional Legacy

Abraham Lincoln's views of constitutional power generally aligned with what was called the "adequacy of the Constitution" theory at the time.[126] This theory held that the antebellum South's arguments had distorted constitutional analysis by discussing only the rights protected by the Constitution, obscuring its implied commands to maintain the government and protect the general welfare. Proponents of the adequacy theory stressed the president's duty to ensure faithful execution of the laws and his oath to preserve the Constitution. Lincoln agreed with all this. His message to Congress on July 4, 1861, referred to the need to steer between a government too strong for liberty and one too weak for order. And Attorney General Bates's opinion defending Lincoln's suspension of habeas corpus explicitly relied on the theory.[127]

Lincoln's constitutional analysis always tied his assertions of power to particular constitutional text, even if it was no more specific than the command of the oath to preserve the Constitution. The implication of textual reliance was that even prerogative powers were bounded in two ways. They were subject to applicable textual limits and to other powers in the government, such as those of Congress. Jefferson's thinking about the Louisiana Purchase had detached executive prerogative from the text in a failed effort to constrain its application, leaving a legacy that suggested unbounded power, even if Jefferson made no such assertion.

Lincoln accurately described Jefferson's acceptance of Louisiana as a yielding of scruples "on the plea of great expediency."[128] Here their conceptions of prerogative overlapped. Both presidents were prepared to yield to great expediency when driven to that ground. Thus Lincoln was prepared to defend all of his actions, even if unauthorized or unconstitutional, as justified by the overriding need to preserve the Union and the Constitution.[129] And he was perfectly willing to submit his decisions to Congress and the people, whose judgments he would abide. A product of the Whig tradition, which had stressed the power of Congress to control the executive, he could do no other.

The Civil War, having altered the nation, also altered constitutional interpretation permanently. Lincoln's thinking about the Constitution mixed textual grounding with conceptual flexibility. In the Gettysburg Address, he united the values of democracy and equality (in a more inclusive sense than Jackson's) and tied both of them to reliance on the federal government.[130] His opponents among the Democrats, rejecting these connections, clung to nostalgia for a polity that died in the ashes of Richmond. The war made the constitution Hamiltonian. Antebellum constitutional amendments, such as the Bill of Rights, had limited federal power; the Reconstruction amendments and many later ones would increase it.

Lincoln's behavior shows that a president's interpretation of executive power is a function both of the conditions and politics of the day and of his interpretation of other constitutional provisions. Thus constitutional interpretation is quite contingent and dependent on facts. It is conventional to think of judicial interpretation of the Constitution as legitimate only when it is grounded in the facts of the case; interpretation by presidents should be appraised similarly. Lincoln's interpretations were always based on facts rather than the airy imaginings of theorists.

The Supreme Court contributed little to the process of interpretation. Aside from the *Prize Cases*, not many questions about the legality of war measures came to the Court either during the war or afterward, so that the legal nature of the war was never clarified judicially. By the end of the war, Lincoln had appointed five justices, completely recasting the Court. The substitution of Chase for Taney in the chief's chair at the end of 1864 ended an era and finally freed the Court from its thralldom to slavery. There was even a bit of court packing, as Congress authorized a temporary tenth justice in 1863 in an effort to assure the safety of wartime legislation.

Binding the Wounds: Pardons, Slavery, and Reconstruction

As the Civil War's conclusion became apparent, Abraham Lincoln had both the temperament and the moral stature to be merciful to the defeated South. Not everyone in the North shared his magnanimity. Three major issues took center stage: what to do with defeated rebels, what to do about slavery, and what to do about the former Confederate states. A person's position on these issues usually reflected (or generated) an underlying theory about the nature of secession. Lincoln always held that secession was illegal—that the southern states remained in the Union but were temporarily ruled by rebels. Therefore, replacing the rebels with loyal officers would reconstruct the states. Radical Republicans such as Thaddeus Stevens contended that secession destroyed the states as legal entities, leaving them "conquered provinces" subject to plenary reconstruction. Others thought the seceded states had reverted to territories subject to readmission by Congress under its power to admit new states.

Separation of powers issues pervaded this theoretical debate. Lincoln's theory implied reconstruction via the president's military and pardon powers; the alternate theories implied reconstruction by Congress. Equally important, the debate concerned whether to reconstruct only the state governments or southern society in general. The issues of a permanent end to slavery and suffrage for the freed slaves were central to the latter question.

Lincoln's thoughts about reconstruction were always dominated by the more immediate need to finish the war successfully. He was explicitly tentative and experimental about the endgame. His initial approach sought to restore the allegiance of former rebels and to secure the return of those seceded states where Union occupation presented an opportunity to resume civil government.[131] In December 1863, Lincoln issued a proclamation offering amnesty to rebels (except the leaders of the Confederacy) who were willing to swear allegiance to the United States and to federal laws and proclamations about slavery. Once 10 percent of the 1860 voters in a state had taken the oath, they could form a state government that the president would recognize. Congress could then decide whether to seat the representatives and senators elected by the restored state.

Lincoln based his plan on the Constitution's requirement that the United States "guarantee to every State . . . a Republican Form of Government."[132] Because the guarantee clause does not specify which branch of the federal government shall do the guaranteeing, Lincoln was exercising presidential initiative and hoping for congressional acquiescence.[133] He recognized Congress's power to modify his plan and admitted that with peace, executive power would diminish. This initial proposal was quite sketchy; it omitted the explosive issue of suffrage for the freed slaves and would not have forced a social revolution on the South.

In its 1864 session, Congress tried to override Lincoln's proclamation with the Wade-Davis bill. Much harsher than the president's policy, it would have raised the necessary percentage of initial oath takers to 50 percent and would have required delegates to state constitutional conventions to take an "ironclad oath" that they had never supported the rebellion (not just that they no longer did so).

At the end of the session, Lincoln killed the bill with a pocket veto.[134] He explained that the bill's attempt to abolish slavery by statute in the seceded states was unconstitutional under his theory about secession; the pending Thirteenth Amendment to the Constitution was needed for that. Implicitly conceding congressional power to determine the course of reconstruction, he also said that he did not want to be "inflexibly committed to any single plan of restoration."[135] Wade and Davis rejoined bitterly with charges of executive "usurpation," of an "outrage on the legislative authority" that would allow the Confederacy's leaders to return to power and preserve slavery.[136] The Republicans in Congress were trying to extend their control of the process of reconstruction for a maximum period before the reformed states could send new delegations to Congress. The former rebels would demand admission and threaten to dilute the political control of the radicals. With the battle lines between the branches thus drawn, reconstruction would have to await military victory.

Before Lincoln and his unfortunate successor Andrew Johnson had finished, the presidential pardon power would reach a prominence never approached before or since. Lincoln, wanting to restore the nation, rejected retribution against the leaders of the Confederacy; he said he favored just chasing them out.

As the war concluded, Lincoln pressed Congress hard to adopt the proposed Thirteenth Amendment to end slavery and ensure the permanence of his legacy—he said it would "wind up" the problem of slavery.[137] More than at any other time in his presidency, he intervened in Congress by making promises of patronage to secure favorable votes.[138] Once he had secured passage of the amendment through Congress, Lincoln signed it (although there was no constitutional need to do so) and happily sent it to the states for ratification, which was completed by the end of 1865.

The Civil War finally settled a fundamental question that Americans had debated since the founding: was the United States a nation or a confederacy of sovereign states? That issue was decided by Lincoln's conduct as president and sealed at Appomattox Courthouse. In the Gettysburg Address, Lincoln shifted from traditional and ambiguous references to the Union to the word *nation* "to invoke a new birth of freedom and nationalism for the United States."[139] The war had sped the replacement of the decentralized community of Jefferson's dreams with Hamilton's nationalized economy.[140] The internal improvements and financial legislation enacted during the war helped to integrate the national economy, and the Republican administrations that followed were ready to support business. The Army mostly demobilized after the war but remained well above historic levels because of responsibilities in Reconstruction and Indian control. The permanent federal bureaucracy grew with new pension programs for veterans (and patronage opportunities for presidents).

As long as it was shackled by slavery, the United States could never take a leading place in the world. Thus, just as the Emancipation Proclamation transformed the war (the war having already transformed Lincoln), it also transformed America's role in the world. Now the nation was poised to become a great power. Another, equally fundamental question remained, however: what *kind* of nation had the Civil War created? That was the issue to be addressed in Reconstruction and, as it happened, for a long time afterward.

CHAPTER SIX

Unmindful of the High Duties

Andrew Johnson

Unmindful of the high duties of his office, of his oath of office, and of the requirement of the Constitution that he should take care that the laws be faithfully executed, did unlawfully . . . commit . . . a high misdemeanor in office.—Article I of the impeachment articles against Andrew Johnson, 1868[1]

When John Wilkes Booth pulled the trigger, he replaced our greatest president with our worst. The assassination vividly demonstrated the vulnerability that the Constitution created by assigning executive responsibility to one person. Andrew Johnson's great failure was that he squandered a brief opportunity to reconstruct the defeated South in a way that would have meaningfully aided the freed slaves and could have reduced many future tribulations for the nation. He engaged in an unnecessary and debilitating struggle with Congress over the control of Reconstruction policy. Finally, he provoked a failed impeachment effort that set a bad precedent about the use of the ultimate means of redress against a president.

The Prisoner of His Prejudices[2]

Andrew Johnson's presidency shows how radically the personal character of the president affects the exercise of the constitutional powers of the office.[3] Johnson was a self-made tailor who rose from poverty. He clung to traditional Jacksonian views: devotion to majority rule, belief that secession was "treason," unabashed racism, a hatred of privilege, and adherence to states' rights on such matters as suffrage. Obdurate and confrontational, Johnson took conflict personally as Lincoln never did. A governor of Ohio summed him up: "He is obstinate without being firm, self-opinionated without being capable of systematic thinking, combative and pugnacious without being courageous. He is always *worse* than you expect."[4] He was the exact opposite of Lincoln along each of these axes of character.[5]

Before the war, Johnson's ambition drove him to become Democratic governor of Tennessee, a congressman, and a senator. Although a slave-holder, he supported emancipation as a way to win the war. As the lone senator from a seceded state to remain in Congress, he was rewarded by Lincoln, who made him the vice presidential candidate on the Union (Republican) ticket in 1864. He embodied the southern Unionist that Lincoln was always seeking, with the foreseeable disadvantage that he was both Unionist and *southern*; he said, "I am of the Southern people, and I love them and will do all in my power to restore them."[6]

Johnson lacked both the political acumen and the moral stature to command the reuniting nation—he had not been elected to the presidency, had not endured Lincoln's "fiery trial," and as a war Democrat had few ties to the ascendant Republicans in Washington. Instead of proceeding cautiously once thrust into the presidency, he adamantly pressed policies contrary to those of Congress and eventually discovered the consequences.

Presidential Reconstruction

Andrew Johnson's debut on the national stage was a disaster. After having a few medicinal drinks to staunch a lingering illness, he was visibly drunk at his vice presidential inaugural, disgracing himself by delivering a rambling, incoherent speech. That put him on the sidelines for the brief time remaining to the Lincoln administration. Amid the shock of the assassination, Johnson assumed the presidency in April with Congress in adjournment until December.

Wanting to be free to set Reconstruction policy and seeing no need for new statutory authority, the new president did not call a special session of Congress. Here he missed an opportunity to use the goodwill that he enjoyed in the aftermath of the assassination to work with Congress on the unprecedented issues of Reconstruction. More ominously, he saw himself in Jacksonian terms as a tribune of the whole people who little needed input from the local representatives in Congress. Had he embraced its implications, this attitude might have suited him to heal a nation deeply divided between a triumphant and thriving North and a defeated and ruined South. But, like Buchanan, he made no effort to bridge the gap between his own southern point of view and the national majority. The election mandate of 1864 had swept the northern Republicans to power.

As president, Johnson worked incessantly to the point of exhaustion, concentrating on Reconstruction and leaving most departmental issues to the secretaries. He suffered the usual crowds of patronage seekers and visitors. The cabinet, which he had inherited from Lincoln, usually discussed generalities in its two meetings a week. Johnson kept the *National Intelligencer* as the administration's house organ but had it playing a new tune.

Reconstruction presented the president an essentially blank constitutional slate. How much could he have accomplished? In the midnineteenth century, notions that the historically weak federal government could engineer a grassroots social revolution or that it could supervise state governments closely were alien. (Proposals of this kind remain deeply controversial.) The trauma of the Civil War had eroded the old assumptions, but no one knew how much. Racism north and south pressed hard against black suffrage. Redistribution of land to the freedmen would have been an extraordinary step (land reform has rarely succeeded worldwide).[7] Revision of the system of federalism would require amending the Constitution in some fundamental way. Not knowing what might have happened, we do know that Andrew Johnson made the least, not the most, of the opportunities glimmering before him.

When Johnson took office, Lincoln had initiated his 10 percent plan, but Congress had refused to seat anyone elected from the first three states. The fierce congressional reaction to Lincoln's veto of the Wade-Davis bill had signaled an intention to insist on strict requirements for Reconstruction, but Johnson was not paying attention. For a few weeks the new president considered his options while revealing his plans to none of the anxious national leaders who came to press their conflicting advice on him. He had three goals in mind. First, he wanted a quick restoration of southern state governments upon minimum conditions not including black suffrage. Second, his populist side wanted to shift power from southern aristocrats to his own political base, the "plebeians" as he called them. Third, he sought his own election as president in 1868. For that he would need to form a new coalition of moderates and conservatives and would need to cement the support of the Democrats, who had wandered in the political wilderness during the war.

The period after Appomattox was a crucial opportunity that Lincoln would have perceived with his acute sense of political timing.[8] Action to change the power structure in the South or to aid the freed slaves had to happen before the old elites recovered from the shock of defeat and lost their fear of being punished for rebelling. Southerners looked to the president for cues—they had little information about national politics and the attitudes of the North. Johnson heartened white southerners by signaling that he was on their side and would restore them to power, including control over the blacks.

Johnson implemented his Reconstruction policy in two ways. First, he used his plenary power to issue pardons to reattach southerners to the Union, an action that also paved the way to restoring the states to the control of the former rebels. Johnson issued a broad amnesty that, like Lincoln's, excluded Confederate leaders. Because Johnson's pardons included restoration of property rights (except in slaves), they ended the possibility that land temporarily abandoned by rebel owners would be distributed to the freed slaves.

Johnson retained his lifelong populist hatred for the southern planter aristocracy. Hence, his initial amnesty plan differed from Lincoln's by excluding the rich so that he could decide about their pardons individually. Johnson had long thought that pardons should be issued after consideration of the individual circumstances, not as amnesties in bulk. He may also have intended to obtain gratitude and political support or just to have the pleasure of the groveling that attends requests for pardons. But after struggling with the flood of pardon applications for a time, he grew careless, issuing them wholesale and eventually even delegating the job to a clerk. The president expanded his pardon program in September 1867, offering pardons to most remaining rebels who would take an oath of future loyalty. He explained that a vindictive policy would do more harm than good. That judgment was probably correct, and Johnson certainly shared the underlying impulse of magnanimity with Lincoln, but the wholesale pardons contained no conditions that would advance specific goals of Reconstruction. Eventually, Johnson forgave every rebel.

In using the pardon power to alleviate the effects of rebellion on the functioning of the nation, Johnson was on firm constitutional ground. His predecessors Washington, Adams, and Madison had employed general amnesties to restore order after local disruptions. Nothing in the scale or nature of the Civil War demanded a rethinking of the established doctrine that presidents could employ clemency at their discretion. The relatively civilized conduct of the war under Lincoln, with adherence to the international law of war and the taking of prisoners of war, reflected an assumption that wholesale treason prosecutions would not follow a Union victory.

After the war, Congress did try to limit the effects of presidential pardons in various ways, for example by barring former rebels from citing pardons to prove their loyalty as a basis for claiming property that had been seized by the Army.[9] In a series of cases the Supreme Court rejected these limits, insisting that legislation may not limit the normal effect of a pardon in removing all legal disabilities that attend criminal prosecution.[10] Once Johnson moved beyond pardons to other methods of Reconstruction, however, Congress would be able to assert its own powers to guide the process.

Johnson's approach to the state governments was guided by his belief that there was "no such thing as reconstruction."[11] That is, he thought that secession was unconstitutional and that the Confederate states had never left the Union. Combined with the new president's strong states' rights values, and especially his view that the states could determine suffrage, this was a formula for permissive and partial Reconstruction. He was prepared to restore any state that would nullify its ordinance of secession, accept the end of slavery, and repudiate Confederate war debt.[12] Once a state demonstrated its loyalty in these ways, the president thought it was entitled to be represented in Congress.

Given the Constitution's silence concerning secession, civil war, and reconstruction, Johnson's constitutional position was plausible enough. Yet it contained the seeds of a disastrous confrontation with Congress. During the Civil War, twenty-five of the thirty-six antebellum states were represented in Congress. After Appomattox, when the former Confederate states sent new delegations to Congress, would Congress be required to seat them? Johnson's theory held that Congress could not refuse readmission and retain its own legitimacy once his basic conditions were satisfied.

Congress was not likely to agree. Even its moderate members would likely believe that the power of Congress to control its own membership under Article I of the Constitution gave it plenary authority to reject anyone appearing at its door pretending to represent a state or district.[13] Since 1862, Congress had insisted that it would seat only persons who could take the "ironclad oath" that they had never supported the rebellion.

Any president should understand that his own departmentalist reading of the Constitution is likely to be met by the equally departmentalist position of another branch when its core powers are involved. Here the institutional interests of Congress in its own autonomy overlapped with theories about the nature of Reconstruction. Therefore, when the president determined unilaterally what the conditions for readmission should be, he challenged Congress to substitute its own, competing vision of Reconstruction and to enforce that vision through its exclusion power, which Johnson could not control. The president lacked the intellectual subtlety to realize that he was advancing over very bad ground.

Johnson began by trying to revive Lincoln's 10 percent plan, which Congress had rejected during the war. Relying on the commander in chief power, on May 9 Johnson issued a proclamation recognizing the three state governments that had been created under Lincoln's plan. In an effort to lure some states back into the Union in the last days of the war, Lincoln had not demanded either abolition of slavery or black suffrage. By war's end, Tennessee, Arkansas, and Louisiana had formed new governments by holding constitutional conventions that abolished slavery. These cobbled-together governments had little popular support and did nothing for the freed slaves. Under the Wade-Davis approach that Lincoln had vetoed, Congress was very unlikely to seat anyone they sent to Washington.

Johnson hoped to complete Reconstruction before Congress convened in December.[14] In May, with the support of the cabinet he issued his own model procedure and applied it to North Carolina. A provisional governor appointed by the president would call a state constitutional convention that must abolish slavery and ratify the Thirteenth Amendment. For all other purposes, the old elites could simply resume control of the reconstructing states. Freedmen were assured no rights, although Johnson did suggest that the new state governments grant some black suffrage. He was trying to appease northern feelings, which were aroused by the elemental injustice of hurrying to confer votes on former rebels while denying it to the freedmen, many of whom had fought for the Union. Ignoring Johnson's suggestion, the states complied minimally with his conditions and began adopting the infamous black codes, which did grant freed slaves some basic civil rights but tied them economically to a dependent status closely resembling slavery.

With the war at an end, the constitutional basis for Johnson's policy was most unclear. Relying on the commander in chief power to justify domestic action in peacetime was wholly unprecedented, but for the time being there was little alternative to military government in a chaotic region where both civil authority and economic activity had collapsed. Moreover, the Constitution's republican guarantee clause provided a plausible basis for paternalistic control. Because the clause does not specify roles for the three branches, Johnson cannot fairly be criticized for taking the initiative to stabilize the South. Still, guarantee clause precedents had established only that the courts were not inclined to enforce the clause, not that Congress was excluded from a role.[15] Firing a warning shot, Senator Carl Schurz told Johnson that he had no power either to appoint civilian governors of states or to call for state conventions.

With Johnson's support, the newly reconstructing states took several actions that were sure to infuriate the heavily Republican Congress once it assembled. In addition to enacting the black codes, some states refused to ratify the Thirteenth Amendment. And in the fall elections, they elected Confederate Vice President Alexander Stephens and ten Confederate generals to Congress. Johnson, himself hostile to northern opinion, had not conveyed its angry tone southward. A collision impended.

Meanwhile, the president failed to ensure the faithful execution of the law in the South. Under conditions of anarchy, southern whites were enforcing white supremacy with brutal and widespread violence, in an effort to prevent the former slaves from receiving anything more than nominal freedom. As a former southern governor said, "With reference to emancipation, we are at the beginning of the war."[16] Clearly, the president could not eradicate these vast injustices short of placing a soldier on every southern street corner. But he could have alleviated some of the worst repression. The Army was still in place in the South, providing the president a ready means of information and response.

Instead of moving to redress the situation, Johnson made it worse. He ignored insistent reports of widespread southern violence against blacks that were coming from General Grant and Senator Schurz (whom Johnson had sent on a fact-finding mission). The president's racist rhetoric inflamed emotions already raw. He took steps to withdraw black Union troops from the South, where they were often the freedmen's best protection. Instead, Johnson wanted to grant civil control to local militias and police, which consisted of former rebels. He ignored the fact that early and unconstrained restoration of civilian rule in the South would surely harm the freed slaves, toward whom he was entirely callous.

Andrew Johnson's War with Congress

In December 1865, Congress convened, and the struggle that would end in impeachment began. Johnson greeted them with his first annual message, which clearly stated his constitutional theory of Reconstruction.[17] He sounded his usual themes of restoration and states' rights and claimed that his plan was sufficient. Celebrating the imminent ratification of the Thirteenth Amendment, he argued that it would "heal the wound" that caused disunion. Accordingly, he called for seating the new representatives from the South. He reported peaceful and cooperative conditions in the former Confederacy. He was badly misreading the climate of opinion in the North, where widespread opinion held that the South was not accepting the outcome of the war and that Johnson was welcoming new members of Congress who might as well have been clad in Confederate gray.

Days after the president's message, Secretary of State Seward, acting pursuant to his statutory authority to announce successful ratifications of constitutional amendments, issued a proclamation declaring the Thirteenth Amendment to have been ratified.[18] Following the president's theory that secession was a nullity, he found just enough ratifications, including eight former Confederate states, to make the requisite three-quarters of the antebellum total of thirty-six states. Congress would soon acquiesce in the amendment's validity by enacting legislation to aid the freedmen under its enforcement provision. Meanwhile, the constitutional issue whether any state could be forced to ratify an amendment lay dormant but was fated to arise another day.

Organizing itself to contest the president for control of Reconstruction, Congress formed a Joint Committee on Reconstruction. The committee's composition signaled Johnson that there was room for compromise. The committee was centrist, mixing radical Republicans, moderates, and Democrats. With his insensitivity to political subtlety, however, Johnson always saw all Republicans as radicals. Immediately Congress signaled its firmness by insisting on the ironclad oath and refusing to seat the butternut delegations from the reconstructing states. Partisan considerations certainly played a role in congressional reluctance to accept new southern members. They would be Democrats, reducing Republican control all the more because the freed slaves would henceforth be counted as full persons for apportionment even if they could not vote. Control of

Reconstruction legislation and the survival of wartime statutes promoting internal improvements were both at stake.

A wearying pattern soon emerged: Congress would enact Reconstruction legislation, the president would veto it, Congress would override the veto, and the president would resist enforcement of the law. Nothing approaching this standoff has occurred at any other time in American history. The surprising fact is not that the confrontation ended in impeachment but that the president escaped conviction and removal.

Doubting the president's version of conditions in the South, the joint committee initiated an investigation. To the surprise of few, the hearings revealed dismaying levels of mistreatment of blacks and resistance to Reconstruction. Even if one corrected for bias in the investigation, it remained clear that in return for Johnson's laxity toward the South, "defiance had been his portion."[19] Angered from the outset, Congress rolled up its sleeves and began to set Reconstruction policy independent of the president's wishes.

The first important bill reacted to the black codes by extending and strengthening the Freedmen's Bureau Act of 1865. The bureau was a temporary agency that was meant to improve the lot of the freedmen by means of civil rights protections, land grants, and education.[20] The extension had the support of all Republicans. With the war at an end, Congress based the constitutionality of the bureau on its power to spend for the general welfare, relying on the tradition of spending for disaster relief.[21] Ignoring history, Johnson vetoed the bill, arguing that the framers never contemplated "a system for the support of indigent persons in the United States" and objecting to special treatment for blacks, which he thought unwarranted.[22]

The most confrontational part of the veto message was Johnson's argument that a rump Congress, having improperly excluded qualified representatives of reconstructed states, could not validly legislate.[23] He drew a contrast to his Jacksonian claim to be the sole representative of the whole people. He said explicitly that he was speaking for the unrepresented South. One congressman remarked sarcastically that this position was "modest for a man . . . made President by an assassin."[24] Leaving no enemy unmade, Johnson followed up with an inflammatory speech appealing to the southern white supremacists who hated the bureau. This veto narrowly survived an override attempt. The war between the branches was on.

Against increasing congressional pressure, the president fought every effort to improve the welfare of the freedmen. He thought racial equality

in any form was radical. Correctly perceiving that the northern states generally opposed black suffrage, he could not see that the North did support
basic civil rights for the freed slaves. He had interfered with the operation
of the Freedmen's Bureau since taking office in 1865. His failure to protect the freedmen, many of them veterans, from the ravages of the black
codes caused resentment in the North. General Grant finally issued an order to protect blacks from prosecution for offenses that were not pursued
equally against whites.

The first important congressional override of a presidential veto in
American history occurred after Johnson vetoed the Civil Rights Act,
which gave blacks sweeping legal protections.[25] The bill defined citizenship for the first time in American history, rejecting *Dred Scott* by declaring everyone born in the United States a citizen. It gave all citizens
equal rights regarding such fundamental matters as contracts, property,
and litigation. And it provided for federal punishment of state officials
who violated its guarantees. Here was the promise of essential elements
of equality for the freedmen, to be enforced by the federal government. It
was all too much for Johnson, who vetoed it.[26] He considered it premature
to grant citizenship to all blacks so soon after emancipation and thought
that some forms of state discrimination against them were appropriate.

Johnson's strongest objections, though, were to the provisions of the
civil rights bill that would "sap and destroy" the traditional relations between the federal government and the states. The president's interpretation of the Constitution's structure of federalism was true to antebellum
principles. The premise of his position was that the Civil War left the federal system as it had been, that the Constitution was a constant despite
the conflagration of a war caused by states taking up arms against the
federal Union. Overriding the veto by a narrow margin, the president's
opponents in Congress adopted a competing interpretation based on the
transformational nature of the war. No one could know, however, which
position the courts would endorse. Accordingly, Congress formulated
what would become the Fourteenth Amendment to erase all doubt and to
evade Johnson's veto opportunity.

The proposed constitutional amendment largely paralleled the Civil
Rights Act.[27] Along with overruling *Dred Scott* by providing citizenship to
the native born, it recast federalism. The amendment forbade the states
to deprive citizens of federal "privileges or immunities" or to deny them
due process or the equal protection of the laws. For the first time, Americans would be able to assert sweeping federal constitutional rights against

the state governments. As it had evolved so far, the congressional plan for Reconstruction omitted any requirement for black suffrage, but it would have secured basic civil rights for the freedmen without punishing the South harshly or attempting a full social revolution. In the North, it seemed quite gentle; in the South, unbearably harsh.

For the remainder of the growing constitutional crisis, each branch retreated to its most primal powers. For Congress, the prospect of presidential vetoes and the need to override them meant that bills had to be formulated to garner two-thirds support in both houses. The president fell back on the veto, on his power to determine how to execute the law, and on patronage. He employed all three powers in ways sure to infuriate Congress. Johnson thought Congress should not mind vetoes, once calling the veto power "wholly negative and conservative in its character."[28] His interference with execution of laws that were passed over his vetoes was often blatant. For example, he removed Freedmen's Bureau agents who vigorously enforced the law. Gathering his control over the executive branch, Johnson removed more than a thousand federal officers and said he would replace them with his supporters.[29] Congress, ever alert to the balance of power over patronage, was incensed.

In June 1866, the joint committee issued a report accompanying the proposed Fourteenth Amendment, stating a desire for sectional reconciliation but making ratification a condition on the readmission of states.[30] Asserting that the seceded states had forfeited their constitutional rights, the committee invoked the constitutional power of Congress to admit new states. It promised to allow the three presidential state governments representation in Congress upon ratification of the amendment. From the entire Confederacy, only Tennessee ratified and was readmitted. The other ten states rejected it overwhelmingly.

President Johnson sent Congress a message objecting to the transmission of the proposed amendment to the states, arguing that Congress needed two-thirds majorities based on representation of all thirty-six states.[31] The battle lines between president and Congress were now clearly drawn for the impending congressional elections of 1866. Two starkly different views of the nation and its Constitution offered themselves to the voters—Johnson's restored Jacksonian republic versus Congress's emerging vision of a nation knit together by new constitutional rights and relationships.

In hopes of recasting Congress, the president decided on an unprecedented tactic. He would make an extended tour, a "swing around the circle" he called it, taking the case for his Reconstruction policy directly to the people and campaigning against his congressional opponents. Today such a step is normal and expected, but this was a time when presidents still did not campaign openly for themselves or others.[32] It is a grand irony that such a momentous step in the evolution of the president's connection with the people produced a political disaster of such magnitude.

Johnson's undignified behavior on the swing suited the politicking of his backwoods origins but not the office he now held. He descended to trading insults with hecklers. General Grant, forced to come along, said he was "disgusted at hearing a man make speeches on the way to his own funeral."[33] The Republicans, crying that Johnson was squandering the fruits of victory, captured veto-proof majorities in both houses. Characteristically, Johnson reacted to the electoral drubbing with renewed defiance.

The Congress elected in November 1866 would normally convene in December 1867, but the outgoing Thirty-Ninth Congress had provided for its successor to meet in March 1867 to keep Johnson from acting alone for most of the year. Even before the new veto-proof Congress assembled, the old Congress responded to the election returns by moving both to take formation of Reconstruction policy away from the president and to restrict his control over the executive branch.

Congress was reacting not only to Johnson's opposition to ratifying the Fourteenth Amendment but also to continuing bad news from the South. In the summer of 1866, severe race riots in Memphis and New Orleans, in which local police were prominent participants, had caused many deaths and injuries to freedmen and Unionists.[34] The president's leniency toward the South had created a climate fostering violence; he had done nothing in response to the riots. The outbreak of violence, together with the enactment of the black codes, gave the lie to the president's claims that all was well in the reconstructing states.

In February 1867, Congress passed the First Military Reconstruction Act.[35] This was singularly drastic legislation. Reciting that no legal governments existed in ten states, it created five military districts to administer them, each to be headed by a general appointed by the president.[36] The commanders could suspend previous presidential governments. To end military government a state would have to allow black suffrage and ratify the Fourteenth Amendment. Congress now saw the suffrage requirement as central to the success of Reconstruction. Support for it came from considerations of equal treatment, the protective potential of black political power, and an expectation that these would be new Republican voters.

Johnson vetoed the bill, calling it despotic and unconstitutional, and was overridden the same day.[37] His veto message invoked the Supreme Court's 1866 decision in *Ex parte Milligan*, which had held martial law unconstitutional in places where the civil courts were open and functioning.[38] That case had arisen in Indiana, however, which was a far cry from Mississippi. For good measure, Johnson threw in an objection to granting blacks the vote.

As its time ran out, the furious Thirty-Ninth Congress overreached by invading the president's command relationships with the executive branch.[39] In part, Congress was irritated by Johnson's use of patronage. Unable to get confirmation of most nominations, the president was building his own political base by appointing Democrats to offices that did not require confirmation (such as postmasters). More seriously, Congress was seeking to protect conduct by senior executive officers that, although provoked by Johnson's misbehavior, was insubordinate and would have brought dismissal in ordinary times. Secretary of War Stanton had been defying the president and undermining him with Congress. Even General Grant had been advising legislators on ways to control the president.

Congress responded with the Tenure of Office Act, which was enacted over an immediate veto that had the ostensible support of the entire cabinet.[40] The act broadly required the Senate's advice and consent to presidential removal of officers. There was a curious special provision for the cabinet. These officers were to serve for the term of the president who had appointed them unless sooner removed with the consent of the Senate. Concerned about the possible unconstitutionality of the bill, Congress had introduced a fatal ambiguity to obtain passage: did the restriction apply to the current cabinet? Since Stanton was serving during Lincoln's second term, the act might restrict his removal. But Johnson had not appointed Stanton; therefore, perhaps the act did not apply to him. As we shall see, on such minutia might an impeachment turn.

This veto stood on very firm constitutional ground. Ever since the Washington administration, the conventional understanding of the Constitution had been that the president possessed an unfettered removal power for at least the constitutional cabinet and senior military officers. Johnson's uncharacteristically calm veto message pointed out that the unconstitutionality of senatorial participation in removals had been "settled . . . by construction, settled by precedent, settled by the practice of the Government, and settled by statute."[41] Everyone knew this was a strong argument. When the final confrontation between the president and

Congress centered on this statute, Congress would be fighting on very bad ground.

In a second bill that was framed with the aid of Stanton and Grant, Congress interfered with the normal military chain of command. A rider to the Military Appropriations Act of 1867 required the commanding general of the Army, who was Grant, to be stationed at Washington, required the president to forward all orders to the Army through him, and forbade his removal without Senate approval.[42] Andrew Jackson would have ignored so blatant an intrusion on the daily command of the Army. Andrew Johnson, wanting the appropriations in the bill, signed it and appended a signing statement objecting to the constitutionality of the rider.

As the Thirty-Ninth Congress wound down in early 1867, it considered whether to impeach the president. The House Judiciary Committee began holding hearings, but the time was not ripe. Impeachment was still too fateful a step—it was unprecedented, subject to deep uncertainty about the appropriate grounds for removal, and obviously risky for those who pursued it and for the nation. Much of the clash between the branches was due to strong and legitimate disagreement about the principles that should govern Reconstruction. Simply exercising the constitutional veto power surely could not be an impeachable offense. If the president was failing in his duty of faithful execution of the law, he was not the first to do that, and none of his predecessors had faced serious impeachment jeopardy.

Johnson was cagey enough to behave in ways that made it difficult to identify any clear violation of his duties. Instead of refusing outright to enforce statutes enacted over his veto, he followed the forms of the law by appointing the military commanders Congress had created. If he chose commanders who were unsympathetic to congressional desires or instructed them in ways members of Congress would not approve, he was still within the ordinary bounds of the political system.

As the new Congress took the still-warm seats of the expiring one, it enacted a Second Military Reconstruction Act to add some details to the initial one.[43] Of course veto and override followed. Johnson did, however, accept General Grant's suggestions as he chose the military commanders to implement the legislation. The military began enrolling black voters, and new governments featuring carpetbaggers, scalawags, and freedmen took shape.[44] Now the president counterattacked from a different direction.[45] He obtained opinions from Attorney General Henry Stanbery that took a very narrow view of the statutory criteria for disenfranchising former rebels and for federal removal of local officials.

General Grant, thinking that these interpretations would emasculate military Reconstruction, encouraged the regional commanders to take a broad view of the statutes rather than follow the attorney general's opinion. Johnson had a confrontation with Stanton over the matter but did not dismiss him. No matter who was right about the interpretive issues, under the Constitution the president and not his subordinates is responsible for the legal positions the executive branch takes.

Congress intervened in the dispute with the Third Military Reconstruction Act, which overruled Stanberry's specific interpretations of the law and contained an extraordinary provision, drafted with Stanton's help, explicitly freeing military commanders from any duty to follow "any opinion of any civil officer of the United States."[46] Correctly denouncing this provision as unconstitutional for stripping him of essential elements of command over his military subordinates, Johnson vetoed it and was overridden.[47]

President Johnson's fierce departmentalism was not directed solely toward Congress. When the State of Mississippi challenged the constitutionality of military Reconstruction in the Supreme Court, the Johnson administration convinced the Court not to intervene in the intensely political maelstrom of Reconstruction.[48] Attorney General Stanbery found himself arguing for the president's sole power to decide how to execute laws that he had vetoed and despised and that the attorney general himself was busily undermining. A president who had shown himself willing to defy Congress certainly would not welcome intrusions from the judiciary.

With his principal civilian and military subordinates in league with Congress against him, Johnson was in peril of complete loss of control over the executive branch. He decided to assert his constitutional authority. In August, with Congress in recess, the president finally asked Stanton for his resignation.[49] When Stanton refused pending the return of Congress, Johnson suspended him and designated a reluctant Grant to serve as acting secretary as well as commanding general. This action was consistent with the Tenure of Office Act, but the president refused to admit compliance with it, vaguely citing the "Constitution and laws" as his authority. At the same time Johnson removed three of the regional commanders for overly vigorous enforcement of their statutory duties and replaced them with generals who were Democrats.

As Congress reassembled in December 1867, Johnson sent an incendiary annual message disparaging the readiness of blacks for suffrage and

claiming that military Reconstruction was tyrannical and unconstitutional.[50] He also sent a more politic message justifying the suspension of
Stanton.[51] The Tenure of Office Act required such a communication, but
again Johnson complied without conceding the validity of the statute. The
message was a persuasive litany of Stanton's perfidies. The president particularly emphasized Stanton's failure to convey to him a telegram from
New Orleans authorities asking for instructions before the riot there. The
president had been blamed, unfairly he thought, for the violence. Predictably, the Senate was unimpressed. By a large margin, it disapproved
Stanton's suspension.

A bit of comic opera ensued within the executive, confirming that the
president had lost control of both the cabinet and the military. Grant,
uncertain of his legal status and disgusted, resigned as acting secretary of
war and locked the office behind him. A lurking Stanton seized the keys
and reoccupied the office. A squabble erupted in the press, with Johnson
accusing Grant of lying. General William T. Sherman, who never pulled
a punch, compared Johnson to "a general fighting without an army."[52] In
February 1868, Johnson finally defied the Tenure of Office Act by removing Stanton without asking the Senate's consent and replacing him with
the undistinguished general Lorenzo Thomas.[53] Setting new records for
insubordination, Stanton had Thomas arrested briefly for violating the
Tenure of Office Act. No one could bear any more of this; impeachment
loomed.

Impeachment

The Johnson impeachment demonstrated that any effort to remove a
president presents two fundamental issues that tend to confound each
other.[54] First, there is the immediate issue whether the incumbent's behavior merits conviction and removal. Second, the precedent has a separation
of powers effect: the outcome of an impeachment necessarily increases
or decreases the relative strength of president and Congress, perhaps for
a long time. Even if the president be a scoundrel, some in Congress will
quail at the thought of removing the head of state, a step that risks harm
to the nation. In 1868, the members of Congress who pressed for Johnson's removal were also explicitly attempting to reduce the power of the
presidency, which had so vastly expanded under Lincoln, toward the more
Whiggish model that had often preceded the Civil War. Reflecting this

concern, the impeachment process focused mostly on the allocation of control over the executive branch between president and Congress, and especially on the removal question. But larger questions about the fate of the Republic could not be excluded from what often appeared to be just a nasty interbranch squabble.[55]

For Congress and the president alike, impeachment was completely untrodden ground in 1868.[56] Fundamental questions abounded. These included both the substantive meaning of the Constitution's reference to "high Crimes and Misdemeanors" and the requisite procedures for impeachment by the House of Representatives and trial by the Senate. The constitutional history of the impeachment clauses suggested strongly that serious abuses of office would suffice for removal—that technical proof of a crime was not necessary (or perhaps not sufficient, if the crime did not relate to official business).[57] At the same time, the framers were concerned to protect the autonomy of the office, lest the president serve "at the pleasure of the Senate." There was also a curious practical problem. There was no vice president, and the succession statute placed the president pro tem of the Senate next in line.[58] That was the irascible Benjamin Wade, an uncompromising radical who had offended many in his own party. Moreover, Wade's identity as successor made any impeachment effort resemble a congressional coup.

Congress made a fundamental strategic error in the Johnson impeachment. Although the best ground for removal was his refusal to execute the statutes governing Reconstruction, Congress deemphasized that charge in an apparent desire to avoid "political" grounds for impeachment rather than legal ones.[59] Accordingly, violation of the Tenure of Office Act took prominence. The act revealed that it was an impeachment trap by specifically providing that violation of its provisions would be a crime and a "high misdemeanor." Three days after the Stanton removal, the House impeached Johnson on a straight party-line vote of 128–47. A special committee then drafted the articles after the impeachment decision had already been taken. This procedural irregularity revealed that the House wanted Johnson removed but was not quite sure why.

Most of the eleven counts charged various violations of the Tenure of Office Act.[60] One article even sought to remove Johnson for his lurid speeches on the swing around the circle. Only the final, catchall article XI included both of the real reasons for impeachment: Johnson's denial of the legitimacy of the rump Congress and his consequent resistance to congressional Reconstruction. This article recited his efforts to undermine

enforcement of the statutes, including the Tenure of Office Act, in violation of the president's faithful execution duty. The House then approved
the articles, forwarded them to the Senate, and named seven managers to
prosecute the case, including three radicals.

The Senate trial began in March, presided over by Chief Justice
Chase.[61] Johnson was saved by the better performance of his lawyers, the
reluctance of some Republican moderates to take the fateful step of removing a president, and the looming presence of Wade as successor to the
office. The fact that the charges focused on the removal of an officer contrary to a statutory restriction invited litigating all the uncertainties and
precedents that had long attended that issue. Muddying the waters was
the question whether the Tenure of Office Act even applied to Stanton.
Johnson's lawyers argued these points capably and claimed boldly that the
Tenure of Office Act was unconstitutional and that Johnson was therefore
entitled to disobey it:

> If the law be upon its very face in flat contradiction of plain expressed provi-
> sions of the Constitution, as if a law should forbid the President to grant a
> pardon in any case, . . . I say the President, without going to the Supreme Court
> of the United States, maintaining the integrity of his department . . . is bound to
> execute no such legislation; and he is cowardly and untrue to the responsibility
> of his position if he should execute it.[62]

This was a strong argument: presidents had long asserted the power to
refuse to enforce unconstitutional statutes, especially ones that infringe
executive prerogatives.[63] Johnson's attorneys went on to argue that he was
merely creating a test case by disobeying the law and would obey a Supreme Court ruling.

The managers browbeat the witnesses; the defense tried the legal
case.[64] The president helped his own cause considerably by conducting
a strategic retreat from his most extreme positions during the trial—he
promised to stop interfering with Reconstruction.[65] He had enough sense
not to appear in person. The Senate eventually authorized the chief justice to decide issues of law, evidence, and procedure subject to override.
Because of the nature of the charges, the trial did not focus effectively
on Johnson's interference with Congress's overall Reconstruction policy;
instead, it often bogged down in minutia. The House managers, going
against the legalistic grain of the charges in their overall effort to confine
presidential power, sometimes claimed that impeachable offenses were

essentially political, that they could extend to anything "subversive of some fundamental or essential principle of government, or highly prejudicial to the public interest."[66] So unconfined a definition of impeachable misconduct was bound to alarm many senators. Johnson's lawyers hewed strictly to legal issues and insisted that only an indictable offense would permit removal.

In May, the voting began with the last, omnibus article, which failed to reach the two-thirds needed by a single vote, with seven Republicans voting nay.[67] (More nay votes may have been available if needed.) Besmirching the process, president-in-waiting Wade voted for conviction. After that, the impeachment dribbled to an end. Stanton finally resigned and was replaced by the widely respected general John Schofield.

For the most part, Johnson did leave Reconstruction alone for his remaining months in office. After the trial, Johnson may have concluded that although he had lost many battles, he had won the war over Reconstruction. He could see that his acquittal fed southern resistance and that his own intransigence had forestalled any sweeping social reconstruction. He left office satisfied that he had never wavered from his own principles.

The legacy of the Johnson impeachment is complex and full of irony. Congress, having baited an impeachment trap for the president by enacting the Tenure of Office Act, fell into the trap itself because many in Congress knew that Johnson's constitutional objections were sound enough to undermine the conclusion that he should be removed for violating the act. The judgment of history has been that Johnson was right, that the act was an unconstitutional infringement on the president's control over the executive branch.[68] It is very difficult to argue that either the vesting clause or the commander in chief clause would permit Congress to saddle a president with a secretary of war against his will (a postmaster might present a different question). Hence the Johnson acquittal provided some precedential support for the constitutional unity of the executive branch under presidential command.

More broadly, many observers have drawn the conclusion that the failed impeachment was beneficial because it provided future presidents necessary autonomy from political removal for mere unpopularity. A modern chief justice, William Rehnquist, has argued that the impeachment trial of President Johnson fundamentally threatened one of the framers' "original contributions to the art of government"—the independent, not parliamentary, executive.[69]

There is much to be said for this point of view. One can easily imagine an alternative history in which unpopular presidents would regularly be removed for their political "crimes and misdemeanors." Such a development would indeed have worked a fundamental change in a system that had survived the Civil War in part because President Lincoln enjoyed the protection of the four-year term that he needed to make his often unpopular policies prevail. A "parliamentary" presidency might be better than the one the Constitution created, but it is not the one bequeathed to us by the events of 1868.

The full context of the Johnson impeachment reveals that Congress was not trapped between the illegitimate alternatives of removing the president for violating an unconstitutional statute or doing so over general political disagreements. The offense for which Johnson *did* deserve removal was his refusal to discharge his faithful execution duty. He was entitled to employ his veto as he saw fit, but once overridden on Reconstruction policy, he should have accepted defeat by acknowledging the legislative primacy of Congress.

Granted, Johnson's claims that the rump Congress was illegitimate and that military Reconstruction was unconstitutional were sincerely held and were not fanciful. Many legal problems of the era were essentially extraconstitutional, because the Constitution says nothing about secession, civil war, or reconstruction. Both Presidents Lincoln and Johnson thought that their military and pardon powers gave them initial command of many Reconstruction issues. Where they differed was in Lincoln's explicit willingness to defer to the will of Congress and Johnson's defiance of it. Lincoln's legal posture was not destabilizing to our constitutional system; Johnson's was. By extending his departmentalist arguments to encompass a challenge to Congress's fundamental authority to legislate, Johnson initiated a confrontation about the ultimate powers of the constitutional branches. Only his retreat in the face of impeachment prevented resolution of the confrontation through the only constitutional mechanism available to resolve it—Johnson's conviction and removal.

If supported by adequate development of the facts, removing Johnson for his refusals to execute congressional Reconstruction would not have created a precedent that simple political disagreement can ground impeachment. Still, if misused or misunderstood, such a precedent would have tended to support impeachment for general laxity or reluctance to execute the law as Congress might prefer. Understandably, in 1868 Congress was loath to impeach a president for what he did *not* do. Even the mighty Jackson had failed his constitutional duties by ignoring the plight of the Indians. The precedent of a removal for nonfeasance, then, would have had an unavoidably uncertain and troubling scope. The case is close, but I think Johnson had crossed a line that justifies removal if the ultimate legislative authority of Congress is to be maintained.

Although the impeachment failed, its practical effect was to reduce the power of successor presidents in the remainder of the nineteenth century. To that extent the broadest purposes of the advocates of impeachment were realized. Of course, Johnson's failures as president were as personal as they were institutional. Accordingly, even the weakened presidents that followed had their successes, as the nation waited for the long national nightmare of the Civil War era to end.

With President Johnson neutralized by the impeachment effort against him, the centerpiece of congressional Reconstruction, the Fourteenth Amendment, achieved the remaining number of needed ratifications from southern states. Secretary Seward, well aware of the president's objections to the amendment, issued a proclamation equivocating about whether ratification had succeeded.[70] In an action without precedent, both houses of Congress immediately passed resolutions declaring ratification. Seward then issued another proclamation reciting the events and announcing adoption of the amendment. Congress had prevailed in the end.

Beset by the domestic crises that culminated in impeachment, the Johnson administration had neither time nor attention for the aggressive conduct of foreign affairs.[71] Still, Secretary of State William Seward, a committed expansionist, remained in office. President Johnson, having a full domestic agenda, left diplomacy mostly to Seward, although he did announce in an annual message that any American acquisition of territory would take place "peacefully and lawfully, while neither doing nor menacing injury to other states."[72] Seward's negotiation of the treaty with Russia to acquire Alaska for $7.2 million was the major foreign policy achievement of the United States during Reconstruction. He negotiated the treaty in secret and presented the final product to a surprised Senate, which accepted the deal.

The end of the Civil War also allowed the Johnson administration to address some unfinished business concerning the invasion of Mexico by Napoleon III of France, who sent troops there in 1861 and later installed Austria's Archduke Maximilian as ruler. In no position to fight two wars at one time, the Lincoln administration had confined itself to

some Monroe Doctrine bluster. After Appomattox, Secretary Seward issued more credible warnings that the United States would not tolerate
reinforcing Maximilian with European troops. Cast adrift by his erstwhile
sponsors, Maximilian fell to the Mexicans in 1867. It was clear that "the
temporary suspension of the Monroe Doctrine as a result of the Civil War
had ended."[73]

"Let Us Have Peace"

"Let us have peace" was the successful (and carefully ambiguous) campaign slogan for Ulysses S. Grant in 1868, signifying an understandable
national weariness after eight years of bloodshed and strife.[74] Before the
election, seven states were readmitted to Congress, reducing the federal
government's leverage on them. Signs were visible, however, that the
struggle continued. In the South, the Ku Klux Klan was rising to enforce
white supremacy with private violence. Of course, President Johnson's
military did not respond.

Ulysses Grant was so popular that he could safely follow the tradition
of avoiding a campaign for the presidency. He did not hunger for the post
but thought he was better suited than an ordinary politician to preserve the
results of the war. The election returns gave him a 53 percent majority, a figure bolstered by the black vote in newly reconstructed states. The Electoral
College magnified Grant's popular majority, and Republicans won sweeping majorities in both houses of Congress. The effect was to consolidate the
formal gains of Reconstruction, including the Fourteenth Amendment.[75]

Grant immediately distanced himself from his predecessor, announcing in his inaugural that "all laws will be faithfully executed whether they
meet my approval or not."[76] Naively, Grant began by trying to rule above
party.[77] With his military background, the new president had neither aptitude nor appetite for the kind of bargaining and coalition building that
any successful president must employ. He chose an undistinguished cabinet that he viewed more as staff than as bridges to the party's constituencies. He provided little guidance to the cabinet, leaving patronage to
them. Naturally, because the cabinet was weak, patronage control gravitated to the Senate. Thus, even with a former general at its head, the executive branch was not under firm control.

It was a bad time for the Republican Party to be without leadership.
The salient national issues were shifting from Reconstruction to economic

development and civil service reform. Bitter intraparty divisions surfaced between the new reformers and the party "Stalwarts," who represented the emergent urban political machines and wallowed happily in the politics of spoils. By 1870, in response to widespread demands that he assert control and unify the cabinet, Grant changed its composition as he allied with the Stalwarts. Now he used patronage to feed the demands of the political machines and even tried to curry favor in the South by giving some posts to Democrats.

Grant did have an important success in recasting the Supreme Court.[78] In an odd episode, President Johnson and Congress together had done a bit of unpacking of the Supreme Court. In July 1866, Congress reduced the number of justices from ten to seven to deny Johnson any appointment opportunities.[79] The vote on the bill crossed party lines, and Johnson signed it, never trusting the judiciary. In early 1869, Congress voted to put the number back to nine. Johnson vetoed the bill on his last day in office. It was soon reenacted as an inaugural present for President Grant; the number has remained at nine ever since.

By 1870, Grant had obtained confirmations of his two nominees, and just in time. As they arrived at the Court, it had just partially invalidated the Civil War "greenback" law that made paper money official legal tender of the United States.[80] Wasting no time, the new justices immediately set out to reverse the decision and succeeded the next year.[81] A piece of wartime legislation with long-term economic effects was safe. Grant's judicial selections had already cast a long shadow into the future.

Generally undistinguished as it was, Grant's presidency has been unfairly condemned by historians.[82] Notwithstanding his best efforts, Grant was never able to solve the clash between the two great political demands of Reconstruction: reconciliation with the South and equality for the freedmen.[83] Of course, it was impossible to satisfy both. The president found himself in a reactive posture that had never characterized him in war. He was aware that he could not invoke the powers of a wartime commander in chief. For both constitutional and political reasons, he was reluctant to use force and anxious to justify doing so—he said that "I want to avoid anything like an unlawful use of the military."[84] When he did use the troops to enforce the law, he was vilified as a military dictator; when he did not, he was excoriated for failing his duty of faithful execution.

Grant also had the bad luck to preside over the blossoming corruption of the Gilded Age, as a nation weary of strife settled down to getting rich. Corruption repeatedly touched Grant's administration but not the president personally. It did come close. The "whiskey ring" scandal, which involved bribes to corrupt federal tax officials, reached Orville Babcock, one of the president's personal secretaries. Loyal to a fault, Grant tried to protect him and was spattered with tar. Secretary of War William Belknap was driven from office for taking kickbacks on corrupt contracts for Indian supplies.[85] (Meanwhile, Congress was no fount of virtue—the Credit Mobilier scandal involved bribing congressmen with stock to support the transcontinental railroad.)

Yet there were positive aspects to Grant's presidency. Although he could tell that northern support for vigorous Reconstruction policy was waning, he did try to protect the freedmen from the worst abuses against them.[86] By 1870, with the president's support the Fifteenth Amendment was in place, forbidding the states to deny suffrage on grounds of race. The amendment was a curiously partial response to problems of voting equality. It left women out entirely and did nothing to prevent ostensibly neutral barriers to black suffrage such as literacy tests. But it allowed the North to leave the freedmen, finally armed with at least theoretical voting rights, on their own to protect themselves. Congress did follow up with three Enforcement Acts, which forbade interference with voting rights, imposed federal supervision over elections, and outlawed the main Ku Klux Klan atrocities.[87] Grant's attorney general, Amos Akerman, proved to be an aggressive enforcer of these federal protections. With the newly formed Department of Justice at his disposal and the president at his back, Akerman brought prosecutions in the South that broke the power of the Klan for the time being. Unhappily, however, Grant possessed neither the political will nor the enforcement mechanisms that would have been needed for sustained and effective suppression of southern violence.

As president, Grant "instinctively sought to project American power abroad."[88] Of course, the need to complete Reconstruction meant that Grant's main projection of power was into the defeated South. Still, his able and expansionist secretary of state, Hamilton Fish, negotiated an important treaty of reciprocity with Hawaii that effectively extended the Monroe Doctrine to the central Pacific and paved the way for later annexation. On the negative side of the ledger, Grant negotiated an ill-advised treaty to annex the Dominican Republic that fell far short of Senate ratification. The purpose of the treaty, to give the freedmen leverage against southern whites by providing them a colonization outlet in case of continued mistreatment, was too unrealistic.

Grant was the first president to serve a second term since Jackson.[89] Reconstruction withered further under a political realignment that would produce party stalemate and divided government for the next two decades. The Democrats took the House of Representatives in 1874, signaling the South that the way was clear for white "redeemer" governments to displace the Reconstruction state governments and to begin dismantling the gains that the freedmen had made. As a last gasp of Reconstruction effort, with Grant's support the lame duck Congress passed the Civil Rights Act of 1875, forbidding discrimination in public accommodations such as inns and railroads but not providing for enforcement by the federal government.[90] Yet the tide was ebbing. The president's agonized annual message at the end of 1874 had called for additional enforcement authority that was not forthcoming. Grant complained to Senator Wade that he could not "get Congress to help him."[91]

Violent displacement of Reconstruction governments was under way. In Louisiana, a massacre in Colfax killed about a hundred blacks. Grant sent troops to restore order, knowing that he was supporting a flagrantly corrupt Reconstruction government against white supremacists who were determined to seize power. The unsatisfactory outcome led Grant to stay his hand in Mississippi, where the Reconstruction government was toppled. The old elites were securing their coveted redemption.

Grant's second term was also haunted by a severe depression that began in 1873 and lingered for two decades. Labor conflict induced by wage cuts took center stage in American politics and became a central concern of presidents. At the end of Grant's unlucky and discredited presidency the Republican Party denied him a third term in hopes of holding the White House with another candidate. And so they did, but only by means of political machinations that ended Reconstruction in an appropriately dismal fashion.

Rutherford Hayes was a safe candidate, a Civil War veteran and governor of Ohio who was free of corruption, enemies, or distinction. The 1876 election, which was marred by fraud and violence, gave Democrat Samuel Tilden a majority of the popular vote and an apparent majority in the Electoral College. Yet Hayes was awarded the presidency by the one-vote majority of a special commission that Congress appointed to resolve challenges to electoral votes in three southern states that held the election in balance.[92] During this tortured process, Hayes gathered the support he needed by promising to follow a "let alone policy" toward the South.[93] Conservative whites in the North and South had reconciled at the expense of the blacks.

As president, Hayes had a mixed record regarding his duty of faithful execution of the law. Like Grant, he hoped for both conciliation and equality in the South. Good-hearted and naive, he tried to achieve these goals by forming alliances with white southerners. They accepted his promises to "put aside the bayonet" in return for empty promises to protect the freedmen.[94] When evidence surfaced that the redeemer governments were continuing their course of repression, there was no remaining will in the North to respond. The president contented himself with rhetorical gestures. He demonstrated more vigor when the great railroad strike of 1877 broke out, sending federal troops to restore order in some places, although he left most of the task to state militias.[95]

The principal battles of the Hayes administration were not with recalcitrant southerners or angry workers but with the Stalwart wing of the Republican Party. Hayes installed a cabinet that was prepared to accommodate southern interests. In selecting his cabinet, Hayes ignored the wishes of the Senate oligarchs, touching off a war over control of appointments.[96] In an effort to undermine the Stalwart political machines and promote a merit system, the president forbade federal officers to hold party offices also. Picking a fight with New York senator Roscoe Conkling, Hayes removed Conkling's man Chester Arthur from the lucrative post of collector of the port of New York after widespread allegations of corruption. Toward the end of his term, Hayes claimed victory: "My sole right to make appointments is tacitly conceded."[97] Victory was not won without cost, however. Exhausted by his "continual struggle" with the Stalwarts, Hayes did not stand for a second term.[98] Meanwhile, the squabbling Republicans lost control of the Senate to the Democrats in 1878, giving the coup de grâce to Reconstruction.

Hayes won one more political battle with Congress that also translated into a separation of powers standoff. After the 1878 elections, an emboldened Congress tried to repeal Reconstruction enforcement legislation by adding riders to the Army appropriations bill and the general civil appropriations bill.[99] Congress knew Hayes would veto any separate effort to repeal the statutes and hoped he would not dare to risk shutdown of the Army or the government by vetoing the money bills. Dare he would. The president vowed to stop this "unconstitutional and revolutionary attempt to deprive the Executive of one of his most important prerogatives" by making him "approve a measure which in fact he does not approve."[100] After Hayes vetoed repeated versions of the riders and was sustained each time, Congress receded. As with patronage, Hayes had avoided surrendering to congressional efforts to poach on executive power.

Hayes left office with the presidency—and the nation—intact if battered. Somehow the federal government had weathered what Lincoln called the "mighty scourge" of the Civil War. The war itself had recast the nation. Reconstruction, largely a failure, did leave a legacy of promises in the three constitutional amendments and in some surviving civil rights legislation. But redemption of those promises would be a long time coming. As Reconstruction ended, darkness settled over the South.

PART III
Steward of the People

[I insisted] upon the theory that the executive power was limited only by specific restrictions and prohibitions appearing in the Constitution or imposed by the Congress under its Constitutional powers. My view was that every executive officer . . . was a steward of the people bound actively and affirmatively to do all he could for the people. . . . I declined to adopt the view that what was imperatively necessary for the Nation could not be done by the President unless he could find some specific authorization to do it. My belief was that it was not only his right but his duty to do anything that the needs of the Nation demanded unless such action was forbidden by the Constitution or by the laws. . . . I did not usurp power, but I did greatly broaden the use of executive power.—Theodore Roosevelt, 1913

CHAPTER SEVEN

Facing the Lions

McKinley, Theodore Roosevelt, and Wilson

He goes to face the lions, if ever a man did.—A diplomat's remark about President Wilson's trip to the Paris Peace Conference, 1918[1]

The Civil War accelerated America's passage into the industrial age. As the heartbreak of Reconstruction receded, business corporations proliferated until the United States had become the world's largest economy by the dawn of the twentieth century. Yet working conditions did not keep pace, and conflict between labor and management produced constant strikes. The presidency lay in the doldrums, as if resting from the cataclysm of the 1860s. But at the turn of the century, as imperial dreams stirred the nation, presidents reawakened the office and began its twentieth-century transformation.

Congressional Government

In 1885, an acute young political scientist named Woodrow Wilson titled his treatise *Congressional Government* to capture and applaud the essential nature of the federal government as he saw it.[2] Professor Wilson, who wanted power to be linked to accountability in ways characteristic of parliamentary government, was not friendly to multiple checks on majority will. Yet only two decades later, his revision of the book, retitled *Constitutional Government*, praised Alexander Hamilton and celebrated the presidency toward which he was beginning his own ascent. Wilson now thought that political parties could bridge formal separations of power and assure the necessary political responsibility under the guidance of an active president. Clearly, something had happened in the interim.

The presidency's nadir may have been when the assassination of James Garfield in 1881 brought Chester Arthur to the presidency with the odor of the corrupt New York Customs House still clinging to him.[3] Arthur had been placed on the ticket to secure the electoral votes of New York and to appease his mentor, Senator Roscoe Conkling. Garfield, an intelligent and able former congressman (and of course a Civil War veteran), had served only four months when a deranged office seeker shot him. Perhaps prophetically, as Garfield entered office he had seen the presidency as a "bleak mountain" he must climb.[4] When he failed to reach the top, a lesser mountaineer would take his place.

The wounded president lingered painfully for eighty days until infection brought on by his doctors' malpractice finally finished him. During that time, he was lucid but conducted no important public business. Within the administration, there was some inconclusive discussion about the appropriate response to presidential disability, but Vice President Arthur understandably quailed at the thought of assuming power. The tragedy revealed the Constitution's failure to provide for disability, a gap that would not be filled by amendment until many years and several periods of vacuum atop the executive branch had ensued. Meanwhile, disabled presidents clung to office without offering constitutional interpretations about the problem. Vice presidents kept silent to avoid any hint of a coup. The result was a constitutional vacuum at the top of the executive branch, as all three branches of government and the people as well simply waited for the outcome of one man's crisis of health.

Garfield held office just long enough to fight and win a battle over patronage with the crown prince of the Stalwarts, Senator Conkling.[5] The senator, whose man Arthur was now vice president, began by telling Garfield he would like to select the treasury secretary. Garfield declined but did put both Stalwarts and reformers in the cabinet. The president then declared independence and infuriated Conkling by appointing one of the senator's enemies to the lucrative New York Customs House without consulting him. Garfield said the stakes were whether this important office should be "under the direct control of the Administration or under the local control of a factional Senator."[6] Conkling reacted by overplaying his hand. He dramatically resigned from the Senate, hoping for a triumphant reelection by the New York legislature, but suffered a stunning defeat instead. The executive branch remained in the president's hands.

History is never short of irony. Once president, Chester Arthur redeemed himself from his shady origins by conducting the office with dignity and independence and by presiding over passage of the Pendleton Act, which erected a monument to the murdered Garfield by creating a merit-based civil service at long last.[7] The act controlled entry to positions in the "classified service," which did not include senior executive officers. The act did not forbid removals but deterred political dismissals by eliminating the opportunity for political replacements. Presidents were given authority to expand the classified service and did so steadily until it covered about half the executive positions by the turn of the century. Now the modern structure of the executive branch was in place: the president and some layers of political appointees at the top oversaw a growing cadre of permanent civil servants below them.

Although the existence of the civil service appears to reduce presidential control over the executive branch, it actually aids presidents by reducing the power of the Senate over patronage for lesser federal positions.[8] Congress created the service because its own influence was being eroded by the power of the emerging state and local political machines. Hence, instead of the traditional zero-sum appointments game between presidents and the Senate, there was advantage to both branches in limiting the stakes of patronage.

The concept of faithful execution requires a referent to guide presidential choices. Gilded Age presidents found it easy to interpret their faithful execution duty to require them to protect the private property that was gathered in new industrial concentrations. Even the only Democrat to serve between Buchanan and Wilson, Grover Cleveland (elected twice, with an intermission for Benjamin Harrison), exhibited no fine Jacksonian concern for the little man (or woman).[9] Modern scholars argue that a presidential "protective" power to save lives and property is a natural interpretation of the faithful execution duty.[10] This is true, but it can obscure the problem of choosing *whose* lives and property are to be protected from *whom*, as the Pullman strike of 1894 illustrates.

A railway union struck the Pullman rail car company after the company cut wages drastically without reducing rent in company houses or interrupting dividends.[11] Labor leader Eugene Debs called a national sympathy strike against trains carrying Pullman cars; more than one hundred thousand workers responded. As the crisis grew, strikers stopped trains nationwide, and fighting broke out between strikers, strikebreakers, and police.[12] Respectable opinion condemned labor and demanded order. President Cleveland, who combined an aggressive nature with moral certainty, knew what to do. As hysteria mounted, he dispatched federal troops to Chicago, despite protests by Governor John Altgeld.

A constitutional issue lurked here—the Constitution requires the federal government to protect the states against domestic violence on application of the state legislature or executive, and Illinois was declining any help.[13] Could the president intervene anyway, on the theory that either the faithful execution duty to protect lives and property or the commander in chief power provided the necessary authority? If so, these general provisions would be overriding the negative implication from the Constitution's more specific provision concerning domestic violence, which appears to reflect federalist sensitivities. Cleveland's intervention, based on a judgment of necessity, answered this question in the affirmative. The history of Reconstruction had demonstrated that Cleveland's interpretation is correct when the facts support it—states had often proved unwilling to protect their citizens against violations of federally guaranteed rights.[14] In the context of the Pullman strike, however, Cleveland was relying on looser conceptions of the need to ensure law and order and to deliver the mails. This made his case weaker but not fictive—there was a lot of disorder.

Cleveland's military intervention killed or injured scores of strikers, broke the strike, and destroyed the union. To end the strike, the administration obtained a federal court injunction against it. There was no explicit statutory authority for the issuance of such an injunction. The Supreme Court decided that the executive had an inherent constitutional right "to apply to its own courts for any proper assistance" in performing its duties.[15] The Court correctly thought that it is preferable to encourage the executive to resort to judicial process instead of immediate violence when public order is threatened. Going to court provides both the possibility of a judicial check on executive action and the need for the executive to make its claim of necessity in public so that Congress and the people can evaluate it.

In the event, the Court upheld Debs's criminal conviction for violating the injunction, in the process delivering a ringing endorsement of broad presidential power to use force to secure "all rights" protected by the Constitution, without making it particularly clear which ones it had in mind.[16] Thus Cleveland's intervention was forceful, successful—and one sided. His predecessor Washington had shown more restraint in dealing with the Whiskey rebels, as had Hayes in responding to the great railroad strike of 1877. His successor Theodore Roosevelt would throw workers' interests into the balance in settling the coal strike of 1902.

Underlying any president's interpretation of the Constitution in general and law enforcement duties in particular is a conception of the proper role of government. For Cleveland, that role was to protect the private property of business enterprises. He revealed his conception of his duty to the people at large in his first term. As he vetoed a bill to buy seed for impoverished Texas wheat farmers, Cleveland argued that the appropriation would promote dependency: "Though the people support the Government, the Government should not support the people."[17] This was the second veto of federal aid to disaster victims in American history, following Johnson's veto of the Freedmen's Bureau Act.[18] It had the same mean spirit. Abraham Lincoln, free of the insensitive social Darwinism of the Gilded Age, had said that government should do for the people what they could not do, or not do as well, for themselves. It is hard to improve on that formulation, although of course one must decide when it applies.

Grover Cleveland initiated the practice of presidential dissimulation about personal health issues. In a curious episode, he foreshadowed the efforts that some of his successors would make to hide disability. In the summer of 1893, he boarded a friend's yacht and disappeared for five days while he had a secret operation to remove a tumor from his jaw.[19] Cleveland successfully suppressed news of the operation by attacking a journalist who discovered it, and the story stayed secret for decades. Although Cleveland prized his reputation for honesty, the incentive for any president to lie about ill health overcame him.

Most nineteenth-century presidents were not active managers of legislation, despite Jefferson's early example of the potential of the art. Cleveland made the typical remark that he "did not come here to legislate."[20] Still, like the others, he found himself intervening actively with patronage promises when the stakes were high enough—the silver coinage issue in his case. Systematic presidential pressure on Congress to legislate would arise under Theodore Roosevelt. Gilded Age presidents did, however, actively employ the veto pen, especially against what they regarded as special-interest legislation.

In the realm of foreign policy, the Gilded Age featured presidential diplomacy that was driven largely by the interests of American business in developing international markets for its burgeoning production.[21] Without pursuing any grand theory of empire, presidents advanced American interests in opportunistic ways. President Benjamin Harrison and his secretary of state, James G. Blaine, were "aggressive and sometimes bellicose" (especially Harrison).[22] The president, cold and aloof, and the secretary, dynamic and charismatic, were not close personally, but they overcame their tensions to begin a decade of expansionism.[23] They energetically reasserted American hemispheric leadership, aggressively pursued Caribbean and Pacific bases, and encouraged a coup against the Hawaiian monarchy.

The coup occurred when the American minister to Hawaii allied with American sugar interests as they plotted to seize control.[24] The minister's order to land troops from a cruiser at a crucial moment helped the coup succeed, whereupon representatives of the new government hustled to Washington and quickly negotiated a treaty of annexation. Harrison denied responsibility for the coup but urged annexation to keep Hawaii away from other circling powers. (A century later Congress would apologize for the coup.)

Presidential foreign policy can change sharply. Showing his stubborn, moralistic streak and his antiexpansionist values, the incoming Grover Cleveland withdrew the Hawaiian treaty from the Senate, saying correctly that the United States was complicit in the coup.[25] Nonetheless, after withdrawing the treaty Cleveland did recognize the new Hawaiian government to appease its supporters in Congress. In his first term, Cleveland had withdrawn a Nicaraguan canal treaty negotiated by Arthur on grounds it would create an entangling alliance. Traditional values always lay ready for invocation.

That most traditional of American foreign policy values, the Monroe Doctrine, received vigorous assertion even under the usually restrained Cleveland. When Great Britain got into a boundary dispute with Venezuela involving British Guiana, the president had his aggressive secretary of state, Richard Olney, send a very sharp note to the British pressing them to arbitrate rather than to intervene, and they receded.[26] Increasingly, presidents were behaving as the heads of a great power, at least within the neighborhood. Their reach was about to expand.

Dreams of Empire

William McKinley surprised everyone, including himself, with his initiation of a modest empire for the United States.[27] The 1898 war with Spain was a pivotal event in the nation's emergence as a world power. Affable, benign, and intelligent, McKinley made his way to the presidency as a reliable supporter of Republican tariffs, all the while disclaiming imperial intentions. John Hay, who had known everyone who mattered since his time serving Lincoln, said that McKinley had "one of the sweetest and quietest natures I have ever known among public men."[28] Then and now,

McKinley's considerable political skill and decisiveness have been under-estimated because of his unassuming nature. Nonetheless, "in many ways the first modern President, he used the instruments of his office as no one had since Lincoln, dominating his cabinet, controlling Congress, and skillfully employing the press to build political support for his policies."[29] Having seen combat in the Civil War, McKinley was not bellicose. A prac-tical politician and not a theorist, he was alert to seize the considerable opportunities that came before him.

As the United States became a player on the world stage under McKin-ley, the presidency required some organizational changes. Grover Cleve-land had run the White House like his Buffalo law office, concentrating on keeping the paper flowing and the press at bay. Fortunately, among the handful of personal secretaries that McKinley inherited was the most gifted aide since John Hay, George Cortelyou. As the prototype for the modern chief of staff, Cortelyou organized the new president's office, giv-ing it much greater capacity to respond to events.[30] An important compo-nent of that capacity was press relations. Cortelyou gave journalists space within the White House for the first time, keeping them close at hand and feeding them the president's views.

As McKinley took office, he was urged to renew efforts to annex Ha-waii. He was soon persuaded that the lure of a link to Asian markets for American goods and the imperatives of Mahan's sea power theories justi-fied annexation.[31] It appeared, however, that there was enough antiannex-ation sentiment in the Senate to doom the treaty. It was the outbreak of war with Spain that revealed the strategic importance of Hawaii. Relying on Polk's precedent of annexing Texas by joint resolution, McKinley suc-cessfully turned to that option, which needed only a simple majority in both houses.[32] In victory, the president happily invoked Manifest Destiny, which he had now extended thousands of miles into the Pacific. Where else might it lead?

Some Americans had dreamed of annexing Cuba ever since the ante-bellum push for a tropical empire for slavery. At the end of the nineteenth century, Spain's doddering and abusive rule of the island renewed impe-rialist urges. President Cleveland had resisted the impulses, saying that there would be no war in Cuba during his presidency and that if Congress declared one he would refuse to mobilize the Army.[33] His attachment to the Monroe Doctrine meant keeping other nations from making acqui-sitions in the Americas; his anti-imperialism meant keeping the United States from doing so as well.

McKinley opposed intervention also, but not dogmatically. As fever for war with Spain mounted, the president cautiously resisted it, stalling by investigating conditions in Cuba.[34] He did send the *Maine* to Cuba to show the flag, knowing that its presence risked an incident. After the *Maine* exploded, he decided on military intervention, for reasons that have remained unclear. Surely it was tempting to eject Spain from the Americas at long last. To keep his options open, McKinley sent a message to Congress that asked not for a declaration of war but rather for authority to use the armed forces to stabilize Cuba. Congress added a demand for Cuban independence, while renouncing any intent to annex Cuba. Spain declared war; so did Congress.

The "splendid little war," as John Hay called it, soon led to the seizure of Cuba and the Philippines from Spain.[35] As the war wound down, McKinley took Puerto Rico as well to protect the Panama canal project. The one-sided peace treaty, extracting these possessions in return for a token payment of $20 million to Spain, squeaked through the Senate, where anti-imperial sentiment lingered. Meanwhile, the president invoked his power as commander in chief to create military governments in Cuba and the Philippines and ran them with little congressional oversight. But what should the long-term policy of the United States be regarding these conquests?

McKinley was prepared to honor the nation's promise to free Cuba once it had stabilized. After dithering a bit, he decided to advocate annexing the Philippines. As with Hawaii, he was persuaded by desires to open new markets for American goods—China beckoned—and to forestall annexation by another imperial nation. His decision to retain the Philippines and Puerto Rico broke precedent by acquiring overseas territory with no intention of admitting any of it as states. Anti-imperialists claimed the action was unconstitutional.[36] For the fall congressional elections in 1898, McKinley took his case for an American empire to the country in a far more successful swing around the circle than Andrew Johnson's disastrous effort. The issue had faded from national prominence before McKinley's easy reelection in the presidential election of 1900. At Princeton, Woodrow Wilson celebrated the war's triumphal conclusion: "The nation has stepped forth into the open arena of the world."[37]

Once it became clear to the Filipinos that the United States was not leaving after defeating Spain, a rebellion broke out under Emilio Aguinaldo.[38] The three-year revolt previewed the worldwide counterinsurgency horrors of the twentieth century. McKinley sent the able administrator William Howard Taft to govern the Philippines. Taft built some support among the people by doing good works. Yet as would happen so often in counterinsurgency, the military occupiers descended into brutality (including waterboarding) to pacify the recalcitrant natives. Word of abuses by American troops became widespread soon after Theodore Roosevelt became president, by which time the insurgency was ending. Acting only after a furor arose, Roosevelt called for a full investigation of the facts and eventually defused the controversy by dismissing the general who committed the worst atrocities. Dreams of an American empire had somehow turned sour.

China still beckoned.[39] In 1899, Secretary of State John Hay issued the Open Door Note, a circular letter urging the great powers not to discriminate against each other within their spheres of influence in China. Exploitation of the suffering Chinese was not condemned, of course. The following year the Boxer Rebellion erupted, as China's outraged army and citizens besieged foreign legations and killed some diplomats. President McKinley sent twenty-five hundred American troops to China as part of an international relief expedition. Congress was out of session but raised no subsequent objection to this unprecedented intervention so far from the Americas. A second Open Door Note then affirmed the intention of the United States to protect American lives and property and to preserve "equal and impartial trade" in China. As always with intervention, getting in was easier than getting out. American troops remained in China until ejected by the Japanese in 1941. China consented through a series of executive agreements that were not submitted to Congress.

For presidents, the late nineteenth century was a time of stalemate with the Senate over proposed treaties. The Senate rejected every major treaty from 1871 to 1898, leading John Hay to conclude that another important treaty would never pass the Senate.[40] Presidents learned to evade the supermajority requirement for ratification. They would either enter executive agreements with other nations to bypass Congress completely or propose joint resolutions (as for Hawaii) that needed only simple majorities.[41] This persistent tension culminated in the great collision with Woodrow Wilson after World War I. By that time, presidents had formed a modest American empire, overcoming or evading significant congressional resistance along the way.

Early in his second term, William McKinley became the third president to fall to an assassin's bullet. His vice president, Theodore Roosevelt, had been selected because of his own relentless self-promotion and the desire of the New York Republican Party to get him out of the statehouse and out of the way.[42] McKinley's political manager Mark Hanna protested in vain: "Don't any of you realize that there's only one life between this madman and the Presidency?"[43]

"The Meteor of the Age"[44]

Halley's Comet swung close by in 1906, the better to inspect the presidency of its namesake, Theodore Roosevelt. His levels of energy and enthusiasm exhausted everyone and all of their adjectives.[45] A polymath to rival Jefferson, TR read everything and had written enough books to embarrass any university professor. He was an active nationalist whose sense that public interests should prevail over private ones was captured in the name of his signature program, a "square deal" for all. He thought that the "fundamental rule" in our national life was that "in the long run, we shall go up or down together."[46] No Grover Cleveland, he. Roosevelt even declared that "the government is us . . . you and me."[47] To him, the president was more than a Jacksonian tribune of the people—he was a direct amalgam of their will.

Because it is difficult to provide everyone a square deal at the same time, Roosevelt was perfectly willing to determine the necessary angularities himself. In one of his frequent self-referential descriptions of someone else, he once said of Oliver Cromwell: "There certainly never was a more extraordinary despotism than this; the despotism of a man who sought power not to gratify himself or those belonging to him . . . but to establish the reign of the Lord, as he saw it."[48] Tempering TR's sense that he knew what was best for everyone was a surprisingly cautious approach to achieving his goals. Thus he insisted that his reform proposals meet tests of "practicality" and "efficiency."[49]

Theodore Roosevelt possessed a gift for diplomacy that the presidency had not seen since John Quincy Adams.[50] Far more subtle in practice than in rhetoric and enjoying close personal ties to the international political and literary elite, Roosevelt reveled in conducting summit diplomacy secretly through his network of contacts. Often neither Congress nor the public knew of his initiatives.[51] His personal dominance of foreign policy would come to characterize much of the twentieth century, for good or ill. Although he often evaded official channels of analysis and communication in the State Department, he did begin the professionalization of the foreign service, reducing the nation's dependence on the often loutish amateur diplomats of the nineteenth century.

Taking office in September 1901, at the tender age of forty-two and in the wake of yet another beloved president's assassination, Roosevelt had the good judgment to begin cautiously. He retained the two stars of McKinley's cabinet, Secretary of State John Hay and Secretary of War Elihu Root, and let others drift away after a time. He also kept George Cortelyou. Understanding the value of Cortelyou's cultivation of good relationships with the press, Roosevelt included a press room in his renovations of the White House, the better to manipulate the scribes.

By December, Roosevelt had compiled a massive annual message to Congress that opened the great themes of his presidency.[52] This missive commenced TR's unprecedented bombardment of Congress with messages calling for legislation on this and funding of that. For the first time, he was interpreting the president's constitutional power to recommend legislation to justify open, active, and constant participation in the legislative process. Roosevelt's new practice had limited effectiveness, because his relentlessness and bombast displaced the more subtle and deferential approaches that the barons of Capitol Hill expected. Eventually he learned to work his way indirectly, urging his views on the people until they were ready to pressure their legislators.

The first theme of the annual message revealed Roosevelt's approach to the massive concentrations of economic power that had arisen in the form of legal trusts holding multiple companies together. Social unrest about the great corporations had mounted sufficiently to convince the new president that the federal government needed to control them somehow. There were considerable uncertainties, however, about the extent to which the Constitution permitted regulating corporations and about the government's political and practical power to do so. The annual message stated TR's operating distinction between good trusts that increased efficiency and should be left alone and bad ones that abused the public (for example by charging unfair or discriminatory prices). Telling them apart would be a presidential responsibility under the duty to enforce the laws. The pertinent laws, the Sherman Antitrust Act and the Interstate Commerce Act, lay dormant. Both legislation and executive action would be necessary. The message tentatively called for compiling and disclosing information about the activities of the trusts so that the public could evaluate them.

The second theme of the message introduced Roosevelt's greatest contribution as president, conservation of the nation's natural resources. The idea that the federal government should be an active steward of the environment was new, but it ran deep with a president whose love of the outdoors was legendary. Roosevelt had two main priorities. First, he wanted to reclaim the arid West by forming large water projects that the private sector could not finance. Second, he wanted to manage the nation's public lands in a sustainable way. This meant preventing the sale of substantial portions of the forests for private ownership and development and preserving some public land from any material impairment (even the controlled logging or grazing that would be permitted generally). Again, both legislation and executive action impended.

In foreign policy, the new president wanted to promote balance among the great powers. Therefore, the United States would need to remain a force in international affairs. In particular, Roosevelt wanted to build up the Navy, to continue McKinley's policy toward America's new foreign possessions, and to eliminate obstacles to creation of a transoceanic canal in Central America. Although Roosevelt continued many policies of his late predecessor, he also struck out on his own. He would surmount controversy to achieve each of his three main goals.

Executing the Laws, Rough Rider Style

For many issues, Theodore Roosevelt's presidency featured a more circumspect exercise of constitutional duties than his frenetic style suggested. Thus his famous motto for foreign affairs, "Speak softly and carry a big stick," describes his practice accurately if it is understood that he was genuinely cautious about wielding the stick. Roosevelt saw politics as the art of the possible and was willing to compromise on most issues. He never dominated Congress, because although both houses were Republican, the leadership was conservative. Hence he accomplished more through executive action than through legislation.

In early 1902, the president moved against the trusts in the most visible way possible.[53] He preferred to regulate, not destroy them, but he lacked statutory power to do that. Hence he decided to revive the Sherman Act. He instructed Attorney General Philander Knox to sue to dissolve the Northern Securities Company, a huge holding company for three railroads controlled by James J. Hill, E. H. Harriman, and J. P. Morgan. It was the national symbol of monopoly. The president was interpreting his constitutional duty of faithful execution in an aggressive way. In 1904, the Supreme Court upheld the suit.[54]

Emboldened by this result and his election in 1904, Roosevelt also sued Standard Oil and some other companies, with mixed results.[55] His trust busting was restrained and selective, directed only against trusts he thought bad. Thus the president made antitrust enforcement into theater, gaining a reputation as a trust buster "without actually harming any trusts."[56] Still, he had slowed the creation of new ones. Roosevelt increased the practical power of the presidency by reaching private understandings with business owners in the shadow of his power to pursue formal enforcement measures.

Eventually, the president induced Congress to enact the first Progressive statutes, which regulated the national economy.[57] He was attacking the nineteenth-century understanding of the Constitution as creating a federal government with only tangential impact on a citizen's daily life. In 1906, after lurid disclosures by muckraking journalists about the food industry, TR signed the Meat Inspection Act and the Pure Food and Drug Act. He also signed the Hepburn Act, giving the Interstate Commerce Commission power to set railroad rates. Now episodic intervention against railroad abuses by the Justice Department would be replaced by continuous supervision by an expert commission, as a new organizational model for federal regulation emerged. Having himself served as a civil service commissioner, the president was imbued with the Progressive faith in government by experts.[58]

Roosevelt created a new presidential role in keeping the economy running when he intervened in a major coal strike in 1902, not to break the strike as prior presidents had done but to mediate a "square deal" for both sides.[59] Although admitting that he lacked any clear constitutional right or duty to act, he refused to adopt "the Buchanan principle of striving to find some constitutional reason for inaction."[60] Informed by his attorney general that he lacked any power to intervene forcefully in the absence of an outbreak of violence, Roosevelt turned to more informal uses of his high office. After exerting considerable personal pressure on both sides, Roosevelt brokered an arbitrated settlement before the onset of winter could leave the nation without heat. During the crisis, the president made preparations to have the Army operate the mines if necessary. He later explained that using the Army would have formed an "evil precedent" but that he was prepared to invoke "the Jackson-Lincoln theory of the presidency" to resolve a great crisis through "immediate and vigorous executive action."[61] Roosevelt eventually generated his "stewardship" theory of the presidency to justify his behavior in the coal strike.

Roosevelt's success in ending the coal strike built his popularity. Encouraged by his example, later presidents often intervened in industrial disputes without any specific statutory authority to do so. They could claim a power of the presidency to protect the national economy as part of a loose conception of the faithful execution duty that relied on safeguarding the public. After World War II, Congress and the Supreme Court would rein in the practice, fearing its abuse.

"Leave It as It Is"

Visiting the Grand Canyon for the first time, Theodore Roosevelt uttered the credo of the conservation movement: "Leave it as it is. The ages have been at work on it, and man can only mar it."[62] His use of what he called the "bully pulpit" of the presidency to shape public opinion was never more effective than in this context.[63] By creating political support for conservation, the president also laid the basis for expanding his constitutional power to promote this new national value.

TR's technique for expanding presidential power was to read existing statutory authority very broadly. He knew that Congress could rarely muster the votes necessary to override his actions. Roosevelt implemented his statutory interpretations by issuing various executive orders to the bureaucracy. Signing almost as many orders as all of his predecessors combined, he brought the executive order to its modern prominence as a means of managing the executive.[64] This practice had great consequences for twentieth-century presidents as the nation entered an era of statutory empowerment of the federal government. As the corpus of statutes grew, so did the opportunities for presidential interpretive activity. Roosevelt's expanded use of executive orders created a "new norm" for his successors, who continued frequent use of the practice once Roosevelt had demonstrated its utility.[65] After issuing orders, presidents would rely on their veto power to stop Congress from retracting or modifying delegations of power that they had treated expansively.

Most of President Roosevelt's conservation accomplishments depended on executive orders.[66] An early decision epitomized his style. In response to a request to form a wildlife refuge on federal land in Florida, he responded: "Is there any law that will prevent me from declaring Pelican Island a Federal Bird Reservation? Very well, then I so declare it."[67] During his presidency, TR formed federal conservation reserves of many kinds and even took steps to save the buffalo from extinction.[68]

Any president's actual constitutional power of faithful execution depends on the aggressiveness of his statutory interpretations. Roosevelt, true to his nature, pushed toward the limits but kept within hailing distance of statutory text. But freewheeling statutory interpretation is of little use to presidents if the courts can be expected to invalidate it. Early in the twentieth century, as statutes accumulated, federal courts were evolving the rudiments of administrative law and testing techniques for controlling executive officers by requiring them to abide statutory restrictions. Presidents have always known, however, that courts are less likely to overturn statutory interpretations when they bear the president's own signature rather than that of a subordinate administrator.[69]

The president's lieutenant in the conservation project was the head of the Forest Service in the Department of Agriculture, Gifford Pinchot, who became a useful lightning rod for criticism. A sharp controversy with Congress arose over a rider to the agriculture appropriations bill barring the creation of new or augmented forest reserves in six western states without the approval of Congress.[70] The bill had passed easily. The president could not veto it without shutting down the department. Pinchot hurriedly drafted an executive order reserving sixteen million acres under the existing statute. Roosevelt signed the order, and two days later he signed the appropriations bill. Defending his "midnight proclamation," he challenged Congress to rescind the order, acknowledging its power to do so if it could override his veto. He prevailed. Repeatedly the president tested what Congress would tolerate. Development interests charged that Pinchot had violated a statute when he reserved twenty-five hundred water-power sites by designating them ranger stations. Critics denounced presidential "dictatorship."[71] Congress tried to override the order, but TR vetoed the bill.

Roosevelt also preserved the public lands by invoking the apparently innocuous Antiquities Act of 1906.[72] This statute, which has itself become an antiquity, authorizes the president to designate as national monuments "historic landmarks, historic and pre-historic structures, and other objects of historic or scientific interest." The act requires, however, that the reserved parcels "be confined to the smallest area compatible with the proper care and management of the objects to be protected." The act appears to envision small parcels such as Indian burial mounds. Nonetheless, when commercial development threatened the Grand Canyon and Congress refused to protect it as a national park, Roosevelt invoked the act to designate the entire Canyon as a national monument.[73] If the Grand Canyon could qualify, what could fail? Later presidents have relied on the precedents set by Roosevelt and have treated the act as broad authority to create monuments; Congress has usually acquiesced in these orders.[74]

President William Howard Taft continued Roosevelt's policy of large
federal land reservations, but at a less frenetic pace. In 1915, the Supreme
Court endorsed this activity in a decision with wide application to executive legal interpretations.[75] The Court announced an "acquiescence doctrine," according to which long-standing presidential practices, known
to and not overridden by Congress, may be regarded as authorized by
unclear statutes. This doctrine held out the prospect that presidential actions could prove to be self-reinforcing. If one president has the courage
to start down a road that leads from the text of a statute into uncharted
territory, others can follow, their confidence increasing with time and repetition. Thus presidential statutory interpretation, like constitutional interpretation, is accretive.

Waving the Big Stick

The Monroe Doctrine has always implied American hegemony over the
Western Hemisphere. Theodore Roosevelt made that claim explicit and
put it into action. The president watched closely as Great Britain and
Germany attempted to force Venezuela to honor its debt obligations to
them.[76] The two great powers blockaded Venezuela in late 1902, while
assuring the United States that they would honor the Monroe Doctrine
by making only "temporary" territorial incursions. Without consulting
Congress, a distrustful president moved naval forces into the Caribbean
and secretly threatened Germany with intervention. Roosevelt's pressure eventually forced Britain and Germany to agree to arbitration of
their claims. The president later codified this approach by announcing
the "Roosevelt Corollary" to the Monroe Doctrine: the principle that if
a nation in the Western Hemisphere needed policing, the United States
would do it.[77]

The president had an opportunity to put his corollary to use when
European creditor nations pressed the Dominican Republic in a time of
local unrest.[78] Saying that he "would do what a policeman has to do,"
Roosevelt sent several ships to prop up the regime and offered to run its
customhouses to ensure that revenues reached the creditors. When the
Senate refused to ratify his policy with a treaty, he made an executive
agreement with the Dominican government. He kept ships offshore until
the Senate relented and approved. Thus presidential "protection" under
the Roosevelt Corollary could closely resemble imperialist domination at
presidential discretion.

Theodore Roosevelt's most controversial and consequential intervention in the Americas was in Panama.[79] When he took office, Congress was considering both Nicaragua and Panama (then a province of Colombia) as sites for an interocean canal. Roosevelt persuaded Congress to favor Panama, whereupon it fell to him to negotiate a treaty with Colombia to acquire the rights to dig. The president negotiated a treaty that he thought fair and was outraged when the Colombian legislature balked at ratification. He was not inclined to deal further with the Colombian government. Meanwhile, signs of a rebellion for independence emerged in Panama.

With a wink and a nod, Roosevelt encouraged the separatists. "He did not instigate the rebellion—he knew he did not have to."[80] He claimed authority to guard an existing railroad across the isthmus under an old treaty with Colombia that called on the United States to assure safe transit. And when the Panamanians rose, the president had a gunboat on hand to prevent Colombian reinforcements from taking control. He quickly recognized the new regime and signed a favorable treaty with its representative, clearing the way for the canal. Amid debate over the legality of the president's action, the Senate ratified the treaty in early 1904.

Roosevelt mounted a spirited defense of the morality and legality of his conduct in his annual message and another special message.[81] He was asserting three kinds of foreign policy powers. First, he correctly claimed authority to interpret the meaning of existing treaties and to determine how and whether to negotiate new ones. Second, and again correctly, he claimed authority to determine when to recognize a revolutionary regime as the legitimate government of a new nation. To these powers he added his discretion as commander in chief to deploy the military to enforce treaty obligations and to constrain violence in the Western Hemisphere. These were all tenable legal arguments. Nonetheless, Roosevelt's actions remained morally vulnerable because he engaged in both imperialist bullying of a weaker nation and intervention into its control over its own territory. Roosevelt dismissed the complaints—he had his canal. In the fall elections, the people signaled their approval by electing him along with substantial majorities for his party in Congress.

As the Panama episode revealed, Theodore Roosevelt's role as commander in chief was never far in the background of his foreign policy. He sought to modernize the organization of both the Army and Navy for their new responsibilities. The president's own combat experience in Cuba had shown him the need to create a professional army in place of the traditional model of a small body of regulars supplemented by a large number of volunteers. The Army's commanding general, Nelson Miles, was a Civil War veteran whose insubordination and rivalry for the presidency evoked McClellan.[82] The president rebuked him roughly for the former, and that ended the latter.

After this initial success, Roosevelt committed the worst blunder of his presidency, which occurred in his supervision of the Army. An incident between black troops and civilians in Brownsville, Texas, led to allegations that the troops had shot up the town.[83] The president accepted the Army's precipitate findings that all of the troops were guilty (based in part on their refusal to incriminate one another). Although the evidence against them was murky at best, Roosevelt ordered them all summarily dismissed from the Army and refused to reconsider his action. By the standards of the time, TR was no racist and did press for some advancements for blacks. But his judgment and humanity deserted him in the Brownsville matter.

The president's buildup of the Navy was a happier experience. He got appropriations from Congress to build the "Great White Fleet." Toward the end of his time in office, he decided to send it around the world to announce the emergence of the United States among the great powers.[84] Meeting resistance to the tour in Congress, he asserted an absolute constitutional right to deploy the Navy as he chose and pointed out that he had enough money on hand to send the fleet halfway around. Congress could bring them home if it so chose. It did, and a soon-to-retire president proudly greeted the fleet's return. During his tenure, despite not a little gunboat diplomacy and waving of the big stick, he had committed no troops to combat except for the final phases of the Philippine campaign that he inherited.

Theodore Roosevelt's greatest foreign policy achievement was his skillful and successful mediation of a peace settlement in the Russo-Japanese War in 1905, for which he justly received the Nobel Peace Prize.[85] He pursued the effort as part of his policy to encourage a balance of power among nations. He used his characteristic diplomatic methods of secrecy and reliance on his informal network of international contacts to work through the maze of conflicting interests of the combatants. The United States was ascending toward the first rank among nations.

President Roosevelt's last annual message, headily awash in self-congratulation, contained a celebration of executive power: "Concentrated power is palpable, visible, responsible, easily reached, quickly held to account."[86] This assertion certainly echoed Professor Woodrow Wilson's revised opinion of the state of the presidency. Roosevelt's critics could answer that an energetic and popular president is rather difficult to control. The writer H. G. Wells summed up his presidency: "Never did a President so reflect the quality of his time."[87] TR's capacity to both embody and shape public opinion is shared by all effective presidents. In such hands and at the intersection of constitutional and political power does the fate of the Republic lie.

On the night of his triumphant election in 1904, Roosevelt invoked Washington's two-term precedent. Having served most of McKinley's second term, he renounced any desire to run for another. Thus Roosevelt had combined Washington's and Tyler's precedents. If a vice president who succeeded to the presidency by death of the incumbent became a real president, it was natural to apply the informal two-term limit to him at some indefinite point. The reason for Roosevelt's self-denial was probably his understanding that a lame duck president gains freedom of action to act aggressively, no longer suffering the debilitating effects of constant speculation about reelection intentions as a motive for supposedly public-regarding actions.[88]

Ambition did overcome Roosevelt in 1912, when he tried for the presidency once again.[89] But he held to his promise in 1908 and was even allowed to designate his successor, the ponderous, amiable, and efficient William Howard Taft. It should not have surprised Roosevelt that Taft would be his own man once in office—even Chester Arthur had managed that much. No one is the same after taking the oath. Taft did continue Roosevelt's general approach to antitrust and public lands issues, but to Roosevelt he committed the unforgivable sin of not being TR himself.

President Taft was too much the lawyer and not enough the statesman to be a really effective president.[90] He never engaged the public imagination as had Roosevelt. As president, he behaved like the judge he had been and would be again, working through problems analytically. Taft thought that doing good deeds was enough and that everyone would understand. Hence he neglected the press and did not manage the news, giving his opponents a field day. He even delivered his annual messages in dry installments, assuring that no one would heed them.[91]

Taft's strong managerial skills served him better.[92] He began steps toward preparation of an executive budget to coordinate departmental requests and enhance presidential control over the growing bureaucracy. But Congress, fearful of interference with its control over the purse strings, forbade this useful initiative, and Taft desisted. Soon enough, Roosevelt was attacking him and the three-way presidential contest of 1912 loomed ahead.

After leaving office and becoming a law professor, Taft attacked Roosevelt's "stewardship" theory of the presidency:

> The true view of the Executive functions is, as I conceive it, that the President can exercise no power which cannot be fairly and reasonably traced to some specific grant of power or justly implied and included within such express grant as proper and necessary to its exercise. Such specific grant must be either in the Federal Constitution or in an act of Congress passed in pursuance thereof. There is no undefined residuum of power which he can exercise because it seems to him to be in the public interest.[93]

Taft's critique of Roosevelt's stewardship theory is the correct one—that it is detached from constitutional text and contains no apparent limits.[94] Taft justified his more lawyerly approach by citing Lincoln, who "always pointed out the source of authority" that justified his actions.[95] By contrast, Roosevelt's theory would set up the president "to play the part of a Universal Providence and set all things right." Thus Taft identified the danger that inheres in a stewardship theory of presidential powers—that a president as sure of his own rectitude as was TR would be subject to no internal constraint.

Roosevelt himself implemented his stewardship theory with some restraint. Although he had derived it by study of Jackson and Lincoln, he knew that he faced no crisis on the scale of the Civil War and could not justify an attempt to replicate Lincoln's precedents.[96] Nevertheless, he had also absorbed the Progressives' vision of a vigorous federal government led by a powerful president.[97] By personally demonstrating the potential for that vision to succeed, he initiated an association between presidential power and liberal politics that would endure for most of a century, until Ronald Reagan showed the potential for a strong president to serve conservative ends.

Taft sought consolation for his concerns about Roosevelt's theory by noting that, unlike a court, a president "does not consider himself bound by the policies or constitutional views of his predecessors."[98] He could, and did, evolve his own approach, affected but not directed by his predecessors. Taft's lawyerly search for constitutional authority was not disabling, as it was not for Lincoln. Applied with sensitivity to the facts and constrained by historical precedent, it was the most legitimate path to take. There is even a stewardship element in it, as Lincoln had demonstrated. That is, statesmanship enters the calculus in realms of constitutional or statutory silence. For both constitutional and statutory interpretation, the entire set of commands the text imposes must be considered and reconciled.

Thus, for statutory interpretation, Taft emphasized that he could infer power from the "general code of duties under the laws" even if it was nowhere explicit in any one of them.[99] But there were limits. Although Taft continued Roosevelt's conservation program, he could not abide Pinchot's aggressiveness and dismissed him, explaining that the forester was "quite willing to camp outside the law to accomplish his beneficent purposes."[100] Taft's laudable effort was to tether presidents, albeit loosely, to their governing texts. His successor, another morally self-assured steward of the people, may have absorbed some of Professor Taft's instruction, for he adopted a style of governance that was more reliant on Congress than was Roosevelt's.

From Schoolboy to Schoolmaster

Among the similarities between Theodore Roosevelt and the man who defeated him for the presidency in 1912 was a steep rise to power. In 1910, Woodrow Wilson was already a president—of Princeton University. After a stopover as governor of New Jersey, he was again a president. The aggressive certainty that Roosevelt and Wilson shared could surface either in "the schoolboyish bellicosity of Theodore Roosevelt or the schoolmasterish moralism of Woodrow Wilson."[101] Descriptions of Wilson often echo those of Roosevelt: "No other President has combined such varied and divergent elements of learning, eloquence, religion, and war"; he was "bold, extremely sure of himself, and often stubborn."[102] Within Wilson a disciplined intellect warred with deep passions.[103] Ironically, the seemingly restrained Wilson was more willing than Roosevelt to take large risks in search of big solutions to problems. Focused, driven, and lacking TR's release in ebullience, he was wound very tight (perhaps accounting for his history of strokes).

Wilson was a child of the South, having grown up in Virginia and Georgia during the Civil War and Reconstruction. His experience with the dysfunctional state governments of his youth left him a Hamiltonian nationalist with little regard for his fellow Virginian Jefferson. His approach to the Constitution was guided by a conviction that after the Civil War the nation needed federal solutions to such social problems as regulation of the great corporations, instead of the decentralized approach of the antebellum years.[104]

Unlike most presidents, Woodrow Wilson had thought deeply about American government before reaching its pinnacle. He helped to invent the academic field of public administration. Like many of his contemporaries, he somewhat naively thought that politically neutral experts could reliably perform most policy-making functions. (In fact, politics pervades most administration.) For high-level issues that obviously involved politics, Wilson urged executive rather than congressional responsibility because of its coherence. With Roosevelt in mind, he said in 1908 that if the president "rightly interpret the national thought and boldly insist upon it, he is irresistible"; he believed, though, that the cabinet departments could "proceed with their business for months and even years" without needing the president's attention.[105]

Wilson's theory of government artificially bifurcated his responsibility for administration in a way that would hamper his performance of his faithful execution duties. Like Lincoln, he tried to clear his desk of matters he considered minor so that he could concentrate on great affairs of state.[106] He went too far. He paid insufficient attention to the selection of his cabinet. He held weekly cabinet meetings that were like Lincoln's—consultative, but not usually reaching the largest issues. By letting the cabinet members run their departments, Wilson serendipitously built a system that could run in his absence in the final years when he was consumed with Versailles or lying disabled.

The president delegated power freely and often excessively. This characteristic is revealed by one of the great blots on his record, racial segregation in the civil service, which was promoted by undersupervised underlings. Woodrow Wilson had a blind spot for race relations. Showing his southern roots, he once said that "time is the only legislator" that could improve race relations.[107] Somehow, Wilson "did not equate segregation with subjugation."[108] He never showed the least urgency about improving life for blacks, responding to their needs only when criticized. In his cabinet southerners William McAdoo at Treasury and Albert Burleson at the post office enforced segregation in the civil service with Wilson's acquiescence. Presidents are constitutionally responsible for the conduct of the executive branch that they head; Wilson failed his duty in this regard.

As president, Wilson imported his decisional style from university life: collegial and open discussion, followed by solitary formulation of a decision. In essence, he functioned much like a judge—he "heard the arguments . . . and retired to ponder his decision."[109] And like a judge, he was unwilling to revisit decisions once made, although he would accept some guidance on details. This characteristic meant that it was very difficult to correct his errors.

Like Roosevelt, Wilson could do good work very quickly. He composed his own speeches and messages. Both men conducted very active and ultimately personal presidencies, lacking the institutional support that later presidents would enjoy. Understanding the value of good press relations, Wilson was the first president to hold regular press conferences. Yet he let the White House organization languish. Fortunately, his principal secretary, Joseph Tumulty, was able enough to run the operation. Wilson's most powerful aide was a private citizen. Edward M. House, a rich Texan whose only title was an honorific "Colonel," was so perfectly attuned to Wilson's thinking that he served both as principal adviser and freelance representative for the president. Wilson called House his "second personality."[110] In American history, Colonel House remains a unique figure, combining great power with complete unaccountability.[111] He even negotiated directly with foreign diplomats during World War I. Essentially, he provided Wilson a way to refine and implement his own will through an entirely confidential and trustworthy personal agent.

Progressive Legislator in Chief

Woodrow Wilson built on Theodore Roosevelt's precedents that expanded the president's constitutional power to recommend legislation. Going beyond TR's precedent of greeting Congress with an ambitious outline of his intentions, Wilson had a complete legislative program ready for presentation to Congress by the time of his inauguration. And present it he did. Abjuring the usual period of initial freedom from the presence of Congress, Wilson called a special session for April 1913. He then restored a precedent dating from the Federalist era by appearing personally to urge passage of his program.[112] (Thomas Jefferson, a poor public speaker, had abandoned the earlier practice of speaking directly to Congress, replacing it with written messages.) With Wilson, the often dry annual message would give way to the theatrical opportunity of the State of the Union address. The imminent rise of the electronic media would amplify every later president's words and the leverage they exerted.

Wilson's new role as president-in-Congress would have meant little had the nation not been ready for new levels of federal statutory intervention in the economy. Roosevelt had prepared the ground with his group of early Progressive statutes. Wilson rekindled and increased the momentum, revealing a skill at appealing to the people over the heads of Congress that any successor could profitably emulate. From the Progressive era forward, statutes increasingly displaced or supplemented the traditional common law, placing a premium on presidential power to manage legislation. The complementary constitutional role of faithful execution would also expand in scope and importance as the twentieth century wore on.

Wilson worked the Sixty-Third Congress hard. He kept it in session for almost eighteen months to take advantage of his majorities in both houses. He achieved major victories for his three main priorities: tariff reform, central banking, and antitrust regulation.[113] By reducing the tariff, the president attempted to subject American corporate power to the disciplining effects of foreign competition and to bring consumers lower prices. The creation of the Federal Reserve System filled the gap at the heart of American banking that had existed since Andrew Jackson. With the combination of public and private elements in the Fed, Wilson empowered the federal government to respond to financial crises instead of waiting for J. P. Morgan to bail the markets out in times of panic, as had happened twice before under Cleveland and Roosevelt. The two antitrust statutes filled important gaps in existing law. The Clayton Act forbade specified predatory practices, and the Federal Trade Commission Act created an agency charged with continuous supervision of the economy to prevent unfair competitive practices generally. The federal presence in the lives of Americans was growing.

Displaying his tendency to think of the presidency in parliamentary terms and saying he must be "prime minister," the president followed lines of party support, not formal separation of powers.[114] Unlike Taft, who would not intrude in the legislative process, Wilson often negotiated with congressional leaders. When the tariff bill ran into trouble under intense lobbying pressure in the Senate, he denounced special interests. A congressional investigation then drove the lobbyists underground, and the bill passed. The bully pulpit was in strong hands with this minister's son. Politics was a moral crusade for Wilson: because his opponents were stupid or evil, compromise could elude him.[115] He was aided, though, by the public clamor for legislation that he induced.

Creation of the Federal Trade Commission embodied Wilson's faith in neutral expertise, but at substantial eventual cost to the unity of the executive branch. The FTC became the model for the independent regulatory commissions that would eventually perform much of the federal government's economic regulation.[116] In an effort to ensure bipartisan, "apolitical" administration, the act created an agency that would have multiple membership at the top, requirements for political party balance among the members, long statutory terms, and a prohibition of presidential removal without cause.[117] These structural features necessarily hampered presidential supervision of the independent agencies. The wisdom and constitutionality of insulating administration from presidential supervision have been debated ever since, as we shall see. The meaning of the restriction on presidential removal of the members was unclear at the time, but the Supreme Court would eventually provide an answer.

Woodrow Wilson was never able to replicate the heady days of 1913–14. In 1916 there was a second pulse of Progressive legislation, including restrictions on child labor and an eight-hour day for railroaders, but the president's relations with Congress were eroding.[118] Soon he would turn his energies to saving the world. His reelection victory over Charles Evans Hughes was narrow, but he kept party control of both houses of Congress until 1918, when he lost both houses in a harbinger of the coming confrontation with the Senate.

Wilson had achieved most of his domestic priorities, which were broad but did not initially include women's suffrage. As his reelection campaign began, he finally supported what became the Nineteenth Amendment, and he did help tease it through Congress, but he cannot be given much credit in the long struggle to secure the vote for women.[119]

Protecting Liberty Abroad

Like many presidents, Woodrow Wilson came to prize his freedom of action in foreign affairs, as contrasted with the daily frustrations of coaxing domestic legislation from Congress. In 1908 he had taken a broad view of presidential power: "The initiative in foreign affairs, which the President possesses without any restriction whatever, is virtually the power to control them absolutely."[120] This statement accurately described the behavior of Wilson's predecessors, who had so often conducted foreign relations without consulting or even informing Congress in advance. Suddenly a treaty would be presented to the Senate, an executive agreement announced, or a new nation recognized. Wilson understood that this control of initial (and often determinative) policy formation stems from two institutional sources, the unitary nature of the executive branch and the president's supervisory control over the nation's diplomats. Congress is left to exercise its seemingly impressive list of foreign policy powers reactively and often ineffectively, by legislating restrictions that the president might veto or denying him appropriations or treaty ratification.

Once in office, Woodrow Wilson acted "like a divine right monarch in foreign affairs."[121] Believing deeply in American exceptionalism, he was insensitive to the self-regard of other cultures. Not as widely traveled or connected as Theodore Roosevelt had been and having no experience in diplomacy, he had a poor sense of its limits. Like TR, however, he did much of his own diplomatic correspondence and handled some major issues without involving the cabinet. Both Wilson and his first secretary of state, William Jennings Bryan, were "given to grandiose visions of America's role in the world."[122] The moralistic strain in American foreign policy that Wilson revived still surfaces regularly. He rode it to achieve his greatest accomplishment in foreign policy, the elevation of the United States to full and equal membership in the community of nations.[123]

Like Theodore Roosevelt, President Wilson felt free to intervene within the Western Hemisphere.[124] He held the insensitive view that Latin American nations should not mind the presence of a few American troops as long as there was no attempt to annex territory permanently. The result was a strongly interventionist version of the Monroe Doctrine and the Roosevelt Corollary. Wilson's "moral imperialism" attempted to spread democracy rather than to conquer territory. He tried it out unsuccessfully on the hemispheric stage before attempting it worldwide, also unsuccessfully.[125]

Wilson began his crusade in nearby Mexico. In 1914, he helped oust the Mexican dictator Victoriano Huerta in favor of an insurgent, Venustiano Carranza.[126] Wilson stationed warships off the coast of Mexico to interdict arms to Huerta. The Senate approved his intervention in Mexican affairs. After an incident with local authorities, he ordered bombardment of Veracruz and sent in the Marines to occupy the city, losing nineteen Americans. After another insurgent, Pancho Villa, shot up the town of Columbus, New Mexico, Wilson ordered General John Pershing into "hot pursuit" of Villa without asking Congress for authority, whereupon the Army roamed northern Mexico for about a year without locating Villa. Wilson also sent troops into Haiti and the Dominican Republic; an American military presence continued in both nations for decades. This record should not have encouraged an interventionist stance. Wilson displayed far more caution before he advocated sending American troops to Europe.

When the guns of August 1914 roared in Europe, the Wilson administration immediately issued a neutrality proclamation.[127] For the remainder of his time in office, the president tried to determine the great issues
of neutrality, war, and peace by himself. It was a one-man operation.
Certain of his own moral compass and fully trusting no one else's judgment, Wilson involved Congress—and even his own cabinet—only as he
deemed necessary. Perhaps because of his deeply religious nature, Wilson
was more inclined to consult his own conscience for guidance than public
opinion.

The American commitment to neutrality was tested by the large appetite of the Allies for American goods, combined with revulsion over
Germany's submarine warfare against the Atlantic trade in violation of
traditional understandings of international law. After the sinking of the
Lusitania in 1915 took many American lives, the administration conducted a long series of diplomatic exchanges with Germany, pushing for
reparations and assurances that unrestricted submarine warfare would be
abandoned. For a time, the Germans desisted.

The early conduct of neutrality policy led Secretary of State Bryan to
resign because he thought the United States was risking war by pressing
Germany too hard. His departure removed an important check on Wilson. Deciding to create his own foreign policy from then on, the president
replaced him with Robert Lansing, whom he treated like a clerk. Lansing
got even by repeatedly disobeying and undermining Wilson, who did not
remove him despite ample cause.[128] Meanwhile, Wilson used House for
shuttle diplomacy in Europe, giving him only loose instructions. Increasingly supportive of the Allies, House also tended to undermine the president's neutrality.

Wilson rode to a narrow reelection victory in 1916 on the slogan "he
kept us out of war."[129] Not for long. In February 1917, Germany resumed
unrestricted submarine warfare. Soon came the leak of the Zimmermann
telegram, a foolish message from the German foreign secretary to the
Mexican government suggesting an alliance in case of war, with Mexico's
recovery of the southwestern United States as the prize. Although tensions were rising, "a clear majority of Americans" still opposed entering
the war.[130]

Hemmed in by his earlier strong statements against submarine warfare, the president proposed arming merchant ships. When a bill authorizing this step was filibustered in the Senate, a petulant Wilson denounced
the senators as "a little group of willful men," revealing his arrogance
and badly straining congressional relations.[131] The president then issued

an executive order to arm the ships, having been advised by his attorney general that he had constitutional power to do so without legislation.[132] Several of the ships were promptly sunk. Options were narrowing.

Trying to chart his course, President Wilson consulted with the cabinet and congressional leaders to test their inclinations and then announced a diplomatic break with Germany to a joint session of Congress, which approved. With the cabinet urging a declaration of war, Wilson characteristically isolated himself and made the final decision for war alone and without informing anyone about his intentions.[133] He then called a special session of Congress in April and asked it for a declaration of war against Germany.

Displaying his usual rhetorical gifts, Wilson invoked both of his primary foreign policy goals in his war speech.[134] Fearing the destabilizing effects of a German collapse, he still wanted the "peace without victory" that he had pursued throughout the period of neutrality. At the same time he wanted to "make the world safe for democracy." He never admitted the intrinsic difficulty of waging a hard war to achieve a soft peace. Putting that question off for the future, Congress declared war.

Entering World War I required unprecedented steps both to raise a large army and to send it overseas. In his war message, President Wilson told Congress he would send over bills to expand the Army and Navy and to mobilize the economy. The next day Wilson had a list of statutes for them.[135] The president claimed that the commander in chief power made the president responsible for war planning. Although he had worked closely with Congress in enacting his domestic agenda, now he demanded congressional cooperation, or else he would appeal to the people. Members of Congress, including Democrats, expressed resentment that they were expected to pass the bills as submitted. But they acquiesced, enacting statutes that heaped power on the executive.[136]

Congress gave Wilson "infinitely more power" than it had ever granted any president in wartime.[137] As in the Civil War, there was authority to conscript soldiers. In addition to power to mobilize the military, Congress granted the president sweeping authority to control the economy—to regulate food distribution, to control mines and factories, to fix prices, and more. Eventually, the railroads were temporarily nationalized. Wilson had broad latitude to create and control the administrative entities needed to perform these novel tasks. After many difficulties, an army of two million men was raised and sent to France, where it contributed to the decisive final offensive against Germany in 1918.

In reality, neither Congress nor the president was in full control of the chaotic mobilization effort, which often relied on private volunteers to aid government functions such as war production. Since the Civil War was beyond most living memories and remained unique in American history, the generation that fought World War I muddled its way along to solve problems that were outside its experience.

Congress struggled to oversee the burgeoning executive effectively. At one point Wilson beat back a proposal to create a joint committee to superintend the war effort. Although the Civil War provided a clear precedent for this step, Wilson claimed it would be congressional assumption of executive powers. There was even a proposal in the Senate to create a war cabinet of "three distinguished citizens of demonstrated ability" (to include ex-president Roosevelt) to direct the war effort.[138] Wilson fought off this proposal as well.

These controversies revealed that as broad as the wartime delegations to Wilson were, there was no true constitutional dictatorship in the classic sense, because Congress kept ultimate control and was constantly involved in managing the war.[139] In World War I, a more flexible and accountable response to crisis than constitutional dictatorship had emerged. This was a model of a continuing partnership of the political branches, featuring wide executive discretion that remained subject to legislative modification or retraction—unless the president's veto intervened. After the war had ended, in 1920 Congress passed a bill terminating sixty wartime delegations to the president. Wanting to retain his powers to the end of his term, Wilson pocket vetoed it.[140] Republicans complained about "executive dictatorship"; Congress successfully repealed the delegations the next year.[141]

Dreams of Peace

Woodrow Wilson had shifted his stance from neutrality to war because he concluded that it was necessary for the United States to enter the war in order to structure the peace and avert future wars. Here he "yielded to his own messianic impulses," believing that only he could lead the way.[142] Since messiahs do not work on committees, he would attempt, heroically and ultimately fatally, to carry the world on his shoulders. Congress and the American people would just have to go along.

In January 1918, Wilson outlined his peace plan to Congress as the

Fourteen Points.[143] This idealistic formula included open covenants, freedom of the seas, self-determination of peoples, and an international organization to enforce peace.[144] It was still "peace without victory." Once battlefield victory had been won in late 1918, however, Wilson discovered that the Allies, who had been bled white winning the war, wanted to carry away the spoils. Clearly it would take monumental efforts to bend the world to the president's will.

Believing that he needed to control the process of negotiating a peace treaty, Wilson made two important errors. First, departing from his earlier practice for legislation, he did not carefully prepare a coalition in Congress and the nation that would favor the startling new proposals he would bring them. By the time he went to the people belatedly in 1919, negative opinion had coalesced. Second, in order to present a unified front to other nations, he formed a negotiating team without including senators and Republican leaders, who would be critical to ratification. Unwisely, he also called for election of a Democratic Congress to ratify his efforts. This injection of partisanship into affairs of state helped the Republicans capture both houses of Congress in 1918. In one of the parliamentary systems that Wilson had long admired, he would have lost his office; perhaps he now saw the advantages of a prescribed term in times of trouble.

In late 1918, Wilson sailed for Europe, becoming the first American president to leave the Western Hemisphere.[145] He stayed away for about half a year, with a brief return to conduct domestic business at the end of the congressional session. The president's arrival in Europe met an ecstatic public reception. The adulation fed his sense that the peoples of the world depended on his judgment, whatever their designated leaders might think. At Versailles, Wilson spent many months in detailed, intense, complex bargaining with the heads of the allied powers and representatives of sundry other nations.[146]

No other president has ever tried to negotiate a treaty of this scope personally. He saw no alternative—while he was back in the United States, Colonel House, as usual lacking clear instructions, had made concessions to the Allies that Wilson repudiated upon his return to the table. This episode sundered the president's relationship with House. And because Wilson disliked and distrusted Lansing, he was essentially on his own in formulating American policy.

The product of all this angst, the Treaty of Versailles, has never had many admirers. It was too punitive toward Germany and too compromised on other issues to provide a stable platform for peace. Knowing this, President Wilson tied his hopes to its provision for a League of Nations to secure peace in the future. He also knew that the league would be the sticking point with the Senate and the American people. As Felix Frankfurter observed, the concept of a powerful international organization was "too new, too vast to enlist the understanding and the faith of the American people, in view of our traditional isolation."[147]

Returning to the United States, Wilson presented the treaty to the Senate and met with both individual senators and the Foreign Relations Committee, which was chaired by his enemy Henry Cabot Lodge. No congressional committee had ever been invited to the White House (and none have since). Wilson spoke freely with them but would not give them the treaty negotiation documents.[148] The senators insisted on amendments or reservations to the treaty to protect American autonomy. The president considered any alteration fatal to the success of the treaty in promoting collective security among nations.[149]

Stalemated and exhausted, Wilson decided to take his case to the people. This swing around the circle had tragic consequences both for Wilson personally and for the United States. It was all a blur—the frenetic speaking tour, the collapse in Colorado that ended the tour, the dolorous train ride home, the stroke that ensued, the disability that shrouded the rest of his term of office.[150] Of course, the treaty was lost as well, at what cost historians debate. With exquisite malice, Lodge conducted the initial negative votes in the Senate while the president lay incapacitated. As he struggled to recover, Wilson could take comfort from his evident impact on the final shape of the peace, but his quixotic pursuit of a world without war was doomed from the beginning.

From his stroke in early October 1919 to the end of his term almost eighteen months later, Woodrow Wilson was partly or wholly unable to discharge the duties of his office.[151] Initially partly paralyzed, he remained physically weak and mentally erratic. The more rigid, moralistic side of his personality dominated the political realist in him. Overall, he was "incapable of leadership on any issue."[152] During this time he was shielded from view by his fiercely protective wife, Edith, and his doctor, Cary Grayson. Edith Wilson controlled and constricted the flow of paper to the president, deciding which issues demanded his attention and which did not. The president's condition was never frankly revealed—the word "stroke" did not appear amid the clouds of euphemisms about his "nervous exhaustion."

As we have seen, Article II of the Constitution provides that in case of the president's "inability to discharge the powers and duties" of the office, they devolve on the vice president. Within the executive branch, the president's stroke produced immediate attention to the question whether Wilson had a constitutional "inability" to continue in office. (His practical inability was substantial but not entire.) Several considerations hampered resolution of this issue. First, it is unlikely that Wilson ever seriously considered resigning or temporarily delegating power to someone else. He was too much the fighter for that. Second, the extent of his possible recovery was unknown, and his condition did improve as time went by. Third, the original Constitution made no provision for temporary disability; hence the legality of a temporary arrangement was doubtful.[153] Fourth, and ironically, John Tyler's precedent complicated matters because he had assumed the office of president after Harrison's death—would Vice President Thomas Marshall similarly become president even if he took control only temporarily?

Soon after Wilson's stroke, Secretary of State Lansing convened the cabinet, with Tumulty's approval, to consider the constitutional issue. When Dr. Grayson provided assurances about the clarity of the president's mind, the cabinet accepted them, ending the inquiry. Vice President Marshall, who had been an "invisible figure in Washington" during his time in office, had the good sense to remain that way, emulating his predecessors in times of presidential disability.[154] After the president had recovered a bit, he quite unfairly fired Lansing for holding cabinet meetings during his illness, although he had been fully informed. The message of the dismissal was that taking any initiative to fill in for a disabled president is a risky endeavor. Somehow the Wilson administration staggered to the finish line, but not without inflicting serious damage to the civil liberties of Americans in the meantime.

Infringing Liberty at Home

No one who is imbued with Woodrow Wilson's level of moral certainty is likely to take dissent kindly. Wilson's restrictions on First Amendment rights were much greater and less justified than those of any previous or subsequent administration, including Lincoln's.[155] Wilson employed the excuse of wartime, but in an ominous new way. He intended to mobilize not just the Army but the nation, as even Lincoln had not tried to do. A clash with civil liberties was inevitable.

The president's war message to Congress warned ominously about the existence of a German fifth column within the United States and revealed his stern attitude toward dissent: "If there should be disloyalty, it will be dealt with, with a firm hand of stern repression."[156] He meant it. In 1917, the constitutional limits of governmental control of dissent were still quite unclear. The First Amendment had received little judicial interpretation, and no federal statute had tried to control dissent since the Sedition Act of 1798. The essential problem was (and is) that wartime dissent *does* hamper the effectiveness of any nation's war effort. Therefore, a democracy must decide what it will tolerate to gain the benefits of free speech.

The president began with an apparently benign initiative. He issued an executive order forming a Committee on Public Information, a propaganda unit headed by a journalist and charged with publicizing positive information about the war in order to "arouse ardor and enthusiasm" among the people.[157] Falling to its task with a vengeance, the committee and its network of agents extolled American virtue and condemned German villainy. Its propaganda soon whipped up both governmental and private persecution of dissenters and nonconformists.

Unlike Lincoln, Wilson sought and received statutory authority to restrict speech and used the courts rather than the military for enforcement. In enacting the Espionage Act of 1917 and the Sedition Act of 1918, Congress showed some awareness of the lessons of 1798 but nevertheless crafted broad statutes that were ripe for abuse under aggressive executive enforcement. The Espionage Act prohibited spying, sabotage, refusing military service, and obstructing recruitment.[158] It also authorized the postmaster general to exclude seditious material from the mail.[159] The Wilson administration proposed the Sedition Act a year later to fill perceived gaps in the earlier statute. Echoing its 1798 predecessor, it prohibited "any disloyal, profane, scurrilous, or abusive language about the form of government of the United States, or of the Constitution of the United States . . . or any language intended to bring [them] into contempt, scorn, contumely, or disrepute."[160]

No one could safely criticize the government under the Sedition Act's standard. Former president Theodore Roosevelt trenchantly said that Congress was making it a crime to tell the truth.[161] Modern constitutional analysis would hold it unconstitutional on its face. Wilson's signature on the bill adopted an indefensible interpretation of the First Amendment. The founding generation had known that free speech is an important check on the daily operation of the federal government and must therefore be protected. Wilson was blind to this central constitutional value.

Needing an enthusiastic public to meet military quotas, the president aggressively stifled dissent. He had a lot of help. His intolerance was shared by the cabinet, federal prosecutors, judges, and juries. The public pressure to suppress disloyalty was fierce, even erupting into vigilante justice at times. Quite simply, no check on repression was operating inside or outside the federal government.

President Wilson communicated his aggressive policy to three main subordinates, all of whom were inclined to extreme measures and insensitive to the value of dissent: Postmaster General Albert Burleson and Attorneys General Thomas Gregory and A. Mitchell Palmer. During Wilson's times of distraction or disability, these men rampaged freely, secure in the knowledge that the president approved of their general approaches.[162]

Burleson, described by Upton Sinclair as a man of "pitiful and childish ignorance," set out to cleanse the nation's mail of socialist or otherwise malign publications.[163] Wilson looked on like an indulgent father, gently chiding Burleson to be cautious as the furor over his censorship grew. The postmaster resisted what little control the president exercised, threatening to resign if he could not execute the law as he chose.[164] Wilson retreated, overruling Burleson only when he foolishly banned the liberal *Nation* magazine for some imagined sin.

Attorney General Gregory, lacking a major investigative arm because the future Federal Bureau of Investigation was still in its infancy, accepted help from a reactionary private group, the American Protective League.[165] Together they assailed a radical union, the Industrial Workers of the World, at one point arresting over a thousand of its members and later prosecuting hundreds of them in an effort to break the union. Gregory also ordered "slacker raids" to find draft evaders in various cities. Federal and local law enforcement officers stopped and interrogated thousands of young men, detaining many of them without charges or warrants.[166]

Prosecutions under the new statutes rose to a wartime total of over two thousand. The socialist leader Eugene Debs was sentenced to ten years in prison under the Espionage Act for a speech that criticized overenforcement of the act and implied that the United States was no longer a democratic nation.[167] If a prominent political leader like Debs could be silenced, no one was safe. Under pressure from local leaders and without any serious monitoring by the attorney general, federal prosecutors brought charges against dissenters who seemed dangerous to someone. After the armistice, most but not all pending charges were dropped.

Attorney General Gregory was replaced by A. Mitchell Palmer in 1919, just in time for the height of the "red scare" that was first triggered by the Russian Revolution and then inflamed by a series of domestic strikes and terror bombings (including one at Palmer's house). Palmer fanned the existing hysteria against radicals of all kinds. He employed the young and zealous J. Edgar Hoover to gather information about dissenters. Often ignoring the constitutional warrant requirement, federal agents raided suspected radical organizations nationwide, arresting about four thousand suspected subversives.[168] The Palmer raids targeted vulnerable aliens, who could be deported summarily under the wartime statutes. In his weakened condition, President Wilson may not have known about all the abuses, but there was plenty of smoke to reveal the fire.

Thus, in World War I and its aftermath, the lines of command that are essential to the faithful execution of the law broke down. The president neither chose his subordinates with wisdom nor supervised them adequately. In turn, the Justice Department did not constrain its decentralized prosecution system (including its affiliated private vigilantes). The president was certainly generally aware of what was happening but did not intervene. He even tolerated urban race riots in the summer of 1919 that killed or burned out many blacks.[169]

The courts did not step up to protect civil liberties. The Supreme Court kept quiet until after the armistice and then upheld convictions under the statutes. Eventually, the repression of dissent was too much for Justice Holmes, whose dissenting opinions in the later cases showed the way to the future.[170] No president can be excused for his own failures of interpretation, however, on the grounds that the courts did no better. The power to engage in departmentalist interpretation carries responsibility also.

Woodrow Wilson displayed an unseemly vindictiveness toward dissenters that Abraham Lincoln never did. During the Civil War, most arrests were for short durations to gain control of local populations. In World War I, arrests often led to deportation or long prison terms. Late in his presidency, Wilson even rejected an opportunity to repair some of the damage when he refused to consider proposals that the dissenters be granted amnesty.[171] He granted some pardons, but denied one to Debs.[172]

As the discredited Wilson administration wound down at last, the Republicans campaigned for their restoration to the presidency on a platform of limiting excessive executive power. Their nomination of Warren Harding guaranteed that nothing too bold would occur. The journalist

William Allen White uttered an apt epitaph for the era: "After eight years of Wilson and the four short years of breathing space with Taft . . . and seven years of Roosevelt," the nation was "tired of issues, sick at heart of ideals and weary of being noble."[173] The roaring twenties would provide just the antidote, with presidential torpor as prescribed.

CHAPTER EIGHT

What Must Be Done

Franklin Roosevelt

[Franklin Roosevelt] was never theoretical about things. What must be done to defend the country must be done. . . . The Constitution has never greatly bothered any wartime President.—Attorney General Francis Biddle[1]

Twelve years after the American electorate happily conferred its highest office on the overmatched Warren Harding, it desperately cast its lot with Franklin Delano Roosevelt in hopes of a vigorous response to the Great Depression. During his twelve years in office, FDR transformed both the presidency and the place of the United States in the world. The Constitution eventually caught up to the rapidly unfolding twentieth century, but not without a fight.

Interlude

Woodrow Wilson once cruelly said of Warren Harding that he "has nothing to think with."[2] His sins were those of omission, his excuses those of incapacity. His talents well suited him to the career of small-town newspaper owner from which he rose to the United States Senate and then to the presidency, borne along by his warm geniality and a consequent lack of enemies. His campaign touched America's need for "not nostrums but normalcy."[3] Once in the White House, he sadly realized that "I am not fit for this office and I should never have been here."[4] A merciful heart attack relieved him of his burdens after two and a half years in office, just as his administration's scandals were about to erupt.

Known today only as a synonym for scandal, the Harding administration did manage some accomplishments. A weak man, Harding did not favor a strong presidency and could not have conducted one. He abjured "personal government, individual, dictatorial, autocratic, or what not."[5] Yet the cabinet had some stars in Charles Evans Hughes at State, Andrew Mellon at Treasury, and Herbert Hoover at Commerce. Not surprisingly, it was in those portfolios that the accomplishments occurred. In foreign affairs, Hughes initiated a policy that lasted throughout the twenties of promoting American trade while avoiding overseas provocations or entanglements. In finance, at long last Congress provided authority for the executive branch to form a federal budget, ending the long-standing practice of separate and uncoordinated submission of departmental requests and laying the basis for greater presidential control of the executive. And business found a responsive government, as it would throughout the 1920s.

Yet Harding also selected two knaves (Attorney General Harry Daugherty and Interior Secretary Albert Fall) and one fool (Navy Secretary Edwin Denby). Worse, he supervised them not at all, leading to the Teapot Dome scandal that wrecked his historical reputation.[6] As fate closed in on Warren Harding, the scandals started to surface.[7] First, he discovered that his veterans' bureau administrator had looted the bureau. Teapot Dome arose after Albert Fall induced an unsuspecting Harding to approve transfer of naval petroleum reserves to Interior while Navy Secretary Denby slept. Fall then leased the lands on very favorable terms with heavy kickbacks. Harding revealed his own level of acuity by saying that "if Albert Fall isn't an honest man, I am not fit to be President."[8] Both were true. Meanwhile, the "Ohio gang" operated out of the Justice Department (of all places), taking bribes to settle cases and war claims. Toward the end, Harding lamented that he could take care of his enemies and that his troubles were with his friends. The president's faithful execution duty includes a component of watchfulness; Harding failed it utterly.

His successor, Calvin Coolidge, had been chosen as vice presidential candidate because as governor of Massachusetts he had broken a police strike in Boston and therefore appealed to advocates of law and order.[9] Coolidge certainly had the gift of timing. Shocked by the lurid Harding scandals, the nation coveted Coolidge's virtues, which were those of "a small-town New England bank clerk."[10] The new president was honest, frugal, conservative, and conscientious.[11] He never used two words where none would do. Seeing the preservation of law and order as the essence of government responsibility, Coolidge quickly cleaned up Harding's messes. The president soothed business by appointing its allies to oversee its activities. For example, he appointed William Humphrey to the Federal Trade Commission after Humphrey had disparaged the agency as "an instrument of oppression and disturbance and injury."[12] In the hands of such stewards, the laws would receive minimal faithful execution.

Coolidge kept the national purse as closed as his mouth. He had the fortitude to veto a veterans' bonus and was overridden. When the Mississippi flooded disastrously in 1927, he initially refused direct federal aid but did send Herbert Hoover to coordinate private efforts.[13] All of this fitted the mood of the times. Coolidge left office after six years, happy in the knowledge that he could have won another term.

Under Secretary of State Hughes, foreign policy in the Harding and Coolidge years was essentially seamless.[14] Knowing little of the world, these two presidents let their capable secretary take the lead. The United States followed a strategy dictated by its status as the world's greatest economic power but not as a leading military power. The executive's caution in foreign affairs was increased by Congress's assertiveness in this era in the wake of its victory over Wilson. The Washington Naval Conference in 1921 did limit the naval arms race among the great powers and was the first major international arms reduction agreement. Meanwhile, American refusal to reduce the burdensome war debts of the Allies poisoned postwar relations with them and helped set the table for the Depression.

In Latin America, the executive shifted away from gunboat diplomacy and military intervention. Relations improved with much-abused Mexico. A treaty paid Colombia $25 million for the loss of Panama. Hughes also disclaimed the Roosevelt Corollary, denying American intentions to exert hegemony in the hemisphere.[15] American troops finally left the Dominican Republic in 1924, but in Nicaragua the Marines struggled against local unrest and did not leave until 1933.

Hughes's successor Frank Kellogg was a cautious man who was often mired in detail. He negotiated the naive Kellogg-Briand pact in 1928, outlawing war as an instrument of national policy. Its toothlessness was revealed when all the European great powers signed it and the Senate easily ratified it. Real collective security was still off the table.

Herbert Hoover, the man with the perfect résumé, ascended gracefully to the presidency. He had risen from an early orphaning to become a highly successful mining engineer and businessman and then turned to public service. In World War I he skillfully provided food relief to Belgium and coordinated food production in the United States. His tenure as secretary of commerce was a triumph. Indeed, he had "never known failure."[16] Stiff and formal, he was respected rather than loved. As president, he was too much the engineer and too little the politician—it was said that "he can understand vibrations but cannot hear tone."[17]

Hoover's conception of the role of the federal government, although firmly anchored in the values of the progressive wing of the Republican Party that he inhabited, was inadequate to the economic crisis that was about to overwhelm him. Hoover's roots among the Quakers explain his deep sense of the importance of combining individual responsibility with voluntary community cooperation. The president's lifetime of achievement had confirmed the value of his approach; he would not modify it under the pressure of conditions that volunteerism could not remedy. Thus, as the Great Depression came on, he opposed direct aid to individuals as destructive of responsibility. He thought that the congressional power to spend for the general welfare did not extend to relieving the people from natural or economic disasters, which he considered a local responsibility.[18] He did, though, approve of aid to corporations, especially banks. This ideologically incoherent position proved politically disastrous for a president who soon lost the faith of the people.

As the stock market crash of late 1929 was followed by the successive tsunamis of the onset of the Great Depression, the United States lacked both a tradition of strong federal intervention in the economy and the bureaucratic apparatus to administer large government programs.[19] With the federal government still a remote presence in most Americans' lives, the steps Hoover did take were unprecedented, although too tentative in modern theory. He began by trying to support agriculture, a sector in which a period of persistent depression in the 1920s had worsened dramatically. President Coolidge had vetoed farm export subsidies; Hoover called a special session of Congress and got a farm bill providing for cooperatives and some government purchases of crops as a last resort.

Hoover did not favor high tariffs, but in 1930 Congress rolled him with the disastrous Hawley-Smoot tariff, the highest in American history, and the president swallowed it. The special-interest steamroller that tariff legislation embodies was too much for his limited political skills to surmount. This selfish tariff provoked retaliation by the Europeans and accelerated the onset of the Depression by stifling international trade.

By 1931 both the economy and the Hoover presidency were in freefall. The second phase of his response to the Depression prefigured the New Deal by promoting a secondary mortgage market, creating the Reconstruction Finance Corporation to provide emergency loans to banks, and initiating some public works projects. Yet he vetoed legislation providing relief for individuals in a nation where many were starving. When the Bonus Army of veterans camped out in Washington to appeal for early payment of a promised bonus for service in World War I, he insensitively rousted them with the real Army. Many ordinary Americans had been left out of the prosperity of the 1920s and were now destitute. Visibly, Hoover's philosophy of the government's duty under the Constitution did not extend to them. Trapped by his own limitations of vision, he complained that Americans "cannot legislate ourselves out of a world economic depression."[20] The landslide election of Franklin Roosevelt in 1932 rejected the traditional values that Hoover espoused but did not, in itself, replace them with anything new.

Transformations

When Hamilton and Jefferson first offered their competing views of the American polity to the nation's people, they could not have foreseen that the essential tension between them would persist for more than 225 years. In terms of presidential politics, the parties that formed from the seeds they sowed have enjoyed extended periods of dominance, lasting until some political *frisson* shifts the balance of power from advocates of a relatively powerful federal government to those favoring a relatively weak one, or back the other way. From the demise of the Federalists in 1800 to 1860, the Democrats held the presidency and promoted decentralization for all but the eight years of the ill-starred Whigs. After the disruption of the Civil War, laissez-faire government prevailed until 1932 except for the activist presidencies of Theodore Roosevelt and Woodrow Wilson. The watershed election of 1932 shifted the balance again. The next thirty-six years until the bitter election of 1968 saw Democratic presidents except for Eisenhower. Since then, the balance has swayed mostly to the Republicans in the age of Nixon and Reagan.[21]

In the election season of 2016, the foundational choice will be before the nation again. Of course, the baseline has changed—that is, today even a relatively restrained federal government is far larger and more active than anything in the vision of the framers. The largest single shift in the baseline, which occurred in the New Deal, remains the focus of debate about the role of the government under the Constitution.

Except for George Washington, no president has taken office with a wider range of permissible action than Franklin D. Roosevelt, whose personality ideally suited him to making maximum use of the opportunity. "He was not especially gifted in any field except politics. But in politics he had no equal."[22] His struggle with polio in the 1920s had altered and deepened FDR, transforming him into an empathetic man and a superb political actor who was always serenely optimistic and positive on the surface and completely inaccessible underneath. An early adviser said that he was playing a lifetime part and "no one would ever see anything else."[23] He was sly, devious, secretive—sometimes too much so—and immensely practical and flexible. A talker, not a reader, Roosevelt gathered facts and opinions from a wide range of advisers but rarely disclosed his own thinking.

FDR lacked any detailed political philosophy, resisting theory as an excessive constraint on his freedom of action.[24] His "untroubled conception of the presidency consisted quite simply of the thought of himself in it."[25] He did follow a few simple, powerful political principles. Like his cousin Theodore he thought government should subordinate the private to the public good and help the underdog. Soon after his election, FDR said he sought "to provide work and economic security to the mass of the people."[26] His enduring commitment to having the federal government ensure a New Deal for the common American led to his greatest contributions as president to the nation and to its Constitution.

As president, Franklin Roosevelt encountered many questions of law. Although trained as a lawyer, he did not think like one.[27] As had been true of Woodrow Wilson, his legal education bored him and he found law practice stifling. He was impatient with the lawyer's focus on detail, deliberation, and process. Politics, not law, was his art. His mind ran in broad channels of right and wrong; political opportunity and feasibility dominated his calculations. By taking steps to ensure the political acceptability of his actions, he expected to prevent successful assaults on their legal legitimacy.

In his inaugural speech, President Roosevelt claimed that "our Constitution is so simple and practical that it is possible always to meet extraordinary needs by changes in emphasis and arrangements without loss of essential form." Throughout his long presidency, he never wavered from the judgment that the existing, "marvelously elastic" Constitution needed no amendment to support the remedies for the Great Depression that he sought.[28] He would fight a great battle with the Supreme Court over his vision of a Darwinian Constitution that evolved with the life of the nation, in contrast to the Court's lingering Newtonian interpretation of a fixed set of governmental orbits.

Enacting a New Deal

In 1933, Franklin Roosevelt became the last president to be inaugurated in March. The just-ratified Twentieth Amendment would henceforth bring the congressional schedule into modern times, eliminating the long gap between the election of a Congress and its first assembly over a year later. Presidential terms would begin on January 20. Hence FDR would enjoy the last extended window of opportunity to govern in the absence of Congress. He did not take it. Unlike Lincoln, Roosevelt needed immediate legislation to address the crisis before him. Accordingly, he quickly called the new Congress into special session, and the storied "hundred days" began.

The nation was near standstill. The economy was operating at about half capacity, and about a quarter of the workforce was unemployed. Thirty-eight states had closed their banks to stem the tide of failures. On Inauguration Day banks in New York and Illinois and the New York Stock Exchange closed as well.[29] Widespread calls for Roosevelt to assume "dictatorial" powers had been aired for weeks, even in respectable places.[30] FDR's inaugural, after its stirring call to hope, remarked that he might have to ask Congress for a sweeping grant of power "to wage a war against the emergency," but only if it first denied him the particular tools he needed.[31]

FDR set to work. On his first day in office he called Congress into immediate session and invoked a dubiously relevant statute to declare a four-day national bank holiday.[32] He used the Trading with the Enemy Act, a leftover World War I authority that was designed to allow financial controls in wartime. The act provided more symbolic than real authority for the bank holiday, but relying on it saved FDR from making a stark constitutional claim of power and closed the banks long enough for the president to ask for emergency banking authority as Congress convened. Thus he began with what amounted to an exercise of the Lockean prerogative and signaled his willingness to interpret his faithful execution duty aggressively, as he would often do.

On its first day in session, Congress ratified FDR's bank holiday by passing an Emergency Banking Act that was hurriedly cobbled together by the executive.[33] The outpouring of legislation that followed in the hundred days—fifteen major statutes—was unprecedented then and is unmatched since.[34] In this first phase of the New Deal, FDR was in his most experimental mood.[35] Ideas were drawn from World War I emergency authorities, from programs initiated or considered by Hoover, and from the brains of the gifted flock of advisers who descended on Washington. The ideas coalesced as legislation that was not intellectually or economically coherent.

With the president setting the agenda much as a prime minister might do, Congress delegated sweeping powers to him through a hurried and informal legislative process.[36] Lawyers in the executive branch quickly vetted the proposals for constitutionality. The bills rested with varying degrees of comfort on the federal power over interstate commerce or the power to tax and spend for the general welfare. The spending bills rested on venerable precedents concerning disaster relief, extending their logic from natural to economic disasters in a way that President Hoover would never have countenanced.[37] Taken together, they asserted FDR's view that the powers of the federal government were adequate to meet the crisis.

The Emergency Banking Act ratified the bank holiday and successfully reopened the banks under federal supervision. The Agricultural Adjustment Act provided farm price supports. Congress ended gold clauses in public and private contracts as the president took the nation off the constraining gold standard. Aid to the unemployed arrived with the Civilian Conservation Corps and major public works programs such as the Tennessee Valley Authority and the Public Works Administration. Direct relief programs supplemented the employment efforts. The federal government was beginning to affect ordinary Americans as never before (except for wartime conscription).

The flagship statute, the National Industrial Recovery Act, was an astonishing delegation of power to regulate the economy.[38] In an attempt to satisfy everyone, it called on business and labor to cooperate in a grand scheme to boost the economy.[39] It allowed industries to create codes regulating competition in order to increase wages (but also prices) and to reduce hours of work to increase employment. The president, after supposedly reviewing the voluminous codes to ensure they were not too anticompetitive, would sign them into law. The National Recovery Administration, created to administer the NIRA, swiftly became the nation's first large federal civilian bureaucracy. Thrown together in crisis conditions, the NRA was always chaotic and eventually became unpopular.

Interior Secretary Harold Ickes summed it all up: "It's more than a New Deal. It's a new world."[40] Broad as the statutory delegations to Roosevelt were, however, they never constituted a constitutional dictatorship in the classic sense, because the legislature retained active control, and individual rights were never suspended.[41] Many of the statutory authorities were expressly temporary. Nevertheless, normal constitutional controls on executive discretion were slackened if not abandoned. And an executive edifice began to arise that remains in place today.

No president had ever shown such capacity for legislative leadership. FDR involved himself in the legislative process more constantly and in more detail than had either Theodore Roosevelt or Woodrow Wilson.[42] Franklin Roosevelt once estimated that he spent three to four hours a day working with legislators during congressional sessions.[43] He used the veto pen mostly to prevent spending that he did not favor and to keep Congress in line.[44] In his first two terms, he never denied Congress information it demanded.[45] As the initial crisis eased, the normal obstacles to legislating reappeared, but on a new baseline. Henceforth the White House would be the focal point of the federal government and Congress would expect— and come to depend on—each administration's legislative program as an organizing plan for its own efforts. The president's constitutional power to recommend legislation had moved to a new level of engagement.

Seeing that his cousin Theodore had overdone his hectoring of Congress, FDR vowed to limit his calls to action. He did not try to cure all national ills. The constitutional vision that a president's legislative program embodies is as important for what it omits as what it contains. Needing the support of southern Democrats, he was always hesitant on civil rights (he moved forward largely at Eleanor's instance). To his credit, though, he issued an executive order banning race discrimination in government civilian employment and procurement.[46] This was the first of what would become a series of executive orders by successive presidents, addressing discrimination in activities performed or supported by the federal government.

To induce the public to prod Congress, Roosevelt became the first master of the electronic media. He gave a total of about twenty of his conversational "fireside chats" with the public on the radio, connecting with ordinary citizens in a new way. (When FDR died, a grief-stricken man was asked if he had known Roosevelt. The response was: "No, but he knew me.")[47] The deep reservoir of support that FDR enjoyed protected him from the fierce opposition that his initiatives generated.

New roles for the federal government required an expanded presidential apparatus to control a burgeoning executive branch. Franklin Roosevelt is conventionally credited with (or blamed for) creating the "institutional presidency" in place of the small personal staff that preceded his tenure.[48] Yet like much else in the New Deal, this process proceeded in fits and starts and was completed only on the eve of World War II.

The early Roosevelt presidency had no more organizational than policy coherence. The president's governing style favored the creation of multiple units with overlapping or competing responsibilities, all of which converged at FDR's desk. This "penchant for administrative profligacy" maximized the president's discretion while maddening his subordinates.[49] It also reflected his reluctance to fire anyone who performed poorly—he simply gave the same job to someone else. While the wheels of this unwieldy machine churned, FDR bided his time and watched the progress of public opinion, judging the right moment for action. It was not a way to manage the executive branch that could be operated successfully by anyone other than FDR, and not always by him.

In his first cabinet, Roosevelt installed two Republicans, the prickly Harold Ickes at Interior and the mystical Henry Wallace at Agriculture. For attorney general, he chose Homer Cummings, whose willingness to please outran his legal and political gifts.[50] FDR was happy with Cummings, calling him "a great fellow. He can always find a way to do things."[51] This lack of lawyerly detachment in the attorney general would ill serve the president.

An expansion of the executive branch increases the president's patronage opportunities. But as appointments proliferate, the practical capacity of the president to supervise his subordinates attenuates. At the outset of his presidency, FDR held back about a hundred thousand patronage appointments to retain his leverage over Congress.[52] Later on, he used patronage to build support for a lasting Democratic coalition in place of the fragile one the party had so long relied on, a step that led eventually to statutory controls to protect the independence of the civil service.

President Roosevelt understood the importance of coordinating his administration's legal arguments as they would be advanced in federal litigation. The success of departmentalist constitutional interpretation depends on the extent to which the executive branch sings with a single voice. In early American history, the part-time attorney general was unable to supervise federal litigators. Creation of the Justice Department in 1870 led to partial but not complete unification of litigation control, as some agencies successfully lobbied Congress for their own authority. FDR issued an executive order in 1933, calling for Justice to conduct all litigation involving the United States to the extent that statutes permitted it.[53] This action led to greater but not complete presidential control over litigation, as Congress continued its episodic practice of granting separate authority to some agencies.

The core of the New Deal as Americans experience it today resulted from a second wave of legislation in 1935.[54] In a fireside chat FDR identified his guiding principle. He quoted Lincoln's maxim that government should do what people could not do for themselves and said he was trying to provide "greater security" for the average American.[55] Now he was going beyond his earlier efforts, which had extended old precedents for providing relief after natural disasters to the new context of relieving economic distress. He offered the modern idea of a social safety net, citing the statement in the Preamble to the Constitution that the purpose of the federal government is to "promote the general Welfare." He understood that the Depression had increased widespread and chronic poverty that the boom of the twenties had hidden. Thus in his second inaugural he referred to "one-third of a nation ill-housed, ill-clad, ill-nourished."[56] As his first term proceeded, he moved from the quick fixes that the initial crisis demanded to an attempt to restructure American society.

The core of the "second New Deal" was the Social Security Act, containing unemployment insurance, aid to dependent children, and old age pensions.[57] The act was carefully drafted under the leadership of Labor Secretary Frances Perkins, with close attention to constitutional issues. Other important and enduring statutes such as the securities acts structured the marketplace to make it work fairly and openly.[58] All of this was, in the words of John Maynard Keynes, a "reasoned experiment within the framework of the existing system." Failure of FDR's experiment would leave "orthodoxy and revolution to fight it out."[59] For all that Roosevelt's nostrums displeased the real revolutionaries to his left, they outraged the forces of orthodoxy to his right, who soon fought back in the courts.

Struggling Over the Constitution

In the late nineteenth and early twentieth centuries, the Supreme Court frequently but erratically invalidated federal and state social legislation for unconstitutionality.[60] The Court's activism once again demonstrated the power presidents have to cast a long legal shadow by nominating justices who share their conception of the Constitution. Justices appointed by conservative presidents who believed in a limited role for federal regulation and a wide scope for private property rights brought those values into their resolution of cases, and thus into formal constitutional doctrine.

By writing a Jeffersonian conception of the role of government into the Constitution, the Court responded to deep impulses in American political life and constitutional thought. The Court set its face against the more active, Hamiltonian style of government that was struggling to emerge in the Progressive era. Two kinds of arguments proved fatal to federal statutes. The Court often held that even such activities as mining and manufacturing were too local in nature to come within the congressional power over interstate commerce. Alternatively, the Court invoked a concept of substantive liberty guaranteed by the due process clauses in the Bill of Rights to forbid government interference in private contracts for employment, ignoring the practical disparities in bargaining power that were often present.

The essential premises of New Deal legislation were antithetical to these doctrines. To Franklin Roosevelt and his allies in Congress, the twentieth-century economy was so integrated that local activity often had interstate effects, and regulation of private bargaining was essential to individual security.

In 1933, the Court was delicately balanced. On the right were four stalwart conservatives, Justices Butler, McReynolds, Sutherland, and Van Devanter—the "Four Horsemen." On the left were three reliable liberals, Justices Brandeis, Cardozo, and Stone. The two swing justices were the chief, Charles Evans Hughes, and the somewhat captious Owen Roberts. The Court's precedents in recent decades had provided threads from which widely variant opinions could be woven. The precedents wobbled somewhat, as occurs in the sequential decision making of any collective body. But the Court had never confronted a president and struck down the heart of his legislative program.

The great collision of constitutional views occurred on "Black Monday" in May 1935, when the Court unanimously decided three cases against the New Deal.[61] One of the decisions followed the old-time religion by invalidating an urgently needed farm bankruptcy statute on grounds it infringed the constitutional rights of creditors.[62] The other two were landmark attempts to constrain presidential power. Both were quite unfair to FDR personally.

In *Schechter Poultry Corp. v. United States*, the Court invalidated the NIRA on two grounds: that the act extended into local activities beyond the federal commerce power and that it delegated excessive and unconstrained power to the president.[63] The decision swept more broadly than necessary by stating two grounds for invalidating the statute when one would do. Worse, the Court's decision occurred only a month before the NIRA was due to expire anyway. Obviously, the Court was warning both other branches to stop the nonsense.

In *Humphrey's Executor v. United States*, the Court held that Congress could constitutionally limit the president to specified causes such as misconduct for removing independent commissioners.[64] This decision rebuked the president for removing the egregious William Humphrey from the Federal Trade Commission without asserting any reason except general political disagreement. The Court ignored FDR's reliance on one of its recent decisions that had seemed to establish that Congress could not constitutionally limit presidential removal of senior executive officers.[65]

The Court's holding in *Humphrey's Executor* is defensible because in that era the commissioners of the FTC were mainly adjudicators, for whom political supervision is questionable. Ever since the founding period had left uncertainty surrounding the "decision of 1789," it had been possible that Congress could set valid limits to plenary presidential removal of officers outside the core "constitutional cabinet."[66] Even so, the result in the case did not foreclose the possibility that a president could assert a real need to remove a recalcitrant commissioner in order to fulfill his own constitutional duty to superintend execution of the laws.

The subsequent importance of the Court's decision in *Humphrey's Executor* lay in some extremely broad and unsupported statements in the opinion. The Court asserted that independent regulatory commissions like the FTC were somehow entirely outside the executive branch and wholly insulated from presidential supervision except for the constitutional power to nominate the officers.[67] These statements, evidently triggered by the justices' alarm about FDR's freewheeling managerial style, have caused trouble ever since.

Congress relies on *Humphrey's Executor* to shield the independent agencies from presidential political supervision, and all presidents from 1935 on have known that. Beginning with FDR, presidents have signed bills creating independent agencies, notwithstanding their constitutional doubts about restrictions on their removal power. Presidents have acquiesced in this way whenever the particular bill including such restrictions seems otherwise desirable to them. FDR began the retreat by signing bills that restructured the Federal Reserve Board and created the National Labor Relations Board and other agencies.[68] To Roosevelt, the game seemed worth the candle, but his precedent of signing statutes creating independent commissions has fragmented the executive branch in a fundamental way, as we shall see.

As if the rout on Black Monday were incomplete, the Court went on in succeeding months to eliminate other New Deal statutes. Both the Agricultural Adjustment Act and the Guffey Coal Act fell, leaving the administration unsure how it could provide farm price supports or regulate wages and hours in critical industries.[69] Ironically, the Court's decision on the Agricultural Adjustment Act adopted the Hamiltonian position that the federal power to spend for the general welfare is independent of other congressional powers—but then went on to strike down the act as a disguised form of regulation that invaded reserved powers of the states.[70]

The president fought back with his only available weapon, rhetoric, deriding the NIRA decision in a press conference for adopting a "horse-and-buggy definition of interstate commerce."[71] The question, he said, was whether the federal government had "control over any national economic problem." He was right, but that was cold comfort. The Court's decisions had hamstrung parts of the New Deal and now threatened the rest, especially the Social Security Act.

As the 1936 election approached, various proposals to control the Supreme Court were debated inside and outside the Roosevelt administration.[72] Many of them had been around for years. There were four categories of proposals. First, the Constitution could be amended to confine the Court's power to review the constitutionality of statutes, for example by requiring a supermajority vote of justices to invalidate a statute. But that step might give Congress too much power. Second, an amendment could alter the Constitution's grants of authority to Congress, by broadening the definition of the commerce power, for example. But the justices might undermine an amendment by interpretation. Third, an amendment could set term limits or age limits for justices. But age and longevity correlate poorly with judicial philosophy. Finally, there was a statutory avenue—packing the Court by adding to the number of justices and thus giving the president immediate opportunities to nominate people who shared his view of the Constitution.

Among these alternatives, court packing had several advantages. Since it could be accomplished by statute, the delays and uncertainties that attend constitutional amendment would be avoided. The Constitution's amendment process posed a seemingly insuperable barrier to reform—any thirteen states could defeat ratification of a proposal. Moreover, time was of the essence if the remaining New Deal legislation were to survive.[73] If a statutory experiment proved unwise, another statute could correct the problem.[74] Precedent did not seem to stand in the way. The Court's membership had fluctuated somewhat over the years.[75] Some of these alterations were starkly political—to deny Jefferson and Johnson nomination opportunities, and to give Lincoln and Grant additional ones. The British historian James Bryce had observed that the Constitution's failure to specify the number of justices was "a weak point, a joint in the court's armor through which a weapon might some day penetrate."[76] As early as 1935, Roosevelt's lawyers had reminded him about the Grant precedent, which had saved the Civil War greenbacks by inducing the Court to reverse a decision.[77] Now might be the time to strike.

Yet court packing had a central—and ultimately fatal—disadvantage. Since long before the founding, Anglo-American law had emphasized that "no one should be a judge in his own cause."[78] The very source of judicial power lay in its neutrality. Even if, as everyone knew, judges cannot entirely escape their own personal values, it is one thing to disagree, even stridently, with court decisions and quite another to try to control interpretation by choosing the interpreters. Of course, our constitutional system has always allowed presidents to nominate judges, but only when vacancies arise by happenstance and only with the Senate's approval. Along with the constitutional guarantees of life tenure and guaranteed salary for the judges, these simple checks in the appointments process ordinarily furnish acceptable levels of judicial neutrality. Any form of court packing threatens neutrality by allowing one of the players to select the referees in the middle of the game.

Throughout 1936, President Roosevelt and Attorney General Cummings gave sustained attention to alternatives for controlling the Court.[79] The problem seemed to come down to the "nine old men" (as they were often called) on the present Court. Yet the traditional form of court packing by adding a justice (or two?) did not seem sufficient, because many of the important decisions had been unanimous or by substantial majorities. FDR, frustrated by having had no opportunity to name a justice in his first term, characteristically sifted his choices and guarded his cards.

Meanwhile, the campaign for reelection contained plenty of presidential rhetoric assaulting the tyranny of the "old order" and urging a modern approach to the Constitution. The departmentalist disagreement between the branches about the contours of the Constitution was evident, but FDR advanced no remedy beyond his retention in office. He was unwilling to confront the Court too directly and unready to press a particular plan for reforming it. His oblique attack surely reflected his understanding that the American public generally had considerable esteem for the Court as an institution, even when disagreeing with its decisions. The cost of FDR's muted approach was that any mandate he received from the election would not signify popular support for any specific change in the Court.

The president personally and the New Deal generally certainly did garner mandates from FDR's landslide victory in 1936, which swept large Democratic majorities into both houses of Congress and fed Roosevelt's tendency to hubris.[80] Since early in the year he had been referring to himself as the people's tribune in an explicit comparison to Andrew Jackson. Now he said that he had been the issue in the campaign, and having made no promises, he was free to act as he chose. Unfortunately, it was in this expansive atmosphere that Homer Cummings had a bright idea. He realized that Woodrow Wilson's attorney general had crafted a plan to expand the size of the federal judiciary.[81] Best of all, the plan's author was James McReynolds, now one of the conservative stalwarts on the Supreme Court. Cummings brought the idea to the president, who endorsed it. Neither man discussed it with anyone else in the cabinet or anyone in Congress.

In February 1937, the president sprung the court-packing plan on the nation in a radio address, stunning everyone with its scope and implications—and with the fact that there had been no warning of it during the campaign.[82] Whenever any lower court judge or Supreme Court justice reached the age of seventy, had served for at least ten years, and did not retire, the president would be authorized to appoint another judge to that court.[83] The Supreme Court could reach a maximum of fifteen members. The plan was a cumbersome and excessive response to the current struggle with the Court.

FDR offered a transparently dishonest rationale for the bill. He explained that promoting judicial efficiency was his purpose—the courts needed more judges to discharge their caseload. As delicately as possible, he also suggested that judicial capacity declines with age. Nowhere did he say that he meant to alter the direction of the Court's decisions with a flood of new justices, and no one did he fool.

The plan was in trouble from the start. Having failed to gather support in advance, the president tried to force the bill through Congress, clumsily using the lever of patronage to try to keep the legislators in line. Conservatives who detested and feared FDR mobilized and found allies in his Democratic opponents, especially in the South. Even the president's natural allies were deeply discomfited. Passage of the bill would set a precedent for manhandling the Court that could someday profit their adversaries. It was not fanciful to suggest that the rule of law itself was at stake. In Congress, hostile and extended hearings on the bill paraded the arguments of the opposition. A letter from Chief Justice Hughes arrived, demolishing the president's fabricated efficiency claims.

In March, the president belatedly gave a fireside chat that revealed the actual impetus for the plan. He said that the Court had set itself up as a "super-legislature" that read concepts into the Constitution that were never there. Therefore, the nation "must take action to save the Constitution from the Court and the Court from itself." He called for justices with "a present-day sense of the Constitution." Remarking that the Constitution "is what the Justices say it is rather than what its framers or you might hope it is," he was indirectly making a departmentalist offer to substitute his interpretations for those of the sitting justices. Disclaiming any intent to appoint puppets, however, he promised to seek judges who would not override Congress on policy issues.[84] There was much force to these arguments, and they might have earned the president an extra justice or two from Congress, but an increase of up to six was going too far.

Into the midst of the controversy, the Supreme Court dropped a bombshell of its own. In late March, it began issuing a series of decisions that *upheld* state and federal social legislation.[85] First came a case allowing state minimum wage regulation and overruling a crabbed decision from the year before.[86] Then major decisions upheld the National Labor Relations Act and the Social Security Act.[87] The Court's retreat, known ever since as the "switch in time that saved nine," was not actually a response to the court-packing plan. The crucial votes of the justices in these cases had occurred in December, before announcement of the plan.[88] Instead, the switch appears to have been caused by the landslide outcome in the 1936 election. The election's sharp repudiation of the "old order" had moved Justice Roberts and Chief Justice Hughes into a new majority for upholding the statutes.

The Court's retreat from activism would prove to endure for many decades, but no one could know that in 1937. The justices might have made a tactical withdrawal until the furor subsided. Still, the new decisions took much of the remaining steam out of the plan. And when one of the conservative justices announced his retirement in May, finally giving FDR an appointment opportunity, the outcome was clear. The Senate Judiciary Committee wrote the obituary for the court-packing plan in a very hostile report, condemning it for "applying force to the judiciary."[89]

Franklin Roosevelt's own assessment of the court-packing debacle was that he had "lost the battle but won the war."[90] It appears, however, that he won the war before he lost the battle. Popular pressure on the Court as expressed in a national election is a better basis for judicial reconsideration than presidential threats. FDR once said that the Constitution "was a layman's document, not a lawyer's contract."[91] He also said that the Constitution is worthy of reverence "not because it is old, but because it is ever new."[92] The national debate over the fate of the "old order" that occurred in 1936 resulted in a people's updating of their Constitution, one that would last for generations.

Yet the president's victory was ultimately contingent and temporary. The Court's about-face in 1937 ended whatever hope there was for a constitutional amendment ratifying the New Deal vision of federal power.[93] Someday the constitutional battle could—and would—be renewed. Meanwhile, President Roosevelt went on to recast the Supreme Court by making transformative appointments to it.[94] The eight nominations he enjoyed in the remainder of his long term of office were almost all strong New Dealers; their influence on American constitutional law lasted for decades.

The president's defeat over the court-packing plan resulted in unanticipated collateral damage to the presidency. On the eve of sending the plan to Congress, Roosevelt submitted an important bill to reorganize the sprawling executive branch.[95] A study group had recommended centralizing the executive, by integrating the independent regulatory commissions into cabinet departments where they could be supervised by the president, for example.[96] In the superheated atmosphere of the Court fight, the reorganization bill was unfairly tarred as the "dictator bill." That doomed it. In the late 1930s, real dictators stalked Europe; the imagery of an American version was unfair to FDR but too powerful to overcome.[97]

Two years later a weak substitute passed, granting the president some reorganization authority subject to close congressional control, and exempting the independent agencies. Roosevelt then issued an executive order creating the Executive Office of the President and moving the Bureau of the Budget into it from Treasury. This action began building the organizational skeleton for the modern presidency, but an opportunity for broader consolidation of the executive branch had been lost.[98]

In another organizational step with long-term consequences, Roosevelt bifurcated his legal hierarchy by creating the office of White House Counsel.[99] FDR's attorneys general had usually demonstrated the detachment from political ends that is intrinsic to a lawyer's professional duties. Having chafed under this constraint, the president created an in-house counsel, not subject to Senate confirmation, who could be expected to provide fully sympathetic legal advice. The existence of the counsel has produced tensions with the Department of Justice ever since. Now presidents enjoy the opportunity, so appealing to FDR himself, of playing off one legal adviser against another, in search of the most welcome view of the Constitution and statutes.

First Steps beyond Our Borders[100]

During most of the 1930s, while the attention of Americans was held by the crisis of the domestic Depression, foreign affairs barely registered as a national priority. In his first term, Franklin Roosevelt mostly shared the people's inattention. In his inaugural address, he reversed his earlier call for the United States to join the League of Nations but promised benignly to be a good neighbor to other nations. He soon ignored even this bromide, however, by wrecking the London Economic Conference, which was convened in 1933 to pursue currency stability. FDR, in the process of freeing American monetary policy from the confining gold standard, told American delegates that he would not support meaningful stability measures. The effect was to end international cooperation in response to the worldwide Depression, as the United States and other nations shrank into their own protective shells.

The primary accomplishments of Franklin Roosevelt's second term were in foreign policy, not domestic. By his second inaugural, the enduring legislation of the New Deal was in place, and the collapse of the court-packing plan soon left his relationship with Congress in disarray. The story of the second term is that of a president successfully educating and nudging the American people and their Congress toward an increasing commitment to international engagement on the side of the Allies, even though the risk of involvement in another devastating world war was evident.

As the 1930s unfolded, the gathering menace of the Nazis and the Japanese Empire impressed the president. Sharing his cousin Theodore's international outlook and possessing his own cosmopolitan set of contacts, FDR found himself at odds with prevailing sentiment among the American people. Although he believed that national security demanded international engagement, a substantial majority of the public was hardening into an uncompromising isolationism. The twenties had seen deep disillusionment with the Wilsonian values that had led to American involvement in World War I. To many, it now seemed that the war had been a mistake initiated by excessive interdependence with the Allies. As Europe staggered toward another cataclysm, American isolationists stood guard to prevent another slide into the morass.

Franklin Roosevelt inherited a traditional foreign policy apparatus centered on the State Department. He left a greatly expanded establishment that included several of his characteristic ad hoc and overlapping creations, such as the Office of Strategic Services (the precursor of the Central Intelligence Agency). The creation of these new units that reported directly to him enhanced the president's control of both policy and information as compared to the ponderous and often leaky bureaucracy at State. FDR decided all major foreign policy issues personally. His secretary of state, the Tennessee politico Cordell Hull, held office for all twelve years of the presidency but enjoyed only limited influence. Hull clashed with his oily and patrician undersecretary, Sumner Welles, who often superseded him at the president's side. Meanwhile, Harry Hopkins served as the president's minister without portfolio, carrying his personal communications secretly to foreign leaders in a way reminiscent of Wilson's Colonel House.

FDR early displayed his taste for personal initiative in his negotiations for recognition of the Soviet Union. To avoid anticommunist hardliners in the State Department, the president conducted the negotiations himself in the form of an exchange of letters with Soviet foreign minister Maxim Litvinov that dealt with such complex matters as the settlement of claims held by citizens of either nation against the other. Congress voiced no objection, and the Supreme Court subsequently upheld the president's unilateral power to settle claims in the process of recognizing a revolutionary government.[101] Thus, almost 150 years after George Washington first entered an executive agreement, the Supreme Court endorsed the constitutionality of the practice. Given the accumulated weight of executive branch precedent and congressional acquiescence in the practices of recognition and claims settlement, it would have been difficult indeed for the Court to override so much history.

President Roosevelt did honor his good neighbor pledge in Latin America, where he was soon highly regarded. Herbert Hoover's goodwill had paved the way. In 1933, FDR disavowed the (Theodore) Roosevelt Corollary to the Monroe Doctrine by stating that the United States opposed armed intervention in the hemisphere.[102] Showing that he was serious, he withdrew remaining troops in Central America and refused appeals to intervene in Cuba and Mexico.

Roosevelt's reading of the Constitution's foreign policy powers and their concentration in the presidency went beyond even Wilson's. FDR's precedents would eventually provide the constitutional underpinning for the emergence of the United States as a superpower after the war. At the beginning, the primary technique he used to promote a broader conception of America's role in the world was aggressive statutory interpretation, often embodied in executive orders. Appropriately enough, this tactic owed much to precedents set by Theodore Roosevelt's willingness to find enough elasticity in statutes to promote his own values. In FDR's long tenure he issued more than thirty-five hundred executive orders on a wide variety of subjects, the most by any president.[103]

Ironically, as FDR turned to foreign policy he found an ally in his erstwhile nemesis, the Supreme Court. *United States v. Curtiss-Wright Export Corp.*[104] was a harbinger of the Court's change of course. The Court's holding in the case is no longer controversial; instead, it has become a fundamental precept of modern constitutional analysis. In approving the constitutionality of a statute delegating power to the president to stop some foreign arms sales, the Court decided that it is constitutionally permissible for Congress to grant the executive more discretion in foreign policy than in the domestic realm. That sensible precedent confined the implications of *Schechter Poultry* and liberated both Congress and the president to deal with the international crises soon to come.

The Court's opinion by Justice Sutherland had another, more startling aspect as well, one that has caused constitutional controversy ever since. In a discussion that was not necessary to its decision and therefore not formally binding, the Court described the president's constitutional foreign policy powers in sweeping terms. It referred to

the very delicate, plenary, and exclusive power of the President as the sole organ of the Federal Government in the field of international relations—a power which does not require as a basis for its exercise an act of Congress, but which, of course, like every other governmental power, must be exercised in subordination to the applicable provisions of the Constitution.

Both as professor and president, Woodrow Wilson would certainly have agreed with this formulation. Many presidents had taken initiatives in foreign affairs without asking Congress for authority, consulting it in advance, or, at times, even informing it afterward.

The Court's endorsement of these precedents encompassed several ambiguities. Referring to "exclusive" power implies that Congress cannot control it. But subordination to "applicable" constitutional provisions could mean that the general legislative powers of Congress are controlling or only that specific limitations such as advice and consent to treaties pertain. The characterization of the president as the "sole organ" of American foreign policy alluded to John Marshall's famous argument in Congress during the Adams administration. The phrase could mean that the president alone determines the policy. More modestly, it might mean that as head of state the president communicates to other nations policy that may be generated by Congress. (Marshall meant it in the latter sense.) Thus this celebrated passage contains what the reader wants to find in it.

From that day to this, presidents searching for justification of their actions have hummed the *Curtiss-Wright* hymn to executive power. For Franklin Roosevelt, however, the immediate problem of his second term was not one of employing possibly overbroad statutory grants but rather one of evading obviously restrictive neutrality legislation.

Overcoming Neutrality

Congress has not often tied the president's hands in foreign affairs. Yet between 1935 and 1939, Congress enacted and President Roosevelt signed a series of restrictive statutes that attempted to guarantee American neutrality in the escalating conflicts around the world.[105] The legislation tried to avert the perceived mistakes that had drawn the United States into World War I—lending money to belligerents, treating them unequally, and risking American ships to submarines. Like generals, however, legislatures often make the mistake of trying to fight the last war. Because some of the statutes forbade American aid to any belligerent nation, they benefited aggressors attacking weak nations that the president wanted to protect.

Franklin Roosevelt administered the neutrality acts to suit his own purpose of attempting to avoid war by deterring the aggressive regimes in Germany, Italy, and Japan. Consequently, he complied grudgingly and often minimally with the statutory restrictions until the outbreak of war in Europe gave him an opportunity to interpret his faithful execution duty to harmonize yesterday's policies with today's conditions.

The 1935 Neutrality Act required an embargo on arms sales to all belligerents whenever the president found that a state of war existed. FDR unhappily applied the act to Italy's attack on Ethiopia. But after he declined to do so for the Spanish Civil War, on grounds that the act did not apply to internal conflicts, Congress overrode him with an amendment. In 1937, as isolationist opinion grew, Congress added restrictions on bank loans to belligerents. In a compromise, however, Congress allowed the export of goods other than munitions on a "cash-and-carry" basis.[106] To avoid benefiting Japan, though, Roosevelt declined to apply the cash-and-carry provisions to the Sino-Japanese conflict on the pretext that Japan had not declared war on China.

In September 1939, Europe went to war, and the president, after an immediate declaration of neutrality, had to invoke the embargo against both the Allies and the Axis nations. Later that month, FDR called Congress into special session and received the Neutrality Act of 1939, which repealed the arms embargo and allowed belligerents to purchase war goods on the cash-and-carry basis. Because Britain and France still had a transatlantic trade and Germany and Italy did not, the modified policy let the United States begin its role as the "arsenal of democracy." Congress was emerging from its isolationist shell, but slowly. The president was dismayed by the woeful unpreparedness of the United States for war but could do little about it until Congress supplied the funds to upgrade the military. Roosevelt said he was "walking on eggs."[107]

In the spring of 1940, the fall of France to the Nazis finally brought home to many Americans the presence of real danger to their security. The threat was palpable to the president.[108] Calling for a major expansion of the military, he told a joint session of Congress that Americans must "recast their thinking about national protection."[109] Public and congressional sentiment was shifting: Congress provided the requested funds and authorized the first peacetime draft in American history.[110]

Saying he wanted to promote "national solidarity at a time of world crisis," Roosevelt installed two internationalist Republicans in his cabinet, the venerable Henry Stimson at the War Department and Frank Knox at the Navy Department.[111] This step did not form a true coalition government, however, because the two officers reported to the president, not their party. The experiment proved successful—both men served effectively and cooperatively in the difficult times to come.

More momentously, FDR decided to breach the two-term limit that had stood as precedent since George Washington. Throughout the second term, endless speculation over the president's reelection intentions pleased Roosevelt by keeping everyone guessing and blocking potential party rivals from emerging. By 1940, the two-term tradition appeared to have attained the sacred status of its originator, but Roosevelt was ready to break the mold. Characteristically, he did so deviously, without ever directly asking for and justifying his request for a third term. Instead, he allowed supporters to manipulate the Democratic convention that summer, producing a "draft" of the president that he graciously accepted.[112] The conventional explanations of the decision for a third term are that Roosevelt was unwilling to step aside during a world crisis and that he saw no available successor who could be relied on to preserve the New Deal.[113] Perhaps so, but FDR also found it very difficult to imagine anyone other than himself as president. The third-term issue was prominent throughout the fall campaign; Roosevelt's clear but not landslide victory over Wendell Wilkie confirmed his claim to be the best candidate to help the nation weather the coming storm.

As the American people and their representatives eased toward supporting preparedness, the British presented an urgent need. With the Nazis directly across the English Channel and invasion preparations visibly underway, Britain needed immediate naval help. Winston Churchill, newly anointed as prime minister, sent a message to Roosevelt with a list of "immediate needs," including "the loan of forty or fifty of your older destroyers to bridge the gap" until new naval construction in Britain could bolster defense.[114] FDR replied that he would need statutory authority to send them.

The wily Churchill may have been less interested in the ships themselves than in entangling the two nations "beyond possibility of separation and divorce."[115] In fact, both Roosevelt and Churchill knew that the destroyers "had more psychological and political utility than they had naval value."[116] They were creaky relics of World War I that would take months to refit for action. Hence, large issues of statesmanship rather than mundane ones of military supply lay at the heart of the destroyer proposal.[117] The blossoming direct relationship between Roosevelt and Churchill was fostered by their many shared values—and also, ironically, by the presence of the arch Nazi appeaser Joseph Kennedy as the American ambassador in London. Both national leaders detested and avoided Kennedy, drawing them closer to each other.[118]

For both legal and political reasons, however, FDR could not simply accede to the proposal, no matter how much he favored helping the British. The neutrality legislation appeared to stand in the way. A provision banning transfer of ships that were essential to national defense signified that America's own security could not be disregarded—sending warships to an ally would undermine our own defense capacity. Moreover, although American isolationism was softening, it would remain a potent force until the attack on Pearl Harbor. FDR was entering his tense reelection campaign for an unprecedented third term and did not relish providing ammunition for his opponents.

For legal advice, the president turned to his gifted attorney general, Robert Jackson, who was as close to FDR personally as anyone was allowed to come.[119] Jackson informally advised the president that statutory authorization would be necessary for any gift, loan, or sale of warships to Britain. When the cabinet met to consider the issue, Knox broached the idea of trading the old destroyers for some British naval bases. This proposal changed Jackson's mind, because it would strengthen rather than impair American defenses.

The president then informed the attorney general that he had decided to make the destroyer deal by an executive agreement instead of a statute.[120] Jackson concurred that a combination of the commander in chief power and the foreign affairs powers would supply the necessary authority. "On the basis of this advice, which is what Roosevelt wanted to hear, he decided to complete the deal, and then and only then tell Congress."[121] Roosevelt would be relying on the recent precedent of recognizing the Soviet Union by executive agreement and the Supreme Court's endorsement of that action. The contexts were different, but no clear precedent stood in the way.

On September 3, 1940, Roosevelt announced that he had made an executive agreement to send Great Britain fifty destroyers in return for long-term leases on some British bases in the western Atlantic and the Caribbean. Before doing so, he grumbled that "he might get impeached for what he was about to do."[122] As he expected, there was sharp criticism of the deal's legality.[123] There was certainly a risk to American neutrality. Churchill later wrote that Germany would have been justified in declaring war in response to the deal. But a strong majority of the American people approved of it.[124] The president had won the political battle.

Jackson provided an official opinion supporting the use of an executive agreement to trade destroyers for bases.[125] After review, editing, and approval by the president, the opinion was sent to Congress and released to the public. Jackson's opinion said that the president's role as commander in chief carried a "responsibility to use all constitutional authority which he may possess to provide adequate bases" for the military. In addition, world conditions "forbid him to risk any delay that is constitutionally avoidable." Jackson then turned to "that control of foreign relations which the Constitution vests in the President as a part of the Executive function." He quoted the Supreme Court's broad language in *Curtiss-Wright* but relied on it in only a limited and tentative way. Conceding that the president's foreign affairs powers are "not unlimited," he emphasized the traditional distinction between agreements that create future commitments involving legislation, which would ordinarily require a treaty, and those that do not create any extended commitments, such as the destroyer deal.

The attorney general also found sufficient statutory authority, although it took some strained construction to reach that conclusion. He concluded that the trade was legal under the statute forbidding transfer of ships that were essential to national defense because trading them for the British bases "will strengthen rather than impair the total defense of the United States." That was correct, but other statutory arguments were more labored.

Both Roosevelt and Jackson surely knew that the destroyer deal would be extremely provocative to Germany. The whole point of the neutrality laws was to avoid such risks of war. The opinion threaded its way through the letter of the statutory restrictions, with mixed success. What FDR and Jackson ignored was the spirit of the statutes. The president had decided to skirt the edges of the neutrality laws in an effort to aid the British.

It may be that the destroyer deal was a "rather circumspect application of the Locke-Jefferson-Lincoln doctrine" of emergency power.[126] Still, on the constitutional side, Roosevelt's loose interpretation of his military and foreign affairs powers could be adapted to many other circumstances—and would be.[127] And the president's willingness to minimize statutory restrictions, which was reminiscent of Theodore Roosevelt's cavalier treatment of the public land statutes, showed how difficult it could be for Congress effectively to confine an aggressive executive with legislation.

The president continued to nudge Congress toward his point of view. At FDR's prompting, the Lend-Lease Act of 1941 repealed the cash-and-carry provisions of 1939 and allowed the president to procure any item needed for the defense of any country that was vital to American interests and then to sell, lend, or lease it to that nation as he saw fit. Lend-Lease would prove to be the great engine of supply to the Allies in the coming war. In a last burst of caution, the act provided that nothing in it authorized naval convoys, whereupon Stimson and Knox asserted that the president's commander in chief power would allow convoying.[128]

The undeclared naval war in the Atlantic, "the War before the War," ensued.[129] Like General Jackson in Florida, President Roosevelt engaged in some quite offensive "defense."[130] In May 1941, the president proclaimed an "unlimited national emergency," thereby activating ninety-nine statutes granting the executive special powers.[131] Soon Roosevelt moved from naval patrols to outright escorting of convoys, on the premise that authority to supply the Allies implied the power to get the supplies safely to the buyers. He steadily expanded the defense perimeter of the United States eastward, eventually sending troops to Greenland and Iceland.

In September 1941, after a torpedo attack on an American destroyer, the president ordered the Navy to hunt U-boats. More clashes followed, including the loss of a destroyer. Churchill's later report that Roosevelt told him he "would wage war, but not declare it" rings true.[132] During this period, the president was devious and secretive, gauging public opinion. Like both Polk and Lincoln, he was calibrating his provocations of a future enemy. In late November, the president and his aides discussed "how we should maneuver them into the position of firing the first shot without allowing too much danger to ourselves."[133] In the faraway North Pacific, a fleet was assembling to fire the shot.

As American neutrality slowly eroded after the outbreak of war in Europe in 1939, President Roosevelt formed and implemented a secret alliance with Great Britain.[134] The United States shared the fruits of British intelligence, which gave FDR information on Hitler's plans and the activities of Nazi agents in the United States. Returning the favor, FDR supplied the British with vital intelligence that helped them find and sink the *Bismarck*.[135] The president engaged in secret war planning exercises with the British, which led to agreement on a "Europe first" strategy in the event of a two-front war. This vastly important decision was unknown to Congress or the American public. In August 1941, FDR met with Churchill in Newfoundland, where they issued the Atlantic Charter, a broad set of general principles upon which the two nations agreed.

Given their naval interests, it cannot surprise that both Theodore and Franklin Roosevelt were alert to the Japanese threat in the Pacific. In his first week in office, FDR warned the cabinet of the possibility of war with Japan; he used early NRA funds to build warships.[136] During the thirties, as Japan moved from purloining Manchuria to invading China proper, American policy increasingly tried to cabin Japanese aggression.[137] Toward the end of the decade, the Roosevelt administration terminated the 1911 commercial treaty with Japan.

As tension with Japan escalated, Roosevelt imposed trade embargoes in stages under his statutory authority to hold back commodities vital to national defense. He moved from scrap metal and aviation gasoline to all steel and then all oil. In July 1941, he froze Japanese assets in the United States under a World War I statute, producing a complete barrier to trade. Japan began planning to strike back.

During the neutrality period, Franklin Roosevelt took the lead in educating the American public about world affairs. Amid all his maneuvers and obfuscations, he still delivered the primary message that the nation must act abroad to be safe at home. That judgment has been the basis of American globalism ever since. With the perfect wisdom of hindsight, later Americans have seen isolationism as a foolish blindness to foreign perils. Congress, blamed for embodying the foolishness, suffered a long-standing loss of respect for its foreign policy expertise, and presidents enjoyed lasting benefits derived from FDR's greater vision.[138] Thus the real power of a branch of government depends in part on the historical reputation of those who inhabit it.

Not a Strong Civil Libertarian[139]

Although he lacked Woodrow Wilson's self-righteousness, Franklin Roosevelt was no friend of civil liberties.[140] He combined general insensitivity to such matters with occasional outbursts of outright repression. "He supported [civil liberties] in the abstract, but not when they got in his way."[141] Although his suppression and prosecution of free speech was not nearly as widespread and systematic as the World War I precedent, it was unnecessary in a war that enjoyed great popular support. In the greatest blot on his presidency, FDR ordered the mass internment of Japanese Americans in World War II without the slightest justification. Roosevelt's unconstitutional internment stands as one of the gravest breaches of the duty of faithful execution in the nation's history.

As storm clouds gathered over Europe in 1937, the sorry career of the House Un-American Activities Committee (HUAC) began. Initially chaired by Martin Dies of Texas, HUAC soon earned its spurs for distorting facts and blasting reputations. In the early years, it happily pursued communists and fascists alike. Like several of his successors, President Roosevelt was ambivalent about the committee, which was busily impugning some of his own enemies. Nor could he be seen to intervene in the internal affairs of Congress. Accordingly, he practiced "the rhetoric of condemnation and the politics of appeasement."[142] The seeds of much future unhappiness were being sown.

Within the executive branch, in 1936 FDR secretly authorized J. Edgar Hoover of the Federal Bureau of Investigation to investigate suspected fascists and communists within the United States, even though in the wake of the World War I abuses Attorney General Harlan Fiske Stone had warned against assigning the FBI to policing loyalty. Consummately able to protect his own power, Hoover kept his assembly of extensive files on suspect individuals and groups secret to avoid criticism. From time to time, Roosevelt sent Hoover the names of those opposing his foreign policy. More substantial justification for investigation came from intelligence about German fifth column activities in the United States.[143]

In 1940, Congress enacted a sedition act for modern times. The Alien Registration Act, known as the Smith Act, required all aliens to register with the government and forbade anyone to advocate overthrowing any government in the United States by force.[144] The president declined to veto the bill, saying that its ban on speech was not an improper encroachment on civil liberties given world conditions. There were only two prosecutions under the Smith Act during the war because all three of FDR's attorneys general opposed it. Thus, in contrast to the Wilson administration, the president's subordinates resisted his excesses instead of themselves running amok.

After Francis Biddle replaced Robert Jackson at Justice, Roosevelt ominously wondered whether Biddle "was 'tough enough' to deal with the subversive element."[145] The president hectored Biddle to prosecute dissent, repeatedly asking when he would bring prosecutions: "He was not much interested in . . . the constitutional right to criticize the government in wartime. He wanted this anti-war talk stopped."[146] Yielding, Biddle eventually prosecuted the ludicrous William Pelley, a fascist leader and admirer of Hitler, under the Espionage Act for false statements interfering with the military.[147]

In 1942, under pressure from the press and the president, Biddle indicted thirty American fascist leaders, charging them under the Espionage Act and the Smith Act with a conspiracy to undermine the morale of the military.[148] Roosevelt even pursued Father Charles Coughlin, the radical radio priest who attacked FDR and praised Hitler. The president ordered Coughlin's journal (with a circulation of over a million) barred from the mail, putting it out of business.

Although Franklin Roosevelt stayed mostly in the shadows as the Japanese American internment was planned and executed in 1942, he bears full responsibility for it.[149] Perhaps surprisingly, in the immediate aftermath of Pearl Harbor the West Coast was relatively calm. Then the Japanese Empire brutally overran the Philippines and other American and Allied possessions in the Pacific. Long-standing racial hostility against the Japanese population on the West Coast, fueled by greed for their property and hysterical press coverage of false reports of sabotage and espionage, put pressure on the western congressional delegations and the military to remove the threat by relocating the people.

Neither military nor civilian officers sufficiently resisted this pressure or carefully probed its factual basis. General John DeWitt, a small-minded man who commanded the western defenses, deeply imbibed the rising hysteria in the West, crediting every crazy rumor of impending sabotage. The secretary of war, Henry Stimson, had the gravitas to curb excesses. For a while he demurred to a mass evacuation on constitutional grounds. Those grounds were obvious. Although some of the Japanese were aliens, most were American citizens, born in the United States. Both citizens and aliens were constitutionally entitled to equal protection, due process of law, and the writ of habeas corpus.

Attorney General Biddle also objected to evacuations as unconstitutional, calling them "ill-advised, unnecessary, and unnecessarily cruel."[150] Reports from J. Edgar Hoover at the FBI cast serious doubt on the military necessity arguments. The FBI had arrested about two thousand Japanese aliens soon after Pearl Harbor; these were the known threats to security. Biddle told Stimson there was no evidence of any plans for attacks or sabotage.

Yet as time went by, subordinate officers in the War Department, including DeWitt and Assistant Secretary John McCloy, put increasing pressure on Stimson and Biddle to approve some form of evacuation of the Japanese Americans. In early 1942, DeWitt's "Final Report" called for mass evacuation, laid out various unsupported scenarios of sabotage and espionage, called the Japanese "an enemy race," and even asserted that "the very fact that no sabotage has taken place to date is a disturbing and confirming indication that such action will be taken."[151] It was not a document that deserved deference from anyone.

Secretary Stimson sent President Roosevelt a memo asking whether he supported various options, including extensive evacuations. Stimson tried to make an appointment with FDR, who was "too busy" to see him.[152] The president was either stalling or evading responsibility for the decision. FDR eventually responded by telephone to Stimson to "go ahead in the line [he] thought best" but to "be as reasonable as you can." The president wanted to regard the evacuation question as one of military necessity, not one of fundamental rights of citizens and others.[153] In fact, there was no necessity, and constitutional rights were manifest.

The War Department drafted a proposed executive order to authorize evacuations, the Justice Department approved it, and Roosevelt signed it.[154] The order was not discussed in cabinet "except in a desultory fashion."[155] FDR thought that in wartime, he could take any action he thought necessary to defend the nation.[156] Yet he never probed the factual basis for the order, nor did he consult General George Marshall or other senior military officers. Aside from DeWitt, most advocates of evacuation were civilians.

Congress soon ratified the order by enacting a brief and thinly deliberated statute that made violating military relocation orders a crime.[157] Neither the executive order nor the statute mentioned Japanese Americans. Both simply allowed the War Department to control the movement of individuals within designated military zones. Nor did they mention internment, although the program evolved into long-term incarceration after inland western governors heatedly refused to resettle the Japanese in their states.

Eventually, the Supreme Court upheld the evacuation and internment orders.[158] The majority opinions accepted the executive's claims of military necessity at face value, despite clear signals in the record that they were baseless. For that reason, the internment cases have frequently been cited for the proposition that the Supreme Court will not challenge the executive during a war, although the Court sometimes finds more courage afterward.

The president never expressed any regret about his approval of the program, although his shadowy role, like the lack of explicitness in the order and statute, may reveal a certain sense of shame. Roosevelt had long considered the Japanese to be unsuited to assimilation in the United States and was receptive to baseless claims about the threat they posed to security.[159] This moral blind spot haunts his legacy still. His cabinet officers showed more sensitivity to the legal issues and to the terrible precedent that was being set than he did, but without assistance from the president they did not hold out against strong and persistent forces calling for removal of the Japanese Americans.

Another episode in the early stages of World War II carried an important civil liberties precedent for the future. This is the tragicomic story of the Nazi saboteurs.[160] Their trial by military commission in 1942 later served as a precedent for President George W. Bush's order concerning military trials of suspected terrorists. Yet it was no fit model for anyone to emulate.

In June 1942, eight German soldiers (one of them a naturalized American citizen) were landed off Long Island and Jacksonville by submarines. They buried their uniforms and went inland bent on sabotaging industrial facilities. Their blundering soon led to their capture. What to do with them? Along with their uniforms, they had shed the legal protections of prisoner of war status. They could be tried as ordinary criminals, but Attorney General Biddle concluded that they could not be convicted of major crimes.[161]

An alternative offered itself: trial by military commission. Spies and saboteurs had suffered that fate ever since General Washington hanged British Major Andre for spying in the Revolutionary War. A military tribunal could act secretly, swiftly, and informally. Biddle soon pressed Secretary of War Stimson to convene a special military commission. The president revealed his own hand by sending Biddle a note expressing his belief in the guilt of the saboteurs and saying the death penalty was "almost obligatory."[162] A memo to FDR from Biddle that day summarized the advantages of a tribunal: that espionage and treason carried the death penalty but probably could not be proved in court, and that the president's order could forbid judicial review. Excluding the courts would not, he advised, unconstitutionally suspend the writ of habeas corpus, since it was "traditional to deny our enemies access to the courts in time of war."[163]

Both men were happily prejudging the case and manipulating the process to ensure their favored outcome. Ordinary federal criminal trials are well insulated against these sins by the executive; military commissions are not.[164] Less than a week after the saboteurs were arrested, FDR issued a proclamation creating a seven-member military tribunal to try them under the law of war.[165] After informal proceedings, the record was to be transmitted directly to the president for his final review. The president's order forbade judicial review. He fumed, "I won't give them up. . . . I won't hand them over to any United States marshal armed with a writ of habeas corpus. Understand?"[166] The long shadow of *Merryman* had fallen over the case.

As the trial proceeded, lawyers for the accused reached the Supreme Court with a petition for a writ of habeas corpus. The Court issued a short opinion upholding the jurisdiction of the military tribunal.[167] The trial concluded with death sentences for all the saboteurs under the law of war against espionage and sabotage. The voluminous record went to Roosevelt, who cannot have studied it in detail. The president approved six of the sentences and reduced the other two to prison terms. Executions followed immediately. President Roosevelt showed little interest in the rule of law in disposing of the saboteurs, and the Supreme Court did little better. Unfortunately, the bad precedent would come to the forefront again.

Conducting a World War

Franklin Roosevelt's challenge as commander in chief in World War II was far more complex than Woodrow Wilson's in World War I. Wilson had kept his stern distance from the Allies, insisting on the separate functioning of the expeditionary force. Roosevelt had to manage close cooperation with the other two members of the "big three," Churchill and Stalin, as they conducted a war over multiple fronts. As in World War I, Congress conferred no unlimited constitutional dictatorship on the president but rather rejected many of FDR's requests while conferring broad authority overall.[168]

Roosevelt rose brilliantly to the immense task.[169] Avoiding Wilson's mistake of excessive partisanship in wartime, he had made bipartisanship integral with the appointments of Stimson and Knox. As leader of the military, he had the granitic and gifted General George Marshall, who soon persuaded him to create the Joint Chiefs of Staff as a management tool. The president knew that efficiency gains from creating the JCS would come at a potential cost to his own power, because a unified military front could more easily challenge or manage their commander in chief than could the traditionally separate service chiefs.

The United States entered the war with a clear strategy because of the "Europe first" decision that Roosevelt had reached with the British years before. National outrage sparked by Pearl Harbor tested the strategy's staying power, but it held together in a somewhat compromised form. In 1942, FDR had to balance Stalin's insistent demands for a second front in Europe to relieve pressure on the Soviet Union against Churchill's resistance to a continental invasion that might repeat the agony of World War I. Stalin's position was supported by American Army officers who had the straight-ahead attitude of U. S. Grant, Churchill's by American Navy officers who needed resources for their Pacific war.

In dealing with the powerful personalities around him, FDR "certainly got his way more often" than did Churchill or Stalin.[170] The president approved the North African and Italian campaigns to appease Churchill and to get American troops into action against the Germans and Italians. Then he shifted and pressed successfully for the invasion of France in 1944, finally pleasing Stalin somewhat. Roosevelt's famous personal relationship with Churchill provided a lesson for world history in what an alliance could be. He badly misread Stalin, though, treating him like a Chicago mayor whom he could charm into cooperation. Ironically, a president who always operated behind a mask could not detect a mask even more impenetrable than his own.[171]

The president was comfortable dealing with strong military subordinates. He chose Marshall in part because he would stand up to Churchill, as he did to FDR himself (while always acknowledging who was boss). Moreover, Marshall could control General Douglas MacArthur as well as anyone could.[172] MacArthur did bare his fangs once with Roosevelt. At a meeting with Admiral Chester Nimitz and the president in 1944 to determine strategy for the Pacific war, the general said that if FDR had the temerity to abandon the Philippines, he could expect electoral revenge from the American people. He should have been relieved of command for that, but the president, aware of MacArthur's domestic political support, let him have his photo opportunity wading ashore in triumph.

As the war progressed, the "big three" adjusted their strategy in a series of meetings held far from any prying eyes, including any in the United States Congress. The meetings suited FDR's taste for personal diplomacy. He used Harry Hopkins as his personal envoy to the other two leaders.

As the State Department receded into the background, Secretary Hull was not even invited to the major conferences, and the military took on an enhanced role in forming foreign policy.[173]

After meetings at Casablanca in 1943, Roosevelt stated the central allied war aim, the unconditional surrender of the Axis nations. The announcement met with approval back home. Well aware of the cost of Woodrow Wilson's rigidity, FDR was characteristically pragmatic about his postwar goals. He broadly favored the self-determination of peoples, the end of colonization, free trade, and a world organization to maintain peace. He did know that the United States could not prevent Soviet hegemony in eastern Europe and conceded as much at Yalta near the end of his life. After the Yalta meeting he misled Congress about the status of postwar Poland and kept secret his deal with Stalin to bring the Soviets into the war against Japan.[174]

As World War II wound toward a close, large international rearrangements were in prospect. An important question was whether the United States should enter them through the traditional mechanism of treaties or by the statutory equivalent of congressional-executive agreements.[175] With the reputation of the Senate still in eclipse after the League of Nations debacle following World War I, a serious movement arose to amend the Constitution to replace the treaty mechanism entirely with ordinary statutory process. But the Senate would not likely support submitting such an insult to the states for ratification. President Roosevelt, knowing this and having other things on his mind, simply finessed the issue. Without explanation, he sent the United Nations proposal along as a treaty but submitted the Bretton Woods monetary agreements for passage as a congressional-executive agreement. Congress went along with both, leading to the "triumph of interchangeability" between these constitutional alternatives.[176]

Throughout his presidency, Franklin Roosevelt barely acknowledged his physical disability. Toward the end, he denied his mortality as well. The president was a sick man in 1944, when he almost casually took on a fourth term to finish his work. Democratic Party leaders wanted Vice President Henry Wallace off the ticket because he would lose votes, and because they quailed at the thought of him as president. After an extensive canvass of possible candidates, they settled on Senator Harry Truman, who had a solid record and was "the man who would hurt [the president] least."[177] They knew they were choosing a president as well, but the American public did not.

Like Woodrow Wilson before him, Franklin Roosevelt hid the extent of his decline behind a wall of doctors and obfuscations.[178] By the end of his third term, he could not work for sustained periods. The photos taken at Yalta in early 1945 show a dying man. Still, he soldiered on until he fell, like Lincoln, as one of the last casualties of a war that he had dominated.

PART IV

One Single Man

[President Kennedy] was hoping to be able to meet with [the Executive Committee] early enough to decide on a course of action and then broadcast it to the nation Sunday night. . . . I called the President . . . and told him we were ready to meet with him. It was now up to one single man. No committee was going to make this decision. — Attorney General Robert Kennedy, recounting the Cuban missile crisis of 1962

CHAPTER NINE

Going to Hell

Truman and Eisenhower

The president has the power to keep the country from going to hell.—President Harry Truman, 1952[1]

In April 1945, the weight of the presidency fell suddenly on a singularly unprepared man.[2] Franklin Roosevelt had done nothing to prepare Harry Truman for the probability that he would assume the presidency. The vice president, omitted from the councils of state, was ignorant of the president's thinking about the war's endgame, including his intentions regarding the almost completed atomic bomb. Having masked his disability for so long, Roosevelt had also hidden and denied the signs of impending death at the end. Preparing Truman to assume office would have eroded the president's shield of denial.

Modern vice presidents do not have the luxury of time to adapt to a presidency thrust upon them by the death of a president. As late as 1901, Theodore Roosevelt had months after the McKinley assassination to prepare himself to deal with Congress and the issues of the day. Not so for new presidents after World War II. Yet most presidents continue to hold their vice presidents at a distance, reducing their preparedness. Three reasons probably account for this tendency. First, because vice presidents are chosen to balance a ticket and not to duplicate the presidential candidate, personal and political chemistry may be absent. Second, if the vice president hopes to succeed to the office, a certain rivalry may be present—"soon enough, my friend." Third, and sadly, the constant threat of assassination forces presidents to block out the danger if they are to function. A hovering vice president can provide an unpleasant reminder of the risks. Hence, Truman's unpreparedness may dismay us but should not surprise us.

Harry S Truman was "as straightforward as a sentence without commas."[3] Emblematic of his simplicity was his lack of a middle name—he made do with the initial *S*. Truman was an honest man—and a shrewd enough politician to emerge from the corrupt Kansas City machine without being ruined by it. His varied experience, which included combat in World War I, business, farming, and political service from local government to the Senate, nurtured his innate good judgment. Unlike his predecessor, he did not temporize; he said, "I am here to make decisions."[4] If Roosevelt erred on the side of postponing commitments, his successor erred on the side of rushing them. A prodigious worker, Truman exuded vitality and warmth.

Largely self-educated, Truman read widely and said that each president "ought to know his American history," explaining that if ever there was a "clean break from all that had gone before," the result would be chaos.[5] The new president had absorbed a strong view of executive prerogative from his study of Andrew Jackson and Woodrow Wilson and saw himself as their heir.[6] Sounding rather like Theodore Roosevelt, he proposed to do whatever would be best "for the welfare of all of our people," often referring to the general welfare clause in the Constitution's Preamble and viewing the document overall as "a living force," "a growing thing."[7]

In his first cabinet meeting, President Truman asked everyone to stay on for the time being, welcomed their advice, and said he would make the decisions and would expect their support afterward.[8] The new president wanted to have a cabinet with his own people, free of ties to FDR, but he did not want to proceed abruptly while his predecessor was still being mourned.[9] Some changes were visible right away. Truman did not allow the White House staff to make policy. Disliking FDR's loose administrative style, Truman instilled some discipline, working with the staff of the Bureau of the Budget to conform spending to his policies.[10] Comfortable around strong, accomplished people, Truman eventually brought such luminaries as Dean Acheson and George Marshall into his cabinet. Yet he was not always a good judge of character and kept some politically damaging cronies around, such as military aide Harry Vaughn.

Truman needed to find an immediate replacement for the secretary of state, the time-serving Edward Stettinius, who was now next in line for the presidency. His choice of James Byrnes was a misstep. Byrnes had expected the vice presidency for himself in 1944 and soon revealed his view that he should be sitting in Truman's chair by ignoring instructions and failing to keep the president fully informed of his activities. Truman, correctly calling Byrnes "able and conniving," did not sack him immediately.[11] The president was not afraid to exert control, however. When Treasury Secretary Henry Morgenthau demanded a role in the upcoming Potsdam conference, Truman refused and accepted his resignation. Soon he had replaced half the cabinet, often with former congressmen. He had the courage to resist patronage pressure on appointments.[12]

Dropping the Bomb

During President Truman's first days in office, he spoke to Congress, reiterating FDR's demand for unconditional surrender of the Axis forces and stating his support for a United Nations.[13] Secretary of War Henry Stimson dropped by to inform him about the atomic bomb project, then nearing its initial test firing.[14] Truman accepted a suggestion to create a select committee to study the implications of using the bomb. The committee, consisting of eight distinguished citizens chaired by Stimson and aided by an advisory group of physicists, recommended use of the bomb in hopes that the shock would end the war.

Of his decision to use the bomb against Japan, Truman later said: "I regarded the bomb as a military weapon and never had any doubt that it should be used."[15] Given the available options, this conclusion was nearly inevitable.[16] As American forces neared Japan, casualties were soaring. Estimated casualties for the planned invasion of Japan reached a half million. No Japanese unit had surrendered during the war, and there was little evidence Japan would accept defeat now. There was no confidence that a warning demonstration of the unproved atomic technology would be feasible or effective. And the bureaucratic momentum produced by a $2 billion project was immense. In the event, of course, the use of the bombs did end the war, at horrific cost to their victims. It was also the single most far-reaching exercise of the commander in chief power in American history, affecting the course of world history during the entire period of the Cold War.

After the surrender of Germany, Truman, Churchill, and Stalin met in Potsdam to plan for the final assault on Japan and the end of the war.[17] As an Army veteran who had now seen the devastation of Berlin firsthand, Truman knew the power of conventional warfare. He had scant experience in foreign affairs and had not met either Churchill or Stalin. Like

FDR, he took a liking to Stalin and considered him amenable to reasoned negotiation. Apparently, the wolf never bared his teeth. Truman received the promise he most wanted from Stalin, a confirmation of the Soviet commitment to enter the war against the Japanese, but like FDR at Yalta, he got nowhere on his efforts to ensure a democratic future for eastern Europe. Together, the leaders issued the Potsdam Declaration, demanding the unconditional surrender of Japan and promising "prompt and utter destruction" if it were not forthcoming.[18] Soon afterward, the atomic bombs produced both the utter destruction and an almost unconditional surrender, allowing only for retention of the emperor subject to the will of a higher emperor, Allied commander Douglas MacArthur. Truman's first four months in office were a whirlwind.

Giving Them Hell

With war's end, President Truman confronted the domestic effects of rapid demobilization. He soon discovered that the United States was no better prepared to end the war than it had been to begin it.[19] He knew that Congress would likely be a balky partner. Since 1938, a coalition of Republicans and conservative southern Democrats had formed an effective majority to stifle progressive legislation. This coalition would prove extremely durable, holding sway until 1964. As a result, presidents during this period were tempted to avoid Congress by using their executive order power wherever possible.

Throughout his tenure, Truman was quite combative toward Congress. He vigorously employed his power to recommend legislation.[20] Shortly after the war ended, the president sent up a comprehensive program of domestic legislation that included health care and aid to education and housing. Although it met a cool reception, he later resubmitted it repeatedly. When he received a bad bill, he wielded the veto pen enthusiastically. After the Republicans regained control of both houses of Congress in 1946 for the first time since Hoover, there were many bills he disliked. Truman vetoed a total of 250 bills, the third most among all presidents (after FDR and Cleveland). He was overridden twelve times, the most since Andrew Johnson. The overall result was a standoff that left the essential elements of the New Deal in place but not extended.

The feisty president also had an adversarial relationship with the press. Many publishers were conservative; reporters wistfully contrasted FDR's capacity to charm them. At odds with both Congress and the press and lacking his predecessor's radio magic, Truman was quite unpopular with the public during much of his presidency. It is no accident that his popularity at the one moment that counted, Election Day in 1948, resulted from the frenetic whistle-stop campaign in which the people could see the real Harry Truman.

The postwar period saw a record level of strikes, as labor and management fought over the spoils of the great economic boom that was beginning.[21] Emulating Theodore Roosevelt, Truman took a personal role in settling threatened strikes in critical industries. He too adopted an aggressive view of the faithful execution duty by acting to preserve public order without statutory authority any more specific than the reserve power to call up the troops to suppress civil disorders.

The president saw himself as an ally of labor, but he was not willing to tolerate economic chaos. Through White House negotiations, he succeeded in heading off a steel strike. Even more ominously, a national railroad strike threatened to paralyze commerce.[22] To stop the strike, Truman signed an executive order authorizing the government to seize the railroads, a probably illegal tactic that delayed the strike while Truman jawboned both sides at the White House.[23] He could not bring them together, and the ensuing strike caused massive disruption. An angry president informed the cabinet that he would draft striking workers into the Army. When Attorney General Tom Clark objected to the legality of that step, Truman is reported to have said: "We'll draft them and think about the law later."[24]

The president spoke to the nation, warning that he would call out the Army and use it to break the strike. Implicitly accepting Clark's advice, Truman proceeded to make a dramatic address to Congress, asking for legislation authorizing him to draft striking workers. During his speech, the strike settled. Truman's determination had prevailed. The president also ended a disruptive coal strike by obtaining an injunction against the powerful miners' union.

Harry Truman earned a more enduring legacy in the field of civil rights. In early 1948, he sent Congress the first special presidential message on civil rights, stressing that the government had a duty to enforce the sleeping constitutional guarantees of the post–Civil War amendments and calling for comprehensive statutes protecting voting rights, ending poll taxes, and assuring nondiscrimination in travel.[25] Knowing that Congress would not likely comply anytime soon, the president then issued two executive orders forbidding segregation in the military and the civil service.[26] The orders had thin public support, and it took time to implement them fully, but the Korean War would be fought by mostly integrated forces.[27] More important, no president since the Civil War era had taken significant steps to aid black Americans. Later presidents would build on Truman's precedent by issuing a series of antidiscrimination executive orders.[28] His action was one of the sparks that ignited the civil rights movement of the following decades.

Unsurprisingly, Harry Truman was determined to be elected president in his own right. At the convention that nominated him, Truman showed little interest in selecting the vice presidential nominee, notwithstanding his own path to the presidency. Saying that he "never did care much" who ran with him, Truman accepted the party favorite Alben Barkley, an old New Deal warhorse who showed clear signs of coveting the presidency.[29] Thus he continued the casual approach that had produced many presidents, from "his accidency" John Tyler to Truman himself.

Once nominated, Truman strategically called a special session of Congress to press them to enact his program, knowing they would refuse. That set up the whistle-stop campaign that covered almost twenty-two thousand miles, the president saying, "I want to see the people."[30] He ran against the "do-nothing Congress," saying the battle was the special interests against the people. On Election Day the underdog president won by a clear margin over his wooden opponent, Governor Thomas Dewey, and carried his party back to nominal control of both houses of Congress as well.[31]

Although Harry Truman was now safely out of the shadow of Franklin Roosevelt, trouble brewed. Some lax presidential supervision of the White House staff led to scandals involving influence peddling at a government agency. No illegality surfaced, but it was apparent that cronyism was rampant. Like many presidents, Truman viewed attacks on his people as attacks on himself, but he did mount an internal investigation. The air of impropriety surrounding the administration increased when real corruption in tax administration came to light.[32] Amid revelations of bribes and shakedowns by tax collectors, the commissioner of internal revenue and the head of the Justice Department's tax division resigned. Soon after, Truman dismissed Attorney General McGrath for botching and blocking the investigation. The president then took effective action to fire the miscreants and moved federal tax collectors into the civil service to avoid repetition of the problem.

Waging a Global Cold War

World War II fundamentally altered the stature of the United States, which now possessed unmatched military and economic strength. Nevertheless, victory was accompanied by a frightening loss of security because of the emergence of the atomic bomb and long-range delivery systems for it. The challenge was to transform the war's wreckage into "half a world, a free half . . . without blowing the whole to pieces in the process."[33] No one knew how to do that.

Simultaneously empowered and threatened as never before, the postwar United States reacted in two fundamentally new ways.[34] First, the nation abandoned its traditional isolationism in favor of a web of international commitments that contemplated the use of military force around the world. Second, the nation abandoned its traditional practice of full demobilization after a war in favor of creating a permanent military and intelligence establishment that could project force and respond to threats. These developments rejected the warnings of the Constitution's framers against entangling alliances and standing armies, both of which they feared as nursemaids of war and tyranny. The mechanisms of the eighteenth-century Constitution would just have to adapt. Or not.

Before long, the Truman administration "turned traditional U.S. foreign policy assumptions upside down" by abandoning the unilateralism that had been gospel since the time of George Washington in favor of a multilateral approach to assuring national security.[35] Congress provided support in needed statutes, treaty ratifications, and funding, but the impetus came from the executive. National unpreparedness was no longer acceptable. Pearl Harbor, never again.

As a neophyte in foreign policy, Harry Truman had the good judgment to gather a distinguished set of advisers. These figures, who would become known as the establishment, dominated American foreign policy for decades. With Henry Stimson as their exemplar, the group included Averill Harriman, Robert Lovett, George Marshall, Dean Acheson, George Kennan, and James Forrestal.[36] They shared a general worldview that fit well with President Truman's inclinations. The result was a self-sustaining approach to foreign policy and especially to the Soviet Union that would shape the emerging Cold War for its duration. Truman's tendency to see a highly complex world in simple terms, as contrasted with FDR's more nuanced approach, propelled him toward a quite Manichean stance that was captured and confirmed by Winston Churchill's "iron curtain" speech in Truman's presence in 1946.

The core of the emerging policy was a highly pessimistic view of the Soviets and of the prospects for meaningful negotiation with them, which soon took official form in the containment policy first articulated by George Kennan.[37] Containment condemned the appeasement of totalitarian systems that had preceded World War II—reference to Munich quelled potential appeasers as the establishment sought the credibility of the nation's power and commitments. Now it was America's Manifest Destiny to be the worldwide guarantor of freedom from communism. The premises of containment required that the United States possess overwhelming military power and be prepared to use it as needed to halt communist expansion.[38] The doctrine's limits were not evident.

In its early years, the containment policy tended to be rigid. Truman, despising communism, showed little interest in reaching accommodation with the Soviets. Yet Stalin's approach was generally cautious, not seeking war but probing for advantage and leaving openings for negotiation that the administration did not pursue. As the Cold War evolved from an acute to a chronic affliction, American policy makers would eventually learn the advantages of a more subtle set of approaches.

New global responsibilities required new structures for the executive branch.[39] The National Security Act of 1947 was the "Magna Charta of the national security state."[40] Congress unified the armed services under the new Department of Defense, using the Joint Chiefs of Staff as the coordinating mechanism. Within the White House it created the National Security Council, which would contest the State Department for primacy in foreign affairs. And it formed the Central Intelligence Agency, which would soon become a secretive "government within a government."[41] The CIA would operate with few substantive limits on its activities and without detailed accounting to Congress for its expenditures.[42] Adding bureaucracies made the process of forming foreign policy more complex and conflicted, destabilizing old constitutional relationships. Close presidential supervision would be imperative if the new structure were to cohere and succeed.

With help from Congress, President Truman successfully resolved the first crisis of the new era. The governments of both Greece and Turkey were tottering, in danger of collapse and Soviet domination.[43] Told by a senator that he would have to "scare hell" out of the American people to get a military aid package through Congress, Truman responded eagerly.[44] The president announced the Truman Doctrine, saying it must be American policy to support free peoples who were resisting subjugation by "armed minorities or by outside pressures." The columnist Walter Lippmann presciently protested the doctrine's apparent breadth, indiscriminateness, and rejection of diplomacy.[45] Congress approved the aid, and the two governments did not fall. The era of Cold War intervention was under way. Presidents could learn that overselling the communist threat worked with Congress and would rarely err in the opposite direction.

By 1947, as George Marshall became secretary of state, the department began a period of preeminence in making foreign policy, although always under presidential supervision. The Marshall Plan helped to revive the economy of Europe.[46] President Truman, who was deeply involved in crafting the plan, had the grace and good sense to give the credit to the eminent former general to ensure passage in Congress. At a final expenditure of $13.3 billion, this generous gesture made friends and confounded foes, contrasting with the selfish posture of the United States in the aftermath of World War I.

Postwar Palestine presented highly sensitive issues.[47] As the British took their leave, the State of Israel declared its existence in May 1948. The question of recognition produced a heated clash within the Truman administration. The leaders of the establishment, stressing American dependence on Arab oil, counseled holding back, but President Truman forged ahead and accorded Israel immediate de facto recognition. Secretary Marshall, who had bitterly opposed recognition, gave soldierly acquiescence, and the storm passed. To the president, it was the right thing to do for the survivors of the Holocaust, and it served his domestic political interests as well.

A very dangerous crisis followed, as the Soviets blockaded land access to West Berlin in June. Stalin, alarmed by American support for a reinvigorated West Germany, was trying to drive the Allies out of the Berlin enclave to perfect his control over East Germany. The president stood firm: "We stay in Berlin, period."[48] But how? In consultation with Marshall, he chose an approach midway between withdrawing and sending an armed convoy overland.[49] There would be no Munich here. An airlift began to supply Berlin.[50] It went on around the clock for almost a year, with hundreds of daily air missions. Stalin backed down and raised the blockade when he saw that it had become politically counterproductive. Truman's combination of firmness and restraint had prevailed.

In early 1949, Dean Acheson became Truman's last secretary of state, replacing the retiring George Marshall. Having no Edward House or Harry Hopkins, Truman drew close to Acheson. They made an odd couple—the plainspoken midwestern politician and the ultimate establishment figure. But there was great mutual respect and affection. Acheson told the president what he needed to hear, and Truman had enough personal security to listen.[51] This relationship was emblematic of the president's approach to his staff—he was fair and open and prepared to give discretion in return for loyalty. In the end, though, Truman said: "I make American foreign policy."[52]

The Berlin blockade spurred "the most radical U.S. step of the early postwar era," the formation of the North Atlantic Treaty Organization, ratified in 1949.[53] Now the containment policy became international law. In the first military alliance that the nation had entered in peacetime, the signatories agreed that after an attack on any of them, each of them would take "such actions as it deems necessary, including the use of armed force." One hopes that the president took the time to journey out to Mount Vernon to explain it to George Washington.

The year 1949 was a time of international alarums and excursions with long-standing effects, including domestic ones.[54] The Soviet Union proudly exploded its first atomic bomb, ending the brief American monopoly. The communists took over in China. With the Soviets newly empowered and the Chinese newly hostile, Americans wondered how the triumph of the war had turned so sour.[55] Imagining conspiracies, they began the second Red scare.

Adding to the jitters, the administration decided to build the hydrogen bomb, dramatically ratcheting up the arms race.[56] Once again, President Truman was crisply decisive. When told by a study group that the Soviets would eventually build H-bombs, Truman approved development, saying he had no choice. No one could think that the world was adequately under control. The onset of the Korean War raised tensions still higher.

Korea

In June 1950, stunning news arrived that North Korea had suddenly launched a massive invasion into South Korea. The Korean peninsula, which had seemed a strategic backwater, had been omitted from the defense perimeter previously announced by the United States.[57] This naked aggression provoked a vintage response from Harry Truman: "By God, I'm going to let them have it."[58] Cooling down, the president quickly convened a group of his national security advisers (rather than the cabinet) to consider the administration's response.[59] The team included Dean Acheson, Defense Secretary Louis Johnson, JCS chair Omar Bradley, and Averell Harriman as a general troubleshooter. All concurred with the president's instinct that a strong response by the United States was imperative. This was a flagrant border crossing that could not be allowed to stand—it reminded everyone of Hitler's moves in Europe. All thought that Stalin had likely ordered the invasion (in fact, he had merely tolerated the proposal by the chronically addled North Koreans). Cold War imperatives created by newly shouldered American responsibilities for global security were working overtime.

In a series of long meetings over the next few days, President Truman hammered out his position.[60] An initial decision to use air and sea power to protect American dependents in Korea was easy. As North Korean forces swept forward, a consensus developed that air and naval power should also be used to slow the advance but that introduction of ground troops was a much graver step. "In a seemingly routine manner," Truman approved a full commitment of American air and naval forces to defend South Korea.[61] General Bradley suggested waiting a few days to decide about troops. Truman asked the chiefs to ponder it. War momentum was building.

The president then met with congressional leaders and reviewed his decisions so far.[62] They responded rather inconsistently. A senator asked whether the president would request congressional authority for military action in Korea. Truman said he would consider that. After two full days of meetings, the question had not come up within the executive. When the president asked the chair of the Senate Foreign Relations Committee whether he should seek congressional approval, the answer was no. Both inside and outside the meeting, Republican and congressional leaders issued warnings that the president was merely informing Congress of his actions and not truly consulting with it or asking for authorization.[63]

Public reaction to this first military action in Korea was generally favorable.[64] There were cheers on the floor of Congress when the decision to send military aid was announced. The applause may have lulled the administration into thinking that more formal congressional support was unnecessary. Averill Harriman advised President Truman to obtain formal congressional authorization for the intervention in Korea.[65] Secretary

Acheson disagreed because of the need for speedy and flexible response; he urged relying directly on the commander in chief power.

Notwithstanding his background in Congress, Truman tilted toward Acheson's position. The president vividly recalled his constant struggles with enemies in the Senate and did not want to slow the decision-making process. Perhaps equally important, Truman feared that appealing to Congress for authority now would make it harder for future presidents to deal with emergencies. Harriman recalled this stance as characteristic: "He always kept in mind how his actions would affect future presidential authority."[66] One adviser suggested obtaining a congressional resolution for the political support it would provide. This was good advice: as Truman would learn later, unilateral executive action left members of Congress without responsibility and free to find fault.

In a news conference, President Truman argued that the United States was "not at war"; rather, the nation was suppressing "a bandit raid."[67] Taking up a reporter's suggestion, the president agreed that it was a "police action" under the United Nations Charter. This terminology doubtless captured the president's intention to wage a limited war in Korea rather than a general one against China and the Soviet Union.

At the time of Truman's initial use of air and naval power, it may have seemed that the scale of the commitment could be confined in ways that resembled earlier presidential uses of force without declarations of war. There was a crucial difference here, however. Resisting an invasion in force by a modern army in a nation thousands of miles from our shores is very likely to lead to a full-scale war, as this one soon became. Thus the president's initial intervention should have been treated as war in the constitutional sense, requiring authorization by Congress.

Meanwhile, Douglas MacArthur had made a quick tour of Korea. Warning of the imminent collapse of South Korea, he called for bringing in two Army divisions from Japan as quickly as possible. As so often in war, this early estimate of military needs would turn out to be woefully inadequate. When word of the request reached the president on June 30, he immediately approved it without consulting anyone. He later explained: "I just had to act as commander in chief, and I did."[68] Although the fateful decision to commit ground troops was an impulsive decision by an impulsive man, it may also have seemed a natural next step after earlier actions had met general approval.

By this time, the president did have in his pocket a United Nations authorization to use force, approved in a Security Council vote. That would provide him some cover in international law but no domestic constitutional support. No president has treated the presence or absence of UN support as affecting his power under the Constitution, for the simple reason that no president can control the UN and ensure that its endorsement will occur. If the UN declines to act, no president will concede that his constitutional power is thereby diminished.

Again Truman's actions met with initial approval in Congress and the nation. Congress easily approved an emergency appropriation, extended conscription authority, and granted the executive various war powers.[69] Thus the use of force in Korea was eventually, if not initially, a joint action of the branches.

President Truman's decision for unilateral intervention in Korea owed much to his sense of the historical role of the presidency. The State Department sent him a list of precedents for unilateral presidential use of the military. "Truman, impressed by the appearance of precedent and concerned not to squander the power of his office," went forward.[70] In this case, however, the president did not need to forgo prior congressional authorization. This was not an emergency like the outset of the Civil War, when Lincoln had to fight without Congress for a time. Congress could have supplied a speedy and unconfining authorization, as it would do repeatedly in the future. Truman appeared to be worried that formal congressional support would have been delayed or opposed, thus sending embarrassing signals of national division to the enemy. But that is a necessary price of the Constitution's placement of the power to declare war.

The Korean War presented President Truman with two great challenges: he had to overcome both the enemy and his own commanding general, Douglas MacArthur. MacArthur, who had been a general since 1918, was a supreme egotist with a long record of insubordination toward civil authority. His better side, "so truly intelligent, creative, and audacious," clashed with "the part of him that was so vainglorious, selfish, and arrogant."[71]

Initially the war went badly, as American and South Korean forces made a long retreat to the Pusan perimeter.[72] MacArthur then turned the war around with his brilliant but risky flanking landing at Inchon, which Truman had approved. Soon the front lines were back to the 38th parallel, where the conflict had begun. MacArthur pressed to continue the offensive. Without consulting Congress, President Truman made another fateful decision: to expand the objective of the war from expelling the invaders to creating a free and united Korea.[73] Still hoping to avoid drawing the Chinese into the conflict, however, he ordered MacArthur not to use American troops near the Chinese border. This third stage of Truman's unilateral war making in Korea was probably even more important than the first two, because it clearly risked involvement by the Chinese and possibly the Soviets in a regional war.

The general, unmanageable after his dramatic victory at Inchon, swept far north toward the Chinese border along the Yalu, ignoring both his orders and Chinese warnings to stay back.[74] Late in the year, Chinese forces surged into the war, sending the Americans reeling backward until MacArthur's subordinate Matthew Ridgway stabilized the front near the 38th parallel again. A bloody military standoff ensued that lasted until termination of the war in 1953.

As the war settled into stalemate, MacArthur's misbehavior increased.[75] His disagreement with the president was fundamental. The general rejected the concept of limited war and was ready to attack China. He began issuing statements insulting the Chinese and continued to do so after Truman ordered him to desist. At one point MacArthur derailed a presidential peace initiative by mocking the Chinese just as Truman was initiating some sensitive negotiations. Furious, the president awaited the right moment to relieve the general. Revealing the extent to which he had lost his mental balance, MacArthur wanted to use nuclear weapons against China and to seal off the Korean peninsula with a zone poisoned by radiation.

Turning on his superiors, MacArthur charged the administration with a failure of will because it did not seek what he regarded as a real victory. His fatal move was dispatching a letter to the Republican leader in the House of Representatives, airing his complaints.[76] When the letter became public, the president prepared the ground by obtaining the unanimous agreement of the Joint Chiefs to MacArthur's removal. With his eye on history as usual, Truman even had an aide do some research into the relationship between President Lincoln and General McClellan, which confirmed Truman's impression that he needed to dismiss the general.[77] Meeting with his civilian advisers to inform them about his decision, Truman rejected a suggestion that his announcement say the decision had unanimous senior civilian and military support: "I'm taking this decision on my own responsibility as President of the United States and I want no one to think I'm trying to share it with anyone else."[78] Perfect.

Knowing he would ignite a political firestorm, Truman fired MacArthur, saying he had to act to maintain civilian control of the military. The expected dramatics—and more—ensued. MacArthur returned to the United States and gave a grandiose speech to Congress, followed by ecstatic ticker-tape parades, denunciations of Truman galore, and even threats of impeachment. But when congressional hearings rolled around, MacArthur's own testimony revealed the extent of his instability, and the Joint Chiefs devastated him with their analysis of the war. The time had come for him to "just fade away."[79] The greatest threat to civilian control of the military in American history had passed.[80] The president took the long view: "The American people will come to understand that what I did had to be done."[81]

The precedents that Harry Truman set in Korea could be, and would be, cited in the future for the proposition that the president may send the military into a conflict of any scale at his discretion. His unilateral intervention in Korea, which produced a conflict in which over 36,500 Americans died, is generally and correctly regarded as a precedent different in kind and not just degree from earlier presidential uses of the military.[82] To an extent, though, this assessment relies on hindsight. The president escalated the conflict in three stages: first, air and naval forces; second, ground troops; third, the push to unify Korea. Each stage built on perceived necessity and general support provided by conditions at the time. There was also a persistent underestimation of the commitment it would take to subdue the enemy. Of course, that is a feature of most wars, or we would have many fewer of them. None of this excuses Truman's failure to seek congressional authorization at any of his stages of escalation, but it is not as though he made a single decision to launch a war that he knew would someday merit a monument on the Washington Mall. The Vietnam War would see a similar pattern of escalating engagement, as later presidents would fail to learn the lessons Korea could teach.

The constitutionality of President Truman's actions was debated vigorously at the time.[83] Dean Acheson, having been a primary sponsor of unilateral war making, had his department prepare an extended legal defense that tried to fit Korea within earlier presidential uses of the military, such as the adventures in Latin America.[84] Congress, having climbed aboard the train as it departed the station, never seriously rebuked the president for ignoring its institutional perquisites. Today the Korean precedent stands as an outlier in presidential use of war-making powers, ready for invocation by any president with the fortitude to endure the criticism that will inevitably follow.[85]

The Truman presidency shaped another precedent that has been a foundation stone of the modern national security state: the state secrets privilege that shields military and foreign policy secrets from judicial inquiry.[86] In 1948, an Air Force B-29, the aging workhorse of the strategic bomber fleet, exploded in midair in Georgia. Families of some civilians who had been on board sued the government for negligence, but their suit died when the executive branch successfully resisted disclosure of the crash report on national security grounds. In *United States v. Reynolds*, the Supreme Court held that where a "reasonable danger" of exposure of national security secrets exists, a court should decline to order release of government information if the head of the executive department personally certifies the need for secrecy.[87] The Court said that a reviewing court could sometimes examine the evidence *in camera* (secretly) to verify the claim of privilege, but that the privilege was absolute if military secrets were truly present. It saw no need to probe the government's assertions in the case at hand. That was unfortunate—many years later, release of the records showed the absence of any military secrets and the presence of much negligence in the crash. Thus *Reynolds* places control of government secrecy squarely in the unchecked discretion of the executive branch unless a court presses hard enough to determine whether the subject matter is justifiably secret, a matter that judges often regard as beyond their competence. This sweeping decision, born of Cold War fears, has lasted into today's era of terrorist threats.

Steel Seizure

Late in his presidency and with the Korean War still dragging along, Harry Truman took control of the nation's steel mills to avert a strike that he thought would threaten essential war production. The steel seizure presented starkly clashing issues concerning the demands of national security and the sanctity of private property. The controversy soon wound up in the Supreme Court, which issued a landmark opinion, *Youngstown Sheet & Tube Co. v. Sawyer*, rebuffing the president by enjoining the seizure.[88] *Youngstown* still stands as the most important Supreme Court decision defining the limits of the president's constitutional authority in relation to statutes. Modern presidents ordinarily follow its guidance as they interpret the Constitution.

In the spring of 1952, steel industry unions wanted a wage increase, and management wanted a compensating price increase. President Truman favored higher wages but opposed price increases as inflationary.

After mediation, a strike loomed. Truman could have invoked authority granted him by the Taft-Hartley Act to stop the strike for eighty days but declined to do so, claiming that the act's "cooling-off period" would provide no permanent solution.[89] The act, which had passed over his veto in 1947, was anathema to Truman. Hence, the president faced more of a political than a legal emergency.[90]

"From his reading of history, Truman was convinced his action fell within his powers as President and Commander in Chief. In a state of national emergency, Lincoln had suspended the right to *habeas corpus*, he would point out."[91] Although a steel strike in wartime is no trifle, the situation in 1952 was not nearly as dire as the crisis Lincoln faced in 1861. Truman had the ready option of seeking authority from Congress, as Lincoln did not. Nevertheless, the president forged ahead, telling his staff: "The President has the power to keep the country from going to hell."[92] Sympathetic as one might be with that proposition, the question of methods remains.

President Truman's breezy confidence was probably reinforced by his experience of having sent American troops into Korea unilaterally without suffering any subsequent penalty from Congress, the courts, or the people. If Truman relied on his unilateral war making to justify the more modest action of the steel seizure, he failed to see that the courts would be more willing to review a domestic seizure of industry than a military response to an overseas invasion. The president may have succumbed to the seductive lure of the common legal argument that a greater power always includes a lesser one. Instead, the better analysis is that context counts and each action needs its own sufficient justification. He was also encouraged by the earlier success of his forceful approach to settling the national railroad strike.[93]

In April 1952, Truman announced in a nationwide radio address that he was seizing the steel mills to stop the strike. His executive order placed the mills under government supervision and directed them to continue production. The companies immediately sought an injunction against the order. Like many separation of powers cases, *Youngstown* was litigated under great time pressure and in the glare of intense national publicity. Such trying circumstances can cloud the judgment of advocates. In the trial court, the government erred by suggesting that presidential power is unlimited.[94] The argument made the Hamiltonian claim that the vesting clause in Article II is a grant of all powers that are executive in nature. More effectively, the government urged that the seizure was necessary and placed it against the background of other emergency actions by past presidents. Alarmed by the sweep of the arguments it had heard, the trial court issued an injunction.

The Supreme Court, in a six-to-three vote, upheld the injunction. Justice Black wrote the majority opinion in his characteristically broad strokes. Black began by noting that the government had argued that the president was acting within "the aggregate of his constitutional powers" and had asserted no statutory authority for the order. He concluded that seizures were not merely unauthorized by statute. Instead, in 1947, Congress had "refused to adopt" that remedy by rejecting an amendment to the Taft-Hartley bill that would have authorized emergency seizures.

Without specifying the consequences of this statutory posture, Justice Black moved on to reject the government's constitutional arguments. First, the Court refused to extend the president's broad powers over troops in combat to domestic seizures of private production facilities. That decision was for Congress, said Justice Black, not for the military. Nor did either the vesting clause or the faithful execution clause provide authority, because "the President's power to see that the laws are faithfully executed refutes the idea that he is to be a lawmaker." Only Congress could authorize the taking of private property for public use. Therefore, the executive order was illegal.

Justice Robert Jackson, who had joined the Court in 1941 after his tenure as attorney general, wrote a brilliant concurrence that has been the most influential opinion in the case. He began by offering a framework for analyzing the relative legal postures of president and Congress in a particular instance:

1. When the President acts pursuant to an express or implied authorization of Congress, his authority is at its maximum, for it includes all that he possesses in his own right plus all that Congress can delegate. . . . If his act is held unconstitutional under these circumstances, it usually means that the Federal Government as an undivided whole lacks power. . . .

2. When the President acts in absence of either a congressional grant or denial of authority, he can only rely upon his own independent powers, but there is a zone of twilight in which he and Congress may have concurrent authority, or in which its distribution is uncertain. Therefore, congressional inertia, indifference or quiescence may sometimes, at least as a practical matter, enable, if not invite, measures on independent presidential responsibility. In this area, any actual test of power is likely to depend on the imperatives of events and contemporary imponderables rather than on abstract theories of law.

3. When the President takes measures incompatible with the expressed or implied will of Congress, his power is at its lowest ebb, for then he can rely only
upon his own constitutional powers minus any constitutional powers of Congress over the matter. Courts can sustain exclusive presidential control in such
a case only by disabling the Congress from acting upon the subject. Presidential
claim to a power at once so conclusive and preclusive must be scrutinized with
caution, for what is at stake is the equilibrium established by our constitutional
system.[95]

Jackson concluded that this case fell into the third category. Therefore,
he inquired whether the executive possessed any constitutional power
sufficient to override congressional denial of seizure authority. He could
find none. Jackson disparaged arguments for broad and vague presidential powers of an "inherent" nature. He noted that Congress could grant
and later retract emergency authority and had often done so in time of
war or domestic crisis. Experience suggested that "emergency powers are
consistent with free government only when their control is lodged elsewhere than in the Executive who exercises them." The framers had included only one emergency power, to suspend the writ of habeas corpus
in times of rebellion or invasion. He would not imply others.

Chief Justice Vinson and two other Truman appointees dissented.
They concluded that a review of history demonstrated that "with or
without explicit statutory authorization, Presidents have . . . dealt with
national emergencies by acting promptly and resolutely to enforce legislative programs, at least to save those programs until Congress could act."[96]
Vinson argued that Truman's action was necessary to preserve an opportunity for Congress to legislate. Here, the president had acted to reconcile
two statutory programs, the ones for military procurement and inflation
control: "Unlike . . . the head of a department when administering a particular statute, the President is a constitutional officer charged with taking
care that a 'mass of legislation' be executed."[97] Moreover, Truman had
sent two messages to Congress, reporting his action and offering to abide
by any congressional instructions.

The opinions in *Youngstown* provide much guidance for separation
of powers analysis. First, a correction: Justice Black's assertion that the
executive never legislates was simplistic. He ignored the large number of
executive orders that rest on no clear statutory authority. When these orders have a sufficient constitutional basis and do not contravene any statute, they have the force of law.[98] Still, the majority opinion had salutary
elements that it shared with the five concurrences. None of the majority

justices were willing to imply broad, "inherent" presidential powers to respond to domestic emergencies in a context where Congress had recently
legislated. As Justice Jackson trenchantly noted, such powers "tend to
kindle emergencies." Similarly, the justices were unwilling to transform
the president's broad power to commit troops to combat into control over
the domestic economy and the rights of private citizens.

The majority justices concluded that both houses of Congress had
actively considered and rejected proposals to authorize presidential seizures of the kind that Truman ordered. In that situation it is important for
courts to enforce the congressional policy rather than to expect Congress
to write everything into text. It would be impractical to expect every statutory policy to be explicit. Most controversies over statutory restrictions
on the executive concern implied statutory meaning. It is most unlikely,
for example, that President Truman would have seized the mills if a statute had forbidden the action explicitly.

Youngstown has created a vital principle within the executive branch:
that the president may not contravene statutes setting domestic policy
on the basis of weak claims of necessity. (Claims of necessity are readily
credited in the White House.) The decision warns against executive over-
reaching, whether in action or in argument. Nevertheless, the principle
has not proved very confining to presidents, because the courts are usually
loath to find that presidential action has contravened a statute. Thus the
dissent's willingness to look for creative ways to uphold executive authority opened a path that later courts have often followed.

After the Supreme Court upheld the injunction, the president, having promised to abide the outcome of the case, returned the mills to the
custody of the owners. After a seven-week strike, Truman brokered a
settlement. No disruption to the wartime supply of steel occurred. The
president had made a misstep, but not one that dealt a successful blow to
the rule of law.

The Home Front in the Cold War

The global contest against communism induced American governments
at all levels to restrict civil liberties within the United States.[99] A second
Red scare blossomed. Adding to the unsettling world events, domestic labor unrest implied subversion to many. The House Un-American Activities Committee revived, energized by the young Richard Nixon. Senator
Joseph McCarthy began his rampage. President Truman and his successor

Dwight Eisenhower had to decide what stance to take toward congressional destruction of both private citizens and civil servants. They also had to decide how far to go in rooting out any subversives from the executive branch. Both presidents had mixed records regarding civil liberties. Overall, the Constitution had a rough time of it.

Fears of communist subversion naturally empowered the FBI and other executive watchdogs—J. Edgar Hoover had his *second* Red scare to orchestrate. When Harry Truman became president, he learned that Franklin Roosevelt had secretly authorized electronic surveillance of suspected subversives by the FBI. At the urging of Attorney General Tom Clark, Truman agreed to continue the secret program. With his tendency to see the contest with the Soviets in stark, moral terms, Truman was easily persuaded. Unbeknownst to the president, the program would be expanded—Clark did not say that FDR's original authorization had applied only to aliens; now citizens would be watched also.[100]

In fact, there was not much to the Red menace. The American Communist Party, driven underground in the first Red scare, never had more than a hundred thousand members and usually many fewer.[101] Ominously, though, many Americans had flirted with communism during the Depression and World War II, exposing them to danger if their past affiliations were probed, as they would be. After the 1946 elections gave control of Congress to the Republicans, they discovered that alleging subversion within government was a handy stick with which to beat the Roosevelt and Truman administrations in hopes of unraveling the New Deal. Harry Truman found himself wavering between efforts to appease his tormentors and stands based on his own more liberal principles. It did not work very well. To prove that he was tough on communism, he began by dismissing Secretary of Commerce Henry Wallace for urging accommodation with the Soviets.

In early 1947, the president issued an executive order establishing the Federal Employees Loyalty and Security Program.[102] Meant to satisfy security concerns, it would have the unintended effect of feeding the Red scare.[103] Truman was trying to build on the past. In 1939, the Hatch Act had forbidden federal employees to be members of organizations that advocate overthrow of the government. Roosevelt had authorized dismissal if there were "reasonable doubt" of a person's loyalty. The act was lightly enforced, because FDR's attorneys general were strong civil libertarians who resisted abuses. Truman had no one around him who wanted to play that role.

An inquiry committee that Truman appointed announced that the presence of "even one disloyal" employee would be a "serious threat . . . to the security of the United States."[104] This bald statement revealed the temper of the times. It would be accurate only if the cost of finding and eliminating the subversive were near zero, and it was not.[105] Truman's executive order set the balance far toward overprotectiveness. The order recited that it sought "maximum protection" against disloyalty in the civil service in search of "absolute" security.[106] The loyalty of every applicant and current employee would be reviewed without regard to the sensitivity of the post. A person would be ineligible if "reasonable grounds exist for belief" of disloyalty to the government. The order specified implementing procedures, including FBI investigation of derogatory information and a hearing before a loyalty review board, procedures for which were fundamentally defective.[107]

Many of the hearings had an Alice in Wonderland quality. Under the program, 4.7 million employees were investigated, about five hundred discharges were ordered, and another two thousand people resigned to avoid the process.[108] No evidence of espionage was found.[109] The chilling effect on the federal workforce's exercise of its First Amendment rights cannot be measured, but it was undoubtedly substantial. The program did no credit to President Truman's exercise of his constitutional duty of faithful execution, which includes a duty to protect the constitutional rights of those who serve the executive branch.

In February 1950, Senator McCarthy announced the first of his fictitious lists of communists in the federal government.[110] Truman, to his credit, "issued a furious statement declaring that there was not a word of truth in McCarthy's charges."[111] He also resisted McCarthy's assaults by refusing to give him some federal personnel files.[112] But the witch hunt was on, and the outbreak of war in Korea amplified it. Truman vetoed the McCarran Internal Security Act of 1950, which barred government employment of persons who had joined subversive organizations listed by the government, saying he would "veto any legislation . . . which adopt[s] police-state tactics and unduly encroache[s] on individual rights."[113] Congress swiftly overrode the veto. Tacking to his right, Truman then strengthened his own program by altering the dismissal standard from reasonable grounds for belief of disloyalty to the mere existence of a reasonable doubt about loyalty. Overall, he was trying to limit the damage to civil liberties, but not very effectively.

Having served almost two full terms in office, Harry Truman was ready to retire. He did not have to. In 1947, the Republican Congress had proposed the Twenty-Second Amendment to the Constitution, limiting presidents to two terms in order to forestall the rise of any more Franklin Roosevelts. Apart from the dubious merit of getting even with a dead man, the amendment had some virtues. It did prevent presidents from hanging on beyond their period of useful service. FDR was certainly worn out at the end of three terms, Wilson after two, and Polk after one. But by converting each reelected president to a lame duck the next morning, the amendment deprived the people of their choice for president and reduced presidential power and accountability in the second term. FDR himself had found new energy and support in his third term by changing his emphasis from repairing a broken economy to winning a world war.

The new amendment would not have applied to Truman. Nonetheless, after his election in 1948 he wrote and kept private a message declining to run again, saying that the old two-term precedent should continue— not by constitutional amendment but by custom.[114] In 1952, he announced that he was honoring his promise to himself.

I Like Ike

"I Like Ike" was not just a campaign slogan but an accurate gauge of the mood of the United States in the fall of 1952. After twenty years of turmoil under the Democrats, the nation was ready for a quieter time. The genial and reassuring general who had liberated Europe could be expected to ensure safety in a threatening world and stability in matters domestic.[115]

Dwight Eisenhower glided into the presidency with a résumé that included his distinguished career in the Army, the presidency of Columbia University, and the leadership of NATO. He had a remarkably engaging personality that radiated sincerity and openness, combined with a dominating presence. Nonetheless, he has often been underestimated, in part because he was not given to self-promotion. (Most presidents avoid this hazard.) He was more ambitious and crafty than he appeared. He liked to let subordinates take the heat for decisions while he floated above politics, enhancing his role as head of state.[116] Under his soothing placidity and sometimes fractured syntax were "a clear mind, a firm grasp of issues, instinctive political skills, and a fierce temper."[117]

In domestic politics, President Eisenhower's view of the constitutional role of the federal government was moderately conservative. He often quoted Lincoln's aphorism that government should do what people could not do for themselves, but he applied it narrowly.[118] He sought what he called a "middle way" between political extremes, which would protect basic security for citizens but would avoid the "socialistic experiment."[119] This meant that he would not attack the New Deal (he even supported a broadening of Social Security coverage). He was devotedly conservative in fiscal policy. Having inherited an $8 billion deficit, he was determined to eliminate it and did so, leaving a surplus of $500 million as he retired.

Ike's view of the role of the federal government implied a rather Whiggish view of presidential powers.[120] In foreign policy, he did not share Truman's inclination to use the military without congressional authorization.[121] Having seen the political consequences of Korea for his predecessor, the former general did not want to extend his flanks without support. He began a practice that would continue, of asking for Congress to endorse an action that was claimed to be already within the president's constitutional power.[122] The hope was that political ground would be gained while surrendering no constitutional territory.

Having been more of a managerial than a fighting general, Eisenhower organized the White House along lines of a military staff.[123] In an effort to settle minor issues at lower levels and reserve his time for major ones, he assigned tasks to specialists, not the shifting groups of generalists that Franklin Roosevelt and Harry Truman used. He created the chief of staff position for the White House and filled it with Sherman Adams, a tireless, icy paragon of efficiency. He also created an office of congressional relations that would become permanent; it processed requests for patronage from members of Congress. His approach to Congress was nonconfrontational, even after 1954 when the Democrats controlled both houses. Like FDR, he tracked public opinion by polling.

Eisenhower held regular weekly cabinet meetings despite their limited value, as a way of signaling support for his team and interest in their doings. The president had an orderly, prudent style of decision making that emphasized hierarchy and consultation. This style reduced both mistakes and innovation. It was clear who was in charge. His closest partner was the austere and arrogant John Foster Dulles at State, who like Woodrow Wilson was the son of a minister. Charles Wilson from General Motors was at Defense, signifying the president's comfort with the business community. At Treasury was the appropriately thrifty George Humphrey. Attorney General Herbert Brownell would play a prominent role as the civil rights movement accelerated. Not on the team was Vice President Richard Nixon, whom the president disliked (in a comment that revealed both men, Ike said Nixon seemed to have no friends).[124]

In 1955, Eisenhower suffered a major heart attack just as planning started for reelection.[125] There followed the usual efforts to minimize public awareness of the president's real condition. Press Secretary James Hagerty screened the release of information, giving out floods of trivia to obscure the seriousness of the situation. An informal committee took temporary operational control of the executive branch, with Sherman Adams acting as conduit to the president, keeping him informed and minimizing his workload. Dulles oversaw foreign policy, Brownell watched domestic policy, and Nixon, involved for once, coordinated the cabinet in a carefully deferential way that pleased the president. After months in the hospital Eisenhower went home to Gettysburg to convalesce for the rest of the year.[126]

So Long, Joe

As a leading hero of World War II, Dwight Eisenhower had the perfect credentials to contain the anticommunist fury of the right wing of his party. Yet even he struggled to do so. He began badly by failing to deliver a planned defense in a campaign speech of his mentor George Marshall, then under a particularly scurrilous attack by Joseph McCarthy.[127] News of the deletion only encouraged the senator.

Once in office, Ike bolstered his right flank by substituting his own, even stricter, employee loyalty program for Truman's. The new standard condemned "any behavior, activities or associations which tend to show that the individual is not reliable or trustworthy."[128] How many of us could survive strict application of that standard? More dismissals and resignations followed. There was still no sign of actual espionage or subversive misbehavior.[129]

The president also gave the FBI a free hand to investigate radicals and did not stop some prosecutions that Truman had initiated against American communist leaders under the Smith Act for "conspiring to advocate" the violent overthrow of the government. The Supreme Court upheld convictions of the leaders.[130] The Court enunciated a test for assessing free speech claims: "whether the gravity of the 'evil,' discounted by its improbability, justifies such invasion of free speech as is necessary to avoid the danger." This balancing test, if applied fairly to the prosecutions and the Truman/Eisenhower loyalty programs, would surely have condemned them all. Neither president made any such judgment in a careful way. Both failed their responsibility to protect free speech.

None of this mollified "Tail-Gunner Joe," as McCarthy called himself. Now that he could control investigations from his position as chair of a Senate subcommittee, he turned on the administration.[131] The president took no action when McCarthy forced the State Department to purge "subversive" books from its overseas libraries, including works by such incendiaries as Jean Paul Sartre and Arthur Schlesinger Jr. Eisenhower refused to condemn McCarthy in public, saying it would demean the presidency to enter a mudslinging contest with him. The president did quietly try to undermine McCarthy behind the scenes by urging party leaders to abandon him.[132] Finally McCarthy went too far, in part by attacking the Army, to which the president remained loyal.

As McCarthy probed the Army, looking for mud to sling, the president asked Attorney General Brownell for legal advice about executive privilege to withhold information.[133] Brownell replied that no precedent existed to support refusing congressional subpoenas. The president decided to create one. He made a sweeping claim of executive privilege by writing the secretary of the Army that it was not in the public interest for any conversations or documents about advice given within the executive branch to be disclosed and instructing him not to reveal any such materials.[134] The justification was the standard one that if advice is not kept confidential, it will not be candid and therefore will be unreliable.

This justification reflects common sense. Groups of all kinds inside and outside of government form policy in shielded internal discussions before they announce it to the world. The problems of posturing or sycophancy that undermine the candor of publicly available advice are particularly acute in the superheated political zone near the president, but they occur as well at lower levels in the bureaucracy, as in the Army. Equally important, in government power flows where information goes. Every president wants to determine who has access to information and advice bearing on a pending decision, as a way to control the decision itself. Of course, the shield provided by executive privilege is leaky, and important public interests in accountability offset the interests underlying the privilege. As we shall see, modern presidencies have been marked by controversies akin to the one in the Army-McCarthy hearings.

President Eisenhower's assertion of executive privilege worked at the time. The Army stood its ground, and the senator raved on, his reputation imploding as he finally exposed his true nature to a fascinated and re-pelled public.[135] This was an early instance of the moral power of televi-sion; before long, presidents would learn its full potential. Eisenhower finally had his victory, but McCarthy had ravaged the executive branch for years before the president finally stood up to him.

Massive Retaliation

President Eisenhower inherited a Cold War that had settled into the pat-tern it would follow for almost four decades. Superpower contests oc-curred around the fringes without many direct confrontations between them. Ike, having experienced a great deal of war, knew the effects and limits of military power. He shared the establishment view of the intrac-tability of the communists and the need to contain them. Hence, like Truman, he would strive to maintain the credibility of American power without resorting to its use unless necessary.

At the outset of Eisenhower's presidency, the death of Joseph Stalin presented an opportunity to engage constructively with the Soviet Union, but the new administration was too devoted to Cold War orthodoxy to ex-plore the opening.[136] Besides, there was the pressing matter of the Korean War. Eisenhower had kept his campaign promise to go to Korea and had concluded that the war must be ended. In his first achievement as presi-dent, he managed to obtain a cease-fire within six months.[137]

The Eisenhower administration soon evolved its own distinctive na-tional security policy as the president worked out his own definition of his duties as commander in chief.[138] Early on, Eisenhower expressed a casual attitude toward atomic bombs, saying that they were just another tool to destroy an enemy, like bullets. He then shifted to his enduring position that massive retaliation for an enemy nuclear strike was the only suitable use for atomic weapons. This policy tended to stabilize the Cold War, because it rejected the constant desire of the military to initiate small nuclear wars on the premise they could be somehow contained. The presi-dent once said that "I'm the only Army general to have disassociated my-self from Army thinking."[139] A president having less credibility with the military or less confidence in his military judgments would have found it difficult to sustain such a policy.

Happily for Eisenhower, the massive retaliation policy furthered his re-lated aim to protect national security by keeping military spending within bounds that could be sustained for a long Cold War. However expensive, atomic bombs were cheaper than the proliferated arsenal the Joint Chiefs preferred. Against constant pressure to do more, Ike kept the lid on spending throughout his presidency and exited the office with his famous warning about the growing power of the military-industrial complex and its threat to democratic processes. He had seen that when presidents try to control military spending with veto threats, they encounter the pork barrel frenzy that attends many military spending bills.

The Eisenhower administration fended off persistent efforts in Congress to hamper the presidential use of executive agreements and to reduce the impact of the treaty power.[140] The Bricker Amendment would have altered the Constitution to make all executive agreements subject to congressional approval and to forbid treaties from having domestic effect without implementing legislation.[141] The genesis of the proposal was negative congressional reaction to Franklin Roosevelt's use of executive agreements for subjects of such magnitude as recognition of the Soviet Union and the destroyer deal. There was also concern that the treaty power could be used to erode the rights of the states. When the administration finally squelched the proposal in 1954, presidential power that had accumulated since 1789 had been preserved. Congress had, however, sent a cautionary signal.

President Eisenhower spent much time and effort sparring with communist regimes around the globe, usually without significant commitment of American military forces. His aggressive partner in this effort was Secretary Dulles. The president himself held a tight rein on the military. He created the office of national security adviser to provide an honest broker of information flowing within the executive branch, but not to be the independent center of power that would evolve.

In hindsight, the most ominous foreign policy issues concerned Vietnam.[142] President Truman had put his toe in the water in 1950 by providing military aid to France. As their colonial effort collapsed at Dien Bien Phu in 1954, the French asked Eisenhower for air support for the besieged garrison.[143] He refused, thinking that it would be ineffective. The Geneva Accords followed, temporarily dividing Vietnam. The United States was not a signatory but pledged to abide the accords. In a fateful step, the Eisenhower administration supported the refusal of the South Vietnamese government to hold elections required by the accords. Soon the administration was providing both money and military advisers to the South Vietnamese government of Ngo Dinh Diem, in a commitment that daily made withdrawal more difficult politically. Although Eisenhower did not see Vietnam as having intrinsic strategic importance, he subscribed to the "domino theory," that if one nation in Southeast Asia fell to the communists the others would follow.

In Asia, the communist and nationalist Chinese repeatedly squabbled over the offshore islands Quemoy and Matsu, with episodic gunfire and constant threats.[144] The Joint Chiefs wanted to let nationalist leader Chiang Kai-Shek bomb bases in China and to use nuclear weapons against the communists if they responded. The president repeatedly refused to authorize this dangerous escalation of an essentially meaningless conflict. It remained only a local irritant.[145]

Europe and the Middle East presented more substantial challenges, in response to which President Eisenhower had mixed success.[146] In 1956, Hungarians encouraged by a decade of liberation rhetoric emanating from the United States rose against their Soviet oppressors. Eisenhower could only look on in frustration as Red Army tanks put down the rebellion. He had more success with the curious Suez Canal crisis. President Nasser of Egypt seized the canal, in part because the United States canceled funding for his Aswan dam project. America's usual allies Israel, Britain, and France attacked him to regain control of it. The president firmly opposed the use of force against Egypt. After applying some economic pressure, he managed to stand the allies down. Eisenhower, who regarded Truman's intervention in Korea as unconstitutional, thought that he would need advance congressional authorization to commit major forces to Suez.[147]

In 1958, for the only time in his administration President Eisenhower sent American troops to occupy foreign soil, using authority granted by Congress to send the Marines into Lebanon at the request of its government to stop unrest there. The troops came out after restoring order at the cost of a single casualty.

Relations with the Soviet Union were never far from President Eisenhower's mind. Two developments raised the ante of possible negotiation: America's first H-bomb explosion in 1954 and the Soviet Union's Sputnik satellite in 1957. A rather profitless summit meeting in Geneva in 1955 was the first since Potsdam—a beginning, at least. As the United States mobilized to begin the space race, Soviet premier Nikita Khrushchev made one of his periodic threats to take Berlin. Eisenhower deftly defused the situation by inviting the premier to visit the United States for a summit meeting, at which they scheduled further talks. With mutual restraint by the two superpowers, Cold War jousting was staying under control.

The Road to Little Rock

Having been raised in segregated Kansas and Texas and having spent his career in a segregated military, Dwight Eisenhower could live with segregation. He thought that an end to segregation would have to begin locally and could not be accomplished by government compulsion. His attorney general, Herbert Brownell, who believed in integration, perceived that the president "would not lead the charge" to change American race relations.[148] Before long, the awakening civil rights movement pressed him to take a stand.[149]

In 1953, a major challenge to segregation in the nation's public schools was pending in the Supreme Court when Chief Justice Vinson suddenly died. President Eisenhower's first Supreme Court appointment would have momentous implications. The president had already promised former California governor Earl Warren the first Court vacancy, but there had been no mention of the chief's chair.[150] Warren pressed for the nomination, and Eisenhower acceded. To his surprise, he had appointed a great chief justice whose views would often be at odds with the president's preferences.[151] In the pending litigation, Attorney General Brownell filed a brief favoring desegregation after the president had reviewed and approved it. In May 1954, the Court issued its surprisingly unanimous decision in *Brown v. Board of Education*, holding that segregation violated the equal protection clause in the Constitution.[152]

Eisenhower's instinct for the middle way did not work in the context of civil rights. He thought that segregationists fighting against constitutionally guaranteed rights and people seeking enforcement of those rights were morally equivalent extremists.[153] On this issue above all, a firm moral commitment was needed from the president. It was not forthcoming. To be fair, Eisenhower did take some positive steps. He extended the executive order program banning race discrimination in federal functions that Presidents Roosevelt and Truman had begun.[154] He implemented Truman's order to desegregate the military, supported integration in the District of Columbia, and gave Brownell latitude to pursue civil rights by selecting strong federal judges in the South.

In his campaign for reelection, President Eisenhower said tepidly that he accepted the *Brown* decision. His victory with 57 percent of the votes was another personal triumph for him, but it produced no identifiable mandate on this issue. Meanwhile, the Democrats made some slight additions to their control of Congress, and of course the southern Democrats formed an immovable bloc against integration. At Attorney General Brownell's urging, the administration successfully sponsored a modest civil rights bill in 1957. Even though its final version merely gave the Justice Department some added authority to pursue voting rights, it was the first civil rights bill of any kind to pass since Reconstruction.

In the fall of 1957, Southern intransigence triggered a crisis.[155] Central High School in Little Rock, Arkansas, was under a court-ordered integration plan. In late September, Governor Orval Faubus mobilized the National Guard on the pretext of preserving order but used it to turn the black children away, defying federal authority. Faubus then withdrew the Guard and let mob violence rule. Little Rock's mayor called for the president to send federal troops under his venerable statutory authority to suppress disorder. President Eisenhower, out of options, conferred with Brownell and sent the Army into Little Rock. They were the first federal troops to be used to protect blacks in the South since Reconstruction.

The president's televised address to the nation said that the court orders required obedience.[156] He gave no sign that he acted out of personal support for civil rights; he simply could not allow a state governor to defy federal court orders. Some of Andrew Jackson's genes were stirring in him—this was nullification all over again. He was also aware of the effects of the crisis on world opinion. Secretary Dulles told him that the situation in Little Rock was "ruining our foreign policy."[157] Before long, the crisis eased. The children went to school, and by November the troops could leave.

Covert Legacy

President Eisenhower both endorsed the foreign policy of containment and extended it in an effort to roll communism back where it already had a foothold. The way to do that cheaply and without confronting the Soviet Union was covert action. Ike grew very fond of it, and his penchant for seeking congressional authorization for military action did not extend to it. His expansion of the CIA and of the newly created and still secret National Security Agency for electronic surveillance produced large bureaucracies that were ready to follow presidential whims. The CIA was a particularly attractive tool for Cold War use. It was far more nimble and secretive than the encrusted Departments of State and Defense. Its "black budget," by which it obtained funds via secret transfers from other agencies rather than in open appropriations, could hide a great deal, including, as time went on, many sins.[158]

In 1953, covert action toppled the left-leaning leader Mohammad Mossadegh in Iran.[159] Harry Truman had refused to participate with the British in a coup against him. Eisenhower took the issue up with the National Security Council and decided to go forward via the CIA in the person of Kermit Roosevelt. The coup succeeded, placing the friendly if erratic shah in power, as Iranians would well remember when they rose against him decades later. But the CIA's participation was an official secret and was not acknowledged for decades.

Speedy success in Iran encouraged more interventions. In Guatemala, Eisenhower authorized the CIA to help overthrow a ruler thought to be associating with communists.[160] A sporty little rebellion installed a brutal regime that the administration had chosen. There were also interventions in the Congo and Indonesia, but with less effect. In all these cases, the administration tended to underestimate indigenous forces of nationalism and anticolonialism, blaming all ferment on monolithic communism.[161] In the process values of self-determination that the United States had promoted since Woodrow Wilson were sacrificed.

The Eisenhower administration's most important covert program eventually came a cropper. From 1956 on, secret U-2 spy planes overflew the Soviet Union, with the president personally approving each flight.[162] The program was a spectacular success, giving the United States precise information on the progress of Soviet arms. In 1960, the Soviets finally shot down a U-2 and recovered the pilot alive. Knowing only that the aircraft had gone missing, President Eisenhower embarrassed himself by lying repeatedly about the flight until Premier Khrushchev gleefully revealed that he had the pilot and the truth in hand.[163] The episode wrecked a planned summit meeting and forced discontinuation of the flights, but only after much had been learned.

After Fidel Castro took over Cuba in early 1959 and veered leftward, President Eisenhower began unlimbering covert forces, leaving what would prove a bitter legacy for his successor.[164] As he left office, Ike was training Cuban exiles for a planned countercoup against Castro. Once encouraged and armed, this dedicated band would have been very difficult to dissolve. Ike also imposed a trade embargo on Cuba and worked to mobilize opposition to its regime within Latin America. He was the first president to oppose Castro unsuccessfully, but not the last.

CHAPTER TEN

Bear Any Burden

Kennedy and Lyndon Johnson

Let every nation know, whether it wishes us well or ill, that we shall pay any price, bear any burden, meet any hardship, support any friend, oppose any foe to assure the survival and the success of liberty.—John F. Kennedy, 1961[1]

The soaring rhetoric of John F. Kennedy's inaugural, which seemed to promise an unlimited Wilsonian commitment to worldwide freedom, masked the intensely pragmatic politician beneath. But then, Kennedy was fond of masks. He was "intelligent, detached, curious, candid if not always honest, and he was careless and dangerously disorganized."[2] He was very impatient, addicted to excitement, and quite willing to use his great charm to manipulate others. His aides thought that "he felt almost nothing but tried to figure out everything."[3] No passionate liberal, he was an ambitious politician who displayed little ideology beyond anticommunism and a faith in active, pragmatic government. For dogma he substituted an approach, striving to use tough-minded intelligence to solve problems in a world full of irony. He was decisive enough, usually choosing the most moderate of available options. His approach to reading the Constitution would be equally pragmatic.

Reckless Youth[4]

During his political career, Kennedy hid two great personal secrets: his poor health and his reckless sex life. Revelation of either would have stopped him short of the presidency or vitiated his effectiveness in office. Immediately after his election to the presidency he declared himself in "excellent" health and denied rumors of Addison's disease, a serious disorder of the adrenal system.[5] But he lied about his condition and hid his medical records. In fact, he took daily injections of steroids for Addison's, along with a pharmacopeia of medications for his severe back pain, intestinal problems, and other difficulties. It may be that all the pain and medication did not interfere with Kennedy's performance as president.[6] But like some of his predecessors, he did not care to share the truth with the people so that they could judge.

At least Kennedy was healthy enough to have sex with the dozens of women who came to him through elaborate artifices that were known to many around him. Here he was risking blackmail, scandal, or both. Soon after the inauguration, J. Edgar Hoover fired a warning shot by sending the new president a report about a liaison, simultaneously guaranteeing his own tenure.[7] The president did not desist.

Kennedy began the practice of live televised press conferences. Soon these provided him a powerful connection to the people, who could see his gifts on display. He wanted to control the news. Behind the scenes, he rebuked publishers for press coverage that displeased him. He also wiretapped friends and enemies to plug information leaks. Meanwhile, he was happily leaking information himself to manipulate the press, leading someone to remark that "the ship of state is the only ship that leaks from the top."[8] He used polls by Lou Harris to stay abreast of public opinion. The transformation of the presidency into a continuous campaign was beginning and would mature in the presidencies to follow.

Kennedy thought that Eisenhower's White House was too formal and structured, stifling new ideas and fresh thinking. He quickly dismantled the existing hierarchy, replacing it with a wheel with himself at the hub, rather as FDR had done.[9] He would be his own chief of staff. He never had the patience to work with large, formal groups that would include too many dullards and too much trivia. Meetings with the cabinet or the National Security Council irritated him. Instead, he wanted a cloud of very smart generalists around him, working on whatever he assigned them with the tools of critical thinkers.[10] For example, he gave power to his national security adviser, McGeorge Bundy, to avoid the slow processes of the State Department. Bundy's "arrogance and hubris" might have made him the "perfect dean" at Harvard, but they boded ill for the nation.[11] This system was prone to chaos and error, as Kennedy would soon learn.

From the outset, Kennedy intended to focus his presidency on foreign affairs, where the dominant coalition in Congress could not easily block his desire for immediate achievements. He wanted to draw on both Woodrow Wilson's idealism and Franklin Roosevelt's pragmatism.[12] Calling the presidency "the vital center of action in our whole scheme of government," he said that the president must "be prepared to exercise the fullest powers of his office—all that are specified and some that are not."[13]

The first requisite for an effective foreign policy was protection on the right flank, where the anticommunist hardliners lurked. Therefore, the president sought Republicans for his team and found them in Bundy and Secretary of Defense Robert McNamara. He also kept Eisenhower's CIA director, Allen Dulles. The colorless Dean Rusk would do at State, where Kennedy wanted an officer who would faithfully execute his own policies.

John Kennedy had little appetite or aptitude for the grinding congressional negotiations that were necessary to legislate, as he had revealed in his own lackluster congressional career. He once remarked to his erstwhile opponent Richard Nixon that "foreign affairs is the only important issue for a president to handle, isn't it?"[14] For domestic political cover after his razor-thin electoral victory, Kennedy chose Douglas Dillon from the Eisenhower administration to serve at Treasury, where he stewarded the emerging boom of the 1960s. Eisenhower advised Dillon to secure a written promise of independence before accepting; Kennedy responded that "a President can't enter into treaties with cabinet members."[15] He balanced the moderately conservative Dillon by placing the liberal Walter Heller at the head of the Council of Economic Advisers. Of course, Kennedy's closest associate on matters both domestic and foreign was his brother Robert, who was installed as attorney general. In response to well-founded complaints about this nepotism, Kennedy answered revealingly that "I need someone I know to talk to in this government."[16]

Unlike his predecessor, President Kennedy always had to struggle to keep the military short of open revolt. He had little rapport with the Joint Chiefs, thinking they were much too aggressive. He soon found an ally in General Maxwell Taylor, who had opposed Eisenhower's reliance on massive retaliation, favoring a policy of flexible response. In essence, Kennedy chose to pursue both strategies at once, building both nuclear and conventional arsenals at a cost that Ike would never have tolerated.

When the chairman of the Joint Chiefs, General Lemnitzer, briefed the new president on the military's nuclear attack plan in the event of war, Kennedy was horrified to learn that it called for a total, undiscriminating, obliterating attack on the entire communist bloc.[17] It betrayed the kind of rigid thinking that the president detested. During the tenure of Presidents

Eisenhower and Kennedy, the chiefs made regular requests for authority to use nuclear force; both presidents rejected every such request. This ultimate authority remained securely in presidential hands.

Soon after Kennedy's inaugural, the CIA began pressing him to approve the Cuban exiles' proposed invasion to overthrow Castro. The new president was boxed in. If he called off the operation, a chance to remove Castro would evaporate, and Kennedy would face charges of appeasing communists at the very moment he wanted to prove his toughness to the world. By assembling a private army that could not be closely controlled by any American president, Eisenhower had both taken covert warfare to a dangerous new level and made a commitment that could not easily be retracted, because the Cuban exiles would not likely accept an order to abandon their dreams.[18]

But how could Kennedy know that the invasion would succeed? Both the CIA and the Joint Chiefs assured him of success without the use of American armed forces. The CIA in particular was vastly overoptimistic, predicting without any evidence that the Cuban people would rise against Castro. Some military advisers were more dubious but held their tongues, assuming that if the operation was failing the president would do whatever was necessary to make it succeed.[19] Everyone in sight was busily manipulating the new president.

Throughout the planning, everyone seems to have assumed that the president's participation in supporting the invasion was within his power as commander in chief. Since it was to be a covert operation, no formal request to Congress for authority was considered. Kennedy's prime concern was to reduce the political risk of the operation by somehow hiding the role of the United States. In early April 1961 final approval of the "least covert military operation in history" was pending.[20] The president then shocked his military and civilian advisers by including Senator William Fulbright in a meeting with them.[21] This breach of separation of powers norms by involving an outsider from Congress in executive deliberations produced a defensive reaction in the group as Fulbright opposed their plan. When the executive advisers stood their ground, Kennedy approved the operation. The president then responded to a press inquiry about an imminent invasion by stating that there would be no intervention in Cuba by United States armed forces "under any conditions."[22] The stage was set for the disaster that followed.

The Bay of Pigs invasion by fourteen hundred Cuban exiles was supported ineffectually by some old CIA airplanes with false markings.[23] As Castro overwhelmed the invaders, Kennedy held to his promise not to involve regular American armed forces. In the aftermath, President Kennedy correctly announced: "I am the responsible officer of this government."[24] Privately, he was furious, knowing that he had been deceived by the CIA and the Joint Chiefs, who, he said, "were sure I'd give in to them" by intervening with American forces to save the exiles.[25] Trying to regain his command of the executive branch and doing damage control, the president refused to allow his military adviser, General Taylor, to testify before a congressional committee that was investigating the disaster.[26]

The Bay of Pigs experience reinforced Kennedy's inclination to rely on generalists whom he trusted.[27] It did not, however, incline him to bring members of Congress into sensitive deliberations in the future—he thought Fulbright would have reacted as he himself did if exposed to the same barrage of advice. Kennedy realized that he had to control his military and intelligence subordinates more closely and needed to ensure fuller internal debate before he made critical decisions.

The Bay of Pigs disaster did not deter the Kennedy administration from efforts to unseat Castro. It simply drove those efforts into even more covert avenues that could be kept secret from all but a few executive officials. The president soon approved Operation Mongoose, an operation to remove Castro by fair means or foul, including various CIA assassination plots that often descended into the absurd.[28] The operation was chaired by Robert Kennedy, whose loyalty to his brother was unquestioned and who would be understood to speak for the president while preserving presidential deniability of knowledge about misdeeds.[29]

Mongoose was a step beyond the covert interventions of the Eisenhower administration. Only a notion that deposing communist regimes was always within the president's commander in chief powers could have provided legal support for this line of policy. The argument would have been severely overextended, and of course it was never advanced in public. In recognition of the dubious legality of Mongoose, its seamiest aspects were kept from the written record entirely.[30]

Watching the Bay of Pigs debacle with interest from Moscow, Premier Nikita Khrushchev decided to test the new president's mettle and even to bully him a little. Now began an extended period of superpower confrontation at the height of the Cold War, with the fate of the civilized world often resting on the shoulders of two men, operating under the very different constitutional systems of the two nations. The bullying occurred at a June 1961 summit at Geneva.[31] Thinking Kennedy weak as well as inexperienced, the wily but erratic Khrushchev hectored him unmercifully and threatened to sign a peace treaty with East Germany that would leave western access to West Berlin in jeopardy.[32] The president replied coldly that such a step could lead to war: the United States was prepared to fight for Berlin.

The testing followed as Khrushchev made public his threat to Berlin. Kennedy was prepared to make a first use of nuclear weapons to keep the United States from being driven from Europe by the massive Red Army. In August, he gave an address on television saying that an attack on West Berlin would be an attack on us all. Congress increased defense spending. The crisis eased when the Soviets built the Berlin Wall to stop the flow of refugees to the West and receded from their threats. Reducing the tension, Khrushchev initiated a private, direct correspondence with Kennedy that went on for years and would eventually take on supreme importance.

Soon after the wall went up, Khrushchev announced the resumption of atmospheric nuclear tests, which both nations had discontinued temporarily. Kennedy had sought unsuccessfully to discuss a test-ban treaty at Geneva, and this was a step backward. Unwilling to appear weak, he reluctantly resumed first underground and then atmospheric testing that fall.

The Missiles of October [33]

The Cuban missile crisis of October 1962, was the most dangerous passage in the long history of the Cold War. For an agonizing thirteen days, decisions made by "one single man," President John Kennedy—and by his lonely counterpart in Moscow—determined whether a devastating nuclear war would commence.[34] During the crisis, the American constitutional system effectively devolved absolute power on the president and his small circle of executive branch advisers to decide questions of war, peace, and national survival. This devolution, unimaginable to the framing generation, occurred because of a combination of Cold War political imperatives and the force of modern circumstance. The president's stewardship of national security under his power as commander in chief became the nation's only practical recourse under the urgency of events. In perilous times to come, the same may be true again.

During the Cuban missile crisis, the United States was under a constitutional dictatorship in the classic sense that the president and his advisors were acting in the absence of "timely legal checks to their authority."[35] After the denouement, the president would have to throw himself on the mercy of the nation or its survivors, but during the period of maximum jeopardy there would be no effective outside controls on executive discretion. The crisis was brought on not only by the Soviet move to place missiles near our shores but also by domestic political forces that President Kennedy could not easily resist.[36] Whatever the mix of causation, however, once events presented the president with stark choices to make about the missiles, responsibility centered in him. He was exercising the constitutional commander in chief power as it had evolved to his time, under conditions that did not make seeking congressional authorization feasible.

The outcome of the missile crisis depended not only on whether President Kennedy and Premier Khrushchev made correct decisions but also on whether their choices would be implemented. As John Kennedy knew from his experience in World War II, large bureaucracies such as armies inherently suffer "friction" between commands issued at the top of the pyramid and actions taken at the bottom. Yet it may be an action at the bottom—a decision to shoot down an airplane or to fire a nuclear missile—that drives the overall course of history. Both Kennedy and Khrushchev struggled with this problem, ultimately with success. This outcome supports robust constitutional lines of command and control between the head of state and officers in the field, although no legal arrangements can eliminate human error or folly.

In September 1962, the escalating Cold War tensions that had resulted in the building of the Berlin Wall began to focus on revelations of Soviet shipments of arms and troops to Cuba.[37] Within Congress and especially from Republicans, pressure built for the administration to do something about this nearby threat. Even former president Eisenhower joined the fray, suggesting that the new president was weak on foreign policy.[38] Congress passed a joint resolution declaring the determination of the United States to prevent Cuba from either exporting its revolution or creating a military capability "endangering the security of the United States."[39] The resolution did not authorize the president to take any action, but it certainly signaled that support existed for an aggressive executive stance. At a press conference, Kennedy assured the nation that if Cuba were to become "an offensive military base," the United States would do "whatever must be done" to protect its security.[40]

The missile crisis began on the morning of October 16, when the first photographs of Soviet missile sites in Cuba, taken by CIA overflights, reached President Kennedy.[41] In September, concerned by information that the Soviets might be placing surface-to-air missiles in Cuba, he had publicly warned the Soviets not to install offensive missiles. They had responded that they would do no such thing. The photos, however, showed construction of launchpads for surface-to-surface missiles that could reach much of the United States, along with some of the missiles themselves. The project appeared to be nearing operational status.

The presence of Soviet missiles in Cuba would have reduced but not eliminated the overwhelming American strategic advantage in intercontinental missiles. A midrange missile located nearby is the equivalent of an intercontinental one located overseas. Thus the Soviet move was destabilizing, especially if Cubans were allowed access to the triggers, but it was not a fundamental alteration in the strategic balance of power. Probably more important to Kennedy, it directly challenged his pledge to prevent the placement of offensive military capacity in Cuba.

The president immediately convened an advisory group with about thirteen members, soon to be known as the ExComm.[42] At its heart were his principal national security advisers: his brother Robert, Secretaries McNamara and Rusk, chairman of the Joint Chiefs Maxwell Taylor, National Security Adviser Bundy, and CIA Director McCone. Along with some of the core group's subordinates, the president added some people who were normally outside the inner circle to obtain a wide range of views. Vice President Lyndon Johnson, who had been almost ignored previously, was included for his knowledge of Congress. UN Ambassador Adlai Stevenson, who always irritated the Kennedys, would be the conduit to world opinion. And former secretary of state Dean Acheson provided institutional memory stretching back to the Truman administration.

For the next two weeks, the ExComm would meet in long, intensive sessions that drove everyone to the point of exhaustion. Its style was nonhierarchical, as all searched for solutions to present to the president. President Kennedy attended some but not all of the sessions; he understood that "personalities change when the President is present."[43] (That is, sycophancy overcomes candor.) Ominously, Kennedy's doctors increased the dosage of some of his medications to help him deal with the immense stress.[44]

At the initial ExComm meeting, the "dominant feeling . . . was shocked surprise"; the repeated Soviet promises had all been lies, "one gigantic fabric of lies."[45] When the president asked the ExComm why Khrushchev was doing this, the group accurately inferred his purposes: to redress the strategic missile imbalance and to force the United States to make concessions on Berlin and to remove midrange American missiles from Turkey. The perception of betrayal immediately eliminated one option. Letting the construction proceed while negotiation with the Soviets proceeded leisurely would be dangerous and would appear weak to the world. It would also expose the president to a fierce domestic political reaction, with the Bay of Pigs precedent being trumpeted as another example of Kennedy's weakness.

Challenged in the most primal way, Kennedy initially responded aggressively: "We're going to take out those missiles" with an air strike.[46] As the meeting went on, McNamara suggested a naval blockade to prevent more missiles or supplies from reaching Cuba. Robert Kennedy soon concurred, saying that he hated the idea of a surprise attack by a "very large nation against a very small one."[47] The question of the historical importance of the president's action, which always resonated with John Kennedy, had entered the calculus. Equally important, the two main options, air strike or blockade, had surfaced. Meetings over the next several days thrashed out the implications of both.

The ExComm operated in great secrecy. Participants later said they could never have reached sound decisions if their deliberations had been public.[48] That conclusion is surely correct. As it was, they had time to explore every option, to reflect (if hurriedly), to disagree, to refine their views. The president, trying to hide the crisis by maintaining the semblance of a normal schedule, could debrief them, consider, and return. It was an advantage to have the president's brother on the ExComm. Because he could articulate JFK's presumed views without himself being the president, the group was spared the intimidating effect the presidency had gathered over the years.

Within the ExComm (and presumably in the president's own mind), constant tension was produced by the aggressive position of the Joint Chiefs as articulated by Maxwell Taylor, who was himself in tension with his even more aggressive colleagues. Hardest to control was Air Force general Curtis LeMay, the firebomber of Tokyo, who revealed his insubordination by raising the specter of Munich with the president.[49] The chiefs had long sought an invasion of Cuba, on grounds that a communist government in the hemisphere was intolerable (a kind of super Monroe Doctrine). Now, reflecting their training and experience, they focused on the fact that Soviet missiles in Cuba would soon be aimed at the United States, only minutes away. In their view, the threat must be removed in the way they knew, by an air strike followed by an invasion. They constantly emphasized the danger of allowing the missiles to become operational and the limited time available to prevent that.

What the Americans did not know was that Soviet forces on the island already possessed tactical nuclear cruise missiles that could easily reach the American base at Guantanamo or any invasion beaches.[50] Air strikes, then, would produce dangers both known and unknown. The known danger was that air power might not eliminate every Soviet missile aimed at the United States, resulting in a nuclear counterstrike from Cuba. The unknown and more immediate one was that an air strike would trigger tactical nuclear counterstrikes against Guantanamo and any other American forces in range. The event everyone most feared was the first explosion of a nuclear weapon somewhere, after which all control of the crisis might be lost.

Left out of the discussion was Congress. In the first days, the question of a declaration of war on Cuba was raised in the ExComm and rejected by the president as implying an intention to invade.[51] Deputy Attorney General Nicholas Katzenbach concurred, arguing that the question was one of national self-defense needing no congressional authorization.[52] So did Dean Acheson, repeating his performance years before regarding Korea.[53] The vice president, whose knowledge of Congress was unsurpassed, recommended ignoring Congress: "We're not going to get much help out of them."[54] The ExComm, feeling an acute need for secrecy while a response was formulated, needed little persuasion to leave leaky and balky legislators out of the discussion. Keeping information within the restricted group also kept control of the decision within that group. No one knew what would happen if a general debate broke out in the nation.

By October 20, the president had chosen a blockade, to be restyled a "quarantine" to make it seem less an act of war and to evade comparison with the Soviet's 1948 Berlin blockade. Kennedy said that he would not push the Soviets "an inch beyond what is necessary."[55] He thought that an attack on Cuba would produce a Soviet attack on Berlin, and then what? He told the group he wanted to give Khrushchev room to back down. Kennedy told General Taylor that he knew the chiefs would be unhappy with the decision but he expected their support.[56]

The president had in hand a Justice Department opinion that a quarantine would be legal.[57] In response to a suggestion that the Monroe Doctrine be invoked to justify it, Kennedy responded that he had never liked the doctrine and would not talk about it. Instead, he obtained a vote of the Organization of American States endorsing the quarantine, for whatever support it would provide him in international law and politics.

As the president prepared to address the nation on television on October 22, he informed three startled groups of his decision: the cabinet, the

Soviets, and congressional leaders. The congressional meeting was "the most difficult" so far.[58] JFK made it clear he was providing information, not seeking formal advice and consent.[59] Powerful senator Richard Russell objected strenuously to the quarantine and called for a strike. Kennedy, angered, later said that if Russell had been through all the meetings, he might have understood. Senator William Fulbright echoed Russell. Both of these seasoned legislators, presented unprepared with the decision, reacted just as Kennedy had when he was first informed of the presence of the missiles. The president understood that.

Kennedy's televised message explained the situation, declared the quarantine, and included the ominous warning that any nuclear missile launched from Cuba at the United States would be regarded as an attack by the Soviets, "requiring a full retaliatory response upon the Soviet Union."[60] Here was the policy of massive retaliation, generated by presidents and acquiesced in by Congress, at its most chilling. Its explicit invocation raised the stakes to the maximum. If a tactical nuclear warhead had exploded over Guantanamo, would Kennedy have ordered the Air Force's obliterating strategic attack plan loosed at the Soviet Union?

As the president knew, the quarantine would soon apply to several Soviet ships presently nearing Cuba with more missiles and supplies. The Navy was ready to intercept and board any vessel reaching the forbidden zone. Issues about boarding procedure and whether to use force to overcome resistance now challenged civilian control of the military. When Secretary McNamara pressed the chief of naval operations for detail on how he planned to stop ships, the admiral replied that "this is none of your goddamn business" and that the Navy had been carrying out such operations since the days of John Paul Jones. McNamara told the admiral that the Navy would not fire a shot at anything without his permission and walked out of the room.[61]

Something fundamental had changed since Jones sailed into harm's way. It was no longer enough to send a capable commander faraway with discretion to act. Now nuclear war might ensue. As Secretary McNamara understood, the president's active command had to reach all the way to the scene of confrontation. Early in his presidency, Kennedy had installed the Situation Room in the White House, with advanced communications capacity to extend the reach of his personal command. The admiral did not understand what had changed; he was trying to protect military expertise, including traditional deference to the commander on the scene. In the event, the president selected the first ship to be boarded, an old freighter that was unlikely to be carrying contraband materials, to make the point to the world that the United States was serious. That worked.

In Moscow, Premier Khrushchev decided to retreat. Having witnessed one devastating war, he had no desire for another. On October 24, American reconnaissance saw that the Soviet freighters had turned around. Said Dean Rusk, "We're eyeball to eyeball and the other fellow just blinked."[62] But the crisis was far from resolved. Many missiles were still in Cuba. Without consulting the president, the Air Force raised its alert level to one step short of actual war, sending the message uncoded so the Soviets would read it. With the two great nuclear arsenals set on hair trigger, American forces mobilized for a projected invasion of Cuba the following week.

The crisis peaked on Saturday, October 26.[63] Almost no time was left—the Joint Chiefs were reacting to new evidence that the missiles in Cuba were nearing readiness by demanding massive air strikes as early as the following Monday. A message from Premier Khrushchev arrived, offering to remove the missiles in return for an American promise not to invade Cuba. While the ExComm was digesting this, a second message from Khrushchev was broadcast in Moscow. This one added a condition: removal of the American missiles from Turkey. Kennedy thought that was a reasonable trade, but Bundy objected that it would sell out NATO allies for American interests. McNamara, although unpersuaded that the missiles in Cuba presented a grave strategic threat to the United States, concurred.[64] Cold War needs for the reliability of American commitments had come to the fore.

As the exhausted executive officers pondered an American response, events threatened to spin out of control. Bulletins arrived confirming that one American U-2 had accidentally strayed over Soviet airspace in Siberia and that another had been shot down over Cuba by a surface-to-air missile. The ExComm had previously agreed that if a U-2 were destroyed, the United States would attack the offending missile site. But for the time being, the president "pulled everyone back" from retaliating.[65]

As the day wound down, Kennedy adjourned the depleted ExComm in favor of a smaller meeting including his brother, McNamara, Rusk, and Bundy to decide among the recommendations on the table.[66] A consensus had been emerging to respond to Khrushchev's first message in order to avoid the complications created by a promise to remove the missiles from Turkey. Rusk suggested that a secret promise could be made regarding Turkey. The president agreed. He dispatched his brother Robert to see Soviet ambassador Anatoly Dobrynin, bearing a letter officially promising not to invade Cuba if the missiles were removed and offering to discuss "other armaments." The attorney general delivered the letter and made the oral promise to remove the missiles from Turkey, conditioned on continued secrecy about the matter. He also rattled Dobrynin (and Khrushchev) by stressing that it was increasingly difficult to keep the American military under control—time was of the essence.

The two-part strategy succeeded. On Sunday the relieved Americans received Khrushchev's response promising that he would dismantle, crate, and retrieve the missiles from Cuba. Nothing was said in public about the American missiles in Turkey. Thus the missile crisis was settled by a secret arrangement that was carefully withheld from the American people. When Dobrynin later tried to formalize the oral promise by an exchange of letters, Robert Kennedy told him the president would not correspond on the subject but would keep his word.[67] There would be no paper trail. After a decent interval, the missiles were removed. Lying, the president denied that the action was a quid pro quo for Cuba.[68]

The shield of lies with which President Kennedy hid his trade of missiles in Turkey for missiles in Cuba was constructed to meet both international and domestic political considerations.[69] Perhaps NATO would not see that its security had been compromised to protect the United States. At home, Kennedy faced condemnation from the right wing for any negotiations with the Soviets regarding Cuba—revealing a seemingly even strategic deal would appear a surrender to many. The midterm elections for a delicately poised Congress were in immediate prospect, and the 1964 campaign was not very far away.[70] The American people could see that the Soviets had retreated, but they did not know the full story.

Amid general applause for the successful outcome of the missile crises, there was one chilling episode. When Kennedy met with the Joint Chiefs to thank them for their help, he was amazed at their intransigence. They were "openly contemptuous" of the president.[71] The egregious LeMay objected that the deal was the "greatest defeat in our history" and called for an invasion. Down that road lay World War III. The chain of civilian control, although strained, had held.

President Kennedy's resolution of the missile crisis certainly deserves praise. It has been called "perhaps the greatest personal diplomatic triumph of any President in our history."[72] Certainly it was a "close run thing," as Wellington said of Waterloo. Fortunately, Kennedy's blend of forcefulness and restraint was matched by Khrushchev's own flexibility and restraint. Of course, the crisis never needed to happen and probably would not have happened had Kennedy not blundered at the Bay of Pigs, impressing Khrushchev with both his visible desire for Cuba and his apparent weakness. So the premier had matched the president's blunder with one of his own, and to everyone's good fortune they recovered their senses in time.

Throughout the crisis the members of Congress were kept in ignorance or given only a courtesy briefing about imminent executive actions. After the sour meeting on the eve of the quarantine it was not likely they would be brought into the process of presidential decision making. The only way they could have been usefully involved would have been to add some congressional leaders to the ExComm, so that they would have been fully briefed about the issues. Perhaps that could have worked, although confidentiality concerns assured that it would not be tried. In any event, such an experiment would not have meaningfully involved Congress as an institution.

Resolution of the Cuban missile crisis had several positive consequences. The "hotline" between Washington and Moscow was soon set up to speed communications and avoid miscalculations. The direct and private correspondence between president and premier that resolved the crisis continued and often took a friendly tone. The two men had been through a trial of fire together. Negotiations toward a nuclear test-ban treaty went forward, leading to the first arms limitation of the nuclear age, the Limited Test Ban Treaty of 1963, which ended atmospheric explosions.[73] In the end, the crisis was the last direct confrontation between the superpowers in the Cold War, although the proxy wars around the world went on—and on.

To the Schoolhouse Door

Having been born into a life of great wealth, John Kennedy always demonstrated a certain lack of empathy for those less fortunate, the nature of whose daily lives he could scarcely imagine. Early in his presidency, civil rights engaged him mostly for its effect on world opinion. He knew that significant domestic legislation was blocked by the dominant coalition of southern Democrats and Republicans and was unwilling to spend much political capital taking positions that would further alienate the South. Civil rights was "a source of ongoing irritation to him rather than an opportunity to reform historic wrongs."[74] He would quote Thomas Jefferson's observation that "great innovations should not be forced on slender majorities."[75]

Kennedy did take some executive actions to promote civil rights that did not require legislation. He continued the executive order program forbidding race discrimination by government agencies and contractors that dated from FDR. He even expanded the reach of the program by requiring the controversial practice of affirmative action, in order to expand opportunities for minorities in the federal sphere.[76] Yet he delayed a promised executive order protecting civil rights in federally supported housing until after the 1962 election.[77] All of these activities occupied the twilight zone where Congress had neither authorized nor forbidden executive action, and Kennedy knew that congressional deadlock would prevent any statutory override.

There was a darker side to Kennedy's actions. He nominated four segregationist federal judges in the South to please Senator James Eastland of Mississippi, the chair of the Senate Judiciary Committee. He traded that acquiescence for the confirmation of black civil rights attorney Thurgood Marshall to a circuit court. And he sent Congress a mild civil rights bill regarding voting rights. Perhaps correctly, he thought that the nation was not ready for more aggressive action and that if he pushed too hard, he would jeopardize his reelection.

The one domestic issue that did engage Kennedy fully was the health of the economy, which undergirded everything. Although he soon increased military spending substantially, he tried to limit spending overall and to combat inflation. In 1962, he was outraged when steel companies raised their prices without warning and in the immediate wake of a wage settlement with the unions that had constrained raises.[78] Feeling betrayed, Kennedy jawboned the companies into rescinding the price increase. He denounced the companies on television and unleashed the Justice Department and the FBI on them. Noisy investigations of possible antitrust violations commenced, along with some ruthless tactics such as wiretapping and late-night telephone calls to steel executives from the FBI. The pressure succeeded; the companies retreated, and whatever threat of inflation they had posed was gone.

President Kennedy soon found himself trapped in the middle between civil rights leaders clamoring for progress and even moderate southerners dragging their feet. Feeling unappreciated for his efforts, whenever possible he had his brother take the lead on preventing or resolving the disorders of the early 1960s. The first flare-up, violence against the Freedom Riders who were trying to desegregate southern bus lines in 1961 in response to court orders, caught him by surprise.[79] Knowing that the law was on the side of the riders but calling the crisis a "civil rights mess," Kennedy hesitated. His options were unappealing. He did not want to inflame the South by sending in the Army, but state and local authorities could not be trusted. He accepted a suggestion to create a civilian force of US marshals and dispatched them unenthusiastically to restore order. Kennedy was angered when told to his face that there was a need for his moral leadership. He made no televised statement, leaving that to his attorney general.

In the early 1960s, civil rights leaders moved to integrate the last two state universities that were still resisting the Supreme Court's school desegregation orders from 1954 and earlier. When James Meredith, armed with a federal court order, sought entry to the University of Mississippi in 1962, Governor Ross Barnett blocked his admission.[80] Both the attorney general and the president negotiated with the governor in an effort to obtain peaceful compliance with the order. JFK informed the governor he would enforce the order and sent in hundreds of marshals. Severe riots ensued, as the state provided no protection. After going on television to say that his constitutional obligation was to enforce the court orders, Kennedy sent in both the federalized National Guard and the regular Army. At the end of the violence, two people were dead, two hundred federal agents were injured, two hundred rioters were arrested, and Meredith was admitted.

Next a frightening set of civil disorders broke out in Birmingham after civil rights leaders started demonstrations in hopes of desegregating the city. Horrified, the American people watched televised scenes of the Birmingham police using fire hoses and dogs against the demonstrators, many of whom were teenagers, while hauling them off to jail. President Kennedy's initial reaction was to say incorrectly that there was no federal statute involved in the Birmingham disorders and that he had no power to intervene in a state matter.[81]

Actually, the president's faithful execution authority was sufficient. He had the traditional statutory authority to use the militia or the Army to quell disorder. Also, local authorities were violating the constitutional rights of the demonstrators to free speech and assembly, to equal protection of the law, and to due process. Thus the constitutional component of the faithful execution duty filled any gaps in the statutes. To his displeasure, the president was immediately corrected by Dean Erwin Griswold of the Harvard Law School, who said that Kennedy "hasn't even started to use the powers that are available to him," and by Dr. Martin Luther

King, who pointed to ongoing blatant violations of basic constitutional rights.[82]

The president did negotiate with local leaders behind the scenes to have demonstrators released from jail and to obtain promises of desegregation in Birmingham. As disturbances continued, he put the Army on alert and prepared to federalize the National Guard. On television, he stated that he had obtained a fair agreement that was being sabotaged by extremists on both sides. As the waters calmed, the president saw that he would have to propose a strong civil rights bill, whatever his inclinations. He had been accurately measuring the temper of Congress but not "the dynamism of a revolutionary movement."[83]

At the University of Alabama, Governor George Wallace promised to stand in the schoolhouse door to prevent integration under another court order.[84] Sounding like Eisenhower, the president responded that he was "obligated to carry out the court order. . . . There is no choice in the matter." Vice President Johnson, who understood civil rights issues, told Kennedy that what blacks wanted most from him was a moral commitment to their cause, not a discussion of court orders.[85]

On the scene at Tuscaloosa, Deputy Attorney General Katzenbach approached Governor Wallace, standing defiantly in the schoolhouse door. Katzenbach communicated Kennedy's order that he desist from unlawful obstruction; Wallace refused. Here was the old southern doctrine of state interposition against federal authority. Andrew Jackson would have offered to hang him from the nearest tree. President Kennedy, invoking his power to suppress domestic violence, again federalized the National Guard and put the Army on alert. When a Guard general told Wallace to stand aside, he did so, having made his political point. The students registered.

At long last, an American president now spoke to the people about civil rights as a matter of conscience. On television, Kennedy said it was "not even a legal or legislative issue alone. . . . We are confronted primarily with a moral issue." He called for congressional action to integrate public accommodations, to enforce desegregation, and to protect the right to vote. He knew that this stand would jeopardize his legislative program and might cost him reelection. He did introduce a strong bill, which was stalled in Congress when he died. Yet Kennedy's ambivalence continued in the summer of 1963. He kept a public distance from the March on Washington in August, while maneuvering behind the scenes to prevent disorder.[86] Seeing the triumphs of the march and of King's great speech, Kennedy gave his cautious endorsement. He was growing in office, if slowly.[87]

Slipping into Vietnam

President Kennedy gazed upon an unstable scene in Southeast Asia. His first important initiative there involved Laos, and he handled it skillfully. Confronted by the possibility of a communist takeover, Kennedy conducted a successful bluff. He threatened to send in American troops while having no intention of doing so and pressured the Soviets to rein in their clients in Laos.[88] (Meanwhile, the Joint Chiefs urged the use of land and air forces in Laos, with nuclear bombs as needed should the Chinese intervene.) Somehow, a coalition government was formed, and when it unraveled later, Kennedy was able to shunt the Laos question to negotiations in Geneva.

Vietnam would be another matter. Like Eisenhower, Kennedy knew that Vietnam had little intrinsic strategic importance to the United States, but he also subscribed to the domino theory. Thinking that he could not both allow Vietnam to fall to the communists and win reelection, he attempted to hold the South Vietnamese government together without a large military commitment.

Kennedy began by approving Eisenhower's last counterinsurgency plan for Vietnam, which provided funds for their military. He then created a secret Vietnam task force in the executive and charged it vaguely to prevent communist domination of South Vietnam.[89] As ambassador, he chose his former political opponent for the Senate, Henry Cabot Lodge Jr., covering his own right flank. Before long, Kennedy took the first step down what would prove to be a long, tragic road for the United States by accepting a recommendation from his task force to send in more military advisers, this time exceeding the limit of 685 advisers set in the 1954 Geneva Accords. No more stop signs lay ahead.

Kennedy concluded that letting Vietnam collapse would injure America's international standing and would expose him to right-wing calumny. He then exchanged prearranged letters with President Diem of South Vietnam in which Diem asked for more support and Kennedy joined him in a "sharply increased joint effort" against the communists. Before the end of the year, more than two thousand advisers had arrived. Some of them became the first American troops to be sent into battle in Vietnam. The administration tried to hide both the extent and nature of the

American role.[90] But the first American casualty provided a name that would someday appear on Maya Lin's stark granite wall in Washington.

From the outset of American involvement in Vietnam, American presidents struggled to obtain good intelligence about actual conditions there. A pattern soon emerged. The president would send (another) fact-finding mission charged to dispel doubts about the progress of the war. It would be unable to do so, because every optimistic assessment, usually from somewhere in the Defense Department, was offset by a pessimistic one, usually from somewhere in the State Department. After one such clash, a frustrated Kennedy asked: "The two of you did visit the same country, didn't you?"[91] With the facts always contested, ideology tended to dominate decisions.

For lack of an acceptable alternative, President Kennedy muddled along, caught between his fear of a Vietnamese collapse and his desire to keep the American commitment limited enough to preserve the political option of an exit. By 1963, the administration had lost faith in the ability of President Diem to preserve his nation. Kennedy accepted recommendations that the United States support a coup against Diem by signaling approval to the plotters. In early November, the coup began amid dishonest statements that the American government was not involved in any way.[92] When the insurgents assassinated Diem, President Kennedy was genuinely shocked at his own handiwork. Unwittingly, he had bequeathed to his successor a new level of American involvement and difficulty in Vietnam.

As he prepared for a political trip to Texas, Kennedy asked an aide for an exploration of all options concerning Vietnam, a review of "the whole thing from the bottom to the top."[93] It appears that he would have attempted to preserve the status quo until his reelection. After that, no one knows. His last words on the subject, in an undelivered speech scheduled for November 22, were "We dare not weary of the task."[94] Weary we would, and more than he could have imagined.

"Let Us Continue"[95]

Like Harry Truman before him, Lyndon Johnson knew he had a legacy to face as he assumed the presidency at a moment of national trauma. Two legacies, actually. On the domestic side, there was a stalled legislative program that included a vital civil rights bill. In foreign affairs, Vietnam was unstable in the wake of the coup against Diem. Johnson's own two legacies would be a nearly unparalleled record of success in enacting domestic legislation and a tragic record of failure in Vietnam. Today, his large achievements are unfairly obscured by his one great failure, for which he does bear full responsibility.

John Kennedy selected Lyndon Baines Johnson as his running mate after defeating him for the nomination in a bitter contest. The choice of Johnson was driven by electoral considerations—Kennedy's best chance for victory lay in capturing some of the South, especially Texas.[96] There was substantial opposition to Johnson within the party and Kennedy's circle, however, because LBJ's Senate career was substantially more conservative than his presidency would become.[97] A general point about the predictability of presidential performance lurks here: the positions a person takes while climbing the ladder toward the presidency reflect pressures that may fall away once the goal is attained.

For Johnson, the vice presidency seemed the only available route to the presidency he so deeply coveted. Once installed in the post, he made two unsuccessful attempts to capture significant power.[98] First, he made overtures to his former colleagues in the Senate, hoping to combine his ceremonial role as presiding officer with a continuing role as head of the party caucus and thus de facto majority leader. The Senate Democrats rebuffed this attempt to blur the separation of powers. Not incidentally, if successful the move would have given Johnson the power to contest the president by asserting his command of the Senate. Second, Johnson asked Kennedy for an office in the White House (which no vice president had enjoyed) and for a supervisory portfolio over various national security issues—a deputy president, perhaps. Kennedy took a lesson from Lincoln's deft deflation of Seward's early move for shared power. He gave LBJ an office across the street and assigned him to advisory boards that entailed no command responsibility. For the remainder of Kennedy's administration, Johnson sank into a depressed but loyal silence, a visibly invisible man. His presence on the periphery carried the constant, intrinsic vice presidential intimation of presidential mortality.[99]

Master of Congress[100]

Lyndon Johnson's transition into the presidency amid national shock and horror after the Kennedy assassination may have been his finest hour. He knew that the mood of Congress and the country would support completion of JFK's legislative program. LBJ certainly possessed the experience to succeed in that task. Over a span of twenty-three years, he had served in both houses of Congress and had risen to become the greatest majority leader in the modern Senate. Therefore he also knew the obstacles.

Between the assassination and his first State of the Union address seven weeks later, Johnson skillfully built "a platform from which to launch a crusade for social justice on a vast new scale."[101] On his first night in office, he remarked that "every issue on my desk tonight was on my desk when I came to Congress in 1937."[102] Thus the scale of his ambition was not merely to fulfill his martyred predecessor's agenda but to complete and even outdo the agenda of his revered mentor, Franklin Roosevelt. Time would tell whether the American people were ready for a fundamental expansion of the role of the federal government in their lives.

Of course, pushing bills along from the White House differs from doing so within Congress. Johnson was aware that he would have both more and less power over legislation than any single member of either chamber. Although he could not wield any of the various internal levers possessed by congressional leaders, he could offer anyone in Congress some of the myriad gifts within his command, such as patronage and post offices. More important, the immense power of his veto let him inform the members which provisions he would tolerate and which he would not.

Lyndon Johnson's extraordinary personality held both advantages and disadvantages for him as president. His volcanic energy led him to drive himself and others unmercifully. One observer said, "I never thought it was *possible* for anyone to work that hard."[103] Nothing less would have brought him from the grinding poverty of his youth in central Texas to the heights of power. Yet his deep insecurity made him insist on total loyalty and subservience from his subordinates. His vast ambition to achieve more than any predecessor could not be satisfied—no amount of approval was ever sufficient. He capriciously displayed both greatness of spirit and dismaying pettiness.[104] Robert Kennedy, with whom he had a spectacular feud, summed him up as "the most formidable human being I've ever met."[105]

Johnson's political focus was the obverse of John Kennedy's. Each of them preferred to operate in the arena where he could exercise the most control over events. LBJ's talents and interests centered on domestic issues, not foreign policy. He cared about the lives of ordinary Americans in ways Kennedy never did, and he was comfortable engaging deeply with

Congress, as Kennedy never was. Johnson drew both his political philosophy and his legislative approach from his mentors, Franklin Roosevelt
and House Speaker Sam Rayburn. The essence of his political philosophy
was his faith in the state as an engine of social progress. In 1964 he said,
"Hell, we're the richest country in the world, the most powerful. We can
do it all."[106] He was sure the Constitution was adequate to the task.

With his penchant for dominating every issue he could reach, Johnson
served as his own chief of staff most of the time. He installed a set of able
and devoted generalist aides, most of them Texans. Like FDR he assigned
the same problem to several people at once, leaving issue resolution at his
own desk. More darkly, he saw opposition as betrayal. Hence he followed
JFK's practice of using the Internal Revenue Service to investigate and
discomfit his enemies.[107]

LBJ gave closer attention to moving legislation through Congress than
any other president in American history, not excepting FDR. Like his
hero, Johnson revealed the immense potential of the president's seemingly innocuous constitutional power to recommend legislation to Congress. He boasted that he planned to "crack the wall of separation enough
to give the Congress a feeling of participation in creating my bills without
exposing my plans . . . to advance congressional opposition."[108] Accordingly, he saw that "there is but one way for a President to deal with the
Congress, and that is continuously, incessantly, and without interrup-
tion."[109] Possessed of shrewd political instincts and a master at negotiation and persuasion, the president knew that timing and preparation were
essential to legislative success. His aides were everywhere on Capitol
Hill, and he was in constant direct contact with individual members of
Congress, hectoring, cajoling, bullying, prevailing.[110] His style was most
memorably on display in his herculean and ultimately successful effort to
secure passage of the Civil Rights Act of 1964.[111] Johnson tended not to
make explicit promises in return for votes, but the mutuality of cooperation was understood all around.

There was an intrinsic disadvantage to all this frenetic activity in pursuit of completing—and surpassing—FDR's New Deal. Johnson wanted
to get as many bills passed as possible in the two brief windows of opportunity he perceived, one after he took office in 1963 and another after his landslide victory in 1964. He would worry about implementation
and adjustments later on. In consequence, much of the legislation over
which Johnson presided was sloppy and riddled with unintended effects.
It shared these characteristics with much of FDR's legislation from the

Hundred Days, which at least had crisis conditions as an excuse. But because it is as difficult constitutionally to amend as to enact legislation, repairs often proved difficult or impossible to make. Unhappily, Johnson's legacy fostered an enduring skepticism in the American political process about whether federal legislation can be expected to achieve its purposes. As a result, no later president would be able to spur Congress to action with comparable success.

Johnson quickly put his own stamp on the presidency.[112] His first State of the Union address declared war on poverty. Having been raised in poverty and having seen the ravages of the Depression firsthand, LBJ had a natural sympathy for the downtrodden. Only FDR had shown a similar willingness to include the most powerless Americans in his concept of the Constitution's faithful execution duty.

Congress was compliant. It quickly enacted a tax cut bill that Kennedy had promoted unsuccessfully for years. Then it passed the main war on poverty bill, which focused on education and job training. Many structural causes of poverty remained untouched, however, and funding was insufficient. Unhappily, the war on poverty was intrinsically unwinnable. The president's program combined vast expectations with modest means in a recipe for disappointment that he would repeat.

A greater triumph was the civil rights bill, which absorbed most of Johnson's efforts for the first half of 1964. He told people he would be the president who finished what Lincoln began.[113] Believing deeply in civil rights, LBJ would not settle for a weak bill. When advisors counseled him not to spend scarce political capital on a lost cause, Johnson asked, "What the hell's the presidency for?"[114] He surmounted a three-month filibuster in the Senate, the longest ever, and happily signed the landmark Civil Rights Act of 1964.[115] It prohibited discrimination in public accommodations and employment and bolstered enforcement of desegregation orders. The president later expanded the act's protections by issuing an executive order prohibiting sex discrimination in federal functions.[116]

Enforced with vigor, the Civil Rights Act began the transformation of the South. Its passage required moral presidential leadership of a high order, along with great practical political skill. Johnson knew that his sponsorship of civil rights legislation would hurt him and his party in the South, but he willingly paid the price. There is greatness in that.

A war on poverty and the first important civil rights legislation since Reconstruction were not enough for Johnson. Next came his signature goal, the creation of a Great Society. This proposal resonated with Jefferson's inaugural call for a republic of civic virtue in which all Americans could join, although on a grandiose scale that would have staggered Jefferson himself. Johnson's plan was to begin by repairing the cities and the environment. He also promised to bolster education, which was always important to him because it had lifted him out of poverty. To have any hope of accomplishing his great dreams, Johnson needed to be elected in his own right, along with a supportive Congress.

In the November election, LBJ won a landslide victory, garnering 61 percent of the popular vote and sweeping large Democratic majorities into both houses of Congress on his coattails. Liberalism stood at high tide, controlling all three branches of the federal government. Knowing that the tide would someday ebb, in the first half of 1965 Johnson assailed the new Congress with sixty-five messages proposing legislation.[117] The four most important initiatives, all of which passed, were Medicare/ Medicaid, aid to education, immigration reform, and voting rights. There was more—wilderness protection, clean air regulation, highway beautification. Not since FDR's most important legislative achievements in 1935, the year of Social Security, had there been such transformative domestic legislation.

The Voting Rights Act of 1965, which eventually changed the face of southern governance, was enacted following the march for voting rights in Selma, Alabama, and the violent response it received.[118] Showing that he meant business, Johnson sent US marshals into Alabama to ensure that the march would be completed peacefully; he also threatened Governor Wallace with the use of federal troops. Passage of the act followed Johnson's impassioned statement on television that "we shall overcome." For the first time since Lincoln, a president had associated his own fate with that of American blacks.[119] Later on, he also nominated the first black Supreme Court justice, Thurgood Marshall. It has been well said that "dedication to social justice has not been one of the hallmarks of the modern presidency."[120] Except for Lyndon Johnson.

Most of the steam had gone out of LBJ's great legislation machine by the fall of 1965. The war in Vietnam was increasingly occupying national attention as the president escalated it while quietly cutting back on funding requests for his Great Society programs. A deadly riot in the Watts section of Los Angeles initiated a series of urban riots in the late 1960s, which soon produced a political backlash against social programs in general and blacks in particular. The president continued to press for new legislation, but he had to settle for a few scattered victories in the remainder of his term. These were not trivial—they included the Head Start program for early education, the creation of new cabinet departments for housing and transportation, a civil rights bill forbidding discrimination in housing (which responded to the shock of the assassination of Martin Luther King), and a crime control bill to reduce urban disorder and rising crime rates.

The tragedy of Lyndon Johnson's presidency was in part a domestic one. As the sixties thundered along, there were signs of "an overarching political consensus shattered in a rush of extraordinary achievements," that is, of a disintegration of the New Deal settlement that LBJ had yearned to extend, not destroy.[121] A Republican sweep in the 1966 midterm elections heralded the birth of the conservative movement that would soon recast American politics.[122] Well before that, the formation of a Great Society in America had been put on hold indefinitely while the president wrestled with his nemesis, Vietnam.

War without Consent

Conflict in Vietnam touched six American presidencies, Truman through Ford.[123] It damaged several of them, most of all Lyndon Johnson's. The consistent thread of presidential self-injury was deception about the incumbent administration's actual intentions and activities in Vietnam. When Congress and the American public discovered the deceptions, as they always did, debate about the dubious wisdom of the Vietnam engagement was elevated into a necessary but debilitating debate about its constitutional legitimacy.

By this era, Americans generally accepted the need for some kinds of covert executive activity in foreign affairs. As we have seen, dating at least from Franklin Roosevelt there has been substantial precedent for secret executive action that has been tolerated after its discovery. Still, it is impossible to fit the scale of the Vietnam deceptions into our constitutional scheme. By overstretching their constitutional power as commander in chief, presidents produced reactions from Congress and the public that have had long-standing, largely negative effects.

Like John Kennedy, Lyndon Johnson took office with an urge to prove himself in foreign affairs and a determination to avoid any national defeat or demonstration of weakness. Like Andrew Jackson, he emerged from the American hinterland with an outlook that was parochial, nationalistic, touchy about national honor, suspicious of foreigners, and inclined to military solutions.[124] LBJ's congressional service had given him some background in foreign policy. Once president, Johnson received immediate help—he soon forged close ties to Robert McNamara and Dean Rusk and also relied on McGeorge Bundy. Seduced by the obvious intelligence and legendary tough-mindedness of his aides, Johnson accepted the commitments he inherited.[125]

The cold warriors around Johnson had overdrawn three historical lessons in a way that would impel the new president into Vietnam.[126] First, the nation's unpreparedness before Pearl Harbor led them to perceive no sufficient limits to American military power. Second, the specter of Munich deterred any action that might "appease" communists. Third, the domestic havoc that followed the "loss" of China to communism taught that any retreat in foreign policy would receive domestic political punishment. Vividly recalling Joe McCarthy's rampage, which was fueled by charges that the United States had lost China to the communists, LBJ was determined not to be the president who lost Vietnam.[127]

Thus, from the outset of his presidency, Lyndon Johnson was trapped by the dominant political currents of his time.[128] Unhappily, it was already becoming evident that the strategic situation in Vietnam was nearly intractable. North Vietnam justifiably considered the conflict a civil war—it saw South Vietnam as an illegitimate creature that had refused to hold the elections required by the Geneva Accords. Determined to reunify the nation, North Vietnam was disinclined to negotiate and was prepared to absorb considerable punishment in order to supply its insurgent allies in South Vietnam, the Vietcong. For its part, the South Vietnamese government was an ongoing stew of corruption, incompetence, and intransigence that tottered on the edge of collapse because of a lack of popular support and saw negotiating with the North as a prelude to ultimate defeat. The United States wanted to preserve South Vietnam from communist domination but had to do so by means of a limited war that would not forfeit support at home or bring the Chinese or the Soviets into the war directly (here the Korean experience was instructive).

In retrospect, "LBJ appears less a fool or a knave than a beleaguered executive attempting to maintain an established policy against an immediate threat in a situation where there was no attractive alternative."[129] That said, he made a crucial mistake near the outset that eventually undermined the constitutional underpinning of his efforts. Johnson's sponsorship of the Tonkin Gulf Resolution to authorize the war involved deception about both the facts and the president's intentions, setting the stage for a repetition of these sins that would eventually destroy his presidency. It is one thing to find oneself in a strategic bind and quite another to try to work out of it behind a bodyguard of lies.

At first, Johnson temporized with Vietnam while he pushed his domestic agenda through Congress. By the spring of 1964, the president was uneasy about "messing around" in Vietnam without congressional approval.[130] Recalling Korea, he understood the constitutional and political value of a congressional commitment. Here lay an irony. Harry Truman had avoided seeking a resolution of support for the Korean intervention in order to keep his successors' hands free. But the heavy political price that Truman paid for his unilateral action reversed the effective force of the precedent, at least politically. Johnson would make a different mistake by seeking authorization without giving Congress enough information to make it meaningful.

Complicating Johnson's calculus was the looming presidential election. For most of the summer he hesitated, not wanting to send a war message to Congress in this season. Then an opportunity arose that he decided to seize.[131] He had authorized secret raids on the North Vietnamese coast by South Vietnamese commandos while US destroyers patrolled nearby in the Gulf of Tonkin. In early August, the North Vietnamese sent torpedo boats to attack the destroyers.[132] The *Maddox* fired at the boats after receiving reports that they had loosed torpedoes. Days later came inconclusive reports of a second attack on the *Maddox*. The president, after launching air attacks at the bases from which the boats had sallied, decided to seek a congressional resolution. There was some confusion within the administration about whether a second attack had occurred, but no matter, Johnson presented it as a fact. Remarking that he did not think congressional authorization for retaliation was necessary, he preferred it in light of the Korean precedent.[133]

Neither at this time nor later did Johnson consider a declaration of war against North Vietnam. After World War II, formal declarations have fallen out of use, because they imply an intent to invade and subjugate the enemy. Limited wars do not seek that goal. For example, Truman did not begin his intervention in Korea intending to occupy and unite the peninsula. In the post–World War II era, presidents request and Congress grants resolutions authorizing the use of force for stated purposes. Suiting an era of shadow wars against lesser nations or even terrorists, the resolutions are usually phrased broadly to meet all eventualities. They are the constitutional equivalent of declarations of war.[134]

President Johnson wanted an authorization unencumbered by any embarrassing congressional debate that might signal disunity to the enemy. Congress complied, except for some portentous grumbling. Addressing the nation on television, LBJ misleadingly described acts of unprovoked aggression on the high seas. He did not mention the commando raids, and he assured the people that "we still seek no wider war."[135] The resolution, drawn from earlier ones, had been on hand for months, ready for submission at the right time. It authorized the president to use "all necessary measures to repel any armed attack against the United States and to prevent further aggression." When the sweeping text of the resolution raised questions in Congress, the administration sent soothing assurances that the president did not intend to escalate the war.[136] Johnson campaigned for election on that explicit representation, saying that he did not propose to have American boys do what Asian boys should do for themselves.

The Tonkin Gulf Resolution passed overwhelmingly, as have most war authorizations in American history. Members of Congress, presented with a presidential claim that an aggressor has attacked the nation, are loath to oppose a military response. Johnson had exaggerated the facts, but so had Polk many years before with no adverse consequences; a crisis seems no time for nice distinctions. There is, however, likely to be a disconnect between what Congress approves and what Congress intends in these situations. The problem arises from the dual roles of the congressional action. Congress wants to address the foe in fierce and unyielding terms of national unity and resolve. At the same time, it is addressing the president and usually trying to express both support and caution. In short, the message is likely to be mixed and muddled if the nation is uncertain about the wisdom of war or the extent of an appropriate commitment. Hence, a president who takes Congress at its literal word risks outrunning the underlying level of national support, as Johnson would do. He signaled his insensitivity to the unsteadiness of the base he stood on by crowing in private about the breadth of the resolution: "Like Grandma's nightshirt, it covered everything."[137] In the end, it would not be Grandma who stood exposed.

"The election over, the President during the first seven months of 1965 incrementally and often after hours of agonizing internal deliberations committed the United States to war."[138] Air attacks against North Vietnam began, increased, and moved north. Taking the Tonkin Gulf Resolution at its word, Johnson said he had "no uncertainty" about his authority to increase the bombing.[139] The introduction of Marines to guard air bases in South Vietnam was followed by steadily increasing numbers of Army troops. By the end of 1965, United States armed forces in South Vietnam numbered 185,000; by early 1968, over 500,000.[140]

Throughout Johnson's time in office, Congress supported the war with the large supplementary appropriations that were needed. By separating funding for Vietnam from other appropriations bills, the president was forcing Congress to share responsibility for continuation of the war, as he explicitly reminded the legislators.[141] The funding bills often passed by large margins, amid protests by many legislators that they no longer supported the administration's war policy but would not abandon the troops in the field. For a long time it had been a principle of American politics that voting against supplies for the military in wartime is political suicide, as the Federalists had established by opposing the War of 1812. Hence congressional control of the purse is a weak constitutional lever in wartime, and every president since Madison has known that. Congress follows the flag. Its appropriations under the duress of presidential faits accomplis provide constitutional ratification, but it is thinner than Grandma's nightshirt.

As he escalated the war, LBJ repeatedly denied doing so, in an effort to protect the viability of his domestic initiatives and to preserve the option of withdrawing without seeming defeated.[142] Soon the press discovered a "credibility gap" between his statements and the facts. Like Kennedy, LBJ tried to manipulate the press by planting stories and bullying media executives, with only middling success. A vital and enduring loss of the American people's trust in their presidents was occurring.[143]

Johnson took criticism of the war personally and soon stopped listening to dissenting views. Loyalty substituted for analysis in his councils. Tormented, he did sometimes call on the establishment "wise men" who had provided advice to presidents since Truman. This group, whose membership evolved over the years, offered the benefit of free-ranging wisdom at the cost of restricted background on the issues they considered. When they finally turned against the war in 1968, Johnson knew that the game was up.[144]

As the war escalated, the Joint Chiefs constantly pressed for more troops while assuring Johnson that this time it would do the trick. The president generally credited their views and gave them latitude to run the ground war as they chose. In contrast, he micromanaged the air war, personally picking targets in an effort to achieve maximum results without drawing the Chinese into the conflict. He forced the generals to make optimistic statements to the public, whatever their actual views. He did resist predictable pressure from the chiefs to employ even greater force against North Vietnam.

As American casualties mounted without a resolution in sight, the largest antiwar movement in American history gathered steam.[145] By 1967, hundreds of thousands were taking to the streets, and college campuses erupted. The president had two kinds of reactions, one of them positive. He made no effort to prosecute peaceful dissent. The First Amendment's guarantees of freedom of speech and assembly had acquired enough force through Supreme Court interpretation in the years following World War I to forestall any such effort.

Less creditably, LBJ concluded that domestic dissent must have roots in foreign sources such as the enemy in North Vietnam. He simply could not believe that so many Americans would disagree so fundamentally with him in good faith. He loosed all the investigative agencies of the executive branch to infiltrate the dissenters and to intercept their communications, in a vain hope of proving the international connection.[146] Much of this activity violated statutory or constitutional limitations.[147] When the CIA directly informed him that no such connection could be shown, he ignored it. Thus his widespread violations of the First Amendment were indirect and surreptitious, but no less illegal than the cruder forms he eschewed.

After years of what one observer called "all-out limited war," nothing better than stalemate was in prospect.[148] The president's strategy shifted from achieving victory to holding on and punishing the North Vietnamese until they could be forced to negotiate an acceptable settlement.[149] Of course, Johnson did not share his diminishing expectations with Congress or the people. In late 1967, a deeply frustrated Robert McNamara called for scaling back the American effort and left office, to be succeeded by Clark Clifford. The stunning Tet offensive by the North Vietnamese in early 1968 was a military defeat for them but a political victory, because it ended the patience of the American people with the war and the president.

At the end of March 1968, President Johnson went on television and announced that he would restrict the bombing and renew his efforts for negotiations with the North Vietnamese. At the end of his speech he surprised the nation by saying that he would decline to run for a second elected term. He had been privately contemplating retirement for about a year. There was little prospect for more of the domestic legislation he treasured. And his mind was turning to history. He had suffered a severe heart attack while in the Senate and did not want to subject the nation to a repeat of Wilson's last years, with a crippled president lingering in office.[150] An unwinnable war had crushed his dreams.

The Vietnam obsession was not President Johnson's only foreign policy problem. Of course, everything else went at least somewhat better. In this hemisphere, he made a unilateral decision to send troops into the Dominican Republic in 1965 after a coup occurred there. Instability in that unhappy nation was partly the fault of the United States, which had earlier helped to oust dictator Rafael Trujillo.[151] Johnson misled Congress and the public by claiming the intervention was an attempt to protect American lives, when it was in fact actuated by a concern that the new government might be leftist.[152] This poorly conceived intervention gave way to an authoritarian regime that lasted a quarter century.

The six-day war between Israel and its neighbors in 1967 produced a more subtle and successful American response.[153] President Johnson pressed Israel to accept a cease-fire as the price of holding off possible intervention by the Soviet Union in the region. LBJ also stayed his hand when Israeli forces attacked the American spy ship *Liberty*, killing and wounding many sailors. He accepted an apology and reparations. What passes for calm in the Middle East was restored.

In another spy ship incident oceans away, the USS *Pueblo* was seized on the high seas by the erratic North Korean regime in early 1968, prompting widespread calls for a military response. Having enough war on his agenda already, Johnson conducted a patient diplomatic campaign that produced release of the crew at the end of the year, as the president prepared to lay down his burdens.

Lyndon Johnson's two constitutional legacies produced mixed results for the presidency. His expansion of the power to recommend legislation still stands as the model for maximum use of the potential lurking in the president's role in Congress. Unlike Jefferson, who first energized the president's role via a stealth campaign, or Jackson, who used the force of his veto to impose his view of the Constitution on Congress, LBJ worked openly and cooperatively with legislators. He deserves full credit for the legislative record he compiled, which stands second in importance to that of FDR.

Of course, the Vietnam War dominates Johnson's constitutional legacy regarding the commander in chief power. Here, his habit of deception ultimately reduced the power of his successors by squandering the traditional trust of the people in their presidents. Richard Nixon would add to the mistrust. The presidency has never fully recovered from the damage they inflicted on it. Johnson always thought he was on firm constitutional ground as he expanded the Vietnam War, because of the Tonkin Gulf Resolution and continuing appropriations for the war. The tenacity of the antiwar movement's claim that the war was illegal and unconstitutional, however, shows that something more was afoot than translation of moral and political objection to the war into constitutional argument.

The problem was twofold. First, LBJ expanded the war far beyond the expectations of the Congress that enacted the resolution. He did so despite explicit promises to show restraint. Second, his consistent pattern of deception forfeited the connection to popular support that would otherwise be implied by such actions as continuing appropriations. Contrast the pattern of Lincoln's actions. Having begun to conduct the Civil War in the absence of Congress, he asked for its explicit ratification of what he was doing and gave his justifications. That was a much sounder basis for sweeping presidential action than the thin support Johnson obtained. Unfortunately, his successor would compound his errors.

CHAPTER ELEVEN

Not Illegal

Nixon, Ford, and Carter

DAVID FROST: Can [the president] decide whether it's in the best interests of the nation or something, and do something illegal?

RICHARD NIXON: Well, when the president does it, that means it is not illegal. . . . If the president, for example, approves something because of the national security, . . . then the president's decision in that instance is one that enables those who carry it out, to carry it out without violating a law. —David Frost interview, televised May 19, 1977[1]

I s it true that every presidential interpretation of the Constitution is legal, at least unless Congress either overrides it by legislation or impeaches the president? That vision of a growing "imperial presidency" alarmed Arthur Schlesinger in the 1970s.[2] At its grandest, the vision would give the United States a "constitutional" dictator, but one who would be mostly free of the constitutional shackles that justify the old republican idea of a temporary grant of nearly unlimited power. Worst of all, the extent of the dictator's power would lie only in his or her own mind and not in a grant from the nation's other representative institutions. In that sense, the power would not be constitutional at all. The Johnson administration, for all its secrecy, duplicity, and grandiosity, never approached this precipice. But his successor would do so, until thrown backward and out of office by the other republican institutions of the nation.

The Oddest Man[3]

Each president's interpretation of the Constitution has been shaped by his own character and values. Because Richard Nixon's nature was unlike that of any other president, some of his approaches to the Constitution were idiosyncratic. Nixon, who once described himself as an introvert in an extrovert's occupation, was deeply shy, suspicious, and negative. Unlike other politicians, he seemed unable to relate to other people in any natural way and often seemed at a distance even from himself.[4]

Yet Nixon's powerful analytic mind operated easily at the level of geopolitics. He understood American politics deeply enough to initiate a national political restructuring that still prevails. His ascension to the presidency after many political reverses was a triumph of his political sagacity and determination. Once there, he instituted the modern characteristic of the presidency as a continuous political campaign, with emphasis on constant fund-raising and maneuvering against political opponents.[5]

There were two principal constitutional consequences of Richard Nixon's odd character. First, his approach to governance, especially in foreign policy, was highly secretive and even personal. He excluded Congress, the people, and most of the executive branch from his decision making. Like Woodrow Wilson he would listen to his advisers and then retire alone to make a decision, often after hours of deliberation. Also like Wilson, he regarded consultation beyond his circle as a waste of time. Like both Wilson and Lyndon Johnson, he saw disagreement as disloyalty. Second, seeking to counter the enemies that he perceived all around him, Nixon transgressed both constitutional and statutory boundaries to an extent that left him disgraced and stripped of office by a resignation that averted a pending impeachment.

A Two-Man Operation[6]

In 1968, Richard Nixon took the presidency in a narrow victory over the shattered Democrats. Having no particular mandate and having made few promises, he was free to chart his own course. Campaigning, he had claimed to have a secret plan to end the Vietnam War, but that was a lie. Nixon was the first incoming president since 1848 to face a Congress dominated by the opposing party, but he could work around that. The new president's career in Congress had left him with an abiding—and dangerous—contempt for the institution. His memoirs argued that "the alternative to strong Presidential government is government by Congress, which is no government at all."[7] He explained that modern presidents had not "stolen" power from Congress; instead, "modern Presidents had merely stepped into the vacuum created when Congress failed to discipline itself sufficiently to play a strong policy-making role."[8] A collision impended.

Nixon thought the foreign policy bureaucracies at State and Defense were filled with enemies and incompetents. He would work around them also. He installed William Rogers at State and Melvin Laird at Defense and promptly cut them out of the policy loop, where they remained. No other president had done that. He would forgo the expertise available at many levels of the federal bureaucracy in favor of his own capacity to figure out facts and policy.

President Nixon's partner in foreign affairs would be the redoubtable Henry Kissinger, his national security adviser.[9] Like Nixon, Kissinger was brilliant, egocentric, brittle, and secretive. This odd couple would conduct American foreign policy from the White House for the duration of the Nixon presidency. The central premise of their partnership was that the Constitution permitted the president to determine and conduct national security policy at his own discretion.

Many previous presidents had been willing to exercise broad powers of initiative in setting foreign policy or deploying the military. John Kennedy and Lyndon Johnson were only the most recent examples. Nixon and Kissinger took these precedents and extended them by their exclusion of outside influences on decision making. Gone were the checks of bureaucratic resistance within the executive, congressional critiques during consultation, and palpable public disquiet from knowledge of executive activity. Nixon relished governing by surprise, announcing steps already taken and held secret in the preparation. This pattern of faits accomplis was almost impossible for anyone to control.

From the outset, President Nixon intended to focus his efforts on foreign policy. Domestic policy, he thought, was about "building outhouses in Peoria."[10] John Kennedy might have agreed, but not Lyndon Johnson. Nixon had once opined that the cabinet could run domestic affairs without a president but "you need a President for foreign policy."[11] Given this outlook, Nixon was prepared to make an implicit bargain with the Democratic Congress. He would mount no assault on existing New Deal statutes and would even sign liberal legislation if Congress would give him a free hand in foreign policy. He kept the bargain—his acceptance of bills on subjects ranging from environmental protection to auto and occupational safety has led to his characterization as the "last liberal President."[12] Apart from his constitutional function of signing or vetoing bills, however, Nixon showed little interest in Congress.

To isolate himself effectively, Nixon installed H. R. Haldeman as a powerful chief of staff. Haldeman rigorously controlled access to the president and executed Nixon's written commands, saving him from the distasteful task of personal supervision of the government. As a domestic analogue to Kissinger, Nixon chose John Ehrlichman. Only these three men and congressional liaison Bryce Harlow had unrestricted access to the president. In this hothouse atmosphere, secrecy, intrigue, lies, and manipulation thrived, and eventually conspiracy arose.

Richard Nixon soon became the third successive president to follow a Vietnam strategy that he would not share with the American people. He too was unwilling to "lose" Vietnam to the communists. Yet because the strategy that he soon adopted was likely to do just that, he could not be honest about it. By the spring of 1969, Nixon had decided to make a gradual withdrawal of American land forces, transferring the burden of ground combat to South Vietnam.[13] To forestall immediate defeat, he would increase aerial bombing in the region. The bombing would drive the enemy to the conference table, where a settlement of some kind could be negotiated and styled "peace with honor" for domestic consumption. Taking a leaf from Kennedy and Johnson, Nixon would cover this retreat with clouds of misleading claims of military success.

To stop North Vietnamese infiltration of the South, Nixon and Kissinger decided to bomb parts of Cambodia (and later Laos) that the enemy used as sanctuaries.[14] Secretary Rogers opposed the action and was ignored; Secretary Laird learned about it later. The United States was not at war with either of these neutral nations, and Congress had provided no explicit authority to extend the war to them. Only the most strained reading of the Tonkin Gulf Resolution (now almost four years old) or an essentially unlimited reading of the constitutional commander in chief power could provide authority for this step.[15] As the bombing started, the president informed a few sympathetic congressmen about it and later notified the pertinent committees, but never Congress as a whole.[16]

Nixon tried to solve the legal difficulty by keeping the bombing secret and ordering military records falsified to conceal it.[17] This tactic foreclosed any possibility that approval by Congress or the people legitimated the action. Of course, the bombing was known to the nations suffering it and to the enemy; it was hidden only from Americans. The secret bombing began in Cambodia in March 1969 and went on for over a year, totaling more than four thousand sorties. The bombing destabilized Cambodia, contributing to its later descent into the horrors of the Khmer Rouge.

President Nixon's conduct of the war soon settled into separate public and private positions.[18] He gave a speech claiming that defeat in Vietnam would produce a collapse of confidence in American leadership and calling on the "silent majority" of Americans for continued support. He scaled back America's foreign policy goals by proclaiming the Nixon Doctrine, which avoided the indefinite commitments of the Truman Doctrine and of some of Kennedy's statements by declaring that the United States would support lesser allies with supplies but not troops. Meanwhile he sent Kissinger to Paris to open secret back-channel negotiations with North Vietnam. Secretary of State Rogers was ignorant of the talks. Reduction of troop levels in Vietnam began quietly and continued steadily.

In the spring of 1970, Nixon and Kissinger planned a ground invasion of the Cambodian sanctuaries.[19] Obviously this could not be concealed. Secretary Laird suggested consulting Congress and was ignored. Nixon's speech to the nation announcing the "incursion" did not mention the secret bombing and promised withdrawal after clearing out the sanctuaries. Congressional leaders were informed hours before the speech. Cambodian premier Lon Nol, informed after the operation began, supported it.

For constitutional justification, the president offered the need to protect American troops fighting in the region.[20] Nixon obtained a Justice Department memorandum supporting the incursion on that ground.[21] Although there is some obvious practical force to such an argument, it could supply a justification for the indefinite expansion of any commitment of the armed forces.[22] Holding on firmly to his bootstraps, the president sought no congressional ratification of his decision.

There ensued the most serious challenges to executive war making since the Vietnam War began.[23] Nixon's prior consultation with a few legislators did not appease Congress. The Senate moved to cut off funds for the war; the House disagreed. The Senate also repealed the Tonkin Gulf Resolution as its Foreign Relations Committee denounced the "constitutionally unauthorized presidential war in Indochina."[24] President Nixon hunkered down to weather the storm.

Plumbers

Richard Nixon's obsessive desire to maintain secrecy produced an increase in assertions of executive privilege against congressional attempts to learn about the administration.[25] It also led him to adopt unconstitutional measures to stop leaks of secret information from within. In his first months in office, the president began hiring White House agents to detect the sources of leaks.[26] They called themselves the Plumbers and were paid from secret political funds that the president immediately began to accumulate. Initiating a covert and often illegal operation within the White House was eventually fatal to the Nixon presidency. Nixon believed that both JFK and LBJ had spied on him and thought that dirty politics was normal. That it might also be illegal seems not to have concerned him.

The bombing of Cambodia was a secret too big to keep for very long. In May of 1969, the *New York Times* published a report about it. Nixon and Kissinger, furious, initiated wiretaps by the FBI and the Plumbers of several national security aides and journalists.[27] Under conventional constitutional doctrine, this activity was illegal. The Fourth Amendment requires that searches be reasonable, which ordinarily means that they are conducted pursuant to a warrant. Yet presidents had ordered warrantless national security surveillance ever since FDR initiated the practice on the eve of World War II, first spying on aliens and later on American citizens. The legitimacy of this line of precedent depended on a delicate balancing of national security and privacy interests.

Unfortunately, presidents had yielded to temptation and had abused this sensitive power by spying on their political enemies. Because the targets of Nixon's wiretaps were not suspected of espionage or other crimes, his action was another abuse of power unless the president's determination that national security necessitated the surveillance was self-justifying. This explains Nixon's later assertion to journalist David Frost that if the president does something for (asserted) national security purposes, that means it is not illegal. To that argument there is no limit.

The full implications of President Nixon's stance on protecting his secrets and spying on his enemies emerged in the "Huston plan" for a new system of domestic intelligence.[28] Presented by an aide who understood Nixon well, the plan envisioned a secret White House operation that would include burglary, electronic intelligence (both international and domestic), and mail opening. Nixon happily approved the plan and presented it to the intelligence community. He would later claim that he had constitutional authority for it, invoking Lincoln's assertions of power to preserve the nation.[29] This distortion of the comparative levels of threat to the nation in the two eras could not have survived exposure to public criticism.

An unlikely defender of American civil liberties temporarily blocked implementation of the Huston plan. J. Edgar Hoover knew it was too dangerous and far reaching. Besides, it would undercut the FBI. When Hoover demanded written orders from the president for anything he considered illegal, the plan was quietly withdrawn. It would be implemented piecemeal later on by the Plumbers in league with operatives in Nixon's Committee for the Reelection of the President. Nixon had set up the exquisitely acronymed CREEP as his own campaign organization separate from the Republican Party, where he could stash his secret cash and now his secret agents as well.

An impetus for the Huston plan was widespread and sometimes violent opposition to the Vietnam War, heightened by the Cambodian invasion.[30] Many campuses were closed. Students had died from National Guard bullets at Kent State University. During massive demonstrations in Washington, troops guarded the White House and other government buildings. Like Lyndon Johnson, Richard Nixon was persuaded that domestic dissent had foreign connections and could not be disabused by the contrary views of the intelligence agencies. Again he was prepared to convert his personal view of what national security required into secret constitutional power. Hence he continued LBJ's illegal practice of widespread secret surveillance of the domestic antiwar movement.

During the Vietnam War, both Presidents Johnson and Nixon usually avoided criminal prosecutions of dissidents in favor of investigation by the intelligence agencies. The few trials were lurid and ultimately unsuccessful.[31] In that sense Nixon's presidential suppression of free speech was milder than that of President Wilson after World War I.

Realigning Politics and Law

Richard Nixon wanted to reformulate American politics. He had two related strategies to make the Republican Party dominant in the long term. To a large extent, they succeeded.[32] Both of them influenced his exercise of his constitutional powers. First, Nixon hoped to capture from the Democrats the "silent majority" of Americans who believed in law and order and national strength. To weld that new majority, he conducted a politics of division that aligned him against urban protesters and the antiwar movement. He loosed Vice President Spiro Agnew on a campaign to intimidate the press for its negative coverage of his administration by appealing to ordinary Americans' patriotism and resentment of the eastern establishment. Agnew became the administration's poster child for pressure against the freedom of the press. Thus, Nixon joined a long line of presidents who had been willing to bully and manipulate the press to affect its communications with the people.

Second, Nixon wanted to realign the traditionally Democratic South as a Republican bastion. Many southern whites had voted for George Wallace in 1968, revealing backlash against LBJ's promotion of civil rights. Nixon's "southern strategy" minimized civil rights enforcement to send a signal of solidarity to southern conservatives. The president made clear that to him the faithful execution duty meant that "we do what the law requires—nothing more."[33] He pressed the Departments of Justice and Health, Education, and Welfare to ease their enforcement of desegregation orders and forced the resignation of some bureaucrats who resisted.[34]

In a development with long-term effects, Nixon pursued political realignment by strategically using his constitutional power to nominate judges.[35] Another (and far more astute) memo from Huston reminded the president that he could influence the nation for a quarter of a century through his judicial choices, if only they were vetted carefully for congruence with the president's values. The memo noted that lower court appointments had traditionally been ceded to senators and urged Nixon to recapture the power of selection. Although sympathetic to that proposal, the president did not pursue it for the usual reason—he needed senatorial support for other matters.

A more immediate task was to fill two Supreme Court vacancies in 1969. The president nominated circuit judge Warren Burger to be the new chief justice, having liked the law-and-order flavor of a speech Burger had given. Characteristically, Nixon held the choice close until he could announce it as a surprise. Confirmation went smoothly, but Burger turned out to be more moderate than Nixon had wished.

For the other slot, the president was determined to pursue his southern strategy. He nominated two southerners who were rejected by the Senate. After his first choice failed because of some minor financial conflicts of interest, Nixon tried a Jacksonian strategy of retaliation by nominating the unqualified G. Harrold Carswell, who was rejected for his endorsement of segregation and his high reversal rate as a lower court judge. Bitterly, Nixon then fell back to Harry Blackmun, who was suggested by Burger and who also disappointed his conservative backers once confirmed.[36]

The visible tendency of judicial nominees to display more independence than predictability would lead to ever-increasing efforts at political vetting as the years went by, in an alteration of the traditional practice of choosing most nominees for relatively neutral reasons such as competence and experience. Politicizing the process of judicial selection has had two constitutional effects. First, it altered the confirmation process, which became more political, confrontational, and ultimately dysfunctional. Second, it eroded the departmentalist barriers between the executive and judicial branches to the extent that judges could be selected for their predictable positions on constitutional issues.

Presidents now use their constitutional power of nomination to try to secure judicial ratification of their interpretations of the Constitution. That is not an illegitimate use of the nomination power—it is one of the tools that the Constitution grants presidents, and it does encounter the check of confirmation—but it had been employed only sporadically in American history, as in FDR's choice of new justices. Presidents have also turned increasingly to relatively young nominees, to lengthen the shadow of their own constitutional views.

Unifying the Executive

Richard Nixon, knowing that he could not do everything through his arrangement of a personal presidency, sought more formal and enduring methods of conforming the sprawling executive branch to presidential command. This project advanced Nixon's political purposes via constitutional technique.[37] He understood that since the turn of the twentieth century, presidential activism had been associated with liberal politics. But Jefferson had demonstrated that a strong president could not only spur but also rein in the federal government. Nixon would build new structures to ensure presidential control of a bureaucracy that he saw as intrinsically liberal and alien to his political views. Once in place, though, the structures would serve conservative and liberal presidents alike. The beneficial effect has been to tie the operation of the executive branch more closely to the president's constitutional and political accountability for administration.

In 1970, President Nixon realized a dream dating from William Howard Taft by using statutory authority for reorganizing the executive to establish the Office of Management and Budget as a presidential bureaucracy to process spending requests from the agencies and to oversee their policy choices.[38] Ever since, OMB has been a powerful force for imposing the president's overall priorities on the executive branch. For example, Nixon began the modern practice of requiring federal agencies to submit their proposed congressional testimony and reports to OMB for clearance.[39]

Presidential supervision of policy making in the executive branch involves a trade-off between political accountability and expertise.[40] Even technical forms of law administration, such as environmental regulation, involve political judgments. Presidents, being accountable to the people for the performance of the executive branch, need to be able to supervise the political component of administration. Moreover, there is a need to coordinate related kinds of policy making that are lodged in the myriad agencies. Still, the technical judgments of fact, policy, and law that underlie much modern regulation must be respected. OMB, with a generalist staff that is much smaller than any important agency, cannot hope to duplicate the expertise of the agencies. Modern supervisory programs try to accommodate these tensions.

The activities of OMB reflect the constitutional judgment of all presidents from Nixon on that the vesting of executive power in the president and the faithful execution duty constitute substantive grants of power to affect policy making throughout the executive branch.[41] Building on Nixon's efforts, subsequent presidents have required agencies to consult with OMB about their proposed regulations. The purpose of this review is to ensure that the overall perspective that inheres in the presidency is reflected in regulations generated by agencies that tend to have more parochial concerns.

The executive orders that create the management programs have all disclaimed any intent to take statutory authority from the agencies where Congress places it and to vest it in the White House. This limitation reflects the constitutional power of Congress to structure the government under the necessary and proper clause, which includes discretion to place statutory authority either in the president or in a subordinate officer. Obviously, the line between consultation and direction is subtle and is not always honored. Nevertheless, the premise that the statutory administrator must be the one to issue a regulation, not the president or OMB, is generally accepted.[42]

Thus Andrew Jackson's approach in his controversy with Treasury Secretary Duane has become presidential common law.[43] If an administrator refuses to take an action the president prefers, the president's recourse is to dismiss the officer and search for a replacement whom the Senate will confirm, not to assume the authority vested in the officer. Because political considerations constrain presidents in firing and replacing their subordinates, even regulators who serve at the president's pleasure, such as everyone in the cabinet, have some practical autonomy. The executive branch is not a monolith and never has been.

President Nixon's creation of OMB came at just the right moment. In the early seventies, Congress was passing and he was signing a flood of new statutes regulating health and safety. Issues of control and coordination soon arose. In an initial action, Nixon used his reorganization authority to create the Environmental Protection Agency to administer a welter of new and old programs. Significantly, Nixon did not place EPA in a cabinet department but gave it a direct reporting relationship with the White House, the better to oversee it. Nixon then required the EPA (and some other agencies) to submit analyses of the costs and benefits of proposed regulations to OMB.[44] If OMB thought that the costs to be imposed on the private sector were too high for the prospective benefits, OMB could try to persuade the agency to alter its action. More than four decades later, the use of cost-benefit analysis as a presidential management tool remains central to the functioning of the executive branch.[45]

In the wake of his landslide reelection in 1972, Richard Nixon decided to go much further toward the centralization of the executive. The next day, with remarkable ill grace even for him, he demanded resignations from the entire cabinet and White House staff so that he could restructure the executive and purge it of his myriad enemies.[46] Believing that his orders had been widely ignored or subverted, he wanted to place most agencies under four super–cabinet officers who would report to him.[47] He made his criterion clear: "Not brains, we want loyalty."[48] He accepted the resignations of some cabinet members and planned to install loyalists at subcabinet levels to enhance his control. The plan foundered, however, on the rocks of Watergate. The scandal began to erupt shortly after the election, sinking all of Nixon's grandiose plans.

"Peace with Honor"

Throughout his first term, President Nixon tried to eliminate the bothersome distraction of the Vietnam War (as exacerbated by the Cambodia mess). The North Vietnamese remained most uncooperative, however. In 1972, they unleashed a large spring offensive. The president responded with a massive aerial campaign, bombing Hanoi and mining Haiphong harbor.[49] In the summer, the war settled into stalemate again, and both sides finally sought a settlement. Nixon broke the diplomatic impasse by quietly dropping the long-standing American condition that North

Vietnam withdraw its troops from the South. American war goals had shrunk to the return of our prisoners of war and a decent interval of survival for the regime in South Vietnam.[50]

With the American presidential election looming, the pace of secret negotiations in Paris quickened.[51] Kissinger reached an agreement for an exchange of prisoners and a cease-fire and announced that "peace is at hand."[52] Not quite. President Thieu of South Vietnam resisted the deal, knowing it would eventually seal his fate. The talks collapsed temporarily. To drive the enemy back to the table, President Nixon ordered the savage "Christmas bombing," the most intensive air attack of the war. It succeeded. The deal that had been reached tentatively in October was restored and imposed on Thieu.

President Nixon announced his "peace with honor," but there would be no peace and little honor. Some historians think he could have had the same deal four years earlier, with far less blood shed on all sides.[53] The cease-fire did not last, except in Congress. A statutory cutoff of funds for all military operations in Indochina passed in 1973, was vetoed by Nixon, and was then imposed in a compromise with him that delayed its effectiveness temporarily. "For the first time Congress had acted decisively to stop the war."[54] But American troops and prisoners were already home, and no one had an appetite for more war making in Indochina. Because the United States had been fully engaged in Vietnam since 1965, future presidents would not need to regard the Vietnam example as a warning that Congress would terminate funding for military operations at any early stage.

From the first to the last the Vietnam War was a presidential war, fought deceptively by three presidents and supported by a Congress that saw no viable alternative to continuing appropriations. Awash in frustration and determined to recapture the constitutional war powers that had apparently slipped into presidential hands, Congress enacted the War Powers Resolution, a curious and highly qualified attempt to reassert its prerogatives.[55]

The WPR has garnered few admirers over the years (and none in the White House). But serious intrinsic difficulties that Congress faced in framing the resolution should limit both our criticisms of it and our expectations about its potential accomplishments. The general problem is that any statute that directly confronts and tries to define the constitutional separation of powers between the legislative and executive branches is likely to encounter presidential resistance, including both an initial veto and later defiance, and may suffer judicial invalidation. (The war between

Congress and Andrew Johnson springs to mind.) Also, at least in its more sober moods Congress does not wish unduly to shackle the president, upon whom the fate of the nation may depend.

More particularly, any statutory effort to define the allocation of war powers entails severe drafting problems: how can the wide variety of war-making instances in American history be captured and controlled in statutory text without hampering the nation's response to tomorrow's crisis? Constitutional ambiguity is by no means always a disadvantage; statutory clarity is not always a cure.

The resolution begins on a hopeful and appropriate note, stating its purpose to ensure that the "collective judgment" of both Congress and the president will apply to the introduction of American armed forces into actual or imminent "hostilities."[56] Yes, but always? Surely some skirmishes do not deserve constitutional process. And how is the collective judgment to be expressed, always by statute or sometimes less formally? The rest of the resolution struggles with those two issues. It immediately veers off track by asserting that the president's constitutional power to send troops into hostilities is exercised only pursuant to a declaration of war, specific statutory authorization, or an attack on the United States or its armed forces.[57] This formulation omits the central issue: at what point on the spectrum of military actions does a constitutional "war" occur that demands advance authorization by Congress? By 1973, there had been hundreds of large and small presidential uses of the military that had not previously been questioned.

Creating even more uncertainty about the effects of the WPR, Congress included a disclaimer saying that it intended neither to alter the constitutional power of either branch nor to grant the president any new authority.[58] This is constitutional quicksand, and it has left the legal force of the WPR in serious doubt ever since.

Let us retrieve some clear meaning from the resolution's main operative provisions. First, it requires the president "in every possible instance" to consult with Congress before sending American forces into hostilities.[59] Second, it requires the president to report every such instance to Congress and to terminate the engagement within sixty days (or in an emergency, ninety days) if Congress does not provide statutory authority.[60] Third, it authorizes Congress to terminate any such engagement at any time by concurrent resolution of the two branches.[61]

Thus, instead of directly asserting the point at which constitutional war begins (an imponderable if ever there was one), Congress chose an essentially procedural route to preventing more Koreas or Vietnams.

Presidents could gather that they were supposed to consult before striking but had sixty days of freedom to act before seeking formal authorization, unless Congress earlier refused to consent.

President Nixon, although deeply embroiled in his Watergate agonies, promptly vetoed the resolution, denouncing it as a "clearly unconstitutional" effort to take away by legislation "authorities which the President has properly exercised under the Constitution for almost 200 years."[62] If the WPR be read to forbid the myriad uses of the military for rescue or punitive raids that had dotted American history, he was right about that, but perhaps the disclaimer solves that problem. Nixon particularly objected to the sixty-day cutoff and the provision for termination of hostilities by concurrent resolution. Congress overrode the veto, and the WPR is still on the books.

Notwithstanding Nixon's objection, the sixty-day cutoff appears to be constitutional.[63] Pursuant to its own explicit constitutional authority to create and regulate the military, Congress has enacted many substantive limitations on use of the armed forces, and presidents have ordinarily abided by them.[64] This provision, although nominally a restriction on the president, is actually an attempt to bring both branches to the table within sixty days of military action. Under modern conditions, that is ordinarily enough time to hash out an authorization, and we shall see that the WPR has sometimes had the beneficial effect of fostering interbranch cooperation. Ironically, the sixty-day limit does seem to authorize or at least acquiesce in brief presidential wars, unless the disclaimer negates such an effect. Presidents have been happy to take advantage of the sixty-day window, as we shall also see.

President Nixon's objection that the WPR's provision for termination by concurrent resolution unconstitutionally evaded his veto opportunity had more force. His position has since been confirmed indirectly by a Supreme Court opinion invalidating other "legislative vetoes."[65] For present purposes, it is enough to note that the termination provision added rather little to the power Congress always has to forbid future military actions by the refusal of either house to provide appropriations for them. A concurrent resolution, if valid, would simply allow the cutoff to occur immediately.

The third enduring issue about the WPR's operation has concerned its rigid consultation requirement. Presidents have consistently resisted or disobeyed this provision. In some cases, they can make a good constitutional claim that the need for secrecy allows them to forgo consultation to protect national security. Rightly fearing leaks of secret battle plans, presidents invoke a version of the constitutional executive privilege to exclude Congress from meaningful participation.

Yet the problem is not simple. Presidents know that Congress is filled with their opponents, but the senior leaders with whom consultation ordinarily would occur are relatively trustworthy people who are not necessarily any leakier than senior executive officers.[66] The constitutional difference is that the president can exert control over the executive officers but not over members of Congress. At least there is always the subsequent check of the need for congressional acquiescence in the action the president takes, but the point of the consultation requirement is to allow congressional input in advance of a fait accompli that narrows practical options.

By 1973, American history had revealed both the potential advantages and the practical problems with making congressional consultation meaningful. When President Kennedy involved Senator Fulbright in a Bay of Pigs meeting, Fulbright challenged the groupthink that was impelling the executive toward disaster. That is the virtue of an outside perspective, but it came too late. When Kennedy informed congressional leaders of his intended actions in the Cuban missile crisis, they reacted in ways that showed their lack of background about the options. Both examples reveal that if congressional consultation is to be both fully informed and timely, it has to occur early and with full briefing. To date, no president has been willing to breach the wall between the branches to that extent.

A New World Order

For Richard Nixon and Henry Kissinger, the Vietnam War was secondary to a restructuring of American foreign relations to respond to global changes that had occurred since World War II.[67] Both men were realists, not moralists. They wanted to normalize relations with both the Soviet Union and China and then to balance their power against each other. Characteristically, they proceeded in secret, opening back channels to both nations that would eventually bring startling changes to world politics. They did not entrust either Congress or the public with any information about these initiatives until they had matured.

While these two pots were simmering, Nixon moved to alter the world's economic system. He made John Connally, a Democrat and an economic nationalist, his treasury secretary as part of a surprising turn toward Keynesian economics. In the early seventies, the United States was experiencing an alarming drain on its gold reserves because of the traditional convertibility of the dollar into gold. Convertibility was the peg on which the world's currency relationships hung. Connally offered a plan to abandon it along with other steps to aid the economy, such as a ninety-day wage-price freeze (for which statutory authority existed). In August 1971, Nixon convened a secret meeting at Camp David to assess the plan.[68] No one was present but executive branch officers and Arthur Burns, chair of the Federal Reserve Board.

Nixon adopted the plan, calling it "the most significant economic action since World War II."[69] Allowing the dollar to float on world markets would devalue it and would end the Bretton Woods currency regime that had been in place since 1946. The Camp David decisions, which reversed the administration's prior statements on economics, were held in secret to avoid an immediate flight of gold reserves. Nixon announced the actions on television—a summer thunderbolt. More were to come.

Richard Nixon's visit to China in 1972 to sit with Mao and normalize diplomatic relations was so dramatic that an opera has been written about it.[70] The president announced and conducted the trip with his usual mastery of timing and public relations in foreign policy. The way had been paved by Henry Kissinger's secret trips to China, of which no word leaked, not even to the State Department. Once in Beijing, Nixon and Kissinger continued their two-man negotiating operation, resolutely excluding the experts from State.[71] This secrecy produced an error: inadvertently, they abandoned American treaty commitments to defend the longtime Chinese allies now huddled on Taiwan. Some scrambling produced a suitably ambiguous patch in the final communiqué that announced the end of mutual hostility between communist China and the United States. One of America's great Red baiters had exchanged toasts with the greatest Red left on the world stage. If Richard Nixon perceived limits to his personal discretion in reformulating American foreign policy, it would be hard to identify them. With no congressional consultation, he had vitiated a treaty, leaving the old cold warriors of the China lobby fuming.

The other major piece of the world puzzle that President Nixon was rearranging was the Soviet Union.[72] Notwithstanding some requisite anticommunist rhetoric, Nixon took a flexible approach to the Soviets from the start. He accepted rough parity in strategic arms, which went under the charming acronym MAD, standing for mutual assured destruction. The idea was that if each nation had enough power to absorb a first nuclear strike and still devastate the other, deterrence would hold. Early on, the president deceived Congress by seeking funds for an antiballistic missile (ABM) defense system that he had no intention of building.[73] Instead, he sought to use it as a bargaining chip with the Soviets, who might be levered into an arms control agreement out of fear that the Americans might actually build a defense system and destroy the premises of MAD.

The ploy worked. The Soviet Union, already showing signs of the sclerosis that would bring it down a generation later and needing relief from the massive expenditures of the arms race, was ready to negotiate. The back channel from Kissinger to Soviet ambassador Dobrynin hummed with activity.[74] Formal arms limitation negotiations were conducted simultaneously in Helsinki as a sideshow to keep the State Department, Congress, and the public distracted.

In 1972, Nixon and Kissinger reached agreement with the Soviets to restrict ABM development in return for caps on the number of offensive missiles each nation could possess. The deal contained "the most important insight of the nuclear age: that an unconstrained arms race was futile, costly, and dangerous."[75] Carrying proposed agreements secretly drafted in the White House, Nixon and Kissinger set off for Moscow to celebrate détente with the old Cold War foe.[76] Formal announcements to Congress and the press said progress was being made at Helsinki.

The Moscow summit produced an ABM treaty limiting each nation to two sites, a strategic arms limitation executive agreement limiting the number of offensive missiles for five years, and a joint statement of principles to guide détente. President Nixon returned to Washington in triumph. Now he was willing to brief Congress on the summit and to address the nation. Only the ABM treaty was presented to the Senate for ratification, which was painless.

Richard Nixon had overturned decades of American foreign policy in three important realms: international currency controls, relations with communist China, and the arms race with the Soviet Union. Everyone outside his immediate circle of executive advisers had learned about each of these initiatives after the fact. Unsurprisingly, Nixon and Kissinger felt free to extend their spirit of adventuring into other regions of the globe. Here the record was more mixed. Three examples will do.

Richard Nixon cared little about the Western Hemisphere, except that he shared the abiding presidential fixations on Fidel Castro and the danger of more communist regimes in the hemisphere. Hence he reacted immediately when a Marxist, Salvador Allende, was elected president of

Chile.[77] With much urging from Henry Kissinger, Nixon ordered the CIA to attempt to overturn the election. A major covert operation ensued. Eventually, Allende was slain in a coup that the CIA had encouraged. There followed the regime of Augusto Pinochet, monstrous but acceptable to the United States.

In 1971, hostilities began between India and Pakistan following brutal repression against Bengali rebels in East Pakistan who were seeking to secede.[78] Much at fault, Pakistan invaded Kashmir and sent air strikes against India. Although claiming to be neutral in the conflict, the Nixon administration actually "tilted" toward Pakistan, largely because India had ties to the Soviet Union. Nixon secretly dispatched arms to Pakistan, while warning the Soviets away. Congress, the State Department, the press, and the American public supported India. The president, having backed the losing side, wound up recognizing Bangladesh. He and Kissinger had poisoned relations with India to no good end.

In the summer of 1973, Henry Kissinger became secretary of state as well as national security adviser. Whatever his faults, the growing Watergate crisis had made him indispensable. That fall, during the Yom Kippur war, President Nixon ordered a massive resupply of Israel.[79] The Arab nations responded with an oil embargo that caused long lines for gasoline in the United States and spiked inflation. When a temporary cease-fire in the Middle East unraveled and the Soviet Union threatened intervention, Secretary Kissinger usurped the authority of the distracted president by presiding over an emergency meeting of the National Security Council that dangerously raised the alert level of American nuclear forces.[80] Fortunately, the Soviets behaved more soberly than had Kissinger, and the crisis passed. More constructively, Kissinger then conducted some strenuous shuttle diplomacy that helped to arrange a more permanent armistice and an end to the oil embargo.

Impoundment

President Nixon's acquiescence in liberal domestic legislation did not extend to spending bills. When it came to money, he was prepared to resist and even confront Congress and did so in a way that led to a sharp reduction in executive spending authority. Although the Constitution requires a congressional appropriation before the Treasury can spend money, the actual process of expenditure is an executive function laced with discretion and is part of the faithful execution duty.[81] The discretion stems from time, interpretation, and circumstance. That is, appropriations statutes, which respond to a budget submitted by the executive, are usually enacted well in advance of the actual spending of the money. When the time to spend arrives, the executive may find that changed circumstances or realized economies allow meeting the purpose of the appropriation without spending all the money. Also, many appropriations are expressed permissively, as directions to spend "not more than" a certain sum. Hence, the executive often finds that some appropriated funds remain available and "impounds" them while awaiting further instructions.

Presidential actions have sketched the borderline between congressional power to appropriate and executive power to spend.[82] Few controversies arose in the early years of the Republic, when federal spending was low. In an early example of impoundment, Jefferson declined to spend an amount appropriated for gunboats because a "favorable and peaceable turn of affairs" on the Mississippi had rendered the expenditure unnecessary. Thus perhaps every appropriation carries an implied authorization to impound the money if to spend it would not advance the original purpose.

The first controversial impoundment occurred when President Grant refused to spend river and harbor funds for "works of purely private interest," as opposed to national interests. The pork barrel aspects of public works legislation have led several presidents to cancel some projects authorized by Congress while executing others. Congress has not always reacted vigorously. For example, although Grant's action produced some incandescent rhetoric in the House of Representatives ("On what meat hath this our Caesar fed?"), the House later accepted the president's position that the appropriation was not mandatory.

In the modern era, extensive impoundments began when Franklin Roosevelt withheld public works and other funds in response to emergency conditions created by the Depression and World War II. Congress had appropriated vast sums for both domestic and war-making purposes and generally accepted any savings that occurred. After the war, presidents continued to impound funds, sometimes in large amounts. Harry Truman claimed that spending is "the discretionary power of the President" and that he could not be forced to spend.[83] Citing his power as commander in chief as a constitutional justification for impoundment, Truman withheld some funds for an expansion of the Air Force in defiance of an apparently mandatory appropriation, but was otherwise cooperative with Congress.[84]

Much of the postwar controversy concerned defense appropriations for weapons systems, with their large pork barrel component. Here, the executive's special informational advantages in national security helped to thwart congressional opposition. Not surprisingly, presidents usually prevailed, although considerable maneuvering was sometimes required.

President Johnson broadened prior arguments to include inherent authority to impound funds for domestic programs. LBJ, having incurred soaring deficits by trying to conduct the Vietnam War and pursue the Great Society at the same time, was pressing Congress to allow him to decide where the necessary cuts should occur.[85] This kind of self-justifying expansion in executive discretion would find its limits in the hands of his successor.

The controversy finally boiled over when President Nixon extended LBJ's precedent by impounding unprecedented proportions of appropriations, as much as 20 percent of "controllable" federal expenditures.[86] A number of programs were to be terminated outright. Reasons advanced for the Nixon impoundments were usually general ones of fiscal integrity, such as the need to limit inflation. Where particular projects were to be abandoned, such as public works, there was usually no effort to justify the choices as the result of any criteria other than presence in the president's budget.

Nixon's legal arguments consisted of a distortion of the historical record through claims that nothing new was occurring and an oversimplification of previous constitutional arguments in support of a conclusion that the president could impound essentially without limitation.[87] Nixon stressed that his national constituency, as opposed to the parochial concerns of individual legislators, gave him a special right to control spending. He added the need to harmonize competing policies in the various statutes that called either for economizing or for spending.[88] Nevertheless, a future chief justice advised the White House that "it is difficult to formulate a *constitutional* theory to justify a refusal by the President to comply with a Congressional directive to spend."[89] That is correct.

The Nixon impoundments finally provoked both judicial and legislative responses. Neither, however, produced a definitive resolution of the permissible extent of impoundment. The Supreme Court's only foray into the issues concerned federal financing for municipal sewage treatment works.[90] The bill authorized the appropriation of amounts "not to exceed" $5 billion and provided that the authorized sums "shall be allotted" to the states by EPA according to a formula, whereupon grant applications would be invited. President Nixon vetoed the bill as "budget-wrecking."

Congress promptly overrode the veto. The president then instructed EPA to allot no more than $2 billion.

The City of New York sued for a declaration that EPA was required to allot the full amount and prevailed. The case reached the Supreme Court in the wake of Nixon's resignation. The executive had abandoned broad claims of constitutional impoundment power and now claimed only discretion regarding the timing of expenditure. The Court decided that whatever discretion there was should be exercised at the later obligation stage, not for allotments. The Court was correct to disapprove the president's impoundment at the allotment stage, because it amounted to an effort to ignore congressional authorization of the program. That was an issue on which the president had exercised his veto and had been overridden. To uphold that impoundment would have accorded the president an absolute veto, not a conditional one.

Congress responded to the impoundment crisis with the Congressional Budget and Impoundment Control Act of 1974, which set up a procedure for impoundments.[91] Proposals to rescind appropriations entirely were to be submitted to Congress, where they would be without effect unless approved by a bill passed within a specified period. Proposals to defer spending temporarily within the fiscal year were allowed in some circumstances. Congress attempted to avoid any constitutional confrontation over the act, however, by including a statement that it was not to be construed as "asserting or conceding the constitutional powers or limitations of either the Congress or the President." It is difficult to identify the effect of this provision on arguments that the act terminates congressional acquiescence in impoundments.

In any event, the 1974 act, along with its later adjustments, has defused controversy over impoundments. Presidents have avoided renewing the controversy for fear of being compared to Richard Nixon. The executive would be on strongest ground in arguing that Congress may not require particular amounts of money to be spent for foreign affairs or military purposes. And the faithful execution clause may give the president some residual constitutional authority even for domestic spending—Nixon's argument against the dynamics of the pork barrel carries some force.

The impoundment issue lies dormant. Presidents have retreated from ground they once trod, leaving a no-man's land. Richard Nixon pressed constitutional claims past the point of their acceptability to either the courts or Congress. By trying to convert his qualified veto over spending into an absolute one, he produced reactions by both other branches that obscured the real merits of a more constrained constitutional power of impoundment. Any president who desires to revive the power would do well to proceed on the basis of a specific showing of need, not a generalized disagreement with Congress over the nation's spending priorities.

Unindicted Coconspirator

In the conventions of tragic drama, the undoing of the protagonist stems from hubris and other fatal flaws embedded in the person's character. Lyndon Johnson's ultimate failure was tragic. So also was Richard Nixon's disgrace (although the tawdriness vitiated the grandeur). The Watergate scandal produced the only resignation of a president to date. Nixon's grandiose and constitutionally unconstrained conception of his powers combined with his central obsessions to provide ample grounds for his impeachment and removal, which would have occurred had he not resigned. Sad and demeaning to the presidency as the story is, it has provided a rather bracing precedent to later presidents, all of whom have distanced themselves constitutionally and otherwise from Nixon, at least in their rhetoric.

Richard Nixon's obsession with dominating the American political system led to some of the abuses that cost him his office. He systematically used the IRS and FBI to investigate and harass his political enemies, including antiwar activists.[92] He appeared to believe that he could order actions violating statutes whenever he saw a national security need to do so.[93] In fact, however, he greatly expanded prior abuses of this kind, violating his faithful execution duty.

In his relentless search for cash to advance his political goals, Nixon twice stopped inches short of provable involvement in bribery. He traded support for higher federal milk production subsidies for over $2 million in secret campaign funds. In a taped conversation he asserted unconvincingly that he was not exchanging government action for the money he received.[94] Similarly, Nixon pressed the Justice Department to settle an antitrust action against a major donor, having said that money was not to be discussed until afterward.[95] For the most part, Nixon did not seek to profit personally from abuses involving money. The exception is his use of over $3 million in government funds to improve his properties at San Clemente and Key Biscayne.[96]

Nixon's obsession with secrecy initiated the train of events that ended his presidency. In 1971, the *New York Times* began publishing the "Pentagon Papers," a voluminous secret study of decision making in the Vietnam War that Robert McNamara had commissioned in 1967.[97] Daniel Ellsberg, a former Pentagon aide, had leaked the papers in an effort to inform the public about the many deceptions surrounding the war. Because the papers were a historical study that ended before the Nixon administration began, the president was initially delighted by the damage they did to recent Democratic administrations.[98] But Henry Kissinger soon changed Nixon's mind by arguing that the nation would be unable to conduct foreign policy if it could not keep its secrets.

No explicit constitutional or statutory power existed for the president to seek to enjoin a newspaper from printing government secrets. Nixon instructed the Justice Department to file suit anyway. There was a handy Supreme Court precedent: the decision upholding an injunction to stop the Pullman strike in the nineteenth century.[99] The precedent was still sound—an orderly and open appeal to the courts to consider authorizing action not clearly warranted by law is far superior to the use of force to compel obedience to executive branch desires, with judicial consideration coming later.[100] In the *Pentagon Papers* case, however, the president ran headlong into strong judicial disfavor of prior restraints on speech. The Supreme Court summarily denied Nixon's request for an injunction.[101]

The Court's decision not to enjoin publication of the papers was correct. Granted, the constitutional interest in foreign policy secrecy that Nixon invoked was not trivial—the papers contained material that would have impeded diplomacy, such as candid assessments of foreign leaders. But an injunction would also have protected material that simply embarrassed the executive branch and was pertinent to the public's strong interest in understanding the behavior of its presidents. Moreover, there was a practical problem with any effort to enjoin the papers: other newspapers had copies and were rushing them into print. Free speech values overrode national security concerns in this case.

It was not lost on the Nixon administration that once the cat is out of the bag, seeking an injunction is a poor way to cram it back in. After the *Pentagon Papers* decision, Nixon unleashed the Plumbers in an effort to stop leaks from occurring in the first place. He told his aides that his enemies used any means against him and "we are going to use any means."[102] The Plumbers proposed a burglary of the office of Ellsberg's psychiatrist to get his records. The president had John Ehrlichman instruct the Plumbers to do whatever was necessary to probe Ellsberg's motives and plans. The amateur burglars broke into the office and found nothing.[103]

Meanwhile, the administration commenced a criminal prosecution of Ellsberg for purloining and releasing the papers; it was dismissed for government misconduct after the burglary was revealed.

As the 1972 presidential election approached, the Plumbers presented a plan to Attorney General Mitchell for secret surveillance of Democratic National Committee headquarters in the Watergate complex.[104] Mitchell approved it. Although no evidence has ever surfaced that President Nixon knew about the Watergate plan in advance, he had earlier instructed Mitchell to implement whatever parts of the original Huston plan he could. Mitchell was certainly correct to think he had the president's implicit blessing for the scheme.

In June 1972, the Plumbers broke into the DNC offices at the Watergate. Maintaining their record of ineptitude, they left a clue that brought the police to arrest them in the act, and their associates across the street fled in such haste that they left evidence tying the caper to the White House. Now began the cover-up that brought down a president.[105] Mitchell told Haldeman and Ehrlichman that they must protect the president at any cost, which meant stopping investigations that might lead to other operations, the "horrors" as Mitchell accurately termed them.

President Nixon immediately began obstructing justice, both committing a felony and setting a new record for faithless execution of the law. He told Haldeman it would be essential to restrain FBI investigations and added that the burglars would need money. Nixon decided to push the CIA to block the FBI on spurious grounds of national security.[106] (When his order to Haldeman to do that eventually became public, Nixon was finished.) Meanwhile, Nixon gathered some of his secret political cash to buy the silence of the Plumbers. It would be expensive, nearing $500,000, and eventually no amount would be enough.

The cover-up held together for the critical period needed to secure Nixon's landslide reelection.[107] After the Plumbers had been convicted of wiretapping and burglary and were awaiting sentencing, one of them informed Judge John Sirica that the operation had been wider than the current defendants. Sirica reconvened the grand jury and the cover-up fell apart. By the spring of 1973, both criminal and congressional investigations were under way. Elliott Richardson, having been made attorney general, selected Archibald Cox as Watergate special prosecutor and, with the president's approval, authorized him to follow the trail wherever it led, including the Oval Office.

Struggling to retain the presidency, Richard Nixon had one last line of defense: executive privilege.[108] Having foolishly taped the White House conversations that would condemn him and having even more foolishly retained them, he resisted judicial and legislative subpoenas for them on grounds that the Constitution gave him sole discretion to decide which records of the executive branch should be revealed. This position was a considerable stretch beyond existing precedent.

The only court order to a president to produce confidential documents had been by John Marshall, sitting as a circuit judge in the treason trial of Aaron Burr.[109] He issued a subpoena for some of Jefferson's correspondence, and the president complied "voluntarily." Ever since the Washington administration, executive privilege disputes with Congress had been settled by political negotiation, not lawsuits.[110] Nothing approaching a firm constitutional precedent that the president has plenary authority over information in his possession had ever emerged.[111]

When special prosecutor Cox continued to press his subpoenas despite the president's claims of executive privilege, Nixon ordered Attorney General Richardson to fire him.[112] Both Richardson and Deputy Attorney General William Ruckelshaus resigned rather than execute the president's order because they had promised Congress that they would protect Cox's independence. The third-ranking officer in the department, Solicitor General Robert Bork, finally fired Cox on the theory that the president could not bargain away his constitutional authority to supervise the executive branch. Although there was some constitutional plausibility to Bork's position, the political firestorm that followed this "Saturday Night Massacre" drove events. Impeachment became a real possibility.

In March 1974, the federal grand jury indicted seven high officials, including Haldeman, Ehrlichman, and Mitchell. Unsure whether it could indict a sitting president, it labeled Richard Nixon an "unindicted co-conspirator."[113] The endgame began. The House Judiciary Committee considered articles of impeachment. The Supreme Court took up the executive privilege issue at the instance of special prosecutor Leon Jaworski, whom Nixon had appointed to still the controversy over the Cox dismissal. In July, the Court issued a unanimous decision ordering Nixon to comply with the subpoenas.[114] It decided that the president does enjoy a constitutional executive privilege, but a qualified rather than absolute one. The Court said that the president's general interest in confidentiality had to yield to the prosecutor's showing of need for evidence in a pending criminal case.

The House Judiciary Committee voted to send three articles of impeachment to the full House.[115] The first alleged obstruction of justice in the Watergate cover-up. The second alleged illegal abuse of federal agencies

by having them spy on citizens and investigate their taxes for political reasons. The third alleged resistance to congressional subpoenas. Nixon was
clearly guilty on the first two counts, both of which are fair interpretations
of the impeachment standard of "high Crimes and Misdemeanors." The
third alleged an essentially political sin that presidents had often committed. (Defying Congress over a constitutional issue was, of course, the essential ground of the unsuccessful impeachment of Andrew Johnson.)

The House considered but did not adopt some other possible articles
of impeachment—for the secret bombing of Cambodia and the president's personal enrichment from using government funds for his houses.
Excessive impoundment could well have been added; it was a less justifiable defiance of Congress than resistance to subpoenas. As in the case of
Andrew Johnson, the House had settled on charges that would be amenable to readily available proof.

This time, the first two counts were quite solid grounds for removal,
but before the House could act, the president ended the agony. Comply-
ing with the Supreme Court's order, Nixon revealed the "smoking gun"
tape of his initial order to obstruct the Watergate investigation. He had
certainly managed the cover-up actively—in 1973, he had said: "I want
you all to stonewall it, let them plead the Fifth Amendment, cover-up or
anything else."[116] Now he was out of options. Nixon resigned to avoid the
impeachment and removal that would surely have followed.

The constitutional legacy of the Nixon denouement is mixed. Presidential constitutional powers took some blows. Nixon's assertion of an
unlimited executive privilege was unanimously rejected by the Supreme
Court and has not surfaced since. His extreme impoundment claims were
squelched by a framework statute that presidents have abided. His exercise of the commander in chief power in an even more secretive and
unilateral way than Lyndon Johnson produced the conflicted War Powers
Resolution, which has signaled later presidents to wield the military with
more caution.

The Nixon endgame took impeachment off the shelf and appeared to
make it a viable control on presidential excesses. Yet Nixon would likely
have survived the crisis had he not preserved the tapes that confirmed
his guilt in the cover-up. The fact that an impeachment article concerned
his abuse of civil liberties may have cautioned later presidents to be less
casual in misusing the apparatus of government.

Finally, cynical successors could note that the impeachment process
was difficult and uncertain even in Nixon's case. No president whose party
controls either house of Congress need fear this ultimate constitutional

penalty very much. The Nixon presidency did have a sobering effect for a time, though, as two gray and Whiggish presidencies followed to fill out the decade.

A Ford, Not a Lincoln

Former Representative Gerald Ford rose to the presidency in a unique manner. In late 1973, Vice President Spiro Agnew resigned in disgrace after his receipt of bribes before and during his vice presidency was revealed. Happily, the recent Twenty-Fifth Amendment had provided that in case of a vacancy in the vice presidency, the president could nominate a successor to be confirmed by majorities in both houses of Congress. After canvassing the field of possibilities, Nixon turned quickly to Ford, who had been minority leader in the House of Representatives since 1965. Although Nixon held a low opinion of Ford's capacities, it seemed a safe bet to select him.[117] As a well-respected member of the House since 1948, Ford should win easy confirmation, and he was known as a party loyalist. The confirmation sailed through. When Ford assumed the presidency in August 1974, however, he lacked the firm constitutional and political base that comes from election on a national ticket.

Gerald Ford was well suited to healing the nation in the wake of the constitutional crisis over his predecessor. "Modest and easily underestimated," he possessed a straightforward, honest, and sensible character that reassured everyone.[118] He was moderate on domestic issues, conservative on economic and fiscal matters, and internationalist in foreign policy. He held no strong theory of the presidency.

An open and relaxed administrator, Ford dismantled the most imperial aspects of the Nixon administration's apparatus.[119] He kept Henry Kissinger as secretary of state but diminished his influence, eventually easing him out as national security adviser. After experimenting with governing without a chief of staff, he turned to the able Donald Rumsfeld, who imposed discipline on a rather unruly operation.

President Ford began the healing process with two exercises of his constitutional pardon power.[120] Both were well intentioned, but neither had the intended effects. First, he extended an amnesty to Vietnam War draft evaders but imposed conditions that made the amnesty too cumbersome to attract many takers. The amnesty followed the old tradition of using the pardon power to heal social divisions in the nation.

Ford's next pardon, of Richard Nixon, likely cost him election to the presidency in his own right in 1976—at least its unpopularity added fuel to a Democratic sweep in the 1974 midterm elections. In retrospect, the pardon was the right thing to do, because it spared the nation and the presidency the damaging spectacle of the former president, whose health had temporarily broken, sitting morosely or defiantly in the criminal dock.

Ford's error was in failing to condition the pardon, as he could have done, on an admission of responsibility by Nixon for his accumulated sins against his office and the nation. As it was, the pardon looked too much like a corrupt bargain—the presidency in return for a pardon. Ford found himself taking the extraordinary step of testifying in Congress to justify and explain his decision.[121] Ford's general reputation for probity preserved his power to govern, but not without some impairment.

The aftermath of the Nixon presidency consumed much of his successor's time. Although Gerald Ford generally exuded a spirit of cooperative harmony with Congress that was probably compelled by Nixon's pattern of evident contempt, he also showed enough firmness to demonstrate that the presidential chair had changed his former congressional outlook. An example is executive privilege, on which highly sensitive issue Ford "projected a conciliatory tone while affirming presidential authority" by withholding documents when he felt it necessary to do so, all the while avoiding explicit invocation of the privilege whenever he could.[122]

While making the necessary repairs, President Ford struggled with a Congress that was ready to enact a "latticework" of statutes to impose structural controls on the executive.[123] Congress overrode his veto of amendments to the Freedom of Information Act that made it more difficult for the executive branch to withhold information from the public. Hoping to forestall statutory restrictions on covert activity, Ford appointed a commission chaired by Vice President Nelson Rockefeller to investigate recent CIA abuses. Congressional investigating committees in both houses piled on, with the Senate committee characterizing the CIA as a "rogue elephant."[124] Actually, presidents had loosed the elephant. Congress then created the salutary structural reform of creating permanent intelligence committees in both houses, charged with providing more oversight of the intelligence community. To head off additional constraints, Ford issued an executive order to control covert activity, including a ban on assassination of foreign leaders.[125]

The economy was in disrepair in the mid-seventies. Having served as an appropriator in Congress, Gerald Ford took more interest in economic matters than had Richard Nixon. As a believer in free markets, he found himself clashing with a Congress bent on Keynesian spending. In his seventeen months in office, Ford vetoed sixty-six bills, ranking him fourth among all presidents in that department.[126] Despite large Democratic majorities, he usually weathered override attempts, failing only twelve times.

As commander in chief, Gerald Ford had to deal with the humiliating fall of South Vietnam in April 1975. As Saigon fell, he ordered military evacuations of refugees, in contravention of the statutory restrictions that Congress had enacted to end the war. Congress considered providing explicit authority, but while it dithered, Ford went ahead anyway.[127] He asserted his constitutional power as commander in chief and argued that these were rescue operations outside the scope of the restrictions.[128]

The president then ordered a more conventional military operation, which he portrayed as a success. The rogue government of Cambodia seized the American merchant ship *Mayaguez* and imprisoned the crew.[129] Desperate to restore American honor in Indochina, Ford sent in the Marines to raid an island where the hostages were thought to be kept and to bombard the Cambodian coast a bit. The Marines suffered some casualties, the *Mayaguez* crew was released from another place, and the president happily claimed victory. On grounds that the War Powers Resolution was unconstitutional, he had not consulted Congress in advance of the operation. By failing to respond sharply, Congress acquiesced in this first violation of the WPR.

In relations with the Soviet Union, Ford and Kissinger attempted to preserve the Nixon policy of détente but encountered push back from conservatives in Congress (and from within the administration, in the person of Secretary of Defense James Schlesinger).[130] At a summit in Vladivostok, Ford negotiated an extension of the Strategic Arms Limitation Treaty, but Senator Henry Jackson blocked ratification. A subsequent summit in Helsinki in 1975 produced a surprising delayed benefit. The Helsinki Accords were condemned by conservatives for conceding Soviet domination of Eastern Europe, but they contained human rights provisions that would later speed the erosion of Soviet power in that region.

The president finally removed his quarrelsome defense secretary and replaced him with Donald Rumsfeld, who would hold that office again under George W. Bush. Dick Cheney became chief of staff, commencing his rise to power. The Ford administration had limited successes to celebrate, but it did serve as a training ground for future Republican administrations.

Governing without Politics

A president who signed official documents, "Jimmy" Carter was unlikely
to display imperial characteristics. President Carter was a bit deceiv-
ing in this regard. His style exuded Jeffersonian simplicity, befitting his
background as a peanut farmer and one-term Georgia governor.[131] But
his intelligence, confirmed by his career as a nuclear submarine officer,
led him astray as president. Like Herbert Hoover, he was a technocratic
micromanager, delving too far into detail and trying to make too many
decisions himself.[132] Worse, he disdained dealing with the Washington
establishment and the barons of Congress. With a fine Wilsonian self-
righteousness, he intended to do the right thing and to appeal to the people if Congress balked. Of course, this political rigidity severely hampered
his presidency. In domestic matters, he butted heads with Congress as the
economy worsened and inflation spiraled. In foreign policy, he had some
remarkable achievements before his luck ran out and the Iranian hostage
crisis doomed his prospects for reelection.

Jimmy Carter surrounded himself with fellow Georgians in a White
House organized like FDR's, with himself at the center of the wheel. He
resisted appointing a chief of staff but eventually installed Hamilton Jor-
dan in that role. In the cabinet, some nationally known figures, such as
Cyrus Vance at State and Joseph Califano at Health, Education, and Welfare, jostled uneasily with the loyalists, such as Griffin Bell at Justice.

As Congress continued its post-Watergate attempts to control the executive branch, President Carter was willing to support incursions on the
president's authority that few of his predecessors would have stomached.[133]
He toyed with endorsing proposals to convert the Justice Department to
an independent agency but eventually opposed them. He signed both the
Ethics in Government Act, which created a permanent mechanism for
appointing special prosecutors to investigate the executive, and the Inspector General Act, which created inspectors in the agencies to report
misfeasance to Congress. Less controversially, he also signed the Presidential Records Act, which made those papers public property and provided for their control and disposition.[134]

In domestic affairs, President Carter was a faithful if bedeviled executive.[135] He was a fiscal conservative without a strongly articulated domestic
program. He offended Congress at the outset by defunding some western
dam projects and had to retreat.[136] He supported civil rights (including

increasingly controversial affirmative action measures) in making appointments, setting enforcement policy, and proposing legislation. He began serious efforts to make effective energy policy after the price shocks of the 1970s, spurring Congress to create an energy department under James Schlesinger. As he struggled with inflation, he made the crucial choice to nominate Paul Volcker to chair the Federal Reserve Board in 1979. Volcker immediately squeezed the money supply to tame inflation, triggering a recession that lasted well beyond Carter's term.

Jimmy Carter was never able to rally the American people strongly to him. He was trying to adapt the exhausted liberal politics of Lyndon Johnson to an era much less receptive to it.[137] In the summer of 1979, he made an ill-received speech that seemed to blame the people for the nation's woes. He then summarily fired a group of cabinet members including Bell, Califano, and Schlesinger. He appeared to lack a sure-handed grip on his administration and on his job. He did better in foreign policy, partly because he could negotiate on his own and then present a finished product that Congress and the people would accept.

Carter was a Wilsonian internationalist who pursued a moralistic human rights agenda more intensively than has any other president.[138] He began by negotiating a treaty to return the Panama Canal Zone to Panama, making up for Theodore Roosevelt's one-sided bargain. Accepting a couple of amendments, he squeezed the treaty through the Senate. Eager for peace in the Middle East, Carter personally negotiated the Camp David Accords, in which Israel returned the Sinai to Egypt in return for recognition. It was a personal diplomatic triumph reminiscent of TR's settlement of the Russo-Japanese War, but a less durable one.

President Carter finished the process of normalizing relations with communist China, a step that required termination of the existing mutual defense treaty with Taiwan. The Constitution specifies how treaties are formed but says nothing about their termination. Carter relied on occasional prior precedents of unilateral presidential termination. Having announced termination of the treaty, the president fended off an attempt by some members of Congress to litigate the constitutionality of his action.[139] The Supreme Court has neither blessed nor condemned unilateral treaty termination by the president. Carter's success in this instance did not still controversy over the issue, but it smoothed the path somewhat for future presidents.

When Jimmy Carter took office, détente with the Soviet Union was moribund.[140] His pragmatic secretary of state pressed him to revive it;

his hawkish national security adviser, Zbigniew Brzezinski, pushed back. Carter held a summit in Vienna with an aged and ailing Leonid Brezhnev, now heading a "stagnating, hollowed-out, repressive superpower."[141] The summit resulted in updated limits on strategic missiles in a proposed second Strategic Arms Limitation Treaty (SALT II), which then languished in the Senate. Carter aggravated Brezhnev, however, by pressing him to recognize human rights in the Soviet sphere. After the Soviets invaded Afghanistan in 1979, Carter angrily withdrew the treaty. He promulgated the Carter Doctrine, which stated that the United States was prepared to use force to prevent any outside power from domination in the Persian Gulf region.[142] Perhaps overreacting to this Soviet action along its own borders, Carter began the defense buildup that his successor would accelerate.

In November 1979, Iranians seized American diplomats at the embassy in Tehran, and the hostage crisis that would consume the remainder of Jimmy Carter's presidency was under way.[143] The president soon invoked statutory authority to freeze Iranian assets in the United States and initiated a long and painful diplomatic process that eventuated at the very end of Carter's term in a return of most of the Iranian assets as a trade for the freedom of the hostages. He tried one military response, a complicated raid to rescue the hostages that failed in April 1980 in the Iranian desert.[144] The president declined to consult with Congress in advance of the raid as required by the War Powers Resolution, asserting his commander in chief power to ensure that secrecy of the preparations would be preserved.[145]

Settlement of the hostage crisis was by an executive agreement that the Carter administration reached with Iran, with Algeria acting as intermediary because the Iranians would not deal directly with the United States.[146] The agreement erased some claims held by citizens of the two nations against the other nation; others were sent to arbitration. A conventional claims settlement treaty would have been exceedingly difficult to negotiate with the revolutionary Iranian regime in the unstable conditions of the crisis. The Supreme Court subsequently upheld the constitutionality of the president's settlement of the crisis by executive agreement, relying on earlier decisions that had upheld FDR's executive agreement recognizing the Soviet Union and settling claims between the two nations.[147] As a final humiliation for President Carter, the Iranians ensured that it would fall to his newly inaugurated successor to announce that an airplane carrying the hostages to freedom was wheels up at the Tehran airport.

PART V
A New Era

[The Moscow summit created] the hope of a new era in human history, and, hopefully, an era of peace and freedom for all. — Ronald Reagan, 1988

CHAPTER TWELVE

First a Dream

Reagan

The poet Carl Sandburg wrote, "The republic is a dream. Nothing happens unless first a dream." And that's what makes us Americans different. We've always reached for a new spirit and aimed at a higher goal. . . . Who among us wants to be the first to say we no longer have those qualities, that we must limp along, doing the same things that have brought us our present misery.—Ronald Reagan, 1981[1]

R onald Reagan was the best of presidents, he was the worst of presidents. The dichotomy between the two sides of him deeply affected his approach to the Constitution and shaped his legacy. Like Franklin Roosevelt, he possessed an optimistic, genial personality that captured the affection of the American people and empowered his transformative effect on American politics. He achieved most of the goals that he set for himself. Yet because he was "grandly indifferent to detail," his conduct of the presidency regarding most matters of everyday administration was so passive and neglectful that it fostered several scandals, including one that marred his last years in office and might have ended the tenure of a less popular president.[2]

Performing as President

Ronald Reagan reacted to a poverty-scarred childhood during the Depression by developing complete emotional self-sufficiency.[3] He was always popular and considerate (and was even civil to his opponents). But he guarded his inner life even from his closest friends. By the time he had completed a moderately successful career as an actor, he had formed a few settled beliefs from which he never wavered. He believed in American exceptionalism, the reduction of government interference with individuals and markets, and the reduction of the risks of nuclear war.[4] He liked to say that his nostalgic vision of America was a "great rediscovery" of traditional values.[5]

Although Reagan was generously willing to share credit, he would not admit mistakes and was extremely stubborn. Without the stubbornness, he would never have achieved any of his large goals. Below the level of his grand principles, Reagan cared little for the details of policy.[6] He expected his staff to inform him about the government and to generate either policy recommendations that he could ratify or at least clear options. In daily governance, he was almost unbelievably passive, initiating few policies, asking few questions, never probing the performance of the executive branch that he headed.[7] His was the most minimal imaginable devotion to the faithful execution duty. Turning seventy just after his inauguration, he was hard of hearing and often left advisers unsure of his preferences in the routine meetings that so bored him. What he wanted to do, and did superbly, was to perform publicly as president, communicating his simple values to the people in a way that rarely failed. Someone else, though, was writing the detailed parts of the script.

In his conception of the presidency, Reagan was "the opposite of Jimmy Carter, who knew far more and understood far less."[8] Reagan was the hedgehog, knowing a few big things, to Carter's fox, knowing so many little things that he lost focus. Reagan's primary handicap in office was that his ignorance about the government prevented him from taking effective command of the executive branch even when he wanted to. He knew little about the law. The kind of analysis of law and policy that most politicians do was foreign to him. He thought in concrete examples, not abstractions. What he had was "interpersonal intelligence," a gift for understanding the people and their concerns.[9]

As president, Reagan pursued four broad policy goals and achieved three of them while abandoning the fourth.[10] First, to diminish the risk of nuclear war, he wanted to enter a treaty with the Soviet Union that would actually reduce nuclear arms. He did that. Second, to bring the Soviets to the table, he wanted to build up America's defenses sufficiently to alarm them. He did that too. Third, he wanted to reduce the burden of taxes and federal regulations on citizens and businesses. He succeeded partially at that. And fourth, he hoped to balance the budget. He never admitted, though, that to achieve all four aims he would have to slash social programs deeply, including the flagship programs of the New Deal. As a political pragmatist, he had no appetite for a futile war against social programs serving the middle class. Therefore, as taxes went down and military spending soared, his budgets careened out of balance, leaving a disastrous fiscal legacy that almost tripled the national debt.

Minding the Store

The abilities and values of Reagan's aides uniquely defined the nature of his highly delegative presidency.[11] For chief of staff, he made the inspired choice of the pragmatic, tough, and savvy James Baker. Less successful was the disorganized and ethically insensitive Edwin Meese, a free-ranging counselor. The third member of the White House "troika" that set much policy in the first term was Michael Deaver, who was best at conveying the president's personal views to the administration. At the outset, Alexander Haig played the bull in the State Department china shop. At Defense, the wily and stubborn Caspar Weinberger jostled with Haig; he would war incessantly with Haig's replacement after the first year, the pragmatic George Schultz. Wanting to downgrade the office of national security adviser, Reagan went through one nonentity after another until he installed a disastrous admiral who brought on the Iran-Contra scandal and finally induced the president to turn to capable successors.

Overall, the cabinet was a loose coalition of diverse views and widely varying levels of ability. Over this chaotic scene the president reigned benignly but did not rule, hating confrontation and avoiding decisions that would favor one aide's views over the objections of another. The normal tensions between State and Defense can improve policy by bringing competing perspectives to bear, if they are resolved at the presidential level. In the Reagan administration, however, the legal and policy divisions in the administration festered at lower levels, as officers tried to prevent controversy from reaching the Oval Office. The faithful execution duty requires greater presidential engagement than that.

The first half year of Ronald Reagan's presidency saw the triumph of his legislative program, which realized his goals of reducing taxes and social spending while increasing defense spending.[12] Reagan's soaring popularity in the wake of his courageous recovery from an assassination attempt in March drove his bills through Congress. The Republicans had recaptured the Senate after twenty-eight years, and the president was able to form a working majority in the Democratic House. But the alliance was temporary, and the rest of Reagan's tenure boasted few legislative triumphs.

President Reagan's restructuring of the fiscal system initiated his run of deficits and altered American society and politics as well. Because the tax cuts favored the rich and the spending cuts slashed programs benefiting the poor that were left over from Lyndon Johnson's Great Society, the gap between rich and poor widened substantially.[13] After an initial misstep of proposing some immediate cuts in Social Security, which were overwhelmingly rejected by Congress, Reagan accepted recommendations of a commission he appointed, which kept the system solvent for a few decades.[14] He had the fortitude to support the successful effort to curtail inflation that Paul Volcker's Federal Reserve was conducting, even at the cost of a substantial economic recession.

Every president sees his constitutional opportunity to recommend legislation and his associated duty of faithful execution through the lens of his hopes to favor or disfavor certain groups in American society.[15] Ronald Reagan surely thought that achieving his broadest goals of reducing taxes, increasing freedom from government interference, and balancing the budget would diffusely benefit all Americans by restoring the mythic America that lived inside his mind. He did not care to notice that what he wound up doing would benefit the rich, harm the poor, and mortgage the future to produce current prosperity.

Reagan's budget package, with its structural deficits, would also make it far more difficult for future presidents to initiate new social programs or even to continue existing ones, whether he so intended or not. By inculcating millions of ordinary Americans with his hostility to government programs, he brought them into the Republican Party for the indefinite future and posed a fundamental challenge to the premises of the New Deal. The debate he initiated rages still.

President Reagan's legacy in domestic administration was impaired by the fact that although he loved the nation, he did not love its government. His inaugural address declared war on both the inherited political regime and the civil servants who administered it by declaring that "government is not the solution to our problem; government is the problem."[16] He was impervious to Grover Cleveland's maxim that "a public office is a public trust."[17] Having little sympathy for the regulatory and redistributive functions of government, he was careless about nominations to many agencies. Various scandals ensued, and he was lax about correcting them.[18]

Knowing that Congress would resist, Reagan did not try to repeal the health and safety statutes from the Nixon era. Instead, he employed another Nixon legacy in an effort to ensure that administration of the statutes would not be excessively burdensome for affected interest groups. Reagan issued an executive order requiring the executive agencies (but not the independent agencies) to conduct cost-benefit analysis of their regulations, under the supervision of the Office of Management and Budget.[19] Richard Nixon had initiated a milder form of this program; the Reagan order was broader and more mandatory.

Neither authorized nor forbidden by statute, this form of regulatory management has become an enduring legacy of President Reagan's tenure. Presidents of both parties have retained the oversight structure created by his executive order, with minor amendments dictated by experience or presidential preference. The reason for the program's durability is that it has significantly enhanced the control of the president (or at least that of his principal subordinates) over the "ever thicker" executive branch that can resist and frustrate presidential preferences.[20] Every president since Reagan has needed this grip on administration. Congress has acquiesced in the program, which has lasted for over three decades.

In two ways President Reagan exerted close control over information about the executive branch. First, he used his executive order power to restrict disclosure of information, by tightening internal controls of classified information to make nondisclosure easier and taking steps to prevent leaks of national security information.[21] Second, he asserted executive privilege vigorously against Congress, sparking some long-running and eventually ugly controversies with congressional committees over regulatory matters.[22] He won no clear victories on these fronts, however. Leaks continued apace, as they always will, and the committees forced disclosures of contested material whenever they showed enough persistence to wear the executive down.

In 1983, the Supreme Court aided the Reagan administration's efforts to control execution of the law by invalidating all forms of the "legislative veto."[23] Legislative vetoes are attempts by Congress to authorize one or both of its houses to override executive actions by passing resolutions that are not presented to the president for his signature or veto. The Court correctly held that legislative vetoes unconstitutionally evade the president's veto power, because they have legal effects, like statutes, but do not follow the full statutory process in the Constitution.[24] Since the World War II era, Congress had increasingly used the legislative veto device in hopes of controlling the ever-expanding executive branch. The provision in the War Powers Resolution for the termination of military action by concurrent resolution is one among many examples. Presidents had vetoed some bills containing legislative veto authority but had also signed many of them out of desire to obtain other provisions in the bills.

All presidents had taken the departmentalist stance that legislative vetoes were unconstitutional.[25] Hence they often issued signing statements declaring that they would not obey the legislative veto provisions contained in otherwise acceptable bills.[26] But in fact presidents sometimes quietly obeyed legislative veto processes, out of a desire to placate Congress. It is not surprising, then, that after the Supreme Court invalidated the technique, Congress continued to place legislative vetoes in statutes and the executive sometimes informally complied with them. Thus the Court's attempt to shield the executive from congressional intrusions was only partly successful.

The Reagan administration's main statutory deregulatory effort produced a disaster in the savings and loan industry.[27] Pushing to free the savings and loan institutions from tight regulation, the president did not see that his plan created incentives for the managers of the thrifts to make risky investments or simply to loot the till. Widespread collapse and scandal cratered the industry. The president and his aides turned a blind eye to the mounting losses. By the time the nation had finished paying the bill, hundreds of billions of dollars had been wasted. It was a failure of both statutory design and faithful execution.

Like Richard Nixon, Ronald Reagan followed a southern strategy to capture conservative whites for the Republican Party by minimizing civil rights enforcement.[28] He signed an extension of the Voting Rights Act, but the Justice Department did little to enforce it. He sided with discriminatory private schools in a battle they fought with the Internal Revenue Service. Near the end of his term he vetoed a civil rights bill and was overridden. He was no bigot, but he seemed insensitive to discrimination.[29]

Expanding on another Nixon precedent, Reagan prompted his Justice Department to vet judicial nominations more closely than ever before.[30] Justice formed a special unit for the task, interviewed candidates systematically for the compatibility of their views with Reagan's, and usually put forward reliable conservatives with strong credentials. By the end of his tenure, Reagan had appointed a higher percentage of the judiciary than anyone except FDR, just over half. His judges are still leaving their mark on American law. By influencing judicial interpretation of the Constitution and statutes to accord more closely with executive branch interpretations, Reagan realized a potential that had long lain dormant in the nomination power. His practice thinned the separation of powers barrier between the branches.[31]

By intruding more political considerations into nominations, President Reagan invited more political scrutiny in confirmations. It is no accident that modern interbranch wars over the confirmation of judicial nominations began with Reagan's failed nomination of Robert Bork for the Supreme Court.[32] The politicized and torpid confirmation process has produced long-standing vacancies in the federal judiciary, impairing its capacity to function.

At the beginning of President Reagan's second term, his aides induced personnel changes that would have fateful consequences for his presidency.[33] The treasury secretary was Donald Regan, who had followed a successful Wall Street career with a capable term at Treasury. Seeking other avenues and noticing James Baker's exhaustion as chief of staff, Regan proposed that they switch jobs. Baker assented, and the two presented the plan to a bemused president, who casually ratified it. Baker went on to move a general tax reform bill through Congress that has received generally high marks.

Regan, however, had moved to a job that ill suited his skills. As chief of staff he was rigid, hierarchical, and politically maladroit. Lacking Baker's antennae for looming political disaster, he would preside over one in the Iran-Contra affair. Meanwhile, Ed Meese was nominated for attorney general. After a special prosecutor decided there was not enough evidence to indict him for trading government jobs for political favors, he was confirmed by the Senate. During the furor over Meese, the president stuck by his old friend, oblivious to the need for the president's official aide in law interpretation to meet an ethical standard higher than freedom from provable crime.[34] This move would also haunt Reagan in the future.

Heroes, Villains, and Cowboys

Ronald Reagan gazed out upon the world with the simple, patriotic values that he brought to everything. Such a reductionist outlook tends to skew a president's constitutional approach to foreign policy, because a world populated by heroes and villains demands a more aggressive set of reactions than does the muddle of the real thing, and constitutional limits can seem irrelevant or even harmful to the pursuit of virtue.

President Reagan wanted to roll communism back, not merely contain it. In this hemisphere, left-wing guerrillas were assailing an American-backed government in El Salvador, with some help from the sympathetic government of the Sandinistas in neighboring Nicaragua. The president hoped to stop the transit of arms to El Salvador and to undermine the Sandinista regime as well. He faced several obstacles, however. First, as he knew, the United States had a long and deeply resented history of military interventions and occupations in Latin America.[35] Nicaragua in particular had been occupied by American Marines for most of two decades in the early twentieth century.

Complicating the prospects for military action was the state of the American military a decade after the end of the Vietnam War. In sharp contrast to the eagerness for intervention that the Joint Chiefs had displayed from Truman through Johnson, a deeply wounded officer corps now resisted new commitments to potential quagmires, especially in the absence of strong popular support. Moreover, neither Congress nor the public showed much appetite for Central American adventures. There was a nascent resistance to the Sandinistas, the "Contras," who were elevated to "freedom fighters" by Ronald Reagan's imagination. Aiding them and resisting the Sandinistas would, however, sharply expand the Truman Doctrine, which did counsel support for established governments against communist guerillas, as in El Salvador, but did not extend to supporting insurgency against established governments, as in Nicaragua.

These considerations impelled the president toward covert intervention in the region. In November 1981, Reagan began secret support of the Contras. His CIA director, William Casey, misleadingly explained the initiative to Congress as a limited effort to stem the flow of arms to El Salvador, not a direct action against the Sandinistas.[36] Congress eventually approved over $300 million in aid to the Contras, a third of it in military supplies.[37] Congress wanted to micromanage foreign policy after Vietnam but was poorly informed about the administration's aims and activities. The legislators vacillated, sometimes approving the aid and sometimes cutting it off. The administration vacillated as well, as some factions sought to support the Contras and others to negotiate with them, with the president characteristically declining to resolve the dispute. As Central American policy drifted into the shadows, executed by the CIA and NSC staff, the stage was set for the debacle to come.

Meanwhile, various foreign policy crises cropped up around the world to bedevil the president. In Lebanon, a well-intended but poorly conceived intervention led to a "case study of foreign policy calamity."[38] In July 1982, President Reagan agreed to send a contingent of troops to that unhappy nation as part of a multinational peacekeeping force. It was trying to stop the bloodshed after Israel had invaded to destroy Palestine Liberation Organization forces lodged there. The chaotic aftermath of the invasion included a horrific slaughter of refugees.[39] The Joint Chiefs, sensing disaster, opposed the deployment but did not press their objections with the president. One of the few procedural successes of the War Powers Resolution ensued. Because American forces would be deployed for a period longer than the sixty-day deadline in the WPR, the administration and Congress negotiated a grant of statutory authority for their presence for up to eighteen months.[40] Both branches had signed off on the operation.

Hoping to keep the combatants apart, eight hundred American Marines found themselves first in a crossfire and then in the crosshairs of terror groups.[41] In April 1983, a bombing at the US embassy killed scores of people, including some Americans. In October, a truck bomb destroyed the Marine barracks in Beirut, killing 241. This strike drove the United States from Lebanon. President Reagan would not admit defeat, however; to him the retreat was a "redeployment" at sea. There was no retaliation—it was difficult to know whom to strike.

Happily for the administration, another crisis produced a splendid little war that drew national attention away from Lebanon in the wake of the barracks bombing. On the small Caribbean island of Grenada, a violent leftist coup brought fears of an expansion of Castro's power beyond Cuba and concerns for the safety of about a thousand American medical students on the island. President Reagan sent an invasion force, which soon took control at a low cost in casualties.[42] He had nodded perfunctorily toward the WPR by briefing congressional leaders after ordering the invasion but before it occurred. He justified this flexing of muscle by the "colossus of the north" by styling it a humanitarian mission. The troops were out before the sixty-day deadline made it necessary to seek congressional support.

Reagan's only other dispatch of American forces into combat occurred when he sent an air strike against Libya in 1986 in retaliation for a terror bombing.[43] The president notified Congress of the strike while the airplanes were en route, rather than consulting in advance while the operation was under consideration. Reagan was sensitive enough about congressional relations that he would likely have provided these two courtesy notifications even without the presence of the WPR. What presidents have been unwilling to do, however, is to consult in advance of a decision to employ the military, because that would share the decision with Congress. Of course, that is precisely the purpose of the consultation requirement. Presidents are loath to set any precedent that might limit their control over military interventions.

Enter the cowboys. The Iran-Contra scandal was a natural product of the risks created by Ronald Reagan's inattention to his duty of faithful execution. A rogue operation in the White House took the president's presumed wishes as its commands, ignoring the constraints of Constitution and statute alike as its agents concocted a foreign policy embarrassment laced with repeated violations of the statutes that would have averted the farce at the outset.

In 1982 Congress began enacting a series of funding restrictions, the Boland amendments, each of which forbade the use of United States funds to overthrow the Sandinistas. Nevertheless, covert action continued under the guise that it was directed to interdicting arms shipments from Nicaragua to El Salvador rather than regime change.[44] In early 1984, with the president's approval the CIA mined Nicaraguan harbors, and Director Casey hid the agency's participation while briefing the congressional intelligence committees. When the truth came out, Congress reacted angrily. The House attached a new Boland amendment to an appropriations bill, which Reagan signed to avoid losing the funds. It prohibited military or paramilitary support for the Contras by the CIA, the Defense Department, "or any other agency or entity involved in intelligence activities."[45] Representative Boland explained in the House that this provision "clearly ends U.S. support for the war in Nicaragua," with "no exceptions."[46]

With the president and Congress in fundamental disagreement about policy toward the Contras, the administration adopted a new approach that was completely hidden from Congress. The president's landslide reelection in 1984 with 59 percent of the vote probably added to the administration's hubris. Reagan told his national security adviser, Robert McFarlane, that he wanted the Contras kept together "body and soul."[47] Since the agencies that normally performed intelligence activities were disabled by the Boland amendment, the initiative passed to the staff of the National Security Council, which is supposed to be an agency for interpreting intelligence and recommending policy, not for covert action.[48]

Within the NSC, the responsibility for keeping the bodies and souls of the Contras attached fell to McFarlane's deputy (and successor), Admiral John Poindexter, and to the flamboyant Lt. Col. Oliver North of the Marine Corps. North, lacking experience in either covert operations or Latin America, did possess unquenchable optimism, total devotion to the president's desires as he understood them, indefatigable energy, and atrocious judgment. Thus, with the intelligence professionals sidelined by the Boland amendment, an amateur operation was cobbled together by officers trained for other duties.

With the president's encouragement and participation, North and Poindexter began finding secret sources of support for the Contras that did not involve expending federal funds. They obtained "donations" from private American citizens and from foreign governments, prominently Saudi Arabia. Perhaps the American donors expected nothing in return except the president's gratitude, but it stretches credulity to say the same of the Saudis. Hence, even if off-the-books private fund-raising was in technical compliance with the Boland amendments because it did not disburse federal funds, there was surely an expenditure of a less tangible, but no less important, form of the nation's capital.[49]

Meanwhile, a hostage crisis in Lebanon took center stage in the president's mind. By early 1985, Hezbollah, a pro-Iranian terror group that was firmly entrenched in Lebanon, had kidnapped five Americans, including the CIA station chief in Beirut. Reagan clearly and constantly communicated to his staff his deep desire to see the hostages freed. The NSC staff responded by concocting a scheme to sell American antitank missiles to Iran, in return for which Iran would press Hezbollah to release the hostages. After McFarlane informed Reagan of the proposal, the president gave initial approval and then discussed it with some members of the cabinet, not including the attorney general. Secretary of State Schultz and Secretary of Defense Weinberger objected strenuously, reflecting the traditional reluctance of their departments to the arming of rogue regimes. Nonetheless, arms were already flowing toward Iran.

There were serious legal obstacles to the plan to trade arms for hostages. Because Iran was listed as a supporter of international terrorism, a statute barred it from buying American arms. In fact, official American policy was to press nations around the world to deny arms to Iran. Hence the plan, in fundamental tension with American law and policy, would have to be both indirect and secret. Israel was asked to sell the arms to Iran, whereupon the United States would replenish the Israeli arsenal.

With Reagan's approval and active interest, a series of amateurish and often farcical negotiations ensued. The NSC staff drew on some help from the CIA and employed some extremely dubious private arms dealers. No one ever knew who could speak for Iran on the other end. Iran eventually received over two thousand antitank missiles and some spare parts for its antiaircraft missiles. The Americans vastly overcharged the Iranians for the supplies, producing profits in excess of $15 million.[50] Eventually, three Americans were released, but during the negotiations more new hostages than that were taken in Lebanon.[51]

The sale of arms to Iran implicated various statutes that controlled international arms sales pursuant to Congress's power to regulate foreign trade. The statutory scheme was complex, with multiple substantive limits on arms sales. Each statute also contained one or both of two common techniques for controlling the executive.[52] First, Congress required the president personally to make specified findings of the importance of a particular action to national security. Second, Congress required that it be notified of each action, typically by reporting to the intelligence committees of the two houses.

The purpose shared by these two controls was political responsibility. If the president approved an action personally and explicitly, his accountability to the law (and to history) was ensured. And if Congress was notified of an action, it would be accountable for acquiescing in or challenging the action. In the ever-changing realm of foreign affairs, these simple control techniques often replace detailed substantive prescription of policy, which is usually difficult or counterproductive to formulate. In Iran-Contra, the Reagan administration would evade both kinds of limits.

The Arms Export Control Act required presidential consent to the retransfer of arms initially exported to Israel and notification of Congress if the sale exceeded a stated dollar amount.[53] The second possible authority for arms transfers to Iran was pursuant to intelligence operations conducted under the National Security Act, the CIA's principal (and sublimely vague) charter. The act required that the intelligence agencies keep the two congressional intelligence committees "fully and currently informed" of all their activities.[54] Where prior notice of significant intelligence activities was not given, the committees were to be informed "in a timely fashion." In addition, the Hughes-Ryan Amendment to the Foreign Assistance Act required that "significant anticipated intelligence activities" could not be conducted by the CIA unless and until the president found that "each such operation is important to the national security of the United States."[55]

Thus, whether the arms sales were legal "depends fundamentally upon whether the President approved the transactions before they occurred."[56] Some early sales occurred before the president signed the necessary finding to approve them. When executive branch lawyers discovered the omission, they quickly drafted a finding for the president to sign.[57] The finding declared that the hostage release efforts were "important to the national security," attempted to ratify prior actions, and directed the CIA not to brief Congress "until such time as I may direct otherwise."[58] It would not be reported for almost a year.

The secretive, convoluted, and confused decision making concerning the arms sales led to violations of both fundamental congressional controls on covert action. It was later claimed that Reagan had made an "oral finding" approving the initial sales, so that they were legal from the outset.[59] Whether he actually did so is lost in the mists of history; later on, he could not remember. There was no compliance with the National Security Act's requirement that notification of Congress about covert intelligence activities, if not made in advance, be "in a timely fashion." After the first written presidential finding directed that congressional notification be withheld, no one ever seems to have revisited the issue.

In 1985, while deeply embroiled with the Iranian negotiations, North evolved a plan to divert profits from the arms sales to the Contras. Poindexter, having become national security adviser, approved it. They consulted no lawyers, however, and thus were not reminded of the substantial argument that the proceeds of sales of American arms are federal funds that must be spent according to law.[60] Poindexter then made the extraordinary decision not to inform the president about the plan. His rationale was to "insulate him from the decision and provide some future deniability for the President if it ever leaked out."[61] By insulating the president from political responsibility for this reckless scheme, Poindexter made national policy without the participation of any elected official from either branch of government. There was no adult supervision from the president or anyone else, since Secretaries Schultz and Weinberger, having opposed the arms sales, were kept in the dark.

By late 1986, both the Iranian and the Contra sides of the operation stood revealed. President Reagan initially denied that arms had been traded for hostages (instead, he claimed that the effort was to empower Iranian "moderates"). When the inaccuracy of his statement became undeniable, he made the revealing admission that although his heart and mind told him he had not traded arms for hostages, the facts said otherwise.[62] Reagan probably never admitted to himself what he had done—after all, it was not something he would have done.

As the revelations spread, Reagan initially assigned Attorney General Meese to determine the facts. Meese conducted a slow, disorganized, and incompetent investigation. Instead of using the Justice Department's own professional investigators, the FBI, he asked some of his other subordinates to inquire. He took no immediate steps to seal the offices of the miscreant NSC staffers, allowing them to conduct a "shredding party" that destroyed an unknown number of crucial documents. The president made no effort to monitor or prod the Meese "investigation."

Soon Poindexter and North were dismissed, and a season of more formal investigations commenced: the president's own Tower Commission, separate investigations by the two houses of Congress,[63] and an endless criminal inquiry by independent counsel Lawrence Walsh.[64] All of these investigations took place while the president's second term was winding down, with his popularity still strong. President Reagan defended himself by stressing his good intentions and his ignorance of many of the details of the actions of his subordinates. Ironically, his failures of faithful execution were his main defense.

Reagan is said to have told Secretary of State Schultz that "the American people will never forgive me if I fail to get these hostages out over this legal question."[65] The president's attitude that law must be subordinated to results, once communicated to willing subordinates, explains much about the Iran-Contra scandal. Using National Security Council staff to support the Contras clearly violated the Boland amendment's prohibition of using any agency that is "involved in intelligence activities" to support military operations in Nicaragua. Although the NSC staff is not ordinarily an operational intelligence agency, it was so acting in Iran-Contra activities, with the intention of evading the Boland amendment.[66]

The majorities of the House and Senate committees investigating the Iran-Contra affair concluded that the administration had engaged in "an evasion of the letter and the spirit" of the law and laid blame partially with President Reagan, whose solicitation of foreign donations for the Contras "set the stage" for his subordinates' view of the law "not as setting boundaries for their actions, but raising impediments to their goals."[67] The Walsh report concluded that Reagan "knowingly participated or acquiesced in covering up the scandal."[68] All of this is correct. The president repeatedly failed his duty of faithful execution.[69]

The Iran-Contra operation created secret national policies that were supported by funds that had not been appropriated by Congress. In modern times, Congress often prefers to control the executive through the appropriations process, because the executive's need for money minimizes the power of the president's veto as compared to new substantive legislation. Also, the yearly funding cycle fosters regular adjustments of policy (although at the hazard of micromanagement). Thus, the appropriations process "provides the link between government operations and the democratic mandate by requiring that all funding take place by statutes, that is, by the actions of persons who can be turned out by the voters every biennium."[70] Circumventing this process by using unappropriated funds, "no matter how noble the purpose and no matter how beneficent the source, is to strike at the heart of this idea."

After Vietnam and Watergate, Congress had imposed and presidents had mostly accepted a new constitutional settlement of the contested issues.[71] The settlement, arranged by the political branches with only occasional participation by the courts, was wide ranging. It included the War Powers Resolution, impoundment control, freedom of information reform, independent counsels, and the provisions for presidential findings and notice to Congress about sensitive activities that President Reagan's private operation evaded. The Iran-Contra affair, although not threatening the settlement wholesale, approached the heart of it. Once again, a president had sought to place himself beyond effective control by Congress.

The official investigations of Iran-Contra, consumed by the effort to discover who did what, failed to drive home the fundamental unconstitutionality of the secret policies and operations in a way that the public could understand.[72] Thus the scandal ended with a legal whimper, having besmirched President Reagan's second term but not having destroyed the esteem that the American people held for him. In the absence of grave political and criminal penalties for the follies and crimes of Iran-Contra, future presidents could learn that coverups of illegality can work and that well-intentioned statutory violations might be forgiven by Congress and the people.

"Tear Down This Wall"[73]

The Reagan presidency ended on a far happier note than Iran-Contra— the reconstruction of America's relationship with the Soviet Union and the beginning of the end of the Cold War. Few developments could have been more surprising. Tensions with the Soviets remained high during Reagan's first term.[74] Within the administration, conservatives like Haig,

Weinberger, and Casey sought unquestioned American military superiority at any cost. Efforts toward détente ended, as did Jimmy Carter's emphasis on human rights. In 1983, Reagan was just being himself when he referred to the Soviet Union as an "evil empire."

Initial movement on arms control was retrograde. Reagan left Carter's pending SALT II agreement on the shelf and deployed intermediate nuclear force (INF) missiles to Europe. Even more alarming to the Soviets was Reagan's destabilizing scheme for a Strategic Defense Initiative (SDI), a plan to mount antimissile defenses in space that he announced in early 1983 and never abandoned. This was very much a personal initiative. Its announcement surprised not only the Soviets but much of his own administration, including Secretaries Schultz and Weinberger and the Joint Chiefs. Reagan had been appalled when early briefings told him that our only defense against a missile strike was the threat to incinerate the other side; hence his desire to build a shield. Apart from his faith in this program (which eventually grew to $60 billion), he knew little about strategic arms.

On the other side, under the aging and rigid Soviet leadership there were few diplomatic opportunities, and as Reagan later said, "They kept dying on me." Everything changed when Mikhail Gorbachev brought a new Soviet generation to power in 1985. He understood that his nation could no longer sustain the debilitating arms race with the United States. Reagan's arms buildup induced him to seek reductions in nuclear forces, as the president had always expected would eventually happen.[75] Now a breakthrough could occur.

Reagan had shown little interest in SALT II because it merely capped and did not reduce nuclear arms. Any agreement that would include scrapping American missiles would, however, face fierce opposition from right-wingers in his administration, Congress, and the public. Reagan thought he had the anticommunist credentials to survive an assault from his right, and he was correct. No other modern president except Eisenhower could have taken such a step.

The path was not smooth to what would become the first reduction in nuclear arsenals, the 1987 INF Treaty, despite the essential commitment of both principals to find common ground. In 1985, Reagan and Gorbachev opened a direct correspondence that continued for the rest of Reagan's presidency, which comprised more than a score of letters carefully prepared by staff.[76] The president began by turning up the heat on Gorbachev. He ended informal American adherence to Carter's SALT agreement and reinterpreted the 1972 ABM Treaty to allow not only laboratory development of missile defenses but actual testing (so that SDI could proceed).[77]

The two leaders had to establish a more personal relationship than words on a page. After an early summit in Geneva allowed them to feel each other out, the endgame began—strangely—in Reykjavik, Iceland, in 1986. Sitting together, Reagan and Gorbachev began musing about an agreement to destroy all nuclear weapons. This was an impossible dream in a world of rapidly proliferating arsenals in other nations. It terrified the president's staff. But when Gorbachev pressed Reagan to abandon SDI as part of a deal, the president angrily refused and broke off the talks. There was still one road open to a treaty, and Gorbachev took it. He soon decoupled SDI from further negotiations by turning to intermediate and short-range missiles of the kind that threatened Europe instead of intercontinental weapons. The INF Treaty that eliminated these weapons was signed at Washington in late 1987. Reagan, holding the right wing at bay, steered it through the Senate by a wide margin.

Celebrating, the president journeyed to Moscow for a summit late in his term. Here he found himself accurately pronouncing the birth of a "new era" of normalized Soviet-American relations while standing amid the busts of Lenin and Stalin that so signified the old one. He also took the opportunity to lecture the Soviets on the human rights provisions of the much-criticized Helsinki Accords that President Ford had signed. This too was prophetic, as the collapsing Soviet Union would discover in a few years.

Years later, and out of office in a nation that no longer existed, Mikhail Gorbachev called his new friend Ronald Reagan "a really big person . . . a very great political leader."[78] He was that. Reagan "looms over the last quarter of the American Century as Woodrow Wilson the first and Franklin Roosevelt the second."[79] His continuation of long-standing American willingness to combine strength with an openness to negotiation finally bore fruit when he met receptivity on the other side. Although it was Gorbachev's dire need to make a deal that finally broke decades of stalemate, progress could not have occurred had the two leaders not shared a faith that they could accomplish what most of the experts thought impossible.

CHAPTER THIRTEEN

The Vision Thing

George H. W. Bush and Clinton

[A friend] suggested that Bush go alone to Camp David for a few days to figure out where he wanted to take the country. "Oh," said Bush in clear exasperation, "the vision thing."
—Quoted in *Time*, 1987[1]

No president aspires to a role as a transitional figure, yet George H. W. Bush bridged two kinds of eras, and did so with competence and grace.[2] He was the last president to have served in World War II and to have imbued the values of that generation. As a young Navy pilot, he compiled a record of heroism to match JFK's.[3] He was also the last of the moderate Republican presidents, watching as his party moved away from him to the right under the influence of Ronald Reagan, whose charisma he could never match. Like other presidents who have followed reconstructive presidencies (Madison, Van Buren, Andrew Johnson, Truman), Bush was left to clean up after the elephant, with the diminished prospects that the task entails.

Personally, Bush was always gracious and warm, having impeccable manners.[4] Curiously for a politician, he shrank from self-promotion or credit-claiming. It should surprise no one that until far too late he could not take seriously a challenge to his reelection from a brash, draft-evading son of the baby boom. Nor could he fathom the constant negative comparisons of his manhood to that of his predecessor, whose wartime heroics were all celluloid.

The scion of a political Connecticut family, Bush repaired to Texas after finishing Yale with distinction, determined to increase the family fortune on his own in the oil business. Entering politics, he served two terms in the House of Representatives and then became a figure of the late establishment with an impressive series of appointive posts: UN ambassador, CIA director, envoy to China, vice president. As president, although expected by many to serve "Reagan's third term," he set his own, somewhat wavering course.

For there was a deficiency—Bush lacked what he sometimes dismissively called the "vision thing," a sense for where he wanted to lead the nation and a capacity to communicate that dream to the people.[5] The resulting criticism revealed the extent to which every modern president is expected to display a distinctive personal politics to shape the nation and its Constitution to his or her own model. Unhappily, Ronald Reagan, who never lacked for vision, had left a legacy that would sharply confine the options available to his next two successors—an explosion of the national debt that could no longer be ignored.[6] "By saddling later presidents with a monumental governing problem, the deficit condemned liberalism to die slowly of neglect."[7] Playing to the Reagan legacy, Bush made a mistake during his 1988 campaign by promising that he would support no new taxes, thereby constricting his options from the start. In addition, in both houses of Congress he faced Democratic majorities, which increased in the midterm election of 1990.

Unlike Ronald Reagan, Bush intended to keep close personal control of foreign policy. With skill honed by experience, he assembled a highly competent national security team that was designed to avoid the chaotic management that had characterized the Reagan administration.[8] Secretary of State James Baker and national security adviser Brent Scowcroft soon forged close ties to Bush (particularly the trustworthy and self-effacing Scowcroft). Secretary of Defense Dick Cheney, who took the post after the Senate rejected its former member John Tower, completed the team by promoting General Colin Powell for chairman of the Joint Chiefs. Overall, it was a group of realist veterans of the Cold War who initially approached the disintegrating Soviet Union with more skepticism than had Reagan at the end of his term.[9]

The Fall of the Wall

No one knew how to end the Cold War, but Bush's polite nature gave him just the right touch.[10] Mikhail Gorbachev, operating under the shelter of Ronald Reagan's easing of tensions, signaled the eastern European nations of the Soviet bloc that he would not intervene against the rising popular movements there, and a domino effect promptly occurred as they serially ejected the communists.[11] The implosion of the Soviet Union itself was next—Gorbachev could no more still the forces he had loosed at home than he could in other countries. By the end of 1991 Gorbachev was out of office, and the Soviet Union was gone. Russia reemerged under the mercurial Boris Yeltsin.

Throughout these dizzying events, Bush and his aides gave restrained support to the emerging republics and avoided crowing about victory in the Cold War, to provide Gorbachev room to maneuver. The president skillfully brokered the entry of a reunified Germany into the western security complex of NATO, overcoming the ghosts of World War II. He also negotiated a Strategic Arms Reduction Treaty with the Soviets to reduce nuclear arsenals (and then another with Yeltsin). Bush increasingly warmed to Gorbachev himself, as had Reagan. Yeltsin would require special delicacy.

Meanwhile, a democratic uprising in China met its brutal end at Tiananmen Square in 1989.[12] Knowing China well and hoping to ease relations with the Chinese in the long run, Bush responded haltingly. He did impose some statutory sanctions in response to Tiananmen, such as stopping arms sales. When an infuriated Congress passed a bill to keep Chinese students in the United States, Bush vetoed it to preserve his options and extended the same rights to the students by executive order. He used back channels to press China to ease its repression of dissent.[13] Eventually he reduced the sanctions, but better relations with China would have to wait.

Closer to home, in December 1989 Bush sent the US military into combat in Panama while Congress was out of session.[14] With the handover of the Panama Canal looming at the end of the century, Panama's reptilian strongman Manuel Noriega, who was deeply involved in the drug trade, seemed a most unfit custodian. To oust Noriega and restore a previously elected Panamanian government, Bush launched the largest military operation since Vietnam (24,000 troops), under the pretext of responding to some assaults on American servicemen.[15] As the operation commenced, the president sent notice to Congress under the War Powers Resolution, but he did not consult Congress in advance. The operation captured Noriega at the cost of about a score of American lives and was popular in a nation still hungry for military victory.

The president was able to complete this rather tidy operation and remove the troops before expiry of the sixty-day WPR clock raised any awkward questions about a need to resort to Congress for permission. Arguably, the invasion of Panama was not a "war" in the constitutional sense that would require preauthorization. Although the scale of the operation was large and resistance from Noriega's forces was both expected and encountered, the evident mismatch portended little chance of a long-term commitment as in Korea or Vietnam. Still, the president's attitude to the WPR was consistently grudging, as events would soon demonstrate.

"This Will Not Stand"

In early August 1990, President Bush was sojourning in the salubrious air of Aspen, Colorado, with British Prime Minister Margaret Thatcher when word arrived that Iraq's Saddam Hussein had invaded and overwhelmed neighboring Kuwait.[16] Some think that the Iron Lady braced a wavering Bush to eject the thug from the oil fields, but everything in the president's own nature called him to duty. This was the kind of classic military aggression over a border that sounded the alarm for anyone from the World War II generation.

Without asking the widely dispersed members of Congress for their views, Bush announced that "this will not stand," and prepared to make good on his statement. He quickly moved American airborne troops into Saudi Arabia's border region near Kuwait, after receiving the Saudis' consent. The troops were a deterrent in the form of a tripwire. Saddam did not move any farther, but he now controlled 20 percent of the world's oil supply. So far, so good, but how to get him out of Kuwait?

In the months that followed, the president benefited enormously from the skill of his national security team. From the outset of his administration, this group had stressed the need to keep the United States beyond effective military challenge from anyone. Bush had kept defense budgeting at high levels.[17] The means for a response to Iraq existed, but there were disagreements about strategy within the administration.

The uniformed military had reacted to the trauma of Vietnam by embracing the "Powell Doctrine," which was named for the politically astute chair of the Joint Chiefs.[18] The doctrine stated that the United States should go to war only with overwhelming force, clear objectives, popular support, and a firm exit strategy. Any nation's war makers would covet such advantages—here the military was pressing its civilian superiors to share its own caution, acquired at such high cost. The Powell Doctrine, which dominated American military policy for the rest of the twentieth century and beyond, contrasts sharply with the prevailing attitude in the military between World War II and Vietnam. Presidents

Truman through Kennedy had repeatedly found themselves pulling back on the reins against generals who were itching to fight—and with nuclear weapons if needed. The egregious General Curtis LeMay was the icon of that era.

President Bush soon emerged as the most hawkish member of his administration with regard to Kuwait.[19] Baker and Powell held back, worried that a war would be costly and dangerous. Cheney and Scowcroft urged prompt action. Muttering about Hitler, the president sent Secretary of State Baker traveling to form an alliance to oust Iraq.[20] With great success, the administration assembled a coalition of thirty-four nations (including Arab states) and obtained a UN Security Council resolution supporting the use of force to restore Kuwait. More than four hundred thousand American troops massed on the border.

Defense Secretary Cheney urged the president to take action against Iraq without asking for authorization from Congress.[21] Here was the attempt to cement the outlying Korea precedent as normal. Cheney, White House Counsel Boyden Gray, and Bush himself thought that the president could rely on international law instead.[22] Under the Constitution, however, repelling Iraq's invasion of Kuwait would clearly be a war in the constitutional sense, requiring authorization from Congress.[23] Given the scale of the intended allied assault and widespread expectations of substantial resistance to it, the case for requiring congressional assent was at least as clear as it had been for any of the three stages of commitment in Korea. Nevertheless, Bush publicly claimed he had the constitutional authority to go to war with Iraq without congressional action.[24]

Recalling Truman's difficulties in conducting the Korean War without Congress fully subscribed, Bush then decided to ask Congress for authority to act. Political prudence accounts for the move: he wanted to present a united front to the nation and the world and to protect himself against failure. Bush did not concede that the War Powers Resolution forced him to seek congressional consent; after he received it, he said he would have proceeded had authority not been granted.[25] One wonders. Although presidents have often gone to war on their own, none has ever defied a negative vote in Congress.

In the event, in early 1991 the president asked Congress for authority to drive Iraq from Kuwait and obtained it narrowly along largely partisan lines. The Senate majority of 52–47 was the closest Senate vote on war in American history. Those who had favored unilateral presidential action against Iraq may have felt vindicated by the jeopardy the president's proposal encountered, but such a reaction would encourage going to Congress only when its support is most obvious and hence least necessary from a constitutional standpoint.

Once the UN deadline for Iraq to leave Kuwait passed, the United States and its allies launched that rarest of wars, one that goes better than expected. The Powell Doctrine was on impressive display. A stunning barrage of new high-tech aerial weapons staggered the enemy, and the ensuing invasion took a mere hundred hours before the invaders stood down to avoid unnecessary carnage. Bush then adhered to the stated purpose of the alliance by declining to press on to Baghdad to remove Saddam. Another war, and another President Bush, would attend to that. For the time being, though, some ghosts of Vietnam had been exorcised and the administration had put on a Wilsonian demonstration of the power of collective action to stop aggression.

The impressive victory in the Persian Gulf left the United States in a newly dominant position in the world, with a massive advantage in military force against anyone and an economy 40 percent larger than that of the next nation.[26] Yet from the vantage point of an American president, the old world order had given way to a new world disorder. The crude disciplining effects of the Cold War were gone, along with the polestar of containment. Local nationalist movements and nonstate actors surged into the power vacuums; American military force would be too blunt an instrument for effective response to every crisis.

Two trouble spots that did not involve the strategic interests of the United States epitomized the need to rethink presidential foreign policy; in both of them the Bush administration would bequeath escalating problems to its successor. In the former Yugoslavia, deep ethnic hatreds exploded. Serbia's brutal "ethnic cleansing" of Croats and Bosnians was a genocide evoking the Holocaust of World War II.[27] Noting that "we don't have a dog in that fight," Secretary of State Baker successfully counseled the president against intervention.[28] Meanwhile Somalia became a failed state, the province of brutal warlords terrorizing the populace. In places like these, more Vietnams could be glimpsed.[29] Tentatively, the administration invested in a small force of peacekeepers to aid UN efforts to stabilize Somalia.

No New Taxes

A combination of necessity and inclination made for a much more muted Bush legacy in domestic matters than in foreign policy, where his heart lay.[30] The Reagan deficits foreclosed new spending programs, especially once the massive bailout of the failed savings and loan industry occurred on Bush's watch. Bush did sponsor the Americans with Disabilities Act and some important Clean Air Act amendments. He vetoed a bill promoting civil rights in employment. Saddled with Democratic majorities in Congress, he wielded the veto pen actively and successfully, penning forty-four vetoes with only one override.

Divided government led President Bush to assert himself in two other traditional ways. First, where new legislation was unlikely, he issued executive orders to advance party priorities within existing statutory authority.[31] Examples included orders restricting rights of unions in federal activities and confining the use of affirmative action against race discrimination. Second, he tussled repeatedly with the Democratic Congress over its demands for information about his administration.[32] Cautious about invoking executive privilege, which was in bad odor after the Nixon administration, Bush withheld information under other doctrinal labels (such as attorney-client privilege). Like most presidents, he wound up revealing some information and retaining the rest, depending on the persistence of the congressional committees.

In 1990, Bush entered a budget deal with Congress to reduce the deficit by a combination of tax increases and spending reductions. Over the course of the nineties, this structural adjustment helped to bring deficits under control and then to end them during the boom late in the decade. At the time, though, Bush's breach of his commitment against new taxes outraged conservatives. With the nation falling into economic recession, the president vetoed an unemployment insurance increase, hurting him politically. The prospects for his reelection diminished and finally disappeared.

Late in his term, George Bush succumbed to the temptation to abuse the pardon power.[33] He pardoned six officials who had been convicted in the Iran-Contra scandal. Considering the gravity of the offenses involved, this precedent undermined the commitment of his presidency to the faithful execution of the law. Worse, one of the pardons went to former defense secretary Caspar Weinberger, then under indictment for a series of Iran-Contra offenses. An effect of this pardon was to protect President Bush himself from inquiry and possible scandal, because a Weinberger trial might have revealed that Bush's claims to have been uninvolved in Iran-Contra were false. Although the pardon power is plenary, its use as a self-protective device is the least legitimate. This episode left a blot on a presidency that was otherwise both effective and honorable.

The Natural

Bill Clinton brought political skills to the presidency that deserve comparison to those of Ronald Reagan. He was "bright and gifted, a natural politician, and he was absolutely sure of his abilities."[34] In fact, he relied too much on his sharp intuitions about issues and people. Constantly skating at the edge of political or personal disaster, he won some battles he should have lost and vice versa—at least there was never a dull moment. He had a deep resilience, bending but never breaking under adversity. He would need it.

Whereas Ronald Reagan moved the center of American politics toward his position, Bill Clinton fought to identify and occupy that emerging center, bringing his own fragmented party reluctantly along.[35] Clinton's life was a nearly uninterrupted political campaign, as he mined opinion polls constantly to find out what the people were thinking. In return, the people could tell that he cared about them. His essential empathy always showed, in contrast to George Bush's natural reserve. Deeply affected by a childhood in the era of racial change in the South, Clinton was as drawn to domestic politics as his predecessor was to foreign policy.[36]

Not long after completing Yale Law School, where he met and married Hillary Rodham, Clinton was elected Arkansas attorney general at age thirty in 1976 and governor two years later. Politics was his career and his obsession—he displayed an amazing hunger for and command of information but often lacked the discipline to bring his knowledge to bear. He lacked the ironic detachment of a JFK. Instead he was immersed in his performance, earnest, and often self-righteous.[37] His easy informality reduced the mystique surrounding the presidency that so many of his predecessors had carefully nurtured. There would be a cost to this—the constitutional role of head of state confers a substantial aura on a president who is prepared to cultivate it.

Like Jimmy Carter, the Clintons arrived in Washington as reformist outsiders not interested in the views of the establishment, and received the cool reception they had invited. Neither Congress nor the press ever really warmed to them. Moreover, Clinton had the muted mandate of election by a plurality. He had 43 percent of the popular vote to 38 percent for Bush and 19 percent for the maverick third-party candidate, Ross Perot. With comfortable Democratic majorities in Congress, there was opportunity at hand, but it would require navigating the new political terrain of the nineties, which increasingly featured an ugly politics of personal destruction.

Throughout his presidency, Clinton constantly invoked his predecessors. He was a "genuine student of his office" who especially tried to emulate FDR and JFK.[38] As had JFK, Clinton admired Richard Neustadt's influential book on presidential power, which portrayed the presidency as weak on the domestic side, constantly needing Congress and struggling to move it by enlisting public opinion.[39] The new president relished the challenge, which seemed to fit his skills but which turned out to be rather greater than he thought.

Over His Head

Clinton's first two years included a number of accomplishments, but a series of avoidable blunders set the stage for the disastrous midterm election of 1994. The president's work habits undermined efficiency in the executive. Afraid that a hierarchical staff structure would deprive him of a chance to consider all options and would suppress original thought, Clinton veered too far toward disorganization.[40] He ignored schedules in favor of endless, inconclusive meetings. His administration always had "the spirit of a collegiate all-nighter."[41] For chief of staff, he installed a boyhood friend, Mack McLarty, who did not have Clinton's backing to instill the discipline the administration so sorely needed.

Initial staffing decisions made Clinton look indecisive or worse.[42] He precipitously fired the entire White House travel staff after some allegations of peculations surfaced and put a crony in charge of the operation.[43] Determined to appoint the first female attorney general, Clinton made two unsuccessful nominations (both of whom had tax problems) before settling on Janet Reno, whom he did not know and from whom he was soon estranged. He did, however, choose the very capable Lloyd Bentsen as treasury secretary. Bentsen soon became the adult in the room.

The initial national security team was uneven. Clinton once said: "Foreign policy is not what I came here to do."[44] This attitude was foolish, as he would discover—trouble finds presidents, whatever their preferred agenda. Because Clinton did not want an activist secretary of state who would create trouble, he chose Warren Christopher, an intelligent workhorse who would reliably execute the president's orders. The initial secretary of defense, Les Aspin, was an amiable disaster, a former congressman who was too disorganized to run the highly complex Pentagon.[45] The CIA director, James Woolsey, never meshed with Clinton or the rest of the team. As national security adviser, Anthony Lake followed the Scowcroft example of public obscurity.

President Clinton immediately got off on the wrong foot with the military, which was predisposed to dislike him. When a tentative plan to allow gays and lesbians to serve in the military surfaced in the newspapers, Clinton and his political advisers decided to go ahead without consulting the military establishment.[46] The Joint Chiefs of Staff met angrily with Aspin and then Clinton, protesting that the action would devastate morale and discipline. Chairman Colin Powell suggested the "don't ask, don't tell" compromise that the president eventually adopted. The policy managed to offend nearly everyone, demonstrating both weakness in an emerging field of civil rights and an apparent disregard for military views. At best it bought some time for American public opinion to catch up with the president's goal of constitutional equality.

Bill Clinton's inaugural address stated his intention to revitalize the federal government and his disagreement with Ronald Reagan's perception that government is the problem, not the solution. Clinton wanted to help the poor, obtain national health care, cut the deficit, and ease the tax load on the middle class.[47] Hence his agenda had both liberal and conservative elements. Eventually he would build his power by winning the support of the political center. He had to start right away. The departing Bush administration sharply increased its deficit estimates, driving Clinton's legislative agenda at the outset.

Clinton's own tendencies toward fiscal conservatism were reinforced by pressure from Treasury Secretary Bentsen and Federal Reserve Chair Alan Greenspan. Greenspan in particular pressed the need to reassure capital markets to avoid economic disaster.[48] As he cobbled together his deficit reduction plan, Clinton once declared in frustration that "we're the Eisenhower Republicans," fending off the Reagan Republicans.[49] In the summer of 1993 Clinton used the intense personal approach to legislators that LBJ epitomized to steer a bill to a narrow, party-line victory. The bill raised taxes on the wealthy somewhat and cut spending modestly. This structural adjustment built on Bush's 1990 budget deal to produce the unexpected during the boom of the late nineties—an end to deficits and even a surplus, the first in thirty years.

The first legislative project on Clinton's own agenda was health care. The product of a romantic dream to complete the New Deal, it produced

a case study in legislative mismanagement.[50] Hillary Clinton led a task
force to craft a bill. The group operated in secret, excluding members of
Congress and many of the interest groups whose support would be essential for passage. The final proposal was horrendously complex and "ludicrously ill-explained."[51] It was then presented to Congress on a take it or
leave it basis, and Congress left it in 1994, never even holding a floor vote
on the bill. Painfully, the president was learning.

The departure of George Bush after a single term left a crowded foreign policy agenda for a successor disinclined to grapple with it. The overarching question was the nature of a post–Cold War American worldview;
answering that was daunting enough for anyone. More pressingly, crises
in Haiti, Somalia, and the former Yugoslavia demanded decisions. Clinton, aware of his own lack of preparation, initially approached foreign
policy ad hoc, delegating authority to his national security team without clear guidelines.[52] He had the general outlook of a prudent Wilsonian
and usually followed Bush's approaches.[53] Clinton was drawn to the prospects for globalizing foreign trade. In 1993, he managed congressional
passage of the North American Free Trade Agreement that Bush had
negotiated, overcoming the opposition of traditional Democratic constituencies.[54] During his tenure, he negotiated hundreds of trade agreements
of his own.

In the Balkans, Clinton watched the continuing genocide with a horror shared by much of the world. He began badly.[55] Proposals to the
European allies in NATO to use American air power against the Serbs
were resisted by the Europeans, who wanted the United States to commit ground troops, as they had done. But the Powell Doctrine, forcefully
embodied by General Powell himself, strongly opposed any such commitment. Clinton dispatched Secretary of State Christopher on an ill-starred
European round of "consultations" about what to do in the Balkans. Having no forceful brief to present, Christopher got nowhere, and the administration returned to its stance of watching and dithering.

Attention soon shifted to Somalia, where George Bush had dispatched
twenty-five thousand troops to aid UN peacekeepers in stabilizing the
ruined nation. In 1993, the UN shifted its role to rebuilding Somalia and
suppressing its warlords, a much dicier mission.[56] Without reassessing its
own role, the Clinton administration tagged along until disaster struck.
American helicopter troops attacked the stronghold of a warlord in Mogadishu, became trapped, and suffered eighteen dead and scores wounded.[57]
During the Somalia involvement, the administration had never admitted

that hostilities were occurring, which would have triggered the deadline for receiving authorization under the War Powers Resolution.[58] After the losses in Mogadishu, the administration agreed with Congress to withdraw remaining American troops.[59] In the wake of this collapsed policy, Defense Secretary Aspin was relieved and replaced by the highly competent William Perry.

The experience in Somalia deterred President Clinton from responding to tragic developments elsewhere in Africa. The nation of Rwanda exploded into tribal genocide that eventually killed about eight hundred thousand people. Clinton, paralyzed by still-raw memories of Somalia, did nothing to stop the slaughter. Intervention was never seriously discussed within the administration.[60] The visible difficulties of military action in Central Africa suggested that under the Powell Doctrine, the United States could exert its military force only in some carefully selected places.

Haiti then produced a farce followed by a heartening foreign policy success for Clinton.[61] Haitian president Jean-Bertrand Aristede had been driven out by a junta, causing a refugee problem that neither the Bush nor the Clinton administration had solved. When Clinton dispatched a naval vessel to stabilize Haiti, local forces drove it away. Humiliated and looking for an opportunity to show strength in foreign policy, Clinton, together with incoming JCS chair John Shalikashvili, planned an invasion by twenty thousand troops.[62] Members of Congress and public opinion polls vigorously opposed military intervention. Hoping to forestall the need to use force, the president sent a diplomatic team composed of Jimmy Carter, Colin Powell, and Senator Sam Nunn to persuade the junta to leave peacefully. The tactic worked, and American forces arrived peacefully to preserve order. Congress later enacted an ambiguous joint resolution assenting cautiously to the operation. Clinton finally had a victory to claim.

Between the passage of the War Powers Resolution in 1973 and the Haitian intervention in 1994, presidents had sent the American military into harm's way for a wide variety of reasons. These included rescuing American citizens in Indochina and Iran; retaliating for attacks on Americans in Libya; stabilizing other governments in Lebanon, Haiti, and Somalia; and overthrowing existing governments in Grenada and Panama. Often the motives of presidents for these actions were a complex mix of humanitarian or protective considerations with geopolitical ones. Advance presidential consultation with Congress under the WPR was consistently minimal or nonexistent. After the fact, presidents were reluctant to admit that hostilities had commenced for purposes of the sixty-day clock in the WPR. With Congress consistently doing little to insist on its prerogatives under the WPR, presidents were testing the boundaries of its acquiescence in interpretations that stretched or disregarded the statutory text.

Without regard to the WPR, were any of these interventions "war" in the constitutional sense, demanding prior authorization by Congress? Addressing that question, President Clinton's Justice Department attempted to restate the applicable constitutional law. It concluded that whether a president should ask for authorization depended on "the anticipated nature, scope, and duration of the planned deployment, and in particular the limited antecedent risk that United States forces would encounter significant armed resistance or suffer or inflict substantial casualties as a result of the deployment."[63] It would be hard to improve on that statement of the constitutional principle that had emerged over the course of American history. It poses the right questions and provides no unrealistic bright-line answer. More controversies over its application to discrete circumstance lay just ahead and would continue into succeeding presidencies.

As the calendar turned to the election year of 1994, President Clinton made yet another misstep, a more personal one that would nearly end his presidency.[64] The Clintons inhabited a poisonous new political era that has persisted to the present. Their enemies in Congress, the press, and political circles constantly pressed for investigations of their conduct, ranging from the travel office firings to the suicide of the deputy White House Counsel and a failed land development they had invested in called Whitewater.

After resisting various demands for personal documents and enduring the calumny that ensued, Clinton finally asked Attorney General Reno to name a special counsel to investigate the various allegations. She did so. Shortly thereafter, Clinton signed an extension of the authorizing Ethics in Government Act, which had expired. In a politically charged action, the special court that named independent counsels under the act replaced Reno's counsel with Kenneth Starr, who had been advising some of Clinton's many enemies. Starr's portfolio initially included the Whitewater scandal and diverse other allegations. After years of investigation, no charges of misconduct were brought against the Clintons for any of these matters. Yet having an independent counsel in existence would provide the means for Clinton's later sexual misconduct to bring him to the brink of removal.

Meanwhile, the midterm elections produced a smashing Republican victory.[65] Republicans took control of both houses of Congress (the House of Representatives for the first time since 1954). It was a stunning personal rebuke to Bill Clinton. Chastened, he immersed himself in the history of the presidency, examining both his good and bad predecessors in a search for guidance.[66] Apparently, the research project helped, because better days lay ahead for the president.

Seizing the Center

In 1995, the new speaker of the House of Representatives was Newt Gingrich, a fierce, uncompromising, highly partisan conservative who was determined to wrest control of domestic policy from the president and the Democrats. The partisan nature of the new House was symptomatic of a structural change then occurring in Congress.[67] The effects of redistricting in the House and of party primaries in the Senate were to produce increasingly conservative Republican legislators and increasingly liberal Democratic ones. The centrist members who had so often been crucial in forming governing coalitions were fast disappearing.

From then until now, bipartisan legislation has been very difficult to enact. Instead, party leaders in the White House and Congress usually line up their armies and go to battle. This development has proved deeply dysfunctional in our polity, because a constitutional system with separated legislative and executive branches requires mutual cooperation if it is to operate successfully. Historically, the parties have aided the operation of the Constitution by compromising on normal disagreements about policy. No longer.

Launching an early strike in this long and dispiriting war, Speaker Gingrich mounted a frontal assault on the New Deal, intending to roll over the weakened president.[68] Gingrich trumpeted the national budget for 1996 as the largest domestic decision since 1933, fundamentally changing the federal government. He was right about that. The bill had tax cuts for the wealthy and reduced spending for social programs like food stamps, Head Start, college loans, and Medicare and would have moved the welfare and Medicaid programs to the states.

However, Gingrich had underestimated the president's political skill. Rethinking his politics after the stinging defeat in the midterm election, Clinton struggled to integrate his usual jumble of policy ideas. Shrewdly, he accepted advice to triangulate the parties—that is, to appropriate the best ideas from the Republican agenda, leaving Republicans with an unpopular residue.[69] The effect would be to attract parts of the eroding center into the Democratic embrace. Thus he proposed reducing the deficit, shrinking the federal government somewhat, and reforming the welfare system, leaving the Republicans to sponsor relatively extreme measures that would threaten popular benefits programs. Now he had truly become Eisenhower.

Drama ensued as Clinton astonished the Gingrich forces by vetoing their budget twice, causing government shutdowns for six days and then three weeks.[70] The president had found ground on which he could stand. Angrily he told Senate Majority Leader Robert Dole that he did not care what happened to his poll numbers: "I am not going to sign your budget. . . . It is wrong for the country."[71] Clinton was betting that people like the government programs that affect them, and he proved to be right. As it became clear that the public blamed Congress for the shutdowns, congressional leaders yielded and restored funding in amounts that suited the president.

Although Clinton won the initial battle, the war continued. The political restructuring of Congress has produced several lasting effects on presidential power. First, senators have expanded the filibuster from an extraordinary event to a routine check on legislation, so that it requires a practical majority of sixty senators to close debate and pass a bill. Similarly, the Senate's confirmation process has become a major obstacle to routine presidential nominees for executive or judicial office, to say nothing of the unavoidably contentious nominations for the Supreme Court. Individual senators routinely place "holds" on nominations to force executive assent to preferences unrelated to the nominee. Vacancies in both the executive and judiciary have been excessive and long-standing no matter who is in the White House.

Presidents have responded to congressional obstruction by looking for workarounds. For executive or judicial nominees, recess appointments have become more attractive; otherwise, acting executive officers sometimes remain in place for years. A president's inability to gain confirmation for preferred subordinates diminishes his effective control of the executive, because acting officers are placeholders who cannot behave as boldly as confirmed ones.

Where substantive legislation is unlikely, presidents are increasingly drawn to use of their executive order power to fill the interstices in existing statutes. For example, President Clinton hoped to promote NAFTA by securing a loan to ease a crisis in the Mexican peso. When Congress balked, he used an available economic stabilization fund instead.[72] To promote conservation values, he made some major reservations of public lands.[73] Appealing to his labor constituency, Clinton reversed some of George Bush's orders concerning unionization—only to be himself reversed when another George Bush succeeded him in office.[74] Thus, in the policy interstices within statutes, presidents can roam freely, but always at peril of reversal by a differently minded successor.[75]

After winning the battle of the budget, President Clinton approached bills emerging from Congress with the upcoming presidential election of 1996 very much in mind. He tacked to the right again. His State of the Union address staggered liberals by declaring that the era of big government was over.[76] (In fact he had just preserved it.) Late one night he overcame his constitutional conscience and signed the Defense of Marriage Act that forbade federal recognition of same-sex marriages, outraging gays and lesbians but pleasing social conservatives. The centerpiece legislation that year was welfare reform, which the president had promised to accomplish. Congress sent him bills converting welfare to a temporary assistance program and making large block grants to the states to administer it. He vetoed two bills and signed the third despite severe qualms about its fairness to the poor.[77]

Two years after his midterm humiliation, President Clinton cruised to a reelection victory over Robert Dole, winning 49 percent of the vote to Dole's 41 percent and Perot's 9 percent. With the Republicans holding onto their congressional majorities, the president did not sponsor large legislative proposals in his second term. The economy was entering the longest continuous expansion in modern history, with sharp growth, low unemployment, low inflation, and declining rates of poverty. The favorable economic numbers helped him broker successful budget deals with Congress in his second term, further reducing deficits while preserving programs he thought were essential.[78] It was a successful holding operation on the domestic front.

As Bill Clinton began his second term, one small cloud lay on the domestic horizon: the Whitewater investigation churned along, seemingly endlessly. The president had poor relationships with both Attorney General Reno and FBI Director Louis Freeh.[79] Clinton and Reno had been distant ever since he allowed her to absorb responsibility for unexpected deaths in the Waco shootout early in his presidency, although the ultimate responsibility for law execution was his. Freeh seemed rigid and self-righteous to the president. He wanted to be rid of both officers, but the scent of scandal in the air foreclosed any removals. Reno refused to leave voluntarily, so she stayed. Replacing the FBI director, a touchy matter in the best of times, was out of the question. Thus do exigent politics frustrate a president's desire to staff even the core hierarchy in the executive branch with persons of his own selection.

Stopping Genocide

President Clinton's second term featured two successful military interventions in the Balkans. A major genocide on the rim of Europe, one marked by mass deportations, concentration camps, and the slaughter of innocents, finally chased memories of Somalia and impelled action. The personnel changes that normally mark a president's second term also drove policy change. Most important, Colin Powell had rotated out of his post as chair of the Joint Chiefs. His doctrine retained force but was now shorn of the formidable presence of its namesake. At the State Department, Madeleine Albright brought a hawkish attitude toward the Balkans that stemmed from her own European background. (She once asked Powell what the point was of having such a superb military if it was not to be used.)[80] Thus the historic tendencies of the Defense Department to press for military action while the State Department resisted had reversed. Eventually Defense Secretary Perry and JCS chairman Shalikashvili became receptive to action. The Wilsonian national security adviser, Tony Lake, also pressed to form a European alliance to stem the genocide.

The perils of a ground campaign in the Balkans (which many an invader had discovered) initially confined the administration to the option of an air assault on the Serbs.[81] In the summer of 1995 Clinton formed a strategy with NATO partners for a joint air attack on Serbian forces.[82] Neither Congress nor the American public demonstrated any appetite for the project. Although the president consulted with Congress throughout this period, he did not seek its authorization to act.[83] Heavy NATO bombing, dominated by American forces, eventually drove the Serbs to the bargaining table.

Peace talks at Dayton, Ohio, were brokered by roving diplomat Richard Holbrooke.[84] The talks produced tenuous accords that unfortunately did not account for the fate of the Serbian province of Kosovo, where trouble would next erupt. Nevertheless, accomplishing a settlement in the face of great difficulties was the administration's first major foreign policy success. At Dayton, Clinton agreed to send twenty thousand American troops to the Balkans to serve as peacekeepers, although Congress was dubious and polls showed most Americans opposed.[85] The fighting subsided for the time being.

By 1998, guerrilla warfare in Kosovo had sparked renewed Serb atrocities, and pressure mounted for another intervention.[86] By this time, the defense secretary was the quite independent former Republican senator William Cohen. Hugh Shelton chaired the Joint Chiefs, and Sandy Berger was national security adviser. Clinton and the NATO allies threatened Serbian leader Slobodan Milosevic with renewed air assault if he did not desist. Clinton did not seek statutory authority for the bombing.[87] Congress acquiesced informally because American ground forces were not involved.[88] After the NATO deadline passed, another relentless pounding from the air commenced, but Milosevic resisted. Eventually Clinton and British prime minister Tony Blair agreed to increase pressure on the Serbs by threatening to use ground troops.[89] The gamble worked, as Milosevic retreated and was soon driven from power.

None of President Clinton's uses of force exceeded the War Powers Resolution's sixty-day limit until the involvement in Kosovo, which went on for seventy-nine days, the first time a presidential use of the military exceeded the limit.[90] For authority, Clinton relied on congressional passage of an emergency supplemental spending bill to fund the bombing.[91] The WPR dictates that appropriations do not provide the authority it requires, but because any later statute may amend an earlier one, clouds of legal uncertainty swirled around the situation. During the Kosovo crisis, Congress was unable to muster a majority either to clearly authorize or to forbid American intervention. Instead, as in Vietnam, Congress could agree only to provide appropriations to support the military for the time being. In this case, military success went far toward stilling the controversy, but it would be hard to claim that the presence of the WPR had produced much institutional progress in bringing the collective judgment of the branches into agreement.

Less noticed during the Balkan crisis was Osama bin Laden's call in early 1998 for a holy war against the West, including a call for Muslims to kill Americans.[92] The "war on terror" that has been with us ever since soon commenced in earnest. In 1998, bin Laden's forces bombed two American embassies in Africa. In 2000 they badly damaged the USS *Cole*. The CIA sought ways to get at him; cruise missile strikes on Afghanistan and Sudan failed to hit him. Complicating the effort were legal issues stemming from the ban on assassination of foreign rulers in Gerald Ford's executive order, which was still in effect. Did it apply to nonstate organizations such as al Qaeda? Without resolving the issues, the administration gave unclear orders to the field regarding whether it was acceptable to kill bin Laden outright or whether it was necessary to try to capture him.[93] In addition, there was little public clamor for counterterror military actions. Danger mounted.

The end of the American century found a perilous world containing fragmented but lethal terror risks that could not be deterred.[94] For decades, America's obsession with fighting communism had obscured attention to local nationalist forces that employed unconventional warfare, including terror. Bill Clinton compiled a creditable legacy in foreign policy despite a bad start and a personal preference for attending to domestic policy.[95] He used the military eighty-four times, fighting terror mainly with sporadic air strikes. Two of his accomplishments that signaled the transition between eras were Clinton's recognition of the Hanoi government in 1995 (engineered with some cover from Vietnam veterans in the Senate) and the expansion of NATO to former communist nations such as Poland.

Disgrace

Bill Clinton's second term was gravely damaged by the tawdry scandal concerning his sexual affair with White House intern Monica Lewinsky.[96] The scandal produced some inconclusive constitutional precedent concerning a president's amenability to impeachment. The furor lasted from initial press revelations in January 1998 through the president's acquittal by the Senate on two impeachment counts in February 1999.[97] Clinton's recklessness in conducting an affair within the White House with an immature aide who could ruin him was staggering but not out of character.

The episode probably did not damage the presidency generally, although it deprived Clinton of the potential of his second term when he had just demonstrated that he knew how to be president. The turmoil cast the president's motives into question regarding all his official actions, such as military strikes against Iraq that he ordered while the scandal was at its height. At times, Clinton was barely able to perform his normal duties. Fortunately, his experienced cabinet functioned smoothly enough to pick up the slack. During the entire time, the president maintained high job approval ratings in the polls, suggesting strongly that the American people thought him an amiable rogue who conducted the presidency effectively enough to deserve retention.

Clinton met initial revelations of the affair with the usual heated denials of a married person who is so accused, and he continued the denials while under oath and long past the point where anyone believed him. The mechanism that perpetuated the scandal beyond the cycle of claim and denial was the confluence of two legal proceedings. A former Arkansas civil servant named Paula Jones had filed a civil suit against Clinton, alleging sexual misconduct that occurred while he was Arkansas governor. The suit was nurtured and perpetuated by some of Clinton's enemies who were looking for any means to discredit him. Discovering the Lewinsky allegations, lawyers for Ms. Jones called President Clinton to be deposed concerning his behavior toward her and others. Clinton tried to have the *Jones* suit postponed during the remainder of his presidency, but the Supreme Court could find no ground for doing so.[98] Plausible claims that Clinton had lied in the deposition were then added to independent counsel Starr's Whitewater portfolio, and the chase was on.

In August 1998, President Clinton testified before a federal grand jury regarding whether he had obstructed justice by buying Lewinsky's silence with employment recommendations and by encouraging perjury by her and others.[99] His performance was a masterpiece of disingenuous obfuscation and evasion. Starr then crafted an extremely graphic report to the House of Representatives detailing Clinton's sexual adventures and lies and concluding that grounds for impeachment might be present.

The subsequent impeachment and trial of President Clinton had an air of unreality from start to finish.[100] The outcome was never really in question. With forty-five Democrats in the Senate, a two-thirds vote to convict a popular president during an economic boom in peacetime was never in prospect. Nonetheless, conservative Republicans in the House pressed grimly forward, ignoring both the opinion polls and the fact that the Democrats had gained a few seats in Congress in the midterm election during the pendency of the House inquiry. Both the House votes to impeach Clinton on two counts of perjury and obstruction of justice and the Senate votes to acquit him ran strongly along partisan lines.

After his acquittal in the Senate, Clinton apologized to the American people for his misconduct and for the burdens he had placed on Congress and the people.[101] On his last full day in office, the president settled with the independent counsel.[102] There would be no prosecution, but Clinton had to waive potential reimbursement for his substantial legal fees and to admit that he had lied under oath.

A president in jeopardy of impeachment has an opportunity to interpret the Constitution's requirement that guilt of "high Crimes and Misdemeanors" be shown to warrant conviction and removal. This interpretive context is unusual, however, because the president is contravening the ancient common law maxim that no one should judge his or her own cause. Presidential self-interest does affect other interpretations, of course, but usually those involve official, not personal consequences. A president in the impeachment dock forfeits his usual claim to some deference from Congress, the courts, and the people. Similarly, Clinton repeatedly tried to fend off the investigation by invoking varieties of the constitutional executive privilege.[103] Not surprisingly, he met a quite hostile reaction from the courts, which usually forced disclosure of the contested material. Richard Nixon could have warned him about that.

Bill Clinton had his impeachment counsel argue (unconvincingly) that he had not committed the charged offenses of obstruction and perjury and (plausibly) that, given the underlying circumstances, the offenses did not rise to the level of impeachable conduct.[104] The proceedings sparked a vigorous debate inside and outside of Congress concerning whether offenses relating to private sexual conduct could justify impeachment or whether abuses of office had to be present. Because the votes at all stages hewed closely to party lines, it is difficult to tease a clear precedent out of the acquittal. (The presence of substantial numbers of votes crossing party lines, as in the Johnson and Nixon cases, is more readily ascribable to principle.) Perhaps Clinton's continuing popularity with the public throughout confers some precedential weight, however.

How should later presidents understand the constitutional law of impeachment after the Clinton acquittal? Looking back at American history, they might conclude that the real criteria are almost entirely political and that they sort out as follows. First, if the president's party controls the House of Representatives, impeachment is almost unavailable. None has ever commenced when the branches are so aligned. Second, the Johnson impeachment reveals that even an unpopular president who has a serious constitutional defense to the conduct charged can win acquittal. Third, the truncated Nixon proceedings suggest that clear evidence of a felony relating to official conduct may be fatal (the obstruction count); abuse of office not rising to a felony might not be (the abuse of federal agencies count). And fourth, the Clinton impeachment shows that a popular president who is impeached along partisan lines for conduct not clearly related to official duties may be safe.

Since presidents, like the rest of us, tend to think well of their own conduct and are also quite aware of the extent of their power, the specter of impeachment does not appear to be a major constraint on presidential behavior. Instead, the most important constraints are the desire for reelection in the first term, the anticipated verdict of history in the second, and the hope to maintain the party's grip on the presidency.

The extended tussle between Bill Clinton and Ken Starr proved fatal to the independent counsel statute, which expired during the episode and lies unmourned.[105] Starr's relentless attempt to convert sexual misconduct into federal felonies and constitutional misdemeanors did not sit well with the public. To many he seemed an unappealing embodiment of the relentless Inspector Javert of *Les Misérables*.[106] His investigation demonstrated the grave threat that an independent counsel could pose to a president, suggesting to some that the Supreme Court had been wrong in upholding the statute's constitutionality on the premise that it did not impair the president's capacity to perform his constitutional duties.[107]

Expiration of the statute leaves the choice of special prosecutors where it was during Watergate—with the president, acting through the attorney general. Ironically, this structure gives such prosecutors some protection because it is difficult politically for a president to vilify someone chosen under his own auspices, whereas Clinton savagely attacked his court-chosen tormentor without seeming to be inconsistent.[108] The traditional structure also preserves presidential control over the prosecutorial function through the mechanisms of both selection and removal, safeguarding the unitary structure of the core of the executive branch.

The other constitutional presidential control over prosecution, the pardon power, was presumably unavailable to Clinton on grounds that the common law principle against judging one's own cause prevents a president from pardoning himself.[109] (Presidents can sometimes use the power to protect themselves indirectly, however, as George H. W. Bush had done, by pardoning their aides.)

As Bill Clinton left office, he used the pardon power in a different discreditable way. Ignoring recommendations of his staff, he issued pardons willy-nilly, in the atmosphere of "a state fair gambling tent on a Saturday night."[110] A pardon for fugitive financier and tax evader Marc Rich aroused widespread disgust. Clinton's bad example was duly noted by his successor, who carefully circumscribed his own midnight pardons to avoid the lingering bad odor from Clinton's precedent.

PART VI
Deciders

I'm the decider.—George W. Bush

CHAPTER FOURTEEN

No Equivocation

George W. Bush

I had to show the American people the resolve of a commander in chief that was going to do whatever it took to win. No yielding. No equivocation. No, you know, lawyering this thing to death, that we're after 'em.—George W. Bush, 2001[1]

G eorge W. Bush reached the presidency in 2001 only after a five-four vote in the Supreme Court resolved an election dispute in his favor.[2] The constitutional crisis was triggered by a statistical tie in the votes cast in Florida (Al Gore won the national popular vote).[3] As Bush prepared to take the oath of office, Democrats questioned the legitimacy of his presidency. Bush himself did not harbor any doubts. He knew that once he became president, the question was how he would behave in office and how the American people would respond to his leadership.

"I Don't Do Nuance"[4]

George W. Bush's ascent to the presidency followed a somewhat checkered business career and a rapid ascension to the Texas governorship, where he displayed his innate political intelligence. Unlike his predecessor, he was no intellectual. Relatively inexperienced in government, he lacked the background understanding of history and foreign relations that any president needs.[5] During his tenure, he made some efforts to correct this deficiency. For example, he read many biographies of Abraham Lincoln, who had also served in times of crisis.[6] Perhaps overcompensating for a reputation as a lightweight, Bush governed by pursuing a few core values with great persistence.[7] This approach tended to crowd out pragmatism and reassessment of positions. Certainly Bush was disinclined to triangulate policy as had Bill Clinton. Like Jimmy Carter, Bush possessed a strong evangelical Christian faith. His religiosity, like Woodrow Wilson's, contributed to his moral certainty.

The Bush administration was far more audacious than anyone expected. The new president had a simplistic, firmly held vision of the world. He listened to those who agreed with his views and disregarded others.[8] He was prepared to use unilateral executive power to achieve his goals. Ronald Reagan, who served as a role model for Bush, shared these tendencies, although political pragmatism often leavened his ideology.[9] Reagan's presidency had suffered gravely from the Iran-Contra scandal as a result of his single-mindedness, but the lesson was lost on Bush.

When President Bush took office in 2001, he was a neophyte in foreign affairs. To compensate, he assembled an experienced national security team that would dominate the government in the years after the 9/11 terror attacks.[10] These advisers, having experience dating back to the Nixon administration and including service in the Pentagon, shared a worldview that the president soon adopted. They based foreign policy on moral judgments and were inclined to pursue military rather than economic or diplomatic solutions to international problems. Their unilateral rather than multinational approach to international issues tended to reduce their reliance on and respect for international law.

It was natural for two of the leaders, Vice President Dick Cheney and Defense Secretary Donald Rumsfeld, to take a didactic approach to the new president—they had first known him as the child of one of their colleagues. No one, though, should underestimate George W. Bush's confidence in his own judgment.[11] His senior advisers offered him counsel that matched his own predilections. There are no signs that they had to work very hard to persuade him of their wisdom.

The president's unusual method of learning new information reinforced the influence of those closest to him. Most modern presidents have read widely enough to check the views held by those in closest daily contact with them. George Bush, by contrast, received much of his information orally, by meeting with a few senior advisers. His questions revealed a results-oriented mind that looked for the simple solution, toward which he drove.[12] Reliance on oral give and take with a few people tends to obscure complexity and to diminish original thinking, as the period before 9/11 illustrates. In the spring of 2001, CIA Director George Tenet and counterterrorism coordinator Richard Clarke used one of the president's daily briefings to warn of the al Qaeda threat, but the swarm of Arab names and places did not focus the president, who said he did not want to be "swatting flies."[13]

Like Ronald Reagan, George W. Bush tended to evade the massive defense, foreign policy, and intelligence bureaucracies, which both presidents distrusted. Instead, his administration formed and executed policy by means of ad hoc groups of government officials who formed small "shadow governments."[14] These operations displayed a strong neoconservative bias, a passion for secrecy, and a tendency to descend into groupthink, a phenomenon that tends to bring out the most extreme views in an isolated and self-reinforcing group.[15]

One of the defining features of the Bush administration was the extraordinary role played by Vice President Cheney.[16] His predecessors had either been left to molder until the fates intervened, like Truman, or assigned limited policy portfolios, such as Lyndon Johnson's supervision of the space program under Kennedy. As a presidential candidate, George Bush had selected Cheney to provide the experience he so visibly lacked, especially in foreign policy.[17] The vice president soon became the new president's deeply trusted consigliere, exercising wide-ranging influence throughout the administration. After 9/11, Cheney became the most powerful vice president in American history. He "preferred to operate largely in the shadows."[18] His understanding of the levers of power and his ability to manipulate them behind the scenes was unsurpassed.[19]

Cheney's soothing, avuncular manner masked his extreme views about executive power, which he had first articulated in the wake of the Iran-Contra scandal. Through the years, he never wavered. Recall that after Iraq invaded Kuwait in 1990, as defense secretary he tried to persuade the first President Bush to use military force without seeking congressional authorization.[20] In the new Bush administration, Cheney worked to restore executive power after what he saw as unjustified reverses following Vietnam, Watergate, and Iran-Contra. Cheney hoped to roll back the statutory restraints of the 1970s, which he called "unwise compromises" that had weakened the presidency.[21] He made that case to George W. Bush, who agreed with it. Neither man noticed that presidential power had rebounded considerably since the dark days of the Ford administration.

Within the Bush administration, Cheney's devotion to unilateral executive power "had a kind of theological significance that often trumped political consequences."[22] The administration was expanding executive power for its own sake. Cheney understood that a president never knows when a need for broad power may arise. Hence all was claimed and nothing conceded, lest a retreat on one issue imperil the overall drive for power. A corollary to Cheney's general view of executive power was his mania for secrecy. He feared leaks from Congress and was loath to ask it for authority or even to inform it about executive activities. He also favored tightly restricting the flow of information within the executive.

The new secretary of defense, Donald Rumsfeld, had previously held that post in the Ford administration and had also served in Congress and on Nixon's White House staff.[23] Rumsfeld was a fierce bureaucratic infighter who had little patience with the professional military opinions of his generals. Like Cheney, he wanted to transform a reluctant military establishment. The civilians at the Pentagon set out to dominate the military establishment and would succeed to an astonishing and ultimately unfortunate degree.

Condoleezza Rice, the new national security adviser, quickly became a devoted Bush loyalist.[24] She had been a professor and provost at Stanford, specializing in the Soviet military. She did not share the prevailing neoconservative tendency to let ideology trump realpolitick, however, and soon found herself on the sidelines. She was joined there, ironically, by the only senior members of the administration with combat experience, Secretary of State Colin Powell and his deputy Richard Armitage. In an administration that routinely subordinated diplomatic to military responses, State could not expect to be at the center of power, and it was not. Increasingly, Cheney and Rumsfeld shouldered Powell and Armitage out of the way.

Rice later recovered her influence and rose to prominence. As President Bush gained experience in his second term, he tended to turn toward the diplomatic approaches that Rice usually favored. She became a capable secretary of state, displacing Vice President Cheney as the president's principal adviser.[25] In the early days, though, the cowboys rode.

Officials who believe in restoring American power in general and the power of the presidency in particular, and who have great faith in their worldview as well, are quite likely to subordinate law to policy. The rule of law can withstand this pressure only if there is countervailing pressure from somewhere, if not from the president himself, then presumably from the Department of Justice. Instead, the department operated to promote rather than to check the most dubious legal initiatives that arose in the Bush administration.

Hence the behavior of the president's principal legal advisers took on special importance. President Bush's attorney general during his first term was former senator John D. Ashcroft, a man of deep religious devotion, strongly conservative political views, and unquestioned personal integrity.[26] Ashcroft seems never to have earned the full personal confidence of the president. White House Counsel Alberto Gonzales, who enjoyed that confidence, soon eclipsed him as a legal adviser on the most sensitive post-9/11 issues. After the first term, Ashcroft was eased out in favor of the more reliable Gonzales.

Within the Justice Department, the Office of Legal Counsel was formally headed for a time by Jay Bybee but was dominated by his deputy, John Yoo. The forceful and self-assured Yoo had taught foreign relations and international law at the University of California before joining OLC in 2001. Soon after 9/11, he would have the opportunity to press his unconventional legal views on a receptive president, converting them into national legal policy.

Alberto Gonzales had lived a classic version of the American dream, rising from poverty to the Texas Supreme Court.[27] A Bush loyalist, Gonzales was a neophyte in Washington. The day after the inauguration, Gonzales told his staff of lawyers to look for opportunities to expand presidential power. Gonzales quoted President Bush as saying that his predecessors had weakened the office and he wanted to restore it, "to make sure that he left the presidency in better shape than he found it."[28] The president had also instructed Gonzales to be sure nominees for judgeships were reliable conservatives.

The 2000 election had left the Republicans with a ten-vote margin in the House of Representatives and a tied Senate.[29] Bush used tight party discipline to maximize this slight advantage. The new president did not arrive with an extensive legislative agenda. Bush favored, and soon obtained from Congress, deep and regressive tax cuts, forfeiting the surplus he had inherited.[30] His other main domestic programs were the No Child Left Behind initiative (a mandate to the states to improve education, using conditioned federal funding) and a prescription drug plan for seniors. Both were eventually enacted. On his desk when he arrived was the Kyoto Protocol to limit global warming that Clinton had negotiated. The protocol omitted any limits on developing nations like China and India; given that fatal political flaw, Bush discarded it.

In his first week in office, George W. Bush issued an executive order banning federal funding of some abortion-counseling services, reversing a Clinton order that had reversed Bush's father's policy.[31] When Bush's successor Barack Obama took office, he immediately reversed the policy again. Thus, when modern presidents make policy by executive order in statutory interstices, they expose their impermanent decisions to the hazards of future presidential politics. Bush also issued an executive order allowing religious groups to administer federal programs after legislation to authorize it failed. As the administration drifted into the late summer of 2001, disaster struck.

A New Paradigm

The terror attacks of 9/11 imposed immense pressure on President Bush to take strong and effective action in defense of the nation. The term "emergency" was everywhere heard, often to introduce discussion of what responses the Constitution might allow.[32] Amid their own shock, outrage, and pain, Bush and his senior aides began facing these challenges. Existing constitutional precedents were only tangentially relevant. The starting point for their thinking had to be the need for national security.

In the aftermath of 9/11, fears of two kinds distorted judgment within the administration. Fear of another attack "created enormous pressure to stretch the law to its limits in order to give the President the powers he thought necessary" to prevent one.[33] The day after 9/11, President Bush told Attorney General Ashcroft: "Don't ever let this happen again."[34] (Bush later said that preventing another terror attack was the "most meaningful" accomplishment of his presidency.)[35] Everyone in the administration knew that if another attack happened, they would be blamed for not doing enough to stop it. Any lawyerly doubts that had hindered executive authority would be judged with "the perfect, and brutally unfair, vision of hindsight."[36] Yet countervailing pressure flowed from the presence of modern criminal restrictions that might support later prosecution of government officers for decisions they had made under uncertainty.

For Bush and his lawyers, the way out of this dilemma was to adopt expansive interpretations of the president's constitutional powers and restrictive interpretations of possibly confining statutes or constitutional rights. Yet this strategy only deferred the need to identify durable limits to the president's constitutional power and to define the rights of individuals who would be touched by the government's forceful response to terrorist strikes. These questions would demand and receive considered answers eventually.

The president and his legal advisers had to make an initial choice of the theoretical framework to use in analyzing possible responses to the attack. It could be labeled an ordinary, if heinous, crime and pursued through the criminal process. Or it could be labeled an act of war and pursued under wartime authorities and concepts. A substantial argument was available to support either approach. Before 9/11, most acts of terrorism were already federal crimes. Prosecutions of the 1993 World Trade Center bombers and the Oklahoma City bombers had succeeded under these statutes.[37] There was also authority to detain dangerous individuals under immigration and criminal statutes.[38] If gaps remained, Congress could certainly be expected to supplement existing law enforcement authority promptly, as it did with the USA PATRIOT Act.[39] In addition, the Justice Department is full of experienced investigators (the FBI) and prosecutors who stand ready to respond to crimes.

On the other hand, comparisons to wartime arose from the scale of the attack (more Americans died than at Pearl Harbor), the rhetoric of jihad employed by the terrorists, and the widespread national desire for a large-scale response. For the president personally, the experience of standing in the smoking rubble of the World Trade Center in the immediate aftermath of the attack must have left an indelible impression of having visited a battlefield.

There were some problems with the war analogy, though. The legal precedents that had developed in traditional wars would require adaptation to new circumstances. World War II, for example, featured mutual declarations of war by nation-states, extended clashes of arms by soldiers in uniform, and formal instruments of surrender. None of these familiar characteristics of war attend the long twilight struggle with terror. Enemies might include rulers of nations that harbor terrorists, such as the Taliban in Afghanistan, but for the most part they are shifting, shadowy groups of individuals who wear no uniforms, represent no governments, follow none of the conventions that forbid making war against civilians, and cannot be expected to surrender on the deck of the *Missouri*.

Legal responses to terrorism, understanding that terrorists will resort to the ghastliest weapons they can obtain, must concentrate on detecting and preventing future attacks rather than obtaining evidence after the fact and jailing any surviving miscreants. Moreover, since the problem is created by a strategy and not a state, it is bounded by neither place nor time. The challenges this situation poses for the American constitutional system are obvious, difficult, and not fully resolved to this day.

The day after 9/11, President Bush announced a war on terrorism.[40] Now he was resolving to do "whatever it took to win" without equivocation or "lawyering this thing to death."[41] (Lawyering there would be, but not of a conventional nature.) Within a week, Congress enacted the Authorization for Use of Military Force (AUMF).[42] This legal equivalent to a declaration of war authorized the president to "use all necessary and appropriate force" against the 9/11 terrorists wherever found and against nations harboring them.

The war theory had prevailed at the outset. The facts actually lay somewhere between crime and war, as the presidential commission that investigated the attacks later concluded.[43] The administration's legal response to 9/11, as it developed fully, embraced neither the criminal nor the war model in a straightforward way. Instead, there would be a response that employed elements of existing approaches but also struck out into uncharted territory. Four main constitutional issues needed resolution. First, what were the limits to the president's power to conduct electronic surveillance in search of terrorist plots? Second, how should terror suspects be detained—were they prisoners of war under the Geneva Conventions? Third, how aggressively could suspects be interrogated? Fourth, in what courts and by what process should suspects be tried for their crimes?

All of these constitutional issues were difficult. President Bush followed essentially the same strategy in answering all of them: to proceed unilaterally—and to the maximum extent secretly—to the very edge of what complaisant lawyers would identify as legal. Before long, revelations of the administration's activities produced heated public controversies about each of the issues. Eventually, both Congress and the courts set limits on what the administration could do. It is a rich story of overreach and reaction.

Listening for Terrorists

Because intelligence is central to detecting terror threats, President Bush immediately sought the most effective ways to intercept communications among terrorists.[44] He had some precedents to build on and some constraints to consider. Presidents since Franklin Roosevelt had conducted secret electronic surveillance on their own constitutional authority, without ever being more precise about the source of that authority than the president's duty to protect the nation. Recall that FDR initiated the practice to detect alien spies and saboteurs in the tense days preceding World War II, that President Truman expanded it to include citizens, and that

Presidents Johnson and Nixon sparked a scandal by using it to harass antiwar groups during the Vietnam War.

In 1978, President Carter signed the Foreign Intelligence Surveillance Act (FISA), acknowledging at the signing ceremony that FISA required "a prior judicial warrant for *all* electronic surveillance for foreign intelligence or counterintelligence purposes in the United States in which communications of U.S. persons might be intercepted."[45] Carter was conceding that Congress could restrict whatever executive power had existed to conduct surveillance without a warrant. FISA's legislative history explained emphatically that the statute provided the "exclusive means" for conducting electronic surveillance.[46] Congress was recognizing no constitutional executive power.

FISA warrants were issued in secret by a special federal court if there was probable cause to believe that the target was a foreign nation or the agent of one. This probable cause standard was markedly weaker than the one traditionally used in criminal law, which is whether there is probable cause to believe that a crime has been committed. From 1978 until 9/11, the investigative process under FISA worked smoothly, without greatly hampering the executive. Whether any residual executive constitutional authority existed remained unexplored.

In early 2002, President Bush signed a secret order authorizing the National Security Agency to intercept communications within the United States without seeking FISA warrants.[47] The Terrorist Surveillance Program (TSP) remained entirely hidden from the American people and most members of Congress for almost four years, until its existence was revealed by the press in late 2005. Although the administration kept the legal memoranda supporting the program secret, the Department of Justice eventually explained the essential rationale for the TSP.[48] The department invoked the president's constitutional authority to protect the nation against armed attack and claimed that the AUMF's statutory authority to pursue al Qaeda implicitly authorized ignoring FISA's requirements.

The TSP was cobbled together under crisis conditions. Soon after 9/11, President Bush convened his senior intelligence officials to discuss ways to prevent another attack. The president asked whether there was "anything more we could be doing, given the current laws."[49] After some discussions, NSA Director Michael Hayden, CIA Director Tenet, and Vice President Cheney brought a proposal to the president, who approved it.[50] Hayden later explained that the TSP allowed agency employees to eavesdrop if they had a "reasonable basis" to believe one party to a conversation had terrorist connections.[51] This disregarded compliance with FISA's warrant requirement and ignored the underlying constitutional reason for it—to obtain review by a neutral judge of a determination of need made within the agency.

Alberto Gonzales later explained that the administration's lawyers initially concluded that warrantless surveillance could not be squared with FISA, but it was then decided to "push the envelope."[52] The underlying problem was that technological change in telecommunications had rendered FISA seriously obsolete.[53] When FISA was enacted, it was easy to tell whether communications of interest were occurring at least partly in the United States, which was the jurisdictional trigger for the act. By 2001, however, telephones existed in cyberspace. There was an overwhelming flood of telecommunications to monitor—trillions of e-mails and billions of cell-phone calls per day. Old certainties about the points of origin and termination of communications had evaporated, because many purely international communications were routed through switches located in the United States.

Therefore, the TSP inverted the traditional process. Instead of investigating known suspects, it searched to identify the suspects, whereupon FISA methods became more feasible. To do this, NSA had to give some cursory attention to a vast mass of communications, searching for patterns that might reveal a terror plot. Yet probable cause in either the Fourth Amendment or the FISA sense would be present only after the inquiry was well under way.

Under President Bush's order, telecommunications companies gave NSA access to their switching systems, sweeping in vast numbers of international and domestic communications together. The president decided to go ahead on a temporary basis without seeking warrants. No efforts to comply with the statute occurred for several years. The administration rejected any pursuit of statutory change out of fear that the authority might not be granted, choosing to rest on its emergency powers. Revisiting FISA after 9/11 to update the statute would have mixed complex technical questions with sensitive political ones. Moreover, it would have been necessary to address these issues without revealing the nation's actions to its adversaries. The administration chose not to grapple with these thorns. It appears that the program targeted about seven thousand people overseas and about five hundred within the United States.[54]

Under the presidential directive creating the TSP, the attorney general was required to recertify its legality every forty-five days. Eventually, this requirement led to a crisis within the administration. In March 2004, Deputy Attorney General James Comey, standing in for a hospitalized John Ashcroft, refused to reapprove part of the program. After a frenzied flurry of activity that included trips by senior officers to the hospital to see Ashcroft, who backed his deputy, Comey was called to the White House for a confrontation with President Bush.[55] The president told Comey: "I decide what the law is for the executive branch." Comey responded, "That's absolutely true, sir, you do. But I decide what the Justice Department can certify to and can't certify to, and despite my absolute best efforts, I simply cannot in the circumstances." Both men were correctly describing their proper roles. Afterward, the president retreated and authorized the Justice Department to do what it thought was right.

President Bush's confrontation with Deputy Attorney General Comey and the president's eventual acquiescence in the department's legal advice were both prompted by information that if the program continued, the department's entire top echelon would resign in protest. No president would lightly invite comparison to President Nixon's infamous "Saturday Night Massacre" in 1973, in which both the attorney general and his deputy resigned rather than execute Nixon's command to dismiss Watergate special prosecutor Archibald Cox.

In such cases, threats to resign over a matter of principle carry great power because if carried out, they bring internal government disputes into the light of day. President Bush had little practical alternative but to yield to his legal advisers, because his refusal to do so would very likely have revealed the existence of the TSP. In this case, the revolt of the president's subordinates provided an important check on his legal interpretation. President Bush was correct in asserting that he was "the decider," but the combined judgment of his senior legal advisers effectively drove his decision.

Although Congress was not asked to authorize the TSP, a few congressional leaders were briefed in secret by Vice President Cheney and other officials as the program began. The initial briefings were limited to the chairs and ranking minority members of the two intelligence committees.[56] The briefings, which were cursory, said that NSA would hunt terrorists, their supporters, and their financiers. The briefings later expanded to the "gang of eight" that is supposed to receive notice of covert operations: the majority and minority leaders of the two houses, along with the four members of the intelligence committees. This restricted notification to Congress caused considerable resentment once the existence of the program became known to the public. The restricted notification may also have been illegal, under the National Security Act's requirement that the intelligence committees be "fully and currently informed of all intelligence activities." Whether illegal or not, it was certainly begrudging and minimal.

Once the existence of the TSP became public knowledge in late 2005, a sharp debate erupted over its legality. In his State of the Union speech the next month, President Bush defended the program, claiming that "previous Presidents have used the same constitutional authority I have." This statement ignored the significance of FISA. After the midterm elections of 2006 delivered both houses into the hands of the Democrats, who intended to investigate the administration vigorously, the Bush administration decided to seek statutory authorization for the program.

By 2008, Congress and the administration worked out amendments to FISA creating new surveillance authority to supplement the traditional FISA regime.[57] The statute now authorizes NSA to target persons "reasonably believed" to be outside the United States, after the agency receives approval from the Foreign Intelligence Surveillance Court for its procedures on targeting, minimization of acquisition of information about Americans, and compliance with the Fourth Amendment. Thus the political branches eventually came into agreement regarding how the United States should search the airwaves for terrorists.

The constitutional interpretation upon which President Bush based the initial version of the TSP was unpersuasive, however. Granted, his predecessors had built a line of precedents supporting presidential power to conduct electronic surveillance without special statutory authority. But Congress had enacted FISA to end executive abuses of that power. The executive's legal arguments for the TSP downplayed the force of FISA and overstated the implications of the AUMF, in an effort to avoid grappling directly with deep constitutional questions concerning the extent of presidential power in the new world after 9/11.[58] Perhaps the initial version of the TSP was justifiable on an emergency basis, but the president had no sufficient excuse for failing to seek its timely ratification by Congress.

Enemy Combatants

As President Bush initiated the bombing of Afghanistan in October 2001, he sent a letter to Congress claiming that he was acting pursuant to his constitutional authority and thanking Congress for its support, including passage of the AUMF. Thus the modern presidential practice of conceding no ground to Congress regarding war powers continued. The letter implied that the president intended to conduct the war with minimal participation by Congress, the courts, and the public. That he would do, both in Afghanistan and in the later war in Iraq, with unfortunate consequences for the nation and for his own presidency. He would have done well to notice that in the nation's two gravest wartime crises, Presidents Lincoln and Roosevelt had consulted widely and frequently outside the executive branch, involving Congress and important elements of the public in their plans.

The initial assault on al Qaeda was part of a grander scheme in the president's mind, as he revealed in early 2002 by stating the Bush Doctrine, which rejected the multilateralism that had prevailed since World War II in favor of a willingness to undertake preventive war and spreading of democracy anywhere.[59] This sweeping change in foreign policy delighted the neoconservative aides who had promoted it. If the United States stood alone as the world's superpower, its president could become a super-Wilson, bringing the lessons of American exceptionalism to everyone.

As the war started, however, more mundane but unprecedented constitutional issues about its conduct demanded attention. Prisoners soon accumulated, but they wore no uniforms. Unlike conventional wars, it was difficult to distinguish an al Qaeda warrior from a farmer. Those prisoners who were dangerous might have to be held indefinitely. Since this was a war on terror, perhaps its prisoners were entitled to the full protections of the Geneva Conventions. Some of the prisoners possessed valuable information; interrogation methods needed devising. Al Qaeda's very purpose is to commit acts that are war crimes, such as murdering civilians. Prosecutions for war crimes might be in conventional criminal trials, courts-martial, or military commissions.

An important initial question about prisoners was where to hold them. Both legal and practical considerations affected the decision to send many of them to the Navy base at Guantanamo Bay, Cuba.[60] The base offered strong advantages in security and in possible immunity from American legal constraints. If the base were beyond the habeas corpus jurisdiction of the federal courts, prisoners could be held indefinitely without legal recourse.[61] "Gitmo" would be a law-free zone, except for law that applies to executive officers anywhere, such as military law, and constraints that the president might impose.

Two months after 9/11, President Bush issued an executive order providing for detention of suspected terrorists and their subsequent trial for war crimes by military commissions.[62] The order rested on the president's constitutional power as commander in chief and on authority implied by some statutes, including the AUMF. The order was within the longstanding tradition that the president and executive officers control the treatment of prisoners of war, within currently applicable treaty or statutory limits.

Regarding detention, the order authorized the Defense Department to detain aliens when there was "reason to believe" they were members of al Qaeda or other terrorist groups and instructed the secretary to treat them "humanely," with "adequate food, drinking water, shelter, clothing, and medical care." The order did not prescribe any process for deciding who was a terrorist and who was not. Many of the prisoners were held incommunicado for several years, without any opportunity to challenge the grounds for their detention. Some of them were American citizens. The administration soon lumped all of these prisoners together as "enemy combatants," a term without meaning in international or domestic law apart from its casual use by the Supreme Court as a reference to the Nazi saboteurs of World War II. The advantage of this neologism was that it did not clearly imply any legal rights, unlike the term "prisoners of war."

The first prisoners arrived at Guantanamo in January 2002. They eventually reached a maximum of about nine hundred, a number that diminished over the years. (Other prisons were in Afghanistan, in Iraq after that war started, and in undisclosed locations around the world.) Conditions at Guantanamo have been deeply controversial.[63] Some housing has resembled an American maximum-security prison. Dormitories have provided better conditions for cooperative detainees. Perhaps a third of the initial detainees could reasonably be characterized as enemy combatants.[64] Uncertain about the threat posed by those it held, the military simply kept them. They were accorded no process to determine whether they should have been held at all.

President Bush's executive order authorizing detention and creating military commissions differed in a fundamental way from emergency actions taken by prior presidents: he sought no ratification from Congress for his actions, even though it was usually in session and was legislating busily. This omission greatly increased the executive's jeopardy in litigation.

In *Hamdi v. Rumsfeld*, the Supreme Court upheld the habeas corpus petition of an American citizen who had been captured as an alleged enemy combatant during military operations in Afghanistan.[65] When the Supreme Court heard his case, he had been imprisoned without a hearing for about two and a half years. The sole evidentiary basis offered by the government for holding Hamdi was a military affidavit reciting that he had been captured in combat. The government opposed any truly adversarial process.

The Supreme Court rejected the executive's claim that it could hold a citizen indefinitely without meaningful process. The Court decided that Congress had implicitly authorized detaining enemy combatants when it approved using military force against the 9/11 terrorists. The AUMF provided authority for indefinite detention at least while active military operations remained under way in Afghanistan. Nevertheless, a citizen held under that authority had a due process right to a "meaningful opportunity to contest the factual basis for that detention before a neutral decisionmaker," which might be "an appropriately authorized and properly constituted military tribunal."

Hamdi had two companion cases. In *Rasul v. Bush*, the Court held that federal habeas corpus jurisdiction applied to petitions brought by aliens who had been captured during hostilities with the Taliban and who were being detained at Guantanamo Bay.[66] In *Rumsfeld v. Padilla*, the Court considered the petition of an American citizen who had been arrested at O'Hare Airport in Chicago as a suspected terrorist and then designated an enemy combatant and transferred to military authority.[67] The Court dismissed Padilla's petition on a technical ground, deferring any resolution of very sensitive issues involving the executive's conversion of a criminal defendant into an enemy combatant and the resulting transfer of jurisdiction from a federal criminal court to a military commission.[68]

The Court's decisions finally spurred action from Congress, which enacted two major statutes to deal with issues concerning detention. First was the Detainee Treatment Act of 2005 (DTA), which regulated some aspects of detention conditions (for example, forbidding cruelty toward detainees) and restricted the jurisdiction of the federal courts to review challenges to the detention program.[69] Later, the Military Commissions Act of 2006 (MCA) reaffirmed the DTA's restrictions on judicial review of detention.[70] In *Boumediene v. Bush*, the Supreme Court held that Congress had unconstitutionally suspended the writ of habeas corpus without providing an adequate substitute.[71]

This extended minuet among the three federal branches constituted a search for constitutional legitimacy in the long twilight war on terror.[72]

The unspoken premise of the exercise was that a war on terror that is governed by the rule of law will be more effective in the long run, that it will save more lives than might be lost by adhering to the law's constraints. Because that is a risky judgment, it is not easy for elected politicians to make. George W. Bush resisted making it throughout his time in office.

Early in 2002, President Bush made an overarching legal decision that would affect both trials for detainees and the limits of interrogation: whether the Geneva Conventions of 1949 applied to the captives.[73] The four conventions, responding to the horrific lessons of World War II, tried to ensure decent treatment of people held in any form of modern conflict. As ratified treaties, they are binding federal law under the Constitution's supremacy clause.[74] Two of them are centrally important to the war on terror: the one governing treatment of prisoners of war and the one controlling treatment of civilians detained in wartime.[75] Although there are differences in the rights various kinds of prisoners enjoy, Common Article 3, which is present in all of the conventions, requires all prisoners to be treated "humanely" and forbids "cruel treatment and torture." It also prohibits the imposition of criminal sentences "without previous judgment pronounced by a regularly constituted court affording all the judicial guarantees which are recognized as indispensable by civilized peoples."

The Justice Department advised President Bush that he could either suspend the Geneva Conventions in Afghanistan or, in a lesser step, determine that they did not apply to al Qaeda and Taliban prisoners.[76] This advice contravened two prevalent opinions—that human rights treaties may not be suspended and that everyone detained in war is protected by one of the conventions. Another obstacle was the federal War Crimes Act, which criminalizes "grave breaches" of the Geneva Conventions.[77]

The Bush administration wanted to employ harsh interrogation methods, many of which would have violated Geneva strictures. And it wanted to craft its own procedures for prosecuting war criminals. Therefore, to meet the administration's goals the detainees would have to fall outside *all* of the Geneva protections. That is the interpretation the Justice Department offered and the president accepted.

President Bush initially decided against granting POW status to the captives, but that was not the end of the matter. Secretary of State Colin Powell asked for reconsideration of the decision. With his extensive military background, he was uniquely qualified to do so. He and the current JCS chair, Richard Myers, feared that the decision would encourage mistreatment of captured American troops. The Pentagon's military lawyers, the judge advocate generals, shared the desire to preserve reciprocity under Geneva. White House Counsel Gonzales responded that in the "new kind of war" against terrorism, the need to obtain information from captives and to try some of them for war crimes "renders obsolete Geneva's strict limitations on questioning of enemy prisoners and renders quaint some of its provisions."[78]

In February 2002, the president issued an order titled *Humane Treatment of al Qaeda and Taliban Detainees*, mostly adhering to his earlier decision. His order accepted "the legal conclusion of the Department of Justice" that no part of the Geneva Conventions applied to al Qaeda. He decided that parts of Geneva would apply to Taliban detainees but that they were not entitled to full POW status. The president then directed that "as a matter of policy, the United States Armed Forces shall continue to treat detainees humanely and, to the extent appropriate and consistent with military necessity, in a manner consistent with the principles of Geneva."

Like constitutional interpretation, treaty interpretation is a normal presidential function. This particular exercise of that function was extremely strained and met widespread condemnation by international lawyers, military leaders, and others.[79] Bush was ignoring precedents set by all of his predecessors since 1949. None had ever declined to apply the Geneva Conventions to persons captured in armed conflict, including such irregular forces as the Vietcong. In addition, the order's unclarity about when and to what extent the "principles of Geneva" would apply invited the serious problems in implementation that would soon surface in the field.

President Bush's executive order that initially authorized detention also provided for trial by military commission of alien terrorists suspected of war crimes.[80] The order, issued just two months after 9/11, was the product of an intense and pressured process.[81] There were advocates for using regular criminal trials, military courts-martial, and military commissions. Lawyers in the White House Counsel's office then short-circuited the process, opting for military commissions and drafting a proposed order for the president. They modeled the draft order on President Roosevelt's order for military trial of the Nazi saboteurs, which the Supreme Court had upheld. Military lawyers objected to the draft order on grounds that it ignored changes in the law after World War II, but Vice President Cheney overrode all opposition, took the order to Bush, and obtained his signature.

Military commissions differ from civilian courts in several respects. They consist of military officers, not neutral judges, they follow more informal procedures than do criminal courts, and they have no juries. Military courts-martial occupy a middle ground, using military judges and juries but mostly following the rules of evidence used in the civilian courts. In the Civil War, military commissions had played a controversial role.[82] Controversy about the trials produced an important Supreme Court precedent, *Ex parte Milligan*, which stated that citizens may not be tried by the military where the civilian courts are functioning.[83]

Military law had evolved substantially since the trial of the Nazi saboteurs. In 1950, passage of the Uniform Code of Military Justice reformed military law. The UCMJ contemplates the use of military commissions but does not say when they are acceptable. It does say that the commissions must use court-martial procedures unless that is not "practicable." The president's order, however, provided for procedures much less formal than those used in courts-martial. Trials could proceed in the absence of the accused and his counsel when necessary to protect classified information. Evidence could be admitted if it "would have probative value to a reasonable person," even if it were inadmissible in other kinds of American criminal trials. Coerced testimony, also inadmissible in ordinary civilian and military trials, might be allowed.

The president did not consult Congress about the order.[84] After trials began, a challenge reached the Supreme Court in the case of Salim Hamdan, a Yemeni who had served as Osama bin Laden's driver.[85] Hamdan was charged before a military commission with participating in a conspiracy to attack civilians and to commit acts of terrorism. He objected that the structure and process of the military commission violated the UCMJ and the Geneva Conventions. Five justices agreed with this contention, making a majority.

The Court's holding was that neither the AUMF nor the DTA authorized use of the military commissions, and the UCMJ and the Geneva Conventions forbade them. The government had conceded that statutory limits were binding in this case—it was not repeating the attempt in the steel seizure case to rely on exclusive constitutional powers. The Court concluded that three aspects of the trial process violated the UCMJ's restrictions on military commissions: holding closed trials, allowing unreliable evidence, and deciding by nonunanimous votes. Turning to the Geneva Conventions, the Court relied on Common Article 3, which required that any trial of persons detained in conflict be by a "regularly constituted" court giving guarantees "recognized as indispensable by civilized peoples." Courts-martial were regularly constituted; special courts like these were not.

The *Hamdan* ruling invalidated the Bush order and remanded the question of using military commissions to Congress, which could authorize or prohibit them. The decision fits squarely within a line of Supreme Court cases that resolve wartime tensions by seeking congressional authority for executive action instead of articulating sweeping doctrine about executive authority and civil liberties.[86] Congress responded with the MCA. Like the earlier DTA, this statute is friendly to the executive. The MCA authorizes the president to establish military commissions to try "alien unlawful enemy combatants," a category explicitly including members of both al Qaeda and the Taliban.[87]

With statutory authority from the MCA in hand, the administration began planning trials. President Bush eventually brought to Guantanamo fourteen "high-profile" terror suspects who had previously been detained in secret CIA facilities. This group included the notorious Khalid Sheikh Mohammed, the planner of the 9/11 attacks. When Bush left office, the administration was preparing to bring capital charges against KSM and some others.

Of all the legal decisions made by President Bush after 9/11, those concerning the limits to permissible interrogation of suspected terrorists proved to be the most bitterly controversial.[88] The stakes were very high. The administration always understood the crucial importance of gathering information about terror plots from those most likely to possess it. Charges that American officers were torturing suspects soon surfaced. The torture debate has renewed interest in a very old question: when, if ever, is torture permissible in defense of civilized society?[89]

No consensus exists regarding what constitutes torture. Proud of their modern sensibilities, nations have invented "torture lite," techniques such as isolation, stress positions, sleep deprivation, exposure to heat or cold, and exposure to bright lights and constant noise.[90] Much current controversy surrounds waterboarding, in which the subject is strapped down and taken to the point of drowning by pouring water over his or her nose and mouth. American troops used it against insurgents in the Philippines early in the twentieth century and were prosecuted for it. Its victims call it torture; some lawyers disagree.

The events that sent the Bush administration into this quicksand began days after 9/11, as President Bush signed a memorandum authorizing the CIA to capture, detain, and interrogate terrorism suspects. Eventually, the CIA would maintain an entire secret prison system overseas. The president did not want anyone to know whom we held, what we were doing to them, or what we were learning from them. The president's initial directive to the CIA did not contain guidelines regarding interrogation techniques. The agency, which had little experience with interrogation of the unwilling, quickly put a program together. CIA officers in the field soon barraged headquarters with questions about approved methods.

The CIA did not use its own personnel to conduct all interrogations. Instead, it "outsourced" some of them through one of its most secret activities, the "extraordinary rendition" of prisoners. In the wake of 9/11, President Bush authorized rendition. This practice consists of transporting captives to nations other than the United States, where they are held for interrogation and sometimes tortured.[91] The intelligence obtained is then furnished to the CIA. In use at times prior to 9/11, rendition has expanded dramatically since then.[92] The Convention against Torture, which the United States has signed, forbids rendition if there are "substantial grounds" to anticipate torture. The CIA claims that it instructs recipient nations not to torture captives and that it has no knowledge that they do so.

As prisoners and problems accumulated, CIA Director George Tenet considered the use of particular "enhanced interrogation techniques" against individual al Qaeda captives. Khalid Sheikh Mohammed was a subject of intense interest for his possible knowledge of terror plots. Held at a CIA black site in Poland, KSM was initially defiant. In response, he was treated roughly and waterboarded. Interrogators then desisted and asked for advice, fearing they might have crossed the line into torture. He eventually produced a great deal of information, some of it from traditional noncoercive practices.

An obstacle to harsh interrogation lay in the fact that both international and domestic law contained explicit and unconditional bans on torture. Under a federal criminal statute enacted to implement the international Convention against Torture, torture is "an act . . . specifically intended to inflict severe physical or mental pain or suffering."[93] There is no emergency exception.

In the summer of 2002, the administration sought general advice from OLC regarding the legal limits to CIA interrogation methods. OLC responded with a memorandum to White House Counsel Gonzales that has become notorious as the "torture memo."[94] The opinion is an extremely tendentious and ill-reasoned attempt to draw the line of forbidden conduct at an extreme point.[95] The opinion told the president that the federal torture statute would be unconstitutional "if it impermissibly encroached on the President's constitutional power to conduct a military campaign." The premise is that the interrogation of terror suspects is within the "core" of executive war powers. The memo even argues that the president's war-making authority is exclusive, not shared with Congress: "Congress may no more regulate the President's ability to detain and interrogate enemy combatants than it may regulate his ability to direct troop movements on the battlefield."[96]

The "torture memo" could not stand the light of day. Alberto Gonzales disapproved it publicly immediately after its release in 2004, in the wake of the Abu Ghraib prison abuse scandal. A replacement opinion with a more temperate analysis eventually appeared, but the administration never retreated from its underlying stance that "enhanced" interrogation methods were legal.

In the fall of 2005, Congress considered what would become the Detainee Treatment Act. The administration was particularly concerned about the proposed "McCain Amendment," providing that no one in federal custody may be subjected to "cruel, inhuman, or degrading" treatment.[97] The administration vigorously lobbied against the McCain Amendment.[98] President Bush even threatened to veto the entire military budget, to which the DTA was attached, if it were not removed. After tense and protracted negotiations, Congress persisted in including the amendment, and the president yielded momentarily. He signed the DTA into law, but appended a signing statement claiming the authority to disregard any provision in it that impaired his constitutional powers.

In the same spirit, in 2008 President Bush vetoed a bill that would have required the CIA to follow the Army's field manual for interrogations. The bill would have eliminated most harsh techniques, including waterboarding.[99] Even near the end of his tenure, the president was unwilling to accept a prospective limitation that might tie his hands. Whether or not he believed everything about his power that the "torture memo" asserted, he often acted as though he did. What he did not do, however, was openly contravene any of the accumulating statutory limits on conduct of the war on terror.

Adventure in Iraq

From the first moments of his administration, George W. Bush sought another war against Iraq. His very first National Security Council meeting discussed the overthrow of Saddam Hussein. Before 9/11, "dozens of reports were generated" at the Defense and State Departments about invading Iraq, "as the CIA increasingly warned about the threat from al Qaeda."[100] The president was ignoring a grave threat and focusing on a nonexistent one. Iraq was the war that George W. Bush wanted and eventually got. The war that he had not wanted, in Afghanistan, soon took second place in his priorities.

The signs of distraction were evident immediately after the attacks on 9/11. That night, counterterrorism chief Richard A. Clarke "walked into a series of discussions about Iraq," not al Qaeda, in the White House.[101] Vice President Cheney and Defense Secretary Rumsfeld soon pushed for war with Iraq. By the fall of 2002, analysts throughout the executive branch were being ignored or pressed into an inappropriate role: "intelligence and facts were being fixed around the policy."[102] In search of a casus belli against Iraq, the administration made unsupported claims that Saddam Hussein was developing weapons of mass destruction (WMD).[103] There had been virtually no internal debate or analysis of the relationship of an Iraq war to the wider war on terror. The lessons that John Kennedy had learned so painfully at the Bay of Pigs would have to be relearned.

As the midterm elections of 2002 approached, George Bush pressured Congress into authorizing war in Iraq at his discretion.[104] The congressional findings of fact that accompanied the authorization recited the false claims the president had promoted: that Iraq was producing WMD and had links to al Qaeda. As had his father, Bush sought congressional assent to war in Iraq even though his lawyers had advised him he needed no new authority. In 2002, the White House Counsel told the president he could rely on the 1991 congressional authorization and UN resolutions to attack Iraq.[105] Instead, he used patriotic pressures during the first election season after 9/11 to obtain his blank check for a new war. In the election, Republicans gained seats in both houses, easing the president's path forward.

Bush dispatched Secretary of State Colin Powell to the UN to seek international support, subjecting Powell to the indignity of presenting a brief that turned out to be false. A shaky alliance assembled, with none of America's major allies except Great Britain. As the war began, the president took note of the congressional authorization and said he was acting pursuant to his power as commander in chief. The war itself was mostly an American effort and was another impressive display of the nation's military might in conventional warfare.

Within three weeks, American forces stormed into Baghdad, and then the trouble began.[106] There had been almost no planning for the aftermath of military victory. At the Pentagon, "they wanted to focus not on what could go wrong but on what would go right."[107] Clear warnings of impending civil war and chaos were ignored. American military and civilian officers clashed. "No one was really in charge of Iraq."[108] Soon there was a quagmire worthy of comparison to Vietnam, as the United States tried to stabilize Iraq and to find an exit strategy. Of this war it has fairly been said: "It is one of the supreme ironies of recent history that leaders bent on perpetuating U.S. primacy squandered it through reckless use of the nation's power."[109]

Both the Afghanistan and Iraq wars were conducted in the Bush style. "Character is fate. . . . Bush's [Iraq] war, like his administration, . . . was run with his own absence of curiosity and self-criticism, his projection of absolute confidence, the fierce loyalty he bestowed and demanded."[110] This is not an atmosphere that welcomes or even tolerates arguments about the limits to power or that encourages inquiries to see if abuses are occurring. By stretching itself to fight two wars, the administration also stretched the American military in ways that risked a critical loss of control on the ground.

Orders had to be translated into actions, and as analysts of war emphasize, the "friction" between the two can be considerable once an operation begins.[111] Considerable it would be in the war on terror. Yet good generals know that friction must be anticipated and guarded against. There was insufficient attention to this imperative from the highest levels of the Bush administration to the lowest. The scandal involving abuse of prisoners at Abu Ghraib prison was a direct result of this failure to faithfully execute the laws.[112]

President Bush's disengaged approach to his role as commander in chief hampered both the Iraq War and the ensuing occupation. He would tell his generals: "You fight the war and I'll provide you political cover."[113] The president was trying to avoid Lyndon Johnson's mistake of micromanaging the Vietnam War by selecting bombing targets and pushing his generals around.[114] But he went too far in delegating power, allowing generals to select troop levels and occupation authorities to make numerous blunders. Eventually, Bush took a more active role, pushing for the troop surge that finally stabilized Iraq.[115]

Going It Alone

The disturbing tendencies of George W. Bush's administration toward unilateral action marked by excessive secrecy, unrestrained political partisanship, and negligence in operations surfaced in several arenas. The mania for secrecy appeared early with a successful attempt to close the records of an energy task force chaired by Vice President Cheney.[116] After 9/11, many more government records were closed than previously, and classification policy was tightened. Bush issued an executive order restricting access to present and future collections of official presidential records.[117] His administration asserted the state secrets privilege aggressively in litigation, blocking access to information about the war on terror.

Excessive partisan politics marked the brief and troubled tenure of Alberto Gonzales as attorney general. He attempted to politicize the Justice Department in numerous ways, including the use of political tests for career staff attorney positions.[118] He dismissed several United States attorneys for reasons that appeared to be partisan, thereby threatening the integrity of the prosecutorial function. Called to testify before hostile congressional committees, Gonzales repeatedly gave evasive and apparently false answers.[119] The House Judiciary Committee issued subpoenas for White House records concerning the dismissals. The Bush administration released some documents and invoked executive privilege for others, setting off an extended squabble that included inconclusive litigation over the records.[120] The episode demonstrated the capacity of a determined president to shield at least some records long enough to outlast the two-year cycle of a House of Representatives. The turmoil cost Gonzales his post as attorney general.[121]

In a realm of politics that had become more accepted, the Justice Department resumed the practice of prior Republican administrations of vetting judicial prospects carefully for their conservative credentials. President Bush himself paid quite close attention to the selections.[122] This process produced the successful nominations of Chief Justice John Roberts and Justice Samuel Alito, both highly credentialed candidates, along with the gaffe of the failed nomination of the unqualified Harriet Miers.[123]

President Bush's negligent attention to law execution had disastrous consequences in his administration's sluggish response to Hurricane Katrina in 1995.[124] The president appeared to be isolated, uncaring, and unable to take decisive action. The Federal Emergency Management Agency, which his appointments had transformed from a competent agency to a nest of cronyism and incompetence, failed dismally in its response (as did state and local government officials). Bush may have felt constrained in aiding the stricken city of New Orleans by a venerable federal statute forbidding the use of the military for law enforcement.[125] This would have been the time to skirt the edge of a statutory restriction in the style of the two Roosevelts, by sending in the troops to save the people and not to act principally as police.

George Bush almost abandoned use of formal vetoes of legislation in favor of his stealth version in the form of the restrictive signing statement. Having Republican majorities under tight party control for most of his time, he could usually avoid outright confrontation with Congress. Hence he could use signing statements to trim statutes around the edges.

Signing statements had been issued for many years by presidents of both parties.[126] They became bitterly controversial only in the Bush administration.[127] As we have seen, there is good reason to acknowledge a presidential power to refuse to execute unconstitutional provisions in statutes.[128] The problem is one of limits. The Bush administration plowed new ground in two ways.[129] First, it issued many more of these statements than had any earlier presidents, and the statements often contained sweeping boilerplate recitations that any provisions conflicting with executive power would be ignored. That makes it very hard to determine which provisions are the subject of real concern and identify those that actually will not be enforced. Second, the extreme formulations of executive power used in the Bush statements threatened to sweep broadly and without support across statutes of all kinds. Taken seriously, they would disable Congress from legislating meaningful restrictions on the executive in many fields, especially foreign affairs and war.

President Bush's few actual vetoes included funding for stem cell research, an Iraq spending bill that included a troop drawdown requirement, and a renewal of the Children's Health Insurance Program, which he considered to be a dangerous step toward government health care for the public.[130]

To control executive branch regulation, President Bush installed political officers in the agencies to monitor the progress of proposed regulations and conform them more closely to the president's priorities. The administration was particularly unfriendly to vigorous enforcement of environmental statutes. Controversies arose over the administration's attempts to suppress government scientists' arguments that global warming was an environmental crisis requiring government action.[131] Vigorous government responses to climate change would have to wait.

In the last months of George W. Bush's tenure, a financial crisis threatened to swamp Wall Street and then the nation. To many, the onset of another Great Depression appeared to be at hand. Yet the president adopted a strangely passive stance.[132] In the Iraq War, he had deferred to his generals in deciding how to fight; he did that again in the financial crisis. One of the "generals" in this battle was in his direct chain of command: Treasury Secretary Henry Paulson, an energetic Wall Street veteran. The other officer who set the strategy, though, was largely independent of the president's control. This was Ben Bernanke, chair of the Federal Reserve Board and "helmsman of the world economy."[133] Some years before, Bush had nominated Bernanke, at Cheney's urging, to replace the retiring Alan Greenspan.[134] As the nation's central bank, the Fed, an independent regulatory agency, was free of the daily control the president could exercise over Treasury.[135] This meant that two separate lines of command would respond to the crisis. The executive branch would face the worst economic crisis since the 1930s in a fundamentally disunited way.[136]

The crisis that peaked in 2008 had been building for some time, amid some warning signs that few heeded. Deregulation of the financial markets that had begun under Clinton had accelerated under Bush, exacerbated by lax enforcement of the remaining safeguards. A flood of bad loans and the collapse of the bubble produced "by far the deepest global recession since the Great Depression."[137] The bankruptcy of Lehman Brothers froze the capital markets and sent stocks into free fall. Unemployment rose as the economy contracted sharply.

Happily for the nation, the Fed and Treasury cooperated smoothly to stem the bleeding.[138] The president finally took an active role in October 2008, signing a bill funding the first half of a $700 billion stabilization program, which authorized the administration to buy "troubled assets" of "financial institutions."[139] When the automobile industry neared bankruptcy in late 2008, Bush then extended loans to the industry under the statute, although separate authority to bail out the auto companies had not passed in Congress.[140] This obviously strained statutory interpretation did enable the steps that eventually saved the industry. President Obama endorsed and continued the program.

Even as president-elect, Barack Obama worked closely with the Bush administration and with Congress to prepare the ground for funding of the second half of the stabilization program. This unprecedented level of cooperation between outgoing and incoming presidents revealed the depths of the crisis and reflects well on both men. Obama adopted the Bush program even though he knew that it was politically "radioactive" to use the money of innocent taxpayers to save the financial miscreants who had caused the crisis.[141] When the fury of the Tea Party subsequently erupted, Obama bore the political cost of an emergency measure that both presidents had thought necessary and that succeeded in rescuing the American financial system.

CHAPTER FIFTEEN

The Last Mile

Obama

[In difficult cases,] adherence to precedent and rules of construction and interpretation will only get you through the 25th mile of the marathon. The last mile can only be determined on the basis of one's deepest values, one's core concerns, one's broader perspective on how the world works, and the depth and breadth of one's empathy. . . . In those difficult cases, the critical ingredient is supplied by what is in the [interpreter's] heart. — Barack Obama[1]

B arack Obama is fond of noting the unlikelihood that a black man with an unusual name could rise to the American presidency. Small wonder, then, that some of our least stable citizens think his presidency illegitimate, on grounds that he must have been foreign-born and thus ineligible to the office. The truth, though, more befits him—he was born in the only moderately exotic state of Hawaii and is a far more typical American than some believe. True, his ascent to the presidency was sufficiently meteoric to defy convention. He rode to election on the nearly content-free mantras of "hope" and "change." Once installed, however, he induced less change than many would have hoped or feared, and some of what he has done was not signaled by his background.

Born in the U.S.A.

After a boyhood in Hawaii and Indonesia, Obama obtained the elite education that most modern presidents have enjoyed. He excelled at Columbia and Harvard Law School but renounced the lucrative promises of large-firm law practice to become a community organizer in gritty parts of Chicago (and a law professor on the side).[2] Five years after graduation he became a state senator; in 2004, a United States senator. Then followed his first executive office, president of the United States. (At least he could claim a similar career path to that of his hero Abraham Lincoln.)

Obama did have some experience in Washington, although not much regard for its mores. He promised to transcend rather than conduct the toxic partisan warfare that had consumed the capital for years. This stance suited his personality, whether or not it fitted the times. Graceful and highly intelligent, detached and a bit aloof, Obama has an emotional self-sufficiency resembling that of Ronald Reagan.[3] Reveling in policy rather than politics, he is put off by the seamier aspects of modern congressional relations. Confident in the judgments he makes after carefully probing his advisers, he has invited some unnecessary trouble for himself, yet he has risen to some remarkable achievements as president.

Before he took office, Obama had thought about the nature of law, as professors do. Along with the reflections in the epigraph to this chapter, he said: "The law is also memory; the law also records a long-running conversation, a nation arguing with its conscience."[4] Showing his sense for continuity, he identified his four favorite presidents: Lincoln, the two Roosevelts, and Truman.[5] Thus Lincoln's "mystic chords of memory" gain thickness as the nation evolves.

Every president learns, sooner or later, that national security is a bedrock imperative to which his constitutional approach must respond. The end of the Cold War, rather than erasing the danger of atomic weapons, diffused the risk into the hands of shadowy terrorists who would use any weapon available to harm the United States. Within three months of his inauguration, Obama said that his single most important responsibility was "to keep the American people safe."[6] In place of a generalized war on terror, he announced that al Qaeda and its affiliates would be his target.[7]

The new president staffed his administration to supply the experience he lacked, especially in foreign policy.[8] The choice of an insider for vice president, Senator Joseph Biden, was typical for a presidential candidate who lacked broad Washington experience. Biden soon became a valued adviser on many issues. Riskier was the choice of Hillary Clinton, Obama's rival for the nomination, for secretary of state.[9] The move kept her from challenging him from her base in the Senate, but it would be nearly impossible politically to dismiss her later. Fortunately, she quickly turned her considerable abilities to the job and became a very effective secretary with a surprisingly close relationship to the president.[10]

Obama asked George W. Bush's highly capable defense secretary, Robert Gates, to stay on. Along with providing continuity in the midst of two wars, Gates brought cover on Obama's vulnerable right flank.[11] For CIA director, Obama favored counterterror expert John Brennan, but he was too close to the excesses of the Bush era. Obama installed Brennan in the White House as an adviser and relied on him often. The president then turned to a reliable old hand who could steer the CIA through the choppy waters of Washington, Leon Panetta. Obama's friend Susan Rice became UN ambassador.

Surprisingly, Obama controlled foreign policy from the beginning. Because he was not personally close to most of the principals, he installed his own aides on the National Security Council staff to oversee State and Defense.[12] Denis McDonough, who would be a close confidant to Obama as the deputy national security adviser (and chief of staff in the second term), had a background on Capitol Hill. Rahm Emanuel became the White House chief of staff and freelance attack dog. Emanuel did not mesh well with Greg Craig, Obama's first White House Counsel, who left after a year and was replaced by Robert Bauer.

Obama's White House aides were not retreads from the Clinton administration but people of his generation. Because none had been touched by the experience of the Vietnam era, they brought a fresh outlook.[13] Their common goal was to preserve the world leadership of the United States, neither presiding over a decline nor chasing a glimmering hegemony. Their task would be difficult in the midst of the two stalemated wars and a world financial crisis that had not found bottom.

Plus Ça Change[14]

With a victory in the election by a solid margin of 53–46 percent over John McCain, Barack Obama took office with political momentum on his side. He needed to decide which ongoing programs of the Bush administration to change and which to let alone. Obama began with a series of orders that are typical for modern presidents when the party holding the White House changes: a mix of symbolic actions that set a new tone with some outright reversals of existing policies. Wanting to distance himself generally from the secrecy and legal evasions of his predecessor, Obama immediately promised that "transparency and the rule of law will be the touchstones of this presidency."[15] That is a promise easier made than kept.

Obama began by ordering heads of agencies to increase public access to government documents generally, by ordering increased declassification of secret documents, and by eliminating President Bush's restrictions on release of presidential papers.[16] In the latest episode of a long-running drama, the new president reversed his predecessor's policy on abortion counseling and limits on expanding stem cell research.[17]

Much remained the same, however. After some hesitation and a bit of tinkering, Obama reaffirmed the executive order program for OMB review of federal regulations in the shape it had taken during the Clinton administration. Having arisen in its essential current form in the time of Reagan, this program "has become a permanent part of the institutional design of American government."[18] Its administrator, Obama's law professor friend Cass Sunstein, would demonstrate enough devotion to the principles of cost-benefit analysis to aggravate the liberal elements of Obama's base.

At the outset of Obama's presidency, the financial crisis held first claim on his time and energy. The economic team was Timothy Geithner at Treasury, Lawrence Summers as head of the National Economic Council, and Peter Orszag as budget director. This small and sometimes insular group determined the main elements of Obama's initial recovery plan: the auto industry bailout; the second half of the stabilization program begun by President Bush; a $787 billion stimulus package (the largest in American history); and the Dodd-Frank Act, which imposed some renewed regulation on the banking industry.[19] Much remained to be done before recovery could begin, however.

The new president struggled to manage his economic team, with its strong, clashing personalities.[20] Geithner, having a Wall Street background, was sympathetic to the banks and supported them as a way to prevent systemic financial collapse.[21] Paul Volcker, the former chair of the Fed, appeared in a cameo role as eminence gris, calling for tough regulation of the banks to prevent repetition of the sins that had caused the crash. Summers, a former president of Harvard University, was a happy bull in a new china shop. In a chaotic atmosphere reminiscent of the first year of the Clinton administration, the president presided over endless meetings that either failed to result in decisions or even revisited decisions already made. He brought in consumer advocate Elizabeth Warren to set up a new consumer finance agency but was unwilling to challenge the banks' opposition to naming her to head it.

Meanwhile, the independent Federal Reserve Board conducted its own bold economic recovery program, taking steps that the political branches were unwilling to hazard.[22] Under Ben Bernanke's leadership, the Fed began a stimulus program that would last well into Obama's second term, buying many billions of dollars in government securities to release money into the economy. Whatever one might conclude about the exact allocation of responsibility for the economic recovery that has eventually happened, it is clear that from the outset a major role has been played by an independent agency that need not answer to the president's "unitary" command of the executive functions of government.

Obama's early record on national security matters was quite mixed.[23] To distance himself immediately from the Bush administration's handling of the war on terror, he issued a set of executive orders.[24] To end the practice of "enhanced" interrogations, he required questioning to follow the Army Field Manual, having rejected a request by Bush's holdover CIA director for an exception for the agency.[25] In a misstep, Obama promised that Guantanamo would be closed within a year, but he did not reckon with congressional opposition to holding or trying terror suspects within the United States. His politically deaf attorney general, Eric Holder, then served him badly by announcing that the notorious Khalid Sheikh Mohammed would be tried in federal criminal court in Manhattan rather than by a military commission at Guantanamo. Objections immediately arose to providing the worst of the terrorists more process in federal court than smaller fry had received in military commission trials.[26] Spurred by a furious reaction in New York over the costs and risks of securing the courthouse, Congress repeatedly forbade the use of federal funds to transport terror suspects to the United States or to close the prison at Guantanamo.[27] It took most of Obama's first term to commence KSM's trial by military commission, and the prospect of endless proceedings stretched ahead.

Like all presidents, Obama showed little appetite for prosecuting the abuses of the previous administration. Presidents quickly come to understand the pressures that their predecessors faced, and they do not want to establish a precedent that could be turned against them someday. Hence, Obama was quick to say that "we need to focus on the future."[28] He released some of the secret Office of Legal Counsel memos but not the most inflammatory photos of prisoner abuse, invoking the state secrets privilege to shield them.[29] Obama did support Holder's decision to have a special prosecutor perform a criminal investigation of CIA interrogations, notwithstanding objections by Panetta and a number of former CIA directors, who pointed out that the agents had been advised their conduct was lawful. After years of investigation of 101 cases, the prosecutor closed all of them.[30] Whether or not this was a witch hunt, it did not unearth any witches.

Overall, Obama's policy changes from those of the last Bush years in the war on terror were not dramatic.[31] The acceptance by a new president from the other party of Bush's more considered precedents created a new baseline for the conduct of the shadow war. Obama's modifications were meaningful—limiting interrogations, closing the CIA's secret prisons, adhering to the Geneva Conventions. Yet continuity prevailed. Obama soon followed Bush's lead by claiming that the AUMF of 2001 still authorized him to use all necessary force against al Qaeda. A review of detentions showed that Guantanamo held about fifty prisoners who could not safely be released. They would be held indefinitely, with periodic status reviews. Military commission trials resumed after an initial suspension for review. The administration reserved authority to order rendition of prisoners with the usual promises about torture.

To justify his actions, Obama abandoned Bush's tendency to make sweeping claims of unilateral constitutional executive power in favor of finding links to statutory authority and the international law of war.[32] Hence, Obama stressed that he was invoking exclusively statutory authority to pursue al Qaeda.[33] The fact that many of the policies were similar reveals the extent to which Bush's claims of exclusive power had been unnecessary to his goals. Similarly, Obama promised to restrict his use of legislative signing statements and to make his objections to statutory provisions specific.[34] He adhered to that promise, limiting but not abandoning this useful tool.[35]

Toward the end of his administration, President Bush accepted a deadline requested by Iraq to withdraw all American troops by the end of 2011. Barack Obama, who had launched his national political career on the basis of his opposition to the Iraq war as a "dumb war . . . based not on reason, but on passion," was happy to ratify Bush's decision, putting that long war on the road to an end.[36]

Afghanistan would not be as easy. Strategy there might range anywhere from building that wrecked nation into a modern democracy to abandoning it under pretense of victory. Finding an urgent request for more troops on his desk on his first day, Obama initiated an immediate interagency review. He soon announced a counterterror goal to "disrupt, dismantle, and defeat" al Qaeda in Afghanistan and Pakistan.[37] Achieving this goal would, however, imply a broader counterinsurgency strategy of keeping the Taliban out of power and would present special sensitivities regarding operations in Pakistan, a nominal ally.

The president chose General Stanley McChrystal, a counterinsurgency expert, to lead the military effort in Afghanistan and Richard Holbrooke, the hero of the Dayton Accords, as a special envoy for "AfPak." The commander in Iraq, General David Petraeus, was the Army's leading counterinsurgency specialist. His presence there signaled a shift away from the Powell Doctrine of big, short wars toward the grinding contests for control that marked counterinsurgency and also raised the specter of Vietnam.

Aware that Presidents Kennedy and Johnson had never tested prevailing assumptions about the monolithic nature of their adversaries in Vietnam, Obama invited several presidential historians to review the lessons of those times.[38] The discussion suggested that a combination of unclear goals and incremental decisions led to the morass in Vietnam. Obama also thought that George W. Bush's statements that he would listen to his generals and give them what they needed was an abdication of civilian control.[39] To find an exit strategy for Afghanistan, then, Obama had to clarify American objectives and control their implementation.

An immediate decision about Afghanistan was needed because the war there had been starved for resources ever since preparation for the Iraq war began. In February 2009, Obama responded to the urgent Pentagon request by sending seventeen thousand more troops to Afghanistan. By the summer, continuing reverses led the president to initiate another, very extensive strategy review that lasted for months.[40] The problem was that counterinsurgency has a vast appetite for troops (and the dreams of nations). Its advocates in the military leaked their requests for yet more troops to the press, pressuring the president and earning a stiff rebuke. Obama was determined to demonstrate who was boss at the outset of his administration.[41] His eventual decision to add thirty thousand more troops for a total of about one hundred thousand was swayed by Secretaries Clinton and Gates, who presented the rare phenomenon of the departments of state and defense being in agreement on the need for military force.[42]

Obama's announcement of his Afghanistan policy in late 2009 rejected a full counterinsurgency effort, which might well take a decade. To cap the commitment, he required that troop withdrawals begin by 2011, a target that bought domestic political time but gave the enemy an incentive to stall rather than talk.[43] The surge was an attempt to degrade the Taliban sufficiently to allow the Afghan government to handle them.[44] The Afghan president, Hamid Karzai, who combined incompetence, corruption, and instability, then gave Obama a rare gift—a request for an American exit by the end of 2014. The president was only too happy to accede. He had, however, taken political ownership of the war in the meantime.

By the summer of 2011, Obama was ready to accept a recommendation from Gates and Clinton that he begin recovering the surge by the next year. In his first two years, the president had learned that he could not remake Afghanistan. He announced that it was "time to focus on nation building here at home."[45] He hoped eventually to keep only a small force of special operations forces in Afghanistan to bolster the government, monitor Pakistan, and strike at al Qaeda.[46]

During Obama's first term, tensions over Afghanistan induced him to change his national security team.[47] He installed Tom Donilon, an experienced insider who had led the NSC staff for two years, as national security adviser.[48] After General McChrystal rashly gave a magazine interview that included criticisms of Obama and other civilians, the president fired him in favor of Petraeus. Afghanistan would nurture no MacArthurs. Now Obama had a highly politically attuned national security group.[49]

New World Rising

Barack Obama's instincts in foreign policy reflected his detached, analytic personality. He was neither a cynical realist like Henry Kissinger nor a committed moralist like Woodrow Wilson.[50] Instead, he triangulated these positions, drawing from both as suited him. His secretary of state retained the stance of her husband's administration, that the United States was the "indispensable nation" in international affairs.[51] Obama would mute that message—with its implication of indefinite, unilateral commitments—in favor of more reliance on other nations.

Obama's debut on the world stage was a speech in Cairo in mid-2009 that was intended to alter America's relations with the estranged Islamic world, in which he soothingly called for a "new beginning."[52] Early on, Obama was chary of promoting democracy abroad in the aggressive style of his predecessor. At the end of the year, as he received his ludicrously premature Nobel Peace Prize, he jarred the audience by endorsing the concept of just wars, giving the Clinton efforts in the Balkans as an example of a justifiable humanitarian intervention. Noting that the United

States had underwritten global security for six decades since World War II, he invited others to step forward.

Others were indeed stepping forward, at least in terms of economic leadership. China and India were emergent powers. Obama and Clinton sought to shift American foreign policy toward an Asian focus that was intended to cabin China.[53] The difficulty here was America's dependency on China to fund the national debt. It soon became clear that early efforts by Obama to conciliate the Chinese were seen by them as weakness, but the president searched in vain for effective leverage—as Secretary Clinton asked, how do you deal toughly with your banker?[54] In a reversal of historic client roles, China pressed Obama to explain how the United States would control its debt.

It was easier to deal with the fading superpower, Russia, which presented opportunities for cooperation at the start of Obama's tenure. Here Obama followed the path presidents since Reagan had trodden. The George W. Bush administration had entered a treaty with Russia to reduce nuclear warheads.[55] To advance nuclear nonproliferation, Obama negotiated another Strategic Arms Reduction Treaty, reducing warhead ceilings again.[56] It was easily ratified, with some Republican support.

By 2014, however, the bear was stirring again. When Russian president Vladimir Putin took advantage of a crisis in Ukraine to annex Crimea and threaten other parts of the former Soviet Union, a new chill entered the air and talk of containment resumed in the foreign policy discourse in Washington. As he had done elsewhere in the world, Obama took a cautious, multilateral approach to stemming Russia's renewed aggressiveness.[57]

The unexpected foreign policy crisis of Obama's first term was the Arab Spring of 2011, when dictators collapsed like dominoes and the United States tried to help democracy flower without meddling overmuch. Obama had detected signs of restiveness and was pondering his responses when events took charge.[58] After the first upheaval in Tunisia, Egypt took center stage. Remarking that history was moving and the United States needed to be on the right side of it, Obama faced the delicate task of deciding when to pressure longtime American ally Hosni Mubarak to leave office.[59] When the president chose the moment to intercede, he did so against the advice of many of his aides, but he succeeded in easing Mubarak out. Obama was approaching each nation in the region ad hoc, with his actions depending on how the strategic and humanitarian interests of the United States could be advanced.[60]

In Libya, the president chose carefully limited military action.[61] Controversial from the start, Obama's intervention eventually raised serious issues of legality under the War Powers Resolution. The United States had a long history of conflict with Libya's strongman, the delusional and dangerous Gadhafi, including his sponsorship of terror attacks against Americans and President Reagan's air assault against him in retaliation.[62] As Gadhafi's regime fought desperately for survival that spring, his forces closed in on rebel strongholds in Benghazi. A slaughter of civilians appeared likely. The British and French considered military intervention and pressed the president to take part. Because the United States had little strategic interest in Libya, only humanitarian and democratic impulses favored a response.

Obama's national security team was divided over Libya. Defense Secretary Gates, seeing no strategic gain and concerned about the military options, held back while State Secretary Clinton called for action. The president, viewing the decision whether to use military force as his constitutional prerogative, had no plans to consult Congress except in the usual fashion of cursory notification. When Obama was presented with options of declaring a no-fly zone over Libya or doing nothing, he rejected them as unresponsive to the problem of mass civilian slaughter and called for more options immediately. He would not consider using ground troops, lest the United States own the outcome in yet another Islamic nation.

Obama sought and received the support of the UN to use force. He agreed with the British and French that the United States would deliver initial air strikes using its massive capacity and would then assume a role secondary to the allies. His order to strike Libya was his first use of the military in a conflict that he had not inherited. The international intervention helped the rebels to turn the tide against Gadhafi and eventually to oust and kill him. That no such action could be entirely surgical and self-contained was demonstrated by the later murder of four American diplomats in Benghazi by terrorists.

Saying that he needed no congressional authority to join a UN military action that was so limited in scope and duration, Obama met with congressional leaders before the action commenced to assure them that it would be brief but did not ask for their permission.[63] Congress showed little inclination to vote on anything, leaving the matter to the president's sole responsibility. Obama's speech to the nation stressed the need to protect the Libyan people, avoiding any concession that removing a dictator was the goal—that would have evoked George W. Bush in Iraq. Before long, however, regime change was quietly added to the stated purposes of the operation.

President Obama's intervention in Libya raised issues under both the Constitution and the War Powers Resolution. His initial resort to military force against another nation might have been war in the constitutional sense, requiring advance authorization from Congress. If not, the WPR would require seeking authority from Congress if hostilities were to persist past the statutory sixty-day limit. As events unfolded, Obama correctly asserted that he was not engaging in a war under the Constitution and incorrectly asserted that he was not engaging in hostilities under the WPR. The lawyer-president and his executive branch lawyers navigated the tricky legal issues with only partial success.

As the operation began, Obama asked the Office of Legal Counsel for its opinion on whether the Constitution required advance approval from Congress. OLC answered in the negative, following the analysis that the Clinton administration's lawyers had articulated for the Balkan actions.[64] Employing "a fact-specific assessment of the 'anticipated nature, scope, and duration' of the planned military operations," OLC concluded that a war in the constitutional sense was not involved because of the anticipated scale of the intervention.[65] This was correct: it placed Libya squarely among the many precedents for unilateral presidential commitments of the military in American history.

Although large American air strikes did cease after a few days, in the next two months American airplanes struck Libyan air defenses sixty times, and drones fired thirty missiles. As the sixty-day limit for unauthorized hostilities contained in the War Powers Resolution passed, Obama had to decide whether the administration was engaged in hostilities in Libya within the meaning of the WPR. Although the United States had dropped back into a supporting role in the Libyan operation, some American missiles were still being fired.

When the House of Representatives called for the president's justification for not seeking congressional authority, Obama filed a report saying that he was relying on his independent constitutional authority because of the "limited nature, scope, and duration of the anticipated actions."[66] He denied that hostilities were occurring within the meaning of the WPR, because "U.S. operations do not involve sustained fighting or active exchanges of fire with hostile forces, nor do they involve the presence of U.S. ground troops, U.S. casualties or a serious threat thereof, or any significant chance of escalation into a conflict characterized by those factors."

Obama's reasons for denying that hostilities existed in Libya, although persuasive on the constitutional issue, were wrong on the statutory question. The legislative history of the WPR is clear that the clock for seeking congressional authorization of continuing hostilities runs in circumstances like the Libyan intervention.

A conflict that broke out among the president's lawyers revealed the error in his interpretation. The Office of Legal Counsel's initial memo, while arguing that no constitutional war was in prospect, admitted that substantial clashes of arms were expected. Now OLC was boxed in and could not argue that no hostilities were occurring. The Pentagon's chief lawyer, Jeh Johnson, agreed with OLC. But White House Counsel Robert Bauer and State Department Legal Adviser Harold Koh were willing to provide the president the opinion he sought.[67] Both the president and his overly complaisant lawyers knew better. This was an instance in which, in the words of the WPR, the "collective judgment" of Congress and the president should have been brought to bear.

Syria provided another hard case. During its long and bloody meltdown, the president could not see a clear opportunity to intervene at an acceptable cost to the United States and with an acceptable prospect of helping the Syrian people. Everything changed in the summer of 2013, when the Syrian government resorted to chemical weapons against the rebels, with widespread and horrific civilian casualties. Ever since World War I, the international community had recoiled from the use of these weapons and had generated treaty bans on their use. Now pressure mounted for the United States to retaliate, either alone or in concert with other nations. The situation was unprecedented in that an attack on the Syrian government to punish it for a completed atrocity and to deter repetition would not quite fit earlier cases, which had involved urgent present needs to protect civilian lives. Only air strikes were under consideration; no American boots would touch the ground.

For domestic constitutional purposes, humanitarian interventions present considerations somewhat different from traditional strikes to protect American lives or property. Presidents can persuasively assert their constitutional "protective" power when American citizens are in peril and can amass many precedents for immediate use of force in those circumstances, from the Barbary pirates on. Interventions to protect other peoples, however, have no natural limit. This old globe is never short of tragedy, as Rwanda and the Balkans had recently shown. Certainly, the humanitarian impulse is often a component of presidential foreign policy.

Humanitarianism has always been central to American claims of exceptionalism and needs no defense when sincerely presented. The problem is one of constitutional limits—whether American forces can follow wherever the president's heart goes. Syria promised to test the limits.

Past American interventions for humanitarian purposes, as in Libya and Kosovo, had support from either the United Nations Security Council or the NATO allies. By providing support for the foreign policy judgments that underlie decisions to use force, international authorization influences but does not determine domestic constitutional analysis. Thus the commander in chief stands on firmer ground when relevant members of the international community share his determination that forceful action is necessary.

As President Obama considered his options, it became clear that Russian objections would block the UN Security Council from authorizing a strike against Syria. Another blow followed, as the British Parliament rejected an appeal from Prime Minister David Cameron to support British involvement. Grimly, the president initially announced that he was prepared to launch a strike unilaterally, and the Navy moved ships carrying cruise missiles into position.[68] Air strikes on the proposed scale would have been within the president's commander in chief power, well short of an involvement that would constitute war in the constitutional sense. The administration consulted with congressional leaders about the planned operation, pressing the need to enforce international bans on chemical weapons and to prevent their use against American allies in the region. Members of Congress expressed concerns about the efficacy of air strikes, the threat of retaliation by Syria, and the reaction of a war-weary American public.

Within days of his announcement that he would launch military action on his own, the president retreated and said he would seek authorization from Congress.[69] Prospects for a favorable vote looked dim indeed, given Congress's recent record of thwarting the president on many other issues and low levels of public support for a strike. Then an initiative from an unexpected quarter saved the day. Russia proposed that international monitors take control of Syria's stock of chemical weapons, in return for which the United States would forgo resorting to force.[70] Obama leapt at the opportunity to avert a humiliating defeat in Congress. After hurried negotiations, the United States and Russia reached an agreement to neutralize the weapons, imposed it on Syria, and secured the blessing of the UN Security Council.[71]

President Obama's fortunate escape from the Syrian crisis left the constitutional allocation of powers for response to humanitarian disasters unsettled, as before. He did set a precedent by belatedly deciding to seek authorization for intervention from Congress. He explained to the nation that taking this step would mean that "the country will be stronger" and "our actions will be more effective."[72] But he continued to deny that it was constitutionally necessary. Although he was probably right about that, future presidents who forgo congressional authority in similar circumstances can expect Obama's decision to be cited against them.

Machines Making War

Barack Obama greatly expanded two new kinds of warfare that George W. Bush initiated; both employ remotely controlled attacks by machines.[73] The use of unmanned drone aircraft enables a surprise attack almost anywhere in the world. The use of one computer to hack into and disable another, cyber warfare, is stealthier yet, because the victim may be unaware that an attack has even occurred and will likely have great difficulty identifying the source with confidence. Because war by drones and computers is precisely targeted, minimizing the collateral damage that conventional warfare imposes, and is cheap in both American lives and money, its availability provides a constant temptation to overuse, especially in the absence of developed legal constraints.

The consequent constitutional questions are as difficult as they are novel. Does the president's commander in chief power allow him to target and kill any enemy of the United States anywhere in the world? Since cyber war does not involve ordinary violence, is it governed by the domestic and international law of war at all, and if so how? President Obama has been busily working away on both the operational and legal fronts of these two new kinds of war. At the outset, he did so without meaningful participation by Congress, except for whatever consultation was occurring with the relevant committees. Nor did the American people know much about the administration's actions except for the occasional bulletin announcing a completed drone attack.

In his first year in office, Barack Obama stepped up the military campaign against al Qaeda by increased use of drones in both Afghanistan and Pakistan.[74] In his first term, Obama ordered over 250 drone attacks, compared to about 40 by Bush. Strikes within Pakistan particularly re-

quired secrecy to avoid offending the Pakistani government by broadcast-
ing the continuing infringement of its sovereignty. Over four hundred
drones are operated by the Air Force and the CIA from over sixty bases
around the world.

For years, the president would say little more about the program than
that it was on a "tight leash."[75] By that he meant that he was personally
involved in supervising it, along with the executive branch lawyers who
now review many kinds of unconventional warfare.[76] The president, determined to remain responsible for the program, reviewed and approved
the "kill list" of terror suspects.[77]

The constitutional argument for the initial phase of targeted killing
in AfPak was relatively straightforward: Congress had authorized military force against al Qaeda, and the law of war allows self-defense against
those who plan to attack the United States. This argument also countered
criticism that the president was breaking the still-extant promise made
by President Ford in his executive order banning assassination of foreign
leaders. (Because it is politically impossible to rescind Ford's promise
openly, presidents have evaded it when necessary.)

Soon, however, the drones ranged beyond the initial theater in AfPak,
where the AUMF and the law of war had the clearest application. The
drones decimated the leaders of al Qaeda wherever they were found. In
a controversial case, the president approved drone strikes that eventually
killed an American citizen named al-Awlaki, a radical Islamic cleric based
in Yemen who had fomented terror activities against the United States.[78]
The administration formally justified targeting this American citizen overseas as a form of "lawful extrajudicial killing." The Department of Justice
issued a white paper summarizing the analysis contained in earlier classified memoranda.[79] The explanation was that an "informed, high-level official" must determine that the target poses an "imminent threat of violent
attack" against the United States, that "capture is infeasible," and that the
operation will follow "applicable law of war principles."

In some ways, this interim constitutional approach can claim a substantial historical pedigree. For a very long time, presidents have lashed
out at anyone they can reach who seems to threaten Americans, from the
Barbary pirates to the multitude of police actions in Latin America. What
has changed is the exponential growth of a president's capacity to locate,
reach, and destroy persons thought to pose a threat. Thus the old precedents need adaptation to modern conditions. In particular, the drone
program contains a quiet but important shift of emphasis, from capturing

terrorist suspects to killing them outright.[80] Obama inherited the Bush administration's practical and legal travails with detention, interrogation, and trial of terror suspects. Instant aerial executions pose none of these problems. They do, however, raise fundamental issues about due process and the rule of law.

The unilateral nature of the early drone program is particularly troubling. Congressional and public debate about it finally began early in Obama's second term, when he nominated John Brennan, who had been his principal White House assistant for the program, for CIA director.[81] The administration finally supplied Congress with the classified memos supporting targeted killings.[82] Although much of the debate since has occurred behind closed congressional doors, proposals to control the program have surfaced, including requirements for a secret court like the FISA court to review and approve kill lists.[83] When an interbranch control mechanism emerges, it is not likely to resemble the traditional processes of American criminal law.

Barack Obama also sharply increased special operations raids in AfPak, to more than ten per night.[84] Under Presidents Bush and Obama, these raids have blended new technology with more traditional use of American boots on the ground. There has also been increased organizational blending. Of course, the notional distinction that CIA does spying and Defense does operations had blurred long before the war on terror.[85] Presidents since Eisenhower have enjoyed using CIA for covert operations, because doing so avoids the cumbersome military chain of command and is supposedly easier to keep secret. For its part, Defense has assembled its own giant intelligence capacity to guide secret operations and to detect threats generally. Thus presidents command not one but two secret armies and three secret spy shops (including NSA). Controlling this massive military-intelligence complex is a central part of today's faithful execution duty.

One of the commando raids finally killed Osama bin Laden in Pakistan in May 2011.[86] Early in his presidency, Obama instructed the CIA to reinvigorate the hunt for bin Laden, which had gone cold. Once he was tentatively located, planning for the raid was held very close within the administration. Pakistan was not informed because of the mixed loyalties of its government. President Obama actively supervised the plan, personally altering it somewhat.[87] He displayed considerable courage in ordering the raid in the face of uncertainty whether bin Laden would be found in the targeted compound and with the risks of an operational failure as in Somalia or a violent reaction by Pakistan to the presence of American troops. Whether the mission was explicitly to kill bin Laden or to attempt a capture if possible was left uncertain, but the obvious nightmares that would attend a live bin Laden in the dock may have registered with all concerned.

After monitoring the bin Laden raid from the White House with his advisers huddled around him, Obama reacted to the news of success with his characteristic restraint: "We got him."[88] Legal justifications for the killing wove the usual threads of the AUMF, the commander in chief power, international law rights of national self-defense, and the right to kill enemy combatants under the law of war.[89] Surely these were adequate grounds. Eliminating bin Laden gave Obama more freedom to disengage in Afghanistan but exacerbated difficulties with Pakistan. Ironically, whatever be the remaining threat from al Qaeda after bin Laden, the greatest strategic threat to the United States in the region or perhaps the world now lies in the loosely controlled Pakistani nuclear arsenal.

The other trouble spot in the Middle East was Iran, with its nuclear dreams and ingrained hostility to the United States. For both Presidents Bush and Obama, policy options were limited by the two ongoing wars in the region and the need to avoid a third. Obama continued Bush's economic sanctions against the Iranian nuclear program and expanded it to deny Iran's access to international banking.[90] Military action against Iran's well-protected nuclear facilities did not seem feasible, and the president wanted to deflect Israel from attacking the facilities in self-defense.

While pressuring Iran with sanctions, Obama tried to negotiate with its leaders.[91] He sent secret letters to Supreme Leader Ali Khamenei and received the expected torrent of abuse in return. In 2009, in a precursor to the Arab Spring, Iran held an election in which President Mahmoud Ahmadinejad was implausibly declared the winner. As street violence escalated, Obama kept quiet, still hoping for a diplomatic opening, until conditions demanded his condemnation.

The failure of traditional means for influencing or forcing Iran to abandon its nuclear program led Obama to conduct the first major cyber war in history. President Clinton had tried ordinary sabotage against the program, by having defective industrial parts and designs shipped to Iran, for example. President Bush had initiated cyber attacks on the computers controlling Iran's nuclear facilities by sending worms into their software, while trying to prevent collateral damage to civilian facilities like schools or hospitals.[92] Thus analogies to traditional law of war concepts have guided the American approach from the outset.

In a closely guarded operation called Olympic Games, President Obama initiated a new kind of cyber war.[93] A worm called Stuxnet invaded Iranian computers and caused physical damage in factories, for example by causing centrifuges to spin out of control. As a covert intelligence operation, Olympic Games required presidential findings, which were crafted and provided to the intelligence committees on the Hill. The president stayed closely involved as the operation developed, insisting that the worm be kept "unattributable" as long as possible. It appears that Stuxnet did significant damage to the Iranian program before it was revealed after having escaped accidentally into international cyberspace, where it created a furor. Sustained American pressure on the Iranians eventually led to an interim agreement temporarily suspending Iranian nuclear development while negotiators searched for an elusive long range solution.[94]

There now exists a United States Cyber Command, which is a joint National Security Agency and Department of Defense effort with a staff of about thirteen thousand and a budget of about $3.4 billion.[95] Most of its activities are unknown beyond selected precincts in the executive and Congress. The administration admits defending against cyber attacks coming from anywhere. For example, it appears that an attack on computer systems of some large American banks was an Iranian effort to retaliate for Stuxnet. Cyber theft of both government and corporate secrets from the United States by the Chinese government has become an obstacle to harmonious international relations.[96] The administration is developing classified rules for the preemptive use of cyber warfare against anticipated threats.[97] Both domestic and international concepts of lawful warfare must evolve to grapple with this new reality. As Michael Hayden, former director of both the CIA and NSA, observed: "This has the whiff of August, 1945. It's a new class of weapon, a weapon never before used."[98]

Overall, the Obama administration's foreign policy strategy in the first term was to react quickly to opportunities and threats as they presented themselves, eschewing the formation of a grand design that might drive particular decisions. The president was quite willing to use military force to achieve limited objectives. Still, with the United States facing military overstretch abroad and economic crisis at home, Obama's foreign ambitions were limited.

America's lost decade in the Middle East proved especially constraining. At the end of 2011, an American military convoy rolled out of Iraq on the roads it had rolled in on eight years before, leaving behind forty-five hundred American dead and another thirty-five thousand wounded as the human price of a war that cost over a trillion dollars.[99] The war in Afghanistan has its deadlines but not yet its coda.

The global war against terror cost the United States at least \$3 trillion in the decade after 9/11, producing a defense budget that grew by two-thirds in real terms, to half again as much as the Cold War average.[100] Despite all that, with the United States no longer a lone superpower, presidential options have narrowed, and dependence on other nations has increased. Clearly, the costs of American action will matter more than ever. Major world issues concerning debt, energy, trade, immigration, and climate change demand attention. A new world strategy for the United States awaits articulation with the participation of President Obama and his successors.

In the world after 9/11 and the evolution of a reaction to it, an American president faces an altered set of legal controls.[101] The "imperial presidency" of the Vietnam era resulted in at least three kinds of new statutory restrictions on presidential discretion. Accountability controls include the consultation and reporting requirements of the War Powers Resolution and the presidential findings and congressional notification provisions of modern intelligence statutes. Information controls include the presence of inspectors general within agencies and open government statutes that reveal executive branch operations. And direct substantive limitations often exist, including criminal statutes that threaten the president's aides with prosecution if they take certain actions.

Recent presidents have struggled to deal with these restraints, with mixed success. They often treat the WPR as advisory and minimize compliance with other consultation requirements. Unless Congress provokes a confrontation by actually passing a resolution under the WPR to limit a presidential military action or insists on fuller consultation generally, this situation will persist. Nonetheless, the sum total of law applicable to White House action and the efforts of squadrons of lawyers in the executive branch to comply with it is impressive, especially as compared to the simplified legal world that presidents knew as recently as World War II.

At the start of his second term, Obama signaled his awareness of the need to curtail constant military action by his selection of a new national security team including John Kerry at State, Chuck Hagel at Defense, and John Brennan at CIA. In May 2013, the president announced a broad shift in strategy for the war on terror.[102] He called for an end to the emergency-based focus on al Qaeda that had dominated American policy since 9/11 in favor of a more routine search for terror groups threatening the United States. He promised to limit sharply the use of drone strikes, using them only for "continuing, imminent" threats to Americans and only with a "near certainty" of avoiding civilian casualties.[103] He also wanted to shift the CIA away from operations toward its historic role as a spy agency. He was searching for a "new normal" understanding of national security policy, benefiting from the lessons learned after more than a decade of the war on terror.

A World of Secrets

The combination of the war on terror with rapid technological advances has produced another set of thorny issues about the extent of a president's constitutional powers concerning national security. In the twenty-first century, the federal government's large and secret national security apparatus sweeps in vast amounts of information about individuals worldwide and then struggles to control the dissemination of that information.

Behind discrete issues about the constitutionality of particular kinds of information acquisition or retention lies a chilling question: how can a gigantic and secretive national security bureaucracy be controlled by *anyone*? The legitimacy of ordinary administrative agencies is a function of their supervision by the three constitutional branches. The president bears special individual responsibility because of his faithful execution duty. But the size and secrecy of the security bureaucracy attenuates the links to all three branches and threatens to shear them. Today, over 1,200 government organizations and over 1,900 private companies work on counterterror and intelligence programs, employing over 850,000 people with top-secret security clearances.[104] Government expenditures are over $50 billion annually.[105] Vast numbers of intelligence reports ricochet around in cyberspace. Redundancy and waste must be plentiful. Abuse cannot be unknown. How much does the president know, and what can he reasonably hope to do to control this behemoth?

Legal controls do exist, but they are under great stress. Recall that the Bush administration's surveillance program eventually led to statutory resolution providing general oversight of the executive by the secret Foreign Intelligence Surveillance Court. This legal regime tries to control the executive's process for compiling information and then scanning it for clues about terrorism.[106] There are two stages to the surveillance program.

First, the government collects "metadata" from telephone calls made in the United States—phone numbers, time and date of calls, but not content.[107] Second, within this vast haystack it searches for needles—links between communications that may track terrorist activity. Under the statute, with the approval of the FISC the government may target and examine the contents of communications of foreigners "reasonably believed" to be located outside the United States.[108] Thus, if someone on the terrorist watch list receives a call that appears to have a foreign source, the NSA will examine the message. The Obama administration has issued guidelines to control "incidental" examination of communications by Americans that are swept up in the net.[109] Nevertheless, problems of compliance with existing legal controls have dogged this massive program.[110]

Controversy over the surveillance program erupted after a former NSA contract employee, Edward Snowden, leaked information about it to the press.[111] Both the executive branch and the FISC tried to provide assurances that they adequately protect the privacy of citizens while searching for terrorists.[112] Proposed reforms include the provision of a privacy advocate in FISC proceedings to counteract the government's ex parte arguments for approval. Adjustments there may be, but the overall shape of the surveillance program will probably endure.

President Obama has also vigorously used the traditional presidential tools for protecting national security information. He began by relaxing Bush's classification policy somewhat, in an effort to meet his promises about transparency. But before long, he displayed as much sensitivity about leaks as had many of his predecessors.[113] In litigation challenging executive action that occurred both during the Bush administration and his own, Obama effectively asserted the state secrets doctrine to bar disclosures.[114] He persuaded the Supreme Court to deny standing to sue to groups challenging the constitutionality of the NSA surveillance program, barring immediate judicial review of the merits of the program.[115]

Eric Holder's Justice Department has gone very far in its attempts to plug leaks of government secrets.[116] It has prosecuted seven government employees for leaking to the press, including Edward Snowden, more than all previous administrations combined.[117] Sweeping subpoenas for reporters' records have raised the ire of advocates of press freedom and have led to the administration's "review" of its policies.[118] The obvious strain between national security and transparency deserves more sensitive resolution than the Obama administration has accorded it.

Even in the days of a secret security bureaucracy, the Constitution's primal links between the executive and the other two branches and the people remain, although in altered form. Congressional leaders know about the most important presidential initiatives. Eventually, Congress as a whole has its opportunity to exert informal pressure or even to intervene with controlling legislation. Relying largely on retrospective accountability, this is emphatically a second-best form of control. The courts have shown some willingness to play a role in regularizing the war on terror but are often faced with issues they are reluctant or unwilling to adjudicate. The American people do eventually learn about what their presidents have been doing and provide their verdict. Thus presidents act in the expectation that the secrecy shield is temporary and calibrate their decisions accordingly. In a world marked by vast leaks of information, every secret is contingent.

Obamacare

Democratic Presidents since Harry Truman have dreamed about completing the New Deal by sponsoring legislation to create a national health care plan. Lyndon Johnson succeeded in part with Medicare for the elderly, but other Americans remained subject to the vagaries of a patchwork and expensive health care system. Barack Obama stunned many observers by pouring his energies into filling the gap during a time when the economy had by no means recovered from the financial crisis of 2008. By the spring of 2010 the president had demonstrated considerable skill in legislative management by moving the Patient Protection and Affordable Care Act to his desk for signature.[119]

Now the real battle began. Legal challenges to the constitutionality of what was soon called Obamacare began. Ironically, the president's plan drew on earlier Republican plans, and during the early stages of legislative consideration no constitutional objection appeared.[120] Once the constitutional question arose, however, it merged into the popular Tea Party movement, which objected to the entire edifice of the modern American welfare state. To the Tea Party, perversion of the Constitution dated to FDR's New Deal. The constricted version of the commerce clause that was the centerpiece of the New Deal constitutional battle was gospel to them.

While the court challenges to Obamacare percolated along, unrest over the economy and other issues like health care produced a stunning rout for the Democrats in the 2010 midterm elections. To the surprise of many, President Obama had shown a lack of interest in communicating his policy views to the public.[121] Disdaining many of the theatrics of the presidency, he hoped to float above the gritty world of politics, letting his good deeds justify him. George Washington could get away with that, but no modern president can. After the midterm repudiation of Obama's agenda, the challenge to FDR's view of national legislative power was general and fundamental. The presidential election two years later would be fought over this basic issue of the scope and role of the federal government.

The constitutional issue about Obamacare reached the Supreme Court in time for a decision in the midst of the election campaign of 2012. Everyone knew this would be a landmark case—the Court assigned it many more hours of argument than any other case in decades. In late June, the Court upheld Obamacare by a five-four vote.[122] Chief Justice John Roberts played the pivotal role in the outcome with a finesse worthy of his great predecessor John Marshall. First, Roberts joined a majority of five conservative justices in holding that Americans could not be forced to buy health insurance under the power to regulate interstate commerce. But then he joined the four liberals to make a decisive majority upholding the act under the power of Congress to tax and spend. The point of the exercise was to find a way to uphold the statute and avoid placing the Supreme Court at the center of a divisive political campaign while making a precedent that would confine congressional power under the commerce clause in the future.[123] Chief justices, like presidents, respond to institutional considerations about their branch of government in ways that their subordinates do not.

The Court's Obamacare decision left the New Deal constitutional settlement in some disarray. The majority took a "stunningly retrogressive" view of the commerce clause, as a dissent correctly observed.[124] On the taxing and spending power under the general welfare clause, however, the majority was firmly within a tradition predating the New Deal. The president's constitutional position, which he displayed by signing and defending the statute, is far better suited to the modern nation than the majority's "horse and buggy" reading of the commerce clause.[125]

For President Obama, a win was a win, and on he went toward his reelection in November, buoyed by the Court's decision and the belatedly improving economy. Behind the scenes of the reelection effort, Obama and his inner circle considered replacing Vice President Biden with Hillary Clinton, who was completing her tour of duty as secretary of state.[126]

But polling data suggested that her presence on the ticket would not improve the chances of victory, and the move was quietly dropped. Whether she would have made a better choice to stand next in line to the presidency was never the dominant consideration.

Deadlock

For the past two decades, presidents have struggled with an extremely dysfunctional and recalcitrant Congress.[127] For Obama, early difficulties were magnified by the 2010 midterm elections, delivering the House to the Republicans and the Republicans to their fierce right wing of Tea Party insurgents. The conventions of compromise upon which any legislative body must depend have largely evaporated in the increasingly poisonous atmosphere.

From the start of his tenure, Obama faced obstruction in a Senate that routinely required a majority of sixty to move ordinary legislation or nominations.[128] Formerly a method to slow the passage of a few critically important measures by threatening unlimited debate, the filibuster had expanded to encompass almost everything that the Senate must decide.[129] For executive nominations, the problem is that unprecedented numbers of vacancies have hollowed out the executive branch, impairing its capacity to function. Breaking from tradition, senators have threatened filibusters even for core executive branch nominations, such as those of John Brennan for CIA director and Chuck Hagel for secretary of defense. Below the cabinet level, many of the executive branch's critical middle management posts (such as assistant secretaries) have remained without permanent occupants for extended periods.[130] Obama has sometimes resorted to placing favored aides in White House positions that do not require confirmation, as in his selection of Susan Rice as national security adviser after the Senate blocked her nomination for secretary of state, but that is only a patchwork response to a deep structural problem in the Senate.

The filibuster is probably unconstitutional. Article I of the Constitution provides that a majority of each house constitutes a quorum for doing business, such as legislating.[131] This apparent entrenchment of majority rule reflects conventions that antedate the Constitution, regarding the conduct of collective decision-making bodies. But Article I also authorizes each house of Congress to make rules for its internal operations.[132] This provision clearly authorizes such essential housekeeping matters as

the committee system, but the Senate has extended it to develop the unlimited filibuster, which deeply undermines the overall precept of majority rule. Neither presidents nor the federal courts can easily address this
problem. It is the Senate's responsibility.

In his initial judicial appointments, Obama made a mistake that no
recent Republican administration would have replicated. Feeling secure
with fifty-nine Democrats in the Senate, the president tried simultaneously to reduce partisanship in judicial appointments and to increase
his own power relative to the Senate.[133] He asked Democratic senators to
provide three names for each judicial vacancy in their states, rather than
just one. Holding moderate views of the Constitution himself, Obama intended to seek centrist judges. George W. Bush, by contrast, had a full
slate of conservative nominees to present to the Senate within months of
his inauguration. Obama's move stalled the early nominations, and he did
not recover for the balance of his first term. Vacancies in the lower federal judiciary have reached historically high levels. Because of Obama's
"astonishing lassitude" about making lower court nominations and unprecedented levels of obstruction in the Senate, an important opportunity to shape the law evaporated, and everyday efficiency in the judiciary
suffered.[134]

The breakdown in the congressional confirmation process reached
a crescendo of sorts in a bizarre controversy involving presidential recess appointments. As we have seen, when the Senate is in recess, the
president may make a unilateral appointment that lasts until the end of
the Senate's next session.[135] Not surprisingly, recent presidents from both
parties have used recess appointments in an attempt to work around the
Senate. Appointing judges in this way has always been sensitive, but the
practice is well established.[136] Until recently, Congress ordinarily accepted
recess appointments for executive officers.

During the administrations of George W. Bush and Barack Obama,
their opponents in Congress have tried to stop recess appointments almost entirely, and they may have succeeded. When the Senate adjourns
and everyone goes home, an order is entered for "pro forma" sessions
that keep the Senate formally in session, although no business can be conducted because no quorum can be assembled. A single senator stands in
the well of the Senate, "convenes" the body, and adjourns it after a few
seconds. The process is repeated until the real Senate returns. Since the
current Senate has a majority of Democrats, however, why has the majority not stopped the pro forma sessions to let the president make some

recess appointments? The answer is that the House of Representatives, controlled by the Republicans, will not let them. The Constitution provides, in an obscure section, that neither house may adjourn for more than three days without the consent of the other.[137] Therefore, when the *House* adjourns, it forbids the *Senate* to adjourn for more than three days as a way to block recess appointments.

President Obama challenged this practice by making recess appointments during one of the times when the Senate was holding only pro forma sessions. The appointments were necessary to allow two important federal agencies to operate at all. One is the new Consumer Finance Protection Bureau, which was created by the Dodd-Frank Act that responded to the financial crisis of 2008.[138] The others were to the National Labor Relations Board, which enforces the statutes that authorize and regulate unions (it had dropped below a quorum).[139] In both cases, Republicans in Congress have been trying to thwart the implementation of statutes that they oppose by preventing the agencies from taking any legally effective action. Hence Obama could add the force of his faithful execution duty to the rather cloudy recess appointment power.

This controversy led to the first-ever Supreme Court interpretation of the recess appointments clause. In *NLRB v. Noel Canning*, the Court unanimously held that President Obama's recess appointments were ineffective, but split sharply over the rationale.[140] Justice Breyer's majority opinion for five justices began with two conclusions that favored the executive. First, the majority rejected an argument that recess appointments may be made only between the first and second sessions of each Congress (that is, once a year). Modern presidents had often made recess appointments during "intrasession" adjournments within a session, which are frequent and sometimes extend for weeks. Second, the court held that recess appointments could be made for vacancies that had existed during a previous session rather than only for vacancies originating during a recess. Both of these conclusions met strenuous objections on textual and historical grounds from Justice Scalia and three others.

Yet the majority went on to hold that the pro forma sessions of the Senate that were in question did not count as recesses, because the Senate retained the theoretical capacity under its rules to do business (for example under unanimous consent agreements). The majority said that although the three-day adjournments that had occurred in the case were not long enough to constitute recesses in the constitutional sense, a period of about ten days would qualify. Justice Scalia's group objected to the vagueness of this doctrine and thought it would aggrandize executive power. In any event, no justice thought that the president had made valid recess appointments in this case.

The sharp controversy among the justices over historical practice regarding recess appointments demonstrates that no clear constitutional convention had crystallized even after more than two centuries of experience. Justice Scalia objected strongly to the majority's use of an "adverse-possession theory of executive authority" (and of course he disagreed with its application to the facts of the case).[141] He was wrong about the legitimacy of the majority's inquiry. This book has reviewed many kinds of presidential assertions of authority that have been consistent enough and accepted for long enough to deserve deference from the courts.

The *Noel Canning* decision left the president's recess appointments power with little practical utility. As the Bush and Obama presidencies have shown, unless a president has majorities in both houses of Congress, the technique of pro forma sessions of the Senate will be used to block recess appointments. And a president who does have majorities in both houses little needs the power.

In the fall of 2013, an effort to limit the dysfunction of the federal appointments process finally succeeded. For many years, proposals to restrict use of the filibuster for nominations had kicked around in Congress, but they always fell prey to the understanding that today's majority may be tomorrow's minority and to threats of retaliation from the party that currently enjoyed filibuster power. After a series of filibusters blocked nominations to federal appellate courts, the Senate majority erupted in frustration and altered the rules to forbid filibusters of nominations to executive positions and the judiciary, except for the Supreme Court.[142] A predictably furious reaction ensued, but the nation will be better off in the long run if the Senate becomes the majoritarian institution that the Constitution requires it to be.[143]

After the Obama administration's first two years, which featured important legislation addressing the economic crisis and establishing a national medical plan, acrimonious deadlock stifled ordinary legislation. An initial low point occurred in 2011, when the House of Representatives used the need to raise the statutory ceiling on the national debt to accommodate the stimulus as a lever to try to force deep spending cuts. Delicate negotiations between the president and House Speaker John Boehner eventually broke down, with fingers pointing everywhere.[144]

With national default looming, suggestions arose that the president simply ignore the debt limit in favor of enforcing other statutory provisions that appropriated funds. In part, this step would rely on arguments

dating from the *Youngstown* case, that the president has a duty to reconcile conflicts in the statutes.[145] The argument also relied on a heretofore
obscure provision in the Fourteenth Amendment stating that the validity
of the public debt of the United States "shall not be questioned."[146] President Obama rejected these proposals out of hand. The constitutional provision was arguably relevant and controlling—Congress inserted it into
the amendment to foreclose challenges to its Civil War legislation creating
greenback currency and funding pensions.[147] Modern spending legislation
is not fundamentally different. But the president was surely aware that a
practical problem foreclosed any attempt to breach the debt limit. Efforts
by the government to borrow in violation of the limit would be unlikely to
find buyers, given doubts about enforceability of the government's promises to pay. The president and congressional leaders soldiered on.

Congress eventually resolved the crisis for the time being by extending
the debt limit in return for onerous and widespread "sequesters" of spending (that is, budget cuts) to take effect in the future. In an effort to discipline
both branches, Congress was supposing that the approaching deadline for
the unappealing cuts would force another, less draconian compromise. Of
course, no compromise followed, and the sequesters took effect.

Worse was in store. In the fall of 2013, continuing political deadlock
produced a partial shutdown of the government that lasted for sixteen
days and once again threatened default on the national debt. Apparently
chastened by the negative public reaction to this wasteful and debilitating
practice of governing from self-induced crisis to crisis, Congress then managed a small feat of bipartisanship at the end of the year, enacting a budget that will allow the government to operate more normally. Optimism
would be premature. Until a sea change in American politics reduces the
deep partisan conflict that is presently refracted through Congress, it is
difficult to perceive a way out of this mess.

Another story about legislation and litigation has a happier ending.
In 2008, the Obama campaign promised to support equality for gays and
lesbians, but the new president moved quite cautiously on this front.[148] By
the end of 2010, he had enlisted enough military support to obtain repeal
of the "don't ask, don't tell" statute that a temporizing President Clinton
had initiated.[149] The Defense of Marriage Act that Clinton had signed in
1996 presented a greater obstacle. For years, President Obama would not
openly adopt a constitutional interpretation that bans on gay marriage
are unconstitutional. Instead, he attempted an approach like Lincoln's
on slavery—watching the evolution of public opinion while awaiting the

right time to make a commitment. Eventually, Obama instructed his lawyers to abandon their constitutional defense of DOMA in litigation challenging its denial of federal benefits to married gays and lesbians.[150] In mid-2012, the president finally announced his support for gay marriage, but he was following, not leading, the development of this issue. A year later, the Supreme Court invalidated DOMA for infringing constitutionally guaranteed equality.[151] Because the Court's decision did not declare a nationally enforceable fundamental right to gay marriage that would bind the states, however, opportunities remain for presidential leadership on this constitutional issue.

Stymied by a hostile Congress, Obama eventually turned to the traditional presidential response of filling available statutory gaps with executive orders. He announced a "We Can't Wait" campaign of measures as a partial substitute for stalled legislative initiatives.[152] His most important such order invoked prosecutorial discretion to stop deportation proceedings against undocumented young people who had been in the United States since childhood, after Congress had failed to enact legislation to provide relief for them.[153] In an effort to combat climate change, he also ordered the Environmental Protection Agency to move forward with regulations to control power plant emissions of greenhouse gases under existing statutory authority.[154] More comprehensive statutory resolution of the important issues of immigration and climate change awaits a national consensus.

We, the People

Barack Obama's second inaugural address sounded a refrain that "we, the people" had adopted certain broad values that he identified: equality, security, an obligation to posterity. He was engaging in the dialogue that has now continued for two and a quarter centuries, mixing the text of the Constitution, presidential interpretations of it, and the people's responses to both the document and the presidents. Long may this process endure.

Conclusion

The Stream of History

The Constitution of the United States is most significantly not a document but a stream of history. —Felix Frankfurter[1]

Any modern American who would interpret the Constitution faithfully must view it through the stream of history that has flowed into it. Justice Felix Frankfurter, among the most thoughtful American judges, claimed that "the Supreme Court has directed the stream."[2] He was referring to the great battle during the New Deal over the meaning of the commerce clause, a contest in which both justices and the president joined. They were at it once again in the fight over Obamacare, in an argument without end. This book has shown that presidents, while borne along in the stream like the rest of us, have directed it at least as effectively as have the justices. The process is reciprocal—history shapes presidential interpretations, which then guide the future.

Frankfurter's response to Oliver Wendell Holmes's dictum that "continuity with the past is not a duty, it is only a necessity" was that "for judges at least it is . . . not only a necessity but even a duty."[3] This was because "the ties of the Constitution are to the past, and when history calls the justices strain to listen."[4] Holmes had stressed the inescapability of the influence of the past on the present interpreter. Frankfurter was calling on judges to make a self-conscious effort to abide the lessons of history that are crystallized in present understandings of the Constitution. He was invoking the essence of the common-law process of blending continuation and adaptation to form the law.

Presidents, having sworn the same oath as the judges to defend the Constitution, follow an interpretive process that resembles deciding cases but is richer and less constrained than the judicial task. When Barack Obama said that the "last mile" of interpretation depends on what is in the interpreter's "heart," he captured in one word all the main influences on presidential interpretation that I have reviewed in this book: the president's character, experience, and values; the incentives that the office and current politics create; the practical problems that must be solved; and an awareness of the actions of their own predecessors.[5] As presidents gain experience in office and come to understand the uniqueness and complexity of their interpretive responsibilities, it is natural and correct for them to insist that their own departmentalist viewpoint is as legitimate as those of the judges and legislators, each within a sphere assigned by the Constitution.

Both presidents and judges must decide how much guidance to draw from history and how much creativity of their own to add. The great historian Edward Gibbon once said, "I have no way of judging of the future but by the past."[6] Time gone by and time to come are joined by Lincoln's "mystic chords of memory." What we can become is always a function of what we have been. Gibbon's remark, though, identifies a trap: memory can all too easily confine creativity, for presidents no less than others. The stories told in this book reveal that presidents have mostly evaded the trap, being willing to step out onto untrodden ground when their judgment calls on them to do so.

Two personal characteristics have most aided presidents in influencing constitutional development. At the level of goals, presidents need to articulate a firm and clear set of values that the American people will share. Presidents who have reconstructed the politics of their day—and with it the Constitution of their day—have often reached back to restate and reaffirm values they trace to the American founding.[7] Consider Jefferson, Jackson, Lincoln, Franklin Roosevelt, and Reagan. Translation of these goals into constitutional precedent depends more on the gestalt of the president's view about the nature and role of the federal government than it does on his position about the meaning of any particular clause. In selecting means to reach these goals, presidents have been wise to set a pragmatic course that seeks available gains, rather than display a Wilsonian rigidity that courts disaster. An important component of pragmatism is a sense for the strength and limits of available historical precedents.

The Constitution is not a word puzzle to be solved in quiet study but a constituent document whose meaning was contested at its formation and has been ever since.[8] That accounts for both its beauty and its utility.

At any given time, its meaning is a blend of law, politics, and history and is contingent on the necessities that events impose. That is not to say that everything is in flux, however. The ongoing arguments take place in a framework created by what has happened and what issues have been opened or closed by developments in our national life. Presidents, other government officers, and the people all consider the Constitution binding, and because they do, it is. Taking the oath on inauguration day, each president promises to behave within the boundaries of the Constitution as its understanding has come down, with the modifications that he or she can make through personal effort that is accepted by the people.

Presidents generate constitutional law through the process of political ratification that I have traced in this book. Some eminent observers have concluded that modern presidential power is governed solely by political ratification and not by law in any broader sense.[9] This argument omits recognition of the fact that political ratification leads to the development of conventions that bind future presidents within at least broad limits. The precedents that presidents have compiled through their actions are mirrored by a set of precedents that are harder to identify, the roads *not* taken because of presidential judgments that they would exceed constitutional power. There are examples, to be sure. Lincoln denied that he could liberate slaves in regions not in rebellion. No president has claimed a plenary power to attack any other nation anytime at his sole discretion. Presidents usually do not defy clear statutory restrictions without a strong constitutional claim of their own. Hence a largely invisible frame of assumed limitations of power lies somewhere outside the existing set of actions that have been taken and accepted by the people. It has been the role of the president's lawyers to help outline that frame.

Many of our presidents have themselves been lawyers. Has that training improved their constitutional interpretation? Not particularly, because at the level of the presidency interpretation involves so much more than the skills of the tax lawyer or conveyancer. Some of our lawyer-presidents escaped the practice of law for politics at the earliest opportunity (Wilson, Franklin Roosevelt, Clinton). Some have shown scant regard for the rule of law (Jefferson and Franklin Roosevelt at times, Nixon always). The great counterexample is Lincoln, whose long experience as a trial lawyer grounded him in a devotion to actual facts and cogent legal argument.

Let us consider the current state of constitutional law as generated by presidents. First, have we a unitary executive branch headed by a president who enjoys constitutional power to direct and remove officers who execute the law? Yes, to some extent. Presidents have successfully insisted on plenary power to supervise three kinds of executive officers within the limits of discretion that statutes confer. First, from the earliest days, they have exercised full authority over the heads of cabinet departments, and especially the constitutional cabinet (State, Defense, Treasury, Justice).[10]

Second, presidents have always maintained the critical power of civilian control over the military, but not without some very dangerous struggles, especially in the rise of those supreme egotists McClellan and MacArthur. During the early years of the Cold War, presidents resisted constant military pressure to take aggressive action, often involving nuclear weapons. After the searing experience of Vietnam, presidents then struggled to overcome constant military reluctance to take any risky action.

Third, presidents supervise their own White House aides, who coordinate or sometimes execute policy. Through OMB, the institutional presidency now oversees the rest of the increasingly bloated executive branch, employing budgetary controls and the executive order programs for management of regulations.

Yet presidents have conceded two critical features of unitariness to Congress. One is the existence of independent regulatory agencies, in which presidents have acquiesced at least since 1935. The extremely powerful Federal Reserve Board, which has played a central role in financial crises for a century, has a strong claim to be independent of ordinary presidential supervision—the central banks of all developed nations are insulated from political leaders, who tend to inflate the money before elections. Other independent agencies that perform ordinary regulation, such as the Federal Trade Commission, present much less persuasive cases for insulation, but presidents lack the political will to contest their status with Congress.

The other barrier to unitariness is the early (and unavoidable) concession to the Senate of a powerful role in blocking executive and judicial nominations and controlling patronage. Long before the present dysfunction of the confirmation process, the Senate had deeply compromised the prospects of any president to form a politically unified executive branch or to select judges that fit his preferences. We do have the "two-headed monster" for appointments that the framers feared. This explains why presidents exert their command authority down the lines of their clearest constitutional pedigree—over the cabinet, the national security establishment, and their own staff.

Whether Congress and the people acquiesce in or object to presidential actions depends on what information is available to them. Presidents have always kept secrets on their own authority. For many years, executive privilege assertions against Congress were unusual and were resolved through a political process that assumed the routine availability of information, unless it met one of a set of evolving exceptions. Conflict has been sharper in modern times, commencing when Senator Joseph McCarthy sparked presidential assertions of broad power over executive branch information. The sins of Watergate drew attention to the constitutional executive privilege that the Supreme Court recognized, but congressional demands for information remain subject to the tides of politics. Presidents unilaterally assert the state secrets privilege to protect diplomatic and military secrets in litigation. Their record of success in these cases is impressive.

More important is the vast expansion of classification of information after World War II, which attempts to hide large regions of executive activity from everyone. Presidents vary in the transparency of their regimes, but not as much as their rhetoric often suggests—they consistently err on the side of secrecy. The postwar presidents have set classification policy without much input from Congress, relying on some combination of the vesting clause, the commander in chief power, and the faithful execution duty. The same powers, plus the foreign policy powers, account for the continuing efforts of postwar presidents to spy on Americans and foreigners in an effort to identify emerging threats. Congressional attempts to cabin this practice have proved only partly successful.

The core constitutional duty faithfully to execute the laws has received widely variant interpretation depending on how expansively presidents view the role of the federal government and what groups in society they wish to benefit. Lamentably, most presidents have not met this duty vigorously on behalf of relatively powerless people. Some presidents have committed grievous sins against civil liberties (John Adams, Woodrow Wilson, Franklin Roosevelt). Overall, most presidents have not implemented the faithful execution duty in ways that would confirm them as the tribunes of ordinary folk that they so often claim to be. This is because the governing coalitions to which they respond omit the powerless.

The pardon power, which is linked to the faithful execution duty, has always been treated as plenary by presidents. On the positive side, they have employed it to heal social upheavals and to ease the rigors of the criminal law. Less creditably, they have been known to spew forth political favors at the end of their tenure and to protect themselves by pardoning their aides.

The power of the president in the legislative process soon departed from the original understanding in two fundamental particulars. Under the Federalist presidents, the constitutional power to recommend legislation lay dormant because of traditional fears of "corrupting" the sensitive legislators. Jefferson subtly demonstrated the potential for presidential management of legislation, but this power remained underdeveloped until the premodern presidencies of Theodore Roosevelt and Wilson awoke it and Franklin Roosevelt made it an indispensable part of the presidency. Lyndon Johnson, the master of Congress, demonstrated its ultimate reach and its power to help the oppressed.

The president's veto also remained undeveloped until Andrew Jackson transformed it in his war against the Bank, while declaring the independence of his interpretive power from that of the other branches. Ever since, the veto has given presidents great power within Congress, which tries to write bills that the president will accept. (Experience soon proved the difficulty of override, especially once the party system matured.) A strong veto power gives the president's national coalition a way to offset the more parochial concerns that often best Congress.

Development of the president's powers within Congress fostered the maturation of the important power of interstitial legislation through executive orders, because presidents are usually able to forestall statutory overrides of these initiatives. The orders dwell in the twilight zone where Congress has neither clearly authorized nor clearly forbidden executive action. Not surprisingly, it was the audacious Theodore Roosevelt who first demonstrated the capacity of this power as he added conservation to the list of values that American government was committed to pursuing. As the administrative state has grown, the executive order power has grown with it as presidents attempt to harmonize the myriad statutes and to pursue their own programs without new legislation.

Foreign policy powers immediately gravitated to the presidential office, with its powerful natural advantages in exercising them. Washington himself assumed the powers to negotiate treaties in secret, to present them to the Senate for its consent but not advice, and to interpret existing treaties. The executive agreement made an immediate appearance as an escape from the Senate's treaty ratification power, as did the president's sole discretion to recognize the true government of another nation. The use of statutes to avoid the supermajority barrier in the Senate for ratification developed later and is firmly entrenched now.

The basic constitutional pattern in foreign affairs that "the president proposes and Congress disposes" soon emerged. Presidents have long formulated and executed their personal foreign policy, pursuing any course that does not clearly violate existing treaties and statutes. Congress, reduced to a frustrated and reactive stance, tried to get even in its long period of refusing its consent to treaties, capped by breaking Wilson's heart. As Congress attempted to dictate foreign policy on the eve of World War II, FDR showed how a crafty president could dance at the edge of statutes while drawing public opinion his way. After the war, the atomic bomb and the Cold War engendered the national security establishment that has permanently expanded institutional presidential power.

The Constitution's structural tension between the war power of Congress and the president's designation as commander in chief began to migrate toward an executive center of gravity early on, when Jefferson claimed to be deferring to Congress as he pursued the pirates. The decisive break was Polk's deployment of the Army in harm's way in what he called southern Texas and the defenders called Mexico. As the young Lincoln understood, this put it in the power of one man to initiate war through provocation. Lincoln's own greatest emergency actions in the cauldron of the Civil War, the suspension of habeas corpus and the Emancipation Proclamation, were both legally sound in the circumstances. The question ever since has been their utility as precedents for crises less stark. The period through World War I saw constant presidential adventuring with the troops, with Theodore Roosevelt taking the palm by detaching Panama from Colombia for his canal.

The stakes rose after World War II, when the threat of Armageddon emboldened presidents. John Kennedy's unilateral conduct of the Cuban missile crisis appeared to signify that we must allow presidents to serve as temporary constitutional dictators with the fate of the nation or the world in their hands when time and circumstance grant no alternatives. Harry Truman's commitment of troops to Korea without Congress stands as the modern high-water mark of unilateral presidential initiation of hostilities. Later presidents appear to have receded somewhat, having learned some lessons from the tribulations Truman encountered as the war went along. Lyndon Johnson got his initial, fuzzy endorsement for hostilities in Vietnam, but his record of unilateralism and duplicity in conducting the war forfeited the support of both Congress and the people. Richard Nixon, by doubling down on both of LBJ's sins, brought on both his own demise and the congressional risorgimento that asserted control of the "imperial presidency" in so many fields. Later on, the presidents Bush sought congressional authorization for the Persian Gulf wars (over the objections of the obdurate Cheney).

Presidential power has shown its resilience by recovering from the triple traumas of Vietnam, Watergate, and legislation. Presidents have only fitfully obeyed the War Powers Resolution, and Congress has found no better response than complaining. The junior President Bush was even allowed to forget the lessons of Vietnam by fomenting an unnecessary war against Iraq through deception. In the more necessary war, the one against terror, Bush followed his instincts and his advisers into claims of exclusive executive power that were eventually rejected by both Congress and the Supreme Court.

Once shorn of early excesses, claims to executive powers of detention and military trial of terror suspects appear to have stabilized legally. President Obama has followed the precedents of Bush sober on these issues. The question of interrogation—torture—has not settled into any reliable precedent, despite wide rejection of the early Bush practices and Obama's retreat from them. Obama has proved more aggressive in pursuing terrorists than many would have expected, with his expansion of targeted killings. These two presidents have groped for the most effective approach and have called it constitutional. Congress, the courts, and the public follow gingerly along.

Presidents have always taken a stance on the trade-off between national security and individual liberty that lies at the heart of so many national debates. Presidents have consistently favored security over liberty in their calculations. From their point of view, the hazards of a successful blow to the nation naturally loom larger than the costs of temporary incursions on the liberty of some citizens.

It is surprising that there has not been more presidentially initiated repression of dissent in our history. The two worst instances, the sedition controversy under John Adams and the rampage under Wilson, produced enough eventual condemnation to be unthinkable today. Cold War repression was generated by congressional and public hysteria, while presidents tended to brake it a bit.

From the Vietnam era onward, threats to civil liberties from presidents have usually involved their spying on persons who might be subversives or terrorists. As the surveillance capacity of the government multiplies in the cyber age, executive power increases with it, as does the threat of abuse. Because the legitimacy of our system depends so fundamentally on the assent of the people and their representatives to what the executive does, its power to look out upon the people while preventing them from looking in at it presents a central dilemma for our times.

Reviewing all this history, no one should be surprised that an officer who is so largely allowed to define his own powers would do so in an expansive way. The scope of permissible change in the precedents has narrowed somewhat over time, as it does for accretive judicial precedent. Yet the capacity for generation of new lines of precedent is still there, as the war on terror and cyber warfare demonstrate. Presidents can form new precedents far more quickly and easily than the other two branches, which are headed by institutions, not an individual.

As the nation reaches the milestone of 225 years under its Constitution, perhaps the time is ripe for some amendments to reflect experience. Thoughtful observers have suggested many possible improvements.[11] I confess to considerable risk aversion regarding constitutional amendment. This book has shown our government's capacity for adjustment, within limits, to meet the need for change. And every lawyer knows how easy it is for "reform" to make things worse. All that said, the preceding pages suggest at least two simple amendments that could reduce or eliminate present problems.

First, the Electoral College had outlived its usefulness by 1800 and has caused nothing but trouble since. The election crises of 1800, 1824, 1876, and 2000 have demonstrated the Electoral College's capacity to defeat majority rule and its potential to spawn future crises. Given the difficulty of amending the Constitution, though, a work-around may be best. Article I, section 10, of the Constitution authorizes interstate compacts with the assent of Congress. If states holding a majority of votes in the Electoral College pledged to require their electors to vote for the winner of the national election, no constitutional amendment would be necessary.[12]

Second, the constitutional shadow that presidents cast with Supreme Court nominations is too long, and the process of confirming justices is too conflicted. Replacing life tenure with a set term, such as eighteen years, would ameliorate these problems by reducing the stakes.[13] If abolition of life tenure reduced current levels of judicial hubris, that would be a good thing too. This change would require an amendment, and it is difficult to perceive a groundswell of support for it.

Another constitutional dilemma is the role of the vice president.[14] We have seen that the selection of vice presidents is driven by stark electoral considerations, producing wide variability in the quality of those chosen.

Not surprisingly, presidential mortality has produced wide variability in the performance of those succeeding to the office. Moreover, because vice presidential candidates are selected precisely because they are not clones of the presidential candidates, there is likely to be a substantial departure from the dead president's policies and constitutional stances. The disaster of Andrew Johnson proves that point. Mediocrities have abounded. John Tyler self-destructed, Millard Fillmore is a trivia question, Chester Arthur won by exceeding low expectations, Calvin Coolidge cruised through the twenties. Then again, we have had Theodore Roosevelt, Harry Truman, and Lyndon Johnson. But this is a lottery the nation could easily lose again.

Could adjustments to the constitutional text improve the operation of presidential succession? Consider the history of the Twenty-Second Amendment, which codified the two-term tradition. It has had the unfortunate effect of rendering reelected presidents lame ducks, shorn of some kinds of power and accountability. But it appears to have improved the quality of vice presidents somewhat, by confining the time spent waiting in line for the presidency.[15] Thus unambiguous gains are hard to realize by the amendment process.

Supposing, as we must, that outright constitutional change is unlikely, what is the constitutional state of the presidency? I think the office acceptably meets the needs of the United States in the twenty-first century. The most sensitive points concern powers for war or other national emergencies. The unresolved tension between the congressional power to declare war and the president's power as commander in chief is ultimately beneficial, because it leaves articulation of the border to politics and precedent, where it belongs. Presidents should remain free to commit the troops to hostilities that do not clearly constitute war in the constitutional sense. But presidents should obey the sixty-day limit to such commitments in the War Powers Resolution, to bring both political branches into play in a timely fashion.

In situations of ultimate emergency, such as the Cuban missile crisis, our Constitution confers a temporary power of emergency response on the president, as it should. To that extent, he or she is a constitutional dictator, free of proximate restraints but subject to legal responses, such as impeachment, after the fact. Even in ordinary times, our system has recently become similar enough to a permanent constitutional dictatorship to give deep pause. A massive and secret national security bureaucracy supports secret presidential decisions to use force or spy on the world, with only loose controls in congressional or judicial oversight and little public knowledge. The primary constitutional challenge for our time is to construct ways to respond to this development.

The best model for presidential interpretation of the Constitution is still Abraham Lincoln. His exercise of the Lockean prerogative during the emergency of the Civil War was always lawyerly. Grounding his use of power in constitutional text, he never claimed a free-ranging power to do anything that might save the Union. By contrast, the danger that lies in the ever-fashionable Hamiltonian arguments for "inherent" executive power to do whatever the nation needs is precisely that they are not anchored in the text, including its limitations. This prevents the informed dialogue that can ensue when a president claims a particular power under the Constitution's text.

Let us conclude on a hopeful note. Envision the best day in the history of the presidency. It is April 4, 1865. Abraham Lincoln is walking down the street in ruined Richmond, holding the hand of his young son, a guard of soldiers trailing behind, and on all sides freed slaves are joyously reaching out to him. He is just completing his redemption of promises of liberty and equality that this nation made not in the Constitution but in the Declaration of Independence, and is bequeathing a new nation to us all.[16] Hence part of his legacy is the demonstration that not all presidential conceptions of the nation and its Constitution stand on equal footing. A president's highest attainment is, like Lincoln's, to transcend ordinary politics and to set the United States on a better course. Toward that horizon there always lies untrodden ground.

Acknowledgments

B ecause this book reflects my work in separation-of-powers law for decades, my debts for it are deep and diffuse. Among legal academic colleagues, Sandy Levinson, Peter Shane, and Peter Strauss influenced these pages pervasively. At Colorado Law, my successors as dean, David Getches and Phil Weiser, were unfailingly supportive, as were faculty and library colleagues and my student research assistants (especially Brent Owen, Courtney Krause, Rosa Trembour, and Anna Uhls). Gatherings at the universities of Maryland and Richmond road tested the project. At the University of Chicago Press, editors David Pervin and Christopher Rhodes and copy mavens George Roupe and Yvonne Zipter have improved the book while humoring its author. I thank the two anonymous manuscript readers who provided careful and astute critiques.

My labors were eased by the moral support of friends in Boulder, Aspen, and Magnolia. At home, Sherry and Annie gracefully endured my many hours of absence, as did faithful Boomer. Above all, I thank my beloved wife Sherry and dedicate this book to her. One love, one lifetime.

Notes

Introduction

1. Speech at a Dinner of the Harvard Law School Association (June 25, 1895), in The Essential Holmes: Selections from the Letters, Speeches, Judicial Opinions, and Other Writings of Oliver Wendell Holmes, Jr. 184 (Richard A. Posner ed., 1992).

2. Article II, § 1 requires a new president to swear or affirm "that I will faithfully execute the Office of President of the United States, and will to the best of my Ability, preserve, protect, and defend the Constitution of the United States."

3. Because the first forty-four presidents have been men, I usually use the masculine pronoun in this book, with hopeful awareness that on January 20, 2017, the nation will have another opportunity to make it "she." For the importance of presidential interpretation, see Akhil Reed Amar, America's Constitution: A Biography, ch. 5 (2005).

4. I count about twenty-five major Supreme Court precedents on presidential power in the course of over 220 years of our history; they set only loose limits on the executive's interpretive freedom. See Peter M. Shane & Harold H. Bruff, Separation of Powers Law: Cases and Materials (3d ed. 2011).

5. For example, Judge Benjamin Cardozo's great decision in *MacPherson v. Buick Motor Co.*, 111 N.E. 1050 (N.Y. 1916), allowed consumers to sue manufacturers directly for defective products, abandoning the existing requirement that the consumer have a direct contractual relation with the manufacturer. It was soon accepted as new common law.

6. Jack Goldsmith, Power and Constraint: The Accountable Presidency after 9/11 26 (2012).

7. Stephen Skowronek, The Politics Presidents Make: Leadership from John Adams to George Bush (1993), and Presidential Leadership in Political Time: Reprise and Reappraisal (2d ed. 2011).

8. Michael J. Gerhardt, The Forgotten Presidents: Their Untold Constitutional Legacy, chs. 2–5 (2013).

9. "I claim not to have controlled events, but confess plainly that events have controlled me." Letter to Albert G. Hodges (April 4, 1864), 7 Collected Works of Abraham Lincoln 281 (Roy Basler ed., 1953).

10. By "the people" or "the public" I will mean the segments of American society to which a president responds at a given time: elites (including the press), powerful interest groups, members of the president's political party (and some members of the opposition), and likely voters in the next election. Left out are the politically powerless, typically including racial and ethnic minorities, women (until the suffrage movement succeeded in 1920), and the poor.

11. Barry Friedman, The Will of the People: How Public Opinion Has Influenced the Supreme Court and Shaped the Meaning of the Constitution (2009); Lucas A. Powe Jr., The Supreme Court and the American Elite, 1789–2008 (2009).

12. H. Jefferson Powell, A Community Built on Words: The Constitution in History and Politics 6 (2002).

13. Id., 204.

14. E.g., Antonin Scalia, A Matter of Interpretation (1997).

15. E.g., Steven G. Calabresi & Christopher S. Yoo, The Unitary Executive: Presidential Power from Washington to Bush (2008).

16. E.g., John Yoo, Crisis and Command: The History of Executive Power from George Washington to George W. Bush (2009).

17. H. Jefferson Powell, The President's Authority over Foreign Affairs: An Essay in Constitutional Interpretation (2002).

18. For a fine analysis of the tension between presidential initiative and accountability, see Harold J. Krent, Presidential Powers (2005).

19. H. L. A. Hart, The Concept of Law (2d ed. 1994).

20. Kenneth Wheare, Modern Constitutions 179 (1951), quoted in Geoffrey Marshall, Constitutional Conventions: The Rules and Forms of Political Accountability 7 (1984). I believe this to be a standard ("conventional"!) definition of legal conventions.

21. See Keith E. Whittington, Constitutional Construction: Divided Powers and Constitutional Meaning, ch. 1 (1999).

22. See Sanford Levinson, Constitutional Faith (1988).

23. For exploration of these possibilities by leading scholars, see Bruce Ackerman, The Decline and Fall of the American Republic (2010); Sanford Levinson, Our Undemocratic Constitution: Where the Constitution Goes Wrong (and How We the People Can Correct It) (2008).

24. The Path of the Law (1897), in Collected Legal Papers 194–95 (1920).

Chapter One

1. 1 Max Farrand, The Records of the Federal Convention of 1787, 65 (rev. ed. 1966).

2. This chapter draws from Harold H. Bruff, Balance of Forces: Separation of Powers Law in the Administrative State, ch. 1 (2006).

3. Forrest McDonald, The American Presidency: An Intellectual History 92 (1994).

4. Jack Rakove, Original Meanings: Politics and Ideas in the Making of the Constitution (1997); Gordon S. Wood, The Creation of the American Republic, 1776–1787 (1969), and The Radicalism of the American Revolution (1993).

5. The Classick Pages: Classical Reading of Eighteenth-Century Americans (Meyer Reinhold ed., 1975).

6. Garry Wills, Explaining America: The Federalist (1981).

7. For intellectual histories of the development of separation of powers, see M. J. C. Vile, Constitutionalism and the Separation of Powers (1967); and William B. Gwyn, The Meaning of the Separation of Powers: An Analysis of the Doctrine from Its Origin to the Adoption of the United States Constitution (1965).

8. Scott Gordon, Controlling the State: Constitutionalism from Ancient Athens to Today 6 & n.4 (1999); M. N. S. Sellers, American Republicanism: Roman Ideology in the United States Constitution 69–70 (1994).

9. Maurice Ashley, England in the Seventeenth Century (1952); Christopher Hill, The Century of Revolution, 1603–1714 (1961); 2 Simon Schama, A History of Britain: The Wars of the British 1603–1776 (2001).

10. The standard modern edition, with a good introduction, is by Peter Laslett (rev. ed. 1988). For a biography, see Maurice Cranston, John Locke (1985).

11. Second Treatise of Government, ch. 12, § 143, quoted in Laslett, Two Treatises, 364.

12. Id., ch. 14, §§ 159–60 (Laslett, 374–75).

13. Id., ch. 14, §§ 164–68 (Laslett, 377–80).

14. Id., ch. 14, § 166 (Laslett, 378).

15. The classic analysis is Clinton Rossiter, Constitutional Dictatorship: Crisis Government in the Modern Democracies (1948). For an updated treatment, see Sanford Levinson & Jack M. Balkin, *Constitutional Dictatorship: Its Dangers and Its Design*, 94 Minn. L. Rev. 101 (2010).

16. Rossiter, Constitutional Dictatorship, ch. 2; see Levinson & Balkin, *Constitutional Dictatorship*, 103 n.10.

17. His work is often caricatured. For a fine analysis, see Philip Bobbitt, The Garments of Court and Palace: Machiavelli and the World That He Made (2013).

18. Levinson & Balkin, *Constitutional Dictatorship*, 113–16.

19. The standard modern edition is The Spirit of the Laws (Anne M. Cohler, Basia C. Miller & Harold S. Stone eds., 1989).

20. Spirit of the Laws, bk. 11, ch. 6.

21. Charles C. Thach, The Creation of the Presidency, 1775–1789, 27 n.3 (1923).

22. Willi P. Adams, The First American Constitutions: Republican Ideology and the Making of the State Constitutions in the Revolutionary Era (1980).

23. Wood, Creation, 138–40.

24. Gordon S. Wood, Empire of Liberty: A History of the Early Republic, 1789–1815, at 32 (2009).

25. Bernard Bailyn, The Ideological Origins of the American Revolution 35–36 (1967).

26. McDonald, American Presidency, 157.

27. 2 Farrand, Records, 342–43.

28. Forrest McDonald, Novus Ordo Seclorum: The Intellectual Origins of the Constitution 250 (1985).

29. 2 Farrand, Records, 500.

30. Article II of the Committee of Detail's draft constitution had stated that "the Government shall consist of supreme legislative, executive, and judicial powers." Morris, writing the final version, "eliminated this entirely, and simply began his first three articles by announcing that 'all legislative powers,' 'the executive power,' and 'the judicial power' shall be vested in a Congress, a president, and the courts." Richard Brookhiser, Gentleman Revolutionary: Gouverneur Morris, the Rake Who Wrote the Constitution 89–90 (2003).

31. Rakove, Meanings, 130.

32. Vile, Separation of Powers, 153–54.

33. Andrew Rudalevige, The New Imperial Presidency: Renewing Presidential Power after Watergate 28 (2005).

34. Russell K. Osgood, Early Versions and Practices of Separation of Powers: A Comment, 30 William & Mary L. Rev. 209, 284–85 (1989).

35. Art. I, § 9. This authority is listed among congressional powers but is phrased in the passive, leaving room for doubt whether only Congress may exercise it.

36. Thach, Creation, 171.

37. Harold H. Bruff, The Federalist Papers: The Framers Construct an Orrery, 16 Harv. J. of Law & Pub. Pol. 7 (1993).

38. The quotation in text is from The Federalist No. 51 (Madison). The Benjamin F. Wright edition of 1961 has a good introduction.

39. In No. 72, Hamilton chimed in by arguing that eligibility for reelection would temper a president's abuse of office: "his avarice might be a guard upon his avarice."

40. Gwyn, Meaning, 124–27.

41. In No. 55, Madison answered fears of corruption by stressing the incompatibility and ineligibility clauses.

42. Pauline Maier, Ratification: The People Debate the Constitution, 1787–1788 (2010); Herbert J. Storing, What the Anti-Federalists Were For: The Political Thought of the Opponents of the Constitution (1981).

43. Forrest McDonald, E Pluribus Unum: The Formation of the American Republic, 1776–1790, at 211–29 (1965).

44. Maier, Ratification, 231. At 266, she reports Patrick Henry's famous fear that the presidency "squints toward monarchy." Consequently, three states proposed term limits for the president.

45. Mark A. Graber, Dred Scott and the Problem of Constitutional Evil, pt. 2 (2006).

46. "Some words are confined to their history; some are starting points for history." *United States v. Lovett*, 328 U.S. 303, 331 (1946) (Frankfurter, J., concurring).

47. *Youngstown Sheet & Tube Co. v. Sawyer*, 343 U.S. 579, 642 (1952) (Jackson, J., concurring).

48. The quoted phrase is from The Federalist No. 69, in which Hamilton distinguishes the president from the English monarch, who could declare war unilaterally.

49. Leonard W. Levy, Original Intent and the Framers' Constitution 37 (1988).

50. Goldsmith, Power and Constraint, 209.

51. David A. Strauss, The Living Constitution 1 (2010).

52. Akhil R. Amar, America's Unwritten Constitution: The Precedents and Principles We Live By, ch. 1 (2012).

53. 1 William Blackstone, Commentaries on the Laws of England *59–62.

54. The amendment also moved the presidential inaugural date to January 20.

Chapter Two

1. 2 The Papers of George Washington: Presidential Series 173 (Dorothy Twohig ed., 1987).

2. Ralph Ketcham, Presidents above Party: The First American Presidency, 1789–1829, at 8 (1984), says that in 1789, "far from everything being settled, virtually nothing was."

3. Akhil Reed Amar, America's Unwritten Constitution: The Precedents and Principles We Live By, ch. 8 (2012).

4. H. Jefferson Powell, A Community Built on Words: The Constitution in History and Politics (2002). In The Federalist No. 37, Madison said: "All new laws, though penned with the greatest technical skill, and passed on the fullest and most mature deliberation, are considered as more or less obscure and equivocal, until their meaning be liquidated and ascertained by a series of particular discussions and adjudications." In No. 82, Hamilton concurred: "The erection of a new government, whatever care or wisdom may distinguish the work, cannot fail to originate questions of intricacy and nicety. . . . 'Tis time only that can mature and perfect so compound a system, can liquidate the meaning of all the parts, and can adjust them to each other in a harmonious and consistent WHOLE."

5. Glenn A. Phelps, George Washington and American Constitutionalism viii (1993). This section of the chapter draws on Phelps's book.

6. 2 Papers of Washington, 173–77.

7. Gordon S. Wood, The Creation of the American Republic, 1776–1789 (1969), sees the founding period as one of transition from republicanism to Lockean liberalism. Thomas L. Pangle, The Spirit of Modern Republicanism: The Moral Vision of the American Founders and the Philosophy of Locke (1988), finds Lockean principles dominant throughout. Others, e.g., Drew R. McCoy, The Elusive

Republic: Political Economy in Jeffersonian America (1980), find the transition later, in Jeffersonian times.

8. For assessments of Washington's character, see Ron Chernow, Washington: A Life (2010); Richard Norton Smith, Patriarch: George Washington and the New American Nation (1993).

9. Washington's "genius was his judgment." Joseph J. Ellis, His Excellency: George Washington 271 (2004).

10. Forrest McDonald, The Presidency of George Washington ix (1974).

11. Forrest McDonald, The American Presidency: An Intellectual History 213 (1994).

12. Gordon S. Wood, Empire of Liberty: A History of the Early Republic, 1789–1815, ch. 2 (2009) (titled "A Monarchical Republic").

13. Ron Chernow, Alexander Hamilton (2004).

14. Wood, Empire, 65.

15. Pauline Maier, Ratification: The People Debate the Constitution, 1787–1788, epilogue (2010).

16. Hollingsworth v. Virginia, 3 Dall. 378 (1798).

17. Harold J. Krent, Presidential Powers 17–19 (2005).

18. Phelps, Constitutionalism, 152.

19. David P. Currie, The Constitution in Congress, The Federalist Period, 1789–1801, at 296 (1997).

20. Gerhard Casper, Separating Power: Essays on the Founding Period 41–44 (1997).

21. Leonard D. White, The Federalists: A Study in Administrative History, chs. 6, 10–12 (1948).

22. Unlike State and War, for Treasury there was no explicit power in the president to assign the secretary added duties or to direct the performance of those assigned by statute. Instead, Congress specified the internal structure of Treasury in detail, creating a comptroller, auditor, treasurer, and other officers, specifying the duties of each. This structure remained intact throughout the Federalist period.

23. Charles A. Miller, The Supreme Court and the Uses of History, ch. 4 (1969); Currie, Constitution in Congress, 36–41.

24. 1 Annals of Congress 499 (1789).

25. Lawrence Lessig & Cass R. Sunstein, The President and the Administration, 94 Colum. L. Rev. 1, 25–29 (1994).

26. 1 Annals of Congress 611–12 (1789).

27. Stephen G. Calabresi & Christopher S. Yoo, The Unitary Executive: Presidential Power from Washington to Bush 56–57 (2008).

28. He later recanted this uncharacteristic view.

29. Wood, Empire, 87.

30. White, Federalists, 27.

31. Chernow, Washington, 596.

32. Kenneth R. Mayer, With the Stroke of a Pen: Executive Orders and Presidential Power 51 (2001). The first such order, in June 1789, called on heads of offices to submit reports to the president.

33. Jerry L. Mashaw, Creating the Administrative Constitution: The Lost One Hundred Years of American Administrative Law, pt. 1 (2012).

34. Currie, Constitution in Congress, 68, 81. The first yearly appropriation for the War Department was $137,000; the nation was defended by 672 soldiers.

35. White, Federalists, 253–56. By 1801, there were 3,000 federal employees, with only about 150 of them in Washington.

36. The "inferior officers" clause in Article II allows Congress to vest appointment of inferior officers in the president without Senate confirmation, in department heads, or (sometimes) in the courts.

37. Wood, Empire, 107–10.

38. McDonald, American Presidency, 224–25.

39. White, Federalists, 83–87.

40. Chernow, Washington, 591.

41. Id., 717–18.

42. Phelps, Constitutionalism, 167–72.

43. Curtis A. Bradley & Martin S. Flaherty, *Executive Power Essentialism and Foreign Affairs*, 102 Mich. L. Rev. 545, 631–32 (2004).

44. *To the Senate (August 22, 1789)*, 3 The Papers of George Washington: Presidential Series 521–25 (Dorothy Twohig ed., 1989).

45. Later presidents have sometimes sought the Senate's advance advice in writing. McDonald, American Presidency, 386. Of course, presidents often consult informally with individual senators regarding issues in a treaty negotiation.

46. Nancy V. Baker, Conflicting Loyalties: Law and Politics in the Attorney General's Office, 1789–1990 (1992); see also Susan Low Bloch, *The Early Role of the Attorney General in Our Constitutional Scheme: In the Beginning There Was Pragmatism*, 1989 Duke L. J. 561. The Judiciary Act, ch. 20, § 35, 1 Stat. 73, 92–93 (1789), says:

> And there shall be appointed a meet person, learned in the law, to act as attorney general for the United States, . . . whose duty it shall be to . . . give his advice and opinion upon all questions of law when required by the President of the United States, or when requested by the heads of any of the departments, touching any matters that may concern their departments.

47. Bloch, *Early Role*, 567. This provision was deleted for unknown reasons.

48. For a biography, see John J. Reardon, Edmund Randolph: A Biography (1974). Washington later implemented the "decision of 1789" by firing Randolph, who had become secretary of state, for some improprieties concerning France.

49. Harold H. Bruff, Bad Advice: Bush's Lawyers in the War on Terror, ch. 4 (2009).

50. Stanley Elkins & Eric McKitrick, The Age of Federalism: The Early American Republic, 1788–1800, at 232 (1993). The opinions are reprinted in H. Jefferson Powell, The Constitution and the Attorneys General 3–9 (1999).

51. Chernow, Hamilton, 352–53.

52. Leonard W. Levy, Original Intent and the Framers' Constitution 21 (1988); Drew R. McCoy, The Last of the Fathers: James Madison and the Republican Legacy 80–81 (1989).

53. McCulloch v. Maryland, 17 U.S. (4 Wheat.) 316 (1819).

54. See chapter 4.

55. Wood, Empire, ch. 4. John Marshall thought that the debate over the Bank led to formation of the two political parties. Jean Edward Smith, John Marshall: Definer of a Nation 170 (1996).

56. McDonald, Presidency of Washington, 48.

57. Jon Meacham, Thomas Jefferson: The Art of Power, ch. 25 & p. 265 (2012).

58. George C. Herring, From Colony to Superpower: U.S. Foreign Relations since 1776, ch. 2 (2008).

59. Id., 58.

60. Powell, Community, 13–21.

61. For histories of the crisis, see Elkins & McKitrick, Age of Federalism, ch. 8; H. Jefferson Powell, The President's Authority over Foreign Affairs 47–54 (2002); Wood, Empire, 181–89.

62. For analysis of the legal issues, see Martin S. Flaherty, The Story of the Neutrality Controversy: Struggling over Presidential Power outside the Courts, in Presidential Power Stories 21 (Christopher H. Schroeder & Curtis A. Bradley eds., 2009).

63. Chernow, Hamilton, 435.

64. To the Cabinet (April 18, 1793), in 12 The Papers of George Washington: Presidential Series 452–53 (Christine S. Patrick & John C. Pinheiro eds., 2005).

65. Robert J. Reinstein, Recognition: A Case Study on the Original Understanding of Executive Power, 45 U. Richmond L. Rev. 801 (2011).

66. Restatement (Third) of the Foreign Relations Law of the United States § 204 (1987).

67. Neutrality Proclamation (April 22, 1793), 12 Papers of Washington, 472–73.

68. Genet, however, escaped the blade. He stayed in America, became a citizen, married the daughter of New York's governor George Clinton, and lived out the life of a gentleman. This feat of survivorship must have impressed even the world champion at that sport, Talleyrand.

69. For excerpts from the letters and Madison's answering letters, see Peter M. Shane & Harold H. Bruff, Separation of Powers Law: Cases and Materials, ch. 5 (3d ed. 2011).

70. Flaherty, Neutrality Controversy, 42.

71. *Letter from Thomas Jefferson to the Justices of the Supreme Court (July 18, 1793)*, in 26 The Papers of Thomas Jefferson 520 (John C. Catanzariti ed., 1995); *Questions for the Supreme Court*, id., 534–35.

72. *Letter of the Justices of the Supreme Court to George Washington (August 8, 1793)*, in 13 The Papers of George Washington: Presidential Series 392 (Christine S. Patrick ed. 2007). See 1 Charles Warren, The Supreme Court in United States History 108–11 (1923).

73. Currie, Constitution in Congress, 180–81.

74. *Message to the United States Senate and House of Representatives (December 3, 1793)*, in 14 The Papers of George Washington: Presidential Series 462–67 (David R. Hoth ed., 2008).

75. 4 Annals of Cong. 17–18 (1793). The House referred to its "approbation and pleasure," saying the proclamation was justified by the president's duty of faithful execution of the laws. Id., 138 (1793).

76. 1 Stat. 381 (1794), now 18 U.S.C. § 959.

77. Wallace McClure, International Executive Agreements: Democratic Procedure under the Constitution of the United States (1941).

78. Id., 43–44.

79. Louis Fisher, The Politics of Executive Privilege, chs. 1–2 (2004).

80. For the Jay Treaty, see Elkins & McKitrick, Age of Federalism, ch. 9.

81. Herring, Colony to Superpower, 81.

82. Chernow, Washington, ch. 60. When the House demanded the negotiating papers, Washington declared he would "resist the principle" they were seeking to establish. Id., at 741. See Fisher, Executive Privilege, 33–39.

83. *To the House of Representatives (March 30, 1796)*, in Writings: George Washington 930–32 (John Rhodehamel ed., 1997).

84. Joseph M. Lynch, Negotiating the Constitution: The Earliest Debates over Original Intent (1999).

85. Elkins & McKitrick, Age of Federalism, ch. 10.

86. *Proclamation Calling Forth the Militia (August 7, 1794)*, in Writings, 870–73.

87. Phelps, Constitutionalism, 127–35.

88. In Federalist No. 74, Hamilton noted the utility of the pardon power for easing public disorders.

89. Jeffrey Crouch, The Presidential Pardon Power (2009).

90. Michele Landis Dauber, The Sympathetic State: Disaster Relief and the Origins of the American Welfare State 24 (2013).

91. Art. I, § 8.

92. Wood, Empire, 126–28.

93. E.g., id., 206. For overall assessments, see Chernow, Washington, 770–71 ("He was the perfect figure to reconcile Americans to a vigorous executive"); Elkins & McKitrick, Age of Federalism, 516–17 ("The presidency of George Washington was more like a 'reign' than anything we have had since").

94. *Farewell Address (September 19, 1796)*, in Writings, 962–77.

95. Ketcham, Presidents above Party; Phelps, Constitutionalism.

96. Wood, Empire, 37, 42, 78, 207.

97. Id., 524–25.

98. See David G. McCullough, John Adams (2001); Ralph A. Brown, The Presidency of John Adams (1975).

99. Wood, Empire, ch. 7.

100. Powell, President's Authority, 77–88.

101. Eventually, he did so, and they hung him.

102. 10 Annals of Congress 596–618 (1800).

103. Geoffrey R. Stone, Perilous Times: Free Speech in Wartime from the Sedition Act of 1798 to the War on Terrorism, ch. 1 (2004).

104. Wood, Empire, 253.

105. James F. Simon, What Kind of Nation: Thomas Jefferson, John Marshall, and the Epic Struggle to Create a United States (2002).

Chapter Three

1. *Letter to John C. Breckenridge (August 12, 1803)*, 9 The Writings of Thomas Jefferson 244 (Paul L. Ford ed., 1898).

2. For histories of Thomas Jefferson's presidency, see Forrest McDonald, The Presidency of Thomas Jefferson (1976); Leonard D. White, The Jeffersonians: A Study in Administrative History, 1801–1829 (1959).

3. Jeremy D. Bailey, Thomas Jefferson and Executive Power xiii (2007).

4. Susan Dunn, Jefferson's Second Revolution: The Election Crisis of 1800 and the Triumph of Republicanism (2004).

5. Bruce Ackerman, The Failure of the Founding Fathers: Jefferson, Marshall, and the Rise of Presidential Democracy 85 (2005).

6. Bailey, Jefferson and Power, ch. 8; Akhil Reed Amar, America's Constitution: A Biography, ch. 9 (2005). Because he was an interested party and because it was his nature, Jefferson stayed behind the scenes as the amendment was formulated and ratified.

7. During Jefferson's presidency the presidential electors were usually chosen by the state legislatures, not by the people directly. Jefferson's popularity, however, was great enough to collapse the distinction. By the dawn of the age of Jackson, the nation was turning to the direct choice of electors by the voters.

8. Ralph Ketcham, *The Jefferson Presidency and Constitutional Beginnings*, in The Constitution and the American Presidency 5 (Martin L. Fausold & Alan Shank eds., 1991).

9. Thus Jefferson claimed that he alone could "command a view of the whole ground," because he represented the nation and not a state or district. *First Inaugural Address (March 4, 1801)*, in 1 A Compilation of the Messages and Papers of the Presidents 309, 324 (James D. Richardson ed., 1925).

10. Stephen Skowronek, The Politics Presidents Make: Leadership from John Adams to George Bush 71 (1993); David N. Mayer, The Constitutional Thought of Thomas Jefferson, ch. 5 (1995).

11. Ketcham, *Jefferson Presidency*; see also Bailey, Jefferson and Power; Mayer, Constitutional Thought.

12. Daniel J. Boorstin, The Lost World of Thomas Jefferson 190 (1948).

13. For Jefferson's political philosophy, see id.; Joseph J. Ellis, American Sphinx: The Character of Thomas Jefferson, chs. 3–4 (1996).

14. Jon Meacham, Thomas Jefferson: The Art of Power 467–68 (2012).

15. Id., 409.

16. This paragraph draws on Boorstin, Lost World 200–3, and McDonald, Presidency of Jefferson, ch. 1.

17. George C. Herring, From Colony to Superpower: U.S. Foreign Relations since 1776, at 93–94 (2008).

18. Bernard Bailyn, To Begin the World Anew: The Genius and Ambiguities of the American Founders 46 (2003), concludes that Jefferson "had all the qualities of a successful political executive. He balanced decisiveness with accountability; he relied on discussion and persuasion rather than authority; and he was tolerant of dissenting views."

19. White, Jeffersonians, vii: "The Federalists disappeared as a political party, but their administrative system was adopted by their political rivals."

20. White, Jeffersonians, 8. He removed only persons violating "a sort of pernicious political activity rule." Id., 354. See also McDonald, Presidency of Jefferson, ch. 2.

21. Gordon S. Wood, Empire of Liberty: A History of the Early Republic 1789–1815, at 299 (2009); Bailey, Jefferson and Power, ch. 6. About half of the federal offices turned over during Jefferson's first term.

22. "It is of some significance to note that no President before 1829 undertook to buy leadership or legislation with patronage. Congressmen were increasingly eager for influence in appointments and made some inroads on the executive domain, but the practice of using patronage to get votes in either House was rare and would have been thought corrupt." White, Jeffersonians, 43.

23. Forrest McDonald, The American Presidency: An Intellectual History 247, 258, 274 (1994).

24. Mayer, Constitutional Thought, ch. 8.

25. Meacham, Jefferson, 362.

26. Dumas Malone, Jefferson The President, First Term, 1801–1805, 110 (1970).

27. Bailyn, To Begin, 46, notes that Jefferson's actions served "to engrain into American political life the party system, to make party government acceptable, to make party machinery a normal part of political activity, [and] to make party and patronage inseparable." See also Noble E. Cunningham Jr., Jeffersonian Republicans in Power: Party Operations, 1801–1809, 305 (1963).

28. Wood, Empire, ch. 8.

29. Mayer, Constitutional Thought, ch. 8.

30. Wood, Empire, 301.

31. David P. Currie, The Constitution in Congress: The Jeffersonians, 1801–1829 (2000).

32. Geoffrey R. Stone, Perilous Times: Free Speech in Wartime from the Sedition Act of 1798 to the War on Terrorism, ch. 1 (2004).

33. Jeffrey Crouch, The Presidential Pardon Power (2009); Harold J. Krent, Presidential Powers, ch. 5 (2005).

34. New York Times v. Sullivan, 376 U.S. 254, 273–77 (1964).

35. Joseph Wheelan, Jefferson's Vendetta: The Pursuit of Aaron Burr and the Judiciary (2005).

36. Letter to Abigail Adams (September 11, 1804), 8 Writings of Jefferson, 311.

37. Restoration under Treaty with France, 1 Op. Att'y Gen. 114 (June 17, 1802).

38. United States v. Schooner Peggy, 5 U.S. (1 Cranch) 103 (1802).

39. Restoration under Treaty with France, 1 Op. Att'y Gen. 119 (June 25, 1802).

40. The Court's first major assertion of power to bind the executive, Marbury v. Madison (discussed below), was decided the next year.

41. Wood, Empire, ch. 17.

42. Herring, Colony to Superpower, 97.

43. "Our men of war may repel an attack on individual vessels, but after the repulse, may not proceed to destroy the enemy's vessels generally." Noble E. Cunningham Jr., The Process of Government under Jefferson, 48–49 (1978).

44. Meacham, Jefferson, 365; H. Jefferson Powell, The President's Authority over Foreign Affairs: An Essay in Constitutional Interpretation 91–93 (2002).

45. Herring, Colony to Superpower, 99. Herring describes the Barbary pirates episode at 97–101.

46. "Actual practice under the Constitution has shown that, while the President is usually in a position to propose, the Senate and Congress are often in a technical position at least to dispose. The verdict of history, in short, is that the power to determine the substantive content of American foreign policy is a divided power, with the lion's share falling usually, though by no means always, to the President." Edward S. Corwin, The President: Office and Powers, 1787–1984; History and Analysis of Practice and Opinion 201 (5th rev. ed., Randall W. Bland, Theodore T. Hindson & Jack W. Peltason eds., 1984) (emphasis in original).

47. Wood, Empire, ch. 10; MacDonald, Presidency of Jefferson, ch. 3.

48. Letter to Robert Livingston (April 18, 1802), 8 Writings of Jefferson, 143–47.

49. Richard E. Ellis, The Jeffersonian Crisis: Courts and Politics in the Young Republic 280–81 (1971).

50. Mayer, Constitutional Thought, ch. 8.

51. Jon Kukla, A Wilderness So Immense: The Louisiana Purchase and the Destiny of America 301 (2003).

52. Homer S. Cummings & Carl McFarland, Federal Justice: Chapters in the History of Justice and the Federal Executive 56 (1937).

53. McDonald, Presidency of Jefferson, 71.

54. For the quotations in this and the following paragraph, see Kukla, Wilderness, 305–6.

55. Id., at 307; Robert V. Remini, The House: The History of the House of Representatives, 78–79 (2006). The Constitution's Preamble states its purposes: "to form a more perfect Union, establish Justice, insure domestic Tranquility, provide for the common defense, promote the general Welfare, and secure the Blessings of Liberty to ourselves and our Posterity." Perhaps these phrases could provide some authority for the treaty. Article I, § 8 begins by empowering Congress to "provide for the common Defense and general Welfare of the United States." Hence the Federalists argued that Congress had a better claim than the executive to any power to add territory. John Randolph responded for Jefferson by citing the president's function of communication with foreign nations. After "a long and stormy debate," the House approved. *American Insurance Co. v. Canter*, 26 U.S. (1 Pet.) 511 (1828), later upheld the acquisition of territory by treaty.

56. See chapter 1.

57. Mayer, Constitutional Thought, ch. 8.

58. *Letter to the Governor of Louisiana (February 3, 1807)*, 10 The Works of Thomas Jefferson 347 n.1 (Paul L. Ford ed. 1905).

59. *Letter to John B. Colvin (September 20, 1810)*, 9 Writings of Jefferson 279. He went on: "To lose our country by a scrupulous adherence to written law, would be to lose the law itself, with life, liberty, property . . . thus absurdly sacrificing the end to the means."

60. Gary Schmitt, *Jefferson and Executive Power: Revisionism and the "Revolution of 1800,"* 17 Publius 7, 24 (1987).

61. Bailey, Jefferson and Power.

62. Jefferson won 162 of 176 electoral votes. Concludes MacDonald, Presidency of Jefferson, at 87: "The two-party system was all but dead." Jefferson then quickly made himself a lame duck, however, by invoking Washington's example of renunciation of power and announcing he would not seek a third term.

63. See Benjamin A. Kleinerman, The Discretionary President: The Promise and Peril of Executive Power, ch. 6 (2009).

64. The Federalist No. 49 suggests that when the branches disagree on interpretation of the Constitution, an appeal to the people is a normal recourse. Wood, Empire, 452, notes that James Wilson's famous lecture on constitutional law portrays all three branches as stemming from the people—thus all three can appeal to their ultimate source of support in their distinctive ways (members of Congress by speaking to their constituents, presidents by addressing the people generally, the courts by explaining their decisions).

65. Wood, Empire, ch. 12.

66. James F. Simon, What Kind of Nation: Thomas Jefferson, John Marshall, and the Epic Struggle to Create a United States 163 (2002).

67. *Stuart v. Laird*, 5 U.S. (1 Cranch) 299 (1803); see David P. Currie, The Constitution in the Supreme Court: The First Hundred Years, 1789–1888, at 74–77 (1985).

68. Keith E. Whittington, Constitutional Construction, ch. 2 (2001).

69. McDonald, Presidency of Jefferson, ch. 4.

70. Id., 93.

71. Many years later, Chief Justice William H. Rehnquist wrote a book persuasively arguing that the failure of the Chase impeachment was a critical precedent in ensuring the independence of the federal judiciary. Grand Inquests: The Historic Impeachments of Justice Samuel Chase and President Andrew Johnson (1999).

72. 5 U.S. (1 Cr.) 137 (1803). There is a vast literature on *Marbury*. For the story of the case, see Simon, What Kind, ch. 8.

73. The most important case is *McCulloch v. Maryland*, 17 U.S. 316 (1819), upholding the constitutionality of the Bank of the United States.

74. Wood, Empire, 11.

75. McDonald, American Presidency, 271.

76. White, Jeffersonians, chs. 29–30; McDonald, Presidency of Jefferson, ch. 7; at 139, he concludes that "Jefferson conducted a fifteen-month reign of oppression and repression that was unprecedented in American history and would not be matched . . . [until] Jefferson's ideological heir Woodrow Wilson occupied the presidency."

77. David J. Barron & Martin S. Lederman, *The Commander in Chief at the Lowest Ebb—A Constitutional History*, 121 Harv. L. Rev. 941, 974–76 (2008).

78. Meacham, Jefferson, 426. Congress did supply the funds.

79. Wood, Empire, 647–58.

80. Jerry L. Mashaw, Creating the Administrative Constitution: The Lost One Hundred Years of American Administrative Law, ch. 6 (2012).

81. Leonard W. Levy, Jefferson and Civil Liberties: The Darker Side 137 (1963).

82. Wood, *Empire*, 664. In *The Brig Aurora*, 11 U.S. (7 Cranch) 382 (1813), the Supreme Court upheld this grant of discretion to the executive against a challenge that it was an unconstitutional delegation of Congress's legislative powers.

83. Mashaw, Administrative Constitution, ch. 6.

84. 10 F. Cas. 355 (C.C.D.S.C. 1808) (No. 5420). See H. Jefferson Powell, Languages of Power: A Source Book of Early American Constitutional History 230–39 (1991).

85. In those days the justices "rode circuit," sitting part time in the lower federal courts; in that capacity their orders did not carry the force of a Supreme Court opinion.

86. Of course, *Marbury*, discussed above, had asserted the Court's power to bind the executive. And in *Little v. Barreme*, 6 U.S. (2 Cranch) 170 (1804), the Court had enforced its interpretation of a statute through a damages award against an executive officer.

87. A compliant Congress later supplied the presidential authority that the court had thought was missing.

88. Mashaw, Administrative Constitution, 116–17.

89. Harold H. Bruff, Balance of Forces: Separation of Powers Law in the Administrative State 166–67 (2006). The executive does honor court orders for the parties involved in the cases; the nonacquiescence policy denies them any broader effect.

90. McDonald, American Presidency, 428.

91. Andrew Burstein, America's Jubilee 156 (2001): "Heads of departments were not expected to be an extension of the president's policies to anywhere near the degree that they are today; autonomous cabinet members transmitted reports to congressional committees without notifying the president of their contents."

92. Robert A. Rutland, The Presidency of James Madison (1990); Wood, Empire, ch. 18.

93. Herring, Colony to Superpower, 121.

94. Wood, Empire, 673.

95. Powell, A Community Built on Words: The Constitution in History and Politics 98–99 (2002).

96. Leonard W. Levy, Original Intent and the Framers' Constitution 21 (1988).

97. Id.; Powell, Community, 130–35.

98. *Veto Message (March 3, 1817)*, in 8 The Writings of James Madison 386–88 (Gaillard Hunt ed., 1909).

99. *United States v. Butler*, 297 U.S. 1 (1936).

100. Michele Landis Dauber, The Sympathetic State: Disaster Relief and the Origins of the American Welfare State 24 (2013).

101. Rutland, Presidency of Madison, 86.

102. Id., 88, 188.

103. Marcus Cunliffe, *Madison*, in The Ultimate Decision: The President as Commander in Chief 23 (Ernest R. May ed., 1960).

Chapter Four

1. *Veto Message, Re-establishment of the Bank of the United States (July 10, 1832)*, in 3 Messages and Papers of the Presidents 1139 (James D. Richardson ed., 1897).

2. Noble E. Cunningham, The Presidency of James Monroe (1996).

3. George Dangerfield, The Era of Good Feelings (1952).

4. Mary W. M. Hargreaves, The Presidency of John Quincy Adams (1985); Fred Kaplan, John Quincy Adams: American Visionary (2014).

5. Stephen Skowronek, The Politics Presidents Make: Leadership from John Adams to George Bush 100–7 (1993).

6. Don E. Fehrenbacher, The Slaveholding Republic: An Account of the United States Government's Relations to Slavery 296 (Ward M. McAfee ed., 2001).

7. Thus a 2010 biography by Harlow G. Unger is titled The Last Founding Father: James Monroe and a Nation's Call to Greatness.

8. Nancy V. Baker, Conflicting Loyalties: Law and Politics in the Attorney General's Office, 1789–1990, at 55–57, 126–30 (1992).

9. Leonard D. White, The Jeffersonians: A Study in Administrative History, 1801–1829, at 336–38 (1951).

10. "The assertive republic" is the subtitle of chapter 4 of George C. Herring's From Colony to Superpower: U.S. Foreign Relations since 1776 (2008), which covers the period 1815–37. Herring's work informs this section of the chapter.

11. East Florida was most of present Florida. West Florida extended to the Mississippi, and Madison had claimed it was within the Louisiana Purchase. He and Congress snipped off the westernmost portion and added it to the Territory of Louisiana.

12. Daniel Walker Howe, What Hath God Wrought: The Transformation of America, 1815–1848, at 98–117 (2007).

13. Arthur M. Schlesinger Jr., The Imperial Presidency 36 (1973).

14. Herring, Colony to Superpower, 146–47.

15. Donald B. Cole, The Presidency of Andrew Jackson, ch. 4 (1993).

16. Dangerfield, Era, pt. 4, ch. 4.

17. Id., 309.

18. For Jackson's foreign policy, see Cole, Presidency of Jackson, ch. 6.

19. Herring, Colony to Superpower, 170–71.

20. Howe, What Hath God, 669–70.

21. Robert V. Remini, *The Constitution and the Presidencies: The Jackson Era*, in The Constitution and the American Presidency 29 (Martin L. Fausold & Alan Shank eds., 1991).

22. Howe, What Hath God, ch. 9.

23. The quotations in this paragraph are from Remini, *Constitution and Presidencies*, 29, 30, 43. His one-volume biography is Robert V. Remini, The Life of Andrew Jackson (2001). See also Andrew Burstein, The Passions of Andrew Jackson (2003); Fred Anderson & Andrew Cayton, The Dominion of War: Empire and Liberty in North America, 1500–2000, 211 (2005): "The great lesson of his youth was that survival depended on the expression of passion rather than its restraint."

24. Howe, What Hath God, ch. 11.

25. Id., 4–5.

26. Cole, Presidency of Jackson, 4.

27. *Annual Message (December 8, 1829)*, 3 Messages and Papers 1005, 1012.

28. Cole, Presidency of Jackson, 143.

29. Id., ch. 2.

30. The facts in this paragraph are from Cole, Presidency of Jackson, 40–50; see generally Leonard D. White, The Jacksonians: A Study in Administrative History, 1829–1861, chs. 16–17 (1954).

31. Jerry L. Mashaw, Creating the Administrative Constitution: The Lost One Hundred Years of American Administrative Law 150 (2012).

32. Cole, Presidency of Jackson, 74–75.

33. White, Jacksonians, 111.

34. Howe, What Hath God, 414–23.

35. Cole, Presidency of Jackson, chs. 3, 5; Howe, What Hath God, 342–57.

36. Howe, What Hath God, 421; see also Cole, Presidency of Jackson, 110.

37. Alexis de Tocqueville, 1 Democracy in America 340 (Phillips Bradley ed., 1945).

38. 30 U.S. (5 Pet.) 1 (1831).

39. Remini, *Constitution and Presidencies*, 39–40.

40. *Worcester v. Georgia*, 31 U.S. (6 Pet.) 515 (1832).

41. Cole, Presidency of Jackson, 114.

42. Robert V. Remini, Andrew Jackson and the Bank War: A Study in the Growth of Presidential Power (1967); see also Howe, What Hath God, 373–95.

43. Howe, What Hath God, 357–60.

44. Dangerfield, Era, 321.

45. Steven G. Calabresi & Christopher S. Yoo, The Unitary Executive: Presidential Power from Washington to Bush 104 (2008). Monroe had initiated the use of signing statements. Id., at 86.

46. Forrest McDonald, The American Presidency: An Intellectual History 223 (1994). Washington vetoed two bills, John Adams and Jefferson none, Madison seven, Monroe one, and John Quincy Adams none.

47. 17 U.S. (4 Wheat.) 316 (1819).

48. Cole, Presidency of Jackson, ch. 3; Remini, Bank War, ch. 2.

49. Glyndon G. Van Deusen, The Jacksonian Era, 1828–1848, at 63 (1959).

50. Dangerfield, Era, 167–68, 179–82, 187–88.

51. Remini, Bank War, 77.

52. 3 Messages and Papers, 1025.

53. Remini, Bank War, ch. 3.

54. Remini, *Constitution and Presidencies*, 36–37. Jackson's first annual message called for the abolition of the Electoral College in favor of direct election of the president and referred to "the first principle of our system—*that the majority is to govern.*" 3 Messages and Papers, 1101 (emphasis in original).

55. 3 Daniel Webster, The Works of Daniel Webster 446 (1856).

56. The cartoon is reproduced in Akhil Reed Amar, America's Constitution: A Biography 175 (2005).

57. Homer S. Cummings & Carl McFarland, Federal Justice: Chapters in the History of Justice and the Federal Executive 104 (1937).

58. White, Jacksonians, 29.

59. Cole, Presidency of Jackson, ch. 7; Remini, Bank War, ch. 4.

60. Cole, Presidency of Jackson, ch. 9; Remini, Bank War, ch. 5.

61. Cole, Presidency of Jackson, 186.

62. Congress had provided that "the deposits of the money of the United States . . . shall be made in said bank or branches thereof, unless the Secretary of the Treasury shall at any time otherwise order and direct." 3 Stat. 266, 274 § 16 (1816).

63. Howe, What Hath God, 387–88; White, Jacksonians, 36–38, 42, 44.

64. For the full story, see White, Jacksonians, ch. 2.

65. Remini, Life, 262–63.

66. Cummings & McFarland, Federal Justice, 108–9. Jackson's attempt to force Duane to defer to the attorney general's opinion of the law appears to have been little more than a tactical move in the dispute. As Duane's recalcitrance shows, a cabinet secretary who is prepared to resist the president on a point of law will certainly ignore the attorney general.

67. *Memorandum (September 18, 1833)*, 3 Messages and Papers, 1224, 1237–38.

68. Schlesinger, Imperial Presidency, ch. 3.

69. Remini, Bank War, 124.

70. Register of Debates, Twenty-Third Congress, First Session, 220 (January 13, 1834).

71. White, Jacksonians, 42.

72. Register of Debates, 1187 (March 28, 1834).

73. Jerry L. Mashaw, *Governmental Practice and Presidential Direction: Lessons from the Antebellum Republic?*, 45 Willamette L. Rev. 659, 691 (2009). Senators Clay, Calhoun, and Webster argued that the general purpose of the statute was to ensure safety of the funds, and because the Bank was safe, there was no power to remove them. Taney pointed out that the statute contained no such explicit condition, leaving the matter to his discretion. With matters in this posture, Taney was probably right. During this era, the Supreme Court held that an officer could be ordered to do a duty made mandatory by statute (*Kendall v. United States*, 37 U.S. (12 Pet.) 524 (1838)), but this statute appeared to give the secretary discretion.

74. Remini, Bank War, 142–44.

75. 7 The Writings and Speeches of Daniel Webster, 143–44 (1903).

76. Cole, Presidency of Jackson, 264–66; Remini, Bank War, 174.

77. White, Jacksonians, 44. The eminent Edward Corwin later wrote: "Never before and never since has the Senate so abased itself before a President." The President: Office and Powers 267 (1941).

78. Skowronek, Politics, ch. 5, pt. 1.

79. Cole, Presidency of Jackson, ch. 12.

80. Remini, Bank War, 125.

81. For example, President Monroe was unable to force Treasury to desist from its practice of sending its funding requests directly to Congress without consulting him. Calabresi & Yoo, Unitary Executive, 85.

82. Peter L. Strauss, *Overseer, or "The Decider"? The President in Administrative Law*, 75 Geo. Wash. L. Rev. 696 (2007).

83. *The President and Accounting Officers*, 1 Op. Att'y Gen. 624 (1823).

84. *The Jewels of the Princess of Orange*, 2 Op. Att'y Gen. 482 (1831).

85. The quoted phrase is Jefferson's reference to the Missouri Compromise of 1820, but more than one alarm was sounding in these years. For the nullification story, see Cole, Presidency of Jackson, ch. 8; Howe, What Hath God, 395–410; Keith E. Whittington, Constitutional Construction: Divided Powers and Constitutional Meaning, ch. 3 (2001).

86. Van Deusen, Jacksonian Era, 72.

87. *Proclamation of December 10, 1832*, 2 Messages and Papers 540.

88. Cole, Presidency of Jackson, 160.

89. Whittington, Construction, ch. 3.

90. Cole, Presidency of Jackson, 42–43.

91. Jeffrey K. Tulis, The Rhetorical Presidency 73–75 (1987).

92. Howe, What Hath God, ch. 13 (titled "Jackson's Third Term").

93. Major Wilson, The Presidency of Martin Van Buren (1984).

94. Howe, What Hath God, 508.

95. Michael J. Gerhardt, The Forgotten Presidents: Their Untold Constitutional Legacy, ch. 1 (2013).

96. Id., chs. 2–3.

97. *March 4, 1841*, 4 Messages and Papers, 1860.

98. Norma Peterson, The Presidencies of William Henry Harrison and John Tyler (1989).

99. Gerhardt, Forgotten Presidents, 28.

100. Howe, What Hath God, 572.

101. Michael J. Gerhardt, The Power of Precedent 113–16 (2008).

102. Richard M. Pious, The American Presidency 63 (1979).

103. McDonald, American Presidency, 319.

104. Leonard D. White with Jean Schneider, The Republican Era 1869–1901: A Study in Administrative History, 31–32 (1958).

105. Previous attorney general opinions had wobbled between the broad and narrow views of the power. Gerhardt, Forgotten Presidents, 73. Tyler's selected the line of precedent supporting the broad view. Id., 49.

106. Id., 41–47.

107. Id., 64–66.

108. *Luther v. Borden*, 48 U.S. 1 (1849).

109. Howe, What Hath God, 677–90, 698–700.

110. Art. IV, § 3.

111. Mark Graber, *How the West Was Settled: The Louisiana Purchase, the Annexation of Texas, and* Bush v. Gore, in The Louisiana Purchase and American Expansion, 1803–1898 (Sanford Levinson & Bartholomew Sparrow eds., 2005); see also David P. Currie, *Texas*, id., 111.

112. Paul H. Bergeron, The Presidency of James K. Polk (1987).

113. Van Deusen, Jacksonian Era, 197.

114. In 1845, the editor of a popular magazine celebrated "our manifest destiny to overspread the continent." The term took hold. Howe, What Hath God, 702–3.

115. Skowronek, Politics, 160.

116. Howe, What Hath God, 708. Regarding banking, Polk engineered a statute creating an "Independent Treasury," a system of depositing federal funds in government offices scattered around the nation instead of the state banks that Jackson used. Mashaw, Administrative Constitution, 172–73.

117. Robert W. Merry, A Country of Vast Designs: James K. Polk, the Mexican War, and the Conquest of the American Continent 130 (2009).

118. Id., 269.

119. Bergeron, Presidency of Polk, ch. 2.

120. Id., 175–76.

121. Id., ch. 6.

122. Id., 210.

123. Cong. Globe, 29th Cong., 1st Sess. 680 (April 16, 1846).

124. In 1842, Tyler had extended the doctrine as far as Hawaii. Howe, What Hath God, 706.

125. Van Deusen, Jacksonian Era, 215.

126. 3 Messages and Papers, 2292–93.

127. Van Deusen, Jacksonian Era, 224.

128. Cong. Globe, 30th Cong., 1st Sess. 64, 95, App. 93–95.

129. Similar sentiments were expressed by Daniel Webster and John Quincy Adams. Howe, What Hath God, 763, 812.

130. Merry, Vast Designs, 308–9.

131. Howe, What Hath God, 750.

132. White, Jacksonians, 113–14.

133. Howe, What Hath God, 808.

134. Merry, Vast Designs, 433.

135. Van Deusen, Jacksonian Era, 245.

136. The Wilmot Proviso of 1846, a failed congressional effort to forbid slavery entirely in the newly acquired territories, was yet another fire bell in the night. Merry, Vast Designs, ch. 18.

137. Howe, What Hath God, 813.

138. Pity the Whigs. Gerhardt's Forgotten Presidents covers six antebellum presidents: Van Buren, Pierce, and the four Whigs.

139. Gerhardt, Forgotten Presidents, ch. 4.

140. David J. Barron & Martin S. Lederman, *The Commander in Chief at the Lowest Ebb—A Constitutional History*, 121 Harv. L. Rev. 941, 988–91 (2008).

141. McDonald, American Presidency, 393.

142. Gerhardt, Forgotten Presidents, ch. 6; Skowronek, Politics, ch. 5, pt. 3.

143. Gerhardt, Forgotten Presidents, 99.

Chapter Five

1. Ward H. Lamon, Recollections of Abraham Lincoln, 1847–1865, 221 (2d ed., Dorothy Lamon Teillard ed. 1911).

2. *Dred Scott v. Sandford*, 60 U.S. (19 How.) 393 (1857); see Don E. Fehrenbacher, The Dred Scott Case: Its Significance in American Law and Politics (1978); Earl M. Maltz, Slavery and the Supreme Court, 1825–1861, chs. 19–24 (2009).

3. Article IV, § 2, of the Constitution provided that slaves escaping into free territory were not thereby rendered free and must be returned to their owners. If a slave owner could capture runaway slaves in free territory and haul them home, it was most unlikely that the master's travel into free territory while accompanied by slaves would free them.

4. Mark A. Graber, *Dred Scott* and the Problem of Constitutional Evil, introduction (2006).

5. R. Kent Newmyer, The Supreme Court under Marshall and Taney, ch. 5 (1968). At 94, Newmyer paints a sympathetic portrait of Taney—a states' rights patriot, a Jacksonian democrat, and a smart, kind, and humble man who freed his own slaves. His decisions as chief justice, however, always supported slavery.

6. Kenneth M. Stampp, America in 1857: A Nation on the Brink 91–93 (1992).

7. Van Buren once remarked that Buchanan was "amply endowed with . . . clear perceptions of self-interest." Elbert B. Smith, The Presidency of James Buchanan 11 (1975). He was not, however, equally endowed with self-knowledge. The day before he died in 1868, Buchanan told a friend he had "discharged every public duty imposed on me conscientiously. I have no regret for any public act of my life, and history will vindicate my memory." Id., 196.

8. He was elected with 45 percent of the popular vote, over the Republican candidate Fremont and the American Party candidate Fillmore.

9. After saying the executive could not free Scott, Lincoln said:

> We nevertheless do oppose [*Dred Scott*] . . . as a political rule which shall be binding on the voter, to vote for nobody who thinks it wrong, which shall be binding on the members of Congress or the President to favor no measure that does not actually concur with the principles of that decision. . . . We propose so resisting it as to have it reversed if we can, and a new judicial rule established upon the subject. (3 Collected Works of Abraham Lincoln 255 [Roy Basler ed., 1953])

10. For arguments favoring this proposition, see David A. Strauss, *Presidential Interpretation of the Constitution*, 15 Cardozo L. Rev. 113 (1993); for arguments against it, see Thomas W. Merrill, *Judicial Opinions as Binding Law and as Explanations for Judgments*, id., 43.

11. Frank Easterbrook, *Presidential Review*, 40 Case West. L. Rev. 905, 926 (1990). H. Jefferson Powell, A Community Built on Words: The Constitution in History and Politics 174–77 (2002), contrasts Lincoln's Attorney General Bates's opinion supporting the citizenship of blacks with Taney's position.

12. Nevertheless, if the courts had reversed Lincoln's directives as applied to particular patent claimants, the executive would have been bound to comply, however odious the court orders.

13. Maltz, Slavery, ch. 24; Bruce Chadwick, 1858: Abraham Lincoln, Jefferson Davis, Robert E. Lee, Ulysses S. Grant, and the War They Failed to See, ch. 16 (2008).

14. James M. McPherson, Battle Cry of Freedom: The Civil War Era 225–26 (1988).

15. Smith, Presidency of Buchanan, ch. 13.

16. *Power of the President in Executing the Laws*, 9 Op. Att'y Gen. 516 (1860).

17. McPherson, Battle Cry, 247.

18. 2 Bruce Ackerman, We The People: Transformations 34 (1998). For the contrary argument that the Constitution forbade unilateral secession, see Akhil Reed Amar, America's Constitution: A Biography, ch. 1 (2005).

19. Graber, Constitutional Evil, 165–67.

20. Ironically, the Thirteenth Amendment that *was* ratified in 1865 abolished slavery unconditionally.

21. Eric Foner, The Fiery Trial: Abraham Lincoln and American Slavery xvi (2010).

22. Id., xix.

23. Allen C. Guelzo, Lincoln's Emancipation Proclamation: The End of Slavery in America 3 (2004).

24. Phillip S. Paludan, The Presidency of Abraham Lincoln, ch. 1 (1994).

25. Stephen Skowronek, The Politics Presidents Make: Leadership from John Adams to George Bush, ch. 6, pt. 1 (1993).

26. Mark E. Neely Jr., Lincoln and the Triumph of the Nation: Constitutional Conflict in the American Civil War, ch. 1 (2011).

27. McPherson, Battle Cry, 250, 312–14.

28. Daniel Mark Epstein, Lincoln's Men: The President and His Private Secretaries (2009).

29. Id., 31.

30. Paludan, Presidency of Lincoln, ch. 2.

31. Doris Kearns Goodwin, Team of Rivals: The Political Genius of Abraham Lincoln, chs. 10–11 (2005).

32. Of Cameron it was once said, "I do not think he would steal a red hot stove." When the secretary objected, he received an exquisite apology: "I said Cameron would not steal a red hot stove. I withdraw that statement." Paludan, Presidency of Lincoln, 43.

33. David H. Donald, Lincoln 449, 479 (1995).

34. In 1863, John Hay recorded: "He is managing this war, the draft, foreign relations, and planning a reconstruction of the Union, all at once. I never knew with what tyrannous authority he rules the Cabinet, till now. The most important things he decides & there is no cavil." Goodwin, Team of Rivals, 545.

35. Id., ch. 18.

36. In 1864, Chase clumsily tried to have himself substituted for Lincoln on the Republican ticket. Lincoln's supporters attacked and subdued him this time. The president finally got rid of him by nominating him to replace Chief Justice Taney, who had died.

37. This famous sentence from Lincoln's second inaugural reveals that he was reluctant to assign blame even after four years of civil war. For analyses of the legal issues about the Civil War, see Daniel Farber, Lincoln's Constitution (2003); William H. Rehnquist, All the Laws but One: Civil Liberties in Wartime (1998); J. G. Randall, Constitutional Problems under Lincoln (rev. ed. 1951).

38. 4 Works of Lincoln, 268. He did concede that court orders bind the parties and that they should receive "very high respect and consideration" in parallel cases.

39. Article II, § 3.

40. For the debate about Lincoln's intentions in the Sumter episode, see McPherson, Battle Cry, 272 n.78.

41. 1 Stat. 424; see Stephen I. Vladeck, *Emergency Power and the Militia Acts*, 114 Yale L. J. 149 (2004).

42. Farber, Lincoln's Constitution, ch. 6; David J. Barron & Martin S. Lederman, *The Commander in Chief at the Lowest Ebb—A Constitutional History*, 121 Harv. L. Rev. 941, 997–1005 (2008).

43. When the blockade was challenged in the Supreme Court in the *Prize Cases*, discussed below, the president's lawyers argued that the blockade was authorized by an 1807 amendment to the militia statute that allowed the use of federal armed forces to suppress insurrection. The Court's opinion mentioned the argument but did not clearly rely on it.

44. James M. McPherson, Tried by War: Abraham Lincoln as Commander in Chief 24 (2008).

45. See Nelson D. Lankford, Cry Havoc! The Crooked Road to Civil War, 1861 (2007).

46. Art. I, § 9. The power is located in Article I, where the powers of Congress reside. At the Constitutional Convention, without explanation the Committee on Style moved the suspension clause from Article III (on the judiciary) to Article I. Perhaps, then, the suspension power belongs exclusively to Congress. Still, the

framers knew that Congress could be prevented from assembling, since in their memory the Continental Congress had been chased out of Philadelphia by the British, and they knew that Congress could not assemble quickly during its long recesses. The better argument is that the power is shared, with ultimate control in Congress. Amar, *America's Constitution*, 122.

47. Farber, *Lincoln's Constitution*, 158; see also Rehnquist, *All the Laws*, 23.

48. When the justices sat in the lower federal courts, their orders did not carry the force of a Supreme Court opinion.

49. *Ex Parte Merryman*, 17 F. Cas. 144 (C.C.D. Md. 1861) (No. 9487). See James F. Simon, *Lincoln and Chief Justice Taney: Slavery, Secession, and the President's War Powers*, ch. 6 (2006).

50. Taney said: "It will then remain for that high officer, in fulfillment of his constitutional obligation to 'take care that the laws be faithfully executed,' to determine what measures he will take to cause the civil process of the United States to be respected and enforced." 17 F. Cas. at 153.

51. Merryman was indicted for treason and released on bail. The charges were never resolved.

52. Edwin Meese III, *The Law of the Constitution*, 61 Tul. L. Rev. 979 (1987).

53. *Message to Congress in Special Session (July 4, 1861)*, 4 Works of Lincoln, 421.

54. Id., 430.

55. *Youngstown Sheet & Tube Co. v. Sawyer*, 343 U.S. 579, 653 (1952).

56. *Note to Edward Bates (May 30, 1861)*, 4 Works of Lincoln, 390.

57. Rehnquist, *All the Laws*, 44, pointing out the inconsistency of this argument with the Supreme Court's foundational opinion in *Marbury v. Madison*.

58. *Suspension of the Privilege of the Writ of Habeas Corpus*, 10 Op. Att'y Gen 74 (1861).

59. Neely, *Triumph*, ch. 2.

60. An Act to Increase the Pay of the Privates in the Regular Army and of the Volunteers in the Service of the United States, ch. 63, § 3, 12 Stat. 326 (1861), declared Lincoln's actions "hereby approved and in all respects legalized and made valid, to the same intent and with the same effect as if they had been issued and done under the previous express authority of the Congress."

61. Habeas Corpus Act, 12 Stat. 755 (1863).

62. Barron & Lederman, *Constitutional History*, 1005–6.

63. 71 U.S. 2 (1866). See Curtis A. Bradley, *The Story of* Ex Parte Milligan, in Presidential Power Stories 93 (Christopher H. Schroeder & Curtis A. Bradley eds., 2009).

64. 67 U.S. (2 Black) 635 (1863). See Thomas H. Lee & Michael D. Ramsey, *The Story of the* Prize Cases, in Schroeder & Bradley, Presidential Power Stories 53.

65. See chapter 1. Clinton Rossiter, Constitutional Dictatorship: Crisis Government in the Modern Democracies (1948), so concludes, ch. 15, while expressing some doubt, 209. See also Sanford Levinson & Jack M. Balkin, *Constitutional Dictatorship: Its Dangers and Its Design*, 94 Minn. L. Rev. 101, 128 (2010). Scholars

rejecting this characterization include Benjamin A. Kleinerman, The Discretionary President: The Promise and Peril of Executive Power, ch. 7 (2009); Michael Les Benedict, *The Constitution of the Lincoln Presidency and the Republican Era*, in The Constitution and the American Presidency 45 (Martin L. Fausold & Alan Shank eds., 1991); Farber, Lincoln's Constitution.

66. Richard Pious, The American Presidency 57 (1979).

67. 6 Messages and Papers of the Presidents 78 (James D. Richardson ed., 1897).

68. Pious, American Presidency, 60: "Lincoln's prerogative government rested on the consent of the governed. If the framers had not anticipated the exercise of emergency powers, they had provided a system of government supple enough to accommodate both their assertion and their use in authentic crises."

69. Epstein, Lincoln's Men, ch. 6.

70. McPherson, Battle Cry, 559–60.

71. Paludan, Presidency of Lincoln, ch. 4.

72. McPherson, Battle Cry, 362–63.

73. George C. Herring, From Colony to Superpower: U.S. Foreign Relations since 1776, ch. 6 (2008).

74. The *Trent* episode, in which a Navy captain seized two Confederate diplomats heading for Europe, caused a crisis with the British, which was defused by releasing the diplomats. Id., 232–33.

75. Mark E. Neely Jr., The Fate of Liberty: Abraham Lincoln and Civil Liberties (1991).

76. Id., 209.

77. Id., ch. 6.

78. Id., 65.

79. 6 Works of Lincoln, 265–66, 303.

80. Randall, Constitutional Problems, 518: "There is a striking contrast between the great number of arbitrary arrests and the almost negligible amount of completed judicial action for treason, conspiracy, and obstructing the draft."

81. Neely, Fate of Liberty, ch. 3.

82. John F. Witt, Lincoln's Code: The Laws of War in American History (2012); Barron & Lederman, *Constitutional History*, 994–97.

83. *To Edwin M. Stanton (March 18, 1864)*, 7 Works of Lincoln, 254, 255.

84. Neely, Fate of Liberty, 14–18.

85. McPherson, Battle Cry, 289.

86. Id., ch. 20.

87. *Letter to Erastus Corning (June 12, 1863)*, 6 Works of Lincoln, 266–67. Lincoln answered his own question: "I think that . . . to silence the agitator, and save the boy, is not only constitutional, but, withal, a great mercy."

88. Neely, Fate of Liberty, 104–5; Geoffrey R. Stone, Perilous Times: Free Speech in Wartime, ch. 2 (2004). At 133, Stone concludes that, all things considered, there was "only a very limited—and largely unsystematic—interference with free expression during the Civil War."

89. Goodwin, Team of Rivals, 523.

90. Foner, Fiery Trial, 193.

91. Louis P. Masur, Lincoln's Hundred Days: The Emancipation Proclamation and the War for the Union 28 (2012).

92. *Letter to Albert G. Hodges (April 4, 1864)*, 7 Works of Lincoln, 281.

93. Guelzo, Emancipation Proclamation, ch. 1.

94. McPherson, Battle Cry, 352–54.

95. Id., 499.

96. Masur, Hundred Days, 57.

97. 12 Stat. 319. For the Confiscation Acts, see Barron & Lederman, *Constitutional History*, 1009–16; Henry L. Chambers Jr., *Lincoln, the Emancipation Proclamation, and Executive Power*, 73 U. Md. L. Rev. 100 (2013).

98. Charles Royster, The Destructive War: William Tecumseh Sherman, Stonewall Jackson, and the Americans 102–6, 274–75, 279 (1991).

99. Chambers, *Lincoln*.

100. 12 Stat. 589 (1862).

101. Goodwin, Team of Rivals, 460.

102. Masur, Hundred Days, ch. 3.

103. *Letter to Orville Browning (September 22, 1861)*, 4 Works of Lincoln, 531–32.

104. McPherson, Battle Cry, 504.

105. Goodwin, Team of Rivals, 464.

106. *To Horace Greeley (August 22, 1862)*, 5 Works of Lincoln, 388–89.

107. McPherson, Battle Cry, 555.

108. Masur, Hundred Days, 93.

109. *Annual Message to Congress (December 1, 1862)*, 5 Works of Lincoln, 529–37.

110. Guelzo, Emancipation Proclamation, 174.

111. January 1, 1863, reprinted in Peter M. Shane & Harold H. Bruff, Separation of Powers Law: Cases and Materials 1201 (3d ed. 2011).

112. 6 Works of Lincoln, 428.

113. Foner, Fiery Trial, 243.

114. Id., 233, 247.

115. Id., ch. 7; Guelzo, Emancipation Proclamation, ch. 4.

116. Randall, Constitutional Problems, 371–404.

117. McPherson, Battle Cry, ch. 25.

118. Skowronek, Politics, ch. 6, pt. 1.

119. Guelzo, Emancipation Proclamation, ch. 5.

120. McPherson, Battle Cry, 804–5.

121. Phillip S. Paludan, A Covenant with Death: The Constitution, Law, and Equality in the Civil War Era 3 (1975).

122. For some reflections, see Sanford Levinson, Constitutional Faith 139–42 (1988).

123. *Letter to Albert G. Hodges (April 4, 1864)*, 7 Works of Lincoln, 281.

124. Later in 1863, in the *Prize Cases*, the Supreme Court provided implied support for the Proclamation when it upheld Lincoln's unilateral power to blockade the South, with the effect of making property on blockade runners subject to uncompensated seizure.

125. Foner, Fiery Trial, 157.

126. Harold M. Hyman, A More Perfect Union: The Impact of the Civil War and Reconstruction on the Constitution, ch. 8 (1975).

127. The strongest arguments in Bates's opinion invoked the adequacy theory and cited the faithful execution clause, the president's oath of office, and the need to put down rebellion if the Constitution were to be preserved.

128. Neely, Triumph, 119.

129. Hyman, More Perfect Union, 127, 139; Randall, Constitutional Problems, 513–14: "It would not be easy to state what Lincoln conceived to be the limit of his powers." At 517, "Neither Congress nor the Supreme Court exercised any very effective restraint upon the President."

130. Paludan, Presidency of Lincoln, ch. 11.

131. McPherson, Battle Cry, 698–713.

132. Art. IV, § 4.

133. President Tyler's willingness to take some actions to suppress the Dorr Rebellion in the 1840s provided Lincoln a bit of precedent for his actions. See chapter 4.

134. Article I § 7, of the Constitution provides that if Congress prevents the president from returning a vetoed bill to it by adjourning, he can prevent it from becoming law by failing to sign it, or "pocketing" it. See Harold H. Bruff, Balance of Forces: Separation of Powers Law in the Administrative State 227–28 (2006). This was Lincoln's only important veto of any kind; Jackson and Tyler had employed pocket vetoes vigorously.

135. 7 Works of Lincoln, 433.

136. McPherson, Battle Cry, 713.

137. Brooks D. Simpson, The Reconstruction Presidents 56 (1998).

138. Goodwin, Team of Rivals, ch. 25.

139. McPherson, Battle Cry, 859.

140. Eric Foner, Reconstruction: America's Unfinished Revolution, 1863–1877, ch. 1 (1988).

Chapter Six

1. Michael Les Benedict, The Impeachment and Trial of Andrew Johnson, appendix A (1973).

2. This phrase is a characterization of Andrew Johnson by Brooks D. Simpson, The Reconstruction Presidents 76 (1998).

3. Albert Castel, The Presidency of Andrew Johnson (1979).

4. Simpson, Reconstruction Presidents, 110.

5. For a comparison of the character of the two men, see Eric Foner, The Fiery Trial: Abraham Lincoln and American Slavery 334 (2010).

6. Simpson, Reconstruction Presidents, 51.

7. I use the term "freedmen" here because it was the contemporary term for the freed slaves, who of course included many women and children.

8. Simpson, Reconstruction Presidents, ch. 3.

9. Jeffrey Crouch, The Presidential Pardon Power, ch. 2 (2009); Harold J. Krent, Presidential Powers, ch. 5 (2005).

10. The principal case is United States v. Klein, 80 U.S. 128 (1872).

11. Simpson, Reconstruction Presidents, 75.

12. James E. Sefton, Andrew Johnson and the Uses of Constitutional Power, ch. 7 (1980).

13. Art. I, § 5: "Each House shall be the Judge of the Elections, Returns and Qualifications of its own Members."

14. For the period of presidential Reconstruction, see 2 Bruce Ackerman, We the People: Transformations, ch. 5 (1998); Eric Foner, Reconstruction: America's Unfinished Revolution 1863–1877, ch. 5 (1988).

15. See chapter 4.

16. Foner, Reconstruction, 123.

17. 6 Messages and Papers of the Presidents 356 (James D. Richardson ed., 1898).

18. Ackerman, Transformations, 153–54.

19. Sefton, Uses of Power, 123.

20. Foner, Reconstruction, 68–70.

21. Michele Landis Dauber, The Sympathetic State: Disaster Relief and the Origins of the American Welfare State 35–43 (2013).

22. Veto Message (February 19, 1866), 8 Messages and Papers, 3597. A later bill extending the bureau passed over Johnson's veto.

23. Ackerman, Transformations, 170–71.

24. Foner, Reconstruction, 248.

25. 14 Stat. 27 (1866); see Harold M. Hyman, A More Perfect Union: The Impact of the Civil War and Reconstruction on the Constitution, ch. 25 (1973). Tyler's war with Congress had produced overrides; see chapter 4.

26. Veto Message (March 27, 1866), 8 Messages and Papers, 3603.

27. Richard B. Bernstein with Jerome Agel, Amending America: If We Love the Constitution So Much, Why Do We Keep Trying to Change It?, ch. 6 (1993).

28. Foner, Reconstruction, 145.

29. Id., 137.

30. Id., ch. 6.

31. Ackerman, Transformations, 177–78.

32. Jeffrey K. Tulis, The Rhetorical Presidency 87 (1987). (Johnson's tour was "the stark exception to the general practice" of nineteenth-century presidents, who avoided giving policy speeches.)

33. Simpson, Reconstruction Presidents, 108.

34. Foner, Reconstruction, 261–64.

35. Act of March 2, 1867, 14 Stat. 428; see Castel, Presidency of Johnson, ch. 6.

36. Ackerman, Transformations, ch. 7.

37. *Veto Message (March 2, 1867)*, 8 Messages and Papers 3696.

38. 71 U.S. 2 (1866).

39. For vivid examples of the extent of congressional interference with executive command relationships, see Ackerman, Transformations, ch. 8.

40. Act of March 2, 1867, 14 Stat. 430; see Benedict, Impeachment, 51–52.

41. Sefton, Uses of Power, 149.

42. Army Appropriations Act, 14 Stat. 485 (1867); David J. Barron & Martin S. Lederman, *The Commander in Chief at the Lowest Ebb—A Constitutional History*, 121 Harv. L. Rev. 941, 1022–23 (2008).

43. Act of March 23, 1867, 15 Stat. 2.

44. Carpetbaggers were northerners governing in the South; scalawags were southerners cooperating with Reconstruction.

45. Castel, Presidency of Johnson, ch. 7.

46. Act of July 19, 1867, 15 Stat. 14.

47. Sefton, Uses of Power, 157.

48. *Mississippi v. Johnson*, 71 U.S. 475 (1867).

49. Steven G. Calabresi & Christopher S. Yoo, The Unitary Executive: Presidential Power from Washington to Bush 181–82 (2008).

50. *Annual Message (December 3, 1867)*, 8 Messages and Papers 3756.

51. *Message to the Senate (December 12, 1867)*, id., 3781.

52. Castel, Presidency of Johnson, 168.

53. Calabresi & Yoo, Unitary Executive, 184.

54. For a fine exploration of these problems in the Johnson impeachment, see Keith E. Whittington, Constitutional Construction: Divided Powers and Constitutional Meaning, ch. 4 (2001).

55. For popular accounts of the impeachment, see Gene Smith, High Crimes and Misdemeanors: the Impeachment and Trial of Andrew Johnson (1977); David O. Stewart, Impeached: The Trial of President Andrew Johnson and the Fight for Lincoln's Legacy (2009).

56. Article II, § 4 of the Constitution provides: "The President, Vice President, and all civil Officers of the United States, shall be removed from Office on Impeachment for, and Conviction of, Treason, Bribery, or other high Crimes and Misdemeanors." See Michael J. Gerhardt, The Federal Impeachment Process: A Constitutional and Historical Analysis (2d ed. 2000); Charles Black, Impeachment: A Handbook (1974).

57. Harold H. Bruff, Balance of Forces: Separation of Powers Law in the Administrative State, 312–13 (2006).

58. The Senate's president pro tem is the senior senator of the majority party.

59. Foner, Reconstruction, 333–36.

60. The articles of impeachment are in Benedict, Impeachment, appendix A.

61. Id., ch. 5; Castel, Presidency of Johnson, ch. 9.

62. 2 Trial of Andrew Johnson 200 (1868).

63. See chapter 3; Walter Dellinger, *Presidential Authority to Decline to Execute Unconstitutional Statutes*, reprinted in H. Jefferson Powell, The Constitution and the Attorneys General 411–18 (1999).

64. Castel, Presidency of Johnson, 185, summarizes the legal defenses.

65. Ackerman, Transformations, 227–30.

66. Benedict, Impeachment, 144–45.

67. The acquittal was partly the result of an action that formed one of the future president John F. Kennedy's Profiles in Courage (1955), the vote of Kansas senator Edmund Ross against the radicals.

68. Many years later the Supreme Court vindicated Johnson in *Myers v. United States*, 272 U.S. 52 (1926), by holding that a successor statute that conditioned presidential removals on the Senate's consent was unconstitutional. The Court's opinion was written by a former president, Chief Justice Taft. Until the Tenure of Office Act was repealed by the Democrats in 1886, it tended to give Congress control of patronage.

69. Grand Inquests: The Historic Impeachments of Justice Samuel Chase and President Andrew Johnson 278 (1999).

70. Ackerman, Transformations, 233–34; Akhil Reed Amar, America's Constitution: A Biography, ch. 10 (2005).

71. George C. Herring, From Colony to Superpower: U.S. Foreign Relations since 1776, ch. 6 (2008).

72. *December 3, 1867*, 13 The Papers of Andrew Johnson 304 (Leroy P. Graf & Ralph W. Haskins eds., 1967).

73. Herring, Colony to Superpower, 253.

74. Jean E. Smith, Grant 457 (2001).

75. Ackerman, Transformations, 234–38.

76. Smith, Grant, 467.

77. Foner, Reconstruction, ch. 9.

78. Ackerman, Transformations, 239–41.

79. Calabresi & Yoo, Unitary Executive, 176.

80. *Hepburn v. Griswold*, 75 U.S. 603 (1870).

81. *Legal Tender Cases*, 79 U.S. 457 (1871).

82. For a balanced appraisal, see H. W. Brands, The Man Who Saved the Union: Ulysses Grant in War and Peace (2013).

83. Simpson, Reconstruction Presidents, chs. 5–6.

84. Id., 192.

85. Despite the corruption in his War Department, Grant followed a humane, if ineffective, policy toward the Indians that emphasized their assimilation into American society.

86. Fred Anderson & Andrew Cayton, The Dominion of War: Empire and Liberty in North America, 1500–2000, ch. 7 (2005).

87. Smith, Grant, ch. 18.

88. Herring, Colony to Superpower, 259.

89. Foner, Reconstruction, ch. 11.

90. In the ironically named *Civil Rights Cases*, 109 U.S. 3 (1883), the Supreme Court invalidated the act, holding that the Fourteenth Amendment applied only to state, not private, discrimination.

91. Simpson, Reconstruction Presidents, 181.

92. William H. Rehnquist, Centennial Crisis: The Disputed Election of 1876 (2005).

93. Foner, Reconstruction, 558.

94. Simpson, Reconstruction Presidents, 209.

95. H. W. Brands, American Colossus: The Triumph of Capitalism, 1865–1900, ch. 4 (2010).

96. Leonard D. White with Jean Schneider, The Republican Era, 1869–1901: A Study in Administrative History 32 (1958).

97. *July 14, 1880*, 3 Messages and Papers of the Presidents 612–13 (James D. Richardson ed., 1897).

98. Candice Millard, Destiny of the Republic: A Tale of Madness, Medicine and the Murder of a President 31 (2011).

99. Calabresi & Yoo, Unitary Executive, 198.

100. Simpson, Reconstruction Presidents, 221.

Chapter Seven

1. Quoted in A. Scott Berg, Wilson 15 (2013).

2. John M. Cooper Jr., Woodrow Wilson: A Biography, ch. 2 (2009).

3. Justus D. Doenecke, The Presidencies of James A. Garfield and Chester A. Arthur (1981).

4. Candice Millard, Destiny of the Republic: A Tale of Madness, Medicine and the Murder of a President 64 (2011).

5. Id., chs. 7, 9.

6. Id., 109.

7. Michael J. Gerhardt, The Forgotten Presidents: Their Untold Constitutional Legacy, ch. 7 (2013).

8. Jerry L. Mashaw, Creating the Administrative Constitution: The Lost One Hundred Years of American Administrative Law, ch. 13 (2012).

9. Richard E. Welch Jr., The Presidencies of Grover Cleveland (1988).

10. Harold J. Krent, Presidential Powers, ch. 3 (2005); Henry Monaghan, *The Protective Power of the Presidency*, 93 Colum. L. Rev. 1 (1993). For example, in *In re Neagle*, 135 U.S. 1 (1890), the Court upheld the power of the president to assign

a marshal to protect a Supreme Court Justice without special statutory authority. It is hard to imagine *that* case coming out the other way.

11. Barbara W. Tuchman, The Proud Tower: A Portrait of the World before the War, 1890–1914, 423 (1962).

12. Jackson Lears, Rebirth of a Nation: The Making of Modern America, 1877–1920, ch. 5 (2009).

13. Art. IV, § 4.

14. The Fourteenth Amendment, by recasting the nature of federalism, also supports the use of federal power to force states to protect their citizens.

15. Harold H. Bruff, Balance of Forces: Separation of Powers Law in the Administrative State 94–98 (2006).

16. *In re Debs*, 158 U.S. 564 (1895).

17. H. W. Brands, American Colossus: The Triumph of Capitalism, 1865–1900, 484 (2010).

18. Michele Landis Dauber, The Sympathetic State: Disaster Relief and the Origins of the American Welfare State 24–28 (2013).

19. Matthew Algeo, The President Is a Sick Man: Wherein the Supposedly Virtuous Grover Cleveland Survives a Secret Surgery at Sea and Vilifies the Courageous Newspaperman Who Dared Expose the Truth (2011).

20. Robert H. Wiebe, The Search for Order, 1877–1920, 36 (1967).

21. George C. Herring, From Colony to Superpower: U.S. Foreign Relations since 1776, ch. 7 (2008).

22. Id., 265.

23. Homer B. Sokolofsky & Allan B. Spetter, The Presidency of Benjamin Harrison (1987).

24. Tuchman, Tower, 130–31.

25. Herring, Colony to Superpower, 305–6.

26. Wiebe, Search for Order, 258.

27. Ivan Musicant, Empire by Default: The Spanish-American War and the Dawn of the American Century (1998).

28. Scott Miller, The President and the Assassin: McKinley, Terror, and Empire at the Dawn of the American Century 7 (2011).

29. Herring, Colony to Superpower, 312.

30. Lewis L. Gould, The Modern American Presidency, ch. 1 (2d ed. 2009) (titled "The Age of Cortelyou").

31. Alfred Thayer Mahan wrote a highly influential book stressing the importance of sea power, The Influence of Sea Power upon History (1890); among its avid readers was Theodore Roosevelt. See Tuchman, Tower, 131–36.

32. Id., 155–56.

33. Forrest McDonald, The American Presidency: An Intellectual History 396 (1994).

34. For the war with Spain, see Herring, Colony to Superpower, ch. 8; Musicant, Empire by Default.

35. Frank Freidel, The Splendid Little War (2002).

36. In a series of decisions known as the *Insular Cases*, the Supreme Court ratified American imperialism. See Pedro A. Malavet, America's Colony: The Political and Cultural Conflict between the United States and Puerto Rico 38–40 (2004).

37. Herring, Colony to Superpower, 335.

38. Edmund Morris, Theodore Rex, ch. 6 (2001).

39. Herring, Colony to Superpower, ch. 8.

40. McDonald, American Presidency, 388.

41. Bruce Ackerman & David Golove, Is NAFTA Constitutional?, 17–18 (1995).

42. Stephen Skowronek, The Politics Presidents Make: Leadership from John Adams to George Bush 233–34 (1993).

43. Miller, President and the Assassin, 271.

44. The quoted phrase is a friend's description of him. Lewis L. Gould, The Presidency of Theodore Roosevelt 7 (rev. ed. 2011).

45. Roosevelt's best man, Cecil Spring Rice, memorably remarked: "You must always remember that the President is about six." Morris, Theodore Rex, 81.

46. Gould, Presidency of Roosevelt, 31.

47. Morris, Theodore Rex, 140.

48. Benjamin Kleinerman, The Discretionary President: The Promise and Peril of Executive Power 181 (2009).

49. Skowronek, Politics, 232.

50. Herring, Colony to Superpower, ch. 9.

51. For example, a secret Taft-Katsura executive agreement with Japan gave Japan a free hand in Korea despite an American treaty with Korea; Japan renounced any threat to the Philippines or Hawaii. When asked whether to notify the Senate of one such agreement, the president snapped: "Why invite the expression of views with which we may not agree?" Id., 362.

52. 17 Theodore Roosevelt, The Works of Theodore Roosevelt 93–160 (1923); Morris, Theodore Rex, ch. 4.

53. Gould, Presidency of Roosevelt, ch. 3; H. W. Brands, T.R.: The Last Romantic, ch. 17 (1997).

54. *Northern Securities Co. v. United States*, 193 U.S. 197 (1904). The three titans of industry emerged unscathed because the suit was structured to let them profit from dissolution.

55. Roosevelt's refusal to give Congress some documents pertaining to Standard Oil was an early example of the assertion of executive privilege regarding domestic policy. William H. Harbaugh, *The Constitution of the Theodore Roosevelt Presidency and the Progressive Era*, in The Constitution and the American Presidency 63, 75–76 (Martin L. Fausold & Alan Shank eds. 1991).

56. McDonald, American Presidency, 286–87.

57. Gould, Presidency of Roosevelt, ch. 7; Brands, T.R., ch. 21.

58. Edmund Morris, The Rise of Theodore Roosevelt, ch. 16 (1979).

59. Morris, Theodore Rex, chs. 9–11.

60. Gould, Presidency of Roosevelt, 64.

61. Id., 66.

62. Morris, Theodore Rex, 225–26.

63. Doris Kearns Goodwin, The Bully Pulpit: Theodore Roosevelt, William Howard Taft, and the Golden Age of Journalism (2013).

64. Kenneth R. Mayer, With the Stroke of a Pen: Executive Orders and Presidential Power 10, 51–52 (2001).

65. Graham G. Dodds, Take Up Your Pen: Unilateral Presidential Directives in American Politics, ch. 5 & p. 152 (2013). At 25, Dodds has a vivid graph of presidential use of executive orders throughout American history. The graph shows a gradually increasing pace until a sharp rise occurs under Theodore Roosevelt, with successors remaining near or above his levels through the second President Roosevelt.

66. There was also an early legislative victory, as Congress enacted the Newlands Reclamation Act in 1902 to authorize western water projects. Gould, Presidency of Roosevelt, 57–58.

67. Morris, Theodore Rex, 107.

68. Dodds, Pen, 144–50. Had the president failed to save the buffalo, those of us at the University of Colorado would have lost our mascot.

69. Harold H. Bruff, Judicial Review and the President's Statutory Powers, 68 Va. L. Rev. 1 (1982).

70. Nathan Miller, Theodore Roosevelt: A Life 469–72 (1992).

71. Dodds, Pen, 147.

72. 16 U.S.C. § 431.

73. Dodds, Pen, 148. Years later, Congress relented and made it a magnificent national park.

74. Harold H. Bruff, Executive Power and the Public Lands, 76 U. Colo. L. Rev. 503 (2005).

75. United States v. Midwest Oil Co., 236 U.S. 459 (1915).

76. Gould, Presidency of Roosevelt, ch. 4.

77. Morris, Theodore Rex, 325–26.

78. Lears, Rebirth, ch. 7.

79. David McCullough, The Path Between the Seas: The Creation of the Panama Canal, 1870–1914, chs. 12–13 (1977).

80. Herring, Colony to Superpower, 368.

81. Gould, Presidency of Roosevelt, 92.

82. Id., ch. 3.

83. Id., ch. 10.

84. Morris, Theodore Rex, ch. 29.

85. Gould, Presidency of Roosevelt, ch. 8.

86. Morris, Theodore Rex, 541–42.

87. Id., 446.

88. Skowronek, Politics, 252–53.

89. Patricia O'Toole, When Trumpets Call: Theodore Roosevelt after the White House (2005).

90. Paolo E. Coletta, The Presidency of William Howard Taft (1973); Gould, Modern Presidency, ch. 2.

91. Gerhardt, Forgotten Presidents, ch. 11.

92. As Roosevelt's secretary of war, Taft had demonstrated these skills by his prompt and effective use of the military to provide aid to the stricken city of San Francisco in the wake of the devastating earthquake and fire of 1906. Simon Winchester, A Crack in the Edge of the World: America and the Great California Earthquake of 1906, 310–11 (2005).

93. William H. Taft, Our Chief Magistrate and His Powers 139–40 (1925). Note the title, which does not exude imperial pretensions.

94. Donald F. Anderson, William Howard Taft: A Conservative's Conception of the Presidency 291–95 (1968).

95. Gerhardt, Forgotten Presidents, 172–73.

96. Skowronek, Politics, 244–45.

97. Stephen Skowronek, Presidential Leadership in Political Time: Reprise and Reappraisal 21 (2d ed. 2011).

98. Taft, Chief Magistrate, 157.

99. Dodds, Pen, 172.

100. Id., 174.

101. Lears, Rebirth, 2.

102. Cooper, Wilson, 3, 5.

103. Berg, Wilson, ch. 1.

104. Kendrick A. Clements, The Presidency of Woodrow Wilson 2 (1992).

105. Id., 8.

106. Berg, Wilson, ch. 9.

107. Cooper, Wilson, 79.

108. Berg, Wilson, 309.

109. Clements, Presidency of Wilson, 127.

110. Herring, Colony to Superpower, 407.

111. Berg, Wilson, ch. 8.

112. Jeffrey K. Tulis, The Rhetorical Presidency, ch. 5 (1988).

113. Cooper, Wilson, ch. 11.

114. McDonald, American Presidency, 355.

115. An early supporter in the Senate once said: "Wilson had no friends, only slaves and enemies." Berg, Wilson, 5.

116. Conventional legal history dates the origin of the independent agencies to the formation of the Interstate Commerce Commission in 1887. But the ICC was initially put in the Interior Department and only later made a separate entity. In congressional debates in 1910 came the intellectual justification for the ICC's independence, as several members of Congress said it was an "arm of Congress,"

not the executive, because of its "legislative" rate-setting function. The FTC Act brought the developing theories of independence together. Robert E. Cushman, The Independent Regulatory Commissions 101–14 (1941).

117. 15 U.S.C. § 41 et seq.

118. Clements, Presidency of Wilson, 80–81.

119. See Richard B. Bernstein with Jerome Agel, Amending America: If We Love the Constitution So Much, Why Do We Keep Trying to Change It? 128–34 (1993); Akhil Reed Amar, America's Constitution: A Biography, ch. 11 (2005).

120. Cooper, Wilson, 212.

121. Nathan Miller, New World Coming: The 1920s and the Making of Modern America 18 (2003) (quoting Wilson biographer Arthur Link).

122. Lears, Rebirth, 323.

123. Herring, Colony to Superpower, ch. 10.

124. Clements, Presidency of Wilson, ch. 6.

125. Id., 106.

126. Berg, Wilson, 321–23.

127. Clements, Presidency of Wilson, ch. 7. For Wilson's long journey toward war, see Herring, Colony to Superpower, ch. 10.

128. For example, after a Wilson reference to "peace without victory" outraged the Allies, Lansing made an unauthorized public statement to appease them, infuriating Wilson. Herring, Colony to Superpower, 408.

129. Wilson had 49 percent of the popular vote to 46 percent for Charles Evans Hughes. Berg, Wilson, 416.

130. Lears, Rebirth, 339.

131. Cooper, Wilson, 380.

132. Berg, Wilson, 430.

133. Cooper, Wilson, ch. 17.

134. Address to a Joint Session of Congress (April 2, 1917), 41 Papers of Woodrow Wilson 519–27 (Arthur S. Link ed., 1966).

135. Berg, Wilson, ch. 12.

136. Clement, Presidency of Wilson, ch. 8.

137. Clinton Rossiter, Constitutional Dictatorship: Crisis Government in the Modern Democracies, ch. 16 & p. 241 (1948).

138. Id., 247.

139. Id., 245–46.

140. Id., 254.

141. Dodds, Pen, 161. The Supreme Court generally upheld the extraordinary wartime statutes. Rossiter, Constitutional Dictatorship, 254.

142. Lears, Rebirth, 328.

143. Address to a Joint Session of Congress (January 8, 1918), 45 Papers of Wilson, 537.

144. Clements, Presidency of Wilson, ch. 9.

145. See Margaret McMillan, Paris 1919: Six Months That Changed the World (2003).

146. Cooper, Wilson, chs. 20–21.

147. Clement, Presidency of Wilson, 177.

148. Cooper, Wilson, 515.

149. A treaty amendment requires assent of the other nations for the treaty to be effective; a unilateral reservation does not.

150. Gene Smith, When the Cheering Stopped: The Last Years of Woodrow Wilson (1964).

151. Cooper, Wilson, chs. 22–23.

152. Clement, Presidency of Wilson, 205.

153. In 1967, the Twenty-Fifth Amendment was added to fill the gap; it has a complicated procedure for situations of temporary disability that has been invoked when presidents have undergone surgery.

154. Cooper, Wilson, 539.

155. Geoffrey R. Stone, Perilous Times: Free Speech in Wartime, ch. 3 (2004).

156. Id., 137.

157. Clement, Presidency of Wilson, 152.

158. 40 Stat. 217.

159. Stone, Perilous Times, 151.

160. 40 Stat. 553. The act was repealed in late 1920. The Espionage Act remains.

161. Stone, Perilous Times, 189.

162. Berg, Wilson, 497: "Wilson's fingerprints were all over them."

163. Clement, Presidency of Wilson, 153.

164. Stone, Perilous Times, 165 n.

165. Cooper, Wilson, ch. 18.

166. Lears, Rebirth, 341.

167. Stone, Perilous Times, 196–97.

168. Clement, Presidency of Wilson, 212.

169. Cooper, Wilson, 407–8.

170. In *Abrams v. United States*, 250 U.S. 616, 630 (1919), Holmes said that he thought the nation had showed its "repentance" for the 1798 statute by repaying the fines levied under it and that the error should not be repeated.

171. Cooper, Wilson, 573.

172. Debs was eventually pardoned by President Harding, having suffered far more than did Clement Vallandigham in the Civil War.

173. Gould, Modern Presidency, 54.

Chapter Eight

1. In Brief Authority 219 (1962).

2. John M. Cooper Jr., Woodrow Wilson: A Biography 589 (2009). Wilson's

treasury secretary, William McAdoo, added that Harding's "speeches left the impression of an army of pompous phrases moving over the landscape in search of an idea." Kendrick A. Clements, The Presidency of Woodrow Wilson 222 (1992).

3. Nathan Miller, New World Coming: The 1920s and the Making of Modern America 73 (2003).

4. Id., 88.

5. Quoted in Graham G. Dodds, Take Up Your Pen: Unilateral Presidential Directives in American Politics 177 (2013). The contents of the "what not" category remain unexplored.

6. Laton McCartney, The Teapot Dome Scandal: How Big Oil Bought the Harding White House and Tried to Steal the Country (2008).

7. Miller, New World, ch. 5.

8. Id., 108.

9. McCartney, Teapot Dome, ch. 27.

10. Miller, New World, 124.

11. Michael J. Gerhardt, The Forgotten Presidents: Their Untold Constitutional Legacy, ch. 12 (2013).

12. David M. Kennedy, Freedom from Fear: The American People in Depression and War, 1929–1945, 33 (1999).

13. Miller, New World, ch. 17.

14. George C. Herring, From Colony to Superpower: U.S. Foreign Relations since 1776, ch. 11 (2008).

15. Id., 472.

16. Kennedy, Freedom from Fear, 11 (quoting Sherwood Anderson).

17. William E. Leuchtenburg, Franklin Roosevelt and the New Deal, 1932–1940, 13 (1963).

18. Michele Landis Dauber, The Sympathetic State: Disaster Relief and the Origins of the American Welfare State 3 (2013).

19. Kennedy, Freedom from Fear, chs. 1–3.

20. Stephen Skowronek, The Politics Presidents Make: Leadership from John Adams to George Bush 279 (1993).

21. Rick Perlstein, Nixonland: The Rise of a President and the Fracturing of America (2008), explains that the conservative political movement usually attributed to Ronald Reagan was actually initiated by Richard Nixon.

22. Jean E. Smith, FDR x (2007).

23. Kennedy, Freedom from Fear, 112.

24. Lewis L. Gould, The Modern American Presidency, ch. 4 (2009).

25. Kennedy, Freedom from Fear, 95.

26. Skowronek, Politics, 300.

27. Robert H. Jackson, That Man: An Insider's Portrait of Franklin D. Roosevelt 74 (John Q. Barrett ed., 2003): "The President had a tendency to think in terms of right and wrong, instead of terms of legal and illegal. Because he thought

his motives were always good for the things that he wanted to do, he found difficulty in thinking that there could be legal limitations on them."

28. Jeff Shesol, Supreme Power: Franklin Roosevelt vs. the Supreme Court 47 (2010).

29. Leuchtenburg, New Deal, ch. 2.

30. Jonathan Alter, The Defining Moment: FDR's Hundred Days and the Triumph of Hope 5 (2006).

31. Smith, FDR, 302.

32. Id., ch. 15.

33. James MacGregor Burns, Roosevelt: The Lion and the Fox 166–67 (1956).

34. Kennedy, Freedom from Fear, ch. 5.

35. For excellent histories of the New Deal, see Leuchtenburg, New Deal; Burns, Lion and Fox.

36. Clinton Rossiter, Constitutional Dictatorship: Crisis Government in the Modern Democracies, ch. 17 (1948).

37. Dauber, Sympathetic State, ch. 5.

38. 48 Stat. 195 (1933). See 2 Bruce Ackerman, We the People: Transformations, ch. 10 (1998).

39. Skowronek, Politics, ch. 7, pt. 1.

40. Smith, FDR, 332.

41. Rossiter, Constitutional Dictatorship, 263.

42. Leuchtenburg, New Deal, ch. 14.

43. Shesol, Supreme Power, 272.

44. Forrest McDonald, The American Presidency: An Intellectual History 354 (1992).

45. Arthur M. Schlesinger Jr., The Imperial Presidency, ch. 5 (1973).

46. Dodds, Pen, 166; Steven G. Calabresi & Christopher S. Yoo, The Unitary Executive: Presidential Power from Washington to Bush 280 (2008).

47. Jonathan Alter, The Promise: President Obama, Year One 423 (2010).

48. Stephen Hess, Organizing the Presidency 1–3 (1966).

49. Kennedy, Freedom from Fear, 620.

50. The president's bureaucracy for legal advice was expanding. In 1933, Congress created what is now the Office of Legal Counsel in the Department of Justice, headed by an assistant attorney general, to write most formal opinions to the president and other executive officers.

51. Shesol, Supreme Power, 43.

52. Kennedy, Freedom from Fear, 117.

53. Harold J. Krent, Presidential Powers, 58–69 (2005).

54. Leuchtenburg, New Deal, ch. 7.

55. Kennedy, Freedom from Fear, 247. Toward the end of FDR's presidency, his fourth inaugural articulated an "economic bill of rights," revealing his enduring devotion to this theme. Id., 784.

56. Id., 287.

57. Id., chs. 9, 12.

58. For the full list, see Skowronek, Politics, 312. In 1938 the last of the New Deal statutes passed, with minimum wage guarantees and renewed farm supports to replace a program invalidated by the Supreme Court.

59. Kennedy, Freedom from Fear, 337.

60. Barry Friedman, The Will of the People: How Public Opinion Has Influenced the Supreme Court and Shaped the Meaning of the Constitution, introduction (2009).

61. James MacGregor Burns, Packing the Court: The Rise of Judicial Power and the Coming Crisis of the Supreme Court, ch. 8 (2009), Lion and Fox, ch. 15.

62. *Louisville Joint Stock Land Bank v. Radford*, 295 U.S. 555 (1935).

63. 295 U.S. 495 (1935).

64. 295 U.S. 602 (1935).

65. Recall Humphrey's disdain for the FTC at the time of his appointment to it. His subsequent behavior was consistent with his attitude. The decision was *Myers v. United States*, 272 U.S. 52 (1926).

66. See chapter 2.

67. Harold H. Bruff, Balance of Forces: Separation of Powers Law in the Administrative State, ch. 17 (2006).

68. See Calabresi & Yoo, Unitary Executive, ch. 32, lamenting this development.

69. *United States v. Butler*, 297 U.S. 1 (1936); *Carter v. Carter Coal Co.*, 298 U.S. 238 (1936).

70. Dauber, Sympathetic State, ch. 6.

71. Kennedy, Freedom from Fear, 273.

72. Ackerman, Transformations, ch. 11.

73. Burns, Lion and Fox, 295.

74. The recent national experience with Prohibition had shown the perils of constitutional experimentation. (During Prohibition, only President Hoover had shown any willingness to enforce the implementing statute; Harding and Coolidge demurred.)

75. There were six justices at the founding, five in 1801, nine in 1837, ten in 1863, and nine again since 1869.

76. Shesol, Supreme Power, 58.

77. Smith, FDR, 379; see chapter 6.

78. Akhil Reed Amar, America's Unwritten Constitution: The Precedents and Principles We Live By, ch. 1 (2012).

79. Shesol, Supreme Power, ch. 12.

80. Smith, FDR, ch. 17.

81. Burns, Lion and Fox, 296.

82. Shesol, Supreme Power, chs. 14–16; Ackerman, Transformations, ch. 11.

83. For the president's argument for his plan and the Senate report condemning it, see Peter M. Shane & Harold H. Bruff, Separation of Powers Law: Cases and Materials 398–403 (3d ed. 2011).

84. Ackerman, Transformations, 326–27.

85. Id., ch. 11.

86. *West Coast Hotel v. Parrish*, 300 U.S. 379 (1937).

87. *NLRB v. Jones & Laughlin Steel Corp.*, 301 U.S. 1 (1937); *Steward Machine Co. v. Davis*, 301 U.S. 548 (1937); *Helvering v. Davis*, 301 U.S. 619 (1937). In *Cincinnati Soap Co. v. United States*, 301 U.S. 308 (1937), the Court strongly endorsed the Hamiltonian view of the spending power that it had adopted in *Butler*.

88. Shesol, Supreme Power, ch. 14. There is normally a lapse of some months between the votes of justices to affirm or reverse a lower court decision, which are taken after oral argument, and the issuance of final opinions in a case.

89. Reorganization of the Federal Judiciary, S. Rep. No. 711, 75th Cong., 1st Sess. (1937).

90. Burns, Lion and Fox, 315.

91. Burns, Packing the Court, 155.

92. Shesol, Supreme Power, 518.

93. Ackerman, Transformations, ch. 11.

94. Id., 351–53.

95. Barry D. Karl, Executive Reorganization and Reform in the New Deal: The Genesis of Administrative Management, 1900–1939 (1963).

96. Calabresi & Yoo, Unitary Executive, 291–301.

97. Skowronek, Politics, 318–19.

98. In another action with institutional consequences, Congress enacted the Federal Register Act, which requires that unclassified executive orders be published. Dodds, Pen, 183–85. The act responded to the administrative chaos of the NRA, when the orders were often unavailable to the affected public.

99. Harold H. Bruff, Bad Advice: Bush's Lawyers in the War on Terror 66 (2009). FDR chose his trusted longtime adviser, Samuel Rosenman, as the first counsel.

100. This section draws on Herring, Colony to Superpower, ch. 12; Kennedy, Freedom from Fear, ch. 13; Robert Dallek, Franklin D. Roosevelt and American Foreign Policy, 1932–1945 (1995).

101. *United States v. Belmont*, 301 U.S. 324 (1937); *United States v. Pink*, 315 U.S. 203 (1942).

102. Herring, Colony to Superpower, 500.

103. Dodds, Pen, 162. He even made a direct bow to Theodore's legacy by designating Jackson Hole, Wyoming, as a national monument after Congress had declined to protect it by legislation. Id., 167–68.

104. 299 U.S. 304 (1936); see H. Jefferson Powell, *The Story of* Curtiss-Wright Export Corporation, in Presidential Power Stories 195 (Christopher H. Schroeder & Curtis A. Bradley eds., 2009).

105. Herring, Colony to Superpower, ch. 12; Kennedy, Freedom from Fear, ch. 14; Schlesinger, Imperial Presidency, chs. 4–5.

106. Belligerent nations could send ships to take away supplies paid for with cash.

107. Susan Dunn, 1940: FDR, Willkie, Lindbergh, Hitler—the Election amid the Storm, at 35 (2013). At 33, she reports that in September 1939, the US Army of 175,000 troops ranked eighteenth in the world.

108. David Kaiser, No End Save Victory: How FDR Led the Nation into War (2014).

109. Dunn, 1940, 38.

110. Smith, FDR, ch. 21.

111. Dunn, 1940, 98.

112. Id., ch. 10.

113. Leuchtenburg, New Deal, 314–15.

114. Kennedy, Freedom from Fear, 445.

115. James MacGregor Burns, Roosevelt: The Soldier of Freedom 11 (1970).

116. Kennedy, Freedom from Fear, 453–54.

117. For a full exploration of the destroyer deal, see Bruff, Bad Advice, ch. 3.

118. Dunn, 1940, ch. 15.

119. For a biography of Jackson, see Eugene C. Gerhart, America's Advocate: Robert H. Jackson (1958).

120. Jackson later recalled that the summer of 1940 "saw a change in the Roosevelt internal policy. Originally it was to submit any proposal to Congress for specific authorization. It shifted to one of independent executive action." Jackson, That Man, 82.

121. Doris Kearns Goodwin, No Ordinary Time: Franklin and Eleanor Roosevelt; The Home Front in World War II, 142 (1994).

122. Id., 147–48.

123. Bruce Ackerman & David Golove, Is NAFTA Constitutional? 56 n.251 (1995).

124. Smith, FDR, 472.

125. The opinion is *Acquisition of Naval and Air Bases in Exchange for Over-Age Destroyers*, reprinted in H. Jefferson Powell, The Constitution and the Attorneys General 307–14 (1999).

126. Schlesinger, Imperial Presidency, 109.

127. For a summary of Roosevelt's actions based on executive power before World War II, see Mariah Zeisberg, War Powers: The Politics of Constitutional Authority 62–64 (2013).

128. Kennedy, Freedom from Fear, 474.

129. Edward Corwin, Total War and the Constitution: Five Lectures Delivered . . . at the University of Michigan, March 1946, 22 (1947).

130. See chapter 4.

131. Dodds, Pen, 169.

132. Kaiser, No End, 272. FDR compared his behavior to that of President Adams in the quasi war with France and President Jefferson in pursuit of the Barbary pirates. Id., 276.

133. Roberta Wohlstetter, Pearl Harbor: Warning and Decision 239–40 (1962).

134. For the full story, see William Stevenson, A Man Called Intrepid: The Secret War (1976).

135. Id., ch. 28.

136. Leuchtenburg, New Deal, 214–15.

137. Kennedy, Freedom from Fear, ch. 15.

138. Schlesinger, Imperial Presidency, 99.

139. Discussing the wartime internment of Japanese-Americans, Burns, Soldier of Freedom, 215–16, observes that federal officials were "divided, irresolute, and not committed against racism" and that "only a strong civil-libertarian President could have faced down all these forces, and Roosevelt was not a strong civil libertarian."

140. This section draws on Geoffrey R. Stone, Perilous Times: Free Speech in Wartime, ch. 4 (2004).

141. Id., 252.

142. Id., 248.

143. Dunn, 1940, ch. 16.

144. 54 Stat. 670.

145. Stone, Perilous Times, 255.

146. Biddle, Brief Authority, 237–38.

147. Convicted of seditious libel, Pelley was sentenced to fifteen years.

148. The proceedings dragged on for years, ending when the indictments were dismissed after the end of the war.

149. See Peter Irons, Justice at War (1983); Greg Robinson, By Order of the President: FDR and the Internment of Japanese Americans (2001); Page Smith, Democracy on Trial: The Japanese American Evacuation and Relocation in World War II, ch. 8 (ironically titled "The Decision Nobody Made") (1995).

150. Biddle, Brief Authority, 213.

151. For a summary and refutation of DeWitt's Final Report, see Justice Murphy's impassioned dissent in Korematsu v. United States, 323 U.S. 214 (1944).

152. Robinson, Order of the President, 105–6; Smith, Democracy on Trial, 122.

153. Biddle later reflected: "Once, he emphasized to me, when I was expressing my belief that the evacuation was unnecessary, that this must be a military decision." Brief Authority, 219.

154. Executive Order No. 9066, 7 Fed. Reg. 1407 (February 19, 1942).

155. Biddle, Brief Authority, 219.

156. Robinson, Order of the President, 121.

157. Pub. L. No. 503, 56 Stat. 173 (1942). See Irons, Justice at War, 66–68, for the legislative history.

158. The principal case is Korematsu v. United States, 323 U.S. 214 (1944). See

Irons, Justice at War; Report of the Commission on Wartime Relocation and Internment of Civilians, Personal Justice Denied (1983).

159. Robinson, Order of the President, chs. 1–2.

160. See Biddle, Brief Authority, ch. 21; Louis Fisher, Military Tribunals and Presidential Power (2005), and Nazi Saboteurs on Trial: A Military Tribunal and American Law (2003).

161. Biddle, Brief Authority, 328.

162. Id., 330. "Without splitting hairs" he could see no difference between this case and the hanging of Major Andre, and concluded, "Don't split hairs, Mr. Attorney General."

163. Fisher, Military Tribunals, 98.

164. In *Ex Parte Milligan*, 71 U.S. 2 (1867), decided just after the Civil War, the Supreme Court had shown that it understood the difference by refusing to allow trial by military commission of a civilian in Indiana, where the courts were open and functioning. Biddle thought *Milligan* was inapplicable to enemy aliens.

165. Proclamation 2561 (July 2, 1942).

166. Biddle, Brief Authority, 331.

167. The Supreme Court later issued a full opinion, *Ex Parte Quirin*, 317 U.S. 1 (1942).

168. Rossiter, Constitutional Dictatorship, 271.

169. See Burns, Soldier of Freedom; Nigel Hamilton, The Mantle of Command: FDR at War, 1941–1942 (2014); Andrew Roberts, Masters and Commanders: How Four Titans Won the War in the West, 1941–1945 (2009).

170. Roberts, Commanders, 441.

171. During the war Roosevelt once said, "I am perfectly willing to mislead and tell untruths if it will help win the war." Herring, Colony to Superpower, 545.

172. FDR always understood MacArthur's menace. During the New Deal, he once said that radical senator Huey Long was "one of the two most dangerous men in America." When asked for the identity of the other, he replied "Douglas MacArthur." Leuchtenburg, New Deal, 96.

173. Herring, Colony to Superpower, ch. 13.

174. Eric Alterman, When Presidents Lie: A History of Official Deception and Its Consequences, ch. 2 (2004).

175. For this paragraph, see Ackerman & Golove, NAFTA, 45–92.

176. Id., 61.

177. Smith, FDR, 618.

178. Matthew B. Wills, A Diminished President: FDR in 1944 (2003).

Chapter Nine

1. David McCullough, Truman 897 (1992).

2. Eleanor Roosevelt broke the news after Truman was hurriedly called to the White House: "Harry, the president is dead." Robert J. Donovan, Conflict and

Crisis: The Presidency of Harry S Truman, 1945–1948, at 7 (1977). Departing from a White House reception the previous fall, Truman had been told by a friend that he would be living there. Truman responded that he knew that, "and it scares the hell out of me." Id., 9.

3. David M. Kennedy, Freedom from Fear: The American People in Depression and War, 1929–1945, 790 (1999).

4. McCullough, Truman, 384.

5. Id., 558.

6. Lewis L. Gould, The Modern American Presidency, ch. 5 (2009).

7. Donald R. McCoy, *The Constitution of the Truman Presidency and the Post–World War II Era*, in The Constitution and the American Presidency 107, 109–10, 128 (Martin L. Fausold & Alan Shank eds., 1991).

8. McCullough, Truman, ch. 9.

9. Donald R. McCoy, The Presidency of Harry S. Truman, ch. 2 (1984).

10. Gould, Modern Presidency, ch. 5.

11. McCullough, Truman, 479.

12. Truman reappointed David Lilienthal at the Tennessee Valley Authority although he was in trouble for making merit rather than patronage appointments within TVA.

13. McCullough, Truman, ch. 9.

14. Donovan, Conflict and Crisis, ch. 5.

15. McCullough, Truman, 442.

16. Donovan, Conflict and Crisis, chs. 5, 7.

17. Id., chs. 8–9.

18. McCoy, Presidency of Truman, 36.

19. Id., ch. 3.

20. Donovan, Conflict and Crisis, pt. 2.

21. James T. Patterson, Grand Expectations: The United States, 1945–1974, ch. 2 (1996).

22. Donovan, Conflict and Crisis, ch. 22.

23. McCullough, Truman, ch. 11.

24. Id., 501.

25. McCoy, Presidency of Truman, 106–9.

26. Steven G. Calabresi & Christopher S. Yoo, The Unitary Executive: Presidential Power from Washington to Bush 314 (2008).

27. Gould, Modern Presidency, ch. 5.

28. Franklin Roosevelt had initiated the program with a narrower order barring race discrimination in government procurement and civilian agencies. See chapter 8.

29. McCullough, Truman, 638.

30. Id., 654.

31. H. L. Mencken said that Dewey's speeches reminded him of the "worst bombast of university professors." Id., 712. No one who commits *that* sin should reach the presidency.

32. McCoy, Presidency of Truman, 299–300.

33. Dean Acheson, Present at the Creation: My Years in the State Department xvi (1969).

34. For a full exploration of the themes raised in this paragraph, see Stephen M. Griffin, Long Wars and the Constitution (2013). See also Garry Wills, Bomb Power: The Modern Presidency and the National Security State (2010).

35. George C. Herring, From Colony to Superpower: U.S. Foreign Relations since 1776, 595 (2008).

36. Walter Isaacson & Evan Thomas, The Wise Men: Six Friends and the World They Made (rev. ed. 2012) (discussing Averill Harriman, Dean Acheson, Robert Lovett, George Kennan, John McCloy, and Charles Bohlen).

37. Herring, Colony to Superpower, ch. 14.

38. Michael J. Hogan, A Cross of Iron: Harry S Truman and the Origins of the National Security State, 1945–1954, at 415 (1998).

39. Griffin, Long Wars, ch. 3.

40. Herring, Colony to Superpower, 614.

41. Id., quoting Clark Clifford.

42. Tim Weiner, Legacy of Ashes: The History of the CIA (2007).

43. McCullough, Truman, ch. 12.

44. Griffin, Long Wars, 66.

45. Herring, Colony to Superpower, ch. 14.

46. Gould, Modern Presidency, ch. 5.

47. Donovan, Conflict and Crisis, chs. 34, 39; McCoy, Presidency of Truman, 135–37.

48. McCullough, Truman, 630.

49. Herring, Colony to Superpower, ch. 14.

50. Richard Reeves, Daring Young Men: The Heroism and Triumph of the Berlin Airlift, June 1948–May 1949 (2011).

51. McCullough, Truman, 752.

52. McCoy, Presidency of Truman, 119.

53. Herring, Colony to Superpower, 625.

54. Patterson, Grand Expectations, ch. 7.

55. In 1950, a strategic document called NSC-68 responded to President Truman's call for a survey of the Soviet and Chinese threats by summarizing the challenges of containment and calling for a large buildup in American military power to conduct a long worldwide struggle. Robert J. Donovan, Tumultuous Years: The Presidency of Harry S Truman, 1949–1953, ch. 15 (1982).

56. Wills, Bomb Power, ch. 2.

57. McCoy, Presidency of Truman, 221–22.

58. David Halberstam, The Coldest Winter: America and the Korean War 93 (2007).

59. Patterson, Grand Expectations, ch. 8.

60. Griffin, Long Wars, 71–77; McCoy, Presidency of Truman, ch. 10.

61. Donovan, Tumultuous Years, 206.

62. Halberstam, Coldest Winter, 99.

63. Griffin, Long Wars, 72; McCoy, Presidency of Truman, 224.

64. Donovan, Tumultuous Years, ch. 21.

65. Halberstam, Coldest Winter, 99.

66. McCullough, Truman, 789.

67. McCoy, Presidency of Truman, 229.

68. Patterson, Grand Expectations, 213.

69. McCoy, Presidency of Truman, ch. 10.

70. Arthur M. Schlesinger Jr., The Imperial Presidency 132–33 (1973).

71. Halberstam, Coldest Winter, 116.

72. Patterson, Grand Expectations, ch. 8.

73. Donovan, Tumultuous Years, ch. 26.

74. Halberstam, Coldest Winter, 11–12.

75. Id., ch. 48.

76. Donovan, Tumultuous Years, ch.32.

77. Halberstam, Coldest Winter, ch. 49.

78. Id., 605.

79. As MacArthur said in his grandiloquent speech to Congress, "Old soldiers never die, they just fade away." Donovan, Tumultuous Years, 362.

80. Fittingly, William Manchester's 1978 biography of MacArthur is titled American Caesar. Fortunately, MacArthur never crossed either the Rubicon or the Yalu, although he came too close to both.

81. McCullough, Truman, 849.

82. Griffin, Long Wars, ch. 2.

83. Louis Fisher, Presidential War Power, ch. 4 (2d ed. 2004).

84. U.S. Department of State, Authority of the President to Repel the Attack in Korea, 23 Dept. State Bull. 173 (1950).

85. For a chart contrasting Korea with other foreign wars in terms of congressional authorization, see Griffin, Long Wars, 46–47.

86. Louis Fisher, In the Name of National Security: Unchecked Presidential Power and the Reynolds Case (2006).

87. 345 U.S. 1 (1953).

88. 343 U.S. 579 (1952). See Patricia L. Bellia, The Story of the Steel Seizure Case, in Presidential Power Stories 233 (Curtis Bradley & Christopher Schroeder eds., 2009).

89. Donovan, Tumultuous Years, 385.

90. Maeva Marcus, Truman and the Steel Seizure Case: The Limits of Presidential Power 225–26 (1977).

91. McCullough, Truman, 896–97.

92. Id.

93. Griffin, Long Wars, 91–92.

94. Alan F. Westin, The Anatomy of a Constitutional Law Case: *Youngstown Sheet and Tube Co. v. Sawyer*; The Steel Seizure Decision 64 (1958). This argument produced an immediate storm of criticism. President Truman himself issued a disclaimer: "The powers of the President are derived from the Constitution, and they are limited, of course, by the provisions of the Constitution, particularly those that protect the rights of individuals" (id., 67). The broad claims of power caused an adverse public and judicial reaction. William H. Rehnquist, The Supreme Court: How It Was, How It Is 47–53 (1987).

95. 343 U.S. at 635–39.

96. 343 U.S. at 683.

97. 343 U.S. at 702.

98. Harold H. Bruff, Balance of Forces: Separation of Powers Law in the Administrative State 154–62 (2006).

99. Geoffrey R. Stone, Perilous Times: Free Speech in Wartime, ch. 5 (2004).

100. McCullough, Truman, 521.

101. Stone, Perilous Times, ch. 5.

102. Graham G. Dodds, Take Up Your Pen: Unilateral Presidential Directives in American Politics 188 (2013); McCoy, Presidency of Truman, 83–84.

103. Henry Steele Commager called the order "an invitation to precisely that kind of witch-hunting which is repugnant to our constitutional system." Freedom and Order: A Commentary on the American Political Scene 73–74 (1966).

104. Stone, Perilous Times, 342.

105. The optimal number of subversives in any government is a function of their placement (the right number in nuclear laboratories might be zero; in furniture warehouses the number would be higher). One must also consider all costs of finding the subversives, including process costs, the error rate of dismissing loyal people, and the cost of suppressing protected speech by both persons targeted and others.

106. Stone, Perilous Times, 343.

107. The flaw was the absence of identification of complaining witnesses and the right to confront them, a bedrock guarantee of fair process.

108. Stone, Perilous Times, 348.

109. The closest case was the successful prosecution of Alger Hiss for perjury, for lying about spying for the Soviets in the 1930s.

110. Patterson, Grand Expectations, ch. 7.

111. Stone, Perilous Times, 332. In August 1951, Truman referred to McCarthy's "scurrilous work" of smear and accusation. Id., 338.

112. Truman successfully resisted various subpoenas from the loyalty police in both houses of Congress. Mark J. Rozell, Executive Privilege: Presidential Power, Secrecy, and Accountability 38–39 (3d ed. 2010).

113. Stone, Perilous Times, 335. Truman also called the bill a "mockery of the

Bill of Rights." McCoy, Presidency of Truman, 117. He also vetoed the McCarran-Walter Act in 1952, which allowed deporting subversive aliens, and was overridden again.

114. McCullough, Truman, 771.

115. For a balanced biography, see Jean Edward Smith, Eisenhower: In War and Peace (2012).

116. Fred I. Greenstein, The Hidden-Hand Presidency: Eisenhower as Leader (1982).

117. Herring, Colony to Superpower, 656.

118. Patterson, Grand Expectations, 271.

119. Jim Newton, Eisenhower: The White House Years 160 (2011).

120. His successor John F. Kennedy thought Eisenhower "had not understood the real powers of the office." Richard Reeves, President Kennedy: Profile of Power 23 (1993). Actually, the two men just viewed the powers differently.

121. Fisher, War Power, 117–18; Griffin, Long Wars, 104–9.

122. Mariah Zeisberg, War Powers: The Politics of Constitutional Authority 142 (2013).

123. Gould, Modern Presidency, ch. 5.

124. Patterson, Grand Expectations, 252.

125. Smith, Eisenhower, ch. 24.

126. Later in his presidency he would have intestinal surgery and a small stroke, but there would be no crisis to compare with the initial one.

127. Smith, Eisenhower, 543–44.

128. Stone, Perilous Times, 351.

129. By 1956, the totals since Truman began the program in 1947 were twenty-seven hundred dismissals and twelve thousand resignations. Id.

130. Dennis v. United States, 341 U.S. 494 (1951).

131. Newton, Eisenhower, ch. 8.

132. This is often cited as a successful example of Eisenhower's "hidden-hand" presidency.

133. Schlesinger, Imperial Presidency, ch. 6.

134. Rozell, Executive Privilege, 39–40.

135. Smith, Eisenhower, 593–94. McCarthy slunk away, eventually to die in alcoholic disgrace.

136. Herring, Colony to Superpower, ch. 15.

137. Smith, Eisenhower, ch. 20.

138. Newton, Eisenhower, chs. 5, 7, 14.

139. Id., 266–67.

140. Id., ch. 8.

141. Bruce Ackerman & David Golove, Is NAFTA Constitutional? 98–99 (1995).

142. George C. Herring, America's Longest War: The United States and Vietnam, 1950–1975 (4th ed. 2002).

143. Smith, Eisenhower, ch. 22.

144. Newton, Eisenhower, ch. 15.

145. Patterson, Grand Expectations, ch. 10.

146. Newton, Eisenhower, chs. 12, 15.

147. David A. Nichols, Eisenhower 1956: The President's Year of Crisis; Suez and the Brink of War 148 (2011).

148. Id., 56.

149. Patterson, Grand Expectations, ch. 13.

150. Smith, Eisenhower, 602–6.

151. In an equally casual way, he later nominated the liberal William Brennan to the Court. Later presidents would learn to vet nominees with greater care.

152. 337 U.S. 483 (1954).

153. Newton, Eisenhower, ch. 6. Eisenhower deplored "foolish extremists on both sides of the question" of segregation. Id., 174.

154. Calabresi & Yoo, Unitary Executive, 321.

155. Patterson, Grand Expectations, ch. 14.

156. Smith, Eisenhower, 724–27.

157. Herring, Colony to Superpower, 682.

158. William C. Banks & Peter Raven-Hansen, National Security Law and the Power of the Purse 51–52 (1994).

159. Newton, Eisenhower, ch. 5.

160. Id., ch. 9.

161. Patterson, Grand Expectations, ch. 10.

162. Id., ch. 14.

163. Eric Alterman, When Presidents Lie: A History of Official Deception and Its Consequences 18–19 (2004).

164. Griffin, Long Wars, 108–9.

Chapter Ten

1. President Kennedy's inaugural address is reproduced and analyzed in Thurston Clarke, Ask Not: The Inauguration of John F. Kennedy and the Speech That Changed America (2004).

2. Richard Reeves, President Kennedy: Profile of Power 19 (1993).

3. Id., 480.

4. This is the subtitle of Nigel Hamilton's JFK: Reckless Youth, a 1992 biography of Kennedy's early life.

5. Robert Dallek, An Unfinished Life: John F. Kennedy, 1917–1963, ch. 9 (2003).

6. Dallek, Unfinished Life, epilogue, implausibly so concludes.

7. Id., ch. 11.

8. Id., 313.

9. Lewis L. Gould, The Modern American Presidency, ch. 6 (2d ed. 2009).

10. Looking on, Eisenhower acutely observed that Kennedy's people "confuse 'smartness' with wisdom." Jim Newton, Eisenhower: The White House Years 349 (2011).

11. Robert Dallek, Camelot's Court: Inside the Kennedy White House 91 (2013), quoting David Riesman.

12. George C. Herring, From Colony to Superpower: U.S. Foreign Relations since 1776, ch. 16 (2008).

13. Dallek, Unfinished Life, 315.

14. Dallek, Camelot's Court, xi.

15. Dallek, Unfinished Life, 310.

16. Reeves, Kennedy, 29.

17. Id., ch. 20. For the durability of this massive response plan between the 1950s and the early 1990s, see Eric Schlosser, Command and Control: Nuclear Weapons, the Damascus Incident, and the Illusion of Safety (2013).

18. Stephen M. Griffin, Long Wars and the Constitution 111–12 (2013).

19. Id., 112.

20. James T. Patterson, Grand Expectations: The United States, 1945–1974, at 494 (1996), quoting press secretary Pierre Salinger's later assessment.

21. Reeves, Kennedy, ch. 6.

22. Dallek, Unfinished Life, 363.

23. Reeves, Kennedy, ch. 7.

24. Id., 101.

25. Dallek, Unfinished Life, 365.

26. Richard M. Pious, The American Presidency 352 (1979). Kennedy was often firm in exerting executive privilege against Congress as a means to preserve his control over foreign policy. Mark J. Rozell, Executive Privilege: Presidential Power, Secrecy, and Accountability 40–41 (3d ed. 2010).

27. Dallek, Camelot's Court, ch. 4.

28. Reeves, Kennedy, ch. 24. In October 1961, President Kennedy expressed concern with removing Castro "in some way or other." Dallek, Unfinished Life, 438. A congressional investigating committee later uncovered eight schemes to kill Castro between 1960 and 1965. Robert Kennedy would not have attempted an assassination without his brother's assent.

29. Garry Wills, Bomb Power: The Modern Presidency and the National Security State 156–58 (2010).

30. Reeves, Kennedy, ch. 31. When the question of assassination was accidentally mentioned in a memo, CIA Director McCone angrily reacted that it should never even be discussed, so went back underground. Id., 336–37. The initial action memorandum simply referred to planning to follow the oral instructions, whatever they were. Id., 265.

31. Dallek, Camelot's Court, ch. 5.

32. Reeves, Kennedy, chs. 13–15. Khrushchev thought Kennedy "too intelligent

and too weak." Id., 166. The president knew that and vowed to correct the impression of weakness (he couldn't help the intelligence).

33. Both John and Robert Kennedy were familiar with Barbara Tuchman's classic history of the blundering that led to World War I, The Guns of August (1962). At the height of the Cuban missile crisis, the president said to his brother, "I am not going to follow a course which will allow anyone to write a comparable book about this time, *The Missiles of October*." Robert F. Kennedy, Thirteen Days: A Memoir of the Cuban Missile Crisis 105 (1968).

34. See the epigraph to part 4 of this book. See generally Michael Dobbs, One Minute to Midnight: Kennedy, Khrushchev, and Castro on the Brink of Nuclear War (2008).

35. For this definition, see Sanford Levinson & Jack M. Balkin, *Constitutional Dictatorship: Its Dangers and Its Design*, 94 Minn. L. Rev. 101, 117 (2010).

36. Id., 137–38.

37. Mariah Zeisberg, War Powers: The Politics of Constitutional Authority 147–48 (2013).

38. Dallek, Camelot's Court, ch. 8.

39. Louis Fisher, Presidential War Power 126 (2d ed. 2004).

40. Zeisberg, War Powers, 149–50.

41. Dobbs, One Minute, ch. 1.

42. In bureaucratese, the Executive Committee of the National Security Council.

43. Kennedy, Thirteen Days, 11.

44. Dallek, Camelot's Court, 308–9.

45. Kennedy, Thirteen Days, 2, 5.

46. Dallek, Unfinished Life, 547.

47. Kennedy, Thirteen Days, 16.

48. Id., 89.

49. Dallek, Camelot's Court, 316.

50. Dobbs, One Minute.

51. Dallek, Unfinished Life, 553.

52. Reeves, Kennedy, 385.

53. Fisher, War Power, 127.

54. Robert Caro, The Years of Lyndon Johnson: The Passage of Power 208 (2012).

55. Kennedy, Thirteen Days, 105.

56. Dallek, Unfinished Life, 557.

57. Reeves, Kennedy, ch. 35.

58. Kennedy, Thirteen Days, 31–32.

59. Reeves, Kennedy, ch. 34.

60. Dobbs, One Minute, 50.

61. Reeves, Kennedy, ch. 35.

62. Dobbs, One Minute, 88.

63. Id., chs. 8–12; Reeves, Kennedy, ch. 36.

64. Zeisberg, War Powers, 149.

65. Kennedy, Thirteen Days, 76.

66. Dobbs, One Minute, ch. 13.

67. Id., 338. Robert Kennedy's version of the meeting with Dobrynin says that when asked about Turkey, he "said that there could be no quid pro quo or any arrangement made under this kind of threat" but that President Kennedy had wanted to remove the missiles and that it "was our judgment that, within a short time after this crisis was over, those missiles would be gone." Thirteen Days, 86–87.

68. Reeves, Kennedy, ch. 37.

69. For an exploration of this aspect of the crisis, see Eric Alterman, When Presidents Lie: A History of Official Deception and Its Consequences, ch. 3 (2004).

70. Levinson & Balkin, Dictatorship, 138.

71. Dallek, Camelot's Court, 330–31.

72. Patterson, Grand Expectations, 506, quoting Richard Rovere.

73. Dallek, Unfinished Life, ch. 18, notes that Kennedy conducted the negotiations with Wilson's experience after Versailles in mind. Therefore he kept congressional leaders informed throughout, invited a bipartisan delegation to the signing ceremony, and won ratification easily.

74. Dallek, Camelot's Court, 292.

75. Patterson, Great Expectations, 466.

76. Steven G. Calabresi & Christopher S. Yoo, The Unitary Executive: Presidential Power from Washington to Bush 332–33 (2008).

77. Dallek, Unfinished Life, ch. 10.

78. Reeves, Kennedy, ch. 27.

79. Id., ch. 10.

80. Id., ch. 33.

81. Id., 488–90.

82. Dallek, Unfinished Life, 595–96.

83. Id., 513, quoting Arthur Schlesinger.

84. Reeves, Kennedy, ch. 43.

85. Id., 504.

86. Id., ch. 51.

87. Thurston Clarke, JFK's Last Hundred Days: The Transformation of a Man and the Emergence of a Great President (2013).

88. Reeves, Kennedy, chs. 3, 9.

89. Id., ch. 9.

90. Dallek, Unfinished Life, 450.

91. Dallek, Camelot's Court, 407.

92. Reeves, Kennedy, ch. 55.

93. Dallek, Camelot's Court, 419.

94. Patterson, Grand Expectations, 516.

95. This was President Johnson's call for unity in his address to a joint session of Congress on November 27, 1963. Public Papers of the Presidents: Lyndon Baines Johnson 8 (1966).

96. Caro, Passage of Power, ch. 4.

97. Stephen Skowronek, The Politics Presidents Make: Leadership from John Adams to George Bush, ch. 7, pt. 2 (1993).

98. Caro, Passage of Power, ch. 6.

99. See id., ch. 7, for intimations of this phenomenon.

100. This section title alludes to Robert Caro's The Years of Lyndon Johnson: Master of the Senate (2002), the volume in his biography that details LBJ's career as a great leader of the Senate.

101. Caro, Passage of Power, 602.

102. Skowronek, Politics, 335.

103. Caro, Passage of Power, x.

104. LBJ's Aide Joseph Califano said he could be "altruistic and petty, caring and crude, generous and petulant, bluntly honest and calculatingly devious—all within the same few minutes." The Triumph and Tragedy of Lyndon Johnson: The White House Years 10 (1991).

105. Herring, Colony to Superpower, 730.

106. Patterson, Grand Expectations, 531.

107. Gould, Modern Presidency, ch. 6 (2009).

108. Doris Kearns Goodwin, Lyndon Johnson and the American Dream 222 (rev. ed. 1991).

109. Id., 226.

110. Robert Dallek, Flawed Giant: Lyndon Johnson and His Times, 1961–1973, 64 (1998).

111. Caro, Passage of Power, pt. 5.

112. Patterson, Grand Expectations, ch. 18.

113. Dallek, Flawed Giant, 112.

114. Caro, Passage of Power, 428.

115. Clay Risen, The Bill of the Century: The Epic Battle for the Civil Rights Act (2014).

116. Calabresi & Yoo, Unitary Executive, 341.

117. Patterson, Grand Expectations, ch. 19.

118. Almost a half century later, the Supreme Court erected an ironic monument to the act's success by striking down a central provision as no longer necessary. Shelby County v. Holder, 133 S.Ct. 2612 (2013).

119. Watching on television, Martin Luther King was moved to tears. Caro, Passage of Power, 569.

120. Gould, Modern Presidency, 144.

121. Skowronek, Politics, 325.

122. Rick Perlstein, Nixonland: The Rise of a President and the Fracturing of America, bk. 1 (2008).

123. George Herring, America's Longest War: The United States and Vietnam, 1950–1975 (1986). Herring estimates that the war cost the United States $150 billion between Truman's increase of aid in 1950 and the end of congressional funding in 1975 (xi). The conventional grand total of deaths on all sides is 3 million, including more than fifty-eight thousand Americans (and another eight hundred thousand Americans were wounded). See also Stanley Karnow, Vietnam: A History (1991).

124. Herring, Colony to Superpower, ch. 16.

125. David Halberstam, The Best and the Brightest (1972).

126. Griffin, Long Wars, ch. 4.

127. At his first national security meeting after becoming president, Johnson said: "I am not going to lose Vietnam. I am not going to be the President who saw Southeast Asia go the way China went." Dallek, Flawed Giant, 99.

128. Skowronek, Politics, ch. 7, pt. 2.

129. Herring, Longest War, 41–42.

130. Dallek, Flawed Giant, 105.

131. Id., ch. 3.

132. Edwin E. Moise, Tonkin Gulf and the Escalation of the Vietnam War (1996).

133. Dallek, Flawed Giant, 153.

134. Griffin, Long Wars, 126.

135. Alterman, When Presidents Lie, 161.

136. Fisher, War Power, 130–32.

137. Frederik Logevall, Choosing War: The Lost Chance for Peace and the Escalation of the War in Vietnam 204 (1999).

138. Herring, Colony to Superpower, 739.

139. Dallek, Flawed Giant, 373.

140. Patterson, Grand Expectations, ch. 20.

141. William C. Banks & Peter Raven-Hansen, National Security Law and the Power of the Purse, ch. 12 (1994).

142. Dallek, Flawed Giant, ch. 5.

143. Griffin, Long Wars, ch. 4. Citations of studies showing the decline during the 1960s are at 136–37.

144. Herring, Colony to Superpower, ch. 16.

145. Geoffrey R. Stone, Perilous Times: Free Speech in Wartime, ch. 6 (2004).

146. Dallek, Flawed Giant, ch. 9.

147. For example, the CIA is forbidden to engage in domestic surveillance, and the Fourth Amendment requires warrants for many investigations.

148. Herring, Colony to Superpower, 739

149. Dallek, Flawed Giant, chs. 9–10.

150. Id., 528. Johnson died of a heart attack in January 1973, just days after another term would have ended. Of course, he did not suffer the pressures of office during that time and might not have survived another term.

151. Patterson, Grand Expectations, ch. 12.

152. Dallek, Flawed Giant, ch. 5.

153. Herring, Colony to Superpower, Ch. 16.

Chapter Eleven

1. N.Y. Times, May 20, 1977, A16.

2. Arthur M. Schlesinger Jr., The Imperial Presidency (1973).

3. An aide to Richard Nixon once referred to him as "the oddest man I've ever known." George C. Herring, From Colony to Superpower: U.S. Foreign Relations since 1776, 763 (2008).

4. Richard Reeves, President Nixon: Alone in the White House 18 (2001), characterizes Nixon as "a powerful mind voyaging alone in anger and self-doubt." The prologue contains examples of his constant memos to himself containing resolutions about qualities he wanted to display, like compassion, boldness, courage, and strength. At 28–29 is a memo dictated to "Mrs. Nixon" from "The President," referring to himself in the third person and giving instructions on arrangements for his bedside table.

5. Lewis L. Gould, The Modern American Presidency, ch. 7 (2d ed. 2009).

6. Reeves, President Nixon, 325, remarks that Nixon and Henry Kissinger pared national security down to a "two-man operation."

7. Richard M. Nixon, In the Arena: A Memoir of Victory, Defeat, and Renewal 207 (1990).

8. 1 Richard M. Nixon, RN: The Memoirs of Richard Nixon 512 (1979).

9. Robert Dallek, Nixon and Kissinger: Partners in Power (2007).

10. Reeves, President Nixon, 33.

11. Gould, Modern Presidency, 151.

12. Id., 152. The exception to Nixon's cooperation with Congress on domestic policy involved the impoundment controversy, which I discuss below.

13. Dallek, Nixon & Kissinger, ch. 5; Stephen M. Griffin, Long Wars and the Constitution 139 (2013).

14. Reeves, President Nixon, ch. 3. Bombing of North Vietnamese troops in Laos began in February 1970; ever since the Kennedy administration the American military had been observing, training, and sometimes fighting in Laos. Id., ch. 11.

15. John Hart Ely, The American War in Indochina, Part II: The Unconstitutionality of the War They Didn't Tell Us About, 42 Stan. L. Rev. 1093 (1990).

16. Mariah Zeisberg, War Powers: The Politics of Constitutional Authority 152 (2013).

17. William Shawcross, Sideshow: Kissinger, Nixon, and the Destruction of Cambodia (1979).

18. Reeves, President Nixon, ch. 6.

19. Dallek, Nixon & Kissinger, ch. 7.

20. Reeves, President Nixon, 214.

21. The memo, by future Supreme Court justice William Rehnquist, is reproduced in Stephen M. Griffin, *A Bibliography of Executive Branch War Powers Opinions since 1950*, 87 Tul. L. Rev. 649, 686–704 (2013).

22. Schlesinger, Imperial Presidency, ch. 7.

23. Herring, Colony to Superpower, ch. 17.

24. Geoffrey R. Stone, Perilous Times: Free Speech in Wartime 467 (2004).

25. Schlesinger, Imperial Presidency, ch. 8.

26. Reeves, President Nixon, ch. 4.

27. Dallek, Nixon & Kissinger, ch. 5.

28. Reeves, President Nixon, chs. 14–15.

29. Benjamin Kleinerman, The Discretionary President: The Promise and Peril of Executive Power 168 (2009).

30. Stone, Perilous Times, ch. 6.

31. Under Lyndon Johnson, five people including Benjamin Spock and William Sloane Coffin were tried for the curious crime of conspiring to counsel violations of the draft law. Their convictions were reversed on appeal. Richard Nixon prosecuted radical antiwar leaders more actively; the cases were generally reversed on appeal if not dismissed earlier. The most famous trial, of the "Chicago Eight," charged demonstrators with a conspiracy to cross state lines to incite a riot and for doing so. After a tumultuous trial, the convictions and some severe contempt sentences were all overturned. Id.

32. Rick Perlstein, Nixonland: The Rise of a President and the Fracturing of America (2009).

33. Reeves, President Nixon, 158. Nixon did, however, continue the presidential practice of forbidding race discrimination in federal functions by executive order. Steven G. Calabresi & Christopher S. Yoo, The Unitary Executive: Presidential Power from Washington to Bush 349–50 (2008).

34. Reeves, President Nixon, chs. 7, 10.

35. Id., ch. 7.

36. Nixon later had two more opportunities to nominate Supreme Court justices. He chose Lewis Powell and William Rehnquist, thinking that both were reliable conservatives, but Powell turned out to be a moderate.

37. Keith E. Whittington, Constitutional Construction: Divided Power and Constitutional Meaning, ch. 5 (titled "Richard Nixon and the Leadership of the Modern State") (1999).

38. Harold H. Bruff, Balance of Forces: Separation of Powers Law in the Administrative State, ch. 18 (2006).

39. Calabresi & Yoo, Unitary Executive, 348.

40. Harold H. Bruff, *Presidential Power Meets Bureaucratic Expertise*, 12 U. Pa. J. Con. Law 461 (2010).

41. Peter M. Shane & Harold H. Bruff, Separation of Powers Law: Cases and Materials, ch. 4 (3d ed. 2011). In support of these programs, presidents also invoke their otherwise obscure constitutional power to require subordinates to provide opinions in writing about the exercise of their duties. Art. II, § 2.

42. Peter L. Strauss, *Overseer, or "The Decider"? The President in Administrative Law*, 75 Geo. Wash. L. Rev. 696 (2007).

43. See chapter 4.

44. Calabresi & Yoo, Unitary Executive, 348.

45. Cass R. Sunstein, The Cost-Benefit State: The Future of Regulatory Protection (2002).

46. Reeves, President Nixon, ch. 36.

47. He exempted the constitutional cabinet—that is, the Departments of State, Treasury, Defense, and Justice.

48. Reeves, President Nixon, 547.

49. Id., ch. 30.

50. Herring, Colony to Superpower, ch. 17.

51. Dallek, Nixon & Kissinger, ch. 14.

52. Reeves, President Nixon, ch. 35.

53. Among them is James T. Patterson, Grand Expectations: The United States, 1945–1974, ch. 24 (1996).

54. Herring, Colony to Superpower, 803.

55. Pub. L. 93–148, 87 Stat. 555, codified at 50 U.S.C. § 1541 et seq. For the background of the resolution, its subsequent history, and citations to the extensive literature about it, see Shane & Bruff, Separation of Powers Law, ch. 6. Good analyses include John Hart Ely, War and Responsibility: Constitutional Lessons of Vietnam and Its Aftermath (1993); Fisher, Presidential War Power, ch. 6 (2d ed. 2004).

56. Sec. 2(a).

57. Sec. 2(c).

58. Sec. 8(d).

59. Sec. 3.

60. Sec. 4, 5(b).

61. Sec. 5(c).

62. H. Doc. No. 171, 93d Cong., 1st Sess. (1973).

63. H. Jefferson Powell, The President's Authority over Foreign Affairs: An Essay in Constitutional Interpretation 123 (2002).

64. These are collected in David J. Barron & Martin S. Lederman, *The Commander in Chief at the Lowest Ebb—A Constitutional History*, 121 Harv. L. Rev. 941 (2008). The Carter administration later conceded the constitutionality of the sixty-day limitation; other presidents have not. Id., 1077.

65. See chapter 12.

66. Harold H. Koh, The National Security Constitution: Sharing Power after the Iran-Contra Affair 173 (1990).

67. Herring, Colony to Superpower, ch. 17.

68. Reeves, President Nixon, ch. 22.

69. Id., 356.

70. Dallek, Nixon & Kissinger, ch. 10.

71. Reeves, President Nixon, ch. 28.

72. Herring, Colony to Superpower, ch. 17.

73. Reeves, President Nixon, ch. 3.

74. Id., ch 19.

75. Walter Isaacson, Kissinger: A Biography 436 (1992).

76. Reeves, President Nixon, chs. 31–32.

77. Herring, Colony to Superpower, ch. 17.

78. Id.

79. Id.

80. Dallek, Nixon & Kissinger, 530–31.

81. Bruff, Balance of Forces, 257–66.

82. The history in this section relies on Louis Fisher, Presidential Spending Power (1975).

83. Donald R. McCoy, *The Constitution of the Truman Presidency and the Post–World War II Era* 107, 113, in The Constitution and the American Presidency (Martin L. Fausold & Alan Shank, eds. 1991).

84. Barron & Lederman, *Constitutional History*, 1062–63.

85. Akhil Reed Amar, America's Unwritten Constitution: The Precedents and Principles We Live By, ch. 3 (2012).

86. Schlesinger, Imperial Presidency, ch. 8. Controllable expenditures do not include amounts committed in advance, such as the entitlements.

87. Whittington, Constitutional Construction, ch. 5.

88. This was the argument made by the dissents in *Youngstown*. See chapter 9.

89. Schlesinger, Imperial Presidency, 237, quoting a Justice Department memo by William Rehnquist.

90. *Train v. City of New York*, 420 U.S. 35 (1975).

91. Pub. L. No. 93-344, 88 Stat. 297; see Allen Schick, The Federal Budget: Politics, Policy, Process (3d ed. 2007).

92. Stone, Perilous Times, 493.

93. Calabresi & Yoo, Unitary Executive, 354.

94. Reeves, President Nixon, ch. 18.

95. Id., ch. 19.

96. Id., 114.

97. David Rudenstine, The Day the Presses Stopped: A History of the Pentagon Papers Case (1996).

98. Stanley I. Kutler, Abuse of Power: The New Nixon Tapes 3 (1997). This book contains excerpts from the secret White House audiotapes.

99. *In re Debs*, 158 U.S. 564 (1895); see chapter 7.

100. Bruff, Balance of Forces, 94–98, 351–55.

101. *New York Times Co. v. United States*, 403 U.S. 713 (1971).

102. Kutler, Abuse of Power, 8.

103. If Nixon did not quite explicitly order the Ellsberg burglary, he did order a burglary of the Brookings Institution in an effort to find a file that was supposedly embarrassing to the Johnson administration. Id., 6.

104. Stanley Kutler, The Wars of Watergate: The Last Crisis of Richard Nixon, ch. 8 (1990).

105. Reeves, President Nixon, ch. 33.

106. Kutler, Abuse of Power, 67–70. J. Edgar Hoover had recently died in office. Had he been alive, one wonders whether this tactic would have been tried.

107. Reeves, President Nixon, ch. 34.

108. Mark J. Rozell, Executive Privilege: Presidential Power, Secrecy, and Accountability, ch. 3 (3d ed. 2010).

109. See chapter 3.

110. Louis Fisher, The Politics of Executive Privilege (2004).

111. This was the well-supported position of the special prosecutor. Archibald Cox, *Executive Privilege*, 122 U. Pa. L. Rev. 1383 (1974).

112. Kutler, Wars of Watergate, ch. 15.

113. "There is probable cause to believe that Richard M. Nixon . . . was a member of the conspiracy to defraud the United States and to obstruct justice." Reeves, President Nixon, 608.

114. *United States v. Nixon*, 418 U.S. 683 (1974).

115. Shane & Bruff, Separation of Powers Law, 215–17.

116. Patterson, Grand Expectations, 777.

117. Kutler, Wars of Watergate, ch. 16.

118. Sean Wilentz, The Age of Reagan: A History, 1974–2008, 28 (2008).

119. Gould, Modern Presidency, ch. 8.

120. Wilentz, Age of Reagan, ch.1.

121. Rozell, Executive Privilege, 77–78.

122. Id., 78.

123. Andrew Rudalevige, The New Imperial Presidency: Renewing Presidential Power after Watergate, ch. 4 (2006).

124. Id., 50.

125. Shane & Bruff, Separation of Powers Law, 740.

126. James T. Patterson, Restless Giant: The United States from Watergate to *Bush v. Gore*, ch. 3 (2005).

127. Fisher, War Power, 154–56.

128. Barron & Lederman, *Constitutional History*, 1072–74.

129. Herring, Colony to Superpower, ch. 18.

130. Id.

131. Gould, Modern Presidency, ch. 8.

132. Stephen Skowronek, The Politics Presidents Make: Leadership from John Adams to George Bush 364 (1993).

133. Calabresi & Yoo, Unitary Executive, ch. 39. On all of these proposals, he rejected Justice Department complaints that articulated traditional positions.

134. Shane & Bruff, Separation of Powers Law, 341.

135. Michael J. Gerhardt, The Forgotten Presidents: Their Untold Constitutional Legacy, ch. 13 (2013).

136. Skowronek, Politics, 385–86.

137. Id., ch. 7, pt. 3.

138. Patterson, Restless Giant, ch. 4.

139. *Goldwater v. Carter*, 444 U.S. 996 (1979). Congress as a whole acquiesced in Carter's treaty termination by enacting a statute adjusting legal relations with Taiwan.

140. Herring, Colony to Superpower, ch. 18.

141. Wilentz, Age of Reagan, 105.

142. Patterson, Restless Giant, ch. 4.

143. Gary Sick, All Fall Down: America's Tragic Encounter with Iran (1986).

144. Brzezinski had pressed for military action; Vance resigned in protest after the raid.

145. Shane & Bruff, Separation of Powers Law, 858–61.

146. Harold H. Bruff, *The Story of* Dames & Moore: *Resolution of an International Crisis by Executive Agreement*, in Presidential Power Stories 369 (Christopher H. Schroeder & Curtis A. Bradley eds., 2009).

147. *Dames & Moore v. Regan*, 453 U.S. 654 (1981).

Chapter Twelve

1. *Address before a Joint Session of the Congress on the Program for Economic Recovery*, April 28, 1981, Public Papers of the Presidents of the United States: Ronald Reagan 394 (1982).

2. George C. Herring, From Colony to Superpower: U.S. Foreign Relations since 1776, 864 (2008).

3. My portrait of Reagan draws on Lou Cannon, President Reagan: The Role of a Lifetime 709 (rev. ed. 2000), especially ch. 2.

4. His exceptionalism often took the form of reference to the Puritans' concept of America as a "city upon a hill." James T. Patterson, Restless Giant: The United States from Watergate to *Bush v. Gore*, ch. 5 (2005).

5. Stephen Skowronek, The Politics Presidents Make: Leadership from John Adams to George Bush 409 (1993).

6. Cannon, President Reagan, chs. 4, 6. "The paradox of the Reagan presidency was that it depended totally on Reagan for its ideological inspiration while he depended totally on others for all aspects of governance except his core ideas and his

powerful performances." Id., 71. Like FDR he realized that "the decisive aspect of presidential leadership was inspirational rather than programmatic." Id., 85.

7. Reagan "rarely solicited policy options during his eight years in office. In fact, he so rarely made inquiries of his staff about anything that the exceptions were always notable." Id., 262.

8. Id., 78.

9. Id., ch. 8.

10. Id., ch. 1.

11. Lewis L. Gould, The Modern American Presidency, ch. 9 (2009).

12. Sean Wilentz, The Age of Reagan: A History, 1974–2008, ch. 5 (2008).

13. In 1982, a recession forced Reagan to accept tax increases giving back a third of the initial cuts.

14. Patterson, Restless Giant, ch. 5.

15. In August 1981, Reagan opposed a strike by the nation's air traffic controllers. He informed them that their strike was illegal and that they would be fired if they persisted. They did, and they were. The president's action broke the strike and the union. He sought to benefit the traveling public. Graham G. Dodds, Take Up Your Pen: Unilateral Presidential Directives in American Politics 197 (2013).

16. Skowronek, Politics, 414.

17. Cannon, President Reagan, 713.

18. Patterson, Restless Giant, ch. 5.

19. Harold H. Bruff, Balance of Forces: Separation of Powers Law in the Administrative State, ch. 18 (2006).

20. Skowronek, Politics, 413.

21. Dodds, Pen, 191; Mark J. Rozell, Executive Privilege: Presidential Power, Secrecy, and Accountability, ch. 5 (3d ed. 2010).

22. Rozell, Executive Privilege, ch. 5.

23. *INS v. Chadha*, 462 U.S. 919 (1983).

24. Bruff, Balance of Forces, ch. 9.

25. President Reagan tried to expand the scope of the president's "pocket veto" authority by asserting that it applied to congressional intersession adjournments, but the courts did not definitively resolve the issue. Id., 227–31.

26. See Steven G. Calabresi & Christopher S. Yoo, The Unitary Executive: Presidential Power from Washington to Bush, chs. 32–43 (2008), collecting instances of presidential vetoes of bills with legislative veto provisions, signatures of bills containing them, issuance of signing statements refusing to obey them, and occasional informal compliance with them.

27. Patterson, Restless Giant, ch. 5.

28. Wilentz, Age of Reagan, ch. 7.

29. Similarly, he long ignored the burgeoning AIDS epidemic as it killed tens of thousands of gay people and others as well.

30. Cannon, President Reagan, ch. 22.

31. Wilentz, Age of Reagan, ch. 7.

32. Reagan was successful, however, in nominating the first female Supreme Court justice, Sandra Day O'Connor, as well as Justices Antonin Scalia and Anthony Kennedy and the elevation of William Rehnquist to chief justice. It was a distinguished set of nominations, but as usual, not all of them fulfilled the president's expectations about their values.

33. Wilentz, Age of Reagan, ch. 7.

34. Reagan did not dismiss Attorney General Meese even after both the deputy attorney general and the head of the department's criminal division later resigned after complaining to the president that Meese was indictable; another independent counsel cleared him again, and he resigned. Cannon, President Reagan, ch. 22.

35. Id., ch. 14, reporting Reagan's fears of regional hatred against what he called the "colossus of the north."

36. Id.

37. Id., 309 note.

38. Id., 340.

39. Wilentz, Age of Reagan, ch. 6.

40. Louis Fisher, Presidential War Power 160–61 (2d ed. 2004).

41. Cannon, President Reagan, ch. 15.

42. Fisher, War Power, 161–63.

43. Id., 163–64.

44. Theodore Draper, A Very Thin Line: The Iran-Contra Affairs 18–19 (1991).

45. Department of Defense Appropriations Act 1985, § 8066, enacted in Further Continuing Appropriations Act, Pub. L. No. 98-473, 98 Stat. 1935 (1984).

46. Draper, Thin Line, 24.

47. Cannon, President Reagan, ch. 14.

48. At the time of Iran-Contra, President Reagan's Executive Order No. 12,333 defined the NSC as "the highest Executive Branch entity that provides review of, guidance for and direction to the conduct of all national foreign intelligence, counterintelligence, and special activities, and attendant policies and programs."

49. At a meeting Attorney General William French Smith informally approved the fund-raising as long as federal funds were not used either in the initial overtures or to repay donations. Draper, Thin Line, 78–79.

50. Once the Iranians realized they were being overcharged, they balked at the immediate release of hostages; hence, the Americans were undermining their own plan.

51. Draper observes: "So long as the United States was willing to trade arms for hostages, it could be sure that there would be hostages to be traded for arms." Thin Line, 389.

52. David J. Barron & Martin S. Lederman, *The Commander in Chief at the Lowest Ebb—A Constitutional History*, 121 Harv. L. Rev. 941, 1082 (2008).

53. 22 U.S.C. § 2753(a), (d).

54. 50 U.S.C. § 413. This provision was from the Intelligence Oversight Act of 1980, Pub. L. No. 96-450, 94 Stat. 1975.

55. 22 U.S.C. § 2422.

56. John Tower, Edmund Muskie, & Brent Scowcroft, The Tower Commission Report 76 (1987).

57. Draper, Thin Line, ch. 10.

58. Id., 214. Later on, the president signed two more findings that were similar to the first one.

59. Harold Koh, The National Security Constitution: Sharing Power after the Iran-Contra Affair 60 (1990).

60. For cogent arguments that all the Contra evasions were illegal, see William C. Banks & Peter Raven-Hansen, National Security Law and the Power of the Purse, ch. 13 (1994); Philip Bobbitt, Constitutional Fate: Theory of the Constitution, ch. 3 (1984).

61. Draper, Thin Line, 276.

62. Cannon, President Reagan, 608, 655.

63. Report of the Congressional Committees Investigating the Iran-Contra Affair with the Minority Views (Joel Brinkley & Stephen Engelberg eds., 1988).

64. Lawrence E. Walsh, Final Report of the Independent Counsel for Iran/ Contra Matters (1994).

65. Koh, National Security Constitution, 123.

66. Id., ch. 2.

67. Report of the Congressional Committees, 30. The minority report of the Iran-Contra committees contended that the Boland amendments were unconstitutional because they unduly restricted the president's executive authority for foreign affairs. The House minority report was written by Representative Dick Cheney of Wyoming, the future vice president.

68. Cannon, President Reagan, 662.

69. The criminal prosecutions of Poindexter and North ultimately came to little. An appeals court overturned jury convictions of both men for lying to Congress about their activities, because insufficient steps had been taken to ensure that the defendants' compelled testimony to Congress during the Iran-Contra hearings, for which they had been granted immunity from prosecution, did not taint their criminal trials. United States v. North, 910 F.2d 843 (D.C. Cir. 1990), modified, 920 F.2d 940 (D.C. Cir. 1990), cert. denied, 500 U.S. 941 (1991); United States v. Poindexter, 951 F.2d 369 (D.C. Cir. 1991), cert. denied, 506 U.S. 1021 (1992).

70. The quotes in this paragraph are from Bobbitt, Constitutional Fate, 72. At 67, he quotes Director Casey's gloating remark that there existed a "self-sustaining, stand-alone, off-the-shelf covert action capability."

71. Keith E. Whittington, Constitutional Construction: Divided Power and Constitutional Meaning, ch. 5 (2001).

72. Eric Alterman, When Presidents Lie: A History of Official Deception and Its Consequences, ch. 5 (2004); Mariah Zeisberg, War Powers: The Politics of Constitutional Authority, ch. 5 (2013); Koh, National Security Constitution, ch. 1.

73. This was President Reagan's famous 1987 call to Premier Gorbachev to tear down the Berlin Wall. Cannon, President Reagan, 695.

74. Wilentz, Age of Reagan, ch. 6.

75. Cannon, President Reagan, ch. 13.

76. Id., ch. 21.

77. Congress eventually insisted on the original interpretation by attaching a condition to the 1987 INF Treaty. Koh, National Security Constitution, 43.

78. Cannon, President Reagan, 754.

79. Herring, Colony to Superpower, 862.

Chapter Thirteen

1. Robert Ajemian, *Where Is the Real George Bush?*, Time, January 26, 1987.

2. John Greene, The Presidency of George Bush (2000).

3. Herbert S. Parmet, George Bush: The Life of a Lone Star Yankee, ch. 3 (2000).

4. David Halberstam, War in a Time of Peace: Bush, Clinton, and the Generals, chs. 1, 14 (rev. ed. 2002).

5. Patterson, Restless Giant: The United States from Watergate to *Bush v. Gore*, ch. 7.

6. Stephen Skowronek, The Politics Presidents Make: Leadership from John Adams to George Bush, ch. 12 (1993).

7. Steven Skowronek, Presidential Leadership in Political Time: Reprise and Reappraisal 98 (2011).

8. George C. Herring, From Colony to Superpower: U.S. Foreign Relations since 1776, ch. 19.

9. Sean Wilentz, The Age of Reagan: A History, 1974–2008, ch. 10.

10. Halberstam, War, ch. 1.

11. Herring, Colony to Superpower, ch. 19.

12. Id.

13. Wilentz, Age of Reagan, ch. 10.

14. Parmet, George Bush, ch. 20; Patterson, Restless Giant, ch. 7.

15. Louis Fisher, Presidential War Power 165–69 (2d ed. 2004).

16. Id., 169–74; Stephen M. Griffin, Long Wars and the Constitution 174–81 (2013).

17. Patterson, Restless Giant, ch. 7.

18. Herring, Colony to Superpower, ch. 19.

19. Halberstam, War, ch. 7.

20. Patterson, Restless Giant, ch. 7.

21. Id.; Wilentz, Age of Reagan, ch. 10.

22. For a memo from Gray to Bush asserting that the president could legally respond to the invasion "with no formal congressional authorization at all," see Stephen M. Griffin, *A Bibliography of Executive Branch War Powers Opinions since 1950*, 87 Tul. L. Rev. 649, 710–14 (2013).

23. H. Jefferson Powell, The President's Authority over Foreign Affairs: An Essay in Constitutional Interpretation 131 (2002).

24. Michael Glennon, *Too Far Apart: Repeal the War Powers Resolution*, 50 U. Miami L. Rev. 17, 21 n.18 (1995).

25. Fisher, War Power, 172; Griffin, Long Wars, 180.

26. Herring, Colony to Superpower, ch. 20.

27. Serbia had nursed its hatreds for a very long time; they were one of the sparks of World War I. Christopher Clark, The Sleepwalkers: How Europe Went to War in 1914, ch. 1 (2012).

28. Herring, Colony to Superpower, ch. 20.

29. Halberstam, War, ch. 4.

30. Patterson, Restless Giant, ch. 7.

31. Graham G. Dodds, Take Up Your Pen: Unilateral Presidential Directives in American Politics, ch. 7 (2013).

32. Mark J. Rozell, Executive Privilege: Presidential Power, Secrecy, and Accountability, ch. 5 (3d ed. 2010).

33. Wilentz, Age of Reagan, ch. 11.

34. Halberstam, War, 18. Thus the title of Joe Klein's assessment of the Clinton presidency, The Natural: The Misunderstood Presidency of Bill Clinton (2003).

35. Gould, Modern Presidency, ch. 10.

36. Halberstam, War, ch. 16.

37. John F. Harris, The Survivor: Bill Clinton in the White House, ch. 13 (2005).

38. Harris, Survivor, 9.

39. Id., ch. 2.

40. Id., prologue, ch. 5.

41. Gould, Modern Presidency, 219.

42. Id., ch. 10.

43. Harris, Survivor, ch. 3.

44. Patterson, Restless Giant, 334.

45. Halberstam, War, ch. 17.

46. Harris, Survivor, ch. 2.

47. Id.

48. Id., ch. 1.

49. Patterson, Restless Giant, 332.

50. Harris, Survivor, ch. 10.

51. Wilentz, Age of Reagan, 333.

52. Halberstam, War, ch. 22.

53. Herring, Colony to Superpower, ch. 20.

54. Following the frequent practice after World War II, NAFTA was enacted as a congressional-executive agreement rather than a treaty. Bruce Ackerman & David Golove, Is NAFTA Constitutional? 114 (1995) (their answer is "yes"). Entry of the United States into the World Trade Organization followed the same path.

55. Halberstam, War, chs. 18, 20.

56. Id., ch. 23.

57. Mark Bowden, Black Hawk Down: A Story of Modern War (2010).

58. Charlie Savage, Takeover: The Return of the Imperial Presidency and the Subversion of American Democracy, ch. 3 (2007).

59. Peter M. Shane & Harold H. Bruff, Separation of Powers Law: Cases and Materials, 866–67 (3d ed. 2011).

60. Herring, Colony to Superpower, ch. 20.

61. Halberstam, War, ch. 24.

62. Shane & Bruff, Separation of Powers Law, 863–64.

63. *Deployment of United States Armed Forces into Haiti*, 18 Op. Off. Legal Counsel 173, 179 (1994).

64. Harris, Survivor, ch. 9; Wilentz, Age of Reagan, ch. 11.

65. Patterson, Restless Giant, ch. 10.

66. Harris, Survivor, ch. 14.

67. Thomas E. Mann & Norman J. Ornstein, The Broken Branch: How Congress Is Failing America and How to Get It Back on Track (2008).

68. Patterson, Restless Giant, ch. 11.

69. Harris, Survivor, ch. 15.

70. Wilentz, Age of Reagan, ch. 12.

71. Harris, Survivor, 216.

72. Wilentz, Age of Reagan, ch. 12.

73. For example, the creation of the Grand Staircase–Escalante National Monument in Utah. Harold H. Bruff, *Executive Power and the Public Lands*, 76 U. Colo. L. Rev. 503 (2005).

74. Dodds, Pen, 197.

75. Naturally, when Barack Obama took office he reversed the second President Bush's orders. Id., 197–98.

76. Patterson, Restless Giant, ch. 11.

77. Harris, Survivor, ch. 22. He later obtained amendments repairing some of the provisions that offended him most.

78. Id., ch. 25.

79. Id., chs. 24, 27.

80. Id., 50.

81. Herring, Colony to Superpower, ch. 20.

82. Halberstam, War, chs. 29–30.

83. Fisher, War Power, 183–92. Nor did Clinton ask for authority when he later sent peacekeeping troops to the region.

84. Patterson, Restless Giant, ch. 11.

85. Halberstam, War, chs. 31, 34.

86. Herring, Colony to Superpower, ch. 20.

87. Fisher, War Power, 198–201. For the Justice Department memo supporting Clinton's decision, see Shane & Bruff, Separation of Powers Law, 872–78.

88. Halberstam, War, ch. 38.

89. Id., ch. 43.

90. Savage, Takeover, ch. 3.

91. David J. Barron & Martin S. Lederman, *The Commander in Chief at the Lowest Ebb—A Constitutional History*, 121 Harv. L. Rev. 1090 & n.619 (2008).

92. Richard A. Clarke, Against All Enemies: Inside America's War on Terror (2004).

93. Harris, Survivor, ch. 40.

94. Halberstam, War, epilogue.

95. Herring, Colony to Superpower, ch. 20.

96. Harris, Survivor, chs. 30, 33–35.

97. For a good analysis, see Richard A. Posner, An Affair of State: The Investigation, Impeachment, and Trial of President Clinton (1999).

98. *Clinton v. Jones*, 520 U.S. 681 (1997).

99. Patterson, Restless Giant, ch. 12.

100. For a full account, see Peter Baker, The Breach: Inside the Impeachment and Trial of William Jefferson Clinton (2000).

101. Harris, Survivor, 361. The judge in *Jones* held Clinton in contempt for lying and fined him. The underlying lawsuit, which was thinly based, had earlier been dismissed at summary judgment. While it was on appeal, Clinton settled it for $850,000, a multiple of Jones's original claim, thus confirming its large harassment value.

102. Id., ch. 42.

103. Rozell, Executive Privilege, ch. 6; Shane & Bruff, Separation of Powers Law, 287–89.

104. Shane & Bruff, Separation of Powers Law, 224–26.

105. Ken Gormley, The Death of American Virtue: Clinton vs. Starr (2011).

106. Patterson, Restless Giant, ch. 12.

107. *Morrison v. Olson*, 487 U.S. 654 (1988).

108. Akhil Reed Amar, America's Unwritten Constitution: The Precedents and Principles We Live By, ch. 9 (2012).

109. Id.

110. Gould, Modern Presidency, 232.

Chapter Fourteen

1. Bob Woodward, Bush at War 96 (2002).

2. *Bush v. Gore*, 531 U.S. 98 (2000).

3. See Richard A. Posner, Breaking the Deadlock: The 2000 Election, the Constitution, and the Courts (2001). The closest analogue is the disputed election of 1876, settled by a special commission in favor of Rutherford Hayes, who also lost the popular vote. William H. Rehnquist, Centennial Crisis: The Disputed Election of 1876 (2004).

4. George W. Bush early in his presidency, quoted in Stephen Skowronek, Presidential Leadership in Political Time: Reprise and Reappraisal 123 (2d ed. 2011).

5. Lewis L. Gould, The Modern American Presidency, ch. 11 (2009).

6. Peter Baker, Days of Fire: Bush and Cheney in the White House, ch. 27 (2013).

7. Skowronek, Political Time, ch. 4; Robert M. Gates, Duty: Memoirs of a Secretary at War, ch. 3 (2014).

8. For praise of these characteristics, see David Frum, The Right Man: The Surprise Presidency of George W. Bush (2003). For criticism, see Robert Draper, Dead Certain: The Presidency of George W. Bush (2007).

9. Lou Cannon & Carl M. Cannon, Reagan's Disciple: George W. Bush's Troubled Quest for a Presidential Legacy (2008).

10. James Mann, Rise of the Vulcans: The History of Bush's War Cabinet (2004).

11. Thus his famous remark that "I hear the voices, and I read the front page, and I know the speculation. But I'm the decider, and I decide what is best." Sanford Levinson & Jack M. Balkin, *Constitutional Dictatorship: Its Dangers and Its Design*, 94 Minn. L. Rev. 101, 102 (2010).

12. George Packer, The Assassins' Gate: America in Iraq 55 (2005), calls Bush "the most anti-intellectual President since at least Warren G. Harding."

13. Ron Suskind, The One Percent Doctrine: Deep Inside America's Pursuit of Its Enemies since 9/11 185 (2006).

14. James Risen, State of War: The Secret History of the CIA and the Bush Administration (2006); Seymour M. Hersh, Chain of Command: The Road from 9/11 to Abu Ghraib (2004).

15. Irving L. Janis, Victims of Groupthink: A Psychological Study of Foreign-Policy Decisions and Fiascos (1972).

16. Stephen F. Hayes, Cheney: The Untold Story of America's Most Powerful and Controversial Vice President (2007). Baker, Days of Fire, provides a full recounting of Cheney's role in the administration. His power was routinely exercised through David Addington, his aggressive chief of staff and longtime legal counsel.

17. Baker, Days of Fire, ch. 2.

18. Mann, Vulcans, 96.

19. Mindful of his own history of heart attacks and of the fact that although the Constitution now provides a mechanism for replacing a vice president who has died, it does not provide for replacing a disabled vice president, Cheney signed a

resignation letter and left it with aides, for delivery in case of his disability. Baker, Days of Fire, 97–98.

20. Hayes, Cheney, 238–39.

21. Charlie Savage, Takeover: The Return of the Imperial Presidency and the Subversion of American Democracy 75 (2007).

22. Jack Goldsmith, The Terror Presidency: Law and Judgment inside the Bush Administration 212 (2007).

23. At Rumsfeld's side stood his deputy Paul Wolfowitz, an intellectual leader of the neoconservative movement.

24. Elisabeth Bumiller, Condoleezza Rice: A Biography (2007).

25. Baker, Days of Fire, prologue, ch. 20.

26. Nancy V. Baker, General Ashcroft: Attorney at War (2006).

27. Bill Minutaglio, The President's Counselor: The Rise to Power of Alberto Gonzales (2006).

28. Savage, Takeover, 73–76.

29. In May 2001, Senator James Jeffords of Vermont left the Republican Party, and control of the Senate shifted to the Democrats until the 2002 midterm election restored a Republican majority.

30. Sean Wilentz, The Age of Reagan: A History, 1974–2008, epilogue (2008).

31. Graham G. Dodds, Take Up Your Pen: Unilateral Presidential Directives in American Politics 208–9 (2013).

32. Post-9/11 discussions of emergency powers include Bruce Ackerman, Before the Next Attack: Preserving Civil Liberties in an Age of Terrorism (2006); Richard A. Posner, Not a Suicide Pact: The Constitution in a Time of National Emergency (2006); Eric A. Posner & Adrian Vermeule, Terror in the Balance: Security, Liberty, and the Courts (2007).

33. Goldsmith, Terror Presidency, 11–12.

34. Id., 74.

35. Jack Goldsmith, Power and Constraint: The Accountable Presidency after 9/11, x (2012).

36. Goldsmith, Terror Presidency 175, quoting Deputy Attorney General James Comey.

37. 18 U.S.C. chapter 113B—Terrorism, § 2331 et seq.

38. Antiterrorism and Effective Death Penalty Act of 1996, 18 U.S.C. §§ 1531–37.

39. Pub. L. No. 107-56, 115 Stat. 272 (October 26, 2001).

40. Woodward, Bush at War, 17, 45.

41. Id., 96.

42. Pub. L. No. 107-40, 115 Stat. 224 (2001).

43. Final Report of the National Commission on Terrorist Attacks upon the United States, The 9/11 Commission Report 348 (2004): Al Qaeda's "crimes were on a scale approaching acts of war, but they were committed by a loose, far-flung,

nebulous conspiracy with no territories or citizens or assets that could be readily threatened, overwhelmed or destroyed."

44. See Harold H. Bruff, Bad Advice: Bush's Lawyers in the War on Terror, ch. 7 (2009).

45. 50 U.S.C. § 1801 et seq.

46. S. Rep. No. 604, 95th Cong., 1st Sess. (1977).

47. Eric Lichtblau, Bush's Law: The Remaking of American Justice, ch. 5 (2008); Risen, State of War, ch. 2.

48. David Cole & Martin S. Lederman, *Documents Relating to the National Security Agency Spying Program: Framing the Debate*, 81 Ind. L. J. 1355 (2006).

49. Scott Shane & Eric Lindblau, *Cheney Pushed U.S. to Widen Eavesdropping*, N.Y. Times, May 14, 2006, A16.

50. Hayes, Cheney, 486.

51. Shane Harris, *More Than Meets the Ear*, National Journal, March 18, 2006, 28, 32.

52. *Hearing before the Senate Committee on the Judiciary*, Department of Justice Oversight Committee, 110th Cong., 1st Sess., January 18, 2007, 12.

53. Jonathan E. Nuechterlein & Philip J. Weiser, Digital Crossroads: American Telecommunications Policy in the Internet Age (2005).

54. Bruff, Bad Advice, 152.

55. Id., 152–56.

56. Hayes, Cheney, 488.

57. FISA Amendments Act of 2008, 122 Stat. 2436.

58. Trevor W. Morrison, *Constitutional Avoidance in the Executive Branch*, 106 Colum. L. Rev. 1189, 1250–58 (2006).

59. George C. Herring, From Colony to Superpower: U.S. Foreign Relations since 1776, ch. 20 (2008).

60. John Yoo, War by Other Means: An Insider's Account of the War on Terror 128 (2006).

61. A secret Department of Justice opinion so concluded. *Possible Habeas Jurisdiction over Aliens Held in Guantanamo Bay, Cuba*, reprinted in The Torture Papers: The Road to Abu Ghraib 29 (Karen J. Greenberg & Joshua L. Dratel eds., 2005).

62. George W. Bush, Military Order of November 13, 2001: Detention, Treatment, and Trial of Certain Non-Citizens in the War on Terrorism, 66 Fed. Reg. 57831, reprinted in id., 25.

63. Joseph Margulies, Guantánamo and the Abuse of Presidential Power (2006).

64. Benjamin Wittes, Law and the Long War: The Future of Justice in the Age of Terror (2008).

65. 542 U.S. 507 (2004).

66. 542 U.S. 466 (2004).

67. 542 U.S. 426 (2004).

68. Padilla was later transferred back to civilian jurisdiction and convicted of federal conspiracy charges under the criminal code, for participation in a terrorism support cell.

69. Pub. L. No. 109-148, 119 Stat. 2739. The DTA forbade habeas corpus for enemy combatants and replaced it with a quite restricted appeal to the federal circuit court in Washington, DC.

70. Pub. L. No. 109-366, 120 Stat. 2600.

71. 553 U.S. 723 (2007).

72. Philip Bobbitt, Terror and Consent: The Wars for the Twenty-First Century (2008).

73. Bruff, Bad Advice, ch. 9.

74. Article VI provides: "This Constitution, and the laws of the United States . . . and all treaties . . . which shall be made . . . shall be the supreme law of the land."

75. 6 U.S.T. 3316, 75 U.N.T.S. 135 (POWs); 6 U.S.T. 3516, 75 U.N.T.S. 287 (Civilians).

76. Greenberg & Dratel, Torture Papers, 38.

77. 18 U.S.C. § 2441. Grave breaches include "willful killing, torture or inhuman treatment, . . . willfully causing great suffering or serious injury to body or health . . . or willfully depriving a prisoner of war of the rights of fair and regular trial."

78. The memos leading up to and including President Bush's final order are reprinted in Greenberg & Dratel, Torture Papers, 118–43.

79. In another innovative treaty interpretation, President Bush ordered state courts to implement certain judgments of the International Court of Justice. The Supreme Court overrode his decision in *Medellin v. Texas*, 552 U.S. 491 (2008).

80. Bruff, Bad Advice, ch. 10.

81. My account of the order's genesis is drawn from Savage, Takeover, 135–39.

82. Louis Fisher, Military Tribunals and Presidential Power: American Revolution to the War on Terrorism (2005).

83. 71 U.S. (4 Wall.) 2 (1866).

84. *Hearing before the Senate Committee on the Judiciary*, Department of Justice Oversight: Preserving Our Freedoms While Defending against Terrorism, 107th Cong., 1st Sess. (2001) (with testimony for and against the tribunals).

85. *Hamdan v. Rumsfeld*, 548 U.S. 557 (2006).

86. Samuel Issacharoff & Richard H. Pildes, *Between Civil Libertarianism and Executive Unilateralism: An Institutional Process Approach to Rights during Wartime*, in The Constitution in Wartime: Beyond Alarmism and Complacency (Mark Tushnet ed., 2005).

87. The MCA allows the use of coerced confessions in the tribunals under some conditions. Evidence obtained by torture may not be used. Classified information

is subject to controls to preserve fairness to defendants, and judicial review is afforded.

88. Bruff, Bad Advice, ch. 11.

89. For wide-ranging reflections, see The Torture Debate in America (Karen J. Greenberg ed., 2006); Torture: A Collection (Sanford Levinson ed., 2004).

90. Seth F. Kreimer, *"Torture Lite," "Full Bodied" Torture, and the Insulation of Legal Conscience*, 1 J. Nat'l Security L. & Pol'y 187 (2005).

91. Stephen Grey, Ghost Plane: The Inside Story of the CIA's Secret Rendition Programme (2006).

92. Id., ch. 6.

93. 18 U.S.C. §§ 2340–2340A. Torture within the United States has long been illegal under general constitutional and statutory provisions. The Constitution's Eighth Amendment forbids the "cruel and unusual" punishment of prisoners. The due process clause of the Fifth Amendment also forbids federal agents to inflict physical abuse on prisoners. The Convention against Torture is 1465 U.N.T.S. 85 (1987).

94. *Standards of Conduct for Interrogation under 18 U.S.C. §§ 2340–2340A*. The memo is reprinted in Greenberg & Dratel, Torture Papers, 172. Some months later, quite similar advice was rendered to the Pentagon for military interrogations.

95. Bruff, Bad Advice, ch. 11.

96. See Morrison, *Constitutional Avoidance*, 1229–36. For an extensive refutation of this proposition, see David J. Barron & Martin S. Lederman, *The Commander in Chief at the Lowest Ebb—A Constitutional History*, 121 Harv. L. Rev. 941 (2008).

97. As enacted, it is § 1003(a) of the DTA.

98. Harold Koh, *Can The President Be Torturer in Chief?*, 81 Ind. L. J. 1145, 1153–54 (2006).

99. Steven Lee Myers, *Bush Vetoes Bill on C.I.A. Tactics, Affirming Legacy*, N.Y. Times, March 9, 2008, A1.

100. Suskind, One Percent Doctrine, 22.

101. Richard A. Clarke, Against All Enemies: Inside America's War on Terror 30 (2004).

102. Herring, Colony to Superpower, 946–47.

103. Wilentz, Age of Reagan, epilogue.

104. Herring, Colony to Superpower, ch. 20.

105. Savage, Takeover, ch. 6.

106. Thomas E. Ricks, Fiasco: The American Military Adventure in Iraq (2006).

107. Hersh, Chain of Command, 169.

108. Packer, Assassins' Gate, 303.

109. Herring, Colony to Superpower, 960–61.

110. Packer, Assassins' Gate, 390.

111. The term "friction" comes from Clausewitz. See John Keegan, The Second World War 501–2 (1989).

112. Bruff, Bad Advice, ch. 12.

113. Baker, Days of Fire, 458.

114. Id., ch. 17.

115. Id., chs. 29–30; Gates, Duty, ch. 2.

116. Savage, Takeover, chs. 5, 7.

117. Dodds, Pen, 209.

118. Lichtblau, Bush's Law, ch. 9.

119. Id., 295–96.

120. Peter M. Shane & Harold H. Bruff, Separation of Powers Law: Cases and Materials 316–35 (3d ed. 2011).

121. Needing a successor of unquestioned integrity, the president settled on retired federal judge Michael Mukasey, who stabilized the department.

122. Baker, Days of Fire, ch. 1.

123. Id., chs. 22–23.

124. Id., ch. 23.

125. Savage, Takeover, ch. 13.

126. See, e.g., Walter Dellinger, The Legal Significance of Presidential Signing Statements, reprinted in H. Jefferson Powell, The Constitution and the Attorneys General 563 (1999).

127. Peter M. Shane, Madison's Nightmare: How Executive Power Threatens American Democracy 132–42 (2009).

128. Walter Dellinger, Presidential Authority to Decline to Execute Unconstitutional Statutes, reprinted in Powell, Attorneys General, 577.

129. Savage, Takeover, ch. 10.

130. Baker, Days of Fire, chs. 27, 31, 33.

131. Harold H. Bruff, Presidential Power Meets Bureaucratic Expertise, 12 U. Pa. J. Con. Law 461 (2010).

132. Alan S. Blinder, After the Music Stopped: The Financial Crisis, the Response, and the Work Ahead, ch. 1 (2013).

133. David Wessel, In Fed We Trust: Ben Bernanke's War on the Great Panic 1 (2009).

134. Baker, Days of Fire, ch. 24.

135. For development of the independent agencies, see chapter 8.

136. Levinson & Balkin, Constitutional Dictatorship, 152–54 (referring to such split crisis command as a "distributed dictatorship").

137. Wessel, Fed, 265, quoting an International Monetary Fund assessment.

138. Id., chs. 1–4, 11.

139. Emergency Economic Stabilization Act of 2008, Pub. L. No. 110-343. Most of the money was used to keep banks afloat, and all but $32 billion was eventually repaid. Blinder, After the Music, ch. 7.

140. Shane & Bruff, Separation of Powers Law, 523.

141. Jonathan Alter, The Promise: President Obama, Year One 78 (2010).

Chapter Fifteen

1. Jeffrey Toobin, The Oath: The Obama White House and the Supreme Court 36 (2012) (discussing judicial interpretation).

2. For his early years, see David Maraniss, Barack Obama: The Story (2012).

3. Jonathan Alter, The Promise: President Obama, Year One, ch. 9 (2010).

4. Barack Obama, Dreams from My Father: A Story of Race and Inheritance 28 (2004).

5. Jonathan Alter, The Center Holds: Obama and His Enemies 44 (2013).

6. Jack Goldsmith, Power and Constraint: The Accountable Presidency after 9/11, 26 (2012).

7. Alter, Center, ch. 12.

8. James Mann, The Obamians: The Struggle inside the White House to Redefine American Power, prologue (2012).

9. Obama was mindful of Lincoln's precedent of putting his rivals in the cabinet. Alter, Promise, 68.

10. Kim Ghattas, The Secretary: A Journey with Hillary Clinton from Beirut to the Heart of American Power (2013).

11. These considerations also resulted in the choice of national security adviser James Jones, a former commandant of the Marines, and intelligence chief Dennis Blair, an admiral.

12. Mann, Obamians, introduction.

13. Id., ch. 5.

14. " Plus ça change, plus c'est la meme chose," a French proverb meaning "The more things change, the more they stay the same."

15. Goldsmith, Power and Constraint, 17.

16. Graham G. Dodds, Take Up Your Pen: Unilateral Presidential Directives in American Politics 210 (2013).

17. Id. Gesturing to his right, Obama later reaffirmed implementation of the statutory ban on federal funding of abortions (as distinguished from counseling about them) in order to gain votes for his health care plan.

18. Richard Pildes & Cass Sunstein, Reinventing the Regulatory State, 62 U. Chi. L. Rev. 1, 15 (1995).

19. For the financial crisis, see Alan S. Blinder, After the Music Stopped: The Financial Crisis, the Response, and the Work Ahead (2013); Erik F. Gerding, Law, Bubbles, and Financial Regulation (2013); Robert G. Kaiser, Act of Congress: How America's Essential Institution Works, and How It Doesn't (2013).

20. Ron Suskind, Confidence Men: Wall Street, Washington, and the Education of a President (2011).

21. Timothy F. Geithner, Stress Test: Reflections on Financial Crises (2014).

22. David Wessel, In Fed We Trust: Ben Bernanke's War on the Great Panic, ch. 14 (2009).

23. Louis Fisher, Presidential War Power, ch. 10 (3d ed. 2013).

24. Goldsmith, Power and Constraint, ch. 1.

25. Mann, Obamians, ch. 8.

26. William Shawcross, Justice and the Enemy: Nuremberg, 9/11, and the Trial of Khalid Sheikh Mohammed 112–13 (2011).

27. E.g., Pub. L. No. 111-383, 124 Stat. 4351, which Obama signed while complaining about its restriction of "critical" executive authority.

28. Mann, Obamians, 111.

29. Kathleen Clark, *"A New Era of Openness?": Disclosing Intelligence to Congress under Obama*, 26 Const. Comm. 313, 315 (2010).

30. Scott Shane, *No Charges Filed in Two Deaths Involving C.I.A.*, N.Y. Times, August 31, 2012, A1.

31. Goldsmith, Power and Constraint, ch. 1.

32. Id., ch 2.

33. Stephen M. Griffin, Long Wars and the Constitution 248 (2013).

34. Peter M. Shane & Harold H. Bruff, Separation of Powers Law: Cases and Materials 146–48 (3d ed. 2011).

35. For an example, see Charlie Savage, *Ignoring a Law on Foreign Relations*, N.Y. Times, September 16, 2009, A14.

36. Mann, Obamians, 63.

37. David E. Sanger, Confront and Conceal: Obama's Secret Wars and Surprising Use of American Power, ch. 2 (2012).

38. Id.

39. Alter, Promise, 379.

40. Mann, Obamians, ch. 10.

41. Alter, Promise, 379.

42. Robert M. Gates, Duty: Memoirs of a Secretary at War, ch. 10 (2014).

43. Mann, Obamians, ch. 10.

44. Sanger, Confront and Conceal, ch. 2.

45. Id., 56.

46. Id., ch. 5.

47. Mann, Obamians, chs. 15–16.

48. Obama confidant Denis McDonough was his deputy.

49. Odd man out was Richard Holbrooke, whose passionate style clashed with that of his cool president. Holbrooke remained in limbo until his death in 2010.

50. Mann, Obamians, ch 12.

51. Id., ch. 1.

52. Id., ch. 11.

53. Id., chs. 13, 17.

54. Sanger, Confront and Conceal, ch. 15.

55. Peter Baker, Days of Fire: Bush and Cheney in the White House, chs. 10–11 (2013).

56. Mann, Obamians, ch. 14.

57. Mark Landler, *Obama Defends Foreign Policy against Critics*, N.Y. Times, April 29, 2014, A1.

58. Mann, Obamians, ch. 18.

59. Sanger, Confront and Conceal, ch. 18.

60. Mann, Obamians, ch. 19.

61. Id., ch. 20; Gates, Duty, ch. 13; Sanger, Confront and Conceal, ch. 14.

62. In recent years, relations with Libya had warmed somewhat after Gadhafi made some reparations for his terrorism and gave up a nuclear weapons program.

63. Mann, Obamians, ch. 20.

64. See chapter 13.

65. Fisher, War Power, 238–41. The memo is *Authority to Use Military Force in Libya*, April 1, 2011, http://www.fas.org/irp/agency/doj/olc/libya.pdf.

66. Fisher, War Power, 242–43. The report is *United States Activities in Libya*, N.Y. Times, June 15, 2011, 25.

67. Richard H. Pildes, *Law and the President*, 125 Harv. L. Rev. 1381, 1389 (2012); Charlie Savage, *2 Top Lawyers Lost to Obama in Libya War Policy Debate*, N.Y. Times, June 17, 2011, A1.

68. Mark Landler, David E. Sanger & Thom Shanker, *Obama Set for Limited Strike on Syria as British Vote No*, N.Y. Times, August 30, 2013, A1.

69. Peter Baker & Jonathan Wiseman, *Slowing March to Military Action, Obama Seeks Syria Vote in Congress*, N.Y. Times, September 1, 2013, A1.

70. Michael D. Shear, Michael R. Gordon & Steven Lee Myers, *Obama Embraces Russian Proposal on Syria Weapons*, N.Y. Times, September 10, 2013, A1.

71. Michael R. Gordon, *U.S. and Russia Reach a Deal on Dismantling Syria's Chemical Arms*, N.Y. Times, September 15, 2013, at A1; Michael R. Gordon, *Key Nations at U.N. Reach Agreement on Syria Weapons*, N.Y. Times, September 27, 2013, A1.

72. *Remarks by the President in Address to the Nation on Syria (September 10, 2013)*, http://www.whitehouse.gov/the-press-office/2013/09/10/remarks-President -address-nation-Syria.

73. See Sanger, Confront and Conceal.

74. Mann, Obamians, chs. 7–8, 15.

75. Sanger, Confront and Conceal, 252.

76. Alter, Promise, ch. 20.

77. Jo Becker & Scott Shane, *Secret "Kill List" Proves a Test of Obama's Principles and Will*, N.Y. Times, May 29, 2012, A1.

78. Mark Mazzetti, The Way of the Knife: The CIA, a Secret Army, and a War at the Ends of the Earth, ch. 16 (2013); Richard Murphy & Afsheen John Radsan,

Notice and an Opportunity to Be Heard Before the President Kills You, 48 Wake Forest L. Rev. 829 (2013).

79. Fisher, War Power, 264 n.150.

80. Mazzetti, Knife, ch. 12 (2013).

81. Robert F. Worth, Mark Mazzetti & Scott Shane, *Hazards of Drone Strikes Face Rare Public Scrutiny*, N.Y. Times, February 6, 2013, A1.

82. Michael D. Shear & Scott Shane, *Congress to Get Classified Memo on Drone Strike*, N.Y. Times, February 7, 2013, A1.

83. Scott Shane, *A Court to Vet Kill Lists*, N.Y. Times, February 9, 2013, A1.

84. Sanger, Confront and Conceal, ch. 10.

85. This is a theme of Mazzetti, Knife.

86. Sanger, Confront and Conceal, ch. 4; Mann, Obamians, ch. 21.

87. Alter, Center, ch. 12.

88. Sanger, Confront and Conceal, 101.

89. Goldsmith, Power and Constraint, 225.

90. Mann, Obamians, ch. 14.

91. Sanger, Confront and Conceal, ch. 7.

92. Id., ch. 8.

93. Id.

94. Michael R. Gordon, *Long-Term Deal with Iran Faces Big Challenges*, N.Y. Times, November 25, 2013, A1.

95. Gates, Duty, ch. 12; Sanger, Confront and Conceal, ch. 10.

96. David E. Sanger & Nicole Perlroth, *Chinese Hackers Resume Attacks on U.S. Targets*, N.Y. Times, May 20, 2013, A1.

97. David E. Sanger & Thom Shanker, *Broad Powers Seen for Obama in Cyberstrikes*, N.Y. Times, February 4, 2013, A1.

98. John Seabrook, *Network Insecurity*, New Yorker, May 20, 2013, 70.

99. Gates, Duty, ch. 15; Mann, Obamians, epilogue.

100. Sanger, Confront and Conceal, epilogue.

101. This is a major theme of Goldsmith, Power and Constraint.

102. Peter Baker, *Reviving Debate on Nation's Security, Obama Seeks to Narrow Terror Fight*, N.Y. Times, May 24, 2013, A1.

103. Peter Baker, *In Terror Shift, Obama Took a Long Path*, N.Y. Times, May 28, 2013, A1.

104. Dana Priest & William M. Arken, *Top Secret America: A Washington Post Investigation*, http://projects.washingtonpost.com/top-secret-america/articles/a-hidden-world-growing-beyond-control/.

105. Scott Shane, *New Leaked Document Outlines U.S. Spending on Intelligence Agencies*, N.Y. Times, August 30, 2013, A13.

106. The FISC has generated a secret body of law to control the executive. Eric Lichtblau, *In Secret, Court Vastly Broadens Powers of N.S.A.*, N.Y. Times, July 7, 2013, A1.

107. Charlie Savage, *Opinion by Secret Court Calls Collection of Phone Data Legal*, N.Y. Times, September 18, 2013, A1.

108. FISA Amendments Act, 50 U.S.C. § 1881a.

109. Scott Shane, *Guidelines Set for Incidental Capture of Americans' E-mails or Calls*, N.Y. Times, June 21, 2013, A9.

110. Ryan Lizza, *The Political Scene: State of Deception*, New Yorker, December 16, 2013, 48.

111. Luke Harding, The Snowden Files: The Inside Story of the World's Most Wanted Man (2014).

112. Charlie Savage & Michael D. Shear, *President Moves to Ease Worries on Surveillance*, N.Y. Times, August 10, 2013, A1; Charlie Savage, *N.S.A. Plan to Log Calls Is Renewed by Court*, N.Y. Times, October 19, 2013, A11.

113. Alter, Promise, 154–55. For example, in 2011 Obama issued an executive order attempting to stop recurring leaks of classified documents. Dodds, Pen, 210.

114. Shane & Bruff, Separation of Powers Law, 290–311; Clark, *Openness*, 315–16. For example, see *Mohamed v. Jeppesen Dataplan, Inc.*, 614 F.3d 1070 (9th Cir. 2010), dismissing a lawsuit against a company that had provided rendition transport. Attorney General Holder did require that the state secrets privilege be invoked only with "strong evidentiary support" and after high-level reviews. Fisher, War Power, 247–48.

115. *Clapper v. Amnesty Intl. USA*, 133 S.Ct. 1138 (2013).

116. President Obama's assertion of executive privilege in a controversy over a failed undercover operation resulted in his attorney general's citation for contempt of Congress from the House of Representatives. Eric Holder gave the House thousands of pages of documents relating to the operation and withheld only memos relating to internal Justice Department deliberations about dealing with the congressional inquiry. This was a traditional invocation of executive privilege. Charlie Savage, *House Panel's Vote Steps Up Partisan Fight on Gun Inquiry*, N.Y. Times, June 20, 2012, A1.

117. Scott Shane & Charlie Savage, *Administration Took Accidental Path to Setting Record for Leak Cases*, N.Y. Times, June 20, 2012, A17.

118. Mark Landler, *Obama, in Nod to Press, Orders Review of Inquiries*, N.Y. Times, May 24, 2013, A9.

119. 124 Stat. 119, 42 U.S.C. § 18001 et seq.

120. Toobin, Oath, ch. 18.

121. Alter, Promise, chs. 16, 19, Center, ch. 10; Blinder, After the Music, ch. 8.

122. *National Federation of Independent Business v. Sebelius*, 132 S.Ct. 2566 (2012).

123. Toobin, Oath, ch. 23.

124. David A. Strauss, *Commerce Clause Revisionism and the Affordable Care Act*, 2012 Sup. Ct. Rev. 1.

125. See chapter 8.

126. Mark Halperin & John Heilemann, Double Down: Game Change 2012 (2013).

127. Thomas E. Mann & Norman J. Ornstein, It's Even Worse Than It Looks: How the American Constitutional System Collided with the New Politics of Extremism (2012); Symposium, *The American Congress: Legal Implications of Gridlock*, 88 Notre Dame L. Rev. 2065 (2013).

128. Matthew Cooper, *The Tyranny of the Minority?*, National Journal, January 7, 2012, 37.

129. Neil MacNeil & Richard A. Baker, The American Senate: An Insider's History, chs. 12–13 (2013).

130. Michael D. Shear, *Trading Blame as Top Offices Remain Empty*, N.Y. Times, May 3, 2013, A1.

131. Art. I, § 5: "a majority of each [House] shall constitute a Quorum to do Business."

132. Id.: "Each House may determine the Rules of its Proceedings."

133. Toobin, Oath, ch. 9.

134. Id., epilogue.

135. Art. II, § 2; see chapter 4 for early practices.

136. Shane & Bruff, Separation of Powers Law, 405–8.

137. Art. I, § 5: "Neither House, during the Session of Congress, shall, without the consent of the other, adjourn for more than three days."

138. See Kaiser, Act of Congress.

139. Mark Landler & Steven Greenhouse, *Vacancies and Partisan Fighting Put Labor Relations Agency in Legal Limbo*, N.Y. Times, July 16, 2013, A14.

140. 134 S.Ct. 2550 (2014).

141. Id. at 2592.

142. Jeremy W. Peters, *Senate Vote Curbs Filibuster Power to Stall Nominees*, N.Y. Times, November 22, 2013, A1.

143. However, the practice of senatorial courtesy may still allow individual senators to block state-based appointments. Charlie Savage, *Despite Filibuster Limits, A Door Remains Open to Block Judge Nominees*, N.Y. Times, November 29, 2013, A21.

144. Bob Woodward, The Price of Politics (2012).

145. See chapter 9.

146. Woodward, Price of Politics, 327.

147. Sean Wilentz, *Obama and the Debt*, N.Y. Times, October 8, 2013, A25.

148. Alter, Promise, 332.

149. Don't Ask, Don't Tell Repeal Act, 124 Stat. 3515, 10 U.S.C. § 654.

150. Alter, Center, ch. 18.

151. *United States v. Windsor*, 133 S.Ct. 2675 (2013).

152. Charlie Savage, *Shift on Executive Power Lets Obama Bypass Rivals*, N.Y. Times, April 23, 2012, A1.

153. Julia Preston & John H. Cushman Jr., *Obama to Permit Young Migrants to Remain in U.S.*, N.Y. Times, June 16, 2012, A1.

154. Justin Gillis, *Taking a Risk over Climate*, N.Y. Times, June 26, 2013, A1.

Conclusion

1. The Commerce Clause under Marshall, Taney and Waite 2 (1937).

2. Id.

3. *Some Reflections on the Reading of Statutes*, 47 Colum. L. Rev. 534–35 (1947).

4. Charles A. Miller, The Supreme Court and the Uses of History 51 (1969).

5. Perhaps the United States will inaugurate its first female president in early 2017. If so, how will the forty-fifth president interpret her powers? Will her gender inflect her interpretations, as the race of our first black president may have affected his? We do not know. That ground remains untrodden.

6. Jeremy Paxman, Empire: What Ruling the World Did to the British 4 (2011).

7. Steven Skowronek, The Politics Presidents Make: Leadership from John Adams to George Bush (1993).

8. H. Jefferson Powell, A Community Built on Words: The Constitution in History and Politics (2002).

9. Eric A. Posner & Adrian Vermeule, The Executive Unbound: After the Madisonian Republic (2010).

10. Presidents have, however, acquiesced in various statutory limits on their power over inferior officers, for whom supervisory needs are diminished.

11. See especially Sanford Levinson, Our Undemocratic Constitution: Where the Constitution Goes Wrong (and How We the People Can Correct It) (2006); James L. Sundquist, Constitutional Reform and Effective Government (rev. ed. 1992).

12. Levinson, Undemocratic, ch. 3.

13. Id., ch. 4, explains Scot Powe's suggestion of the eighteen-year term to give each president at least two nominees and to reduce opportunities for any single president to name a majority of the Court.

14. Id., 211–12.

15. Akhil Reed Amar, America's Constitution: A Biography 433–38 (2005).

16. For the theme of redemption, see Jack M. Balkin, Constitutional Redemption: Political Faith in an Unjust World (2011).

Index

Adams, John, 27, 32, 35, 50; quasi-war with France, 52–54; sedition, 54–55
Adams, John Quincy, 83–87, 117
Afghanistan, 407, 412–13, 416, 422–23, 432–34, 440, 445
amendments to Constitution. *See specific amendments*
Arthur, Chester A., 182–89
Article II. *See specific powers*
Article V, 23, 237
Articles of Confederation, 12, 15
atomic bomb, 261, 267, 270, 297–98, 306, 360, 374; decision to use, 263–64; hydrogen bomb, 270, 289; massive retaliation, 287–89, 295, 303–4, 340–41
attorney general: creation of, 30, 36–38; departmentalism and, 65–66; institutional records, 84
Authorization for Use of Military Force (AUMF), 408–9, 413–15, 418, 432, 441, 443

Bank of the United States, 38–41, 78, 95–104
Barbary Pirates, 67–68
bin Laden, Osama, 393–94, 442–43
Buchanan, James, 112–13, 120–26
Bush, George H. W., 376–82, 385–86
Bush, George W.: legacy, 429–33, 435–36, 446, 463; presidency of, 401–26, 451; war by machines, 440, 442–43, 463
Bush v. Gore, 401

Cambodia, 328–30, 353
Carter, James E., 354–56, 360, 374, 383, 387, 402, 409

Central Intelligence Agency: George H. W. Bush and, 377; George W. Bush and, 402, 409, 428; Clinton and, 385, 393; creation of, 268; Eisenhower and, 291–92; interrogation and, 419–21; investigation of, 352; Iran-Contra, 366, 368–70; LBJ and, 322; Kennedy and, 296–97, 299; Nixon and, 342, 348; Obama and, 431–32, 441–42, 446, 450
Cheney, Vice President Richard, 353, 377, 380; theory of presidential power, 402–4, 409, 411, 417, 422–24
China, 195, 270, 274, 289, 318, 339–40, 355, 378, 435, 444
Churchill, Winston, 246–48, 250, 255–57, 263, 268
civil liberties, 460, 463–64; Civil War and, 141–45; Cold War, 280–82, 294; Japanese American internment, 252–54; Vietnam War, 322, 331, 347, 350; World War I and, 218–21; World War II and, 250–55
civil rights: Carter and, 354–55; Civil Rights Act of 1964, 314–15; Eisenhower and, 284–85, 290–91; gay rights, 385, 454–55; Kennedy and, 306–10; Lincoln and, 127, 146; Reagan and, 364; Reconstruction and, 154–55, 157, 159, 161, 166, 180–81; Voting Rights Act, 316; Wilson and, 211
Civil War, 120, 131–33
classification of documents, 460
Cleveland, Grover, 189–90, 193, 196
Clinton, Hillary Rodham, 383, 386, 428, 433–35, 449

Clinton, William J.: impeachment of, 394–
97; legacy of, 402, 430, 437, 443, 454, 458;
presidency of, 383–97
Cold War, 267–70, 287–89, 297–98, 373, 377–
78, 381, 428
commander in chief power, 20–21, 462–63,
465; ambiguity of authorizations, 320;
atomic bomb, 263; Balkans, 392–94;
Barbary pirates, 67–68; Berlin, 269;
Cambodia, 353; Civil War, 131–33,
137–40, 146–50; Cleveland, 190; Cuba,
296, 298–306; declarations of war, 319;
Eisenhower, 284, 287–89; Fillmore, 118;
Gulf War, 379–81; Haiti, 387; impoundments, 343, 350; Iran, 356; Iraq, 422–23;
Kennedy, 297; Korea, 271–75; Libya,
367–68, 436–38, 445; McKinley, 194–95;
Monroe, 86; need for authorization,
271–73, 275, 284, 387–88; Obama,
432–34; Panama, 378–79; Polk, 114–15;
Reagan, 366–67; Reconstruction, 162–
63, 170–71, 175, 179; FDR, 247–50; TR,
202–4; steel seizure, 277, 280; Syria, 438–
40; Tonkin Gulf Resolution, 318–20,
324, 328–29; Vietnam, 310–11, 317–22,
335–36, 353; War of 1812, 79–80; Wilson,
212, 214; World War II, 255–58
commerce clause, 230, 234–36, 448–49, 456
Congress: control of membership, 154–55,
159, 161, 164–65; dysfunction, 389–90;
executive corruption of, 15–16, 28; ratification of executive action, 99, 102, 117,
135–38, 149–53, 321, 324, 414; schedule
of meetings, 23, 130–32, 140, 158, 168,
209, 229, 266
Constitutional Convention, 15–17
constitutional dictatorship, 13–14, 18, 137,
215, 231, 255, 298, 325, 462, 465–66
constitutional interpretation, 11, 456–67,
473n4; conventions, 7; First Congress's,
29; Jefferson's, 59; Kennedy's, 293–
95; Lincoln's, 127, 153; Madison's, 78;
Obama's, 427–28; original intent, 5,
48–49; presidential approaches to,
1–5, 127, 153; FDR's, 228–29, 239–40;
TR's, 199, 204–6; textual, 133, 152–53;
Truman's, 262; Washington's, 25
Constitution of the United States: ratification of, 19–20; reform of, 7, 464
Coolidge, Calvin, 224–25

Cuba, 292; Bay of Pigs, 296–97; missile
crisis, 298–306
cyber warfare, 440, 443–44

debt ceiling, 453
Declaration of Independence, 127, 466
deficits, 284, 360–62, 377, 382, 385, 390–91,
405, 435, 453–54
delegation doctrine, 235, 243
departmentalism: defined, 65, 85; Jackson
and, 90, 97–98; Jefferson and, 63–66;
Andrew Johnson and, 162, 171, 176;
Lincoln and, 136; Madison and, 78;
Nixon and, 333; Obama and, 457;
Reagan and, 364; FDR and, 232–33,
238–39; Wilson and, 221
Detainee Treatment Act, 415, 418–19
disability, 188, 191, 217–18, 257–58, 293–94
Dred Scott v. Sandford, 120–22, 135
drones, 440–42, 446

Eisenhower, Dwight D., 281, 283–92, 294–
96, 299, 309, 390
Electoral College, 16, 28, 58, 77, 83, 89, 97,
125, 401, 464
electronic surveillance, 281, 294, 329–31,
408–12, 446–48; FISA, 409–12; terrorist
surveillance, 409–12
emancipation, 145–52, 155; Confiscation
Acts, 147–48, 150; Emancipation
Proclamation, 148–56
embargo, 74–77
emergency powers, 18
exclusive constitutional powers, 5–6, 463;
George W. Bush and, 402–8, 420–21,
425; Curtiss-Wright and, 243–44; Andrew Johnson and, 176; Lincoln and,
136–37, 153; Nixon and, 326; Obama
and, 432
executive agreements, 46–47, 195, 202, 341,
461, 501n51; Bricker amendment, 288;
destroyer deal, 246–49; Iran, 357; recognition of Soviet Union, 242–43
executive branch, 16; budgeting, 205, 224;
civil service, 189, 208, 232, 266, 281–
82; creation of departments, 28–32;
Executive Office of the President, 240–
41; nominations of officers, 34–35, 90–
92, 384, 390; recess appointments to,
109, 118, 451–52; U.S. attorneys, 424;

White House staff, 128, 193, 209, 232, 241–42, 284, 328, 330, 384, 405, 429
executive orders, 33, 198, 243, 264–65, 279, 378, 390–91, 461, 502n65; abortion counseling, 405–6, 429–30; assassination ban, 352, 394; conservation, 197, 200–202; discrimination, 231, 265–66, 299, 307, 315, 382; immigration, 455; loyalty, 281–86; managing regulation, 334, 363, 425, 430; war on terror, 414, 417, 419, 431
executive privilege, 460; John Adams and, 53; George H. W. Bush and, 382; George W. Bush and, 424; Clinton and, 396; Eisenhower and, 286; Ford and, 352; Jackson and, 100; Kennedy and, 297, 339, 519n26; Lincoln and, 140; Nixon and, 348–50; Polk and, 116; Reagan and, 363; FDR and, 231; TR and, 501n55; Truman and, 282; Washington and, 47–49; Wilson and, 217

faithful execution clause, 18, 21, 460; Buchanan, 123–26; George W. Bush, 408; Fillmore, 118; financial crisis, 426; Hayes, 182; Indian removal, 93–95; Iraq, 422–23; Andrew Johnson, 163, 165–68, 170–79; Katrina, 424; Lincoln, 132, 135–36, 145, 152; Obama, 446–48, 460; presidencies of 1920s, 224–29; protective power, 189, 200, 438; Reagan, 359–62, 364, 368, 372; FDR, 231, 245, 251; TR, 197–99, 200–202; segregation, 290, 308–10, 315–16, 327, 332, 334–35, 343–51; steel seizure, 278–80; subversion, 282–84; Truman, 265; Wilson, 208, 210, 221
Federal Bureau of Investigation: Clinton and, 391–92; creation of, 220–21; Kennedy and, 294, 307; Nixon and, 330–31, 346, 348; subversion and, 251–52, 281–82, 285
federal courts, executive nonacquiescence in court orders, 66, 76, 122, 130, 135
Federalist Papers, 19, 32
Federal Reserve Board, 210, 355, 362, 385, 426, 430–31, 459
Federal Trade Commission, 210–11, 225, 235–36, 459
Fifteenth Amendment, 180

Fifth Amendment, 132–33, 145, 234, 252, 414–15
Fillmore, Millard, 118
financial crisis of 2008, 425–26, 430–31
First Amendment, 54–55, 63–64, 282, 285–86, 322
Ford, Gerald R., 351–53, 375, 394, 441
foreign policy, presidential determination of, 461–62; John Adams, 53–54; Arab spring, 435–46; George H. W. Bush, 377–81; Bush Doctrine, 413; Carter Doctrine, 355–56; Clinton, 386–87, 394; Coolidge, 224–25; *Curtiss-Wright*, 267–70; Fillmore, 118; gold standard, 339–40; Grant, 180; Grenada, 367; Harrison, 191–92; Iran, 356–57, 443–44; Israel, 269, 342, 355; Jackson, 87–88; Jefferson, 67–68; Andrew Johnson, 177; LBJ, 323; Kennedy, 294; Lebanon, 289, 367; Lincoln, 141; Marshall Plan, 269; McKinley, 195; Monroe, 85–87; Nixon, 329, 339–42; Obama, 429; Reagan, 365–75; recognition of governments, 44, 203, 242; FDR, 241–50; TR, 196, 198, 202–4; Suez, 289; summit meetings, 289, 292, 297–98, 340–41, 353, 375; Syria, 438–40; Truman Doctrine, 269, 329, 366; Vietnam, 318–21, 327–29, 335–36; Washington, 42–47
Fourteenth Amendment, 166–68, 177–78, 454; equal protection clause, 166, 252, 308, 391; segregation, 266, 290–91, 307–10
Fourth Amendment, 281, 322, 329–31

Garfield, James, 188
general welfare clause, 50, 78–79, 95, 119, 165, 191, 226–30, 233, 236, 449
Geneva Conventions, 408, 413, 416–18, 432
Gorbachev, Mikhail, 374–75, 378
Grant, Ulysses S., 168–71, 178–81, 343
Guantanamo Bay detention facility, 413–15, 419, 431–32
guarantee clause, 110, 154, 163
Gulf War, 379–91

habeas corpus, 18, 134–37, 142, 254–55, 413–15, 491–92n46
Hamilton, Alexander, 27–28, 32–33, 38–45
Harding, Warren G., 221, 223–24

Harrison, Benjamin, 191–92
Harrison, William Henry, 107
Hayes, Rutherford B., 181, 190
head of state, president as, 22, 26–27, 117,
    172, 283, 383
health care reform, 264, 316, 385–86, 405,
    425; Obamacare, 448–49
Hoover, Herbert, 224–27, 230, 354

impeachment, 497n56; Chase, 73; Clinton,
    394–97; Johnson, 170, 172–77; Nixon,
    349–51
impoundment of funds, 342–46
incompatibility clause, 18
independent agencies: creation of, 199, 210–
    11, 459, 503–4n116; removal of officers,
    235–36
independent counsel, 431–32; Clinton, 388,
    391, 395–97; Ethics in Government Act,
    334; Iran-Contra, 372; Watergate, 349
Indian policy, 35, 50, 93–95
internal improvements, 79, 84, 95, 111, 123,
    127, 141, 156
Internal Revenue Service, 314, 346
interrogation, 408, 419–21, 431, 541n93;
    extraordinary rendition, 420, 432;
    torture, 419–20
Iran-Contra scandal, 361–66, 368–73, 382,
    403
Iraq, 421–23, 432–34, 444–45

Jackson, Andrew, 83; legacy of, 122, 124,
    130, 262, 291, 317, 326, 332, 334, 461;
    presidency of, 86–87, 88–105; Texas
    and, 110–11
Jackson, Robert, 136; destroyers for bases
    deal, 247–48, 251; opinion in steel sei-
    zure case, 278–80
Jefferson, Thomas: formation of Republican
    party, 41–45; legacy of, 122, 132, 306,
    323, 343, 349, 461–62; presidency of, 57–
    77; secretary of state, 27–28, 33, 39
Johnson, Andrew, 126, 151, 155, 157–77, 350
Johnson, Lyndon (LBJ): legacy of, 325–28,
    330–32, 344, 346, 355, 385, 409, 423,
    461–62; presidency of, 311–24; vice
    presidency of, 300, 302, 309
Joint Chiefs of Staff: creation of, 255–56,
    268; Eisenhower and, 289; LBJ and, 321–
    22; Kennedy and, 295–97, 301, 304–5,

310; Reagan and, 366–67; Truman and,
    274–75. See also Powell, Colin

Kennedy, John F., 293–317, 327–28, 330,
    339, 376, 380, 383–84, 422, 462
Kennedy, Robert F., 295, 297, 300–301,
    304–5, 313
Khrushchev, Nikita, 289, 292, 297–306
Kissinger, Henry, 327, 329, 336, 339–41;
    secretary of state, 342, 347, 351, 353
Korean War, 266, 270–75, 287, 302, 319, 337,
    380, 462

labor disputes, 181–82, 189–90, 199–200,
    265, 276–80, 307, 530n15
legislative management by presidents, 461;
    George H. W. Bush, 382; George W.
    Bush, 405; Cleveland, 191; Clinton,
    385–86, 390–91; Jackson, 97–98; Jef-
    ferson, 61–62, 77; LBJ, 312–17, 323,
    327, 335; Kennedy, 295; Lincoln, 140;
    Madison, 77; Obama, 428, 448; Reagan,
    361–62, 364; FDR, 229–33; TR, 197;
    Truman, 264–65; Washington, 29;
    Wilson, 209–11, 214
legislative vetoes, 338, 363–64, 530n26
Lincoln, Abraham, 3–4, 105, 183, 208,
    457, 466; civil liberties and, 218–19,
    221; legacy of, 274, 277, 312, 315–16, 324,
    330, 401, 413, 428, 454; Mexican War
    and, 115, 462; presidency of, 122–56;
    Reconstruction and, 176; textual inter-
    pretation, 206, 458; theory of govern-
    ment, 191, 233, 284
Locke, John, 12–14; Lockean prerogative,
    70–72, 75, 132–33, 136, 138, 151–33, 229,
    248, 466
Louisiana Purchase, 68–72

MacArthur, Douglas, 256, 264, 272–73;
    dismissal, 274–75
Madison, James, 27–28, 31, 39, 40, 45,
    60, 77–82, 84–85; Constitutional
    Convention, 15, 17–18, 22; Federalist
    Papers, 19
Manifest Destiny, 111–12, 118–19, 193
Marbury v. Madison, 73–74
Marshall, John, 53–55, 64, 72, 96, 244, 349
mass media, presidential use of, 231, 294,
    309, 316

McCarthy, Joseph, 280, 282, 285–87, 318, 460
McKinley, William, 192–96
Merryman, Ex parte, 134–35
Mexican War, 114–18
military arrests, detentions, and trials, 142–43, 151; Nazi saboteurs, 254–55; war on terror, 408, 412–18, 431–32
Military Commissions Act, 415, 419
Milligan, Ex parte, 169, 418, 512n164
Monroe, James, 83–87
Monroe Doctrine, 87, 113, 141, 177–78, 180, 192–93, 301–2; Roosevelt Corollary, 202, 212, 243
Montesquieu, Baron de, 12, 14

National Industrial Recovery Act, 230, 235
national security adviser, 288, 294, 327, 361, 368, 371, 385, 392–93, 404, 434, 450
National Security Agency, 291, 409–12, 442, 444, 446
National Security Council, 268, 292, 294, 366–70, 372, 421, 429
NATO, 270, 304–5, 378, 386, 392–94, 439
Nazi saboteurs, 254–55, 414, 417–18
necessary and proper clause, 17, 39–40, 79, 97, 140–41
neutrality, 213; Neutrality Proclamation, 42–46; pre–World War II, 242, 244–50
New Deal, 227–33
Nixon, Richard, 280, 285, 324–51, 363, 402, 409, 411, 458, 462
Nullification Crisis, 104–5

Obama, Barack H., 405, 426–55, 457, 463
Obamacare, 448–49
Office of Legal Counsel, 405, 420–21, 431, 437–38, 507n50
Office of Management and Budget, 333–34, 363, 459
opinions clause, 16
oversight of executive branch by presidents: Buchanan, 123; George W. Bush, 411, 424–26; Carter, 354–55; Grant, 178–79; Harding, 224; Hayes, 182; Jackson, 90–91, 99–104; Jefferson, 60; Andrew Johnson, 159, 169, 171–72; Kennedy, 294–97; Lincoln, 128–30; McKinley, 193; Nixon, 327; Obama, 427–30; Polk, 112; Reagan, 360, 363, 365; FDR, 232, 240–42, 246; Truman, 262–63, 266, 268, 270; Tyler, 108–9; Washington, 32–33; Wilson, 208, 213, 220

Panama Canal, 194, 203, 225, 378
pardon power, 460; Adams, 50; George H. W. Bush, 382; Clinton, 397; Ford (of Nixon), 351–52; Jefferson, 63; Andrew Johnson, 160–61; Lincoln, 143, 154; Washington, 50; Wilson, 221
party leader, president as, 22, 61–62
patronage: Arthur, 188–89; Garfield, 188; Grant, 178–79; Hayes, 182; Jackson, 89, 92; Jefferson, 60–61; Andrew Johnson, 167, 169; LBJ, 313; Lincoln, 125; Madison, 77; Polk, 113, 128; Truman, 263; Tyler, 109; Washington, 34
Pentagon papers, 346–47
Philippines, 194–95, 419
Pierce, Franklin, 118–19
political ratification of presidential interpretation, 4, 6–7, 458, 481n64; Jackson, 98–99, 102; Lincoln, 135–38, 149–53; Nixon, 325, 328–29, 339, 345; TR, 203
Polk, James K., 110–17, 131, 193, 320, 462
Powell, Colin, 377, 379, 385, 387, 392–93
Preamble (to Constitution), 233, 262, 481n55
presidential oath, 1, 133, 151–52, 458
presidential papers, 85; Presidential Records Act, 354, 424, 430
press, presidential relations with: Civil War, 144–45; Cleveland, 191; Andrew Johnson, 159; LBJ, 321; Kennedy, 294; Nixon, 331–32; Obama, 447; Polk, 112; TR, 197; Taft, 205; Truman, 264–65; Wilson, 209
Prize Cases, 137
Progressive era legislation, 199, 209–11

Reagan, Ronald: legacy of, 376–78, 382–83, 385, 402–3, 428, 430, 436, 457; presidency of, 359–75
Reconstruction, 153–55, 157–83
Red scare, 221, 270, 280–82
reelection, president's eligibility for, 15–17; single term promises, 112, 116; two-term tradition, 51, 60, 205, 322–23; third term, 181, 246, 282–83. *See also* Twenty-Second Amendment

removal of executive officers, law of, 30–32, 99–101, 169, 173–74, 211

Roosevelt, Franklin D.: electronic surveillance and, 281, 330, 408; impoundment and, 343; LBJ and, 313–15; legacy of, 261–62, 264, 288, 295, 333, 359, 375, 384, 417, 458, 461–62; Obamacare and, 448–49; presidency of, 228–58; third term legacy, 283

Roosevelt, Theodore, 190; legacy of, 212, 219, 243, 248, 262, 265, 461–62; presidency of, 195–207

Russia, 378, 435, 439

Senate, U.S., 16–17; confirmation of officers, 34–35, 90–92, 109, 332–33, 365, 450–53, 459; executive council, 35–36

separation of powers, 12, 14, 17–19, 336

slavery, 20, 51–52, 84, 110–11, 117–19

Spanish-American War, 192–94

spending, as executive function, 30–32; impoundment of funds, 342–46; unauthorized, 75, 132, 371–73

Soviet Union, 242–43, 267–68, 287–89, 291–92, 298–306, 339–42, 353–56, 373–75, 377–78

Stalin, Josef, 255–57, 263–64, 268–69, 271, 287

Stanton, Edwin, 126, 140, 169–75

state secrets privilege, 275–76, 424, 431, 447, 460

statutory interpretation, 200–202, 229, 243, 248–49, 412, 424, 426; acquiescence doctrine, 202, 206–7

steel seizure case (*Youngstown Sheet & Tube Co. v. Sawyer*), 276–80, 418, 453–54

succession to presidency, 108; Arthur, 188; Fillmore, 118; Andrew Johnson, 158; TR, 195–96; Truman, 261; Tyler, 205; Wade, 173; Wilson, 218

Supreme Court, U.S.: advisory opinions, 46; confrontation with FDR, 233–40; Court-packing, 73, 179, 236–40; nominations, 55, 233–34, 240, 290, 332–33, 364, 390, 424; term limit, 464; unauthorized executive litigation, 190, 347

Taft, William Howard, 194–95, 202, 205–7, 210

Taney, Roger, 97, 100–102, 121–22, 130, 134–35, 148, 153

Taylor, Zachary, 117–18

Tenure of Office Act, 169, 171–75

Texas, 87–88, 110

Thirteenth Amendment, 155, 162–64

Tonkin Gulf Resolution, 318–20, 324, 328–29

treaties: ABM, 341; Alaska, 177; Bricker amendment, 288; George W. Bush and, 417; congressional-executive agreements and, 257, 386; Guadalupe Hidalgo, 116; Hawaii, 180, 193–93; INF, 374; Jay, 47–49; Kyoto, 405; Louisiana, 68–70; McKinley and, 195; NATO, 270; Oregon, 113; Panama, 203, 355; Spain, 194; START, 378, 435; termination, 355; Texas, 110–11; Transcontinental, 110–11; UN, 257; Versailles, 215–17; Washington and, 35, 42, 44

Truman, Harry S, 257, 262–84, 287–89, 292, 319, 343, 408, 462

Twelfth Amendment, 58

Twenty-Second Amendment, 283, 465

Twenty-Fifth Amendment, 108

Tyler, John, 107–11

unconstitutional legislation, 63–64, 174–76

Union, theories of, 124–25, 127, 130, 155–56; secession, 123–25, 154

unitary executive, 5, 458–59; Cheney, 404; Clinton, 390, 392; independent agencies, 236; independent prosecution, 397; Andrew Johnson, 175; Nixon, 333–35; Obama, 426, 431; Wilson, 210–11

United Nations, 422, 436, 439

Van Buren, Martin, 90–91, 102, 106

vesting clause, 20, 45, 133, 175, 277, 334

veto power, 17–18, 373, 461; George H. W. Bush, 378, 382; George W. Bush, 421; Cleveland, 191; Clinton, 390–91; Coolidge, 225–26; Ford, 353; Hayes, 182; Hoover, 227; Jackson, 95–99; Andrew Johnson, 165–67, 169–71, 179; LBJ, 313; Nixon, 338, 344; pocket veto, 155, 215, 495n134, 530n25; Polk, 111; FDR, 231; TR, 200; signing statements, 95, 170, 364, 421, 425, 432; Truman, 264, 282; Washington, 28–29

vice presidency, 464–65; Biden, 428, 449–50; Cheney, 403, 537–38n19; Coolidge, 224; Ford, 351; Andrew Johnson, 151;

LBJ, 312; Truman, 257, 266; Tyler, 107; Twelfth Amendment and, 58–59. *See also* succession to presidency
Vietnam War, 288–89, 310–11, 317–24, 328–29, 335–36, 339, 347, 433, 523n123

War of 1812, 79–80
war on terror, 463; 9/11 attacks, 406–9; Afghanistan, 412–13; interrogation, 420–21; military detentions and trials, 414–19
War Powers Resolution, 336–39, 463–65, 526n55; George H. W. Bush, 378–81; Carter, 356; Clinton, 386–88, 392–93;

Ford, 353; Obama, 436–45; Reagan, 364, 367–68, 373
Washington, George, 23, 25–51, 461
Watergate, 346–51
Webster, Daniel, 97–98, 101, 108, 110, 118, 130
Whigs, 3, 98, 106–8, 114, 117–18, 284
Wilson, Woodrow, 187, 223, 228, 243–44, 250, 262; George W. Bush and, 402; legacy of, 292–93, 295, 375, 386, 458, 460–63; Nixon and, 326, 331; precedents for wartime, 255, 257; presidency of, 207–22
World War I, 213–15
World War II, 255–57, 263–64, 407